Exam 70-463: Implementing a Data Warehouse with Microsoft SQL Server 2012

OBJECTIVE	CHAPTER	LESSON
1. DESIGN AND IMPLEMENT A DATA WAREHOUSE		
1.1 Design and implement dimensions.	Chapter 1	Lessons 1 and, 2
	Chapter 2	Lessons 1, 2, and 3
1.2 Design and implement fact tables.	Chapter 1	Lesson 3
	Chapter 2	Lessons 1, 2, and 3
2. EXTRACT AND TRANSFORM DATA		
2.1 Define connection managers.	Chapter 3	Lessons 1 and 3
	Chapter 4	Lesson 1
	Chapter 9	Lesson 2
2.2 Design data flow.	Chapter 3	Lesson 1
	Chapter 5	Lessons 1, 2, and 3
	Chapter 7	Lesson 1
	Chapter 10	Lesson 2
	Chapter 13	Lesson 2
	Chapter 18	Lessons 1, 2, and 3
	Chapter 19	Lesson 2
	Chapter 20	Lesson 1
2.3 Implement data flow.	Chapter 3	Lesson 1
	Chapter 5	Lessons 1, 2, and 3
	Chapter 7	Lessons 1 and 3
	Chapter 13	Lesson 1 and 2
	Chapter 18	Lesson 1
	Chapter 20	Lessons 2 and 3
2.4 Manage SSIS package execution.	Chapter 8	Lessons 1 and 2
	Chapter 12	Lesson 1
2.5 Implement script tasks in SSIS.	Chapter 19	Lesson 1
3. LOAD DATA		
3.1 Design control flow.	Chapter 3	Lessons 2 and 3
	Chapter 4	Lessons 2 and 3
	Chapter 6	Lessons 1 and 3
	Chapter 8	Lessons 1, 2, and 3
	Chapter 10	Lesson 1
	Chapter 12	Lesson 1 and 2
	Chapter 19	Lesson 1
3.2 Implement package logic by using SSIS variables and parameters.	Chapter 6	Lessons 1 and 2
	Chapter 9	Lessons 1 and 2
3.3 Implement control flow.	Chapter 4	Lessons 2 and 3
	Chapter 6	Lesson 3
	Chapter 8	Lessons 1 and 2
	Chapter 10	Lesson 3
	Chapter 13	Lessons 1, 2, and 3
3.4 Implement data load options.	Chapter 7	Lesson 2
3.5 Implement script components in SSIS.	Chapter 19	Lesson 2

OBJECTIVE	CHAPTER	LESSON
4. CONFIGURE AND DEPLOY SSIS SOLUTIONS		
4.1 Troubleshoot data integration issues.	Chapter 10	Lesson 1
	Chapter 13	Lessons 1, 2, and 3
4.2 Install and maintain SSIS components.	Chapter 11	Lesson 1
4.3 Implement auditing, logging, and event handling.	Chapter 8	Lesson 3
	Chapter 10	Lessons 1 and 2
4.4 Deploy SSIS solutions.	Chapter 11	Lessons 1 and 2
	Chapter 19	Lesson 3
4.5 Configure SSIS security settings.	Chapter 12	Lessons 1 and 2
5. BUILD DATA QUALITY SOLUTIONS		
5.1 Install and maintain Data Quality Services.	Chapter 14	Lessons 1, 2, and 3
5.2 Implement master data management solutions.	Chapter 15	Lessons 1, 2, and 3
	Chapter 16	Lessons 1, 2, and 3
5.3 Create a data quality project to clean data.	Chapter 14	Lesson 1
	Chapter 17	Lessons 1, 2, and 3
	Chapter 20	Lessons 1 and 2

Exam Objectives The exam objectives listed here are current as of this book's publication date. Exam objectives are subject to change at any time without prior notice and at Microsoft's sole discretion. Please visit the Microsoft Learning website for the most current listing of exam objectives: *http://www.microsoft.com/learning/en/us /exam.aspx?ID=70-463&locale=en-us*.

Exam 70-463:
Implementing a Data
Warehouse with
Microsoft® SQL Server®
2012

Training Kit

Dejan Sarka
Matija Lah
Grega Jerkič

ISBN: 978-0-7356-6609-2

10   16

Printed and bound in the United States of America.

Microsoft Press books are available through booksellers and distributors worldwide. If you need support related to this book, email Microsoft Press Book Support at *mspinput@microsoft.com*. Please tell us what you think of this book at *http://www.microsoft.com/learning/booksurvey*.

Microsoft and the trademarks listed at *http://www.microsoft.com/about/legal/ en/us/IntellectualProperty/Trademarks/EN-US.aspx* are trademarks of the Microsoft group of companies. All other marks are property of their respective owners.

The example companies, organizations, products, domain names, email addresses, logos, people, places, and events depicted herein are fictitious. No association with any real company, organization, product, domain name, email address, logo, person, place, or event is intended or should be inferred.

This book expresses the author's views and opinions. The information contained in this book is provided without any express, statutory, or implied warranties. Neither the authors, Microsoft Corporation, nor its resellers, or distributors will be held liable for any damages caused or alleged to be caused either directly or indirectly by this book.

Acquisitions and Developmental Editor: Russell Jones
Production Editor: Holly Bauer
Editorial Production: Online Training Solutions, Inc.
Technical Reviewer: Miloš Radivojević
Copyeditor: Kathy Krause, Online Training Solutions, Inc.
Indexer: Ginny Munroe, Judith McConville
Cover Design: Twist Creative • Seattle
Cover Composition: Zyg Group, LLC
Illustrator: Jeanne Craver, Online Training Solutions, Inc.

Contents at a Glance

Introduction   *xxvii*

PART I   **DESIGNING AND IMPLEMENTING A DATA WAREHOUSE**

CHAPTER 1   Data Warehouse Logical Design   3
CHAPTER 2   Implementing a Data Warehouse   41

PART II   **DEVELOPING SSIS PACKAGES**

CHAPTER 3   Creating SSIS Packages   87
CHAPTER 4   Designing and Implementing Control Flow   131
CHAPTER 5   Designing and Implementing Data Flow   177

PART III   **ENHANCING SSIS PACKAGES**

CHAPTER 6   Enhancing Control Flow   239
CHAPTER 7   Enhancing Data Flow   283
CHAPTER 8   Creating a Robust and Restartable Package   327
CHAPTER 9   Implementing Dynamic Packages   353
CHAPTER 10   Auditing and Logging   381

PART IV   **MANAGING AND MAINTAINING SSIS PACKAGES**

CHAPTER 11   Installing SSIS and Deploying Packages   421
CHAPTER 12   Executing and Securing Packages   455
CHAPTER 13   Troubleshooting and Performance Tuning   497

PART V   **BUILDING DATA QUALITY SOLUTIONS**

CHAPTER 14   Installing and Maintaining Data Quality Services   529
CHAPTER 15   Implementing Master Data Services   565
CHAPTER 16   Managing Master Data   605
CHAPTER 17   Creating a Data Quality Project to Clean Data   637

PART VI   ADVANCED SSIS AND DATA QUALITY TOPICS

CHAPTER 18   **SSIS and Data Mining**   667

CHAPTER 19   **Implementing Custom Code in SSIS Packages**   699

CHAPTER 20   **Identity Mapping and De-Duplicating**   735

Index   *769*

Contents

Introduction   **xxvii**

System Requirements   *xxviii*

Using the Companion CD   *xxix*

Acknowledgments   *xxxi*

Support & Feedback   *xxxi*

Preparing for the Exam   *xxxiii*

PART I   **DESIGNING AND IMPLEMENTING A DATA WAREHOUSE**

Chapter 1   **Data Warehouse Logical Design**   **3**

Before You Begin. 4

Lesson 1: Introducing Star and Snowflake Schemas. 4

     Reporting Problems with a Normalized Schema   5

     Star Schema   7

     Snowflake Schema   9

     Granularity Level   12

     Auditing and Lineage   13

     Lesson Summary   16

     Lesson Review   16

Lesson 2: Designing Dimensions 17

     Dimension Column Types   17

     Hierarchies   19

     Slowly Changing Dimensions   21

     Lesson Summary   26

     Lesson Review   26

What do you think of this book? We want to hear from you!

Microsoft is interested in hearing your feedback so we can continually improve our
books and learning resources for you. To participate in a brief online survey, please visit:

www.microsoft.com/learning/booksurvey/

Lesson 3: Designing Fact Tables 27

    Fact Table Column Types   28

    Additivity of Measures   29

    Additivity of Measures in SSAS   30

    Many-to-Many Relationships   30

    Lesson Summary   33

    Lesson Review   34

Case Scenarios. 34

    Case Scenario 1: A Quick POC Project   34

    Case Scenario 2: Extending the POC Project   35

Suggested Practices 35

    Analyze the AdventureWorksDW2012 Database Thoroughly   35

    Check the SCD and Lineage in the AdventureWorks-
    DW2012 Database   36

Answers. 37

    Lesson 1   37

    Lesson 2   37

    Lesson 3   38

    Case Scenario 1   39

    Case Scenario 2   39

Chapter 2   **Implementing a Data Warehouse**   **41**

Before You Begin. 42

Lesson 1: Implementing Dimensions and Fact Tables 42

    Creating a Data Warehouse Database   42

    Implementing Dimensions   45

    Implementing Fact Tables   47

    Lesson Summary   54

    Lesson Review   54

Lesson 2: Managing the Performance of a Data Warehouse 55

    Indexing Dimensions and Fact Tables   56

    Indexed Views   58

    Data Compression   61

    Columnstore Indexes and Batch Processing   62

Lesson Summary 69

Lesson Review 70

Lesson 3: Loading and Auditing Loads 70

Using Partitions 71

Data Lineage 73

Lesson Summary 78

Lesson Review 78

Case Scenarios 78

Case Scenario 1: Slow DW Reports 79

Case Scenario 2: DW Administration Problems 79

Suggested Practices 79

Test Different Indexing Methods 79

Test Table Partitioning 80

Answers 81

Lesson 1 81

Lesson 2 81

Lesson 3 82

Case Scenario 1 83

Case Scenario 2 83

PART II DEVELOPING SSIS PACKAGES

Chapter 3 Creating SSIS Packages 87

Before You Begin 89

Lesson 1: Using the SQL Server Import and Export Wizard 89

Planning a Simple Data Movement 89

Lesson Summary 99

Lesson Review 99

Lesson 2: Developing SSIS Packages in SSDT 101

Introducing SSDT 102

Lesson Summary 107

Lesson Review 108

Lesson 3: Introducing Control Flow, Data Flow, and
Connection Managers 109

Introducing SSIS Development 110

Introducing SSIS Project Deployment 110

Lesson Summary 124

Lesson Review 124

Case Scenarios 125

Case Scenario 1: Copying Production Data to Development 125

Case Scenario 2: Connection Manager Parameterization 125

Suggested Practices 125

Use the Right Tool 125

Account for the Differences Between Development and
Production Environments 126

Answers 127

Lesson 1 127

Lesson 2 128

Lesson 3 128

Case Scenario 1 129

Case Scenario 2 129

Chapter 4   Designing and Implementing Control Flow   131

Before You Begin 132

Lesson 1: Connection Managers 133

Lesson Summary 144

Lesson Review 144

Lesson 2: Control Flow Tasks and Containers 145

Planning a Complex Data Movement 145

Tasks 147

Containers 155

Lesson Summary 163

Lesson Review 163

Lesson 3: Precedence Constraints 164

Lesson Summary 169

Lesson Review 169

Case Scenarios. 170

    Case Scenario 1: Creating a Cleanup Process   170

    Case Scenario 2: Integrating External Processes   171

Suggested Practices. 171

    A Complete Data Movement Solution   171

Answers. 173

    Lesson 1   173

    Lesson 2   174

    Lesson 3   175

    Case Scenario 1   176

    Case Scenario 2   176

Chapter 5   Designing and Implementing Data Flow   177

Before You Begin. 177

Lesson 1: Defining Data Sources and Destinations. 178

    Creating a Data Flow Task   178

    Defining Data Flow Source Adapters   180

    Defining Data Flow Destination Adapters   184

    SSIS Data Types   187

    Lesson Summary   197

    Lesson Review   197

Lesson 2: Working with Data Flow Transformations. 198

    Selecting Transformations   198

    Using Transformations   205

    Lesson Summary   215

    Lesson Review   215

Lesson 3: Determining Appropriate ETL Strategy and Tools. 216

    ETL Strategy   217

    Lookup Transformations   218

    Sorting the Data   224

    Set-Based Updates   225

    Lesson Summary   231

    Lesson Review   231

Case Scenario. 232

    Case Scenario: New Source System   232

Suggested Practices 233

    Create and Load Additional Tables   233

Answers. 234

    Lesson 1   234

    Lesson 2   234

    Lesson 3   235

    Case Scenario   236

PART III   ENHANCING SSIS PACKAGES

Chapter 6   Enhancing Control Flow   239

Before You Begin. 241

Lesson 1: SSIS Variables 241

    System and User Variables   243

    Variable Data Types   245

    Variable Scope   248

    Property Parameterization   251

    Lesson Summary   253

    Lesson Review   253

Lesson 2: Connection Managers, Tasks, and Precedence
    Constraint Expressions 254

    Expressions   255

    Property Expressions   259

    Precedence Constraint Expressions   259

    Lesson Summary   263

    Lesson Review   264

Lesson 3: Using a Master Package for Advanced Control Flow 265

    Separating Workloads, Purposes, and Objectives   267

    Harmonizing Workflow and Configuration   268

    The Execute Package Task   269

    The Execute SQL Server Agent Job Task   269

    The Execute Process Task   270

Lesson Summary 275

Lesson Review 275

Case Scenarios 276

Case Scenario 1: Complete Solutions 276

Case Scenario 2: Data-Driven Execution 277

Suggested Practices 277

Consider Using a Master Package 277

Answers. 278

Lesson 1 278

Lesson 2 279

Lesson 3 279

Case Scenario 1 280

Case Scenario 2 281

Chapter 7   Enhancing Data Flow   283

Before You Begin. 283

Lesson 1: Slowly Changing Dimensions 284

Defining Attribute Types 284

Inferred Dimension Members 285

Using the Slowly Changing Dimension Task 285

Effectively Updating Dimensions 290

Lesson Summary 298

Lesson Review 298

Lesson 2: Preparing a Package for Incremental Load. 299

Using Dynamic SQL to Read Data 299

Implementing CDC by Using SSIS 304

ETL Strategy for Incrementally Loading Fact Tables 307

Lesson Summary 316

Lesson Review 316

Lesson 3: Error Flow 317

Using Error Flows 317

Lesson Summary 321

Lesson Review 321

Case Scenario. 322

    Case Scenario: Loading Large Dimension and Fact Tables   322

Suggested Practices 322

    Load Additional Dimensions   322

Answers. 323

    Lesson 1   323

    Lesson 2   324

    Lesson 3   324

    Case Scenario   325

Chapter 8   Creating a Robust and Restartable Package   327

Before You Begin. 328

Lesson 1: Package Transactions 328

    Defining Package and Task Transaction Settings   328

    Transaction Isolation Levels   331

    Manually Handling Transactions   332

    Lesson Summary   335

    Lesson Review   335

Lesson 2: Checkpoints 336

    Implementing Restartability Checkpoints   336

    Lesson Summary   341

    Lesson Review   341

Lesson 3: Event Handlers. 342

    Using Event Handlers   342

    Lesson Summary   346

    Lesson Review   346

Case Scenario. 347

    Case Scenario: Auditing and Notifications in SSIS Packages   347

Suggested Practices 348

    Use Transactions and Event Handlers   348

Answers. 349

    Lesson 1   349

    Lesson 2   349

Lesson 3   350

Case Scenario   351

Chapter 9   Implementing Dynamic Packages   **353**

Before You Begin. 354

Lesson 1: Package-Level and Project-Level Connection
 Managers and Parameters. 354

Using Project-Level Connection Managers   355

Parameters   356

Build Configurations in SQL Server 2012 Integration Services   358

Property Expressions   361

Lesson Summary   366

Lesson Review   366

Lesson 2: Package Configurations 367

Implementing Package Configurations   368

Lesson Summary   377

Lesson Review   377

Case Scenario. 378

Case Scenario: Making SSIS Packages Dynamic   378

Suggested Practices 378

Use a Parameter to Incrementally Load a Fact Table   378

Answers. 379

Lesson 1   379

Lesson 2   379

Case Scenario   380

Chapter 10 Auditing and Logging   **381**

Before You Begin. 383

Lesson 1: Logging Packages 383

Log Providers   383

Configuring Logging   386

Lesson Summary   393

Lesson Review   394

Lesson 2: Implementing Auditing and Lineage 394

Auditing Techniques 395

Correlating Audit Data with SSIS Logs 401

Retention 401

Lesson Summary 405

Lesson Review 405

Lesson 3: Preparing Package Templates 406

SSIS Package Templates 407

Lesson Summary 410

Lesson Review 410

Case Scenarios 411

Case Scenario 1: Implementing SSIS Logging at Multiple
Levels of the SSIS Object Hierarchy 411

Case Scenario 2: Implementing SSIS Auditing at
Different Levels of the SSIS Object Hierarchy 412

Suggested Practices 412

Add Auditing to an Update Operation in an Existing
Execute SQL Task 412

Create an SSIS Package Template in Your Own Environment 413

Answers 414

Lesson 1 414

Lesson 2 415

Lesson 3 416

Case Scenario 1 417

Case Scenario 2 417

PART IV   MANAGING AND MAINTAINING SSIS PACKAGES

Chapter 11 Installing SSIS and Deploying Packages   421

Before You Begin. 422

Lesson 1: Installing SSIS Components 423

Preparing an SSIS Installation 424

Installing SSIS 428

Lesson Summary 436

Lesson Review 436

Lesson 2: Deploying SSIS Packages 437

    SSISDB Catalog   438

    SSISDB Objects   440

    Project Deployment   442

    Lesson Summary   449

    Lesson Review   450

Case Scenarios 450

    Case Scenario 1: Using Strictly Structured Deployments   451

    Case Scenario 2: Installing an SSIS Server   451

Suggested Practices 451

    Upgrade Existing SSIS Solutions   451

Answers 452

    Lesson 1   452

    Lesson 2   453

    Case Scenario 1   454

    Case Scenario 2   454

Chapter 12 Executing and Securing Packages   455

Before You Begin 456

Lesson 1: Executing SSIS Packages 456

    On-Demand SSIS Execution   457

    Automated SSIS Execution   462

    Monitoring SSIS Execution   465

    Lesson Summary   479

    Lesson Review   479

Lesson 2: Securing SSIS Packages 480

    SSISDB Security   481

    Lesson Summary   490

    Lesson Review   490

Case Scenarios 491

    Case Scenario 1: Deploying SSIS Packages to Multiple
Environments   491

    Case Scenario 2: Remote Executions   491

Suggested Practices 491

    Improve the Reusability of an SSIS Solution   492

Answers. 493

    Lesson 1   493

    Lesson 2   494

    Case Scenario 1   495

    Case Scenario 2   495

Chapter 13   Troubleshooting and Performance Tuning   497

Before You Begin. 498

Lesson 1: Troubleshooting Package Execution 498

    Design-Time Troubleshooting   498

    Production-Time Troubleshooting   506

    Lesson Summary   510

    Lesson Review   510

Lesson 2: Performance Tuning 511

    SSIS Data Flow Engine   512

    Data Flow Tuning Options   514

    Parallel Execution in SSIS   517

    Troubleshooting and Benchmarking Performance   518

    Lesson Summary   522

    Lesson Review   522

Case Scenario. 523

    Case Scenario: Tuning an SSIS Package   523

Suggested Practice 524

    Get Familiar with SSISDB Catalog Views   524

Answers. 525

    Lesson 1   525

    Lesson 2   525

    Case Scenario   526

Chapter 14 Installing and Maintaining Data Quality Services   529

Before You Begin. 530

Lesson 1: Data Quality Problems and Roles. 530

    Data Quality Dimensions   531

    Data Quality Activities and Roles   535

    Lesson Summary   539

    Lesson Review   539

Lesson 2: Installing Data Quality Services. 540

    DQS Architecture   540

    DQS Installation   542

    Lesson Summary   548

    Lesson Review   548

Lesson 3: Maintaining and Securing Data Quality Services. 549

    Performing Administrative Activities with Data Quality Client   549

    Performing Administrative Activities with Other Tools   553

    Lesson Summary   558

    Lesson Review   558

Case Scenario. 559

    Case Scenario: Data Warehouse Not Used   559

Suggested Practices 560

    Analyze the AdventureWorksDW2012 Database   560

    Review Data Profiling Tools   560

Answers. 561

    Lesson 1   561

    Lesson 2   561

    Lesson 3   562

    Case Scenario   563

Chapter 15 Implementing Master Data Services   565

Before You Begin. 565

Lesson 1: Defining Master Data 566

    What Is Master Data?   567

    Master Data Management   569

    MDM Challenges   572

    Lesson Summary   574

    Lesson Review   574

Lesson 2: Installing Master Data Services. 575

    Master Data Services Architecture   576

    MDS Installation   577

    Lesson Summary   587

    Lesson Review   587

Lesson 3: Creating a Master Data Services Model 588

    MDS Models and Objects in Models   588

    MDS Objects   589

    Lesson Summary   599

    Lesson Review   600

Case Scenarios. 600

    Case Scenario 1: Introducing an MDM Solution   600

    Case Scenario 2: Extending the POC Project   601

Suggested Practices 601

    Analyze the AdventureWorks2012 Database   601

    Expand the MDS Model   601

Answers. 602

    Lesson 1   602

    Lesson 2   603

    Lesson 3   603

    Case Scenario 1   604

    Case Scenario 2   604

Chapter 16 Managing Master Data   605

Before You Begin. 605

Lesson 1: Importing and Exporting Master Data 606

    Creating and Deploying MDS Packages   606

    Importing Batches of Data   607

    Exporting Data   609

    Lesson Summary   615

    Lesson Review   616

Lesson 2: Defining Master Data Security 616

    Users and Permissions   617

    Overlapping Permissions   619

    Lesson Summary   624

    Lesson Review   624

Lesson 3: Using Master Data Services Add-in for Excel 624

    Editing MDS Data in Excel   625

    Creating MDS Objects in Excel   627

    Lesson Summary   632

    Lesson Review   632

Case Scenario. 633

    Case Scenario: Editing Batches of MDS Data   633

Suggested Practices 633

    Analyze the Staging Tables   633

    Test Security   633

Answers. 634

    Lesson 1   634

    Lesson 2   635

    Lesson 3   635

    Case Scenario   636

Chapter 17 Creating a Data Quality Project to Clean Data   637

Before You Begin. 637

Lesson 1: Creating and Maintaining a Knowledge Base 638

    Building a DQS Knowledge Base   638

    Domain Management   639

    Lesson Summary   645

    Lesson Review   645

Lesson 2: Creating a Data Quality Project 646

    DQS Projects   646

    Data Cleansing   647

    Lesson Summary   653

    Lesson Review   653

Lesson 3: Profiling Data and Improving Data Quality 654

    Using Queries to Profile Data   654

    SSIS Data Profiling Task   656

    Lesson Summary   659

    Lesson Review   660

Case Scenario. 660

    Case Scenario: Improving Data Quality   660

Suggested Practices 661

    Create an Additional Knowledge Base and Project   661

Answers. 662

    Lesson 1   662

    Lesson 2   662

    Lesson 3   663

    Case Scenario   664

PART VI   ADVANCED SSIS AND DATA QUALITY TOPICS

Chapter 18 SSIS and Data Mining   667

Before You Begin. 667

Lesson 1: Data Mining Task and Transformation. 668

    What Is Data Mining?   668

    SSAS Data Mining Algorithms   670

Using Data Mining Predictions in SSIS 671

Lesson Summary 679

Lesson Review 679

Lesson 2: Text Mining. 679

Term Extraction 680

Term Lookup 681

Lesson Summary 686

Lesson Review 686

Lesson 3: Preparing Data for Data Mining 687

Preparing the Data 688

SSIS Sampling 689

Lesson Summary 693

Lesson Review 693

Case Scenario. 694

Case Scenario: Preparing Data for Data Mining 694

Suggested Practices 694

Test the Row Sampling and Conditional Split Transformations 694

Answers. 695

Lesson 1 695

Lesson 2 695

Lesson 3 696

Case Scenario 697

Chapter 19 Implementing Custom Code in SSIS Packages   699

Before You Begin. 700

Lesson 1: Script Task. 700

Configuring the Script Task 701

Coding the Script Task 702

Lesson Summary 707

Lesson Review 707

Lesson 2: Script Component 707

Configuring the Script Component 708

Coding the Script Component 709

Lesson Summary   715

Lesson Review   715

Lesson 3: Implementing Custom Components 716

Planning a Custom Component   717

Developing a Custom Component   718

Design Time and Run Time   719

Design-Time Methods   719

Run-Time Methods   721

Lesson Summary   730

Lesson Review   730

Case Scenario. 731

Case Scenario: Data Cleansing   731

Suggested Practices 731

Create a Web Service Source   731

Answers. 732

Lesson 1   732

Lesson 2   732

Lesson 3   733

Case Scenario   734

Chapter 20 Identity Mapping and De-Duplicating   735

Before You Begin. 736

Lesson 1: Understanding the Problem 736

Identity Mapping and De-Duplicating Problems   736

Solving the Problems   738

Lesson Summary   744

Lesson Review   744

Lesson 2: Using DQS and the DQS Cleansing Transformation 745

DQS Cleansing Transformation   746

DQS Matching   746

Lesson Summary   755

Lesson Review   755

Lesson 3: Implementing SSIS Fuzzy Transformations 756

    Fuzzy Transformations Algorithm   756

    Versions of Fuzzy Transformations   758

    Lesson Summary   764

    Lesson Review   764

Case Scenario. 765

    Case Scenario: Improving Data Quality   765

Suggested Practices 765

    Research More on Matching   765

Answers. 766

    Lesson 1   766

    Lesson 2   766

    Lesson 3   767

    Case Scenario   768

Index   *769*

Introduction

This Training Kit is designed for information technology (IT) professionals who support or plan to support data warehouses, extract-transform-load (ETL) processes, data quality improvements, and master data management. It is designed for IT professionals who also plan to take the Microsoft Certified Technology Specialist (MCTS) exam 70-463. The authors assume that you have a solid, foundation-level understanding of Microsoft SQL Server 2012 and the Transact-SQL language, and that you understand basic relational modeling concepts.

The material covered in this Training Kit and on Exam 70-463 relates to the technologies provided by SQL Server 2012 for implementing and maintaining a data warehouse. The topics in this Training Kit cover what you need to know for the exam as described on the Skills Measured tab for the exam, available at:

   http://www.microsoft.com/learning/en/us/exam.aspx?id=70-463

By studying this Training Kit, you will see how to perform the following tasks:

- Design an appropriate data model for a data warehouse
- Optimize the physical design of a data warehouse
- Extract data from different data sources, transform and cleanse the data, and load it in your data warehouse by using SQL Server Integration Services (SSIS)
- Use advanced SSIS components
- Use SQL Server 2012 Master Data Services (MDS) to take control of your master data
- Use SQL Server Data Quality Services (DQS) for data cleansing

Refer to the objective mapping page in the front of this book to see where in the book each exam objective is covered.

System Requirements

The following are the minimum system requirements for the computer you will be using to complete the practice exercises in this book and to run the companion CD.

SQL Server and Other Software Requirements

This section contains the minimum SQL Server and other software requirements you will need:

- **SQL Server 2012**   You need access to a SQL Server 2012 instance with a logon that has permissions to create new databases—preferably one that is a member of the sysadmin role. For the purposes of this Training Kit, you can use almost any edition of on-premises SQL Server (Standard, Enterprise, Business Intelligence, and Developer), both 32-bit and 64-bit editions. If you don't have access to an existing SQL Server instance, you can install a trial copy of SQL Server 2012 that you can use for 180 days. You can download a trial copy here:

> *http://www.microsoft.com/sqlserver/en/us/get-sql-server/try-it.aspx*

- **SQL Server 2012 Setup Feature Selection**   When you are in the Feature Selection dialog box of the SQL Server 2012 setup program, choose at minimum the following components:

  - Database Engine Services

  - Documentation Components

  - Management Tools - Basic

  - Management Tools – Complete

  - SQL Server Data Tools

- **Windows Software Development Kit (SDK) or Microsoft Visual Studio 2010**   The Windows SDK provides tools, compilers, headers, libraries, code samples, and a new help system that you can use to create applications that run on Windows. You need the Windows SDK for Chapter 19, "Implementing Custom Code in SSIS Packages" only. If you already have Visual Studio 2010, you do not need the Windows SDK. If you need the Windows SDK, you need to download the appropriate version for your operating system. For Windows 7, Windows Server 2003 R2 Standard Edition (32-bit x86), Windows Server 2003 R2 Standard x64 Edition, Windows Server 2008, Windows Server 2008 R2, Windows Vista, or Windows XP Service Pack 3, use the Microsoft Windows SDK for Windows 7 and the Microsoft .NET Framework 4 from:

  > *http://www.microsoft.com/en-us/download/details.aspx?id=8279*

Hardware and Operating System Requirements

You can find the minimum hardware and operating system requirements for SQL Server 2012 here:

> *http://msdn.microsoft.com/en-us/library/ms143506(v=sql.110).aspx*

Data Requirements

The minimum data requirements for the exercises in this Training Kit are the following:

- **The AdventureWorks OLTP and DW databases for SQL Server 2012**   Exercises in this book use the AdventureWorks online transactional processing (OLTP) database, which supports standard online transaction processing scenarios for a fictitious bicycle manufacturer (Adventure Works Cycles), and the AdventureWorks data warehouse (DW) database, which demonstrates how to build a data warehouse. You need to download both databases for SQL Server 2012. You can download both databases from:

http://msftdbprodsamples.codeplex.com/releases/view/55330

You can also download the compressed file containing the data (.mdf) files for both databases from O'Reilly's website here:

http://go.microsoft.com/FWLink/?Linkid=260986

Using the Companion CD

A companion CD is included with this Training Kit. The companion CD contains the following:

- **Practice tests**   You can reinforce your understanding of the topics covered in this Training Kit by using electronic practice tests that you customize to meet your needs. You can practice for the 70-463 certification exam by using tests created from a pool of over 200 realistic exam questions, which give you many practice exams to ensure that you are prepared.

- **An eBook**   An electronic version (eBook) of this book is included for when you do not want to carry the printed book with you.

- **Source code**   A compressed file called TK70463_CodeLabSolutions.zip includes the Training Kit's demo source code and exercise solutions. You can also download the compressed file from O'Reilly's website here:

   http://go.microsoft.com/FWLink/?Linkid=260986

   For convenient access to the source code, create a local folder called **C:\TK463** and extract the compressed archive by using this folder as the destination for the extracted files.

- **Sample data**   A compressed file called AdventureWorksDataFiles.zip includes the Training Kit's demo source code and exercise solutions. You can also download the compressed file from O'Reilly's website here:

   http://go.microsoft.com/FWLink/?Linkid=260986

   For convenient access to the source code, create a local folder called **C:\TK463** and extract the compressed archive by using this folder as the destination for the extracted files. Then use SQL Server Management Studio (SSMS) to attach both databases and create the log files for them.

How to Install the Practice Tests

To install the practice test software from the companion CD to your hard disk, perform the following steps:

1. Insert the companion CD into your CD drive and accept the license agreement. A CD menu appears.

    NOTE **IF THE CD MENU DOES NOT APPEAR**

    If the CD menu or the license agreement does not appear, AutoRun might be disabled on your computer. Refer to the Readme.txt file on the CD for alternate installation instructions.

2. Click Practice Tests and follow the instructions on the screen.

How to Use the Practice Tests

To start the practice test software, follow these steps:

1. Click Start | All Programs, and then select Microsoft Press Training Kit Exam Prep.

    A window appears that shows all the Microsoft Press Training Kit exam prep suites installed on your computer.

2. Double-click the practice test you want to use.

When you start a practice test, you choose whether to take the test in Certification Mode, Study Mode, or Custom Mode:

- **Certification Mode** Closely resembles the experience of taking a certification exam. The test has a set number of questions. It is timed, and you cannot pause and restart the timer.

- **Study Mode** Creates an untimed test during which you can review the correct answers and the explanations after you answer each question.

- **Custom Mode** Gives you full control over the test options so that you can customize them as you like.

In all modes, when you are taking the test, the user interface is basically the same but with different options enabled or disabled depending on the mode.

When you review your answer to an individual practice test question, a "References" section is provided that lists where in the Training Kit you can find the information that relates to that question and provides links to other sources of information. After you click Test Results to score your entire practice test, you can click the Learning Plan tab to see a list of references for every objective.

How to Uninstall the Practice Tests

To uninstall the practice test software for a Training Kit, use the Program And Features option in Windows Control Panel.

Acknowledgments

A book is put together by many more people than the authors whose names are listed on the title page. We'd like to express our gratitude to the following people for all the work they have done in getting this book into your hands: Miloš Radivojević (technical editor) and Fritz Lechnitz (project manager) from SolidQ, Russell Jones (acquisitions and developmental editor) and Holly Bauer (production editor) from O'Reilly, and Kathy Krause (copyeditor) and Jaime Odell (proofreader) from OTSI. In addition, we would like to give thanks to Matt Masson (member of the SSIS team), Wee Hyong Tok (SSIS team program manager), and Elad Ziklik (DQS group program manager) from Microsoft for the technical support and for unveiling the secrets of the new SQL Server 2012 products. There are many more people involved in writing and editing practice test questions, editing graphics, and performing other activities; we are grateful to all of them as well.

Support & Feedback

The following sections provide information on errata, book support, feedback, and contact information.

Errata

We've made every effort to ensure the accuracy of this book and its companion content. Any errors that have been reported since this book was published are listed on our Microsoft Press site:

http://go.microsoft.com/FWLink/?Linkid=260985

If you find an error that is not already listed, you can report it to us through the same page.

If you need additional support, email Microsoft Press Book Support at:

mspinput@microsoft.com

Please note that product support for Microsoft software is not offered through the addresses above.

We Want to Hear from You

At Microsoft Press, your satisfaction is our top priority, and your feedback our most valuable asset. Please tell us what you think of this book at:

> *http://www.microsoft.com/learning/booksurvey*

The survey is short, and we read every one of your comments and ideas. Thanks in advance for your input!

Stay in Touch

Let's keep the conversation going! We are on Twitter: *http://twitter.com/MicrosoftPress*.

Preparing for the Exam

Microsoft certification exams are a great way to build your resume and let the world know about your level of expertise. Certification exams validate your on-the-job experience and product knowledge. While there is no substitution for on-the-job experience, preparation through study and hands-on practice can help you prepare for the exam. We recommend that you round out your exam preparation plan by using a combination of available study materials and courses. For example, you might use the training kit and another study guide for your "at home" preparation, and take a Microsoft Official Curriculum course for the classroom experience. Choose the combination that you think works best for you.

Note that this training kit is based on publicly available information about the exam and the authors' experience. To safeguard the integrity of the exam, authors do not have access to the live exam.

PART I

Designing and Implementing a Data Warehouse

CHAPTER 1   Data Warehouse Logical Design   **3**

CHAPTER 2   Implementing a Data Warehouse   **41**

Data Warehouse Logical Design

Exam objectives in this chapter:

- Design and Implement a Data Warehouse
  - Design and implement dimensions.
  - Design and implement fact tables.

Analyzing data from databases that support line-of-business (LOB) applications is usually not an easy task. The normalized relational schema used for an LOB application can consist of thousands of tables. Naming conventions are frequently not enforced. Therefore, it is hard to discover where the data you need for a report is stored. Enterprises frequently have multiple LOB applications, often working against more than one database. For the purposes of analysis, these enterprises need to be able to merge the data from multiple databases. Data quality is a common problem as well. In addition, many LOB applications do not track data over time, though many analyses depend on historical data.

> **IMPORTANT**
>
> ### *Have you read page xxxii?*
>
> It contains valuable information regarding the skills you need to pass the exam.

 A common solution to these problems is to create a *data warehouse (DW)*. A DW is a centralized data silo for an enterprise that contains merged, cleansed, and historical data. DW schemas are simplified and thus more suitable for generating reports than normalized relational schemas. For a DW, you typically use a special type of logical design called a Star schema, or a variant of the Star schema called a Snowflake schema. Tables in a Star or Snowflake schema are divided into dimension tables (commonly known as *dimensions*) and fact tables.

Data in a DW usually comes from LOB databases, but it's a transformed and cleansed copy of source data. Of course, there is some latency between the moment when data appears in an LOB database and the moment when it appears in a DW. One common method of addressing this latency involves refreshing the data in a DW as a nightly job. You use the refreshed data primarily for reports; therefore, the data is mostly read and rarely updated.

Queries often involve reading huge amounts of data and require large scans. To support such queries, it is imperative to use an appropriate physical design for a DW.

DW logical design seems to be simple at first glance. It is definitely much simpler than a normalized relational design. However, despite the simplicity, you can still encounter some advanced problems. In this chapter, you will learn how to design a DW and how to solve some of the common advanced design problems. You will explore Star and Snowflake schemas, dimensions, and fact tables. You will also learn how to track the source and time for data coming into a DW through auditing—or, in DW terminology, *lineage information*.

Lessons in this chapter:

- Lesson 1: Introducing Star and Snowflake Schemas
- Lesson 2: Designing Dimensions
- Lesson 3: Designing Fact Tables

Before You Begin

To complete this chapter, you must have:

- An understanding of normalized relational schemas.
- Experience working with Microsoft SQL Server 2012 Management Studio.
- A working knowledge of the Transact-SQL language.
- The AdventureWorks2012 and AdventureWorksDW2012 sample databases installed.

Lesson 1: Introducing Star and Snowflake Schemas

Before you design a data warehouse, you need to understand some common design patterns used for a DW, namely the Star and Snowflake schemas. These schemas evolved in the 1980s. In particular, the Star schema is currently so widely used that it has become a kind of informal standard for all types of business intelligence (BI) applications.

> **After this lesson, you will be able to:**
> - Understand why a normalized schema causes reporting problems.
> - Understand the Star schema.
> - Understand the Snowflake schema.
> - Determine granularity and auditing needs.
>
> **Estimated lesson time: 40 minutes**

Reporting Problems with a Normalized Schema

This lesson starts with normalized relational schema. Let's assume that you have to create a business report from a relational schema in the AdventureWorks2012 sample database. The report should include the sales amount for Internet sales in different countries over multiple years. The task (or even challenge) is to find out which tables and columns you would need to create the report. You start by investigating which tables store the data you need, as shown in Figure 1-1, which was created with the diagramming utility in SQL Server Management Studio (SSMS).

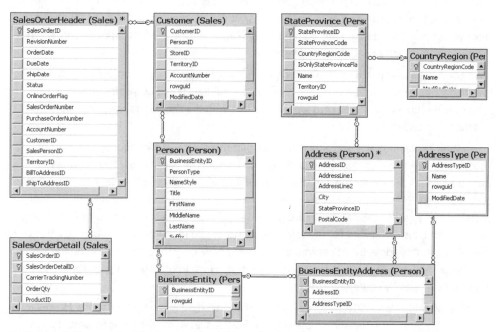

FIGURE 1-1 A diagram of tables you would need for a simple sales report.

Even for this relatively simple report, you would end up with 10 tables. You need the sales tables and the tables containing information about customers. The AdventureWorks2012 database schema is highly normalized; it's intended as an example schema to support LOB applications. Although such a schema works extremely well for LOB applications, it can cause problems when used as the source for reports, as you'll see in the rest of this section.

Normalization is a process in which you define entities in such a way that a single table represents exactly one entity. The goal is to have a complete and non-redundant schema. Every piece of information must be stored exactly once. This way, you can enforce data integrity. You have a place for every piece of data, and because each data item is stored only once, you do not have consistency problems. However, after a proper normalization, you typically wind up with many tables. In a database that supports an LOB application for an enterprise, you might finish with thousands of tables!

Finding the appropriate tables and columns you need for a report can be painful in a normalized database simply because of the number of tables involved. Add to this the fact that nothing forces database developers to maintain good naming conventions in an LOB database. It's relatively easy to find the pertinent tables in AdventureWorks2012, because the tables and columns have meaningful names. But imagine if the database contained tables named *Table1*, *Table2*, and so on, and columns named *Column1*, *Column2*, and so on. Finding the objects you need for your report would be a nightmare. Tools such as SQL Profiler might help. For example, you could create a test environment, try to insert some data through an LOB application, and have SQL Profiler identify where the data was inserted. A normalized schema is not very narrative. You cannot easily spot the storage location for data that measures something, such as the sales amount in this example, or the data that gives context to these measures, such as countries and years.

In addition, a query that joins 10 tables, as would be required in reporting sales by countries and years, would not be very fast. The query would also read huge amounts of data—sales over multiple years—and thus would interfere with the regular transactional work of inserting and updating the data.

Another problem in this example is the fact that there is no explicit lookup table for dates. You have to extract years from date or date/time columns in sales tables, such as *OrderDate* from the *SalesOrderHeader* table in this example. Extracting years from a date column is not such a big deal; however, the first question is, does the LOB database store data for multiple years? In many cases, LOB databases are purged after each new fiscal year starts. Even if you have all of the historical data for the sales transactions, you might have a problem showing the historical data correctly. For example, you might have only the latest customer address (from which you extract customer's current country), which might prevent you from calculating historical sales by country correctly.

The AdventureWorks2012 sample database stores all data in a single database. However, in an enterprise, you might have multiple LOB applications, each of which might store data in its own database. You might also have part of the sales data in one database and part in another. And you could have customer data in both databases, without a common identification. In such cases, you face the problems of how to merge all this data and how to identify which customer from one database is actually the same as a customer from another database.

Finally, data quality could be low. The old rule, "garbage in garbage out," applies to analyses as well. Parts of the data could be missing; other parts could be wrong. Even with good data, you could still have different representations of the same data in different databases. For example, gender in one database could be represented with the letters F and M, and in another database with the numbers 1 and 2.

The problems listed in this section are indicative of the problems that led designers to create different schemas for BI applications. The Star and Snowflake schemas are both simplified and narrative. A data warehouse should use Star and/or Snowflake designs. You'll also sometimes find the term *dimensional model* used for a DW schema. A dimensional model actually consists of both Star and Snowflake schemas. This is a good time to introduce the Star and Snowflake schemas.

Star Schema

Often, a picture is worth more than a thousand words. Figure 1-2 shows a *Star schema*, a diagram created in SSMS from a subset of the tables in the AdventureWorksDW2012 sample database.

In Figure 1-2, you can easily spot how the Star schema got its name—it resembles a star. There is a single central table, called a *fact table*, surrounded by multiple tables called *dimensions*. One Star schema covers one business area. In this case, the schema covers Internet sales. An enterprise data warehouse covers multiple business areas and consists of multiple Star (and/or Snowflake) schemas.

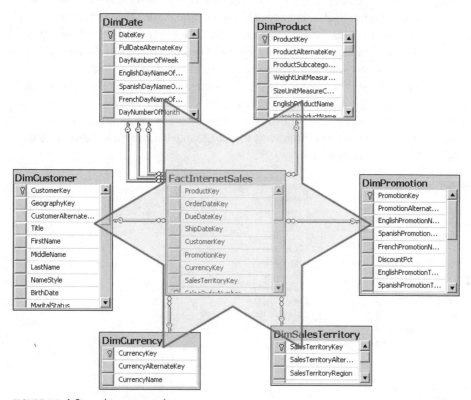

FIGURE 1-2 A Star schema example.

The fact table is connected to all the dimensions with foreign keys. Usually, all foreign keys taken together uniquely identify each row in the fact table, and thus collectively form a unique key, so you can use all the foreign keys as a composite primary key of the fact table. You can also add a simpler key. The fact table is on the "many" side of its relationships with the dimensions. If you were to form a proposition from a row in a fact table, you might express it with a sentence such as, "Customer A purchased product B on date C in quantity D for amount E." This proposition is a fact; this is how the fact table got its name.

The Star schema evolved from a conceptual model of a cube. You can imagine all sales as a big box. When you search for a problem in sales data, you use a divide-and-conquer technique: slicing the cube over different categories of customers, products, or time. In other words, you slice the cube over its dimensions. Therefore, customers, products, and time represent the three dimensions in the conceptual model of the sales cube. Dimension tables (dimensions) got their name from this conceptual model. In a logical model of a Star schema, you can represent more than three dimensions. Therefore, a Star schema represents a multi-dimensional hypercube.

As you already know, a data warehouse consists of multiple Star schemas. From a business perspective, these Star schemas are connected. For example, you have the same customers in sales as in accounting. You deal with many of the same products in sales, inventory, and production. Of course, your business is performed at the same time over all the different business areas. To represent the business correctly, you must be able to connect the multiple Star schemas in your data warehouse. The connection is simple – you use the same dimensions for each Star schema. In fact, the dimensions should be shared among multiple Star schemas. Dimensions have foreign key relationships with multiple fact tables. Dimensions with connections to multiple fact tables are called *shared* or *conformed dimensions*. Figure 1-3 shows a conformed dimension from the AdventureWorksDW2012 sample database with two different fact tables sharing the same dimension.

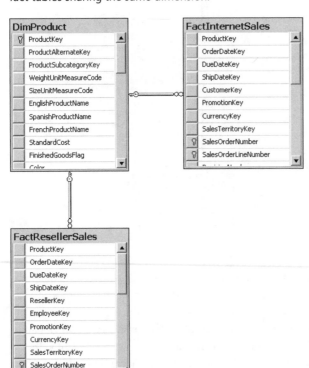

FIGURE 1-3 *DimProduct* is a shared dimension.

In the past, there was a big debate over whether to use shared or private dimensions. Private dimensions are dimensions that pertain to only a single Star schema. However, it is quite simple to design shared dimensions; you do not gain much from the design-time perspective by using private dimensions. In fact, with private dimensions, you lose the connections between the different fact tables, so you cannot compare the data in different fact tables over the same dimensions. For example, you could not compare sales and accounting data for the same customer if the sales and accounting fact tables didn't share the same customer dimension. Therefore, unless you are creating a small proof-of-concept (POC) project that covers only a single business area where you do not care about connections with different business areas, you should always opt for shared dimensions.

A data warehouse is often the source for specialized analytical database management systems, such as SQL Server Analysis Services (SSAS). SSAS is a system that performs specialized analyses by drilling down and is used for analyses that are based on the conceptual model of a cube. Systems such as SSAS focus on a single task and fast analyses, and they're considerably more optimized for this task than general systems such as SQL Server. SSAS enables analysis in real time, a process called *online analytical processing* (OLAP). However, to get such performance, you have to pay a price. SSAS is out of the scope of this book, but you have to know the limitations of SSAS to prepare a data warehouse in a way that is useful for SSAS. One thing to remember is that in an SSAS database, you can use shared dimensions only. This is just one more reason why you should prefer shared to private dimensions.

Snowflake Schema

Figure 1-4 shows a more detailed view of the *DimDate* dimension from the AdventureWorks-DW2012 sample database.

The highlighted attributes show that the dimension is denormalized. It is not in third normal form. In third normal form, all non-key columns should nontransitively depend on the key. A different way to say this is that there should be no functional dependency between non-key columns. You should be able to retrieve the value of a non-key column only if you know the key. However, in the *DimDate* dimension, if you know the month, you obviously know the calendar quarter, and if you know the calendar quarter, you know the calendar semester.

In a Star schema, dimensions are denormalized. In contrast, in an LOB normalized schema, you would split the table into multiple tables if you found a dependency between non-key columns. Figure 1-5 shows such a normalized example for the *DimProduct*, *DimProduct-Subcategory* and *DimProductCategory* tables from the AdventureWorksDW2012 database.

FIGURE 1-4 The *DimDate* denormalized dimension.

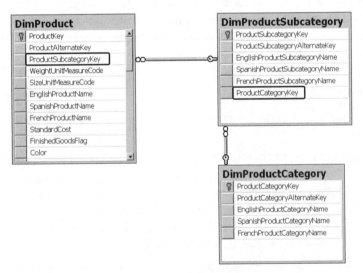

FIGURE 1-5 The *DimProduct* normalized dimension.

The *DimProduct* dimension is not denormalized. The *DimProduct* table does not contain the subcategory name, only the ProductSubcategoryKey value for the foreign key to the *DimProductSubcategory* lookup table. Similarly, the *DimProductSubcategory* table does not contain a category name; it just holds the foreign key ProductCategoryKey from the *Dim-ProductCategory* table. This design is typical of an LOB database schema.

You can imagine multiple dimensions designed in a similar normalized way, with a central fact table connected by foreign keys to dimension tables, which are connected with foreign keys to lookup tables, which are connected with foreign keys to second-level lookup tables.

In this configuration, a star starts to resemble a snowflake. Therefore, a Star schema with normalized dimensions is called a *Snowflake schema*.

In most long-term projects, you should design Star schemas. Because the Star schema is simpler than a Snowflake schema, it is also easier to maintain. Queries on a Star schema are simpler and faster than queries on a Snowflake schema, because they involve fewer joins. The Snowflake schema is more appropriate for short POC projects, because it is closer to an LOB normalized relational schema and thus requires less work to build.

EXAM TIP

If you do not use OLAP cubes and your reports query your data warehouse directly, then using a Star instead of a Snowflake schema might speed up the reports, because your reporting queries involve fewer joins.

In some cases, you can also employ a hybrid approach, using a Snowflake schema only for the first level of a dimension lookup table. In this type of approach, there are no additional levels of lookup tables; the first-level lookup table is denormalized. Figure 1-6 shows such a partially denormalized schema.

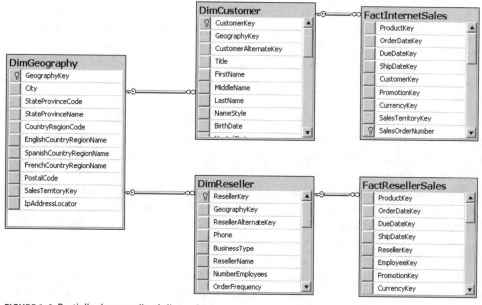

FIGURE 1-6 Partially denormalized dimensions.

In Figure 1-6, the *DimCustomer* and *DimReseller* dimensions are partially normalized. The dimensions now contain only the GeographyKey foreign key. However, the *DimGeography* table is denormalized. There is no additional lookup table even though a city is in a region and a region is in a country. A hybrid design such as this means that geography data is written only once and needs to be maintained in only a single place. Such a design is appropriate when multiple dimensions share the same attributes. In other cases, you should use the simpler Star schema. To repeat: you should use a Snowflake schema only for quick POC projects.

> **✓ Quick Check**
> - How do you connect multiple Star schemas in a DW?
>
> **Quick Check Answer**
> - You connect multiple Star schemas through shared dimensions.

Granularity Level

The number of dimensions connected with a fact table defines the level of granularity of analysis you can get. For example, if no products dimension is connected to a sales fact table, you cannot get a report at the product level—you could get a report for sales for all products only. This kind of granularity is also called the *dimensionality* of a Star schema.

But there is another kind of granularity, which lets you know what level of information a dimension foreign key represents in a fact table. Different fact tables can have different granularity in a connection to the same dimension. This is very typical in budgeting and planning scenarios. For example, you do not plan that customer A will come on date B to store C and buy product D for amount E. Instead, you plan on a higher level—you might plan to sell amount E of products C in quarter B in all stores in that region to all customers in that region. Figure 1-7 shows an example of a fact table that uses a higher level of granularity than the fact tables introduced so far.

In the AdventureWorksDW2012 database, the *FactSalesQuota* table is the fact table with planning data. However, plans are made for employees at the per-quarter level only. The plan is for all customers, all products, and so on, because this Star schema uses only the *DimDate* and *DimEmployee* dimensions. In addition, planning occurs at the quarterly level. By investigating the content, you could see that all plans for a quarter are bound to the first day of a quarter. You would not need to use the DateKey; you could have only *CalendarYear* and *CalendarQuarter* columns in the *FactSalesQuota* fact table. You could still perform joins to *DimDate* by using these two columns—they are both present in the *DimDate* table as well. However, if you want to have a foreign key to the *DimDate* dimension, you do need the DateKey. A foreign key must refer to unique values on the "one" side of the relationship. The combination of *CalendarYear* and *CalendarQuarter* is, of course, not unique in the *DimDate* dimension; it repeats approximately 90 times in each quarter.

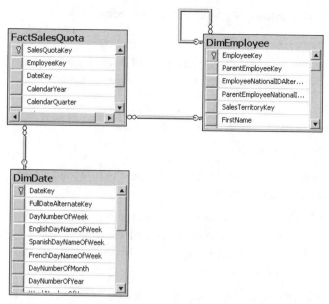

FIGURE 1-7 A fact table with a higher level of granularity.

Auditing and Lineage

In addition to tables for reports, a data warehouse may also include auditing tables. For every update, you should audit who made the update, when it was made, and how many rows were transferred to each dimension and fact table in your DW. If you also audit how much time was needed for each load, you can calculate the performance and take action if it deteriorates. You store this information in an auditing table or tables. However, you should realize that auditing does not help you unless you analyze the information regularly.

Auditing tables hold batch-level information about regular DW loads, but you might also want or need to have more detailed information. For example, you might want to know where each row in a dimension and/or fact table came from and when it was added. In such cases, you must add appropriate columns to the dimension and fact tables. Such detailed auditing information is also called *lineage* in DW terminology. To collect either auditing or lineage information, you need to modify the extract-transform-load (ETL) process you use for DW loads appropriately.

If your ETL tool is SQL Server Integration Services (SSIS), then you should use SSIS logging. SSIS has extensive logging support. In addition, SSIS also has support for lineage information.

Reviewing the AdventureWorksDW2012 Internet Sales Schema

The AdventureWorksDW2012 sample database is a good example of a data warehouse. It has all the elements needed to allow you to see examples of various types of dimensional modeling.

EXERCISE 1   Review the AdventureWorksDW2012 Database Schema

In this exercise, you review the database schema.

1. Start SSMS and connect to your instance of SQL Server. Expand the Databases folder and then the AdventureWorksDW2012 database.

2. Right-click the Database Diagrams folder and select the New Database Diagram option. If no diagrams were ever created in this database, you will see a message box informing you that the database has no support objects for diagramming. If that message appears, click Yes to create the support objects.

3. From the Add Table list, select the following tables (click each table and then click the Add button):

    - *DimCustomer*
    - *DimDate*
    - *DimGeography*
    - *DimProduct*
    - *DimProductCategory*
    - *DimProductSubcategory*
    - *FactInternetSales*

    Your diagram should look similar to Figure 1-8.

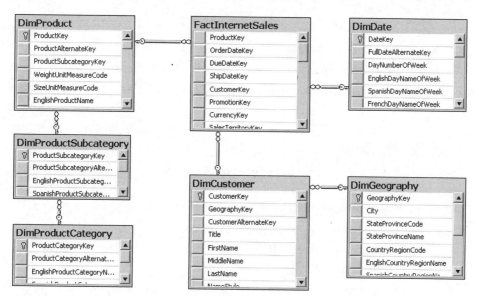

FIGURE 1-8 The AdventureWorksDW2012 Internet Sales Schema.

4. Thoroughly analyze the tables, columns, and relationships.

5. Save the diagram with the name **Practice_01_01_InternetSales**.

EXERCISE 2 Analyze the Diagram

Review the AdventureWorksDW2012 schema to note the following facts:

- The *DimDate* dimension has no additional lookup tables associated with it and therefore uses the Star schema.

- The *DimProduct* table is snowflaked; it uses the *DimProductSubcategory* lookup table, which further uses the *DimProductCategory* lookup table.

- The *DimCustomer* dimension uses a hybrid schema—the first level of the Snowflake schema only through the *DimGeography* lookup table. The *DimGeography* table is denormalized; it does not have a relationship with any other lookup table.

- There are no specific columns for lineage information in any of the tables.

Close the diagram.

NOTE CONTINUING WITH PRACTICES

Do not exit SSMS if you intend to continue immediately with the next practice.

Lesson Summary

- The Star schema is the most common design for a DW.
- The Snowflake schema is more appropriate for POC projects.
- You should also determine the granularity of fact tables, as well as auditing and lineage needs.

Lesson Review

Answer the following questions to test your knowledge of the information in this lesson. You can find the answers to these questions and explanations of why each answer choice is correct or incorrect in the "Answers" section at the end of this chapter.

1. Reporting from a Star schema is simpler than reporting from a normalized online transactional processing (OLTP) schema. What are the reasons for wanting simpler reporting? (Choose all that apply.)

   A. A Star schema typically has fewer tables than a normalized schema. Therefore, queries are simpler because they require fewer joins.

   B. A Star schema has better support for numeric data types than a normalized relational schema; therefore, it is easier to create aggregates.

   C. There are specific Transact-SQL expressions that deal with Star schemas.

   D. A Star schema is standardized and narrative; you can find the information you need for a report quickly.

2. You are creating a quick POC project. Which schema is the most suitable for this kind of a project?

   A. Star schema

   B. Normalized schema

   C. Snowflake schema

   D. XML schema

3. A Star schema has two types of tables. What are those two types? (Choose all that apply.)

   A. Lookup tables

   B. Dimensions

   C. Measures

   D. Fact tables

Lesson 2: Designing Dimensions

Star and Snowflake schemas are the de facto standard. However, the standard does not end with schema shapes. Dimension and fact table columns are part of this informal standard as well and are introduced in this lesson, along with natural hierarchies, which are especially useful as natural drill-down paths for analyses. Finally, the lesson discusses a common problem with handling dimension changes over time.

> **After this lesson, you will be able to:**
> - Define dimension column types.
> - Use natural hierarchies.
> - Understand and resolve the slowly changing dimensions problem.
>
> **Estimated lesson time: 40 minutes**

Dimension Column Types

Dimensions give context to measures. Typical analysis includes pivot tables and pivot graphs. These pivot on one or more dimension columns used for analysis—these columns are called *attributes* in DW and OLAP terminology. The naming convention in DW/OLAP terminology is a little odd; in a relational model, every column represents an attribute of an entity. Don't worry too much about the correctness of naming in DW/OLAP terminology. The important point here is for you to understand what the word "attribute" means in a DW/OLAP context.

Pivoting makes no sense if an attribute's values are continuous, or if an attribute has too many distinct values. Imagine how a pivot table would look if it had 1,000 columns, or how a pivot graph would look with 1,000 bars. For pivoting, discrete attributes with a small number of distinct values is most appropriate. A bar chart with more than 10 bars becomes difficult to comprehend. Continuous columns or columns with unique values, such as keys, are not appropriate for analyses.

If you have a continuous column and you would like to use it in analyses as a pivoting attribute, you should discretize it. *Discretizing* means grouping or binning values to a few discrete groups. If you are using OLAP cubes, SSAS can help you. SSAS can discretize continuous attributes. However, automatic discretization is usually worse than discretization from a business perspective. Age and income are typical attributes that should be discretized from a business perspective. One year makes a big difference when you are 15 years old, and much less when you are 55 years old. When you discretize age, you should use narrower ranges for younger people and wider ranges for older people.

Columns with unique values identify rows. These columns are *keys*. In a data warehouse, you need keys just like you need them in an LOB database. Keys uniquely identify entities. Therefore, keys are the second type of columns in a dimension.

After you identify a customer, you do not refer to that customer with the key value. Having only keys in a report does not make the report very readable. People refer to entities by using their names. In a DW dimension, you also need one or more columns that you use for naming an entity.

A customer typically has an address, a phone number, and an email address. You do not analyze data on these columns. You do not need them for pivoting. However, you often need information such as the customer's address on a report. If that data is not present in a DW, you will need to get it from an LOB database, probably with a distributed query. It is much simpler to store this data in your data warehouse. In addition, queries that use this data per-form better, because the queries do not have to include data from LOB databases. Columns

used in reports as labels only, not for pivoting, are called *member properties*.

You can have naming and member property columns in multiple languages in your dimen-sion tables, providing the translation for each language you need to support. SSAS can use your translations automatically. For reports from a data warehouse, you need to manually select columns with appropriate language translation.

In addition to the types of dimension columns already defined for identifying, naming, pivoting, and labeling on a report, you can have columns for lineage information, as you saw in the previous lesson. There is an important difference between lineage and other columns: lineage columns are never exposed to end users and are never shown on end users' reports.

To summarize, a dimension may contain the following types of columns:

- **Keys**   Used to identify entities
- **Name columns**   Used for human names of entities
- **Attributes**   Used for pivoting in analyses
- **Member properties**   Used for labels in a report
- **Lineage columns**   Used for auditing, and never exposed to end users

Hierarchies

Figure 1-9 shows the *DimCustomer* dimension of the AdventureWorksDW2012 sample database.

FIGURE 1-9 The *DimCustomer* dimension.

In the figure, the following columns are attributes (columns used for pivoting):

- *BirthDate* (after calculating age and discretizing the age)
- *MaritalStatus*
- *Gender*
- *YearlyIncome* (after discretizing)
- *TotalChildren*
- *NumberChildrenAtHome*
- *EnglishEducation* (other education columns are for translations)
- *EnglishOccupation* (other occupation columns are for translations)
- *HouseOwnerFlag*
- *NumberCarsOwned*
- *CommuteDistance*

All these attributes are unrelated. Pivoting on *MaritalStatus*, for example, is unrelated to pivoting on *YearlyIncome*. None of these columns have any functional dependency between them, and there is no natural drill-down path through these attributes. Now look at the *DimDate* columns, as shown in Figure 1-10.

FIGURE 1-10 The *DimDate* dimension.

Some attributes of the *DimDate* dimension include the following (not in the order shown in the figure):

- *FullDateAlternateKey* (denotes a date in date format)
- *EnglishMonthName*
- *CalendarQuarter*
- *CalendarSemester*
- *CalendarYear*

You will immediately notice that these attributes are connected. There is a functional dependency among them, so they break third normal form. They form a hierarchy. Hierarchies are particularly useful for pivoting and OLAP analyses—they provide a natural drill-down path. You perform divide-and-conquer analyses through hierarchies.

Hierarchies have levels. When drilling down, you move from a parent level to a child level. For example, a calendar drill-down path in the *DimDate* dimension goes through the following levels: *CalendarYear* → *CalendarSemester* → *CalendarQuarter* → *EnglishMonthName* → *FullDateAlternateKey*.

At each level, you have members. For example, the members of the month level are, of course, January, February, March, April, May, June, July, August, September, October, November, and December. In DW and OLAP jargon, rows on the leaf level—the actual dimension rows—are called *members*. This is why dimension columns used in reports for labels are called *member properties*.

In a Snowflake schema, lookup tables show you levels of hierarchies. In a Star schema, you need to extract natural hierarchies from the names and content of columns. Nevertheless, because drilling down through natural hierarchies is so useful and welcomed by end users, you should use them as much as possible.

Note also that attribute names are used for labels of row and column groups in a pivot table. Therefore, a good naming convention is crucial for a data warehouse. You should always use meaningful and descriptive names for dimensions and attributes.

Slowly Changing Dimensions

There is one common problem with dimensions in a data warehouse: the data in the dimension changes over time. This is usually not a problem in an OLTP application; when a piece of data changes, you just update it. However, in a DW, you have to maintain history. The question that arises is *how* to maintain it. Do you want to update only the changed data, as in an OLTP application, and pretend that the value was always the last value, or do you want to maintain both the first and intermediate values? This problem is known in DW jargon as the *Slowly Changing Dimension (SCD)* problem.

The problem is best explained in an example. Table 1-1 shows original source OLTP data for a customer.

TABLE 1-1 Original OLTP Data for a Customer

CustomerId	FullName	City	Occupation
17	Bostjan Strazar	Vienna	Professional

The customer lives in Vienna, Austria, and is a professional. Now imagine that the customer moves to Ljubljana, Slovenia. In an OLTP database, you would just update the *City* column, resulting in the values shown in Table 1-2.

TABLE 1-2 OLTP Data for a Customer After the City Change

CustomerId	FullName	City	Occupation
17	Bostjan Strazar	Ljubljana	Professional

If you create a report, all the historical sales for this customer are now attributed to the city of Ljubljana, and (on a higher level) to Slovenia. The fact that this customer contributed to sales in Vienna and in Austria in the past would have disappeared.

In a DW, you can have the same data as in an OLTP database. You could use the same key, such as the business key, for your *Customer* dimension. You could update the *City* column when you get a change notification from the OLTP system, and thus overwrite the history.

This kind of change management is called *Type 1 SCD*. To recapitulate, Type 1 means overwriting the history for an attribute and for all higher levels of hierarchies to which that attribute belongs.

But you might prefer to maintain the history, to capture the fact that the customer contributed to sales in another city and country or region. In that case, you cannot just overwrite the data; you have to insert a new row containing new data instead. Of course, the values of other columns that do not change remain the same. However, that creates a new problem. If you simply add a new row for the customer with the same key value, the key would no longer be unique. In fact, if you tried to use a primary key or unique constraint as the key, the constraint would reject such an insert. Therefore, you have to do something with the key. You should not modify the business key, because you need a connection with the source system. The solution is to introduce a new key, a *data warehouse key*. In DW terminology, this kind of key is called a *surrogate key*.

Preserving the history while adding new rows is known as *Type 2 SCD*. When you implement Type 2 SCD, for the sake of simpler querying, you typically also add a flag to denote which row is current for a dimension member. Alternatively, you could add two columns showing the interval of validity of a value. The data type of the two columns should be Date, and the columns should show the values Valid From and Valid To. For the current value, the *Valid To* column should be NULL. Table 1-3 shows an example of the flag version of Type 2 SCD handling.

TABLE 1-3 An SCD Type 2 Change

DWCId	CustomerId	FullName	City	Occupation	Current
17	17	Bostjan Strazar	Vienna	Professional	0
289	17	Bostjan Strazar	Ljubljana	Professional	1

You could have a mixture of Type 1 and Type 2 changes in a single dimension. For example, in Table 1-3, you might want to maintain the history for the *City* column but overwrite the history for the *Occupation* column. That raises yet another issue. When you want to update the *Occupation* column, you may find that there are two (and maybe more) rows for the same customer. The question is, do you want to update the last row only, or all the rows? Table 1-4 shows a version that updates the last (current) row only, whereas Table 1-5 shows all of the rows being updated.

TABLE 1-4 An SCD Type 1 and Type 2 Mixture, Updating the Current Row Only

DWCId	CustomerId	FullName	City	Occupation	Current
17	17	Bostjan Strazar	Vienna	Professional	0
289	17	Bostjan Strazar	Ljubljana	Management	1

TABLE 1-5 An SCD Type 1 and Type 2 Mixture, Updating All Rows

DWCId	CustomerId	FullName	City	Occupation	Current
17	17	Bostjan Strazar	Vienna	Management	0
289	17	Bostjan Strazar	Ljubljana	Management	1

Although Type 1 and Type 2 handling are most common, other solutions exist. Especially well-known is *Type 3 SCD*, in which you manage a limited amount of history through additional historical columns. Table 1-6 shows Type 3 handling for the *City* column.

TABLE 1-6 SCD Type 3

CustomerId	FullName	CurrentCity	PreviousCity	Occupation
17	Bostjan Strazar	Ljubljana	Vienna	Professional

You can see that by using only a single historical column, you can maintain only one historical value per column. So Type 3 SCD has limited usability and is far less popular than Types 1 and 2.

Which solution should you implement? You should discuss this with end users and subject matter experts (SMEs). They should decide for which attributes to maintain the history, and for which ones to overwrite the history. You should then choose a solution that uses Type 2, Type 1, or a mixture of Types 1 and 2, as appropriate.

However, there is an important caveat. To maintain customer history correctly, you must have some attribute that uniquely identifies that customer throughout that customer's history, and that attribute must not change. Such an attribute should be the original—the business key. In an OLTP database, business keys should not change.

Business keys should also not change if you are merging data from multiple sources. For merged data, you usually have to implement a new, surrogate key, because business keys from different sources can have the same value for different entities. However, business keys should not change; otherwise you lose the connection with the OLTP system. Using surrogate keys in a data warehouse for at least the most common dimensions (those representing customers, products, and similar important data), is considered a best practice. Not changing OLTP keys is a best practice as well.

EXAM TIP

Make sure you understand why you need surrogate keys in a data warehouse.

The AdventureWorksDW2012 sample database has many dimensions. In this practice, you will explore some of them.

EXERCISE 1   Explore the AdventureWorksDW2012 Dimensions

In this exercise, you create a diagram for the dimensions.

1. If you closed SSMS, start it and connect to your SQL Server instance. Expand the Databases folder and then the AdventureWorksDW2012 database.

2. Right-click the Database Diagrams folder, and then select the New Database Diagram option.

3. From the Add Table list, select the following tables (click each table and then click the Add button):

   - *DimProduct*
   - *DimProductCategory*
   - *DimProductSubcategory*

   Your diagram should look like Figure 1-11.

4. Try to figure out which columns are used for the following purposes:

   - Keys
   - Names
   - Translations
   - Attributes
   - Member properties
   - Lineage
   - Natural hierarchies

5. Try to figure out whether the tables in the diagram are prepared for a Type 2 SCD change.

6. Add the *DimSalesReason* table to the diagram.

7. Try to figure out whether there is some natural hierarchy between attributes of the *DimSalesReason* dimension. Your diagram should look like Figure 1-12.

8. Save the diagram with the name **Practice_01_02_Dimensions**.

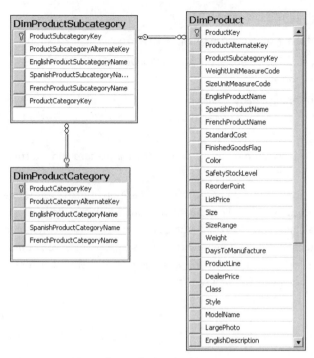

FIGURE 1-11 *DimProduct* and related tables.

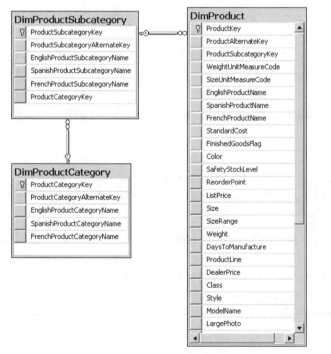

FIGURE 1-12 Adding *DimSalesReason*.

In this exercise, review the database schema from the previous exercise to learn more:

- The *DimProduct* dimension has a natural hierarchy: *ProductCategory* → *ProductSubcategory* → *Product*.

- The *DimProduct* dimension has many additional attributes that are useful for pivoting but that are not a part of any natural hierarchy. For example, Color and Size are such attributes.

- Some columns in the *DimProduct* dimension, such as the *LargePhoto* and *Description* columns, are member properties.

- *DimSalesReason* uses a Star schema. In a Star schema, it is more difficult to spot natural hierarchies. Though you can simply follow the lookup tables in a Snowflake schema and find levels of hierarchies, you have to recognize hierarchies from attribute names in a Star schema. If you cannot extract hierarchies from column names, you could also check the data. In the *DimSalesReason* dimension, it seems that there is a natural hierarchy: *SalesReasonReasonType* → *SalesReasonName*.

Close the diagram.

> *NOTE*   **CONTINUING WITH PRACTICES**
>
> **Do not exit SSMS if you intend to continue immediately with the next practice.**

Lesson Summary

- In a dimension, you have the following column types: keys, names, attributes, member properties, translations, and lineage.

- Some attributes form natural hierarchies.

- There are standard solutions for the Slowly Changing Dimensions (SCD) problem.

Lesson Review

Answer the following questions to test your knowledge of the information in this lesson. You can find the answers to these questions and explanations of why each answer choice is correct or incorrect in the "Answers" section at the end of this chapter.

1. You implement a Type 2 solution for an SCD problem for a specific column. What do you actually do when you get a changed value for the column from the source system?

   A. Add a column for the previous value to the table. Move the current value of the updated column to the new column. Update the current value with the new value from the source system.

    B. Insert a new row for the same dimension member with the new value for the updated column. Use a surrogate key, because the business key is now duplicated. Add a flag that denotes which row is current for a member.

    C. Do nothing, because in a DW, you maintain history, you do not update dimension data.

    D. Update the value of the column just as it was updated in the source system.

2. Which kind of a column is not a part of a dimension?

    A. Attribute

    B. Measure

    C. Key

    D. Member property

    E. Name

3. How can you spot natural hierarchies in a Snowflake schema?

    A. You need to analyze the content of the attributes of each dimension.

    B. Lookup tables for each dimension provide natural hierarchies.

    C. A Snowflake schema does not support hierarchies.

    D. You should convert the Snowflake schema to the Star schema, and then you would spot the natural hierarchies immediately.

Lesson 3: Designing Fact Tables

Fact tables, like dimensions, have specific types of columns that limit the actions that can be taken with them. Queries from a DW aggregate data; depending on the particular type of column, there are some limitations on which aggregate functions you can use. Many-to-many relationships in a DW can be implemented differently than in a normalized relational schema.

After this lesson, you will be able to:

- Define fact table column types.
- Understand the additivity of a measure.
- Handle many-to-many relationships in a Star schema.

Estimated lesson time: 30 minutes

Fact Table Column Types

Fact tables are collections of measurements associated with a specific business process. You store measurements in columns. Logically, this type of column is called a *measure*. Measures are the essence of a fact table. They are usually numeric and can be aggregated. They store values that are of interest to the business, such as sales amount, order quantity, and discount amount.

From Lesson 1 in this chapter, you already saw that a fact table includes foreign keys from all dimensions. These foreign keys are the second type of column in a fact table. A fact table is on the "many" side of the relationships with dimensions. All foreign keys together usually uniquely identify each row and can be used as a composite primary key.

You often include an additional surrogate key. This key is shorter and consists of one or two columns only. The surrogate key is usually the business key from the table that was used as the primary source for the fact table. For example, suppose you start building a sales fact table from an order details table in a source system, and then add foreign keys that pertain to the order as a whole from the *Order Header* table in the source system. Tables 1-7, 1-8, and 1-9 illustrate an example of such a design process.

Table 1-7 shows a simplified example of an *Orders Header* source table. The *OrderId* column is the primary key for this table. The *CustomerId* column is a foreign key from the *Customers* table. The *OrderDate* column is not a foreign key in the source table; however, it becomes a foreign key in the DW fact table, for the relationship with the explicit date dimension. Note, however, that foreign keys in a fact table can—and usually are—replaced with DW surrogate keys of DW dimensions.

TABLE 1-7 The Source Orders Header Table

OrderId	CustomerId	Orderdate
12541	17	2012/02/21

Table 1-8 shows the source *Order Details* table. The primary key of this table is a composite one and consists of the *OrderId* and *LineItemId* columns. In addition, the source *Order Details* table has the *ProductId* foreign key column. The *Quantity* column is the measure.

TABLE 1-8 The Source Order Details Table

OrderId	LineItemId	ProductId	Quantity
12541	2	5	47

Table 1-9 shows the *Sales Fact* table created from the *Orders Header* and *Order Details* source tables. The *Order Details* table was the primary source for this fact table. The *OrderId*,

LineItemId, and *Quantity* columns are simply transferred from the source *Order Details* table. The *ProductId* column from the source *Order Details* table is replaced with a surrogate DW *ProductKey* column. The *CustomerId* and *OrderDate* columns take the source *Orders Header* table; these columns pertain to orders, not order details. However, in the fact table, they are replaced with the surrogate DW keys CustomerKey and OrderDateKey.

TABLE 1-9 The Sales Fact Table

OrderId	LineItemId	CustomerKey	OrderDateKey	ProductKey	Quantity
12541	2	289	444	25	47

You do not need the *OrderId* and *LineItemId* columns in this sales fact table. For analyses, you could create a composite primary key from the *CustomerKey*, *OrderDateKey*, and *Product-Key* columns. However, you should keep the *OrderId* and *LineItemId* columns to make quick controls and comparisons with source data possible. In addition, if you were to use them as the primary key, then the primary key would be shorter than one composed from all foreign keys.

The last column type used in a fact table is the lineage type, if you implement the lineage. Just as with dimensions, you never expose the lineage information to end users. To recapitulate, fact tables have the following column types:

- Foreign keys
- Measures
- Lineage columns (optional)
- Business key columns from the primary source table (optional)

Additivity of Measures

Additivity of measures is not exactly a data warehouse design problem. However, you should consider which aggregate functions you will use in reports for which measures, and which aggregate functions you will use when aggregating over which dimension.

The simplest types of measures are those that can be aggregated with the SUM aggregate function across all dimensions, such as amounts or quantities. For example, if sales for product A were $200.00 and sales for product B were $150.00, then the total of the sales was $350.00. If yesterday's sales were $100.00 and sales for the day before yesterday were $130.00, then the total sales amounted to $230.00. Measures that can be summarized across all dimensions are called *additive measures*.

Some measures are not additive over any dimension. Examples include prices and percentages, such as a discount percentage. Typically, you use the AVERAGE aggregate function for such measures, or you do not aggregate them at all. Such measures are called *non-additive measures*. Often, you can sum additive measures and then calculate non-additive measures from the additive aggregations. For example, you can calculate the sum of sales amount and then divide that value by the sum of the order quantity to get the average price. On higher levels of aggregation, the calculated price is the average price; on the lowest level, it's the data itself—the calculated price is the actual price. This way, you can simplify queries.

For some measures, you can use SUM aggregate functions over all dimensions but time. Some examples include levels and balances. Such measures are called *semi-additive measures*. For example, if customer A has $2,000.00 in a bank account, and customer B has $3,000.00, together they have $5,000.00. However, if customer A had $5,000.00 in an account yesterday but has only $2,000.00 today, then customer A obviously does not have $7,000.00 altogether. You should take care how you aggregate such measures in a report. For time measures, you can calculate average value or use the last value as the aggregate.

> ✔ **Quick Check**
> - You are designing an accounting system. Your measures are debit, credit, and balance. What is the additivity of each measure?
>
> **Quick Check Answer**
> - Debit and credit are additive measures, and balance is a semi-additive measure.

Additivity of Measures in SSAS

SSAS is out of the scope of this book; however, you should know some facts about SSAS if your data warehouse is the source for SSAS databases. SSAS has support for semi-additive and non-additive measures. The SSAS database model is called the *Business Intelligence Semantic Model (BISM)*. Compared to the SQL Server database model, BISM includes much additional metadata.

SSAS has two types of storage: *dimensional* and *tabular*. Tabular storage is quicker to develop, because it works through tables like a data warehouse does. The dimensional model more properly represents a cube. However, the dimensional model includes even more metadata than the tabular model. In BISM dimensional processing, SSAS offers semi-additive aggregate functions out of the box. For example, SSAS offers the LastNonEmpty aggregate function, which properly uses the SUM aggregate function across all dimensions but time, and defines the last known value as the aggregate over time. In the BISM tabular model, you use the Data Analysis Expression (DAX) language. The DAX language includes functions that let you build semi-additive expressions quite quickly as well.

Many-to-Many Relationships

In a relational database, the many-to-many relationship between two tables is resolved through a third intermediate table. For example, in the AdventureWorksDW2012 database, every Internet sale can be associated with multiple reasons for the sale—and every reason can be associated with multiple sales. Figure 1-13 shows an example of a many-to-many relationship between *FactInternetSales* and *DimSalesReason* through the *FactInternetSalesReason* intermediate table in the AdventureWorksDW2012 sample database.

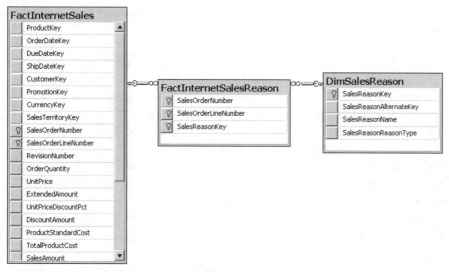

FIGURE 1-13 A classic many-to-many relationship.

For a data warehouse in a relational database management system (RDBMS), this is the correct model. However, SSAS has problems with this model. For reports from a DW, it is you, the developer, who writes queries. In contrast, reporting from SSAS databases is done by using client tools that read the schema and only afterwards build a user interface (UI) for selecting measures and attributes. Client tools create multi-dimensional expression (MDX) queries for the SSAS dimensional model, and DAX or MDX queries for the SSAS tabular model. To create the queries and build the UI properly, the tools rely on standard Star or Snowflake schemas. The tools expect that the central table, the fact table, is always on the "many" side of the relationship.

A quick look at Figure 1-13 reveals that the *FactInternetSales* fact table is on the "one" side of its relationship with the *FactInternetSalesReason* fact table. SSAS with a BISM tabular model does not support many-to-many relationships at all in its current version. In SSAS with a BISM dimensional model, you can solve the problem by creating an intermediate dimension between both fact tables. You create it from the primary key of the *FactInternetSales* table. Let's call this dimension *DimFactInternetSales*. Then you put it on the "one" side of the relationships with both fact tables. This way, both fact tables are always on the "many" side of any relationship. However, you have to realize that the relationship between the *FactInternetSales* and the new *DimFactInternetSales* dimension is de facto one to one.

EXAM TIP

Note that you create an intermediate dimension between two fact tables that supports SSAS many-to-many relationship from an existing fact table, and not directly from a table from the source transactional system.

You can generate such intermediate dimensions in your data warehouse and then just inherit them in your SSAS BISM dimensional database. (Note that SSAS with BISM in a tabular model does not recognize many-to-many relationships, even with an additional intermediate dimension table.) This way, you can have the same model in your DW as in your BISM dimensional database. In addition, when you recreate such a dimension, you can expose it to end users for reporting. However, a dimension containing key columns only is not very useful for reporting. To make it more useful, you can add additional attributes that form a hierarchy. Date variations, such as year, quarter, month, and day are very handy for drilling down. You can get these values from the *DimDate* dimension and enable a drill-down path of year → quarter → month → day → sales order in this dimension. Figure 1-14 shows a many-to-many relationship with an additional intermediate dimension.

FIGURE 1-14 A many-to-many relationship with two intermediate tables.

Note that SSMS created the relationship between *DimFactInternetSales* and *FactInternetSales* as one to one.

PRACTICE **Reviewing the AdventureWorksDW2012 Fact Tables**

The AdventureWorksDW2012 sample database has many types of fact tables as well, in order to show all possible measures. In this practice, you are going to review one of them.

EXERCISE 1 Create a Diagram for an AdventureWorksDW2012 Fact Table

In this exercise, you create a database diagram for a fact table and two associated dimensions.

1. If you closed SSMS, start it and connect to your SQL Server instance. Expand the Databases folder and then the AdventureWorksDW2012 database.

2. Right-click the Database Diagrams folder and select the New Database Diagram option.

3. From the Add Table list, select the following tables (click each table and then click the Add button):

   - *DimProduct*
   - *DimDate*
   - *FactProductInventory*

Your diagram should look like Figure 1-15.

FIGURE 1-15 FactProductInventory and related tables.

EXERCISE 2   Analyze Fact Table Columns

In this exercise, you learn more details about the fact table in the schema you created in the previous exercise. Note that you have to conclude these details from the names of the measure columns; in a real-life project, you should check the content of the columns as well.

- Knowing how an inventory works, you can conclude that the UnitsIn and UnitsOut are additive measures. Using the SUM aggregate function for these two columns is reasonable for aggregations over any dimension.

- The UnitCost measure is a non-additive measure. Summing it over any dimension does not make sense.

- The UnitsBalance measure is a semi-additive measure. You can use the SUM aggregate function over any dimension but time.

Save the diagram using the name **Practice_01_03_ProductInventory**. Close the diagram and exit SSMS.

Lesson Summary

- Fact tables include measures, foreign keys, and possibly an additional primary key and lineage columns.

- Measures can be additive, non-additive, or semi-additive.

- For many-to-many relationships, you can introduce an additional intermediate dimension.

Lesson Review

Answer the following questions to test your knowledge of the information in this lesson. You can find the answers to these questions and explanations of why each answer choice is correct or incorrect in the "Answers" section at the end of this chapter.

1. Over which dimension can you not use the SUM aggregate function for semi-additive measures?

   A. Customer

   B. Product

   C. Date

   D. Employee

2. Which measures would you expect to be non-additive? (Choose all that apply.)

   A. Price

   B. Debit

   C. SalesAmount

   D. DiscountPct

   E. UnitBalance

3. Which kind of a column is not part of a fact table?

   A. Lineage

   B. Measure

   C. Key

   D. Member property

Case Scenarios

In the following case scenarios, you apply what you've learned about Star and Snowflake schemas, dimensions, and the additivity of measures. You can find the answers to these questions in the "Answers" section at the end of this chapter.

Case Scenario 1: A Quick POC Project

You are hired to implement a quick POC data warehousing project. You have to prepare the schema for sales data. Your customer's SME would like to analyze sales data over customers, products, and time. Before creating a DW and tables, you need to make a couple of decisions and answer a couple of questions:

1. What kind of schema would you use?

2. What would the dimensions of your schema be?

3. Do you expect additive measures only?

Case Scenario 2: Extending the POC Project

After you implemented the POC sales data warehouse in Case Scenario 1, your customer was very satisfied. In fact, the business would like to extend the project to a real, long-term data warehouse. However, when interviewing analysts, you also discovered some points of dissatisfaction.

Interviews

Here's a list of company personnel who expressed some dissatisfaction during their interviews, along with their statements:

- **Sales SME** "I don't see correct aggregates over regions for historical data."
- **DBA Who Creates Reports** "My queries are still complicated, with many joins."

You need to solve these issues.

Questions

1. How would you address the Sales SME issue?

2. What kind of schema would you implement for a long-term DW?

3. How would you address the DBA's issue?

Suggested Practices

To help you successfully master the exam objectives presented in this chapter, complete the following tasks.

Analyze the AdventureWorksDW2012 Database Thoroughly

To understand all kind of dimensions and fact tables, you should analyze the Adventure-WorksDW2012 sample database thoroughly. There are cases for many data warehousing problems you might encounter.

- **Practice 1** Check all fact tables. Find all semi-additive measures.
- **Practice 2** Find all hierarchies possible for the *DimCustomer* dimension. Include attributes in the dimension and attributes in the lookup *DimGeography* table.

Check the SCD and Lineage in the AdventureWorksDW2012 Database

Although the AdventureWorksDW2012 database exemplifies many cases for data warehousing, not all possible problems are covered. You should check for what is missing.

- **Practice 1**   Is there room for lineage information in all dimensions and fact tables? How would you accommodate this information?

- **Practice 2**   Are there some important dimensions, such as those representing customers and products, that are not prepared for a Type 2 SCD solution? How would you prepare those dimensions for a Type 2 SCD solution?

Answers

This section contains answers to the lesson review questions and solutions to the case scenarios in this chapter.

Lesson 1

1. **Correct Answers: A and D**

   A. Correct: A Star schema typically has fewer tables than a normalized schema.

   B. Incorrect: The support for data types depends on the database management system, not on the schema.

   C. Incorrect: There are no specific Transact-SQL expressions or commands for Star schemas. However, there are some specific optimizations for Star schema queries.

   D. Correct: The Star schema is a de facto standard for data warehouses. It is narrative; the central table—the fact table—holds the measures, and the surrounding tables, the dimensions, give context to those measures.

2. **Correct Answer: C**

   A. Incorrect: The Star schema is more suitable for long-term DW projects.

   B. Incorrect: A normalized schema is appropriate for OLTP LOB applications.

   C. Correct: A Snowflake schema is appropriate for POC projects, because dimensions are normalized and thus closer to source normalized schema.

   D. Incorrect: An XML schema is used for validating XML documents, not for a DW.

3. **Correct Answers: B and D**

   A. Incorrect: Lookup tables are involved in both Snowflake and normalized schemas.

   B. Correct: Dimensions are part of a Star schema.

   C. Incorrect: Measures are columns in a fact table, not tables by themselves.

   D. Correct: A fact table is the central table of a Star schema.

Lesson 2

1. **Correct Answer: B**

   A. Incorrect: This is Type 3 SCD management.

   B. Correct: This is how you handle changes when you implement a Type 2 SCD solution.

   C. Incorrect: Maintaining history does not mean that the content of a DW is static.

   D. Incorrect: This is Type 1 SCD management.

2. **Correct Answer: B**

   A. **Incorrect:** Attributes are part of dimensions.

   B. **Correct:** Measures are part of fact tables.

   C. **Incorrect:** Keys are part of dimensions.

   D. **Incorrect:** Member properties are part of dimensions.

   E. **Incorrect:** Name columns are part of dimensions.

3. **Correct Answer: B**

   A. **Incorrect:** You need to analyze the attribute names and content in order to spot the hierarchies in a Star schema.

   B. **Correct:** Lookup tables for dimensions denote natural hierarchies in a Snowflake schema.

   C. **Incorrect:** A Snowflake schema supports hierarchies.

   D. **Incorrect:** You do not need to convert a Snowflake to a Star schema to spot the hierarchies.

Lesson 3

1. **Correct Answer: C**

   A. **Incorrect:** You can use SUM aggregate functions for semi-additive measures over the *Customer* dimension.

   B. **Incorrect:** You can use SUM aggregate functions for semi-additive measures over the *Product* dimension.

   C. **Correct:** You cannot use SUM aggregate functions for semi-additive measures over the *Date* dimension.

   D. **Incorrect:** You can use SUM aggregate functions for semi-additive measures over the *Employee* dimension.

2. **Correct Answers: A and D**

   A. **Correct:** Prices are not additive measures.

   B. **Incorrect:** Debit is an additive measure.

   C. **Incorrect:** Amounts are additive measures.

   D. **Correct:** Discount percentages are not additive measures.

   E. **Incorrect:** Balances are semi-additive measures.

3. **Correct Answer: D**

   A. **Incorrect:** Lineage columns can be part of a fact table.

   B. **Incorrect:** Measures are included in a fact table.

   C. **Incorrect:** A fact table includes key columns.

   D. **Correct:** Member property is a type of column in a dimension.

Case Scenario 1

1. For a quick POC project, you should use the Snowflake schema.

2. You would have customer, product, and date dimensions.

3. No, you should expect some non-additive measures as well. For example, prices and various percentages, such as discount percentage, are non-additive.

Case Scenario 2

1. You should implement a Type 2 solution for the slowly changing customer dimension.

2. For a long-term DW, you should choose a Star schema.

3. With Star schema design, you would address the DBA's issue automatically.

## CHAPTER 2

Implementing a Data Warehouse

Exam objectives in this chapter:

- Design and Implement a Data Warehouse
    - Design and implement dimensions.
    - Design and implement fact tables.

After learning about the logical configuration of a data warehouse schema, you need to use that knowledge in practice. Creating dimensions and fact tables is simple. However, using proper indexes and partitioning can make the physical implementation quite complex. This chapter discusses index usage, including the new Microsoft SQL Server 2012 columnstore indexes. You will also learn how to use table partitioning to improve query performance and make tables and indexes more manageable. You can speed up queries with pre-prepared aggregations by using indexed views. If you use your data warehouse for querying, and not just as a source for SQL Server Analysis Services (SSAS) Business Intelligence Semantic Model (BISM) models, you can create aggregates when loading the data. You can store aggregates in additional tables, or you can create indexed views. In this chapter, you will learn how to implement a data warehouse and prepare it for fast loading and querying.

Lessons in this chapter:

- Lesson 1: Implementing Dimensions and Fact Tables
- Lesson 2: Managing the Performance of a Data Warehouse
- Lesson 3: Loading and Auditing Loads

Before You Begin

To complete this chapter, you must have:

- An understanding of dimensional design.
- Experience working with SQL Server 2012 Management Studio.
- A working knowledge of the Transact-SQL (T-SQL) language.
- An understanding of clustered and nonclustered indexes.
- A solid grasp of nested loop joins, merge joins, and hash joins.

Lesson 1: Implementing Dimensions and Fact Tables

Implementing a data warehouse means creating the data warehouse (DW) database and database objects. The main database objects, as you saw in Chapter 1, "Data Warehouse Logical Design," are dimensions and fact tables. To expedite your extract-transform-load (ETL) process, you can have additional objects in your DW, including sequences, stored procedures, and staging tables. After you create the objects, you should test them by loading test data.

> **After this lesson, you will be able to:**
>
> - Create a data warehouse database.
> - Create sequences.
> - Implement dimensions.
> - Implement fact tables.
>
> **Estimated lesson time: 50 minutes**

Creating a Data Warehouse Database

You should consider a couple of settings when creating a data warehouse database. A DW contains a transformed copy of line-of-business (LOB) data. You load data to your DW occasionally, on a schedule—typically in an overnight job. The DW data is not online, real-time data. You do not need to back up the transaction log for your data warehouse, as you would in an LOB database. Therefore, the recovery model for your data warehouse should be Simple.

SQL Server supports three recovery models:

- In the *Full recovery model*, all transactions are fully logged, with all associated data. You have to regularly back up the log. You can recover data to any arbitrary point in time. Point-in-time recovery is particularly useful when human errors occur.

- The *Bulk Logged recovery model* is an adjunct of the Full recovery model that permits high-performance bulk copy operations. Bulk operations, such as index creation or bulk loading of text or XML data, can be minimally logged. For such operations, SQL Server can log only the Transact-SQL command, without all the associated data. You still need to back up the transaction log regularly.

- In the *Simple recovery model*, SQL Server automatically reclaims log space for committed transactions. SQL Server keeps log space requirements small, essentially eliminating the need to manage the transaction log space.

The Simple recovery model is useful for development, test, and read-mostly databases. Because in a data warehouse you use data primarily in read-only mode, the Simple model is the most appropriate for a data warehouse. If you use Full or Bulk Logged recovery models, you should back up the log regularly, because the log will otherwise constantly grow with each new data load.

SQL Server database data and log files can grow and shrink automatically. However, growing happens at the most inappropriate time—when you load new data—interfering with your load, and thus slowing down the load. Numerous small-growth operations can fragment your data. Automatic shrinking can fragment the data even more. For queries that read a lot of data, performing large table scans, you will want to eliminate fragmentation as much as possible. Therefore, you should prevent autoshrinking and autogrowing. Make sure that the Auto Shrink database option is turned off. Though you can't prevent the database from growing, you should reserve sufficient space for your data and log files initially to prevent autogrowth.

You can calculate space requirements quite easily. A data warehouse contains data for multiple years, typically for 5 or 10 years. Load test data for a limited period, such as a year (or a month, if you are dealing with very large source databases). Then check the size of your database files and extrapolate the size to the complete 5 or 10 years' worth of data. In addition, you should add at least 25 percent for extra free space in your data files. This additional free space lets you rebuild or re-create indexes without fragmentation.

Although the transaction log does not grow in the Simple recovery model, you should still set it to be large enough to accommodate the biggest transaction. Regular data modification language (DML) statements, including INSERT, DELETE, UPDATE, and MERGE, are *always* fully logged, even in the Simple model. You should test the execution of these statements and estimate an appropriate size for your log.

In your data warehouse, large fact tables typically occupy most of the space. You can optimize querying and managing large fact tables through *partitioning*. Table partitioning has management advantages and provides performance benefits. Queries often touch only subsets of partitions, and SQL Server can efficiently eliminate other partitions early in the query execution process. You will learn more about fact table partitioning in Lesson 3 of this chapter.

A database can have multiple data files, grouped in multiple *filegroups*. There is no single best practice as to how many filegroups you should create for your data warehouse. However, for most DW scenarios, having one filegroup for each partition is the most appropriate. For the number of files in a filegroup, you should consider your disk storage. Generally, you should create one file per physical disk.

> **MORE INFO** **DATA WAREHOUSE DATABASE FILEGROUPS**
>
> For more information on filegroups, see the document "Creating New Data Warehouse Filegroups" at *http://msdn.microsoft.com/en-us/library/ee796978(CS.20).aspx*. For more information on creating large databases, see the SQL Server Customer Advisory Team (SQLCAT) white paper "Top 10 Best Practices for Building a Large Scale Relational Data Warehouse" at *http://sqlcat.com/sqlcat/b/top10lists/archive/2008/02/06/top-10-best-practices-for-building-a-large-scale-relational-data-warehouse.aspx*. For more information on data loading performance, see the SQLCAT white paper, "The Data Loading Performance Guide" at *http://msdn.microsoft.com/en-us/library/dd425070(SQL.100).aspx*.

Loading data from source systems is often quite complex. To mitigate the complexity, you can implement staging tables in your DW. You can even implement staging tables and other objects in a separate database. You use *staging tables* to temporarily store source data before cleansing it or merging it with data from other sources. In addition, staging tables also serve as an intermediate layer between DW and source tables. If something changes in the source—for example if a source database is upgraded—you have to change only the query that reads source data and loads it to staging tables. After that, your regular ETL process should work just as it did before the change in the source system. The part of a DW containing staging tables is called the *data staging area (DSA)*.

> **REAL WORLD** **DATA STAGING AREA**
>
> In the vast majority of data warehousing projects, an explicit data staging area adds a lot of flexibility in ETL processes.

Staging tables are never exposed to end users. If they are part of your DW, you can store them in a different schema than regular Star schema tables. By storing staging tables in a different schema, you can give permissions to end users on the regular DW tables by assigning those permissions for the appropriate schema only, which simplifies administration. In a typical data warehouse, two schemas are sufficient: one for regular DW tables, and one for staging tables. You can store regular DW tables in the *dbo* schema and, if needed, create a separate schema for staging tables.

Implementing Dimensions

Implementing a dimension involves creating a table that contains all the needed columns. In addition to business keys, you should add a surrogate key to all dimensions that need Type 2 Slowly Changing Dimension (SCD) management. You should also add a column that flags the current row or two date columns that mark the validity period of a row when you implement Type 2 SCD management for a dimension.

You can use simple sequential integers for surrogate keys. SQL Server can autonumber them for you. You can use the IDENTITY property to generate sequential numbers. You should already be familiar with this property. In SQL Server 2012, you can also use sequences for identifiers.

A sequence is a user-defined, table-independent (and therefore schema-bound) object. SQL Server uses sequences to generate a sequence of numeric values according to your speci-fication. You can generate sequences in ascending or descending order, using a defined in-terval of possible values. You can even generate sequences that cycle (repeat). As mentioned, sequences are independent objects, not associated with tables. You control the relationship between sequences and tables in your ETL application. With sequences, you can coordinate the key values across multiple tables.

You should use sequences instead of identity columns in the following scenarios:

- When you need to determine the next number *before* making an insert into a table.

- When you want to share a single series of numbers between multiple tables, or even between multiple columns within a single table.

- When you need to restart the number series when a specified number is reached (that is, when you need to cycle the sequence).

- When you need sequence values sorted by another column. The NEXT VALUE FOR function, which is the function you call to allocate the sequence values, can apply the OVER clause. In the OVER clause, you can generate the sequence in the order of the OVER clause's ORDER BY clause.

- When you need to assign multiple numbers at the same time. Requesting identity values could result in gaps in the series if other users were simultaneously generating sequential numbers. You can call the sp_sequence_get_range system procedure to retrieve several numbers in the sequence at once.

- When you need to change the specification of the sequence, such as the increment value.

- When you need to achieve better performance than with identity columns. You can use the CACHE option when you create a sequence. This option increases performance by minimizing the number of disk IOs that are required to generate sequence numbers. When the cache size is 50 (which is the default cache size), SQL Server caches only the current value and the number of values left in the cache, meaning that the amount of memory required is equivalent to only two instances of the data type for the sequence object.

The complete syntax for creating a sequence is as follows.

```
CREATE SEQUENCE [schema_name . ] sequence_name
    [ AS [ built_in_integer_type | user-defined_integer_type ] ]
    [ START WITH <constant> ]
    [ INCREMENT BY <constant> ]
    [ { MINVALUE [ <constant> ] } | { NO MINVALUE } ]
    [ { MAXVALUE [ <constant> ] } | { NO MAXVALUE } ]
    [ CYCLE | { NO CYCLE } ]
    [ { CACHE [ <constant> ] } | { NO CACHE } ]
    [ ; ]
```

 In addition to regular columns, you can also add *computed columns*. A computed column is a virtual column in a table. The value of the column is determined by an expression. By defining computed columns in your tables, you can simplify queries. Computed columns can also help with performance. You can persist and index a computed column, as long as the following prerequisites are met:

- Ownership requirements

- Determinism requirements

- Precision requirements

- Data type requirements

- SET option requirements

Refer to the article "Creating Indexes on Computed Columns" in Books Online for SQL Server 2012 for details of these requirements (*http://msdn.microsoft.com/en-us/library /ms189292(SQL.105).aspx*).

You can use computed columns to discretize continuous values in source columns. Computed columns are especially useful for column values that are constantly changing. An example of an ever-changing value would be age. Assume that you have the birth dates of your customers or employees; for analyses, you might need to calculate the age. The age changes every day, with every load. You can discretize age in a couple of groups. Then the values do not change so frequently anymore. In addition, you do not need to persist and index a computed column. If the column is not persisted, SQL Server calculates the value on the fly, when a query needs it. If you are using SQL Server Analysis Services (SSAS), you can store this column physically in an SSAS database and thus persist it in SSAS.

Finally, if you need lineage information, you should include lineage columns in your dimensions as well.

Quick Check

- How can SQL Server help you with values for your surrogate keys?

Quick Check Answer

- SQL Server can autonumber your surrogate keys. You can use the IDENTITY property or sequence objects.

Implementing Fact Tables

After you implement dimensions, you need to implement fact tables in your data warehouse. You should always implement fact tables *after* you implement your dimensions. A fact table is on the "many" side of a relationship with a dimension, so the parent side must exist if you want to create a foreign key constraint.

You should partition a large fact table for easier maintenance and better performance. You will learn more about table partitioning in Lesson 3 of this chapter.

Columns in a fact table include foreign keys and measures. Dimensions in your database define the foreign keys. All foreign keys together usually uniquely identify each row of a fact table. If they do uniquely identify each row, then you can use them as a composite key. You can also add an additional surrogate primary key, which might also be a key inherited from an LOB system table. For example, if you start building your DW sales fact table from an LOB sales order details table, you can use the LOB sales order details table key for the DW sales fact table as well.

EXAM TIP

It is not necessary that all foreign keys together uniquely identify each row of a fact table.

In production, you can remove foreign key constraints to achieve better load performance. If the foreign key constraints are present, SQL Server has to check them during the load. However, we recommend that you retain the foreign key constraints during the development and testing phases. It is easier to create database diagrams if you have foreign keys defined. In addition, during the tests, you will get errors if constraints are violated. Errors inform you that there is something wrong with your data; when a foreign key violation occurs, it's most likely that the parent row from a dimension is missing for one or more rows in a fact table. These types of errors give you information about the quality of the data you are dealing with.

If you decide to remove foreign keys in production, you should create your ETL process so that it's resilient when foreign key errors occur. In your ETL process, you should add a row to a dimension when an unknown key appears in a fact table. A row in a dimension added during fact table load is called an *inferred member*. Except for the key values, all other column values for an inferred member row in a dimension are unknown at fact table load time, and you should set them to NULL. This means that dimension columns (except keys) should allow NULLs. The SQL Server Integration Services (SSIS) SCD wizard helps you handle inferred members at dimension load time. The inferred members problem is also known as the *late-arriving dimensions problem*.

Like dimensions, fact tables can also contain computed columns. You can create many computations in advance and thus simplify queries. And, of course, also like dimensions, fact tables can have lineage columns added to them if you need them.

PRACTICE **Implementing Dimensions and Fact Tables**

In this practice, you will implement a data warehouse. You will use the AdventureWorksDW2012 sample database as the source for your data. You are not going to create an explicit data staging area; you are going to use the AdventureWorksDW2012 sample database as your data staging area.

If you encounter a problem completing an exercise, you can install the completed projects from the Solution folder that is provided with the companion content for this chapter and lesson.

EXERCISE 1   Create a Data Warehouse Database and a Sequence

In the first exercise, you will create a SQL Server database for your data warehouse.

1. Start SSMS and connect to your SQL Server instance. Open a new query window by clicking the New Query button.

2. From the context of the master database, create a new database called **TK463DW**. Before creating the database, check whether it exists, and drop it if needed. You should always check whether an object exists and drop it if needed. The database should have the following properties:

    ■ It should have a single data file and a single log file in the TK463 folder. You can create this folder in any drive you want.

    ■ The data file should have an initial size of 300 MB and be autogrowth enabled in 10MB chunks.

    ■ The log file size should be 50 MB, with 10-percent autogrowth chunks.

3. After you create the database, change the recovery model to Simple. Here is the complete database creation code.

```
USE master;
IF DB_ID('TK463DW') IS NOT NULL
  DROP DATABASE TK463DW;
GO
CREATE DATABASE TK463DW
 ON PRIMARY
 (NAME = N'TK463DW', FILENAME = N'C:\TK463\TK463DW.mdf',
  SIZE = 307200KB , FILEGROWTH = 10240KB )
```

```
LOG ON
(NAME = N'TK463DW_log', FILENAME = N'C:\TK463\TK463DW_log.ldf',
  SIZE = 51200KB , FILEGROWTH = 10%);
GO
ALTER DATABASE TK463DW SET RECOVERY SIMPLE WITH NO_WAIT;
GO
```

4. In your new data warehouse, create a sequence object. Name it **SeqCustomerDwKey**. Start numbering with 1, and use an increment of 1. For other sequence options, use the SQL Server defaults. You can use the following code.

```
USE TK463DW;
GO
IF OBJECT_ID('dbo.SeqCustomerDwKey','SO') IS NOT NULL
  DROP SEQUENCE dbo.SeqCustomerDwKey;
GO
CREATE SEQUENCE dbo.SeqCustomerDwKey AS INT
 START WITH 1
 INCREMENT BY 1;
GO
```

EXERCISE 2   Create Dimensions

In this exercise, you will create the *Customers* dimension, for which you will have to implement quite a lot of knowledge learned from this and the previous chapter. In the AdventureWorksDW2012 database, the *DimCustomer* dimension, which will serve as the source for your *Customers* dimension, is partially snowflaked. It has a one-level lookup table called *DimGeography*. You will fully denormalize this dimension. In addition, you are going to add the columns needed to support an SCD Type 2 dimension and a couple of computed columns. In addition to the *Customers* dimension, you are going to create the *Products* and *Dates* dimensions.

1. Create the *Customers* dimension. The source for this dimension is the *DimCustomer* dimension from the AdventureWorksDW2012 sample database. Add a surrogate key column called **CustomerDwKey**, and create a primary key constraint on this column. Use Table 2-1 for the information needed to define the columns of the table and to populate the table.

TABLE 2-1 Column Information for the *Customers* Dimension

Column name	Data type	Nullability	Remarks
CustomerDwKey	INT	NOT NULL	Surrogate key; assign values with a sequence
CustomerKey	INT	NOT NULL	
FullName	NVARCHAR(150)	NULL	Concatenate *FirstName* and *LastName* from *DimCustomer*
EmailAddress	NVARCHAR(50)	NULL	

Column name	Data type	Nullability	Remarks
BirthDate	DATE	NULL	
MaritalStatus	NCHAR(5)	NULL	
Gender	NCHAR(5)	NULL	
Education	NVARCHAR(40)	NULL	*EnglishEducation* from *DimCustomer*
Occupation	NVARCHAR(100)	NULL	*EnglishOccupation* from *DimCustomer*
City	NVARCHAR(30)	NULL	*City* from *DimGeography*
StateProvince	NVARCHAR(50)	NULL	*StateProvinceName* from *DimGeography*
CountryRegion	NVARCHAR(50)	NULL	*EnglishCountryRegionName* from *DimGeography*
Age	Inherited	Inherited	Computed column. Calculate the difference in years between *BirthDate* and the current date, and discretize it in three groups: ■ When difference <= 40, label "Younger" ■ When difference > 50, label "Older" ■ Else label "Middle Age"
CurrentFlag	BIT	NOT NULL	Default 1

> **NOTE** **HOW TO INTERPRET THE REMARKS COLUMN IN TABLE 2-1**
>
> For columns for which the Remarks column in Table 2-1 is empty, populate the column with values from a column with the same name in the AdventureWorksDW2012 source dimension (in this case, *DimCustomer*); when the Remarks column is not empty, you can find information about how to populate the column values from a column with a different name in the AdventureWorksDW2012 source dimension, or with a column from a related table, with a default constraint, or with an expression. You will populate all dimensions in the practice for Lesson 2 of this chapter.

2. Your code for creating the *Customers* dimension should be similar to the code in the following listing.

```
CREATE TABLE dbo.Customers
(
CustomerDwKey  INT            NOT NULL,
CustomerKey    INT            NOT NULL,
FullName       NVARCHAR(150)  NULL,
EmailAddress   NVARCHAR(50)   NULL,
BirthDate      DATE           NULL,
MaritalStatus  NCHAR(5)       NULL,
```

```
Gender          NCHAR(5)       NULL,
Education        NVARCHAR(40)   NULL,
Occupation       NVARCHAR(100)  NULL,
City             NVARCHAR(30)   NULL,
StateProvince    NVARCHAR(50)   NULL,
CountryRegion    NVARCHAR(50)   NULL,
Age AS
  CASE
   WHEN BirthDate IS NULL THEN NULL
   WHEN DATEDIFF(yy,BirthDate,CURRENT_TIMESTAMP) > 50
   THEN 'Older'
   WHEN DATEDIFF(yy,BirthDate,CURRENT_TIMESTAMP) > 40
   THEN 'Middle Age'
   ELSE 'Younger'
  END
 CurrentFlag    BIT            NOT NULL DEFAULT 1,
 CONSTRAINT PK_Customers PRIMARY KEY (CustomerDwKey)
);
GO
```

3. Create the *Products* dimension. The source for this dimension is the *DimProducts* dimension from the AdventureWorksDW2012 sample database. Use Table 2-2 for the information you need to create and populate this table.

TABLE 2-2 Column Information for the *Products* Dimension

Column name	Data type	Nullability	Remarks
ProductKey	INT	NOT NULL	
ProductName	NVARCHAR(50)	NULL	*EnglishProductName* from *DimProduct*
Color	NVARCHAR(15)	NULL	
Size	NVARCHAR(50)	NULL	
SubcategoryName	NVARCHAR(50)	NULL	*EnglishProductSubcategoryName* from *DimProductSubcategory*
CategoryName	NVARCHAR(50)	NULL	*EnglishProductCategoryName* from *DimProductCategory*

Your code for creating the *Products* dimension should be similar to the code in the following listing.

```
CREATE TABLE dbo.Products
(
ProductKey       INT            NOT NULL,
ProductName      NVARCHAR(50)   NULL,
Color            NVARCHAR(15)   NULL,
Size             NVARCHAR(50)   NULL,
SubcategoryName  NVARCHAR(50)   NULL,
CategoryName     NVARCHAR(50)   NULL,
CONSTRAINT PK_Products PRIMARY KEY (ProductKey)
);
GO
```

4. Create the *Dates* dimension. The source for this dimension is the *DimDate* dimension from the AdventureWorksDW2012 sample database. Use Table 2-3 for the information you need to create and populate this table.

TABLE 2-3 Column Information for the *Dates* Dimension

Column name	Data type	Nullability	Remarks
DateKey	INT	NOT NULL	
FullDate	DATE	NOT NULL	*FullDateAlternateKey* from *DimDate*
MonthNumberName	NVARCHAR(15)	NULL	Concatenate *MonthNumberOfYear* (with leading zeroes when the number is less than 10) and *EnglishMonthName* from *DimDate*
CalendarQuarter	TINYINT	NULL	
CalendarYear	SMALLINT	NULL	

Your code for creating the *Dates* dimension should be similar to the code in the following listing.

```
CREATE TABLE dbo.Dates
(
DateKey         INT          NOT NULL,
FullDate        DATE         NOT NULL,
MonthNumberName NVARCHAR(15) NULL,
CalendarQuarter TINYINT      NULL,
CalendarYear    SMALLINT     NULL,
CONSTRAINT PK_Dates PRIMARY KEY (DateKey)
);
GO
```

EXERCISE 3 Create a Fact Table

In this simplified example of a real data warehouse, you are going to create a single fact table. In this example, you cannot use all foreign keys together as a composite primary key, because the source for this table—the *FactInternatSales* table from the AdventureWorksDW2012 database—has lower granularity than the fact table you are creating, and the primary key would be duplicated. You could use the *SalesOrderNumber* and *SalesOrderLineNumber* columns as the primary key, as in a source table; however, in order to show how you can autonumber a column with the IDENTITY property, this exercise has you add your own integer column with this property. This will be your surrogate key.

1. Create the *InternetSales* fact table. The source for this fact table is the *FactInternetSales* fact table from the AdventureWorksDW2012 sample database. Add foreign keys from the three dimensions created in Exercise 2 of this lesson. Add an integer column by using the IDENTITY property, and use it as the primary key. Use Table 2-4 for the information needed to define the columns of the table.

TABLE 2-4 Column Information for the *InternetSales* Fact Table

Column name	Data type	Nullability	Remarks
InternetSalesKey	INT	NOT NULL	IDENTITY(1,1)
CustomerDwKey	INT	NOT NULL	Using the *CustomerKey* business key from the *Customers* dimension, find the appropriate value of the *CustomerDwKey* surrogate key from the *Customers* dimension
ProductKey	INT	NOT NULL	
DateKey	INT	NOT NULL	*OrderDateKey* from *FactInternetSales*
OrderQuantity	SMALLINT	NOT NULL	Default 0
SalesAmount	MONEY	NOT NULL	Default 0
UnitPrice	MONEY	NOT NULL	Default 0
DiscountAmount	FLOAT	NOT NULL	Default 0

Your code for creating the *InternetSales* fact table should be similar to the code in the following listing.

```
CREATE TABLE dbo.InternetSales
(
 InternetSalesKey INT       NOT NULL IDENTITY(1,1),
 CustomerDwKey    INT       NOT NULL,
 ProductKey       INT       NOT NULL,
 DateKey          INT       NOT NULL,
 OrderQuantity    SMALLINT  NOT NULL DEFAULT 0,
 SalesAmount      MONEY     NOT NULL DEFAULT 0,
 UnitPrice        MONEY     NOT NULL DEFAULT 0,
 DiscountAmount   FLOAT     NOT NULL DEFAULT 0,
 CONSTRAINT PK_InternetSales
  PRIMARY KEY (InternetSalesKey)
);
GO
```

2. Alter the *InternetSales* fact table to add foreign key constraints for relationships with all three dimensions. The code is shown in the following listing.

```
ALTER TABLE dbo.InternetSales ADD CONSTRAINT
 FK_InternetSales_Customers FOREIGN KEY(CustomerDwKey)
 REFERENCES dbo.Customers (CustomerDwKey);
ALTER TABLE dbo.InternetSales ADD CONSTRAINT
 FK_InternetSales_Products FOREIGN KEY(ProductKey)
 REFERENCES dbo.Products (ProductKey);
ALTER TABLE dbo.InternetSales ADD CONSTRAINT
 FK_InternetSales_Dates FOREIGN KEY(DateKey)
 REFERENCES dbo.Dates (DateKey);
GO
```

3. Create a database diagram, as shown in Figure 2-1. Name it **InternetSalesDW** and save it.

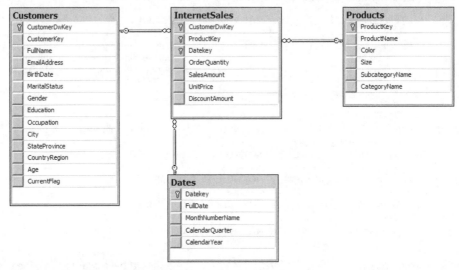

FIGURE 2-1 The schema of the simplified practice data warehouse.

4. Save the file with the T-SQL code.

NOTE **CONTINUING WITH PRACTICES**

Do not exit SSMS if you intend to continue immediately with the next practice.

Lesson Summary

- In this lesson, you learned about implementing a data warehouse.
- For a data warehouse database, you should use the Simple recovery model.
- When creating a database, allocate enough space for data files and log files to prevent autogrowth of the files.
- Use surrogate keys in dimensions in which you expect SCD Type 2 changes.
- Use computed columns.

Lesson Review

Answer the following questions to test your knowledge of the information in this lesson. You can find the answers to these questions and explanations of why each answer choice is correct or incorrect in the "Answers" section at the end of this chapter.

1. Which database objects and object properties can you use for autonumbering? (Choose all that apply.)

   A. IDENTITY property

   B. SEQUENCE object

   C. PRIMARY KEY constraint

   D. CHECK constraint

2. What columns do you add to a table to support Type 2 SCD changes? (Choose all that apply.)

   A. Member properties

   B. Current row flag

   C. Lineage columns

   D. Surrogate key

3. What is an inferred member?

   A. A row in a fact table added during dimension load

   B. A row with aggregated values

   C. A row in a dimension added during fact table load

   D. A computed column in a fact table

Lesson 2: Managing the Performance of a Data Warehouse

Implementing a Star schema by creating tables is quite simple. However, when a data warehouse is in production, more complex problems appear. Data warehouses are often very large, so you are likely to have to deal with performance problems. In this lesson, you will learn how to index DW tables appropriately, use data compression, and create columnstore indexes. In addition, this lesson briefly tackles some T-SQL queries typical for a data warehousing environment.

After this lesson, you will be able to:

- Use clustered and nonclustered indexes on a dimension and on a fact table.
- Use data compression.
- Use appropriate T-SQL queries.
- Use indexed views.

Estimated lesson time: 60 minutes

Indexing Dimensions and Fact Tables

SQL Server stores a table as a heap or as a *balanced tree (B-tree)*. If you create a clustered index, a table is stored as a B-tree. As a general best practice, you should store every table with a clustered index, because storing a table as a B-tree has many advantages, as listed here:

- You can control table fragmentation with the ALTER INDEX command, by using the REBUILD or REORGANIZE option.

- A clustered index is useful for range queries, because the data is logically sorted on the key.

- You can move a table to another filegroup by recreating the clustered index on a different filegroup. You do not have to drop the table, as you would to move a heap.

- A clustering key is a part of all nonclustered indexes. If a table is stored as a heap, then the row identifier is stored in nonclustered indexes instead. A short, integer clustering key is shorter than a row identifier, thus making nonclustered indexes more efficient.

- You cannot refer to a row identifier in queries, but clustering keys are often part of queries. This raises the probability for covered queries. *Covered queries* are queries that read all data from one or more nonclustered indexes, without going to the base table. This means that there are fewer reads and less disk IO.

Clustered indexes are particularly efficient when the clustering key is short. Creating a clustering index with a long key makes all nonclustered indexes less efficient. In addition, the clustering key should be unique. If it is not unique, SQL Server makes it unique by adding a 4-byte sequential number called a *uniquifier* to duplicate keys. This makes keys longer and all indexes less efficient. Clustering keys should also be ever-increasing. With ever-increasing keys, minimally logged bulk inserts are possible even if a table already contains data, as long as the table does not have additional nonclustered indexes.

Data warehouse surrogate keys are ideal for clustered indexes. Because you are the one who defines them, you can define them as efficiently as possible. Use integers with autonumbering options. The Primary Key constraint creates a clustered index by default.

EXAM TIP

Opt for an integer autonumbering surrogate key as the clustered primary key for all DW tables, unless there is a really strong reason to decide otherwise.

Data warehouse queries typically involve large scans of data and aggregation. Very selective seeks are not common for reports from a DW. Therefore, nonclustered indexes generally don't help DW queries much. However, this does not mean that you shouldn't create *any* nonclustered indexes in your DW.

An attribute of a dimension is not a good candidate for a nonclustered index key. Attributes are used for pivoting and typically contain only a few distinct values. Therefore, queries that filter over attribute values are usually not very selective. Nonclustered indexes on dimension attributes are not a good practice.

DW reports can be parameterized. For example, a DW report could show sales for all customers, or for only a single customer, based perhaps on parameter selection by an end user. For a single-customer report, the user would choose the customer by selecting that customer's name. Customer names are selective, meaning that you retrieve only a small number of rows when you filter by customer name. Company names, for example, are typically unique, so when you filter on a company name you typically retrieve a single row. For reports like this, having a nonclustered index on a name column or columns could lead to better performance. Instead of selecting a customer by name, selection by, for example, email address could be enabled in a report. In that case, a nonclustered index on an email address column could be useful. An email address in a dimension is a member property in DW terminology, as you saw in Chapter 1. In contrast to attributes, name columns and member properties could be candidates for nonclustered index keys; however, you should create indexes only if these columns are used in report queries.

You can create a filtered nonclustered index. A filtered index spans a subset of column values only, and thus applies to a subset of table rows. Filtered nonclustered indexes are useful when some values in a column occur rarely, whereas other values occur frequently. In such cases, you would create a filtered index over the rare values only. SQL Server uses this index for seeks of rare values but performs scans for frequent values. Filtered nonclustered indexes can be useful not only for name columns and member properties, but also for attributes of a dimension.

> **IMPORTANT** **MINIMIZE USAGE OF NONCLUSTERED INDEXES IN A DW**
>
> Analyze the need for every single nonclustered index in a DW thoroughly. Never create a nonclustered index in a DW without a good reason.

DW queries involve joins between dimensions and a fact table. Most DW joins use the dimension primary key—the fact table foreign key relationships. SQL Server has a special star join optimization of hash joins for DW queries. SQL Server Query Optimizer recognizes star join patterns and uses bitmap filtered hash joins. Query Optimizer uses hash joins when you join on non-sorted columns from both tables involved in a join. Hash joins can work in parallel threads. With bitmap filtering, they can work on a subset of rows from a dimension and from a fact table in each thread. Bitmap filtered hash joins outperform other types of joins for parallel queries with large scans. Such queries are typical for data warehousing environments. For hash joins, you do not index the foreign keys of a fact table.

Parallel queries are not very frequent when there are many concurrent users connected to a SQL Server, which is common for OLTP scenarios. However, even in a DW scenario, you could have queries with sequential plans only. If these sequential queries deal with smaller amounts of data as well, then merge or nested loops joins could be faster than hash joins. Both merge and nested loops joins benefit from indexes on fact table foreign keys. Achieving merge and nested loops joins could be a reason to create nonclustered indexes on fact table foreign keys. However, make sure that you analyze your workload thoroughly before creating the nonclustered indexes on fact table foreign keys; remember that the majority of DW queries involve scans over large amounts of data. As a general best practice, you should use as few nonclustered indexes in your data warehouse as possible.

> **MORE INFO** **SQL SERVER JOINS**
>
> For more information on different SQL Server joins, see the following documents:
>
> - "Understanding Nested Loops Joins" at *http://msdn.microsoft.com/en-us /library/ms191318.aspx*.
> - "Understanding Merge Joins" at *http://msdn.microsoft.com/en-us/library /ms190967.aspx*.
> - "Understanding Hash Joins" at *http://msdn.microsoft.com/en-us/library /ms189313.aspx*.

Indexed Views

You can optimize queries that aggregate data and perform multiple joins by permanently storing the aggregated and joined data. For example, you could create a new table with joined and aggregated data and then maintain that table during your ETL process.

However, creating additional tables for joined and aggregated data is not a best practice, because using these tables means you have to change report queries. Fortunately, there is another option for storing joined and aggregated tables. You can create a view with a query that joins and aggregates data. Then you can create a clustered index on the view to get an *indexed view*. With indexing, you are materializing a view. In the Enterprise Edition of SQL Server 2012, SQL Server Query Optimizer uses the indexed view automatically—without changing the query. SQL Server also maintains indexed views automatically. However, to speed up data loads, you can drop or disable the index before load and then recreate or rebuild it after the load.

> **MORE INFO** **INDEXED VIEWS IN THE DIFFERENT EDITIONS OF SQL SERVER**
>
> For more information on indexed view usage and other features supported by different editions of SQL Server 2012, see "Features Supported by the Editions of SQL Server 2012" at *http://msdn.microsoft.com/en-us/library/cc645993(SQL.110).aspx*.

Indexed views have many limitations, restrictions, and prerequisites, and you should refer to Books Online for SQL Server 2012 for details about them. However, you can run a simple test that shows how indexed views can be useful. The following query aggregates the *SalesAmount* column over the *ProductKey* column of the *FactInternetSales* table in the AdventureWorks-DW2012 sample database. The code also sets STATISTICS IO to ON to measure the IO.

> **NOTE** **SAMPLE CODE**
>
> You can find all the sample code in the Code folder for this chapter provided with the companion content.

```
USE AdventureWorksDW2012;
GO
SET STATISTICS IO ON;
GO
SELECT ProductKey,
 SUM(SalesAmount) AS Sales,
 COUNT_BIG(*) AS NumberOfRows
FROM dbo.FactInternetSales
GROUP BY ProductKey;
GO
```

The query makes 1,036 logical reads in the *FactInternetSales* table. You can create a view from this query and index it, as shown in the following code.

```
CREATE VIEW dbo.SalesByProduct
WITH SCHEMABINDING AS
SELECT ProductKey,
 SUM(SalesAmount) AS Sales,
 COUNT_BIG(*) AS NumberOfRows
FROM dbo.FactInternetSales
GROUP BY ProductKey;
GO
CREATE UNIQUE CLUSTERED INDEX CLU_SalesByProduct
 ON dbo.SalesByProduct (ProductKey);
GO
```

Note that the view must be created with the SCHEMABINDING option if you want to index it. In addition, you must use the COUNT_BIG aggregate function. See the prerequisites for indexed views in Books Online for SQL Server 2012 for details. Nevertheless, after creating the view and the index, execute the query again.

```
SELECT ProductKey,
 SUM(SalesAmount) AS Sales,
 COUNT_BIG(*) AS NumberOfRows
FROM dbo.FactInternetSales
GROUP BY ProductKey;
GO
```

Now the query makes only two logical reads in the *SalesByProduct* view. Query Optimizer has figured out that for this query an indexed view exists, and it used the benefits of the indexed view without referring directly to it. After analyzing the indexed view, you should clean up your AdventureWorksDW2012 database by running the following code.

```
DROP VIEW dbo.SalesByProduct;
GO
```

Using Appropriate Query Techniques

No join optimization can help if you write inefficient DW queries. A good example of a typical DW query is one that involves running totals. You can use non-equi self joins for such queries. The following example shows a query that calculates running totals on the *Gender* attribute for customers with a *CustomerKey* less than or equal to 12,000 using the *SalesAmount* measure of the *FactInternetSales* table in the AdventureWorksDW2012 sample database. As shown in the code, you can measure the statistics IO to gain a basic understanding of query performance.

```
SET STATISTICS IO ON;
GO
-- Query with a self join
WITH InternetSalesGender AS
(
SELECT ISA.CustomerKey, C.Gender,
 ISA.SalesOrderNumber + CAST(ISA.SalesOrderLineNumber AS CHAR(1))
  AS OrderLineNumber,
 ISA.SalesAmount
FROM dbo.FactInternetSales AS ISA
 INNER JOIN dbo.DimCustomer AS C
    ON ISA.CustomerKey = C.CustomerKey
WHERE ISA.CustomerKey <= 12000
)
SELECT ISG1.Gender, ISG1.OrderLineNumber,
 MIN(ISG1.SalesAmount), SUM(ISG2.SalesAmount) AS RunningTotal
FROM InternetSalesGender AS ISG1
 INNER JOIN InternetSalesGender AS ISG2
  ON ISG1.Gender = ISG2.Gender
    AND ISG1.OrderLineNumber >= ISG2.OrderLineNumber
GROUP BY ISG1.Gender, ISG1.OrderLineNumber
ORDER BY ISG1.Gender, ISG1.OrderLineNumber;
```

The query returns 6,434 rows and performs 2,286 logical reads in the *FactInternetSales* table, 124 logical reads in the *DimCustomer* table, and 5,015 logical reads in a *Worktable*, which is a working table that SQL Server created during query execution.

> **NOTE NUMBER OF LOGICAL READS**
>
> You might get slightly different numbers for logical reads; nevertheless, you should get many more logical reads from the first query than from the second query.

You can rewrite the query and use the new SQL Server 2012 window functions. The following code shows the rewritten query.

```
-- Query with a window function
WITH InternetSalesGender AS
(
SELECT ISA.CustomerKey, C.Gender,
 ISA.SalesOrderNumber + CAST(ISA.SalesOrderLineNumber AS CHAR(1))
  AS OrderLineNumber,
 ISA.SalesAmount
FROM dbo.FactInternetSales AS ISA
 INNER JOIN dbo.DimCustomer AS C
    ON ISA.CustomerKey = C.CustomerKey
WHERE ISA.CustomerKey  <= 12000
)
SELECT ISG.Gender, ISG.OrderLineNumber, ISG.SalesAmount,
 SUM(ISG.SalesAmount)
   OVER(PARTITION BY ISG.Gender
        ORDER BY ISG.OrderLineNumber
        ROWS BETWEEN UNBOUNDED PRECEDING
                  AND CURRENT ROW) AS RunningTotal
FROM InternetSalesGender AS ISG
ORDER BY ISG.Gender, ISG.OrderLineNumber;
GO
```

This query returns 6,343 rows as well, and performs 1,036 logical reads in the *FactInternet-Sales* table, 57 logical reads in the *DimCustomer* table, but no logical reads in *Worktable*. And this second query executes much faster than the first one—even if you run the first one without measuring the statistics IO.

Data Compression

SQL Server supports data compression. Data compression reduces the size of the database, which helps improve query performance because queries on compressed data read fewer pages from disk and thus use less IO. However, data compression requires extra CPU resources for updates, because data must be decompressed before and compressed after the update. Data compression is therefore suitable for data warehousing scenarios in which data is mostly read and only occasionally updated.

SQL Server supports three compression implementations:

- Row compression
- Page compression
- Unicode compression

Row compression reduces metadata overhead by storing fixed data type columns in a variable-length format. This includes strings and numeric data. Row compression has only a small impact on CPU resources and is often appropriate for OLTP applications as well.

Page compression includes row compression, but also adds prefix and dictionary compressions. *Prefix compression* stores repeated prefixes of values from a single column in a special compression information (CI) structure that immediately follows the page header, replacing the repeated prefix values with a reference to the corresponding prefix. *Dictionary compression* stores repeated values anywhere in a page in the CI area. Dictionary compression is not restricted to a single column.

In SQL Server, Unicode characters occupy an average of two bytes. *Unicode compression* substitutes single-byte storage for Unicode characters that don't truly require two bytes. Depending on collation, Unicode compression can save up to 50 percent of the space otherwise required for Unicode strings.

EXAM TIP

Unicode compression is applied automatically when you apply either row or page compression.

You can gain quite a lot from data compression in a data warehouse. Foreign keys are often repeated many times in a fact table. Large dimensions that have Unicode strings in name columns, member properties, and attributes can benefit from Unicode compression.

Columnstore Indexes and Batch Processing

SQL Server 2012 has a new method of storing nonclustered indexes. In addition to regular row storage, SQL Server 2012 can store index data column by column, in what's called a *columnstore index*. Columnstore indexes can speed up data warehousing queries by a large factor, from 10 to even 100 times!

A columnstore index is just another nonclustered index on a table. Query Optimizer considers using it during the query optimization phase just as it does any other index. All you have to do to take advantage of this feature is to create a columnstore index on a table.

A columnstore index is often compressed even further than any data compression type can compress the row storage—including page and Unicode compression. When a query references a single column that is a part of a columnstore index, then SQL Server fetches only that column from disk; it doesn't fetch entire rows as with row storage. This also reduces disk IO and memory cache consumption. Columnstore indexes use their own compression algorithm; you cannot use row or page compression on a columnstore index.

On the other hand, SQL Server has to return rows. Therefore, rows must be reconstructed when you execute a query. This row reconstruction takes some time and uses some CPU and memory resources. Very selective queries that touch only a few rows might not benefit from columnstore indexes.

Columnstore indexes accelerate data warehouse queries but are not suitable for OLTP workloads. Because of the row reconstruction issues, tables containing a columnstore index become read only. If you want to update a table with a columnstore index, you must first drop the columnstore index. If you use table partitioning, you can switch a partition to a different table without a columnstore index, update the data there, create a columnstore index on that table (which has a smaller subset of the data), and then switch the new table data back to a partition of the original table. You will learn how to implement table partitioning with columnstore indexes in Lesson 3 of this chapter.

There are two new catalog views you can use to gather information about columnstore indexes:

- sys.column_store_segments
- sys.column_store_dictionaries

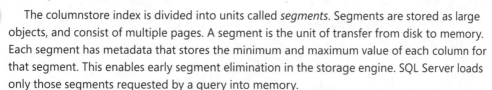 The columnstore index is divided into units called *segments*. Segments are stored as large objects, and consist of multiple pages. A segment is the unit of transfer from disk to memory. Each segment has metadata that stores the minimum and maximum value of each column for that segment. This enables early segment elimination in the storage engine. SQL Server loads only those segments requested by a query into memory.

SQL Server 2012 includes another important improvement for query processing. In *batch mode processing*, SQL Server processes data in batches rather than processing one row at a time. In SQL Server 2012, a batch represents roughly 1000 rows of data. Each column within a batch is stored as a vector in a separate memory area, meaning that batch mode processing is vector-based. Batch mode processing interrupts a processor with metadata only once per batch rather than once per row, as in row mode processing, which lowers the CPU burden substantially.

You can find out whether SQL Server used batch mode processing by analyzing the query execution plan. There are two new operator properties in the Actual Execution Plan: EstimatedExecutionMode and ActualExecutionMode. Batch mode processing is available for a limited list of operators only:

- Filter
- Project
- Scan
- Local hash (partial) aggregation
- Hash inner join
- (Batch) hash table build

Batch mode processing is particularly useful for data warehousing queries when combined with bitmap filtered hash join in a star join pattern.

Columnstore indexes have quite a few limitations:

- Columnstore indexes can be nonclustered only.
- You can have only one columnstore index per table.
- If your table is partitioned, the columnstore index must be partition aligned.

- Columnstore indexes are not allowed on indexed views.
- A columnstore index can't be a filtered index.
- There are additional data type limitations for columnstore indexes.

You should use a columnstore index on your fact tables, putting all columns of a fact table in a columnstore index. In addition to fact tables, very large dimensions could benefit from columnstore indexes as well. Do not use columnstore indexes for small dimensions. Other best practices for columnstore indexes include the following:

- Use columnstore indexes for
  - Read-mostly workloads.
  - Updates that append new data.
  - Workflows that permit partitioning or index drop/rebuild.
  - Queries that often scan and aggregate lots of data.
- Don't use columnstore indexes when
  - You update the data frequently.
  - Partition switching or rebuilding indexes doesn't fit your workflow.
  - Your workload includes mostly small lookup queries.

 Quick Check

1. How many columnstore indexes can you have per table?

2. Should you use page compression for OLTP environments?

Quick Check Answers

1. You can have one columnstore index per table.

2. No, you should use page compression only for data warehousing environments.

PRACTICE **Loading Data and Using Data Compression and Columnstore Indexes**

In this exercise, you are going to load data to the data warehouse you created in the practice in Lesson 1 of this chapter. You will use the AdventureWorksDW2012 sample database as the source for your data. After the data is loaded, you will apply data compression and create a columnstore index.

If you encounter a problem completing an exercise, you can install the completed projects from the Solution folder for this chapter and lesson provided with the companion content.

EXERCISE 1 Load Your Data Warehouse

In the first exercise, you are going to load data in your data warehouse.

1. If you closed SSMS, start it and connect to your SQL Server instance. Open a new query window by clicking the New Query button.

2. Connect to your TK463DW database. Load the *Customers* dimension by using information from Table 2-5 (this is the same as Table 2-1 in the practice for Lesson 1 of this chapter).

TABLE 2-5 Column Information for the *Customers* Dimension

Column name	Data type	Nullability	Remarks
CustomerDwKey	INT	NOT NULL	Surrogate key; assign values with a sequence
CustomerKey	INT	NOT NULL	
FullName	NVARCHAR(150)	NULL	Concatenate *FirstName* and *LastName* from *DimCustomer*
EmailAddress	NVARCHAR(50)	NULL	
BirthDate	DATE	NULL	
MaritalStatus	NCHAR(5)	NULL	
Gender	NCHAR(5)	NULL	
Education	NVARCHAR(40)	NULL	*EnglishEducation* from *DimCustomer*
Occupation	NVARCHAR(100)	NULL	*EnglishOccupation* from *DimCustomer*
City	NVARCHAR(30)	NULL	*City* from *DimGeography*
StateProvince	NVARCHAR(50)	NULL	*StateProvinceName* from *DimGeography*
CountryRegion	NVARCHAR(50)	NULL	*EnglishCountryRegionName* from *DimGeography*
Age	Inherited	Inherited	Computed column. Calculate the difference in years between *BirthDate* and the current date, and discretize it in three groups: ■ When difference <= 40, label "Younger" ■ When difference > 50, label "Older" ■ Else label "Middle Age"
CurrentFlag	BIT	NOT NULL	Default 1

The loading query is shown in the following code.

```
INSERT INTO dbo.Customers
(CustomerDwKey, CustomerKey, FullName,
 EmailAddress, Birthdate, MaritalStatus,
 Gender, Education, Occupation,
 City, StateProvince, CountryRegion)
SELECT
 NEXT VALUE FOR dbo.SeqCustomerDwKey AS CustomerDwKey,
 C.CustomerKey,
 C.FirstName + ' ' + C.LastName AS FullName,
 C.EmailAddress, C.BirthDate, C.MaritalStatus,
 C.Gender, C.EnglishEducation, C.EnglishOccupation,
 G.City, G.StateProvinceName, G.EnglishCountryRegionName
FROM AdventureWorksDW2012.dbo.DimCustomer AS C
 INNER JOIN AdventureWorksDW2012.dbo.DimGeography AS G
  ON C.GeographyKey = G.GeographyKey;
GO
```

3. Load the *Products* dimension by using the information from Table 2-6 (this is the same as Table 2-2 in the practice for Lesson 1 of this chapter).

TABLE 2-6 Column Information for the *Products* Dimension

Column name	Data type	Nullability	Remarks
ProductKey	INT	NOT NULL	
ProductName	NVARCHAR(50)	NULL	*EnglishProductName* from *DimProduct*
Color	NVARCHAR(15)	NULL	
Size	NVARCHAR(50)	NULL	
SubcategoryName	NVARCHAR(50)	NULL	*EnglishProductSubcategoryName* from *DimProductSubcategory*
CategoryName	NVARCHAR(50)	NULL	*EnglishProductCategoryName* from *DimProductCategory*

The loading query is shown in the following code.

```
INSERT INTO dbo.Products
(ProductKey, ProductName, Color,
 Size, SubcategoryName, CategoryName)
SELECT P.ProductKey, P.EnglishProductName, P.Color,
 P.Size, S.EnglishProductSubcategoryName, C.EnglishProductCategoryName
FROM AdventureWorksDW2012.dbo.DimProduct AS P
 INNER JOIN AdventureWorksDW2012.dbo.DimProductSubcategory AS S
  ON P.ProductSubcategoryKey = S.ProductSubcategoryKey
 INNER JOIN AdventureWorksDW2012.dbo.DimProductCategory AS C
  ON S.ProductCategoryKey = C.ProductCategoryKey;
GO
```

4. Load the *Dates* dimension by using the information from Table 2-7 (this is the same as Table 2-3 in the practice for Lesson 1 of this chapter).

TABLE 2-7 Column Information for the *Dates* Dimension

Column name	Data type	Nullability	Remarks
DateKey	INT	NOT NULL	
FullDate	DATE	NOT NULL	*FullDateAlternateKey* from *DimDate*
MonthNumberName	NVARCHAR(15)	NULL	Concatenate *MonthNumberOfYear* (with leading zeroes when the number is less than 10) and *EnglishMonthName* from *DimDate*
CalendarQuarter	TINYINT	NULL	
CalendarYear	SMALLINT	NULL	

The loading query is shown in the following code.

```
INSERT INTO dbo.Dates
(DateKey, FullDate, MonthNumberName,
 CalendarQuarter, CalendarYear)
SELECT DateKey, FullDateAlternateKey,
 FORMAT(MonthNumberOfYear,'00'))
 + ' ' + EnglishMonthName,
 CalendarQuarter, CalendarYear
FROM AdventureWorksDW2012.dbo.DimDate;
GO
```

5. Load the *InternetSales* fact table by using the information from Table 2-8 (this is the same as Table 2-4 in the practice for Lesson 1 of this chapter).

TABLE 2-8 Column Information for the *InternetSales* Fact Table

Column name	Data type	Nullability	Remarks
InternetSalesKey	INT	NOT NULL	IDENTITY(1,1)
CustomerDwKey	INT	NOT NULL	Using the *CustomerKey* business key from the *Customers* dimension, find the appropriate value of the *CustomerDwKey* surrogate key from the *Customers* dimension
ProductKey	INT	NOT NULL	
DateKey	INT	NOT NULL	*OrderDateKey* from *FactInternetSales*
OrderQuantity	SMALLINT	NOT NULL	Default 0
SalesAmount	MONEY	NOT NULL	Default 0
UnitPrice	MONEY	NOT NULL	Default 0
DiscountAmount	FLOAT	NOT NULL	Default 0

The loading query is shown in the following code.

```
INSERT INTO dbo.InternetSales
(CustomerDwKey, ProductKey, DateKey,
 OrderQuantity, SalesAmount,
 UnitPrice, DiscountAmount)
SELECT C.CustomerDwKey,
 FIS.ProductKey, FIS.OrderDateKey,
 FIS.OrderQuantity, FIS.SalesAmount,
 FIS.UnitPrice, FIS.DiscountAmount
FROM AdventureWorksDW2012.dbo.FactInternetSales AS FIS
 INNER JOIN dbo.Customers AS C
  ON FIS.CustomerKey = C.CustomerKey;
GO
```

EXERCISE 2   Apply Data Compression and Create a Columnstore Index

In this exercise, you will apply data compression and create a columnstore index on the *InternetSales* fact table.

1. Use the sp_spaceused system stored procedure to calculate the space used by the *InternetSales* table. Use the following code.

```
EXEC sp_spaceused N'dbo.InternetSales', @updateusage = 'TRUE';
GO
```

2. The table should use approximately 3,080 KB for the reserved space. Now use the ALTER TABLE statement to compress the table. Use page compression, as shown in the following code.

```
ALTER TABLE dbo.InternetSales
 REBUILD WITH (DATA_COMPRESSION = PAGE);
GO
```

3. Measure the reserved space again.

```
EXEC sp_spaceused N'dbo.InternetSales', @updateusage = 'TRUE';
GO
```

4. The table should now use approximately 1,096 KB for the reserved space. You can see that you spared nearly two-thirds of the space by using page compression.

5. Create a columnstore index on the *InternetSales* table. Use the following code.

```
CREATE COLUMNSTORE INDEX CSI_InternetSales
  ON dbo.InternetSales
  (InternetSalesKey, CustomerDwKey, ProductKey, DateKey,
   OrderQuantity, SalesAmount,
   UnitPrice, DiscountAmount);
GO
```

6. You do not have enough data to really measure the advantage of the columnstore index and batch processing. However, you can still write a query that joins the tables and aggregate data so you can check whether SQL Server uses the columnstore index. Here is an example of such a query.

```
SELECT C.CountryRegion, P.CategoryName, D.CalendarYear,
 SUM(I.SalesAmount) AS Sales
FROM dbo.InternetSales AS I
 INNER JOIN dbo.Customers AS C
  ON I.CustomerDwKey = C.CustomerDwKey
 INNER JOIN dbo.Products AS P
  ON I.ProductKey = p.ProductKey
 INNER JOIN dbo.Dates AS d
  ON I.DateKey = D.DateKey
GROUP BY C.CountryRegion, P.CategoryName, D.CalendarYear
ORDER BY C.CountryRegion, P.CategoryName, D.CalendarYear;
```

7. Check the execution plan and find out whether the columnstore index has been used. (For a real test, you should use much larger data sets.)

8. It is interesting to measure how much space a columnstore index occupies. Use the sp_spaceused system procedure again.

```
EXEC sp_spaceused N'dbo.InternetSales', @updateusage = 'TRUE';
GO
```

9. This time the reserved space should be approximately 1,560 KB. You can see that although you used page compression for the table, the table is still compressed less than the columnstore index. In this case, the columnstore index occupies approximately half of the space of the table.

NOTE CONTINUING WITH PRACTICES

Do not exit SSMS if you intend to continue immediately with the next practice.

Lesson Summary

- In this lesson, you learned how to optimize data warehouse query performance.
- In a DW, you should not use many nonclustered indexes.
- Use small, integer surrogate columns for clustered primary keys.
- Use indexed views.
- Use columnstore indexes and exploit batch processing.

Lesson Review

Answer the following questions to test your knowledge of the information in this lesson. You can find the answers to these questions and explanations of why each answer choice is correct or incorrect in the "Answers" section at the end of this chapter.

1. Which types of data compression are supported by SQL Server? (Choose all that apply.)

   A. Bitmap

   B. Unicode

   C. Row

   D. Page

2. Which operators can benefit from batch processing? (Choose all that apply.)

   A. Hash Join

   B. Merge Join

   C. Scan

   D. Nested Loops Join

   E. Filter

3. Why would you use indexed views? (Choose all that apply.)

   A. To speed up queries that aggregate data

   B. To speed up data load

   C. To speed up selective queries

   D. To speed up queries that involve multiple joins

Lesson 3: Loading and Auditing Loads

Loading large fact tables can be a problem. You have only a limited time window in which to do the load, so you need to optimize the load operation. In addition, you might be required to track the loads.

> **After this lesson, you will be able to:**
> - Use partitions to load large fact tables in a reasonable time.
> - Add lineage information to fact table loads.
>
> **Estimated lesson time: 45 minutes**

Using Partitions

Loading even very large fact tables is not a problem if you can perform incremental loads. However, this means that data in the source should never be updated or deleted; data should be inserted only. This is rarely the case with LOB applications. In addition, even if you have the possibility of performing an incremental load, you should have a parameterized ETL procedure in place so you can reload portions of data loaded already in earlier loads. There is always a possibility that something might go wrong in the source system, which means that you will have to reload historical data. This reloading will require you to delete part of the data from your data warehouse.

Deleting large portions of fact tables might consume too much time, unless you perform a minimally logged deletion. A minimally logged deletion operation can be done by using the TRUNCATE TABLE command; however, this command deletes all the data from a table—and deleting all the data is usually not acceptable. More commonly, you need to delete only portions of the data.

Inserting huge amounts of data could consume too much time as well. You can do a minimally logged insert, but as you already know, minimally logged inserts have some limitations. Among other limitations, a table must either be empty, have no indexes, or use a clustered index only on an ever-increasing (or ever-decreasing) key, so that all inserts occur on one end of the index. However, you would probably like to have some indexes on your fact table—at least a columnstore index. With a columnstore index, the situation is even worse—the table becomes read only.

You can resolve all of these problems by partitioning a table. You can even achieve better query performance by using a partitioned table, because you can create partitions in different filegroups on different drives, thus parallelizing reads. You can also perform maintenance procedures on a subset of filegroups, and thus on a subset of partitions only. That way, you can also speed up regular maintenance tasks. Altogether, partitions have many benefits.

Although you can partition a table on any attribute, partitioning over dates is most common in data warehousing scenarios. You can use any time interval for a partition. Depending on your needs, the interval could be a day, a month, a year, or any other interval. You can have as many as 15,000 partitions per table in SQL Server 2012. You can create all the partitions in advance, or you can use a sliding window scenario. For more information on the sliding window scenario and how to automate data loads in this scenario, refer to the SQLCAT whitepaper, "How to Implement an Automatic Sliding Window in a Partitioned Table on SQL Server 2005" at *http://msdn.microsoft.com/en-us/library/aa964122(SQL.90).aspx*.

In addition to partitioning tables, you can also partition indexes. Partitioned table and index concepts include the following:

- **Partition function**   This is an object that maps rows to partitions by using values from specific columns. The columns used for the function are called *partitioning columns*. A partition function performs logical mapping.

- **Partition scheme**   A partition scheme maps partitions to filegroups. A partition scheme performs physical mapping.

- **Aligned index**   This is an index built on the same partition scheme as its base table. If all indexes are aligned with their base table, switching a partition is a metadata operation only, so it is very fast. Columnstore indexes have to be aligned with their base tables. *Nonaligned indexes* are, of course, indexes that are partitioned differently than their base tables.

- **Partition elimination**   This is a Query Optimizer process in which SQL Server accesses only those partitions needed to satisfy query filters.

- **Partition switching**   This is a process that switches a block of data from one table or partition to another table or partition. You switch the data by using the ALTER TABLE T-SQL command. You can perform the following types of switches:

  - Reassign all data from a nonpartitioned table to an empty existing partition of a partitioned table.

  - Switch a partition of one partitioned table to a partition of another partitioned table.

  - Reassign all data from a partition of a partitioned table to an existing empty nonpartitioned table.

EXAM TIP

Make sure you understand the relationship between columnstore indexes and table partitioning thoroughly.

Any time you create a large partitioned table you should create two auxiliary nonindexed empty tables with the same structure, including constraints and data compression options. For one of these two tables, create a check constraint that guarantees that all data from the table fits exactly with one empty partition of your fact table. The constraint must be created on the partitioning column. You can have a columnstore index on your fact table, as long as it is aligned with the table.

For minimally logged deletions of large portions of data, you can switch a partition from the fact table to the empty table version *without* the check constraint. Then you can truncate that table. The TRUNCATE TABLE statement is minimally logged. Your first auxiliary table is prepared to accept the next partition from your fact table for the next minimally logged deletion.

For minimally logged inserts, you can bulk insert new data to the second auxiliary table, the one that has the check constraint. In this case, the INSERT operation can be minimally logged because the table is empty. Then you create a columnstore index on this auxiliary table, using the same structure as the columnstore index on your fact table. Now you can switch data from this auxiliary table to a partition of your fact table. Finally, you drop the columnstore index on the auxiliary table, and change the check constraint to guarantee that all of the data for the next load can be switched to the next empty partition of your fact table. Your second auxiliary table is prepared for new bulk loads again.

 Quick Check

- How many partitions can you have per table?

Quick Check Answer

- In SQL Server 2012, you can have up to 15,000 partitions per table.

Data Lineage

Auditing by adding data lineage information for your data loads is quite simple. You add appropriate columns to your dimensions and/or fact tables, and then you insert or update the values of these columns with each load. If you are using SSIS as your ETL tool, you can use many of the SSIS system variables to add lineage information to your data flow.

If you are loading data with T-SQL commands and procedures, you can use T-SQL system functions to get the desired lineage information. The following query uses system functions that are very useful for capturing lineage information.

```
SELECT
 APP_NAME() AS ApplicationName,
 DATABASE_PRINCIPAL_ID() AS DatabasePrincipalId,
 USER_NAME() AS DatabasePrincipalName,
 SUSER_ID() AS ServerPrincipalId,
 SUSER_SID() AS ServerPrincipalSID,
 SUSER_SNAME() AS ServerPrincipalName,
 CONNECTIONPROPERTY('net_transport') AS TransportProtocol,
 CONNECTIONPROPERTY('client_net_address') AS ClientNetAddress,
 CURRENT_TIMESTAMP AS CurrentDateTime,
 @@ROWCOUNT AS RowsProcessedByLastCommand;
GO
```

Besides lineage information, you might also want to log additional information about the whole load, not just the row-level information. For example, you might want to add the time at which the load execution started, when it ended, the number of rows transferred, and so on. You can create a custom logging table and insert this information at the start and end of the ETL process. If you are using SSIS as your ETL tool, you can use the SSIS built-in logging capabilities to store this load-level information.

In this practice, you test the use of table partitioning for a minimally logged data load.

If you encounter a problem completing an exercise, you can install the completed projects from the Solution folder for this chapter and lesson provided with the companion content.

EXERCISE 1 Prepare Your Fact Table for Partitioning

In this exercise, you will create all the objects you need for partitioning, and then you will load them with data.

1. If you closed SSMS, start it and connect to your SQL Server instance. Open a new query window by clicking the New Query button.

2. Connect to your TK463DW database. Drop the *InternetSales* table.

3. Create a partition function that will split data to 10 partitions for every year from the year 2000 to the year 2009. Use the smallest possible data type for the parameter of the partitioning column. You can use the following code.

```
CREATE PARTITION FUNCTION PfInternetSalesYear (TINYINT)
AS RANGE LEFT FOR VALUES (1, 2, 3, 4, 5, 6, 7, 8, 9);
GO
```

4. Create a partition scheme that will map all partitions to the Primary filegroup, as shown in the following code.

```
CREATE PARTITION SCHEME PsInternetSalesYear
AS PARTITION PfInternetSalesYear
ALL TO ([PRIMARY]);
GO
```

5. Re-create the *InternetSales* table. Add a partitioning column. Use the same data type for this column as you used for the parameter of the partitioning function. Use the following code.

```
CREATE TABLE dbo.InternetSales
(
  InternetSalesKey   INT      NOT NULL IDENTITY(1,1),
  PcInternetSalesYear TINYINT  NOT NULL,
  CustomerDwKey      INT      NOT NULL,
  ProductKey         INT      NOT NULL,
  DateKey            INT      NOT NULL,
  OrderQuantity      SMALLINT NOT NULL DEFAULT 0,
  SalesAmount        MONEY    NOT NULL DEFAULT 0,
  UnitPrice          MONEY    NOT NULL DEFAULT 0,
  DiscountAmount     FLOAT    NOT NULL DEFAULT 0,
  CONSTRAINT PK_InternetSales
    PRIMARY KEY (InternetSalesKey, PcInternetSalesYear)
)
ON PsInternetSalesYear(PcInternetSalesYear);
GO
```

6. Add foreign keys and compress data for the *InternetSales* table.

```
ALTER TABLE dbo.InternetSales ADD CONSTRAINT
 FK_InternetSales_Customers FOREIGN KEY(CustomerDwKey)
 REFERENCES dbo.Customers (CustomerDwKey);
ALTER TABLE dbo.InternetSales ADD CONSTRAINT
 FK_InternetSales_Products FOREIGN KEY(ProductKey)
 REFERENCES dbo.Products (ProductKey);
ALTER TABLE dbo.InternetSales ADD CONSTRAINT
 FK_InternetSales_Dates FOREIGN KEY(DateKey)
 REFERENCES dbo.Dates (DateKey);
GO
ALTER TABLE dbo.InternetSales
 REBUILD WITH (DATA_COMPRESSION = PAGE);
GO
```

7. Load data to the *InternetSales* table. Extract only the year number for the *DateKey* column. Make sure you load years earlier than the year 2008 only. You can use the following code.

```
INSERT INTO dbo.InternetSales
(PcInternetSalesYear, CustomerDwKey,
 ProductKey, DateKey,
 OrderQuantity, SalesAmount,
 UnitPrice, DiscountAmount)
SELECT
 CAST(SUBSTRING(CAST(FIS.OrderDateKey AS CHAR(8)), 3, 2)
      AS TINYINT)
  AS PcInternetSalesYear,
 C.CustomerDwKey,
 FIS.ProductKey, FIS.OrderDateKey,
 FIS.OrderQuantity, FIS.SalesAmount,
 FIS.UnitPrice, FIS.DiscountAmount
FROM AdventureWorksDW2012.dbo.FactInternetSales AS FIS
 INNER JOIN dbo.Customers AS C
  ON FIS.CustomerKey = C.CustomerKey
WHERE
 CAST(SUBSTRING(CAST(FIS.OrderDateKey AS CHAR(8)), 3, 2)
      AS TINYINT) < 8;
GO
```

8. Re-create the columnstore index of the *InternetSales* table.

```
CREATE COLUMNSTORE INDEX CSI_InternetSales
  ON dbo.InternetSales
  (InternetSalesKey, PcInternetSalesYear,
   CustomerDwKey, ProductKey, DateKey,
   OrderQuantity, SalesAmount,
   UnitPrice, DiscountAmount)
  ON PsInternetSalesYear(PcInternetSalesYear);
GO
```

EXERCISE 2   Load Minimally Logged Data to a Partitioned Table

In this exercise, you prepare a table for new data, load it, and use partition switching to assign this data to a partition of your partitioned fact table.

1. Create a new table with the same structure as the *InternetSales* table. Add a check constraint to this table. The check constraint must accept only the year 8 (short for 2008) for the partitioning column. Here is the code.

```
CREATE TABLE dbo.InternetSalesNew
(
 InternetSalesKey    INT       NOT NULL IDENTITY(1,1),
 PcInternetSalesYear TINYINT   NOT NULL
  CHECK (PcInternetSalesYear = 8),
 CustomerDwKey       INT       NOT NULL,
 ProductKey          INT       NOT NULL,
 DateKey             INT       NOT NULL,
 OrderQuantity       SMALLINT  NOT NULL DEFAULT 0,
 SalesAmount         MONEY     NOT NULL DEFAULT 0,
 UnitPrice           MONEY     NOT NULL DEFAULT 0,
 DiscountAmount      FLOAT     NOT NULL DEFAULT 0,
 CONSTRAINT PK_InternetSalesNew
  PRIMARY KEY (InternetSalesKey, PcInternetSalesYear)
);
GO
```

2. Create the same foreign keys and apply the same data compression settings as for the *InternetSales* table.

```
ALTER TABLE dbo.InternetSalesNew ADD CONSTRAINT
 FK_InternetSalesNew_Customers FOREIGN KEY(CustomerDwKey)
 REFERENCES dbo.Customers (CustomerDwKey);
ALTER TABLE dbo.InternetSalesNew ADD CONSTRAINT
 FK_InternetSalesNew_Products FOREIGN KEY(ProductKey)
 REFERENCES dbo.Products (ProductKey);
ALTER TABLE dbo.InternetSalesNew ADD CONSTRAINT
 FK_InternetSalesNew_Dates FOREIGN KEY(DateKey)
 REFERENCES dbo.Dates (DateKey);
GO
ALTER TABLE dbo.InternetSalesNew
 REBUILD WITH (DATA_COMPRESSION = PAGE);
GO
```

3. Load the year 2008 to the *InternetSalesNew* table.

```
INSERT INTO dbo.InternetSalesNew
(PcInternetSalesYear, CustomerDwKey,
 ProductKey, DateKey,
 OrderQuantity, SalesAmount,
 UnitPrice, DiscountAmount)
SELECT
 CAST(SUBSTRING(CAST(FIS.OrderDateKey AS CHAR(8)), 3, 2)
      AS TINYINT)
  AS PcInternetSalesYear,
```

```
        C.CustomerDwKey,
        FIS.ProductKey, FIS.OrderDateKey,
        FIS.OrderQuantity, FIS.SalesAmount,
        FIS.UnitPrice, FIS.DiscountAmount
    FROM AdventureWorksDW2012.dbo.FactInternetSales AS FIS
      INNER JOIN dbo.Customers AS C
        ON FIS.CustomerKey = C.CustomerKey
    WHERE
      CAST(SUBSTRING(CAST(FIS.OrderDateKey AS CHAR(8)), 3, 2)
            AS TINYINT) = 8;
    GO
```

4. Create a columnstore index on the *InternetSalesNew* table.

```
CREATE COLUMNSTORE INDEX CSI_InternetSalesNew
  ON dbo.InternetSalesNew
  (InternetSalesKey, PcInternetSalesYear,
   CustomerDwKey, ProductKey, DateKey,
   OrderQuantity, SalesAmount,
   UnitPrice, DiscountAmount);
GO
```

5. Check the number of rows in partitions of the *InternetSales* table and the number of rows in the *InternetSalesNew* table.

```
SELECT
  $PARTITION.PfInternetSalesYear(PcInternetSalesYear)
   AS PartitionNumber,
  COUNT(*) AS NumberOfRows
FROM dbo.InternetSales
GROUP BY
  $PARTITION.PfInternetSalesYear(PcInternetSalesYear);
SELECT COUNT(*) AS NumberOfRows
FROM dbo.InternetSalesNew;
GO
```

There should be no rows after the seventh partition of the *InternetSales* table and some rows in the *InternetSalesNew* table.

6. Do the partition switching. Use the following code.

```
ALTER TABLE dbo.InternetSalesNew
  SWITCH TO dbo.InternetSales PARTITION 8;
GO
```

7. Check the number of rows in partitions of the *InternetSales* table and the number of rows in the *InternetSalesNew* table again.

   There should be rows in the eighth partition of the *InternetSales* table and no rows in the *InternetSalesNew* table.

8. Prepare the *InternetSalesNew* table for the next load by dropping the columnstore index and changing the check constraint.

9. Save your code and exit SSMS.

Lesson Summary

- Table partitioning is extremely useful for large fact tables with columnstore indexes.
- Partition switch is a metadata operation only if an index is aligned with its base table.
- You can add lineage information to your dimensions and fact tables to audit changes to your DW on a row level.

Lesson Review

Answer the following questions to test your knowledge of the information in this lesson. You can find the answers to these questions and explanations of why each answer choice is correct or incorrect in the "Answers" section at the end of this chapter.

1. The database object that maps partitions of a table to filegroups is called a(n)

   A. Aligned index

   B. Partition function

   C. Partition column

   D. Partition scheme

2. You have inserted data into an unpartitioned table and want to switch the content from this table to a partition of a partitioned table. What conditions must the nonpartitioned table meet? (Choose all that apply.)

   A. It must have the same constraints as the partitioned table.

   B. It must have the same compression as the partitioned table.

   C. It must be in a special *PartitionedTables* schema.

   D. It must have a check constraint on the partitioning column that guarantees that all of the data goes to exactly one partition of the partitioned table.

   E. It must have the same indexes as the partitioned table.

3. Which of the following T-SQL functions is not very useful for capturing lineage information?

   A. APP_NAME()

   B. USER_NAME()

   C. DEVICE_STATUS()

   D. SUSER_SNAME()

Case Scenarios

In the following case scenarios, you apply what you've learned about optimized querying and securing a data warehouse. You can find the answers to these questions in the "Answers" section at the end of this chapter.

Case Scenario 1: Slow DW Reports

You have created a data warehouse and populated it. End users have started using it for reports. However, they have also begun to complain about the performance of the reports. Some of the very slow reports calculate running totals. You need to answer the following questions.

1. What changes can you implement in your DW to speed up the reports?

2. Does it make sense to check the source queries of the reports with running totals?

Case Scenario 2: DW Administration Problems

Your end users are happy with the DW reporting performance. However, when talking with a DBA, you were notified of potential problems. The DW transaction log grows by more than 10 GB per night. In addition, end users have started to create reports from staging tables, and these reports show messy data. End users complain to the DBA that they cannot trust your DW if they get such messy data in a report.

1. How can you address the runaway log problem?

2. What can you do to prevent end users from using the staging tables?

Suggested Practices

To help you successfully master the exam objectives presented in this chapter, complete the following tasks.

Test Different Indexing Methods

For some queries, indexed views could be the best performance booster. For other queries, columnstore indexes could be more appropriate. Still other queries would benefit from non-clustered indexes on foreign keys.

- **Practice 1** Write an aggregate query for Internet sales in the AdventureWorkDW2012 sample database. Create an appropriate indexed view and run the aggregate query. Check the statistics IO and execution plan.

- **Practice 2** Drop the indexed view and create a columnstore index. Run the query and check the statistics IO and execution plan again.

- **Practice 3** Drop the columnstore index and create nonclustered indexes on all foreign keys of the fact table included in joins. Run the query and check the statistics IO and execution plan again.

- **Practice 4** In the *DimCustomer* dimension of the AdventureWorksDW2012 sample database, there is a *Suffix* column. It is NULL for all rows but three. Create a filtered nonclustered index on this column and test queries that read data from the *DimCustomer* dimension using different filters. Check how the query performs when *Suffix* is NULL and when *Suffix* is known (is not NULL).

Test Table Partitioning

In order to understand table partitioning thoroughly, you should test it with aligned and nonaligned indexes.

- **Practice 1** Partition the *FactInternetSales* table in the AdventureWorkDW2012 sample database. Create aligned nonclustered indexes on all foreign keys of the fact table included in joins of the query from the previous practice. Run the query and check the execution plan.

- **Practice 2** Create nonaligned nonclustered indexes on all foreign keys of the fact table included in joins of the query from the previous practice. Run the query and check the execution plan again.

Answers

This section contains answers to the lesson review questions and solutions to the case scenarios in this chapter.

Lesson 1

1. **Correct Answers: A and B**

   A. **Correct:** The IDENTITY property autonumbers rows.

   B. **Correct:** You can use the new SQL Server 2012 SEQUENCE object for autonumbering.

   C. **Incorrect:** Primary keys are used to uniquely identify rows, not for autonumbering.

   D. **Incorrect:** Check constraints are used to enforce data integrity, not for autonumbering.

2. **Correct Answers: B and D**

   A. **Incorrect:** Member properties are dimension columns used for additional information on reports only.

   B. **Correct:** You need a current flag for denoting the current row when you implement Type 2 SCD changes.

   C. **Incorrect:** Lineage columns are used, as their name states, to track the lineage information.

   D. **Correct:** You need a new, surrogate key when you implement Type 2 SCD changes.

3. **Correct Answer: C**

   A. **Incorrect:** You do not add rows to a fact table during dimension load.

   B. **Incorrect:** You do not create rows with aggregated values.

   C. **Correct:** A row in a dimension added during fact table load is called an inferred member.

   D. **Incorrect:** A computed column is just a computed column, not an inferred member.

Lesson 2

1. **Correct Answers: B, C, and D**

   A. **Incorrect:** SQL Server does not support bitmap compression.

   B. **Correct:** SQL Server supports Unicode compression. It is applied automatically when you use either row or page compression.

   C. **Correct:** SQL Server supports row compression.

   D. **Correct:** SQL Server supports page compression.

2. **Correct Answers: A, C, and E**

    A. **Correct:** Hash joins can use batch processing.

    B. **Incorrect:** Merge joins do not use batch processing.

    C. **Correct:** Scan operators can benefit from batch processing.

    D. **Incorrect:** Nested loops joins do not use batch processing.

    E. **Correct:** Filter operators use batch processing as well.

3. **Correct Answers: A and D**

    A. **Correct:** Indexed views are especially useful for speeding up queries that aggregate data.

    B. **Incorrect:** As with any indexes, indexed views only slow down data load.

    C. **Incorrect:** For selective queries, nonclustered indexes are more appropriate.

    D. **Correct:** Indexed views can also speed up queries that perform multiple joins.

Lesson 3

1. **Correct Answer: D**

    A. **Incorrect:** Aligned indexes are indexes with the same partitioning as their base table.

    B. **Incorrect:** The partition function does logical partitioning.

    C. **Incorrect:** The partition column is the column used for partitioning.

    D. **Correct:** The partition scheme does physical partitioning.

2. **Correct Answers: A, B, D, and E**

    A. **Correct:** It must have the same constraints as the partitioned table.

    B. **Correct:** It must have the same compression as the partitioned table.

    C. **Incorrect:** There is no special schema for partitioned tables.

    D. **Correct:** It must have a check constraint to guarantee that all data goes to a single partition.

    E. **Correct:** It must have the same indexes as the partitioned table.

3. **Correct Answer: C**

    A. **Incorrect:** The APP_NAME() function can be useful for capturing lineage information.

    B. **Incorrect:** The USER_NAME() function can be useful for capturing lineage information.

    C. **Correct:** There is no DEVICE_STATUS() function in T-SQL.

    D. **Incorrect:** The SUSER_SNAME() function can be useful for capturing lineage information.

Case Scenario 1

1. You should consider using columnstore indexes, indexed views, data compression, and table partitioning.

2. Yes, it is definitely worth checking the queries of the running totals reports. The queries probably use joins or subqueries to calculate the running totals. Consider using window functions for these calculations.

Case Scenario 2

1. You should check the DW database recovery model and change it to Simple. In addition, you could use the DBCC SHRINKFILE command to shrink the transaction log to a reasonable size.

2. End users apparently have permissions, at least the SELECT permission, on the staging tables. Advise the DBA to revoke permissions from end users on staging tables. In addition, to speed up the security administration, you should put all staging tables in a separate schema, thus allowing the DBA to administer them as a group.

## PART II

Developing SSIS Packages

CHAPTER 3   Creating SSIS Packages   **87**

CHAPTER 4   Designing and Implementing Control Flow   **131**

CHAPTER 5   Designing and Implementing Data Flow   **177**

Creating SSIS Packages

Exam objectives in this chapter:

- Extract and Transform Data
  - Define connection managers.
- Load Data
  - Design control flow.

D ata movement represents an important part of data management. Data is transported from client applications to the data server to be stored, and transported back from the database to the client to be managed and used. In data warehousing, data movement represents a particularly important element, considering the typical requirements of a data warehouse: the need to import data from one or more operational data stores, the need to cleanse and consolidate the data, and the need to transform data, which allows it to be stored and maintained appropriately in the data warehouse.

Microsoft SQL Server 2012 provides a dedicated solution for this particular set of requirements: SQL Server Integration Services (SSIS). In contrast to Line of Business (LOB) data management operations, in which individual business entities are processed one at a time in the client application by a human operator, data warehousing (DW) operations are performed against collections of business entities in automated processes. In light of these important differences, SSIS provides the means to perform operations against large quantities of data efficiently and, as much as possible, without any need for human intervention.

Another difference between LOB and DW data management is *when* the operations are executed; LOB operations are predominantly performed during standard work hours, but DW operations are performed during "maintenance windows": typically, data maintenance in a DW is performed during times of less usage or no usage at all (for example, at night). This is both in order to reduce the impact of resource-intensive operations on the LOB system as well as to reduce the impact of data volatility on the DW.

Based on the level of complexity, data movement scenarios can be divided into two groups:

- *Simple data movements*, where data is moved from the source to the destination "as-is" (unmodified)

- *Complex data movements*, where the data needs to be transformed before it can be stored, and where additional programmatic logic is required to accommodate the merging of the new and/or modified data, arriving from the source, with existing data, already present at the destination

In light of this, the SQL Server 2012 tool set provides two distinct approaches to developing data movement processes:

- The SQL Server Import and Export Wizard, which can be used to design (and execute) simple data movements, such as the transfer of data from one database to another

- The SQL Server Data Tools, which boast a complete integrated development environment, providing SQL Server Integration Services (SSIS) developers with the ability to design even the most complex data movement processes

What constitutes a complex data movement? Three distinct elements can be observed in any complex data movement process:

1. The data is *extracted* from the source (retrieved from the operational data store).

2. The data is *transformed* (cleansed, converted, reorganized, and restructured) to comply with the destination data model.

3. The data is *loaded* into the destination data store (such as a data warehouse).

This process is also known as *extract-transform-load*, or *ETL*. In simple data movements, however, the transform element is omitted, leaving only two elements: extract and load.

In this chapter, you will learn how to use the SQL Server Import and Export Wizard to copy the data from one database to another, and you will begin your journey into the exciting world of SSIS package development using the SQL Server Data Tools (SSDT).

> **NOTE DATA MOVEMENTS IN DATA WAREHOUSING**
>
> In typical data warehousing scenarios, few data movements require no transformations at all; the majority of data movements at the very least require structural changes so that the data will adhere to the data model used by the data warehouse.

Lessons in this chapter:

- Lesson 1: Using the SQL Server Import and Export Wizard
- Lesson 2: Developing SSIS Packages in SSDT
- Lesson 3: Introducing Control Flow, Data Flow, and Connection Managers

Before You Begin

To complete this chapter, you must have:

- Experience working with SQL Server Management Studio (SSMS).
- Elementary experience working with Microsoft Visual Studio or SQL Server Data Tools (SSDT).
- A working knowledge of the Transact-SQL language.

Lesson 1: Using the SQL Server Import and Export Wizard

For simple data movement scenarios, especially when time reserved for development is scarce, using a rich development environment with all the tools and features available could present quite a lot of unnecessary overhead. In fact, all that is actually needed in a simple data movement is a source, a destination, and a way to invoke the transfer. SQL Server offers a simplified development interface—essentially a step-by-step wizard perfectly suitable for simple data movements: the SQL Server Import and Export Wizard.

> **After this lesson, you will be able to:**
>
> - Understand when to use the SQL Server Import and Export Wizard.
> - Use the SQL Server Import and Export Wizard.
>
> **Estimated lesson time: 20 minutes**

Planning a Simple Data Movement

To determine whether the Import and Export Wizard is the right tool for a particular data movement, ask yourself a few simple questions:

- Will the data need to be transformed before it can be stored at the destination?

  If no transformations are required, then the Import and Export Wizard might be the right tool for the job. If transformations are required, you might still be able to use the Import and Export Wizard, if the transformations can all be managed inside the SELECT query that is used when the data is extracted from the source.

- Is it necessary to merge source data with existing data at the destination?

    If no data exists at the destination (for example, because the destination itself does not yet exist), then using the Import and Export Wizard should be the right choice. The same is true if data does already exist at the destination but merging new and old data is not necessary (for example, when duplicates are allowed at the destination).

- If the destination does not yet exist, is there enough free space available at the SQL Server instance's default data placement location?

    Although the Import and Export Wizard will let you create the destination database as part of the process, it will only allow you to specify the initial size and growth properties for the newly created database files; it will not allow you to specify where the files are to be placed. If enough space is available at the default location, then using the Import and Export Wizard might be the right choice.

If you have determined that the Import and Export Wizard fits your data movement requirements, use it; otherwise, you will be better off developing your solution by using SSDT.

EXAM TIP

Plan data movements carefully, and consider the benefits as well as the shortcomings of the Import and Export Wizard.

 Quick Check

1. What is the SQL Server Import and Export Wizard?

2. What is the principal difference between simple and complex data movements?

Quick Check Answers

1. The Import and Export Wizard is a utility that provides a simplified interface for developing data movement operations where data is extracted from a source and loaded into a destination, without the need for any transformations.

2. In simple data movements, data is copied from one data store into another one unmodified, whereas in complex data movements, data is modified (transformed) before being loaded into the destination data store.

Creating a Simple Data Movement

In this practice, you will use the Import and Export Wizard to extract data from a view in an existing database and load it into a newly created table in a newly created database. You will learn how to develop a data movement process by using the step-by-step approach provided by the wizard, you will save the SSIS package created by the wizard to the file system, and then you will execute the newly developed process.

If you encounter a problem completing an exercise, you can install the completed projects from the Solution folder that is provided with the companion content for this chapter and lesson.

EXERCISE 1 Extract Data from a View and Load It into a Table

1. Start the SQL Server Import and Export Wizard: on the Start menu, click All Programs | Microsoft SQL Server 2012. On the Welcome page, click Next.

2. To choose the data source, connect to your server, select the appropriate authentication settings, and select the AdventureWorks2012 database, as shown in Figure 3-1. Then click Next.

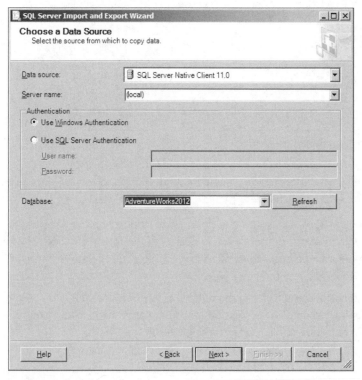

FIGURE 3-1 Choosing a data source.

3. To choose a destination, connect to your server and use the same authentication settings as in the previous step. This is shown in Figure 3-2. One option is to load the data into an existing database; however, in this exercise, the destination database does not exist. Click New to create it.

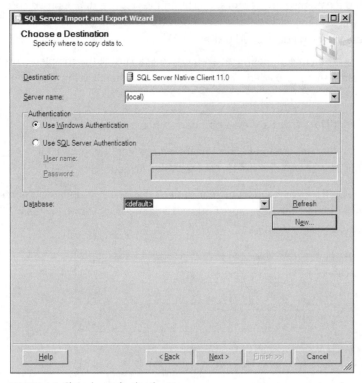

FIGURE 3-2 Choosing a destination.

4. To create a new database, provide a name for it (**TK463**), as shown in Figure 3-3. Leave the rest of the settings unchanged. Then click OK, and then Next.

5. On the next page, shown in Figure 3-4, you need to decide whether you want to extract the data from one or more existing objects of the source database or whether you want to use a single query to extract the data. Select Copy Data From One Or More Tables Or Views, and then click Next.

    The first option allows you to select multiple objects, but it does not allow you to restrict the extracted data; the second option, on the other hand, allows you to restrict the extracted data, but it only supports a single result set.

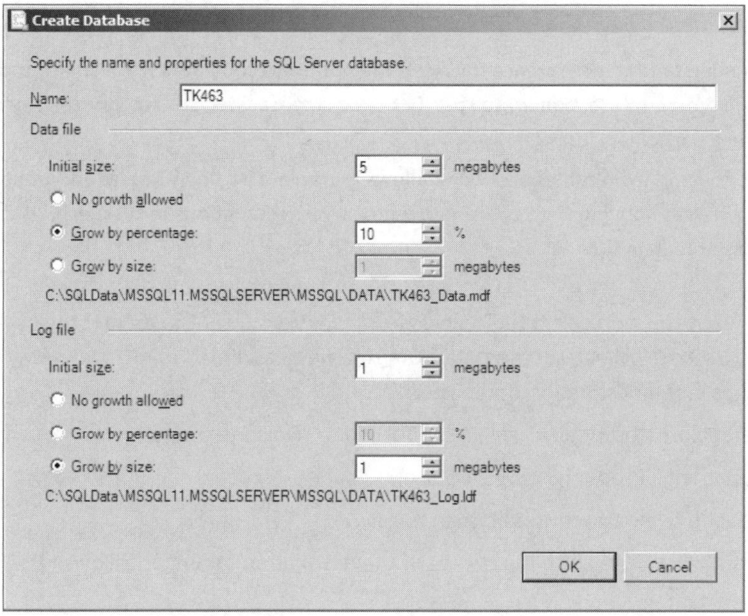

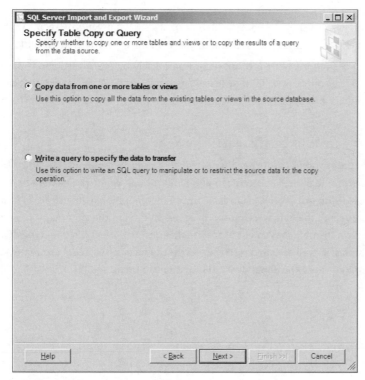

FIGURE 3-3 Creating the database.

FIGURE 3-4 Specifying table copy or query.

6. On the next page, you select the objects from which you want to extract the data. In this exercise, you will extract the data from two views and load it into two newly created tables in the destination database.

   In the left column of the grid, select the following two source views:

   - [Production].[vProductAndDescription]
   - [Production].[vProductModelInstructions]

   In the right column, change the names of the destination tables, as follows:

   - [Production].[ProductAndDescription]
   - [Production].[ProductModelInstructions]

   The result is shown in Figure 3-5.

7. Select the first view, and then click Edit Mappings. As shown in Figure 3-6, you can see that the data extracted from the view will be inserted into a newly created table.

   The definition of the new table is prepared automatically by the wizard and is based on the schema of the source row set. If necessary, you can modify the table definition by clicking Edit SQL. However, in this exercise, you should leave the definition unchanged.

REAL WORLD   **EXTRACTING DATA FROM VIEWS**

Using views as data sources has its benefits as well as some shortcomings. The ability to implement some basic data transformation logic at the source can be beneficial, because it provides an instant "look and feel," inside the operational data store, of how the data will appear in the data warehouse. However, modifying the view might have a negative effect on the data movement process—changes that affect the data type of the view's columns, as well as changes to the view's schema (such as adding or removing columns) might cause the dependent SSIS solutions to break.

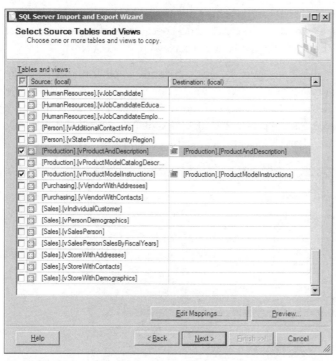

FIGURE 3-5 Selecting source tables and views.

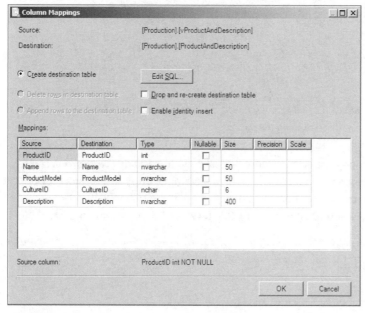

FIGURE 3-6 Column mappings.

8. When you are done, click OK to close the Column Mappings window; if you have made any changes to the table definition, click Cancel because no changes are necessary for this exercise. On the Select Source Tables And Views page, click Next.

9. On the next page, shown in Figure 3-7, you can decide whether to run the package, save it for later, or even do both. Make sure the Run Immediately check box is selected, and also select the Save SSIS Package check box. Then select File System as the destination for the newly created package. Under Package Protection Level, select Do Not Save Sensitive Data. Then click Next.

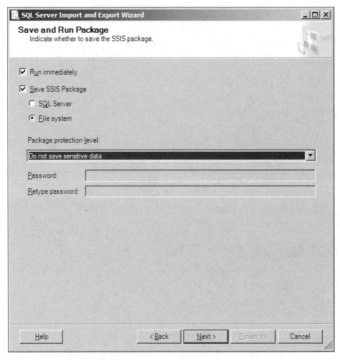

FIGURE 3-7 Saving and running the package.

10. On the next page, shown in Figure 3-8, name your package (**TK463_IEWizard**), provide a description for it if you want (for example, **Copy AdventureWorks2012 Product data to a new database**), and name the resulting SSIS package file (**C:\TK463\Chapter03\Lesson1\TK463_IEWizard.dtsx**). When ready, click Next.

11. On the next page, shown in Figure 3-9, you can review the actions that will be performed when the package is executed. When ready, click Next.

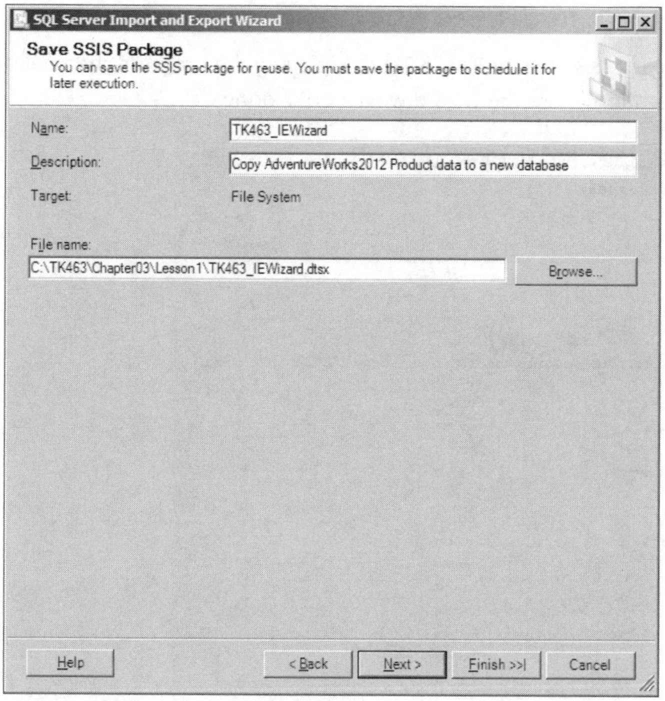

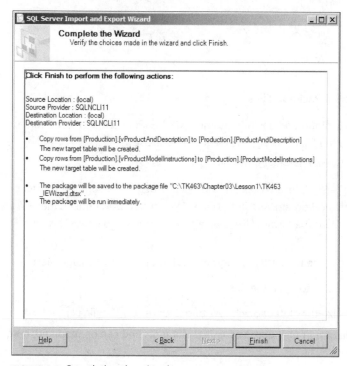

FIGURE 3-8 Saving the SSIS package.

FIGURE 3-9 Completing the wizard.

12. To execute the package, click Finish.

13. A new page appears, as shown in Figure 3-10, displaying the progress and finally the results of the execution. Close the wizard when you're done.

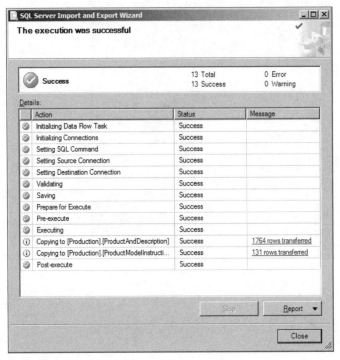

FIGURE 3-10 The execution.

EXERCISE 2   View SSIS Package Files

1. Open Windows Explorer and navigate to the C:\TK463\Chapter03\Lesson1 folder, where you saved the SSIS package file created in Exercise 1.

You will now view the contents of this file.

2. Right-click the TK463_IEWizard.dtsx file and select Open With from the shortcut menu. Click Choose Default Program, and in the Open With dialog box, under Other Programs, select Notepad. Clear the Always Use The Selected Program To Open This Kind Of File check box.

You should not change the default program used to open SSIS package files!

3. When ready, click OK, to open the file.

4. If needed, maximize the Notepad window, and then review the file contents.

SSIS package files are implemented as XML documents and can be modified, if needed, even if SSDT is not available.

Of course, you should not edit SSIS package files manually unless you are familiar with their structure, because you might end up damaging them beyond repair.

5. When done, close Notepad, abandoning any changes.

6. Return to Windows Explorer, and double-click the TK463_IEWizard.dtsx file to open it using the default program, the Execute Package Utility. This utility can be used to configure and execute SSIS packages. The utility cannot be used to make permanent changes to SSIS packages. You will learn more about this utility in Chapter 12, "Executing and Securing Packages."

7. When done, click Close to close the package file without executing it.

8. Close Windows Explorer.

Lesson Summary

- The SQL Server Import and Export Wizard can be used for simple data movement operations.
- The wizard allows you to create the destination database.
- Multiple objects can be transferred in the same operation.
- If the destination objects do not already exist, they can be created by the process.
- The SSIS package created by the wizard can be saved and reused.

Lesson Review

Answer the following questions to test your knowledge of the information in this lesson. You can find the answers to these questions and explanations of why each answer choice is correct or incorrect in the "Answers" section at the end of this chapter.

1. You need to move data from a production database into a testing database. You need to extract the data from several objects in the source database, but your manager has asked you to only copy about 10 percent of the rows from the largest production tables. The testing database already exists, but without any tables. How would you approach this task? (Choose all that apply.)

   A. Use the Import and Export Wizard, copy all tables from the source database to the empty destination database, and delete the excess rows from the largest tables.

   B. Use the Import and Export Wizard multiple times—once for all the smaller tables, and once for each large table, using the Write A Query To Specify The Data To Transfer option to restrict the rows.

C. Use the Import and Export Wizard, copy all tables from the source database to the empty destination database, and restrict the number of rows for each large table by using the Edit SQL option in the Column Mappings window.

D. Use the Import and Export Wizard, configure it to copy all tables from the source database to the empty destination database, save the SSIS package, and then, before executing it, edit it by using SSDT to restrict the number of rows extracted from the large tables.

2. You need to move data from an operational database into a data warehouse for the very first time. The data warehouse has already been set up, and it already contains some reference data. You have just finished preparing views in the operational database that correspond to the dimension and fact tables of the data warehouse. How would you approach this task? (Choose all that apply.)

A. Use the Import and Export Wizard and copy data from the dimension and fact views in the operational database into the tables in the data warehouse, by using the Drop And Re-create The Destination Table option in the Column Mappings window for every non-empty destination table.

B. Use the Import and Export Wizard, configure it to copy data from the dimension and fact views in the operational database into the tables in the data warehouse, save the SSIS package, and then edit it by using SSDT to add appropriate data merging functionalities for all destination tables.

C. Use the Import and Export Wizard and copy data from the dimension and fact views in the operational database into the tables in the data warehouse, by using the Merge Data Into The Destination Table option in the Column Mappings window for every non-empty destination table.

D. Use SSDT instead of the Import and Export Wizard, because the wizard lacks appropriate data transformation and merging capabilities.

3. When SSIS packages are saved to DTSX files, what format is used to store the SSIS package definitions?

A. They are stored as binary files.

B. They are stored as plain text files.

C. They are stored as XML files.

D. They are stored as special Microsoft Word documents.

Lesson 2: Developing SSIS Packages in SSDT

The ability to modify (transform) data before it can be stored at the destination, and the ability to merge the new or modified data appropriately with existing data are not available in the SQL Server Import and Export Wizard; therefore, the wizard is not really suitable for complex data movement scenarios.

Nevertheless, one could, for instance, use the wizard to design an SSIS package in minutes, test it, and deploy it so that the data warehouse could be deployed as soon as possible, and then later use the SQL Server Data Tools (SSDT) to add any missing functionalities in order to improve the reusability and manageability of the solution.

On the other hand, data warehousing scenarios do not generally count among projects to which rapid solution development is paramount; in the majority of cases, data warehousing projects require a lot of research and planning before it would even be reasonable to do any actual development, with the goal of providing a complete, production-ready data move-ment solution. By the time the planning phase is completed, an early and quickly developed data movement process would probably already have become obsolete and would have to be modified significantly for production. It is therefore unlikely that the benefits of early deploy-ment would outweigh the need to revise and possibly redesign the data movement process after the design of the data warehouse has actually matured enough for production.

In other words, SSIS development would usually be done "from scratch"—using SSDT instead of the Import and Export Wizard; but this prospect alone does not render the wizard useless.

SSIS uses a special declarative programming language—or rather, a special programming interface—to define the order and conditions of operations' execution. With a strong em-phasis on automation, DW maintenance applications differ from the majority of applications in that they do not support user interfaces. Monitoring, inspection, and troubleshooting are provided through auditing and logging capabilities.

Techniques used in SSIS design and development may differ significantly from other pro-gramming techniques, appearing especially different to database administrators or develop-ers who are more accustomed to other programming languages (such as Transact-SQL or Microsoft .NET). Most of SSIS development is done graphically—using the mouse, rather than by typing in the commands using the keyboard. A visual approach to design not only allows you to configure the operations, define their order, and determine under what conditions they will be executed, but it also provides a WYSIWYG programming experience.

After they have been deployed, SSIS solutions are usually executed automatically—for example, when using SQL Server Agent—but they can also be invoked on demand, by using utilities provided by the platform or through an application programming interface (API).

Introducing SSDT

SSDT is a special edition of Visual Studio, which is Microsoft's principal integrated development environment. SSDT supports a variety of SQL Server development projects, such as SQL Server Analysis Services Multidimensional and Data Mining projects, Analysis Services Tabular projects, SQL Server Reporting Services Report Server projects, and Integration Services (SSIS) projects. For all of these project types, SSDT provides a complete integrated development environment, customized specifically for each particular project type.

For Integration Services projects, SSDT provides an entire arsenal of data management tasks and components covering pretty much any data warehousing need (a variety of data extraction, transformation, and loading techniques). Nonetheless, in the real world, you could eventually encounter situations for which none of the built-in tools provide the most appropriate solution. Fortunately, the SSIS development model is extensible: the built-in tool set can be extended by adding custom tasks and/or custom components—either provided by third-party vendors or developed by you.

> **NOTE** SQL SERVER BUSINESS INTELLIGENCE STUDIO
>
> In versions of SQL Server prior to SQL Server 2012, the special edition of Visual Studio went by the name SQL Server Business Intelligence Development Studio, or BIDS. In general, the earlier version provides the same kind of experience from a usability perspective—with the obvious exception of the functionalities that do not exist in the previous version of the tool.

 Quick Check

- What is SSDT?

Quick Check Answer

- SQL Server Data Tools (SSDT) is a special edition of Visual Studio used for developing SQL Server 2012 solutions, such as SSIS packages, SSAS multi-dimensional models, and SSRS reports.

PRACTICE **Getting Started with SSDT**

In this practice, you will become familiar with SSDT and have an opportunity to take your first steps in SQL Server 2012 Integration Services solution development.

Compared to the Import and Export Wizard, which you worked with earlier in this chapter, SSIS development in SSDT might at first glance seem like a daunting task; although the wizard does provide a very straightforward development path from start to finish, the overall experience of SSDT is by far superior, as you will soon discover.

The wizard guides you quickly toward results, but SSDT provides you with a complete and clear overview of the emerging solution and unimpeded control over the operations.

If you encounter a problem completing this exercise, you can install the completed projects that are provided with the companion content. These can be installed from the Solution folder for this chapter and lesson.

EXERCISE 1   Create a New SSIS Project

In this exercise, you will familiarize yourself with the SSDT integrated development environment (IDE), create a new SSIS project, and explore the SSIS development tool set.

1. Start the SQL Server Data Tools (SSDT): On the Start menu, click either All Programs | Microsoft SQL Server 2012|SQL Server Data Tools or All Programs | Microsoft Visual Studio 2010 | Visual Studio 2010.

2. Create a new project, either by clicking New Project on the Start Page, via the menu by clicking File | New | Project, or by using the Ctrl+Shift+N keyboard shortcut.

3. In the New Project window, shown in Figure 3-11, select the appropriate project template. Under Installed Templates | Business Intelligence | Integration Services, select Integration Services Project.

4. At the bottom of the New Project window, provide a name for the project and the location for the project files. Name your project **TK 463 Chapter 3**, and set the **C:\ TK463\Chapter03\Lesson2\Starter** folder as the project location. Also, make sure that the Create Directory For The Solution check box is not selected, because a separate folder for the solution files is not needed. Click OK when ready.

5. After the new project and solution have been created, inspect the Solution Explorer pane on the upper-right side of the IDE, as shown in Figure 3-12. The project you just created should be listed, and it should contain a single SSIS package file named Package.dtsx.

   The Solution Explorer pane provides access to solution and project properties and the objects they contain; SSIS projects contain at least one SSIS package. Project-level connection managers and project parameters can be accessed through the Solution Explorer pane.

FIGURE 3-11 Creating a new project.

FIGURE 3-12 Solution Explorer.

6. Save the solution, but keep it open, because you will need it in the following exercise.

> **NOTE PROJECTS AND SOLUTIONS**
>
> The solution itself is not displayed in the Solution Explorer if it only contains a single project, as is the case in this exercise.
>
> You can configure SSDT (or any other edition of Visual Studio) to always display the solution by selecting the Always Show Solution check box in SSDT (or Visual Studio) Options (accessible through the Tools menu), under Projects And Solutions | General.

EXERCISE 2 Explore SSIS Control Flow Design

1. In the Solution Explorer pane, double-click the Package.dtsx package to open the Control Flow designer.

The largest part in the middle of the IDE window is reserved for SSIS package control flow and data flow design.

2. On the left of the SSDT IDE, you can find the SSIS Toolbox, shown in Figure 3-13. In the context of the SSIS package, the SSIS Toolbox lists control flow tasks, allowing you to create and configure the control flow for the SSIS package.

FIGURE 3-13 The SSIS Toolbox in the context of an SSIS package.

Take a minute to explore the toolbox; for now, simply browse through the control flow tasks. You will learn more about them in Chapter 4, "Designing and Implementing Control Flow."

3. Drag the data flow task from the SSIS Toolbox onto the SSIS control flow designer pane, as shown in Figure 3-14.

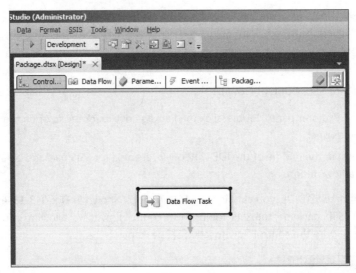

FIGURE 3-14 The SSIS package pane with a Data Flow Task.

4. Double-click the data flow task, or select the Data Flow tab at the top of the SSIS package pane, to access the data flow definition. A newly created data flow task contains no components; however, the contents of the SSIS Toolbox have changed, as shown in Figure 3-15.

   Take another minute to explore the Toolbox; for now, simply browse through the data flow components. You will learn more about them in Chapter 5, "Designing and Implementing Data Flow."

5. When you are finished, save the SSIS project and close SSDT.

FIGURE 3-15 SSIS Toolbox in the context of a data flow task.

Lesson Summary

- SSIS projects are developed by using SSDT, a specialized version of Visual Studio.
- SSDT provides the complete integrated development environment (IDE) required for efficient development of SSIS packages.
- The SSIS toolbox is context-aware and will either allow you access to control flow tasks or data flow components, depending on whether you are designing the control flow or the data flow.

Lesson Review

Answer the following questions to test your knowledge of the information in this lesson. You can find the answers to these questions and explanations of why each answer choice is correct or incorrect in the "Answers" section at the end of this chapter.

1. Which statements best describe SQL Server Data Tools (SSDT)? (Choose all that apply.)

   A. SSDT is an extension of the SQL Server Management Studio that can be used to create SSIS packages by means of a special wizard.

   B. SSDT is a special edition of the SQL Server Management Studio, designed to provide an improved user experience to developers who are not particularly familiar with database administration.

   C. SSDT is a special edition of Visual Studio, distributed with SQL Server 2012, providing a rich database development tool set.

   D. SSDT is a new service in SQL Server 2012 that can be used to perform SQL Server maintenance tasks, such as data movements and similar data management processes.

2. Which of the following statements about simple and complex data movements are true? (Choose all that apply.)

   A. Simple data movements only have a single data source and a single data destination.

   B. Complex data movements require data to be transformed before it can be stored at the destination.

   C. In simple data movements, data transformations are limited to data type conversion.

   D. In complex data movements, additional programmatic logic is required to merge source data with destination data.

3. Which of the following statements are true? (Choose all that apply.)

   A. An SSIS package can contain one or more SSDT solutions, each performing a specific data management operation.

   B. An SSIS project can contain one or more SSIS packages.

   C. An SSIS project can contain exactly one SSIS package.

   D. SSIS packages contain programmatic logic used in data movements and data transformation operations.

Lesson 3: Introducing Control Flow, Data Flow, and Connection Managers

Before you dive into SSIS development, you should be familiar with three essential elements of every SSIS package:

- **Connection managers** Provide connections to data stores, either as data sources or data destinations. Because the same data store can play the role of the data source as well as the data destination, connection managers allow the connection to be defined once and used many times in the same package (or project).

- **Control flow** Defines both the order of operations and the conditions under which they will be executed. A package can consist of one or more operations, represented by *control flow tasks*. Execution order is defined by how individual tasks are connected to one another. Tasks that do not follow any preceding task as well as tasks that follow the same preceding task are executed in parallel.

- **Data flow** Encapsulates the data movement components—the ETL:

  - One or more source components, designating the data stores from which the data will be extracted

  - One or more destination components, designating the data stores into which the data will be loaded

  - One or more (optional) transformation components, designating the transformations through which the data will be passed

---

EXAM TIP

Never confuse the control flow with the data flow. Control flow determines the operations and the order of their execution. Data flow is a task in the control flow that determines the ETL operation.

The role of connection managers is to provide access to data stores, either as data sources, data destinations, or reference data stores. Control flow tasks define the data management operations of the SSIS process, with the data flow tasks providing the core of data warehousing operations—the ETL.

> **After this lesson, you will be able to:**
> - Determine the control flow of an SSIS package.
> - Plan the configuration of connection managers.
>
> **Estimated lesson time: 40 minutes**

Introducing SSIS Development

The integrated development environment (IDE) of SSDT provides a unified and comprehensive approach to database development; Analysis Services, Reporting Services, and Integration Services solutions are all serviced by the same IDE, with obvious and necessary customizations to account for the differences between individual development models.

Even as far as Integration Services solutions are concerned, an SSIS project in its entirety might be more than just a single data movement (and it usually is, quite a lot more). The IDE provides the ability to develop, maintain, and deploy multiple data management processes that in the real world constitute the same complete logical unit of work as one project.

To top that, typically in data warehousing scenarios data movements actually represent just one of several elements of the data acquisition, maintenance, and consumption required to support a business environment. This business need is also fully supported by the SSDT IDE—multiple projects, targeting multiple elements of the SQL Server platform, representing the building blocks of a single business concept, can be developed and maintained as one SSDT solution.

Even though the focus of this chapter is on SSIS development, you should be aware of the larger scope of your work, and plan your development activities accordingly. As you continue on your way through this book, and through data warehouse development, you will gradually begin to realize just how broad this scope really is.

Earlier in this chapter, you developed an SSIS solution—you used a specialized tool, which guided you pretty much straight through all the essential steps of an SSIS development process. By the end of this chapter, you will be able to perform all of these steps on your own, without a wizard to guide you, and after completing this and the following two chapters, you will have learned enough to take on most of what is typically required of an SSIS developer out there, in the real world.

Introducing SSIS Project Deployment

To ensure the isolation of development and testing activities from production operations, SSIS solution development should be performed in dedicated development environments, ideally without direct access to the production environment. Only after the development has been completed and the solutions properly tested should the resulting SSIS packages be deployed to the production environment.

However, even in the planning and development phases, you should not only be aware of the differences between the development and the production environments, but also account for them before even attempting deployment.

Typically, the principal difference between development and production environments is in the configuration of data stores. In development, all data can reside on the same server (even in the same database). In fact, because for development a subset of data is usually all that is needed (or available) to the developer, all stored development data could easily be placed on the developer's personal computer. Therefore, you should account for the following differences between the development and the production environments when developing SSIS solutions:

- **Connections** In production, source and destination data stores would, more often than not, be hosted on different servers.

- **Data platforms** Production versions of the data platforms might be different from the ones used in the development environment (for example, SQL Server 2012 might be used for development, but SQL Server 2008 in production), or the environments could even be on different platforms altogether (for example, SQL Server for development, and another DBMS for production).

- **Security** Generally, a development machine does not need to be part of the same operating system domain as the production servers. Furthermore, the production servers hosting the source or the destination data store could exist in separate domains.

 In previous versions of SQL Server, it was possible to configure SSIS packages by using a configuration file or by storing the configuration data in a table. However, the deployment and maintenance of these configurations proved to be quite a cumbersome task and did not provide very good user experience. In SQL Server 2012, the configuration feature is effectively replaced with *parameterization*, which essentially provides the same functionalities (for instance, the ability to control all of the exposed properties of any configurable object in an SSIS package via the configuration, allowing the administrator to configure the package in compliance with the environment it is being deployed to). The implementation of SSIS parameterization provides a far superior deployment and maintenance experience compared to SSIS configurations. SSIS parameterization will be discussed in more detail in Chapter 4 and Chapter 11, "Installing SSIS and Deploying Packages."

EXAM TIP

SSIS parameterization represents a vital element of SSIS development; its principal role might not be apparent until the SSIS solution is deployed, but it must be considered from the very start of development.

PRACTICE **Modifying an Existing Data Movement**

In Lesson 1 of this chapter, you created a data movement solution using the Import and Export Wizard, the result of which was an SSIS package that you saved as a file to the file system. In Lesson 2, you received an introduction to the SSDT integrated development environment, specifically the SSIS development template (the Integration Services project), and you took a first glance at the SSIS development tool set provided by SSDT.

It has been mentioned several times in this chapter that SSIS packages created by the Import and Export Wizard can be reused and edited by using SSDT; in this third lesson, you will import the SSIS package created in the first lesson into the SSIS project created in the second and modify it with a very important objective in mind: to improve its reusability. You will review the data connections used by the SSIS project and prepare their configuration in order to ensure successful deployment and use in production.

If you encounter a problem completing an exercise, you can install the completed projects from the Solution folder that is provided with the companion content for this chapter and lesson.

EXERCISE 1   Add an Existing SSIS Package to the SSIS Project

1. Navigate to the C:\TK463\Chapter03\Lesson3\Starter\TK 463 Chapter 3 folder in the file system and open the TK 463 Chapter 3.sln solution. This solution is the same as the one you completed in Lesson 2.

2. In the Solution Explorer, right-click the project nodes. Then, in the shortcut menu, under Add, click Existing Package, as shown in Figure 3-16.

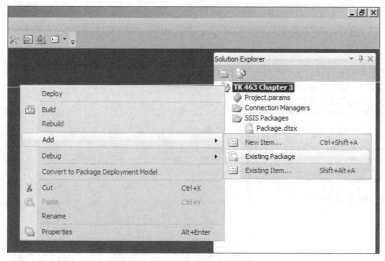

FIGURE 3-16 Adding an existing package to the SSIS project.

3. In the Add Copy Of Existing Package dialog box, shown in Figure 3-17, make sure that File System is selected as the package location, then click the ellipsis button (...) at the bottom of the dialog box. The Load Package dialog box appears. Use it to navigate to the location of the SSIS package you created in Lesson 1: C:\TK463\Chapter03\Lesson1. If for some reason the package is not available, there should be a copy in the C:\TK463 \Chapter03\Lesson1\Solution folder.

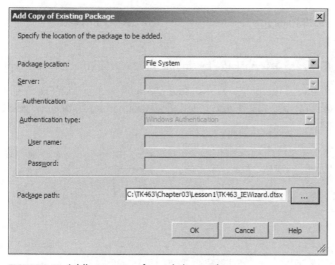

FIGURE 3-17 Adding a copy of an existing package.

4. Select the TK463_IEWizard.dtsx file, click Open, and then click OK. After a few moments, the Solution Explorer should list the newly added package, as shown in Figure 3-18.

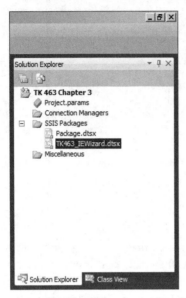

FIGURE 3-18 The SSIS project with multiple SSIS packages.

5. Save the SSIS solution, but keep it open, because you will need it in the next exercise.

EXERCISE 2   Edit the SSIS Package Created by the SQL Server Import and Export Wizard

1. Open the TK463_IEWizard.dtsx package by double-clicking it in the Solution Explorer.

2. Review the control flow of the package. It should contain two tasks: an Execute SQL Task named Preparation SQL Task 1, and a data flow task named Data Flow Task 1, as shown in Figure 3-19.

FIGURE 3-19 The control flow of the SSIS package created in Lesson 1.

3. Double-click (or right-click) Preparation SQL Task 1, and in the shortcut menu select Edit to open the Execute SQL Task Editor. As shown in Figure 3-20, the editor provides access to the Execute SQL Task's settings used in configuring the operation.

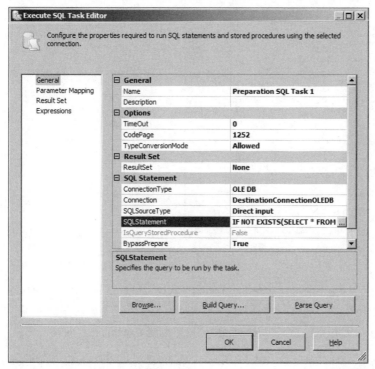

FIGURE 3-20 The Execute SQL Task Editor.

You will learn more about this task in Chapter 4; in this exercise, you just need to review the SQL statement.

4. To see the entire definition, click the ellipsis button inside the value box of the SQLStatement property. Resize the script editor dialog box, shown in Figure 3-21, for better readability, and review the T-SQL script.

As you can see, the task will attempt to create two tables without checking first to see whether they already exist. The failure will not affect the destination database; it will, however, affect the execution of the SSIS package, causing it to fail.

```
Enter SQL Query

IF NOT EXISTS(SELECT * FROM sys.schemas WHERE name =
N'Production')
BEGIN
EXEC(N'CREATE SCHEMA [Production]')
END
CREATE TABLE [Production].[ProductAndDescription] (
[ProductID] int NOT NULL,
[Name] nvarchar(50) NOT NULL,
[ProductModel] nvarchar(50) NOT NULL,
[CultureID] nchar(6) NOT NULL,
[Description] nvarchar(400) NOT NULL
)
GO
CREATE TABLE [Production].[ProductModelInstructions] (
[ProductModelID] int NOT NULL,
[Name] nvarchar(50) NOT NULL,
[Instructions] nvarchar(max),
[LocationID] int,
[SetupHours] decimal(9,4),
[MachineHours] decimal(9,4),
[LaborHours] decimal(9,4),
[LotSize] int,
[Step] nvarchar(1024),
[rowguid] uniqueidentifier NOT NULL,
[ModifiedDate] datetime NOT NULL
)
GO

            OK              Cancel
```

FIGURE 3-21 T-SQL script generated by the Import and Export Wizard.

5. Close the SQL Statement script editor dialog box by clicking Cancel. For the purposes of this exercise, the code does not need to be modified in any way.

6. Close the Execute SQL Task Editor window by clicking Cancel once more.

7. Right-click Preparation SQL Task 1 and select Properties on the shortcut menu. In the lower right of the IDE, you can see the Properties pane, displaying additional settings for the selected object—in this case, the Execute SQL Task. Find the FailPackageOn-Failure setting and make sure its value is False, as shown in Figure 3-22.

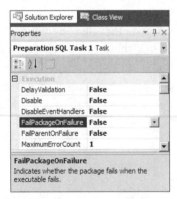

FIGURE 3-22 The Execute SQL Task properties.

This will prevent the possible (or rather, probable) failure of Preparation SQL Task 1 from failing the entire SSIS package.

REAL WORLD (DIS)ALLOWING FAILURE

The purpose of the workaround used in this exercise is to illustrate a point. In actual development work, you should be very careful about when to ignore the failure of individual operations. Focus on preventing failure, rather than exposing your solutions to unpredictability.

8. Select the precedence constraint (the arrow) leading from Preparation SQL Task 1 to Data Flow Task 1. Press Delete on the keyboard or right-click the constraint and select Delete to remove the constraint.

   Precedence constraints are discussed in more detail in Chapter 4.

9. From the SSIS Toolbox, drag another Execute SQL Task onto the control flow pane.

10. Double-click the newly added task, or right-click it and then select Edit, to open the Execute SQL Task Editor. Configure the task by using the information in Table 3-1.

TABLE 3-1 Execute SQL Task Properties

Property	Value
Name	Preparation SQL Task 2
ConnectionType	OLE DB
Connection	DestinationConnectionOLEDB
SQLSourceType	Direct input

11. Click the ellipsis button inside the value box of the SQLStatement property to edit the SQLStatement, and type in the statements from Listing 3-1.

LISTING 3-1 Truncating Destination Tables

```
TRUNCATE TABLE Production.ProductAndDescription;
TRUNCATE TABLE Production.ProductModelInstructions;
```

Optionally, you can copy and paste the statements from the TK463Chapter03.sql file, located in the C:\TK463\Chapter03\Code folder. Click OK when you are done editing the statements.

12. When you have finished configuring the task as defined in steps 10 and 11, confirm the changes by clicking OK. Figure 3-23 shows the configured Preparation SQL Task 2.

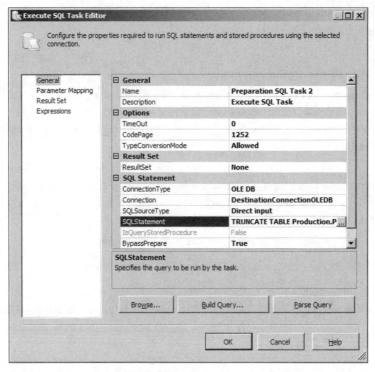

FIGURE 3-23 Preparation SQL Task 2.

13. Select Preparation SQL Task 1. A tiny arrow should appear below it. Drag the arrow over to Preparation SQL Task 2, and then release it to create a precedence constraint between the two tasks, as shown in Figure 3-24.

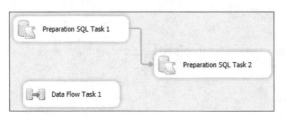

FIGURE 3-24 Creating a precedence constraint.

14. Double-click the precedence constraint you just created, or right-click it and select Edit. In the Precedence Constraint Editor, shown in Figure 3-25, you can configure the conditions of the SSIS package execution.

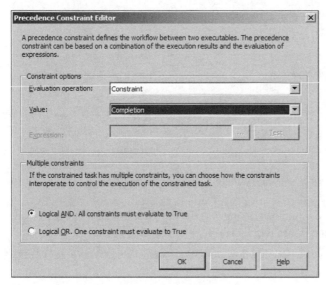

FIGURE 3-25 The Precedence Constraint Editor.

15. Review the options available for the constraint, make sure that Constraint is selected as the evaluation operation, and then select Completion as the new value, as shown in Figure 3-25. Confirm the change by clicking OK.

> **NOTE EVALUATION OPERATIONS**
>
> Precedence constraints are not the only available technique that can be used to control the conditions of SSIS execution. Additional techniques are discussed in Chapter 6, "Enhancing Control Flow."

16. Select Preparation SQL Task 2, and connect it to Data Flow Task 1 with a new precedence constraint. Leave the constraint unchanged. Figure 3-26, shows the amended control flow.

FIGURE 3-26 Modified control flow.

17. Double-click Data Flow Task 1, or right-click it and select Edit, to view its definition, as shown in Figure 3-27.

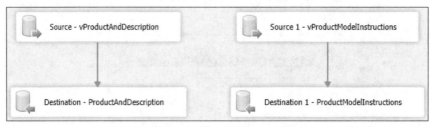

FIGURE 3-27 The definition of Data Flow Task 1.

You can observe two data flows, extracting the data from two views in the source database and loading it into two tables in the destination database.

For now, simply observe the data flow definition. You will learn more about data flow programming in Chapter 6.

> **REAL WORLD**   **COMBINING VS. ISOLATING DATA FLOWS**
>
> In practice, you will rarely see multiple data flows sharing the same data flow task. Although it may seem logical to place data flows that constitute the same logical unit into a single data flow task, it might be more appropriate for maintenance and auditing purposes to place each data flow into its own data flow task.

When done, return to the control flow view by selecting Control Flow at the top of the SSIS package editor.

18. Save the SSIS project, but keep it open, because you will need it in the next exercise.

EXERCISE 3   Configure the Connections and Run the SSIS Package in Debug Mode

1. At the bottom of the SSDT IDE, locate the Connection Managers pane, which provides access to the connection managers used by your SSIS package. There should be two connection managers, as shown in Figure 3-28.

FIGURE 3-28 The Connection Managers pane.

Both connection managers were created by the Import and Export Wizard that you used in Lesson 1 of this chapter.

2. Double-click the SourceConnectionOLEDB connection manager icon, or right-click it and then select Edit, to open the connection manager editor. This editor provides access to the connection manager settings; depending on the type of connection, different variants of the editor are available. The connection managers in this project use the OLE DB data provider.

3. Review the connection properties, as shown in Figure 3-29, and think about which of them would have to be modified for production (Provider, Server Name, authentication, and/or database name).

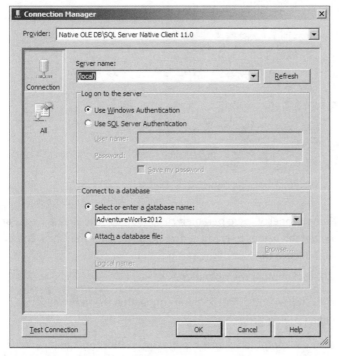

FIGURE 3-29 The OLE DB connection manager.

Here, if you want, you can select the All tab to view more settings and think about what others you have used in the past that would also differ between development and production. This is especially useful if you have worked with SSIS (or Data Transformation Services) in earlier versions of SQL Server.

When done, click Cancel to close the editor. No changes to the connection manager are necessary at this time.

4. Right-click the SourceConnectionOLEDB icon, and then select Parameterize from the shortcut menu. In the Parameterize window, shown in Figure 3-30, you can create new parameters or assign existing parameters to any of the exposed properties of the selected object. Parameterization allows the settings to be modified after the solution's deployment, without requiring a re-design.

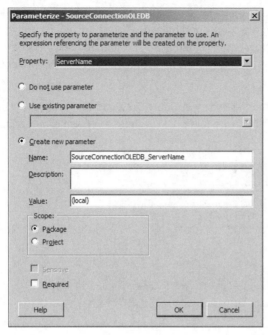

FIGURE 3-30 OLE DB connection manager parameterization.

5. Select the ServerName property to be parameterized first; use the Create New Parameter option with the default values to create a new parameter for the OLE DB connection's server name, and leave the rest of the settings unchanged.

When done, click OK to complete the operation.

6. Repeat the process in steps 4 and 5 for the same connection manager, this time parameterizing the InitialCatalog property.

7. After you finish parameterizing the SourceConnectionOLEDB connection manager, repeat steps 4 through 6 for the DestinationConnectionOLEDB connection manager.

8. After parameterizing both connection managers, save the SSIS solution, and then open the Parameters tab of the SSIS package pane, as shown in Figure 3-31.

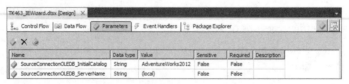

FIGURE 3-31 SSIS Package Parameters

9. When done, return to the Control Flow tab.

10. On the Debug menu, select Start Debugging, or press F5 on the keyboard, to run the package in debug mode.

11. When the package runs, you can observe the order of the operations' execution, governed by the control flow. As each task is completed, it is marked with a completion icon: a green check mark shows successful operations, whereas a red X marks failed ones. Figure 3-32 shows the result of the execution.

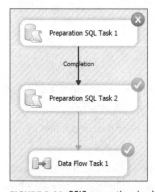

FIGURE 3-32 SSIS execution in debug mode.

Preparation SQL Task 1 failed, as expected, because it attempted to create two tables that already existed in the destination database, but because of a completion precedence constraint instead of the (default) success constraint, and because of a disabled setting that would otherwise cause the package to fail, the rest of the tasks as well as the package itself completed successfully.

12. After the debugging execution has completed, close SSDT.

Lesson Summary

- Existing SSIS packages can be added to SSIS projects in SQL Server Data Tools (SSDT).
- Control flows contain the definitions of data management operations.
- Control flows determine the order and the conditions of execution.
- SSIS package settings can be parameterized, which allows them to be changed without direct access to SSIS package definitions.

Lesson Review

Answer the following questions to test your knowledge of the information in this lesson. You can find the answers to these questions and explanations of why each answer choice is correct or incorrect in the "Answers" section at the end of this chapter.

1. The Execute SQL Task allows you to execute SQL statements and commands against the data store. What tools do you have at your disposal when developing SSIS packages to develop and test a SQL command? Choose all that apply.

   A. SQL Server Management Studio (SSMS)

   B. SQL Server Data Tools (SSDT)

   C. The Execute T-SQL Statement Task Editor

   D. SQL Server Enterprise Manager (SSEM)

2. You need to execute two data flow operations in parallel after an Execute SQL Task has been completed. How can you achieve that? (Choose all that apply.)

   A. There is no way for two data flow operations to be executed in parallel in the same SSIS package.

   B. You can place both data flows inside the same data flow task and create a precedence constraint leading from the preceding Execute SQL Task to the data flow task.

   C. You can create two separate data flow tasks and create two precedence constraints leading from the preceding Execute SQL Task to each of the two data flow tasks.

   D. You can create two separate data flow tasks, place them inside a third data flow task, and create a precedence constraint leading from the preceding Execute SQL Task to the third data flow task.

3. Which precedence constraint can you use to allow Task B to execute after Task A even if Task A has failed?

   A. The failure precedence constraint, leading from Task A to Task B.

   B. The success precedence constraint, leading from Task A to Task B.

   C. The completion precedence constraint, leading from Task A to Task B.

   D. Use two precedence constraints—a success precedence constraint, and a failure precedence constraint, both leading from Task A to Task B.

Case Scenarios

In the following case scenarios, you apply what you've learned about creating SSIS packages. You can find the answers to these questions in the "Answers" section at the end of this chapter.

Case Scenario 1: Copying Production Data to Development

Your IT solution has been deployed to production, version one is complete, and it is now time to start the work on the next version. To keep the data in the development and testing environment as up to date as possible, your manager has asked you to design a data movement solution to be used on a regular basis to copy a subset of production data from the production data store into the development data store.

1. What method would you use to transfer the data on demand?

2. How would you maximize the reusability of the solution?

Case Scenario 2: Connection Manager Parameterization

Data warehousing maintenance solutions have outgrown your company's existing infrastructure, so new servers had to be installed, and this time all data warehousing applications will use a dedicated network. In phase 1, all of your SSIS solutions must be redeployed to new servers, and the system administrator has decided that SSIS projects deserve more network bandwidth, so in phase 2 you will be allowed to dedicate a greater share of the network bandwidth to your data movement processes.

1. How much additional development work will you have to do to complete phase 1?

2. What will you have to do to reconfigure all of the connection managers to use larger network packets for phase 2?

Suggested Practices

To help you successfully master the exam objectives presented in this chapter, complete the following tasks.

Use the Right Tool

If you can combine the benefits of early deployment with the benefits of providing ultimate stability for the entire data warehouse solution, you might be able to achieve "the best of both worlds." For instance, early deployment might allow other members of your team to begin their work sooner (for example, if you deploy an initial version of the data warehouse before the model has been finalized, this might allow report development tasks to start early).

And stabilizing the entire data warehouse solution has obvious benefits (for example, if you implement changes to the data warehouse model in stages, this might allow the iterations in report development to be as reasonable as possible).

- **Practice 1** Develop an initial data movement by using the Import and Export Wizard, using views in the source data store to emulate data transformations.
- **Practice 2** Modify the initial data movement—add proper data transformation logic as well as appropriate logic to merge new or modified data with existing data.

Account for the Differences Between Development and Production Environments

After a final version of a data warehousing solution has been deployed to production, any additional work on the current version, even if these development activities could in fact be reduced to "tweaking," will eventually cause delays in the development of the next version. With good parameterization, the burden of "tweaking" an existing solution is lifted from the shoulders of the developer and is placed on the shoulders of the administrator.

- **Practice 1** Review your existing data movement solutions, and create a list of settings that could be beneficial to their maintenance in production.
- **Practice 2** Create a list of elements in your data movement solution that could be parameterized, but due to their possible effect on the operational characteristics of the solution probably should not be parameterized.

Answers

This section contains answers to the lesson review questions and solutions to the case scenarios in this chapter.

Lesson 1

1. **Correct Answers: B and D**

   A. **Incorrect:** Even though this might seem like the quickest solution, it might only be quick to develop. Copying a large amount of data from the production environment to a testing environment should be avoided, especially if most of the data is just going to be discarded from the destination database afterward.

   B. **Correct:** It might appear cumbersome to design several SSIS packages for a single data movement operation, but this approach will solve the principal problem while also following good data management practices, such as avoiding unnecessary data movements.

   C. **Incorrect:** The Edit SQL option in the Column Mappings window of the Import and Export Wizard cannot be used to modify the data retrieval query, only the destination table definition.

   D. **Correct:** An SSIS package created by the Import and Export Wizard can be edited by using SSDT.

2. **Correct Answers: B and D**

   A. **Incorrect:** Dropping and re-creating tables cannot be used to merge data.

   B. **Correct:** You can use SSDT to add data merging capabilities to an SSIS package created by the Import and Export Wizard.

   C. **Incorrect:** No such option exists in the Import and Export Wizard.

   D. **Correct:** You can use SSDT to design pretty much any kind of data movement processes, especially when you want complete control over the operations needed by the process, but keep in mind that designing SSIS packages "from scratch" may not be as time efficient as possible.

3. **Correct Answer: C**

   A. **Incorrect:** SSIS package files are not stored in binary format.

   B. **Incorrect:** SSIS package files might appear as if they are saved as plain text files, but they are actually well-formed XML files.

   C. **Correct:** SSIS package files are stored in XML format; the DTSX file extension is used for distinction.

   D. **Incorrect:** SSIS packages are not Microsoft Word documents.

Lesson 2

1. **Correct Answer: C**

   A. **Incorrect:** SSDT is not an extension of SSMS. It is a stand-alone application.

   B. **Incorrect:** SSDT is not a special edition of SSMS. It is a special edition of Visual Studio.

   C. **Correct:** SSDT is a special edition of Visual Studio, with a complete database development tool set.

   D. **Incorrect:** SSDT is not a service.

2. **Correct Answers: B and D**

   A. **Incorrect:** Simple data movements can have as many data sources and as many data destinations as needed.

   B. **Correct:** Data transformations are present in complex data movements.

   C. **Incorrect:** Typically, in simple data movements, no transformations are needed, because the data is transferred unchanged. However, it is possible to transform the data at the source—such as by making retrieval queries or by using views or other similar techniques.

   D. **Correct:** Additional programmatic logic to merge source data with destination data is present in complex data movements.

3. **Correct Answers: B and D**

   A. **Incorrect:** SSIS packages cannot contain SSDT solutions.

   B. **Correct:** An SSIS project can contain as many SSIS packages as needed.

   C. **Incorrect:** An SSIS project can contain more than a single SSIS package.

   D. **Correct:** SSIS packages contain the programmatic logic used in data management operations, such as data movements and data transformations.

Lesson 3

1. **Correct Answers: A and B**

   A. **Correct:** SSMS provides all the necessary functionalities to develop and test SQL code.

   B. **Correct:** SSDT does provide a query designer; it is available from the Data menu, under Transact-SQL Editor/New Query Connection. Alternatively, the query editor can also be started from the SQL Server Object Explorer by right-clicking a database node, and selecting New Query... from the shortcut menu.

   C. **Incorrect:** The Execute T-SQL Statement Task Editor is just a text box into which you can type or paste a SQL statement.

   D. **Incorrect:** The Enterprise Manager was replaced with SSMS in SQL Server 2005.

2. **Correct Answers: B and C**

   A. **Incorrect:** Parallel data flow execution is supported.

   B. **Correct:** You can place multiple data flow operations inside the same data flow task.

   C. **Correct:** You can, of course, place data flows in separate data flow tasks, and you can create multiple precedence constraints leading from or to the same task, as long as any two tasks are connected to each other only once.

   D. **Incorrect:** You cannot place a data flow task inside a data flow task, because it cannot contain tasks, only data flow components.

3. **Correct Answer: C**

   A. **Incorrect:** The failure precedence constraint will allow Task B to execute only if Task A has failed.

   B. **Incorrect:** The success precedence constraint will prevent Task B from executing if Task A fails.

   C. **Correct:** The completion precedence constraint will allow Task B to execute regardless of whether Task A has succeeded or has failed.

   D. **Incorrect:** Only a single precedence constraint can be used to connect two distinct tasks.

Case Scenario 1

1. An SSIS package stored in the file system, in the database, or in an unscheduled SQL Server Agent Job would be appropriate.

2. At the very least, the SSIS package would have to be parameterized so that it can be configured appropriately for the specific environment in which it is going to be used. Additionally, the programmatic logic should account for merging new or modified data with existing data.

Case Scenario 2

1. A properly parameterized SSIS package can be redeployed and reconfigured as many times as needed, without the need for any additional development activities.

2. The network packet size property of OLE DB connections is not exposed to parameterization; therefore, the entire connection string would have to be parameterized.

## CHAPTER 4

Designing and Implementing Control Flow

Exam objectives in this chapter:

- Extract and Transform Data
  - Define connection managers.
- Load Data
  - Design control flow.
  - Implement control flow.

In the previous chapter, it was established that Microsoft SQL Server Integration Services (SSIS) facilitate data movement. Of course, the functional capabilities available in SSIS are not limited to data movement alone—far from it! In its essence, SSIS provides a framework for developing, deploying, and automating a wide variety of processes. Setting data movements aside for the moment, here are a few examples of other management processes facilitated by SSIS solutions:

- **File system and FTP access**   For data that resides in or is transported by using files, the complete set of file and file system management operations is supported in SSIS. Whether the files exist in the file system, are accessible through the local network, or reside at remote locations that are accessible via File Transfer Protocol (FTP), SSIS can be used to automate file system operations (such as downloading files from or uploading them to remote locations and managing files in the local file system).

- **External processes**   Processes that exist outside the SQL Server environment can be invoked by using SSIS, for instance, to facilitate data processing that cannot be integrated with internal data processing tasks (perhaps for compatibility reasons) or need not be integrated with those internal tasks (perhaps because the cost of complete integration would outweigh the benefits). An example is an on-demand service that extracts data from an external data store and places it in files that can then be processed with additional programmatic logic implemented in an SSIS package. If such an external process is invoked by using the SSIS package, the resulting solution can be deployed, maintained, and used as a whole, even though its individual parts essentially remain heterogeneous.

- **SQL Server Administration operations** These operations can be automated by using SSIS. A variety of administrative operations (including backups, integrity checks, SQL Server Agent Job invocations, cleanup and maintenance operations, index rebuilds and reorganizations, statistics updates, and various object transfers) are implemented as standard SSIS tasks. In fact, all SQL Server maintenance plans have been implemented as SSIS packages since SQL Server 2005.

- **Operating system inspection** Windows Management Instrumentation (WMI) data is accessible to SSIS (that is, it can be queried), which means that operations on the operating system level can also be automated. In addition, SSIS operations can be controlled with respect to the state of the operating system (for example, you can run a process only when the server is idle or configure a download process based on the current disk queue length).

- **Send mail** SSIS solutions can send email messages (for example, to automate notifications or even to send data or documents automatically via email).

- **SQL Server Analysis Services processing** SSIS can be used to process SQL Server Analysis (SSAS) objects and to execute data definition language (DDL) commands against SSAS databases.

There are two data management operations that have not been mentioned so far; essentially, they are data movement operations, but they deserve special attention:

- **Data profiling** SSIS provides ample possibilities for data cleansing, and data profiling plays an important role in these processes. You will learn more about the Data Profiling Task in Chapter 17, "Creating a Data Quality Project to Clean Data."

- **Data mining queries** SSIS can also be used to extract data from data mining models and load it into the destination database. You will learn more about the Data Mining Query Task in Chapter 18, "SSIS and Data Mining."

Lessons in this chapter:

- Lesson 1: Connection Managers
- Lesson 2: Control Flow Tasks and Containers
- Lesson 3: Precedence Constraints

Before You Begin

To complete this chapter, you must have:

- Experience working with SQL Server Management Studio.
- Elementary experience working with Microsoft Visual Studio or SQL Server Data Tools.
- A working knowledge of the Transact-SQL language.

Lesson 1: Connection Managers

SSIS supports a variety of data stores (such as files, [relational] database management systems, SQL Server Analysis Services databases, web servers, FTP servers, mail servers, web services, Windows Management Instrumentation, message queues, and SQL Server Management Objects). In SSIS projects, a single data store can appear in one or more roles—as a data source, a data destination, or a reference source, for example. Data access is provided to control flow tasks and data flow components through special SSIS objects called *connection managers*.

> **After this lesson, you will be able to:**
> - Understand package-scoped and project-scoped connection managers.
> - Define a connection string.
>
> **Estimated lesson time: 60 minutes**

To simplify development, configuration, and usage, connections and their properties are not defined per each role that a data store appears in but are defined once and can be re-used as many times as needed—for different data store roles, and for different tasks and/or components.

Depending on the data store, and occasionally on the data provider used to establish the connection, connection managers can be used to retrieve or modify data at the data store (for example, to send DML commands and queries to the data store), but also to execute data definition and data control commands against the data store (for example, to send DDL or DCL commands to the data store). For instance, you can use an Execute SQL Task to create a temporary table, use it in a data flow task, and drop it when it is no longer needed.

Most connection manager types are installed as part of the SQL Server instance setup. Additional connection managers are available online, and you can even develop your own custom connection managers if needed. Table 4-1 describes the connection manager types that are installed with SQL Server 2012.

EXAM TIP

Become familiar with all standard connection managers; learn about their purpose, usability, and the benefits and possible drawbacks of their use. Using inappropriate connection managers might prevent you from completing your work or might cause you to run out of time.

TABLE 4-1 The Standard SQL Server 2012 Connection Manager Types

Connection Manager Type	Description	Notes
ADO connection manager	The ADO connection manager enables connections to ActiveX Data Objects (ADO) and is provided mainly for backward compatibility. Consider using an OLE DB or an ODBC connection manager instead.	
ADO.NET connection manager	The ADO.NET connection manager enables connections to data stores using a Microsoft .NET provider. It is compatible with SQL Server.	
Analysis Services connection manager	The Analysis Services connection manager provides access to SSAS databases. It is used by tasks and data flow components that access SSAS data and/or issue DDL commands against SSAS databases.	
Excel connection manager	As the name suggests, the Excel connection manager provides access to data in Microsoft Excel workbooks.	Password-protected Excel workbooks are not supported.
File connection manager and Multiple Files connection manager	SSIS uses a special format to store data in files; the same format is used for SSIS raw files and for SSIS cache files. These two connection managers provide access to a single SSIS data file or to multiple SSIS data files, respectively.	None of the built-in tasks or data flow components support the Multiple Files connection manager; however, you can use it in custom tasks and/or custom data flow components.
Flat File connection manager and Multiple Flat Files connection manager	These connection managers provide access to flat files—delimited or fixed-width text files (such as comma-separated values files, tab-delimited files, and space-delimited fixed-width files). Access is provided through these two connection managers to a single file or to multiple files, respectively.	The Flat File source component supports the use of multiple files when the data flow is executed in a loop container. Multiple flat files will be consumed successfully as long as they all use the same format; otherwise, the execution will fail.
FTP connection manager	The FTP connection manager provides access to files via the File Transfer Protocol (FTP). It can be used to access files and to issue FTP commands against the remote file storage.	Only anonymous and basic authentication methods are supported—Windows integrated authentication is not supported. Secure FTP (FTPS) is also not supported.
HTTP connection manager	The HTTP connection manager provides access to web servers for receiving or sending files and is also used by the Web Service task to access data and functions published as web services.	Only anonymous and basic authentication methods are supported—Windows integrated authentication is not supported.

Connection Manager Type	Description	Notes
MSMQ connection manager	The MSMQ connection manager provides access to Microsoft Message Queuing (MSMQ) message queues. It is used by the Message Queue task to retrieve messages from and send them to the queue.	
ODBC connection manager	The ODBC connection manager provides access to database management systems that use the Open Database Connectivity (ODBC) specification. Most contemporary database management systems, including SQL Server, support ODBC connections.	Microsoft has announced that at some point in the near future, support for OLE DB connections will be removed in favor of ODBC connections. To achieve compliance for the future, you should start using the ODBC connection manager exclusively for those connections for which you would have used the OLE DB connection manager in the past.
OLE DB connection manager	The OLE DB connection manager provides access to database management systems that use the OLE DB provider. It is compatible with SQL Server.	
SMO connection manager	The SMO connection manager provides access to SQL Management Object (SMO) servers, which allows the execution of maintenance operations. It is used by maintenance tasks to perform various data transfer operations.	
SMTP connection manager	The SMTP connection manager provides access to Simple Mail Transfer Protocol (SMTP) servers and is used by the Send Mail task to send email messages.	Only anonymous and Windows integrated authentication methods are supported—basic authentication is not supported.
SQL Server Compact Edition connection manager	As the name suggests, the SQL Server Compact Edition connection manager provides access to SQL Server Compact Edition databases. This particular connection manager is only used by the SQL Server Compact Edition Destination component.	The SQL Server Compact Edition data provider used by SSIS is only supported in the 32-bit version of SQL Server, which means that on 64-bit servers, SSIS packages that access SQL Server Compact Edition must run in 32-bit mode.
WMI connection manager	The WMI connection manager provides access to Windows Management Instrumentation (WMI) data and is used by the WMI Data Reader and the WMI Event Watcher tasks.	

When using stored procedures or parameterized queries against a SQL Server database in an Execute SQL Task, consider using the ADO.NET data provider, because it provides a much better usability and manageability experience compared to the OLE DB data provider:

- With ADO.NET, you can use parameter names in queries, instead of question marks as parameter placeholders.

- When you are using stored procedures, ADO.NET allows you to set the query type appropriately (for example, by setting the IsQueryStoredProcedure property to True) —you provide the name of the procedure and define the parameters in the Task Editor (in any order, with or without the optional parameters), and the query statement is assembled automatically.

- ADO.NET has better support for data types compared to OLE DB (for example, Xml, Binary, and Decimal data types are not available in OLE DB, and there are problems with the SQL Server large object data types VARCHAR(MAX) and VARBINARY(MAX)).

Connection Manager Scope

SQL Server Database Tools (SSDT) support two connection manager definition techniques, providing two levels of availability:

- *Package-scoped connection managers* are only available in the context of the SSIS package in which they were created and cannot be reused by other SSIS packages in the same SSIS project.

- *Project-scoped connection managers* are available to all packages of the project in which they were created.

Use package-scoped connection managers for connections that should only be available within a particular package, and use project-scoped connection managers for connections that should be shared across multiple packages within a project.

If a package connection manager and a project connection manager use the same name, the package connection manager overrides the project connection manager.

In line with the suggested practices of utilizing SSDT (Visual Studio) programming concepts and aligning them with real-world concepts, as discussed in Chapter 3, "Creating SSIS Packages," project-scoped connection managers allow you to use the same set of connections across the entire operational unit represented by multiple SSIS packages, as long as they are grouped inside the same SSIS project.

32-Bit and 64-Bit Data Providers

The SSIS development environment is a 32-bit environment. At design time, you only have access to 32-bit data providers, and as a consequence you can only enlist those 64-bit providers in your SSIS projects that also have a 32-bit version available on the development machine.

The SSIS execution environment, on the other hand, is dictated by the underlying operating system, which means that, regardless of the version of the provider that you used at design time, at run time the correct version will be used. This is true when the package is run by the SSIS service as well as when you run the package yourself from SSDT.

> **IMPORTANT AVAILABILITY OF 64-BIT PROVIDERS**
>
> Not every provider exists in both 64-bit and 32-bit versions. When deploying SSIS packages (or projects) that use 32-bit-only providers to 64-bit environments, you will need to account for the lack of "native" providers by executing the package in 32-bit mode. You will learn more about this in Chapter 11, "Installing SSIS and Deploying Packages," and Chapter 12, "Executing and Securing Packages."

At design time, you can control the version of the providers to be used explicitly, via the Run64BitRuntime project setting. When this setting is set to True, which is the default, 64-bit providers will be used; otherwise, 32-bit providers will be used.

> **NOTE 64-BIT RUN TIME**
>
> The "Run64BitRuntime" setting is project scoped and is only used at design time. It is ignored in 32-bit environments.

Parameterization

As discussed in Chapter 3, to simplify SSIS package deployment and maintenance, plan to parameterize all connection managers, specifically all the settings that might be environment dependent. Typically, one would parameterize the connection string, or individual elements of the connection string that might depend on the environment to which the package will be deployed, such as the name of the instance (ServerName) and the name of the database

(InitialCatalog). Whether parameterizing the entire connection string or its individual elements provides a better deployment and maintenance experience might seem like a matter of personal preference; the important thing is just to parameterize. In fact, parameterization techniques should be aligned to an organization-wide standard. This way, every developer in the organization can rely on being able to use a common method to solve a common problem.

 Quick Check

1. What is the purpose of connection managers in SSIS at design time?

2. What is the purpose of connection managers in SSIS at run time?

3. How does connection manager scope affect their use?

Quick Check Answers

1. At design time, connection managers are used by the SSIS developer to configure a connection to a data source.

2. At run time, connection managers are used by the SSIS engine to establish connections to data sources.

3. A project-scoped connection manager is available to all packages of a particular SSIS project, whereas a package-scoped connection manager is only available to the package in which it was created.

PRACTICE Creating a Connection Manager

In Chapter 3, you viewed an existing connection manager and learned how to parameterize it. In this practice, you will learn how to create a connection manager, how to determine the appropriate type of connection manager to use in a particular situation, and how to configure the connection manager appropriately so that it can be used by SSIS data flow tasks and SSIS data flow components.

If you encounter a problem completing the exercises, you can install the completed projects that are provided with the companion content. They can be installed from the Solution folder for this chapter and lesson.

EXERCISE 1 Create and Configure a Flat File Connection Manager

1. Start SSDT and create a new SSIS project by using the information in Table 4-2.

   After the project has been successfully created, in the Solution Explorer, under SSIS Packages, find the automatically generated SSIS package and change its name to **FillStageTables.dtsx**, and then save the changes.

TABLE 4-2 New SSIS Project Properties

Property	Value
Name	TK 463 Chapter 4
Location	C:\TK463\Chapter04\Lesson1\Starter\
Create Directory For Solution	No (leave unchecked)

2. To initiate the creation of a new connection manager, right-click the empty surface of the Connection Managers pane at the bottom of the SSIS package editing pane.

   You are creating a connection to a delimited text file, so the appropriate connection manager type is the Flat File connection manager.

3. In the Connection Manager's shortcut menu, select New Flat File Connection.

4. In the Flat File Connection Manager Editor, shown in Figure 4-1, click Browse. Then in the File Open dialog box, navigate to the C:\TK463\Chapter04\Code folder, select the CustomerInformation.txt file, and click Open.

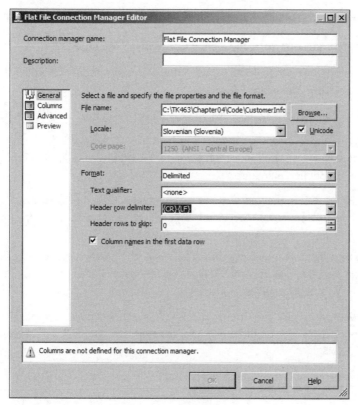

FIGURE 4-1 The Flat File Connection Manager Editor.

5. After selecting the file, review the rest of the settings on the General tab (currently selected), but do not make any changes.

6. Click Columns on the left to open the Columns tab, which allows the editor to parse the file and automatically detect its structure. If everything worked as expected, the warning message Columns Are Not Defined For This Connection Manager should be cleared.

> **REAL WORLD** **FILE FORMATTING**
>
> Always document the structure and formatting of your input files, and do not rely solely on the fact that metadata is stored inside the connection manager. Use proper documentation not only to plan your development, but also to implement validation techniques so that you can detect any changes to the structure or formatting of the input files, especially if they are provided by third parties.

7. If you want, review the rest of the settings, but do not make any changes. Click OK to complete the creation of the Flat File connection manager.

8. Save the SSIS project and keep it open because you will need it in the next exercise.

EXERCISE 2 Create and Configure an OLE DB Connection Manager

1. In the Solution Explorer, right-click the Connection Managers node, and on the short-cut menu, select New Connection Manager.

2. In the Add SSIS Connection Manager dialog box, shown in Figure 4-2, select the OLE DB provider and click Add.

3. In the Configure New OLE DB Connection Manager dialog box, click New to configure a new OLE DB connection manager.

4. As shown in Figure 4-3, in the Connection Manager dialog box, , type **localhost** in the Server Name text box to connect to the default SQL Server instance on the local machine.

   To complete the selection, make sure that Windows Authentication is selected as the authentication mode, and in the Select Or Enter A Database Name combo box select the AdventureWorks2012 database.

5. To test the connection, click Test Connection. The connection should succeed; if it does not, check your permissions on the server—for example, by using SQL Server Management Studio (SSMS).

6. After you have successfully configured the connection manager, click OK to complete its creation.

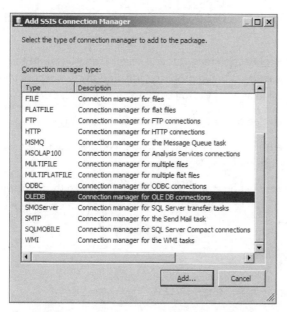

FIGURE 4-2 The Add SSIS Connection Manager dialog box.

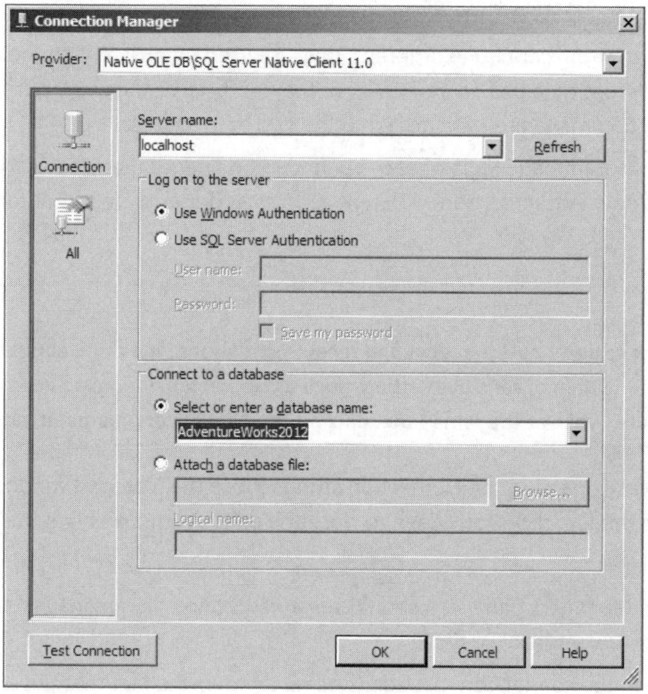

FIGURE 4-3 The Connection Manager dialog box.

7. After returning to the Configure New OLE DB Connection Manager dialog box, click OK to confirm the selection.

8. Right-click the newly added connection manager and select Properties from the shortcut menu to view its properties. In the property grid, find the ConnectionString property. Select the entire value and copy it to the Clipboard by using Ctrl+C.

9. Open Notepad or another text editor, and paste the connection string there.

10. Repeat steps 8 and 9 for the Flat File Connection Manager you created in Exercise 1. Paste the connection string into the same Notepad window.

11. Inspect and compare both connection strings, which should look like those shown in Listings 4-1 and 4-2. They contain key information that is used at run time when the connections are established.

LISTING 4-1 OLE DB Connection String

```
Data Source=localhost;Initial Catalog=AdventureWorks2012;
Provider=SQLNCLI11.1;Integrated Security=SSPI;Auto Translate=False;
```

LISTING 4-2 Flat File Connection String

```
C:\TK463\Chapter04\Code\CustomerInformation.txt
```

The two connection strings are quite different; they are used by different connection managers and different data providers. However, they both serve the same purpose— to provide connection managers with access to the two data sources.

The appropriate programmatic logic of each connection manager then allows the SSIS solution to access data extracted from different sources as if they were not different at all.

EXAM TIP

Learn about SQL Server security best practices and recommendations, and think about how to implement parameterization of sensitive settings such as connection strings to keep your environment secure, while at the same time utilizing the benefits of parameterization.

When you are done inspecting the connection strings, close the Notepad window. If prompted to save the file, click Don't Save to close the editor without saving the data. Return to SSDT.

12. In the Connection Managers pane, you should see a new connection manager named (project) localhost.AdventureWorks2012.

The text (project) in the connection manager's name denotes the fact that this is a project-scoped connection manager.

Right-click the connection manager and, on the shortcut menu, select Rename. Change the name of the new connection manager to **AdventureWorks2012** (without the localhost prefix).

After you confirm the name change, the text (project) is again automatically added to the front of the name. The sole purpose of this is to distinguish between package and project connection managers.

13. Save the SSIS project. Then, in the Solution Explorer, right-click the SSIS Packages node and select New SSIS Package from the shortcut menu to create another SSIS package in the same project.

14. Make sure that the new package, which by default is named Package1.dtsx, is open; this means that you can access its editor pane and see the connection managers available to it.

The AdventureWorks2012 project connection manager should be listed as the only available connection manager.

15. In the Connection Managers pane of the newly added SSIS package, right-click the project connection manager, and then from the shortcut menu, select Convert To Package Connection.

A conversion warning should appear, as shown in Figure 4-4, asking you to confirm the conversion. Do so by clicking OK.

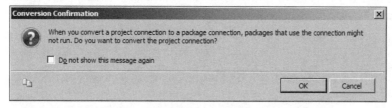

FIGURE 4-4 The Connection Manager Conversion Confirmation dialog box.

16. Open the FillStageTables.dtsx package again. There should now be only one connection manager listed in its Connection Managers pane.

EXAM TIP

Make sure you understand the difference between package and project connection managers and how naming them affects their usability.

17. Open the Package1.dtsx package again, right-click the AdventureWorks2012 package connection manager, and from the shortcut menu, select Convert To Project Connection to return it to its original state.

18. Save the SSIS Project and close SSDT.

Lesson Summary

- Connection managers are used to establish connections to data sources.
- Different data sources require different types of connection managers.
- The usability of a connection manager within an SSIS project or an SSIS package is determined by its scope.

Lesson Review

Answer the following questions to test your knowledge of the information in this lesson. You can find the answers to these questions and explanations of why each answer choice is correct or incorrect in the "Answers" section at the end of this chapter.

1. You need to extract data from delimited text files. What connection manager type would you choose?

   A. A Flat File connection manager

   B. An OLE DB connection manager

   C. An ADO.NET connection manager

   D. A File connection manager

2. Some of the data your company processes is sent in from partners via email. How would you configure an SMTP connection manager to extract files from email messages?

   A. In the SMTP connection manager, configure the OperationMode setting to Send And Receive.

   B. It is not possible to use the SMTP connection manager in this way, because it can only be used by SSIS to send email messages.

   C. The SMTP connection manager supports sending and receiving email messages by default, so no additional configuration is necessary.

   D. It is not possible to use the SMTP connection manager for this; use the IMAP (Internet Message Access Protocol) connection manager instead.

3. You need to extract data from a table in a SQL Server 2012 database. What connection manager types can you use? (Choose all that apply.)

   A. An ODBC connection manager

   B. An OLE DB connection manager

   C. A File connection manager

   D. An ADO.NET connection manager

Lesson 2: Control Flow Tasks and Containers

As a principal element of an SSIS package, control flow defines the operations and the relationships between them, establishing the order and the conditions of their execution. The operations of a control flow are represented by *control flow tasks* (or *tasks*, for short), each task representing a single logical operation (regardless of its actual complexity).

> **After this lesson, you will be able to:**
>
> - Determine the containers and tasks needed for an operation.
> - Implement the appropriate control flow task to solve a problem.
> - Use sequence containers and loop containers.
>
> **Estimated lesson time: 90 minutes**

Planning a Complex Data Movement

In contrast to simple data movements, in which data is moved from the source to the destination "as-is" (unmodified), in complex data movements the data is transformed before being loaded into the destination. Typically, the transformation could be any or all of the following:

- **Data cleansing** Unwanted or invalid pieces of data are discarded or replaced with valid ones. Many diverse operations fit this description—anything from basic cleanup (such as string trimming or replacing decimal commas with decimal points) to quite elaborate parsing (such as extracting meaningful pieces of data by using Regular Expressions).

- **Data normalization** In this chapter, we would like to avoid what could grow into a lengthy debate about what exactly constitutes a scalar value, so the simplest definition of normalization would be the conversion of complex data types into primitive data types (for example, extracting individual atomic values from an XML document or atomic items from a delimited string).

- **Data type conversion** The source might use a different type system than the destination. Data type conversion provides type-level translation of individual values from the source data type to the destination data type (for example, translating a .NET Byte[] array into a SQL Server VARBINARY(MAX) value).

- **Data translation** The source might use different domains than the destination. Translation provides a domain-level replacement of individual values of the source domain with an equivalent value from the destination domain (for example, the character "F" designating a person's gender at the source is replaced with the string "female" representing the same at the destination).

- **Data validation**   This is the verification and/or application of business rules against individual values (for example, "a person cannot weigh more than a ton"), tuples (for example, "exactly two different persons constitute a married couple"), and/or sets (for example, "exactly one person can be President of the United States at any given time").

- **Data calculation** and **data aggregation**   In data warehousing, specifically, a common requirement is to not only load individual values representing different facts or measures, but also to load values that have been calculated (or pre-aggregated) from the original values (for example, "net price" and "tax" exist at the source, but "price including tax" is expected at the destination).

- **Data pivoting** and **data unpivoting**   Source data might need to be restructured or reorganized in order to comply with the destination data model (for example, data in the entry-attribute-value (EAV) might need to be restructured into columns or vice-versa).

EXAM TIP

You should have a very good understanding of what constitutes data transformations. Knowing whether the data needs to be transformed or not will help you determine not only which tasks are appropriate in your work, but also how to define the order and the conditions of their execution.

Another distinguishing characteristic of complex data movements, in contrast to simple data movements, is the need to provide resolution of the relationships between the new or modified source data and any existing data already at the destination. This particular requirement is of principal importance in data warehousing, not only because additions and modifications must be applied to the data warehouse continuously and correctly in order to provide a reliable (uninterrupted and trustworthy) service, but also because all of the organization's historical data is typically stored and maintained exclusively in the data warehouse.

The complexity of a data movement depends on the range of transformations that need to be applied on the source data before it can be loaded into the destination, and on the range of additional operations needed to properly merge new and modified source data with the destination data. As complexity increases, the solution's needs for resources also increases, as do execution times. As mentioned earlier, data warehousing maintenance operations are usually performed during maintenance windows—these may be wide (such as overnight) or narrow (such as a few minutes at specific times during the day). When you are planning data movements, one of your objectives should always be to try to fully utilize as many available resources as possible for the maintenance process so that processing time never exceeds the time boundaries of the relevant maintenance window.

Knowing your workload well will help you determine the design of the control flow of your SSIS packages in order to maximize resource utilization (for example, balancing CPU and I/O operations to minimize latency) and minimize execution time. For instance, by executing CPU-intensive operations with less-than-significant I/O usage (such as difficult transformations and dimension load preparations) in parallel with I/O-intensive operations with less-than-significant CPU usage (such as fact table loads, lookup cache loads, and large updates) could effectively reduce both CPU as well as I/O idle times.

Tasks

The SSIS process can be defined as a system of operations providing fully automated management of data and/or data stores, eliminating the need for human intervention at run time and limiting it to design time and troubleshooting. The principal objective of SSIS could be described as striving to achieve automation in as many deterministic, monotonous, and repetitive operations as possible, so that these operations can be performed by machines, allowing the human participants to focus on what they do best—addressing actual challenges, rather than deterministic procedures; on creative mental processes, rather than repetitive, machine-like execution; and on discovery, rather than monotony.

In SSIS, the role of the human is to design (that is, to determine how specific tasks can be automated), develop (that is, to implement the design), deploy (that is, to commit solutions into execution), and maintain (that is, to monitor execution, solve potential problems, and—most of all—learn from examples and be inspired to design new solutions); execution is automated.

SSIS provides a large collection of the tools required in data management operations. These tools range from simple to quite complex, but they all have one thing in common— each one of them represents a single unit of work, which corresponds to a logical collection of activities necessary to perform real-world tasks.

The SSIS tasks can be divided into several groups, according to the concepts upon which they are based. The following sections describe these groups and the tasks that belong to them.

EXAM TIP

Become familiar with all standard SSIS tasks: understand their intended purpose and their capabilities as well as their limitations, and always think hard about whether the business problem can be solved with just a single task or with a system of two or more tasks.

Data Preparation Tasks

These tasks, shown in Table 4-3, are used to prepare data sources for further processing; the preparation can be as simple as copying the source to the server, or as complex as profiling the data, determining its informational value, or even discovering what it actually is.

TABLE 4-3 Data Preparation Tasks

Task	Description
File System task	This task provides operations on file system objects (files and folders), such as copying, moving, renaming, deleting objects, creating folders, and setting object attributes.
FTP task	This task provides operations on file system objects on a remote file store via the File Transfer Protocol (FTP), such as receiving, sending, and deleting files, as well as creating and removing directories. Typically, the FTP task is used to download files from the remote file store to be processed locally, or to upload files to the remote store after they have been processed (or created) in the SSIS solution.
Web Service task	This task provides access to web services; it invokes web service methods, receives the results, and stores them in an SSIS variable or writes them to a file connection.
XML task	This task provides XML manipulation against XML files and XML data, such as validation (against a Document Type Definition or an XML Schema), transformations (using XSLT), and data retrieval (using XPath expressions). It also supports more advanced methods, such as merging two XML documents and comparing two XML documents, the output of which can consequently be used to create a new XML document (known as a DiffGram).
Data Profiling task	This task can be used in determining data quality and in data cleansing. It can be useful in the discovery of properties of an unfamiliar data set. You will learn more about the Data Profiling Task in Chapter 17.

> **NOTE** **THE FILE SYSTEM TASK**
>
> The operations provided by the File System task target individual file system objects. To use it against multiple objects, you should use the Foreach Loop Container (discussed later in this chapter).

Workflow Tasks

These tasks, shown in Table 4-4, facilitate workflow, which is the structure of the process in terms of its relationships with the environment and related processes; these tasks automate the interaction between individual SSIS processes and/or the interaction between SSIS processes and external processes (processes that exist outside SQL Server).

TABLE 4-4 Workflow Tasks

Task	Description
Execute Package task	This task executes other SSIS packages, thus allowing the distribution of pro-grammatic logic across multiple SSIS packages, which in turn increases the reus-ability of individual SSIS packages and enables a more efficient division of labor within the SSIS development team. You will learn more about the Execute Package task in Chapter 6, "Enhancing Control Flow."
Execute Process task	This task executes external processes (that is, processes external to SQL Server). The Execute Process task can be used to start any kind of Windows application; however, typically it is used to execute processes against data or data stores that cannot or do not need to be more closely integrated with the SSIS process but still need to be performed as part of it.
Message Queue task	This task is used to send and receive messages to and from Microsoft Message Queuing (MSMQ) queues on the local server. Typically, the Message Queue task would be used to facilitate communication with other related processes that also utilize MSMQ, such as other SSIS pro-cesses or external processes. With MSMQ queues, you can distribute your automated data management processes across the entire enterprise.
Send Mail task	The task allows the sending of email messages from SSIS packages by using the Simple Mail Transfer Protocol (SMTP). Typically, the Send Mail task would be used to send information or files, although it could also be used to send messages regarding its execution. You will learn more about notifications related to SSIS solution deployment in Chapter 10, "Auditing and Logging" and Chapters 11 and 12.
WMI Data Reader task	This task provides access to Windows Management Instrumentation (WMI) data, allowing access to information about the environment (such as server properties, resource properties, and performance counters). Typically, the WMI Data Reader task would be used to gather WMI data for further use (to be processed and loaded into a database, for example), or to monitor the state of the environment in order to determine the behavior of SSIS processes or SSIS tasks (whether to run them at all or to configure them dynam-ically in line with the current state of the environment, for example).
WMI Event Watcher task	This task provides access to WMI events. Typically, the WMI Event Watcher task would be used to trace events in the environment, and based on them to control the execution of SSIS processes or SSIS tasks (for example, to detect the addition of files to a specific folder in or-der to initiate the SSIS process that relies on these files).
Expression task	This task is used in the workflow to process variables and/or parameters and to assign the results to other variables used by the SSIS process. Typically, the Expression task is used to assign values to variables without the overhead of using the Script task for the same purpose.
CDC Control task	This task controls the life cycle of SSIS packages that rely on the SQL Server 2012 Change Data Capture (CDC) functionality. It provides CDC information from the data source to be used in CDC-dependent data flows.

Data Movement Tasks

These tasks, shown in Table 4-5, either participate in or facilitate data movements.

TABLE 4-5 Data Movement Tasks

Task	Description
Bulk Insert task	This task allows the loading of data from formatted text files into a SQL Server database table (or view); the data is loaded unmodified (because transformations are not supported), which means that the loading process is fast and efficient. Additional settings (such as using table lock, disabling triggers, and disabling check constraints) are provided to help reduce contention even further.
Execute SQL task	This task executes SQL statements or stored procedures against a supported data store. The task supports the following data providers: EXCEL, OLE DB, ODBC, ADO, ADO. NET, and SQLMOBILE, so keep this in mind when planning connection managers. The SQLMOBILE provider is used for connections to SQL Server Compact Edition instances. The Execute SQL task supports parameters, allowing you to pass values to the SQL command dynamically. Also see the note about ADO.NET connection managers in Lesson 1, earlier in this chapter.
Data flow task	This task is essential to data movements, especially complex data movements, because it provides all the elements of ETL (extract-transform-load); the architecture of the data flow task allows all of the transformations to be performed in flight and in memory, without the need for temporary storage. Chapter 5, "Designing and Implementing Data Flow," is dedicated to this most vital control flow task.

SQL Server Administration Tasks

SQL Server administration can also be automated by using SSIS solutions; therefore, SSIS provides a set of tools that supports typical administration tasks, as shown in Table 4-6. Because these are highly specialized tasks, their names are pretty much self-explanatory.

All of these tasks rely on SMO connection managers for access to the source and destination SQL Server instances. Most of these tasks also require the user executing them to be granted the elevated permissions required to perform certain activities. (For instance, to transfer a database, the user needs to be a member of the sysadmin fixed server role at the source as well as at the destination instance.)

TABLE 4-6 SQL Server Administration Tasks

Task	Description
Transfer Database task	Use this task to copy or move a database from one SQL Server instance to another or create a copy of it on the same server. It supports two modes of operation:
	■ In online mode, the database is transferred by using SQL Server Management Objects (SMO), allowing it to remain online for the duration of the transfer.
	■ In offline mode, the database is detached from the source instance, copied to the destination file store, and attached at the destination instance, which takes less time compared to the online mode, but for the entire duration the database is inaccessible.
Transfer Error Messages task	Use this task to transfer user-defined error messages from one SQL Server instance to another; you can transfer all user-defined messages or specify individual ones.
Transfer Jobs task	Use this task to transfer SQL Server Agent Jobs from one SQL Server instance to another; you can transfer all jobs or specify individual ones.
Transfer Logins task	Use this task to transfer SQL Server logins from one SQL Server instance to another; you can transfer all logins, logins mapped to users of one or more specified databases, or individual users.
	You can even copy security identifiers (SIDs) associated with the logins. The built-in sa login cannot be transferred.
Transfer Master Stored Procedures task	Use this task to transfer user-defined stored procedures (owned by dbo) from the master database of one SQL Server instance to the master database on another SQL Server instance; you can transfer all user-defined stored procedures or specify individual ones.
Transfer SQL Server Objects task	Use this task to transfer objects from one SQL Server instance to another; you can transfer all objects, all objects of a specified type, or individual objects of a specified type.

SQL Server Maintenance Tasks

SQL Server maintenance can also be automated by using SSIS solutions; therefore, SSIS provides a variety of maintenance tasks, as shown in Table 4-7. In fact, SQL Server maintenance plans have been implemented as SSIS packages since SQL Server 2005.

Again, the names of these tasks are pretty much self-explanatory.

TABLE 4-7 Maintenance Tasks

Task	Description
Back Up Database task	Use this task in your maintenance plan to automate full, differential, or transaction log backups of one or more system and/or user databases. Filegroup and file level backups are also supported.
Check Database Integrity task	Use this task in your maintenance plan to automate data and index page integrity checks in one or more system and/or user databases.
Execute SQL Server Agent Job task	Use this task in your maintenance plan to automate the invocation of SQL Server Agent Jobs to be executed as part of the maintenance plan.
Execute T-SQL Statement task	Use this task in your maintenance plan to execute Transact-SQL scripts as part of the maintenance plan. You should not confuse the very basic Execute T-SQL Statement Task with the more advanced Execute SQL Task described earlier in this lesson. The Execute T-SQL Statement Task only provides a very basic interface, which will allow you to select the connection manager and specify the statement to execute; parameters, for instance, are not supported in this task.
History Cleanup task	Use this task in your maintenance plan to automate the purging of historical data about backups and restore operations, as well as SQL Server Agent and maintenance plan operations on your SQL Server instance.
Maintenance Cleanup task	Use this task in your maintenance plan to automate the removal of files left over by maintenance plan executions; you can configure the task to remove old backup files or maintenance plan text reports.
Notify Operator task	Use this task in your maintenance plan to send email messages to SQL Server Agent operators.
Rebuild Index task	Use this task in your maintenance plan to automate index rebuilds for one or more databases and one or more objects (tables or indexed views).
Reorganize Index task	Use this task in your maintenance plan to automate index reorganizations for one or more databases and one or more objects (tables or indexed views).
Shrink Database task	Use this task in your maintenance plan to automate database shrink operations.
Update Statistics task	Use this task in your maintenance plan to automate updates of statistics for one or more databases and one or more objects (tables or indexed views).

Shrinking the database will release unused space from the database files back to the operating system. To achieve this, SQL Server will probably need to rearrange the contents of the file in order to place unused portions at the end of the file. This might cause fragmentation, which in turn may have a negative impact on query performance. In addition, a large modification operation against the database (such as a large insert) performed after the shrinking of the database might require more space than is available, which will require the database to grow automatically. Depending on the space requirements, an auto-grow operation could take a long time, which in turn could cause the modification operation to reach the timeout and roll back, which could effectively render the server unresponsive.

Therefore, you should avoid shrinking databases, and—most importantly—never automate the shrinking process unless absolutely necessary, and even then you should make sure to reserve enough free space to avoid auto-grows!

Analysis Services Tasks

These tasks, shown in Table 4-8, create, alter, drop, and process Analysis Services objects as well as perform data retrieval operations.

All of these tasks use Analysis Services connection managers to connect to SSAS databases.

TABLE 4-8 Analysis Services Tasks

Task	Description
Analysis Services Execute DDL task	This task provides access to SSAS databases for creating, modifying, and deleting multidimensional objects or data mining models.
Analysis Services Processing task	This task provides access to SSAS databases to process multidimensional objects, tabular models, or data mining models.
	Typically, the Analysis Services Processing task would be used as one of the last operations in a data warehouse maintenance process, following data extraction, transformations, loads, and other maintenance tasks, to prepare the data warehouse for consumption.
Data Mining Query task	This task provides access to Data Mining models, using queries to retrieve the data from the mining model and load it into a table in the destination relational database.
	You will learn more about the Data Mining Query task in Chapter 18.

The Script Task

This special task exposes the SSIS programming model via its .NET Framework implementation to provide extensibility to SSIS solutions. The Script task allows you to integrate custom data management operations with SSIS packages. Customizations can be provided by using any of the programming languages supported by the Microsoft Visual Studio Tools for Applications (VSTA) environment (such as Microsoft Visual C# 2010 or Microsoft Visual Basic 2010).

Typically, the Script task would be used to provide functionality that is not provided by any of the standard built-in tasks, to integrate external solutions with the SSIS solution, or to provide access to external solutions and services through their application programming interfaces (APIs).

For script development, VSTA provides an integrated development environment, which is basically a stripped-down edition of Visual Studio. The final script is precompiled and then embedded in the SSIS package definition.

As long as the programmatic logic of the extension can be encapsulated in a single script in its entirety (that is, without any dependencies on external libraries that might or might not be available on the deployment server), and as long as reusability of the extension is not required (that is, the script is used in a single SSIS package or a small enough number of packages), the Script task is an appropriate solution.

> **NOTE WHEN TO USE THE SCRIPT TASK**
>
> Avoid resorting to the Script task until you have eliminated all possibilities of solving the business problem by using one or more standard tasks.
>
> Compared to the Script task, standard tasks provide a much better deployment and maintenance experience. The developers following in your footsteps and taking your work over from you might find it much easier to understand a process that uses standard tasks, however complex, than to "decode" a lengthy Script task.

Custom Tasks

The principal benefit of the Script task is its ability to extend SSIS functionality without the typical overhead of a complete development cycle; the development process for a simple script can just as well be considered part of the SSIS package development cycle.

However, as soon as reusability becomes an important issue (for instance, because the same business logic needs to be implemented in multiple SSIS packages), the deployment and maintenance of SSIS projects depending on a piece of code embedded in an SSIS package file stop being trivial.

Similarly, deployment and maintenance become complicated if the business problem outgrows the ability to encapsulate the business logic inside a single script (for instance, if the developers, purely for practical reasons, decide to reuse existing libraries and reference them in the script instead of embedding even more code into the SSIS package).

To respond to both these concerns, SSIS also supports custom tasks. Compared to the Script task, these do typically require a more significant amount of development effort—a development cycle of their own—but at the same time, they also significantly improve reusability, significantly reduce potential problems with dependencies, and quite significantly improve the deployment and maintenance experience.

Custom SSIS tasks can be developed independently of the SSIS package. This not only allows for a more efficient division of labor among the developers on the team but also allows the custom task to be distributed independently from the SSIS packages in which it is going to be used. Custom SSIS development is discussed in more detail in Chapter 19, "Implementing Custom Code in SSIS Packages."

Containers

When real-world concepts are implemented in SSIS, the resulting operations can be composed of one or more tasks. To allow tasks that logically form a single unit to also behave as a single unit, SSIS introduces containers.

Containers provide structure (for example, tasks that represent the same logical unit can be grouped in a single container, both for improved readability as well as manageability), encapsulation (for example, tasks enclosed in a loop container will be executed repeatedly as a single unit), and scope (for example, container-scoped resources can be accessed by the tasks placed in the same container, but not by tasks placed outside).

EXAM TIP

Although the typical "procedural" approach to programming, in which a single item is processed at a time, should generally be avoided in favor of "set-oriented" programming, in which an entire set of items is processed as a single unit of work, some operations still require the procedural approach— to be executed in a loop.

Study all three containers in SSIS well to understand the differences between them, so that you can use looping appropriately in your SSIS solutions.

Logic is one reason for grouping tasks; troubleshooting is another. In SSDT, the entire SSIS package can be executed in debug mode, as can individual tasks, and a group of tasks enclosed in a container.

SSIS supports three types of containers, as described in Table 4-9.

TABLE 4-9 Containers

Container	Description
For Loop container	This container executes the encapsulated tasks repeatedly, based on an expression—the looping continues while the result of the expression is true; it is based on the same concept as the For loop in most programming languages.
Foreach Loop container	This container executes the encapsulated tasks repeatedly, per each item of the selected enumerator; it is based on the same iterative concept as the For-Each loop in most contemporary programming languages. The Foreach Loop container supports the following enumerators: the ADO enumerator, the ADO.NET Schema Rowset enumerator, the File enumerator, the Item enumerator, the Nodelist enumerator, and the SMO enumerator.
Sequence container	This container has no programmatic logic other than providing structure to encapsulate tasks that form a logical unit, to provide a scope for SSIS variables to be accessible exclusively to a specific set of tasks or to provide a transaction scope to a set of tasks.

 Quick Check

1. What tasks is the Foreach Loop container suited for?

2. How can the current item or its properties be made available to the tasks inside a Foreach Loop container?

3. Is it possible to change the settings of an SSIS object at run time?

Quick Check Answers

1. It is suited for executing a set of operations repeatedly based on an enumerable collection of items (such as files in a folder, a set of rows in a table, or an array of items).

2. You can assign the values returned by the Foreach Loop container to a variable.

3. Yes, it is. Every setting that supports expressions can be modified at run time.

PRACTICE **Determining the Control Flow**

In this practice, you will begin designing a typical SSIS package used in ETL data management processes—loading a data warehouse. The data is transferred to the server in one or more files, and each of the files needs to be processed in the same way: the data must be extracted from them, transformed, and merged appropriately with existing data at the destination data store. After the files have been processed, they must be moved to a secondary location for safekeeping. The data flow task and the extract-transform-load concepts are discussed in full detail in Chapter 5, so in this practice your main objective will be to create the control flow—to determine which tasks correspond to the required operations and to use appropriate containers for maximum efficiency.

If you encounter a problem completing the exercise, you can install the completed projects that are provided with the companion content. These can be installed from the Solution folder for this chapter and lesson.

EXERCISE 1   Use an SSIS Package to Process Files

1. Start SSDT and open an existing project, located in the C:\TK463\Chapter04\Lesson2 \Starter\TK 463 Chapter 4 folder.

   This project is a copy of the project you created in Lesson 1 earlier in this chapter.

2. Open Windows Explorer and explore the project folder; in it you will find two additional folders named 01_Input and 02_Archive.

   Inspect the folders; the first one should contain three files, and the second one should be empty. When you are done, leave the Windows Explorer window open and return to SSDT.

3. Make sure the FillStageTables.dtsx SSIS package is open.

   You will add a control flow into the SSIS package to process the files in the 01_Input folder and move them to the 02_Archive folder after processing.

4. From the SSIS Toolbox, drag a Foreach Loop container to the design surface. Double-click the task, or right-click it and select Edit from the shortcut menu, to open the Foreach Loop Editor.

   Use the editor to configure the task by using the information listed in Tables 4-10 and 4-11.

TABLE 4-10 The Foreach Loop Editor General Settings

Property	Value
Name	Process Input Files

TABLE 4-11 The Foreach Loop Editor Collection Settings

Property	Value
Enumerator	Foreach File Enumerator
Folder	C:\TK463\Chapter04\Lesson2\Starter\TK 463 Chapter 4\01_Input
Files	CustomerInformation_*.txt
Retrieve file name	Fully qualified
Traverse subfolders	No (leave unchecked)

The completed Foreach Loop Editor is shown in Figure 4-5.

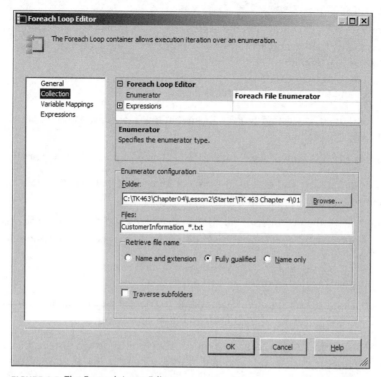

FIGURE 4-5 The Foreach Loop Editor

5. As the Foreach Loop container traverses files in the specified folder, it returns the name of each encountered file (in this case, a fully qualified file name). To use this information later, you need to store it in a variable.

This variable will not be needed outside the Foreach Loop container.

6. On the Variable Mappings tab of the Foreach Loop Editor, create a new variable assignment. In the list box in the Variable column, select <New Variable>.

The Add Variable dialog box opens.

Use the dialog box to configure the new variable by using the information listed in Table 4-12.

TABLE 4-12 Variable Settings

Property	Value
Container	FillStageTables
Name	inputFileName
Namespace	User
Value type	String
Value	None (leave empty)
Read only	No (leave unchecked)

Figure 4-6 shows the completed dialog box.

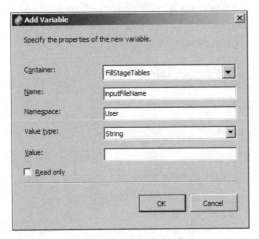

FIGURE 4-6 The Add Variable dialog box.

When done, click OK to complete the creation of a new variable.

7. When you return to the Foreach Loop Editor, verify the value in the Index column of the variable mapping. The Foreach Loop task returns a single scalar value, so the value of the index should be 0 (zero).

When done, click OK to complete the configuration and close the Foreach Loop Editor.

8. Save the project but leave it open, because you will continue editing it in the following exercise.

EXERCISE 2   Assign Property Values Dynamically

1. In Exercise 1, you have configured the Foreach Loop container to enumerate the files in the specified folder and store the name of the file in a variable. Now you need to associate this variable with the Flat File connection manager.

   Right-click the Flat File connection manager and select Properties.

2. In the property grid, find the Expressions property, and in its value box click the ellipsis button (...) to open the Property Expression Editor.

   In the Property column, select the ConnectionString property, and enter the following expression:

   `@[User::inputFileName]`

   This expression assigns the value of the *inputFileName* variable to the connection string of the Flat File connection manager in each iteration of the Foreach Loop container, configuring the connection manager dynamically to connect to a different file each time. The completed dialog box is shown in Figure 4-7.

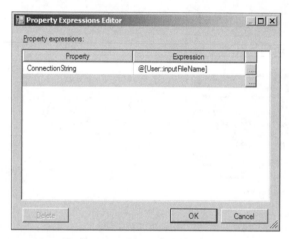

FIGURE 4-7 The Property Expression Editor.

3. The Foreach Loop container is now ready to enumerate files and dynamically control the Flat File connection manager; what it still needs is a few operations that will actually do some file processing.

   From the SSIS Toolbox, drag a data flow task into the Foreach Loop container.

4. Double-click the data flow task to access the data flow editing surface.

   In this exercise, you will not design the entire data flow; these activities are covered in Chapter 5. What you do need to do in this exercise is to configure a data source component; otherwise, you will not be able to complete the rest of the exercises in this chapter.

   Drag a Flat File Source component to the data flow editing surface.

5. Double-click the Flat File Source component, or right-click it and select Edit, to open the Flat File Source Editor.

    Make sure that the correct connection manager is assigned to the component—namely, the Flat File connection manager—and then click OK to complete the configuration of the component.

6. Return to the control flow editing surface and add another task to the Foreach Loop container.

    From the SSIS Toolbox, drag the File System task inside the Foreach Loop container.

7. Define the execution order by creating a precedence constraint between the data flow task and the File System task. The data flow task should be executed first and the File System task last.

8. Double-click the File System task, or right-click it and select Edit, to start the File System Task Editor. Using the information in Table 4-13, configure the task.

TABLE 4-13 File System Task General Settings

Property	Value
IsDestinationPathVariable	False
OverwriteDestination	True
Name	Archive Input File
Operation	Move File
IsSourcePathVariable	True
SourceVariable	User::inputFileName

Configure a new connection for the File System task's DestinationConnection setting. From the list box in the setting's value cell, select <New connection> to open the File Connection Manager Editor.

Use the information in Table 4-14 to configure a new folder connection.

TABLE 4-14 File System Task General Settings

Property	Value
Usage type	Existing folder
Folder	C:\TK463\Chapter04\Lesson2\Starter\TK 463 Chapter 4\02_Archive

The completed dialog box is shown in Figure 4-8.

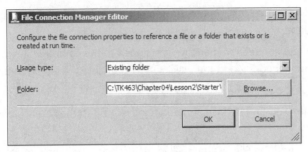

FIGURE 4-8 The File Connection Manager Editor

When done, click OK to confirm the creation.

9.   After you have finished configuring the File System task, click OK to complete the configuration and close the editor.

10. Save the project but leave it open. You will finish editing it in the following exercise.

EXERCISE 3   Prepare and Verify SSIS Package Execution

1.   Now that you have configured the File System task in Exercise 2 to have the Connection-String property assigned dynamically, it should display an error; it cannot validate the source file connection because the *inputFileName* variable has not been assigned.

Right-click the File System task and select Properties from the shortcut menu. Find the DelayValidation property in the property grid and change its value to **True**. This will disable design-time validation, and the variable will only be validated at run time.

> *REAL WORLD*   **NON-DEFAULT SETTINGS**
>
> There are many settings in SSIS solutions that can be controlled, but you will rarely need to change them from their default settings.
>
> Therefore, you should make it a practice to document every non-default setting that you had to implement in your SSIS projects; otherwise, their deployment, maintenance, and consequent development might become extremely difficult, especially over time— and not only for your teammates; even you yourself might eventually forget why some obscure setting in the depths of your SSIS package has one specific value, instead of another one.

2.   Save the SSIS project. If you have followed the instructions correctly, your control flow should now look similar to the one shown in Figure 4-9.

3.   When ready, run the SSIS package in debug mode and observe the execution.

FIGURE 4-9 The SSIS package for processing and archiving input files.

4. After the execution has successfully completed, switch to Windows Explorer and inspect the project's file system.

   The 01_Input folder should now be empty, and the 02_Archive folder should now
   contain all three files.

5. When finished, return to SSDT and close the solution.

Lesson Summary

- A rich collection of tasks supporting the most common data management operations
  is provided by the SSIS design model.
- Control flow is defined by precedence constraints that determine the order and condi-
  tions of execution.
- Tasks representing logical units of work can be grouped in containers.
- Loop containers allow a unit of work to be executed repeatedly.

Lesson Review

Answer the following questions to test your knowledge of the information in this lesson. You
can find the answers to these questions and explanations of why each answer choice is correct
or incorrect in the "Answers" section at the end of this chapter.

1. In your SSIS solution, you need to load a large set of rows into the database as quickly
   as possible. The rows are stored in a delimited text file, and only one source column
   needs its data type converted from String (used by the source column) to Decimal
   (used by the destination column). What control flow task would be most suitable for
   this operation?

   A. The File System task would be perfect in this case, because it can read data from
      files and can be configured to handle data type conversions.

B. The Bulk Insert task would be the most appropriate, because it is the quickest and can handle data type conversions.

C. The data flow task would have to be used, because the data needs to be transformed before it can be loaded into the table.

D. No single control flow task can be used for this operation, because the data needs to be extracted from the source file, transformed, and then loaded into the destination table. At least three different tasks would have to be used—the Bulk Insert task to load the data into a staging database, a Data Conversion task to convert the data appropriately, and finally, an Execute SQL task to merge the transformed data with existing destination data.

2. A part of your data consolidation process involves extracting data from Excel workbooks. Occasionally, the data contains errors that cannot be corrected automatically. How can you handle this problem by using SSIS?

A. Redirect the failed data flow task to an External Process task, open the problematic Excel file in Excel, and prompt the user to correct the file before continuing the data consolidation process.

B. Redirect the failed data flow task to a File System task that moves the erroneous file to a dedicated location where an information worker can correct it later.

C. If the error cannot be corrected automatically, there is no way for SSIS to continue with the automated data consolidation process.

D. None of the answers above are correct. Due to Excel's strict data validation rules, an Excel file cannot ever contain erroneous data.

3. In your ETL process, a few values need to be retrieved from a database at run time, based on another value available at run time, and they cannot be retrieved as part of any data flow task. Which task can you use in this case?

A. The Execute T-SQL Statement task

B. The Execute SQL task

C. The Expression task

D. The Execute Process task

Lesson 3: Precedence Constraints

When it has been determined which tasks to use to provide the required functionality in an SSIS solution, and when it has become clear which multiple tasks constitute individual logical units of work, it is time to define the order of execution, the sequence of operations, and the conditions that need to be fulfilled to allow the execution to proceed from one task (or set of tasks) to the next.

The resulting workflow should not only determine the sequence, but also when to stop the execution in case of failure and how to respond to such situations. After all, SSIS processes are fully automated, and when they are executed there usually is not a user present who would, as soon as failure has been detected, stop the processes, troubleshoot the problem, remove the obstacles, and restart the execution. Also, depending on the business case, failure might or might not be the reason to prevent all tasks that follow the failed one from executing.

> **After this lesson, you will be able to:**
>
> - Determine precedence constraints.
> - Use precedence constraints to control task execution sequence.
>
> **Estimated lesson time: 40 minutes**

To determine the order of execution (also known as the *sequence*), SSIS provides a special object named the *precedence constraint*. Tasks, which must be executed in sequence, need to be connected with one or more precedence constraints. In the SSDT IDE, the precedence constraint is represented by an arrow pointing from the preceding task in a sequence to one or more tasks directly following it.

The way in which the tasks are connected to each other is what constitutes the order, whereas the type of each constraint defines the conditions of execution.

There are three precedence constraint types, all of them equivalent in defining sequences but different in defining the conditions of execution:

- A *success constraint* allows the following operation to begin executing when the preceding operation has completed successfully (without errors).

- A *failure constraint* allows the following operation to begin executing only if the preceding operation has completed unsuccessfully (with errors).

- A *completion constraint* allows the following operation to begin executing when the preceding operation has completed, regardless of whether the execution was successful or not.

Each task can have multiple preceding tasks; a task with multiple precedents cannot begin until all directly preceding tasks have been completed in accordance with the defined conditions. Each task can also precede multiple following tasks; all of these begin after the preceding task has completed in accordance with the defined conditions. However, two distinct tasks can only be connected with a single precedence constraint; otherwise, one of the precedence constraints would be redundant or, if the constraints are conflicting, the execution could not continue anyway.

Precedence constraints can also be extended, allowing dynamic, data-driven execution conditions to be implemented instead of the standard, static conditions inferred by constraint types. You will learn more about precedence constraint customizations in Chapter 6.

Quick Check

1. Can SSIS execution be redirected from one task to another?
2. Can multiple precedence constraints lead from the same preceding task?
3. What is the principal difference between a success constraint and a completion constraint?

Quick Check Answers

1. Yes, by using different conditions in precedence constraints, the order of execution can be directed to the following tasks in one branch or to another branch.
2. Yes, multiple precedence constraints can lead from a single task to the following tasks, but only one precedence constraint can exist between two distinct tasks.
3. A success constraint will only allow the process to continue to the following task if the preceding task completed successfully, whereas a completion constraint will allow the process to continue as soon as the preceding task has completed, regardless of the outcome.

PRACTICE **Determining Precedence Constraints**

In this practice, you will edit the SSIS solution you created in Lessons 1 and 2, earlier in this chapter, to learn about the different types of precedence constraints. You will extend the existing SSIS package with an additional File System task used to move any files that cannot be processed to a special location.

EXERCISE 1 Use Precedence Constraints

1. Start SSDT and open the existing project located in the C:\TK463\Chapter04\Lesson3 \Starter\TK 463 Chapter 4 folder.

   This project is a copy of the project you created in Lessons 1 and 2 earlier in this chapter.

2. Open Windows Explorer and explore the project folder; you should already be familiar with the files named CustomerInformation_01.txt, CustomerInformation_02.txt, and CustomerInformation_03.txt, but there are two additional files named Customer-Information_04.txt and CustomerInformation_05.txt in that folder as well.

   Open the CustomerInformation_04.txt file using Windows Notepad, and inspect its contents. As you can see, it does not contain the correct data and might therefore cause the SSIS package to fail. This is exactly what you will need in this exercise.

   The project folder also contains a new subfolder named 03_Unresolved.

   Leave the Windows Explorer window open for now.

3. Return to SSDT and open the FillStageTables.dtsx SSIS package for editing.

4. Create a precedence constraint between the data flow task and the Archive Input File task.

   To do this, select the preceding task (the data flow task) and then drag the arrow at the bottom of the selected task to the following task (the Archive Input File task).

   When you release the mouse button, a precedence constraint is created.

5. Double-click the newly created precedence constraint, or right-click it and select Edit, to open the Precedence Constraint Editor.

   Review the properties of the precedence constraint you just created. By default, every constraint is a success constraint, meaning that execution will proceed with the following task if the preceding task completed successfully.

6. Open the list box next to Evaluation Operation and review the available constraint types.

   By default, a precedence constraint is a simple constraint, meaning that only the completion of the preceding task is checked when the constraint is evaluated. You can use an expression to include additional checks in the evaluation. You will learn more about this in Chapter 6.

7. When ready, click Cancel to close the Precedence Constraint Editor, abandoning any changes you might have made.

8. Save the project but leave it open, because you will continue editing it in the following exercise.

EXERCISE 2   Redirect Task Execution with Failure Precedence Constraints

1. Drag a new File System task from the SSIS Toolbox into the Foreach Loop container.

2. Double-click the newly added task, or right-click it and select Edit to open the File System Task Editor. Use the information in Table 4-15 to configure this task.

TABLE 4-15 File System Task General Settings

Property	Value
IsDestinationPathVariable	False
OverwriteDestination	True
Name	Exclude Failed File
Operation	Move File
IsSourcePathVariable	True
SourceVariable	User::inputFileName

3. Configure a new connection for the new File System task's DestinationConnection setting. In the list box in the setting's value cell, select <New connection> to open the File Connection Manager Editor.

   Use the information in Table 4-16 to configure a new folder connection.

TABLE 4-16 File System Task General Settings

Property	Value
Usage type	Existing folder
Folder	C:\TK463\Chapter04\Lesson3\Starter\TK 463 Chapter 4\03_Unresolved

When done, click OK to confirm the creation.

4. The File System task should now be in error, for the same reasons as in Lesson 2. Set the task's DelayValidation setting to True to disable design-time validation.

5. Create a precedence constraint between the data flow task and the new File System task; the data flow task precedes the File System task.

6. Double-click the newly created precedence constraint, or right-click it and select Edit, to open the Precedence Constraint Editor.

   Change the value of the constraint to **Failure**. This means that the newly added File System task will only execute if the data flow task has failed. When done, click OK to confirm the change.

7. Right-click the Foreach Loop task and select Properties from the shortcut menu. In the property grid, find the MaximumErrorCount setting and change its value to **100**.

   This setting controls how many times an error can occur during execution before the processing will stop. By increasing the count to 100 you have made it possible for the Foreach Loop task to keep processing files, regardless of whether they can actually be processed or not, until the number of failed files (or other failures) reaches 100.

> *NOTE* **SETTINGS, SETTINGS, SETTINGS...**
>
> This is just another friendly reminder to make it a practice of documenting any and all non-default settings in your SSIS projects for future reference.

8. If you have followed the instructions correctly, your control flow should now look similar to the one shown in Figure 4-10.

9. Save the project, run it in debug mode, and observe the execution.

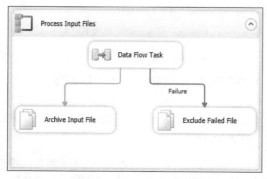

FIGURE 4-10 The SSIS package with redirection.

10. After the execution has completed, switch to Windows Explorer and inspect the file system.

    The 01_Input folder should be empty—all of the files should have been processed.

    The 02_Archive folder should contain four files—these are the four correctly formatted files.

    The 03_Unresolved folder should contain the problematic CustomerInformation_04.txt file that you inspected at the beginning of this exercise.

11. When done, close the solution.

Lesson Summary

- Precedence constraints determine the order of execution and the conditions that must be met for the process to either continue or stop.
- Precedence constraints can even be used to allow the process to recover from failures.

Lesson Review

Answer the following questions to test your knowledge of the information in this lesson. You can find the answers to these questions and explanations of why each answer choice is correct or incorrect in the "Answers" section at the end of this chapter.

1. How is the order of execution, or the sequence of operations, defined in an SSIS package?

   A. The SSIS run time engine determines the order of execution automatically, based on the type of operations, the available software and hardware resources, and the size of data.

   B. The sequence is defined by using precedence constraints.

   C. The sequence is defined by using the Sequence container.

   D. The sequence is defined at design time by using precedence constraints and Sequence containers, but at run time the SSIS engine executes the operations in the order set by the most appropriate execution plan for maximum performance.

2. How does the Failure constraint affect the execution order?

   A. The following task will only execute after the preceding task has failed.

   B. The following task will only execute if the preceding task has not failed.

   C. The following task will never execute, because this constraint is only used at design time.

   D. The following task will execute regardless of whether the preceding task has failed, but an error will be written to the SSIS log.

3. In your ETL process, there are three external processes that need to be executed in sequence, but you do not want to stop execution if any of them fails. Can this be achieved by using precedence constraints? If so, which precedence constraints can be used?

   A. No, this cannot be achieved just by using precedence constraints.

   B. Yes, this can be achieved by using completion precedence constraints between the first and the second and between the second and the third Execute Process tasks, and by using a success precedence constraint between the third Execute Process task and the following task.

   C. Yes, this can be achieved by using completion precedence constraints between the first and the second, between the second and the third, and between the third Execute Process task and the following task.

   D. Yes, this can be achieved by using failure precedence constraints between the first and the second, and between the second and the third Execute Process tasks, and by using a completion precedence constraint between the third Execute Process task and the following task.

Case Scenarios

In the following case scenarios, you apply what you've learned about designing and implementing control flow. You can find the answers to these questions in the "Answers" section at the end of this chapter.

Case Scenario 1: Creating a Cleanup Process

In your data management system, there are two data warehouses (that is, in addition to the operational data store); the principal data warehouse contains all the data, including all historical data, and the secondary data warehouse is used by web applications, exposing your data to customers, and should therefore only contain current data. Your data warehousing solution is already in place, moving data into both data warehouses.

You have been tasked with creating an additional process to determine which data is no longer current and must therefore be removed from the secondary data warehouse.

1. How will you determine which rows need to be removed?

2. What technique would you use to perform the removal as efficiently as possible?

Case Scenario 2: Integrating External Processes

In its data management scenarios, your company uses a mix of proprietary solutions that your team has developed and third party, off-the-shelf solutions that to you, a seasoned developer, appear just like black boxes—you can trust these solutions to work as expected without even a faint clue about how this is actually done.

In your data warehousing solution, you need to consolidate data from a solution of your own and from two diverse black boxes, one of which has a special data extraction tool (a stand-alone application) that retrieves data from the internal store and saves it to files in the file system, while the other one exposes its API layer, providing access to its internal data retrieval functionalities.

1. What functionalities does SSIS provide that can be used to integrate such diverse solutions into a single SSIS process?

2. How would you use the SQL Server platform to solve this problem?

Suggested Practices

To help you successfully master the exam objectives presented in this chapter, complete the following tasks.

A Complete Data Movement Solution

Think about all the processes involved in preparing data to be consumed by the analytical tools used by your managers when determining company strategy. The data must be consolidated, cleansed, loaded into the data warehouse (which includes transforming it appropriately and merging it with existing data), and finally, it must be loaded into the multidimensional SQL Server Analysis Database.

All of these processes need to be performed automatically, at predefined times, and provide current and coherent results in the end. Otherwise, the operations and—eventually— even the future of the company might be at stake.

- **Practice 1** Plan the data consolidation and data cleansing part of your solution. How will you load the data from all the different sources (applications) in your company? What measures will you take to use a unified cleansing process?

- **Practice 2** Plan your data warehouse loading processes. How many separate processes will you require? How will you guarantee the correct execution order to maintain appropriate levels of data integrity inside the data warehouse? When errors are encountered during execution, how will you prevent erroneous data from being available to analysts?

- **Practice 3** Plan the deployment of your solution. What can you do to make it possible to deploy your solution to a production environment? Which properties of the SSIS solution will the database administrator, who is in charge of maintaining it, be able to control?

Answers

This section contains answers to the lesson review questions and solutions to the case scenarios in this chapter.

Lesson 1

1. **Correct Answer: A**

   A. **Correct:** The Flat File connection manager can be used to access data in delimited text files.

   B. **Incorrect:** The OLE DB connection manager cannot be used to connect to text files.

   C. **Incorrect:** The ADO.NET connection manager cannot be used to connect to text files.

   D. **Incorrect:** A File connection manager could be used to access files in the file system, but additional programmatic logic would be required to access the data in delimited text files.

2. **Correct Answer: B**

   A. **Incorrect:** No such configuration setting exists for the SMTP connection manager.

   B. **Correct:** SSIS does not support receiving email messages.

   C. **Incorrect:** SSIS does not support receiving email messages.

   D. **Incorrect:** An IMAP connection manager does not exist in SSIS.

3. **Correct Answers: A, B, and D**

   A. **Correct:** The ODBC connection manager is compatible with SQL Server 2012.

   B. **Correct:** The OLE DB connection manager is compatible with SQL Server 2012.

   C. **Incorrect:** The File connection manager cannot be used to connect to SQL Server.

   D. **Correct:** The ADO.NET connection manager is compatible with SQL Server 2012.

Lesson 2

1. **Correct Answer: C**

   A. **Incorrect:** The File System task does not provide access to the data stored in the file, and therefore cannot be used to extract or convert the data.

   B. **Incorrect:** Although the Bulk Insert task does provide high performance data extraction and loading, it does not facilitate any data transformations.

   C. **Correct:** The data flow task provides all three essential elements of complex data movements—data extraction, data transformations, and data loading. In addition, all three types of operations can be performed in memory and—depending on the data provider used by the destination connection manager—fast loading can also be used.

   D. **Incorrect:** All of these operations can be accomplished in a single task; you just need to be familiar with all of them to determine the most appropriate one.

2. **Correct Answer: B**

   A. **Incorrect:** Though you can use SSIS to run external processes as part of the SSIS solution, even applications with a user interface, SSIS processes are essentially intended for automated execution on a server, without any run-time user intervention. Think of what would happen if you did open each erroneous Excel file in Excel inside an SSIS process—several Excel windows would be open on a server that probably does not even have a screen installed.

   B. **Correct:** Do not create dependencies on user intervention in your automated processes—store any erroneous input files in a safe location and notify the user to correct them, independently of the SSIS process, and return them to the initial location to be processed on the next occasion.

   C. **Incorrect:** SSIS provide several possibilities for recovering from errors, allowing you not only to automate the data management process but also to automate recovery from erroneous states.

   D. **Incorrect:** If there is any "trick" in this question, it is in the statement about Excel's strict data validation rules. Excel is not a data management system and therefore has limited data validation and data integrity functionalities built in.

3. **Correct Answer: B**

   A. **Incorrect:** The Execute T-SQL Statement task cannot retrieve values from the database, nor does it support parameters, both of which are needed in this case.

   B. **Correct:** The Execute SQL task can be used in this case, because it allows values to be passed as input parameters to the SQL statement retrieved as output parameters from the statement.

   C. **Incorrect:** The Expression task cannot be used to retrieve data from a data source.

   D. **Incorrect:** Although arguments can be passed to the external process via the Execute Process task, values cannot be retrieved this way.

Lesson 3

1. **Correct Answer: B**

   A. **Incorrect:** Execution order is not determined automatically. SSIS does not have built-in logic to determine the most appropriate order for executing the operations. If no precedence constraints have been used, SSIS will execute all operations at once.

   B. **Correct:** Precedence constraints determine the execution order.

   C. **Incorrect:** Although Sequence containers allow you to group tasks for execution, they do not directly determine the execution order.

   D. **Incorrect:** Although it is true that an execution plan is created by the SSIS run time engine, the execution order, defined by precedence constraints, is preserved.

2. **Correct Answer: A**

   A. **Correct:** A failure constraint will allow the following task to begin if the preceding task has encountered errors and failed.

   B. **Incorrect:** It is the success constraint that will allow the following task to begin if no errors have been encountered by the preceding task, which in this case has completed successfully.

   C. **Incorrect:** Use of constraints is not limited to design time.

   D. **Incorrect:** The error will be logged, but the following task will begin if and only if the preceding task has failed.

3. **Correct Answer: C**

   A. **Incorrect:** The objective can be achieved by using precedence constraints alone.

   B. **Incorrect:** If a success precedence constraint is used between the last External Process task and the following task, the process will stop if the last External Process task fails.

   C. **Correct:** The External Process tasks will be executed in sequence, and the process will continue, even if one or more of them fail.

   D. **Incorrect:** In this case, the process will continue only if both the first and the second External Process tasks fail.

Case Scenario 1

1. There are several techniques that could be used, but probably the simplest one would be to identify current rows first, and then use an anti-join (for example, by using EXCEPT or NOT EXISTS) against the entire row set, to identify the rows that are not current.

2. To use SQL Server for maximum efficiency when removing a set of rows, you could use a staging table in the same database, fill it with primary key values identifying the rows to be removed, and then issue a set-oriented DELETE statement (such as DELETE... WHERE EXISTS or MERGE...WHEN MATCHED THEN DELETE).

Case Scenario 2

1. To integrate external processes, implemented as individual applications, into an SSIS solution, you could use the Execute Process task or a Script task with the appropriate business logic to control the execution of the external applications. To improve reusability and simplify deployment, a Custom task could also be developed to replace the Script task.

2. The three diverse solutions would probably be integrated by using three different techniques, as follows:

   - To retrieve the data from the data store of the proprietary solution, you could simply create a connection manager to connect to this data store and use standard SSIS tasks to extract the data.

   - To retrieve the data from the second application, the External Process task could be used to execute data retrieval, followed by a Foreach Loop task to process the files and a Bulk Insert task or a data flow task to extract the data from them by using the Flat File connection manager.

   - To retrieve the data from the third application, a Script task could be used to access the application's API, retrieve the data from the application's internal data store, and perhaps save it to a file (for example, an SSIS File or a Flat File) to be processed later.

   To simplify data transformation and loading, all three solutions would only focus on data extraction, loading the data into a staging table, and thus providing a single, unified data source to be consumed by a single transformation and loading process.

## CHAPTER 5

Designing and Implementing Data Flow

Exam objectives in this chapter:

- Extract and Transform Data
  - Design data flow.
  - Implement data flow.

The previous chapter covered control flow tasks that orchestrate the whole extract-transform-load (ETL) process. This chapter looks at the most important control flow task—the data flow task, which is a crucial component in the data warehouse project for ETL operations. All the components in a data flow task operate on rows of data. You can group the elements of the data flow task into three categories: data source adapters, data destination adapters, and data transformations. This chapter shows you how to create data flow tasks and use an appropriate ETL strategy.

Lessons in this chapter:

- Lesson 1: Defining Data Sources and Destinations
- Lesson 2: Working with Data Flow Transformations
- Lesson 3: Determining Appropriate ETL Strategy and Tools

Before You Begin

To complete this chapter, you must have:

- Basic knowledge of Microsoft SQL Server 2012 Integration Services (SISS) control flow features and components.
- Experience working with SQL Server 2012 Management Studio (SSMS).
- A working knowledge of the Transact-SQL language.
- Experience working with SQL Server Data Tools (SSDT) or SQL Server Business Intelligence Development Studio (BIDS).
- An understanding of dimensional design.

Lesson 1: Defining Data Sources and Destinations

The data flow task is one of the most important and complex control flow tasks in SQL Server Integration Services (SSIS). It encapsulates a *data flow engine* that extracts, transforms, and loads data from data sources to data destinations. The data flow engine uses an in-memory, buffer-oriented architecture to efficiently manage different kinds of datasets. The basic unit for all components in a data flow task is a row. Rows are grouped into *buffers*, and buffers are used to move rows through a data *pipeline*. It's called a pipeline because rows flow in, then through, and then out of the data flow task. In this lesson, you will learn how to read data from sources and write data to data destinations.

> **After this lesson, you will be able to:**
>
> - Create a data flow task.
> - Create a data flow source adapter.
> - Create a data flow destination adapter.
> - Implement a simple data flow.
>
> **Estimated lesson time: 70 minutes**

Creating a Data Flow Task

When creating an ETL solution for your data warehouse project, you will spend most of the time building various kinds of data flow tasks. Each package can have zero or more data flow tasks. To add a data flow task to a package, either drag the data flow task from the SSIS Toolbox in the control flow or double-click the task to add it to the control flow area. Now you can select the data flow task and open the Data Flow tab of the SSIS designer, either by double-clicking it or by selecting the Data Flow tab. When you are in the data flow designer, you can browse through multiple data flow tasks by selecting the tasks in the Data Flow Task drop-down list.

There are three types of data flow task components in the SSIS Toolbox:

- Data flow source adapters
- Data flow transformations
- Data flow destination adapters

Data flow adapters provide the ability to extract data from and load data to data sources. *Data flow transformations* use the data provided by data flow adapters to apply a broad range of possible modifications, from simple one-to-one mappings to the application of complex business logic when data is transferred, for example to a data warehouse.

In SQL Server Data Tools (SSDT) 2012, data flow components are grouped by default into five sections in the SSIS Toolbox:

- Favorites

- Common

- Other Transformations

- Other Sources

- Other Destinations

You can move each component between sections by right-clicking it and selecting the section you want. This allows you to personalize your design environment so that you can quickly access the components you use most. If you would like to restore the default values, just right-click anywhere inside the SSIS Toolbox and select Restore Toolbox Defaults. Figure 5-1 shows the Data Flow tab with the SISS Toolbox open. Notice the difference between the SSIS Toolbox components inside the control flow and the ones inside the data flow. Note also that the SSIS Toolbox is a new feature in SQL Server 2012 and that it is different than the Toolbox in previous versions. You can enable it by clicking the icon in the upper-right corner of the designer window.

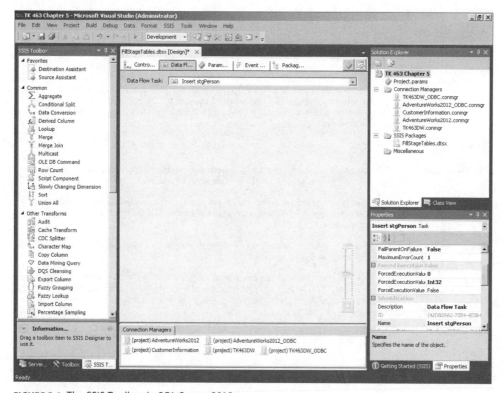

FIGURE 5-1 The SSIS Toolbox in SQL Server 2012.

You can add any data flow component from the SSIS Toolbox to the Data Flow tab in the SSIS Designer either by dragging or by double-clicking them.

EXAM TIP

At run time, the data flow task builds an execution plan from the data flow definition, and the data flow engine executes the plan.

Defining Data Flow Source Adapters

A data flow source adapter is used to extract data from a source and make it available to other components inside a data flow. Data flow source adapters use Integration Services connections, which can be at the package level or at the project level and which point to specific server instances or file locations for the data source. All active connections are listed in the Connection Managers window. The exceptions are the Raw File adapter and the XML adapter, which do not use the package or project connections. Table 5-1 describes the data flow sources and their uses.

TABLE 5-1 Data Flow Sources and Their Uses

Data flow source	Purpose
ADO.NET source	This source provides connections to tables or queries through an ADO.NET provider.
CDC source	Change Data Capture (CDC) is a new component in SQL Server 2012 that allows the retrieval of only changed data (from insert, update, or delete operations) from the source system. It uses an ADO.NET provider to connect to a CDC-enabled table. This source will be explored in more detail in Chapter 7, "Enhancing Data Flow," in the discussion about incremental data load strategies.
Excel source	This source allows extraction from a Microsoft Excel worksheet defined in an Excel file.
Flat File source	This source allows you to extract data from delimited or fixed-width files created with various code pages. It uses a Flat File connection manager.
ODBC source	This source connects to a defined ODBC source by using native ODBC and not the OdbcDataProvider in ADO.NET, as in versions before SQL Server 2012. This is also a new component.
OLE DB source	This source connects to installed OLE DB providers such as SQL Server, SQL Server Analysis Services (SSAS), and Oracle.
Raw File source	The Raw File source reads data from a native SSIS data file that was written by the Raw File destination. Because the representation of the data is native to the source, the data requires no translation and almost no parsing. This means that the Raw File source can read data more quickly than other sources.
XML source	The XML source allows raw data to be extracted from an XML file. It requires an XML schema to define data associations.

To create a data flow source adapter, you can either use a new component called the *Source Assistant* or you can directly choose the specific source adapter from the Other Sources section of the SSIS Toolbox. The Source Assistant helps you create a source adapter and connection manager. It is located in the Favorites section of the SSIS Toolbox.

Adding a Data Flow Source Adapter by Using the Source Assistant

You use the Source Assistant component to add a source adapter by following these steps:

1. Inside the package, on the Control Flow tab of the SSIS Designer, drag the data flow task from the SSIS Toolbox to the Control Flow tab of the SSIS Designer.

2. Double-click the data flow task you just added. From the Data Flow SSIS Toolbox, drag the Source Assistant component onto the data flow designer.

3. In the Add New Source dialog box, you can create and configure the necessary source adapters and connection managers. By default, the assistants will only show the source types that you have installed on your computer. Clear the Show Only Installed Source Types check box to see a larger list of types. Figure 5-2 shows that if you already have a connection manager that will work with a particular type, it will be displayed in the Select Connection Managers list when the corresponding type is selected in the Types list.

4. Select the type of source you need in the Select Source Type list.

5. Select an existing connection manager or select New to create a new connection manager.

6. Click OK.

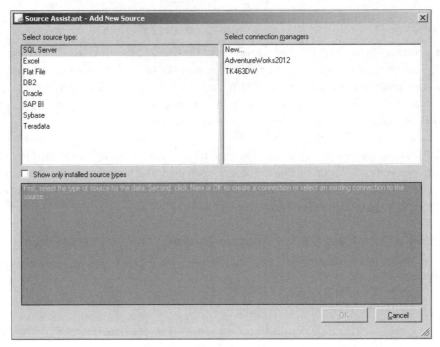

FIGURE 5-2 The Add New Source dialog box.

The Source Assistant component is new in SQL Server 2012 and can be useful when you are just starting to work with SSIS. For real-life projects, however, the best practice is to define the project connections and select the appropriate source adapter under the Other Sources section in the SSIS Toolbox.

Configuring the Data Flow Source Adapter

Most of the data source adapters have similar configuration possibilities. As an example, Figure 5-3 shows the Connection Manager tab of the OLE DB Source Editor dialog box for reading the source data from the *Person.Person* table inside the AdventureWorks2012 database for staging the data later inside the TK463DW database.

In this example, the data access mode is set to Table Or View, and the source table is selected. If the data access mode was set to SQL Command, you could write a custom SQL SELECT statement.

Each row or line (depending on the source) will be converted to SSIS columns inside the source adapter. You can specify the columns to be used in the data flow by selecting them on the Columns tab in each Data Source Editor.

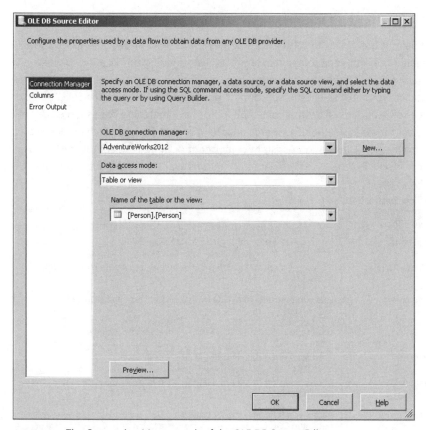

FIGURE 5-3 The Connection Manager tab of the OLE DB Source Editor.

IMPORTANT BEST PRACTICE

The best practice is to extract only the needed columns.

You can also specify properties for each data source adapter by selecting the object and looking at its Properties window. An example would be to set the number of seconds before a command times out by using the CommandTimeout property.

EXAM TIP

Many SSIS objects have a ValidateExternalMetadata property that you can set to False if the object being referenced (such as a table) does not exist when the package is being designed. This property is most commonly used for source or destination adapters when, for example, a destination table is created during package execution.

Defining Data Flow Destination Adapters

Data flow destinations are similar to sources in that they use project or package connections. However, destinations are the endpoints in a data flow task, defining the location to which the data should be pushed. If you want to write data to a flat file or to a specific table inside a SQL Server instance, you must select the appropriate destination adapter. In the SSIS Toolbox, you can also see some additional destinations that do not have matching data source adapters, and vice versa (for example, the CDC source adapter does not have a matching destination). You can use the new Destination Assistant component or directly select the destination adapter you need. Table 5-2 describes the data destinations available in the data flow task.

TABLE 5-2 Data Flow Destinations and Their Uses

Data flow destination	Purpose
ADO.NET destination	Used to insert data through an ADO.NET provider.
Data Mining Model Training	Allows you to pass data from the data flow into a data mining model in SSAS.
DataReader destination	Lets you pass data in a ADO.NET recordset that can be programmatically referenced.
Dimension Processing	Loads and processes a SQL Server Analysis Services dimension.
Excel destination	Used for writing data into a specific sheet in Excel.
Flat File destination	Allows insertion of data to a flat file such as a comma-delimited or tab-delimited file.
ODBC destination	Allows you to insert data by using an ODBC provider. This is a new component in SQL Server 2012. It supports a batch or row-by-row data access mode for inserting the data. In a data warehouse environment, the batch mode is recommended, because of large volumes of data.
OLE DB destination	Uses the OLE DB provider to insert rows into a destination system that allows an OLE DB connection.
Partition Processing	Allows an SSAS partition to be processed directly from data flowing through the data flow.
Raw File destination	Stores data in native SSIS format as a binary file. Very useful in scenarios when you need to temporarily stage data—for example, when the destination server is not available and you do not want to or cannot process the source data again. In SQL Server 2012, the Raw File destination can save all kinds of information (including the comparison flags for string columns).
Recordset destination	Takes the data flow data and creates a recordset in a package variable of type object. The data can be used outside the data flow by other control flow objects.
SQL Server Compact destination	Lets you send data to a mobile device running SQL Mobile.
SQL Server destination	Provides a high-speed destination specific to a local SQL Server database. The SSIS package must be running on the same server as the SQL Server database used for the destination.

EXAM TIP

You can configure the OLE DB destination adapter (and now, with SQL Server 2012, also the ODBC destination adapter) to insert data from the data flow through bulk batches of data, instead of one row at a time. To use this destination-optimization technique for OLE DB, edit the OLE DB destination and set the data access mode to Table Or View—Fast Load. For ODBC, edit the ODBC destination and set the data access mode to Table Name—Batch. If the destinations are not configured with fast load or batch load, only one row at a time will be inserted into the destination table.

Configuring the Data Flow Destination Adapter

Before you configure a data destination adapter, you must have at least one source destination inside the data flow task. Figure 5-4 shows a simple data flow with one source and one destination. The data flow extracts records from the *Person.Person* table inside the Adventure-Works2012 database and inserts them into the *stg.Person* table inside the TK463DW database.

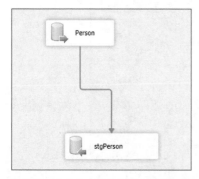

FIGURE 5-4 A simple data flow extracting the data from a source adapter and writing it to a destination adapter.

 Between the source and the destination adapter is a *data flow path*. It connects the output of one component to the input of another component. Paths define the sequence of all components inside the data flow (source adapters, transformations, and destination adapters) and let you add annotations to the data flow, resolve references between columns, or view the source of the column, as you shall see later in this chapter.

Like the source, the destination adapter requires configuration. Usually it is better to first connect the data flow path to the destination adapter so that you can also specify the mappings you want between columns. As shown in Figure 5-5, for an OLE DB destination, you must specify the connection manager and the destination table.

Note that by default an OLE DB destination sets the data access mode to the Table Or View—Fast Load option in the drop-down list. This means that the rows will be processed with bulk insert statements rather than one row at a time. Also by default, the Table Lock check box is selected, which means that at the time of writing the data, a TABLOCK is acquired on the table. This removes the overhead of lock escalation, but if you are simultaneously writing from multiple data flows to the same table, you must disable this option or you will get an error at run time.

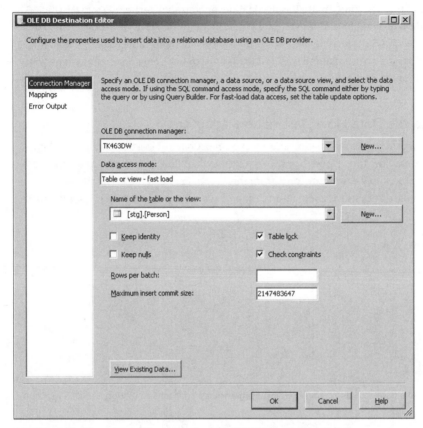

FIGURE 5-5 The Connection Manager tab of the OLE DB Destination Editor.

Figure 5-6 shows the Mappings tab of the same OLE DB Destination Editor. Here you map the columns available for the data flow to the destination columns in the destination adapter. Every destination adapter has a Mappings tab.

If you do not want to map one of the columns, you can set the source value to *<ignore>* in the Input Column area on the Mappings tab. The same applies for destination columns.

> **NOTE** **THE NOT NULL CONSTRAINT**
> If the destination table has a NOT NULL constraint on a specific column and you ignore that column, you can get an error and the package will fail at the destination adapter.

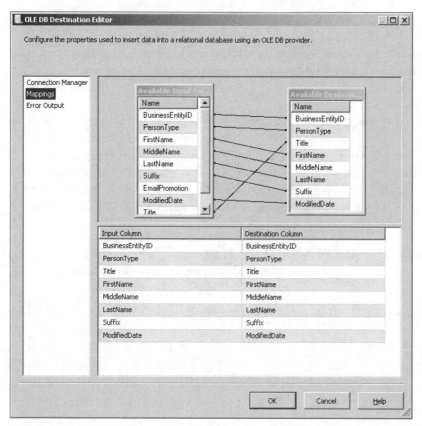

FIGURE 5-6 Mapping columns to the destination adapter in the OLE DB Destination Editor.

SSIS Data Types

To better understand data source and data destination adapters, consider how SSIS manages different data types. When you use a data source adapter, the source data types are mapped to common SSIS data types. This means that after the data source adapter retrieves the data, all operations inside the data flow task are done on SSIS data types. You can have multiple databases, files, and so on, each with specific data types; the data flow engine will convert each data type to an appropriate SSIS data type. For example, numeric data is assigned a numeric data type, string data is assigned a character data type, and dates are assigned a date data type. Other data, such as GUIDs and Binary Large Object Blocks (BLOBs), are also assigned appropriate data types. If the data has a data type that is not convertible to an Integration Services data type, an error occurs.

This means that at design time the data flow knows exactly how much memory it needs for each row from a specific data source adapter. To view or change how data is mapped to SSIS data types, right-click a source adapter and select Show Advanced Editor. Figure 5-7 shows the Input And Output Properties tab of the Advanced Editor for the data source adapter. Here you can expand the Source Output and, under Output Columns, look at or modify each SSIS data type under Data Type Properties. You can see that the *FirstName* column was mapped to a Unicode string [DT_WSTR] SSIS data type with a length of 50 characters.

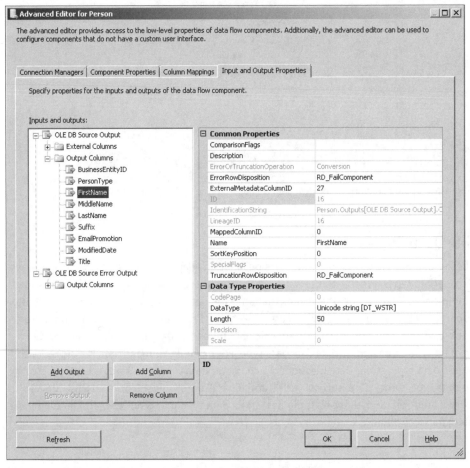

FIGURE 5-7 The Input And Output Properties tab of the Advanced Editor.

✓ **Quick Check**

■ You need to migrate a user-created Microsoft Access database to SQL Server, but the data flow SSIS Toolbox does not contain an Access source adapter. How do you import this data into SQL Server?

Quick Check Answer

■ Although it is not listed in the toolbox, Access is one of the many database sources and destinations that SSIS works with. To extract data from Access, you have three choices: You can use the new ODBC source adapter, create a package connection to the Microsoft Jet OLE DB Provider, or use the OLE DB source adapter.

Using Fast Parse

Fast Parse is a set of operations within SSIS that can be used for very fast loading of flat file data. When you are loading data using the Flat File source adapter and you do not need to parse any locally sensitive data (such as date formats, decimal symbols such as the comma, or currency symbols), SSIS can use the Fast Parse option to load data very quickly. Fast Parse is supported only on a subset of date, time, and integer formats.

To set the Fast Parse property, use the Advanced Editor:

1. Right-click the Flat File source and then click Show Advanced Editor.

2. In the Advanced Editor dialog box, click the Input And Output Properties tab.

3. In the Inputs And Outputs pane, click the column for which you want to enable Fast Parse.

4. In the properties window, expand the Custom Properties node, and then set the FastParse property to True.

This option is available on the column level, which means that some of the columns can be locale sensitive and some not.

> **IMPORTANT** **OPTIMIZING PACKAGES USING FAST PARSE**
>
> Fast Parse has limited functionality, because it works only for specific data types. But if you have a lot of columns of date, time, or integer data types or very large files, Fast Parse is the fastest method for importing data files. On the projects we have worked on, we got more than 20 percent faster loading times, so use it when you have to optimize your packages. Note that Fast Parse is also available in the Data Conversion transformation.

In this practice, you will start building your ETL process to load data into a data warehouse. You will first create appropriate tables for staging the data (the data staging area) from different source systems and then build simple data flows to transfer the data to those stage tables. You will use a specific schema named *stg* inside the TK463DW database for the staging area. The source data will be from the AdventureWorks2012 database and from flat files.

If you encounter a problem completing an exercise, you can install the completed projects from the Solution folder that is provided with the companion content for this chapter and lesson.

EXERCISE 1 Create a Data Flow to Stage the *Person.Person* Table

In the first exercise, you first re-create a SQL Server database called TK463DW for your data warehouse and create a database schema named *stg* to store the tables for a data staging area. Then you will create a data flow task to copy the *Person.Person* table to the staging area.

1. Start SSMS and connect to your SQL Server instance. Open a new query window by clicking the New Query button.

2. You will re-create the database you originally created in Chapter 2, "Implementing a Data Warehouse," because you do not need all of the additional objects that were added in that chapter. Execute the T-SQL code shown here to re-create the database.

```
USE master;
IF DB_ID('TK463DW') IS NOT NULL
  DROP DATABASE TK463DW;
GO
CREATE DATABASE TK463DW
 ON PRIMARY
 (NAME = N'TK463DW', FILENAME = N'C:\TK463\TK463DW.mdf',
  SIZE = 307200KB , FILEGROWTH = 10240KB )
 LOG ON
 (NAME = N'TK463DW_log', FILENAME = N'C:\TK463\TK463DW_log.ldf',
  SIZE = 51200KB , FILEGROWTH = 10%);
GO
ALTER DATABASE TK463DW SET RECOVERY SIMPLE WITH NO_WAIT;
```

3. Create a schema named *stg* and specify the *dbo* as the owner of the schema.

```
USE TK463DW;
GO
-- Create the schema stg to stage all needed source tables
CREATE SCHEMA stg AUTHORIZATION dbo;
```

4. Create the first staging table, *stg.Person*.

```
CREATE TABLE stg.Person
(
BusinessEntityID INT       NULL,
PersonType       NCHAR(2)  NULL,
```

```
Title            NVARCHAR(8)   NULL,
FirstName        NVARCHAR(50)  NULL,
MiddleName       NVARCHAR(50)  NULL,
LastName         NVARCHAR(50)  NULL,
Suffix           NVARCHAR(10)  NULL,
ModifiedDate     DATETIME      NULL
);
```

5. If necessary, start SQL Server Data Tools (SSDT). Then open the TK 463 Chapter 5 project in the Starter folder and open the FillStageTables.dtsx package for editing.

6. On the Control Flow tab of the SSIS Designer, you will notice a sequence container and, under Connection Managers, two connections, one for AdventureWorks2012 and one for the TK463DW database. First drag the Execute SQL task from the SSIS Toolbox into the sequence container object. Edit the Execute SQL task by double-clicking the task icon or by right-clicking the task icon and then clicking Edit.

7. Change the Connection property to use the TK463DW connection.

8. In the SQL Statement property of the Execute SQL Task Editor dialog box, type the following code.

```
TRUNCATE TABLE stg.Person;
```

9. Click OK in the Execute SQL Task Editor dialog box. Right-click the Execute SQL task, click Rename, and type **Truncate Table stgPerson**.

10. Next drag a data flow task from the SSIS Toolbox into the sequence container object. Rename the data flow task to **Insert stgPerson**.

11. Drag the output arrow from the Truncate Table stgPerson task onto the data flow task named Insert stgPerson. The output arrow is green, which means that it represents a precedence constraint (see Chapter 4, "Designing and Implementing Control Flow," for more information about precedence constraints).

12. Click the Data Flow tab at the top of the SSIS Designer. In the SSIS Toolbox, drag OLE DB Source, located under Other Sources, onto the data flow workspace. Right-click the OLE DB source item and then click Edit to open the OLE DB Source Editor dialog box.

13. Select AdventureWorks2012 in the OLE DB Connection Manager list. In the Data Access Mode drop-down list, select Table Or View, and select the *Person.Person* table in the Name Of The Table Or The View drop-down list. Click OK. Rename the OLE DB Source **Person**.

14. In the SSIS Toolbox, drag the OLE DB Destination object onto the data flow design surface. Connect the output of the OLE DB source named Person to the new OLE DB destination object by dragging the blue output arrow from the OLE DB source onto the OLE DB destination adapter. Rename the OLE DB destination adapter **stgPerson**.

15. Double-click stgPerson to display the OLE DB Destination Editor dialog box. Set the OLE DB connection manager to TK463DW and, under Data Access Mode, select Table Or View—Fast Load. Select the *stg.Person* table.

16. On the Mappings tab of the OLE DB Destination Editor, check to make sure that all destination columns are mapped to input columns. Click OK.

17. Execute the FillStageTables.dtsx package. Observe the execution to confirm successful completion of this exercise.

EXERCISE 2 **Use an ODBC Source Adapter to Stage the *Sales.Customer* Table**

In this exercise, you will create a similar data flow task, this time with ODBC data source and destination adapters.

1. Start SSMS and connect to your SQL Server instance. Open a new query window by clicking the New Query button. Select the TK463DW database in the database drop-down list. Create the *stg.Customer* staging table by executing the following SQL statement.

```
CREATE TABLE stg.Customer
(
CustomerID      INT          NULL,
PersonID        INT          NULL,
StoreID         INT          NULL,
TerritoryID     INT          NULL,
AccountNumber   NVARCHAR(20) NULL,
ModifiedDate    DATETIME     NULL,
);
```

2. If necessary, start SSDT. Then open the TK 463 Chapter 5 project and open the FillStageTables.dtsx package from the previous exercise for editing.

3. Add an ODBC connection manager by right-clicking the Connection Managers folder in the Solution Explorer window and selecting New Connection Manager.

   A. In the Add SSIS Connection Manager window, select the ODBC connection manager type and click Add. In the Configure ODBC Connection Manager dialog box, click New. Select the Use Connection String option and then click Build.

   B. Select the Machine Data Source tab and click New. In the Create New Data Source dialog box, select System Data Source, and click Next. Select the SQL Server Native Client 11.0 driver, click Next, and then click Finish.

   C. In the Create A New Data Source To SQL Server dialog box, type **TK463DW_ODBC** as the name and, under Server, type **localhost.** Then click Next. Select With Integrated Windows Authentication and click Next. Change the default database to **TK463DW**, click Next, and then click Finish.

   D. Test the data source and then click OK. In the SQL Server Login window, just click OK. In the Connection Manager window, click OK. You should now see TK463DW_ODBC under Connection Managers in the Solution Explorer window.

4. Repeat the process to add the AdventureWorks2012_ODBC ODBC connection manager. Change the default database to AdventureWorks2012 when you are setting up the ODBC connection manager.

5. Drag the Execute SQL Task from the SSIS Toolbox into the sequence container object. Edit the Execute SQL task by double-clicking the task icon or by right-clicking the task icon and then clicking Edit.

6. Change the Connection property to use the TK463DW_ODBC connection.

7. In the SQL Statement property of the Execute SQL Task Editor dialog box, type the following code.

   TRUNCATE TABLE stg.Customer;

8. Click OK in the Execute SQL Task Editor dialog box. Right-click the SQL Task, click Rename, and type **Truncate Table stgCustomer**.

9. Next drag a data flow task from the SSIS Toolbox into the sequence container object. Rename the data flow task to **Insert stgCustomer**.

10. Drag the output arrow from the Truncate Table stgCustomer task onto the data flow task named Insert stgCustomer.

11. Double-click the Insert stgCustomer data flow task. This will open the Data Flow tab. In the SSIS Toolbox, drag ODBC Source, located under Other Sources, onto the data flow workspace. Right-click the ODBC source item and then click Edit to open the ODBC Source Editor dialog box.

12. Select AdventureWorks2012_ODBC in the ODBC Connection Manager list. In the Data Access Mode drop-down list, select Table Name, and then select the *Sales.Customers* table in the Name Of The Table Or The View drop-down list. Click OK. Rename the ODBC Source to **Customer**.

13. In the SSIS Toolbox, drag the ODBC Destination object onto the data flow design surface. Connect the output of the ODBC source named Customer to the new ODBC destination object by dragging the blue output arrow from the ODBC source onto the ODBC destination adapter. Rename the ODBC destination adapter **stgCustomer**.

14. Double-click stgCustomer to display the ODBC Destination Editor dialog box. Set the ODBC connection manager to **TK463DW_ODBC** and, under Data Access Mode, select Table Name—Batch. Select the *stg.Customer* table.

15. On the Mappings tab of the ODBC Destination Editor, check to make sure that all destination columns are mapped to input columns. Click OK.

16. Execute the FillStageTables.dtsx package. Observe the execution to confirm successful completion of this exercise. If you get an error, please check if you have created a system DSN for the ODBC connection or try to set the project debugging property **Run64BitRuntime** to false.

EXERCISE 3 **Import Data from Flat Files**

In this exercise, you will load additional customer information data that is supplied as a flat file. You will stage this data into the *stg.CustomerInformation* table.

1. Start SSMS and connect to your SQL Server instance. Open a new query window by clicking the New Query button. Select the TK463DW database in the database drop-down list. Create the *stg.Customer* staging table by executing the following SQL statement.

```
CREATE TABLE stg.CustomerInformation
(
PersonID INT NULL,
EnglishEducation NVARCHAR(30) NULL,
EnglishOccupation NVARCHAR(50) NULL,
BirthDate DATE NULL,
Gender NCHAR(5) NULL,
MaritalStatus NCHAR(5) NULL,
EmailAddress NVARCHAR(50) NULL
);
```

2. If necessary, start SSDT. Then open the TK 463 Chapter 5 project and open the FillStageTables.dtsx package from the previous exercise for editing.

3. Drag the Execute SQL task from the SSIS Toolbox into the sequence container object. Edit the Execute SQL task by double-clicking the task icon or by right-clicking the task icon and then clicking Edit.

4. Change the Connection property to use the TK463DW connection.

5. In the SQL Statement property of the Execute SQL Task Editor dialog box, type the following code.

```
TRUNCATE TABLE stg.CustomerInformation;
```

6. Click OK in the Execute SQL Task Editor dialog box. Right-click the Execute SQL task, click Rename, and type **Truncate Table stgCustomerInformation**.

7. Next, drag a data flow task from the SSIS Toolbox into the sequence container object. Rename the data flow task **Insert stgCustomerInformation**.

8. Drag the output arrow from the Truncate Table stgCustomerInformation task onto the data flow task named Insert stgCustomerInformation.

9. Click the Data Flow tab at the top of the SSIS Designer. In the Data Flow Task drop-down list, select Insert stgCustomerInformation. In the SSIS Toolbox, drag the Flat File Source, located under Other Sources, onto the data flow workspace. Right-click the Flat File source item and then click Edit to open the Flat File Source Editor dialog box.

10. Set the new Flat File connection manager by clicking the New button. In the Flat File Connection Manager Editor, type **CustomerInformation** for the Connection Manager Name and, under File Name, click Browse. In the Open dialog box, find the Customer-Information.txt file under Chapter05\Code, and click Open. Set the Locale to English in the drop-down list, and check Unicode. Select the Columns tab in the Flat File Connection Manager Editor and notice that some of the columns are empty, as shown in Figure 5-8.

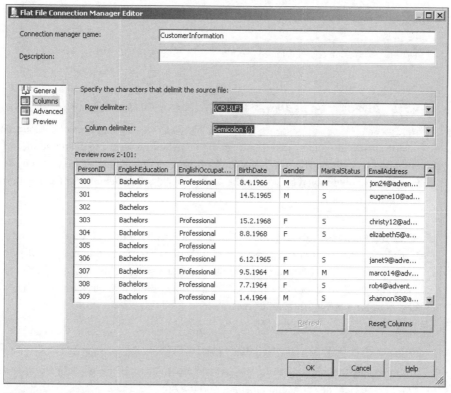

FIGURE 5-8 A preview of loaded columns in the Flat File Connection Manager Editor.

11. Open the source file in Notepad. Note the lack of multiple trailing semicolons after Bachelors in the fourth row for the missing column information, as shown in Figure 5-9. Prior to SQL Server 2012, SSIS would ignore any row delimiter until it believed it was parsing the last column of the row.

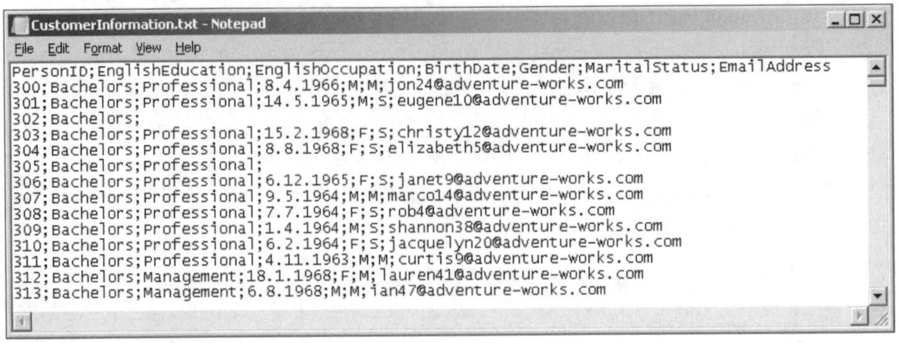

FIGURE 5-9 Missing columns in the text file.

> **NOTE SUPPORT FOR DELIMITED FILES WITH VARYING NUMBERS OF COLUMNS**
>
> The Flat File source now supports delimited files with varying numbers of columns per row (these are sometimes called "ragged-right" delimited files) and delimited files with embedded qualifiers. This new behavior for "ragged-right" delimited files is on by default but can be disabled by setting the AlwaysCheckForRowDelimiters property in the connection manager.

12. Click the Advanced tab and notice that all columns have the same value for the DataType property. Click Suggest Types and, in the Suggest Column Types dialog box, specify that 20,000 rows should be scanned. Click OK. This will now set minimum required DataTypes for all columns. SSIS will now define the minimum length or size of the data type based on 20,000 rows.

> **IMPORTANT ALWAYS DEFINE PROPER DATA TYPES**
>
> When you are loading data using the Flat File source adapter, always define proper data types in the Flat File connection manager on the Advanced tab.

13. Click OK to close the Flat File Connection Manager Editor, and click OK in the Flat File Source Editor. Rename the Flat File source **CustomerInformation**.

14. In the SSIS Toolbox, drag the OLE DB Destination object onto the data flow design surface. Connect the output of the Flat File source named CustomerInformation to the new OLE DB destination object by dragging the blue output arrow from the Flat File source onto the OLE DB destination adapter. Rename the OLE DB destination adapter **stgCustomerInformation**.

15. Double-click stgCustomerInformation to display the OLE DB Destination Editor dialog box. Set the OLE DB connection manager to TK463DW and, under Data Access Mode, select Table Or View—Fast Load. Select the *stg.CustomerInformation* table.

16. On the Mappings tab of the OLE DB Destination Editor, check to make sure that all destination columns are mapped to input columns. Click OK.

17. Execute the FillStageTables.dtsx package. Observe the execution to confirm successful completion of this exercise.

> **NOTE CONTINUING WITH PRACTICES**
>
> Do not exit SSMS if you intend to continue immediately with the next practice.

> **NOTE UNDO AND REDO OPERATIONS NOW SUPPORTED IN SQL SERVER 2012**
>
> Versions of SQL Server before SQL Server 2012 did not support Undo and Redo operations. After you performed an operation, you could not undo it. Now, in SSIS 2012, you can use the Undo and Redo functionality when creating a data flow.

Lesson Summary

- Use appropriate data source or data destination adapters.
- Always extract only the columns you need.
- Use Fast Load or Batch mode when inserting data by using an ODBC or OLE DB destination adapter.
- Use a Raw File destination if you have to temporarily store data to be used by SSIS later.

Lesson Review

Answer the following questions to test your knowledge of the information in this lesson. You can find the answers to these questions and explanations of why each answer choice is correct or incorrect in the "Answers" section at the end of this chapter.

1. Which data flow source adapters can you use if you would like to read data from SQL Server? (Choose all that apply.)

    A. ADO NET source

    B. Raw File source

    C. OLE DB source

    D. ODBC source

2. Which data flow destinations can you use if you would like to temporarily stage data to a file system? (Choose all that apply.)

   A. OLE DB destination

   B. Flat File destination

   C. Raw File destination

   D. Recordset destination

3. Which statements are true regarding data source adapters? (Choose all that apply.)

   A. You can change how source data is mapped to SSIS data types.

   B. You can have only one data source adapter per data flow task.

   C. You must always select all columns from the source adapter.

   D. You can read data from an XML file by using SSIS.

Lesson 2: Working with Data Flow Transformations

 Transformations give you the ability to modify and manipulate data in the data flow. You can perform a wide variety of transformations. It is important that you understand what each transformation does and how it affects the whole data flow in terms of data processing requirements and performance.

> **After this lesson, you will be able to:**
> - Create a data flow task with transformations.
> - Understand the difference between transformations.
> - Use appropriate transformations for specific tasks.
>
> **Estimated lesson time: 80 minutes**

Selecting Transformations

A transformation can operate on one row of data at a time or on several rows of data at once. The operations of some transformations are similar to others; therefore, the transformations can be categorized into natural groupings of similar components. In addition to this natural grouping, this lesson describes the type of blocking that occurs inside the data flow task for each transformation. This foundation will help later in the book when optimization techniques are discussed (in Chapter 13, "Troubleshooting and Performance Tuning"), because blocking behavior has a direct impact on memory consumption.

There are three types of blocking:

- In *non-blocking transformations*, each row is passed through the transformation without any waits.

- A *partial-blocking transformation* waits until a sufficient number of rows is stored and then it passes them through.

- In a *blocking transformation*, all rows must be read into the transformation before the transformation can pass them through.

This book uses the letters *N* for non-blocking, *P* for partial-blocking, and *B* for blocking transformations in the tables in the following sections.

Logical Row-Level Transformations

The most common and easily configured transformations are *logical row-level transformations*, which perform operations on the row level without needing other rows from the source. These transformations, which logically work at the row level, often perform very well. Table 5-3 describes the logical row-level transformations.

Some common uses of this type of calculation in data warehouse scenarios include the creation of calculated columns from multiple source columns, mathematical calculations, conversion of data type values, and the replacement of NULL with other values. In terms of performance and increased workload, the Import Column and Export Column transformations are different than other logical row-level transformations. Both of them allow you to read or write a specific column as a binary data type. For example, by using the Import Column transformation, you can add images stored in separate files to a data flow.

TABLE 5-3 Logical Row-Level Transformations

Data flow transformation	Purpose	Blocking type
Audit	Adds additional columns to each row based on system package variables such as *ExecutionStartTime* and *PackageName*.	N
Cache Transform	Allows you to write data to a cache with the Cache connection manager. The data can then be used by the Lookup transformation. This is useful if you are using multiple Lookup transformations against the same data, because SSIS will cache the needed data only once and not for each Lookup component.	N
Character Map	Performs common text operations such as Uppercase and allows advanced linguistic bit-conversion operations.	N
Copy Column	Duplicates column values in each row to a new named column.	N
Data Conversion	Creates a new column in each row based on a new data type converted from the existing column. An example is converting text to numeric data or text to Unicode text.	N

Data flow transformation	Purpose	Blocking type
Derived Column	Creates or replaces a column for each row based on a specified SSIS expression. This is the most often used logical row-level transformation because it enables the replacement of column values or the creation of new columns based on existing columns, variables, and parameters.	N
Export Column	Exports binary large objects (BLOB) columns, one row at a time, to a file.	N
Import Column	Loads binary files such as images into the pipeline; intended for a BLOB data type destination.	N
Row Count	Tracks the number of rows that flow through the transformation and stores the number in a package variable after the final row.	N

EXAM TIP

When inserting data into data warehouse tables, you should check for NULL inside each column and replace it with a value that represents an "unknown" or default value. With the Derived Column transformation, you can check for NULL by using an SSIS conditional expression. You replace the existing column col1 value with the expression ISNULL(col1) ? 0 : col1. The expression will check first to see whether col1 is NULL and if it is, the expression will put the value 0 for the column col1; if it is not NULL, the col1 column value will stay the same. In SQL Server 2012 SSIS, you can do this more elegantly by using the new REPLACENULL (col1, 0) function.

On the other hand, if you would like to put NULL inside the column, you must use the appropriate SSIS NULL function for the specific data type. For example, if you would like to store NULL inside a 4-byte signed integer column, you must use the NULL(DT_I4) function.

Multi-Input and Multi-Output Transformations

Multi-input and *multi-output transformations* can work with more than one data input or can generate more than one output, respectively. These transformations enable you to combine multiple branches of data flow paths into one or create multiple branches of data flow paths from one. Table 5-4 lists the multi-input and multi-output transformations.

In data warehouse scenarios, you will use these types of transformations a lot. One common scenario is using the Lookup component with Full Cache mode when inserting data into a fact table. The Lookup transformation works very well for acquiring the appropriate surrogate key from the dimension table in these cases (except on very large dimension tables with more than 10 million rows; for these, Merge Join would be a better choice).

TABLE 5-4 Multi-Input and Multi-Output Transformations

Data flow transformation	Purpose	Blocking type
CDC Splitter	Splits a single flow of changed rows from the CDC source component into multiple data flows based on the type of the source data change (that is, whether it is an insert, update, or delete operation). CDC Splitter routes the data based on the __$operation column into three possible outputs. this transformation is like a specific version of the Conditional Split transformation that automatically handles the standard values of the __$operation column.	N
Conditional Split	Routes or filters data based on a Boolean expression to one or more outputs, from which each row can be sent out only one output path.	N
Lookup	Performs a lookup operation between a current row and an external dataset on one or more columns. Additional columns can be added to the data flow from the external dataset.	N
Merge	Combines the rows of two similar sorted inputs, one on top of the other, based on a defined sort key.	P
Merge Join	Joins the rows of two sorted inputs based on a defined join column or columns, adding columns from each source.	P
Multicast	Generates one or more identical outputs, from which every row is sent out every output. This transformation creates a logical copy of the data.	N
Union All	Combines one or more similar inputs, stacking rows one on top of another, based on matching columns. The number of rows in the output of Union All is the combined row counts of all the inputs.	P

As Table 5-4 describes, the Merge and Merge Join transformations require sorted inputs. Both of them are partially blocking, which means that rows might not immediately be sent out the output path. This is because the transformation waits for rows from either input, based on the defined sort order, to preserve the sorted output or match across sorted rows.

EXAM TIP

The Merge Join transformation can match more than one row across the join columns. It behaves the same as the T-SQL Join clause; you can specify an inner join, a full outer join, or a left outer join. Remember that this transformation can be used only if both source inputs are sorted on the same column or columns.

Quick Check

- What is the difference between the Union All and the Merge transformation?

Quick Check Answer

- The Merge transformation is similar to Union All, but with Merge, the sources have to be sorted and the sort position is preserved.

Multi-Row Transformations

Multi-row transformations perform work based on criteria from multiple input rows or generate multiple output rows from a single input row. Multi-row transformations can be more intensive in operation and memory overhead but are crucial for meeting business requirements. Table 5-5 lists the multi-row transformations.

The two most often used multi-row transformations are Aggregate and Sort. The Aggregate transformation is used in data warehousing environments for populating data marts of high granularity. For example, consider an enterprise data warehouse data mart that has daily data and for which the finance department requires a monthly report; for this data mart, you would want to aggregate the data on a monthly basis. As another example, the Sort component is used when you want to use the Merge Join transformation and the source data flow is not sorted.

TABLE 5-5 Multi-Row Transformations

Data flow transformation	Purpose	Blocking type
Aggregate	Associates rows based on defined grouping and generates aggregations such as SUM, MAX, MIN, and COUNT.	B
Percent Sampling	Filters the input rows by allowing only a defined percent to be passed to the output path.	N
Pivot	Takes multiple input rows and pivots the rows to generate an output with more columns based on the original row values.	P
Row Sampling	Generates a fixed number of rows, sampling the data from the entire input, no matter how much larger than the defined output the input is.	B
Sort	Orders the input based on defined sort columns and sort directions. The Sort transformation also allows the removal of duplicates across the sort columns.	B
Unpivot	Takes a single row and generates multiple rows, moving column values to the new row based on defined columns.	P

In the cases of the Sort, Aggregate, and Row Sampling transformations, all the input rows must be read before rows can be sent down the output path. This is why these transformations are fully blocked.

> **NOTE REMEMBER WHICH TRANSFORMATIONS ARE FULLY BLOCKED**
>
> Remember which transformations are fully blocked and try to use them only when absolutely necessary, because they often require more memory and processor capacity. If you are aggregating or sorting a data source input that will not fit into the server memory, the performance will degrade by a factor of 100, because swapping to disk will occur.

The Pivot component has a new user interface in SQL Server 2012 that helps you set up the information more easily than in previous versions. Figure 5-10 shows the new edit window.

In the new Pivot editor, you can specify the Pivot Key, Set Key, and Pivot Value. Each of these is graphically positioned inside the pivot table so that you can understand what each setting will do. Though it is not discussed here, an example package, PivotTransformation.dtsx is provided with the companion content, inside the Visual Studio TK 463 Chapter 5 project.

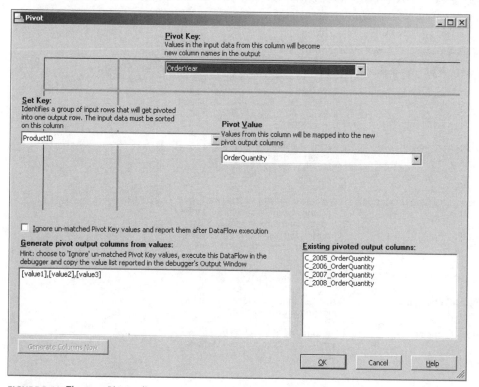

FIGURE 5-10 The new Pivot editor.

IMPORTANT **USING THE NEW PIVOT COMPONENT**

When using the Pivot component, you must explicitly name all new columns based on the distinct values of the column that is specified as the Pivot Key. If you select the Ignore Un-Matched Pivot Key Values And Report Them After DataFlow Execution check box, the component will not produce an error if some of the possible values were not specified as new columns.

You cannot create "dynamic" pivoting (automatically adding new columns) by using this component, because the data flow engine must have exact information about each column that will be present in the data flow. The only workaround is to store all possible values in a single column as XML or as a delimited set of values. In this way, you can create "dynamic" pivoting by using the Script component.

Advanced Data-Preparation Transformations

The last group of transformations lets you perform advanced operations on rows in the data flow pipeline. Table 5-6 lists these advanced data-preparation transformations. Most of these components will be covered in more detail in later chapters.

TABLE 5-6 Advanced Data-Preparation Transformations

Data flow transformation	Purpose	Blocking type
DQS Cleansing	Validates rows by automatically performing data cleansing using an existing knowledge base in Data Quality Services (DQS).	P
OLE DB Command	Performs database operations such as updates or deletions, one row at a time, based on mapped parameters from input rows.	N
Slowly Changing Dimension	Generates transformations necessary to support loading dimension tables in data warehouse scenarios. This transformation handles SCD (Slowly Changing Dimension) Type 1 and Type 2 and also has support for inferred members. Chapter 7 focuses on this transformation.	N
Data Mining Query	Applies input rows against a data mining model for prediction.	P
Fuzzy Grouping	Performs de-duplication based on similarity of string values in selected columns.	B

Data flow transformation	Purpose	Blocking type
Fuzzy Lookup	Joins a data flow input to a reference table based on column similarity. The Similarity Threshold setting specifies the closeness of allowed matches—a high setting means that matching values are close in similarity.	B
Script Component	Applies custom .NET scripting capabilities against rows, columns, inputs, and outputs in the data flow pipeline. This is the most powerful component. Chapter 19, "Implementing Custom Code in SSIS Packages" looks at some of its possibilities.	N
Term Extraction	Analyzes text input columns for English-language nouns and noun phrases.	P
Term Lookup	Analyzes text input columns against a user-defined set of words for association.	P

EXAM TIP

With the Script Component, you can apply almost any kind of transformation to the data flow pipeline. Its application can range from replacing multiple expressions by using multiple Derived Column components to complex transformations using .NET code. You can use Microsoft Visual Basic .NET (VB.NET) and Microsoft Visual C# as programming languages with this component. SQL Server 2012 uses Microsoft Visual Studio Tools for Applications (VSTA) 3.0 as the environment in which to write the scripts, and the component supports Microsoft .NET 4.

Using Transformations

As with the source and destination adapters, you drag transformations from the SSIS Toolbox onto the Data Flow tab of the SSIS Designer. Each transformation has an editor window that defines the way the operation is applied to the data. You can open the editor either by double-clicking a transformation or by right-clicking the transformation and then clicking Edit. For example, the Derived Column transformation specifies an expression that generates a new column in the data flow or replaces an existing column. In Figure 5-11, you can observe that one new column, *FullName*, was added by concatenating the *FirstName* and *LastName* columns by using the following SSIS expression.

```
[LastName] + " " + [FirstName]
```

The Derived Column transformation can also replace existing columns. In this example, the *Suffix* column is replaced with an expression that checks whether the value is NULL and if it is, returns "N/A"; otherwise, it returns the value of the column.

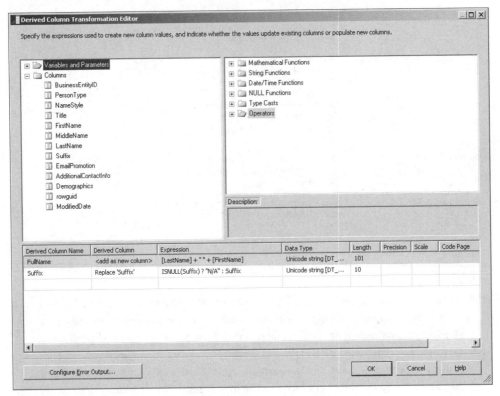

FIGURE 5-11 The Derived Column Transformation Editor.

You apply the whole data flow logic by connecting data source adapters, transformations, and data destination adapters, using data paths that you create by dragging the output arrow onto another component in the data flow. Blue data path arrows are for rows that are successfully transformed, and red output data path arrows are for rows that failed the transformation because of an error, such as a truncation or conversion error. Figure 5-12 shows part of a data flow for updating a customer dimension.

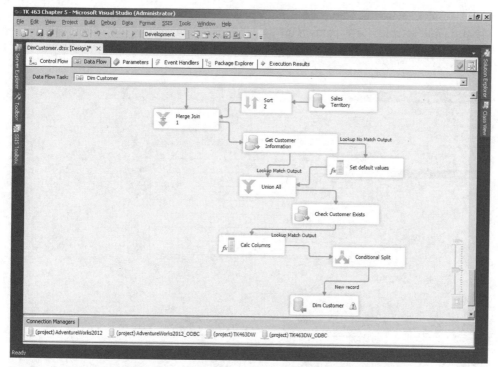

FIGURE 5-12 A data flow showing many transformations connected with data paths.

Resolving Column References

When the metadata about the columns in the data flow task changes, you must correct all the column references. This usually happens when you add new columns from the source, remove some columns inside specific transformations, or even delete specific transformations, requiring you to remap the existing components.

In versions before SQL Server 2012, you had to fix the column reference errors before you could open the transformation. This process of managing metadata in the data flow pipeline is a concept with which many beginners struggle, especially when they make a change early in the data flow that has a ripple effect to downstream components and causes metadata errors. SSIS now includes a Resolve References editor that you can use to quickly resolve the mapping of input and output columns between components. Figure 5-13 shows the new editor, which you can open by right-clicking the data path between two transformations and selecting Resolve Reference.

The Resolve References editor allows you to link unmapped output columns with unmapped input columns for all paths in the data flow path. You can also use it to check that columns are mapped to one another properly and also to see which columns remain unmapped.

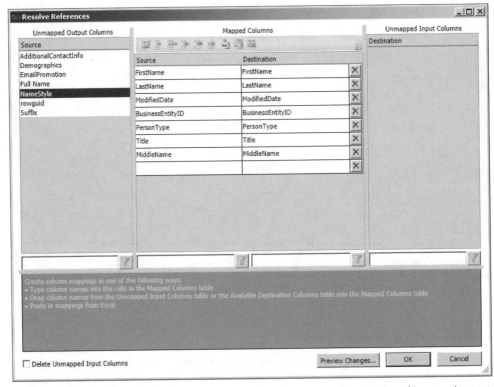

FIGURE 5-13 The Resolve References editor, which helps quickly resolve the mapping of input and output components.

> **NOTE** **RESOLVING A COLUMN REFERENCE ERROR**
>
> If you get a column reference error, you can now open any transformation, because error fixing is done through data paths in the Resolve References editor. The editor also has an option for pasting in mapping information from Excel.

PRACTICE Using Data Flow Transformations

In this practice, you will continue building the ETL process to load data into a data warehouse. You will practice using the multiple transformations needed to load the data into the *dbo.Customers* dimension table.

If you encounter a problem completing an exercise, you can install the completed projects from the Solution folder that is provided with the companion content for this chapter and lesson.

EXERCISE 1 Prepare the *dbo.Customers* Dimension Table for Loading into the Data Warehouse

In this exercise, you use several different transformations to prepare data before loading it into a data warehouse dimension table.

1. If necessary, start SSMS and connect to your SQL Server instance. Open a new query window by clicking the New Query button. Select the TK463DW database in the database drop-down list. Use the following code to create the *dbo.Customers* dimension table and a sequence object, and add a default constraint to the table to map the next value from the sequence to the *CustomerDwKey* column. This will enable automatic insertion of the surrogate key value when you are inserting data through SSIS.

```
-- Drop and create the sequence
IF OBJECT_ID('dbo.SeqCustomerDwKey','SO') IS NOT NULL
  DROP SEQUENCE dbo.SeqCustomerDwKey;
GO
CREATE SEQUENCE dbo.SeqCustomerDwKey AS INT
 START WITH 1
 INCREMENT BY 1;
GO


-- Customers dimension  with a PK
CREATE TABLE dbo.Customers
(
 CustomerDwKey INT          NOT NULL,
 CustomerKey   INT          NOT NULL,
 FullName      NVARCHAR(150) NULL,
 EmailAddress  NVARCHAR(50)  NULL,
 BirthDate     DATE          NULL,
 MaritalStatus NCHAR(5)      NULL,
 Gender        NCHAR(5)      NULL,
 Education     NVARCHAR(40)  NULL,
 Occupation    NVARCHAR(100) NULL,
 City          NVARCHAR(30)  NULL,
 StateProvince NVARCHAR(50)  NULL,
 CountryRegion NVARCHAR(50)  NULL,
 Age AS
  CASE
   WHEN DATEDIFF(yy, BirthDate, CURRENT_TIMESTAMP) <= 40
   THEN 'Younger'
   WHEN DATEDIFF(yy, BirthDate, CURRENT_TIMESTAMP) > 50
   THEN 'Older'
   ELSE 'Middle Age'
  END,
 CurrentFlag   BIT           NOT NULL DEFAULT 1,
 CONSTRAINT PK_Customers PRIMARY KEY (CustomerDwKey)
);
```

```
GO

-- add default constraint to get surrogate key from sequence when inserting
through SSIS
ALTER TABLE  dbo.Customers
  ADD CONSTRAINT DFT_CustomerDwKey DEFAULT (NEXT VALUE FOR dbo.SeqCustomerDwKey)
FOR CustomerDwKey;
Asd
```

2. If necessary, start SSDT, open the TK 463 Chapter 5 project, and then add a new package and rename it **DimCustomer**.

3. Drag a data flow task from the SSIS Toolbox onto the control flow workspace. Rename the data flow task **Dim Customer**.

4. Click the Data Flow tab at the top of the SSIS Designer. In the SSIS Toolbox, drag an OLE DB source adapter onto the data flow workspace. Rename the OLE DB source adapter **StgPerson**. Edit the source adapter and set an OLE DB connection manager to TK463DW, setting the Data Access Mode to Table Or View and selecting the *stg.Person* table.

5. Drag another OLE DB source adapter onto the workspace and rename it **stgCustomer**. In the OLE DB Source Editor, set the OLE DB connection manager to TK463DW and select the *stg.Customer* table.

6. Next you will sort the data from sources on the business key. First, drag two Sort transformations from the SSIS Toolbox onto the data flow design surface. Then connect the output arrow for the stgPerson source adapter to the first Sort transformation and the output arrow for stgCustomer to the second Sort transformation.

7. Edit the first Sort transformation and select the check box on the left side of the *BusinessEntityID* column in the Available Input Columns area. Click OK to save the transformation.

8. Edit the second Sort transformation and select the check box on the left side of the *PersonID* column in the Available Input Columns area. Click OK to save the transformation.

9. From the SSIS Toolbox, drag a Merge Join transformation to the design surface, and then connect the output arrow from the first Sort transformation (stgCustomer) to the Merge Join transformation. When prompted with the Input Output Selection dialog box, choose Merge Join Left Input from the Input drop-down list, and then click OK.

10. Also connect the output arrow of the second Sort transformation to the Merge Join transformation. When prompted, choose Merge Join Right Input from the Input drop-down list, and then click OK.

11. Double-click the Merge Join transformation to display the Merge Join Transformation Editor. Leave the Join Type setting to Inner Join, which will retrieve only matching rows from both sources. Return all the columns from the StgPerson source (the first sort input) by selecting the check box immediately to the left of the Name column header in the left Sort list.

12. In the list of columns on the right, select only the check box next to the *TerritoryID* column. Click OK to save the changes to the Merge Join transformation.

13. Drag another OLE DB source adapter from the SSIS Toolbox to the design surface. Rename it **Sales Territory**. In the OLE DB Source Editor, set the OLE DB connection manager to AdventureWorks2012 and select the *Sales.SalesTerritory* table.

14. The next goal is to join the existing data output from the Merge Join to the Sales Territory source. To be able to use the Merge Join transformation, both sources have to be sorted by the join column. Because the join column is *TerritoryID*, you will have to also re-sort the existing data coming from the existing Merge Join transformation.

    Drag two Sort transformations from the SSIS Toolbox onto the data flow design surface, and then connect the output arrow for the Merge Join transformation to the first Sort transformation and the output arrow from the Sales Territory source to the second Sort transformation.

15. Edit the first Sort transformation (the data coming from the Merge Join transformation) and sort it by the *TerritoryID* column. Edit the second Sort transformation and sort it also by the *TerritoryID* column.

16. Drag a Merge Join transformation from the SSIS Toolbox onto the data flow design surface, and then connect the output arrow from the first Sort transformation (the data from the Merge Join transformation of StgPerson and stgCustomer) to the Merge Join transformation you just added. When prompted with the Input Output Selection dialog box, choose Merge Join Left Input from the Input drop-down list, and then click OK.

17. Also connect the output arrow of the second Sort transformation to the Merge Join transformation. When prompted, choose Merge Join Right Input from the Input drop-down list, and then click OK.

18. Double-click the new Merge Join transformation to display the Merge Join Transformation Editor. Change the Join Type drop-down list setting to Left Outer Join, which will retrieve all the rows from the originating Merge Join transformation of the StgPerson and stgCustomer sources (the left source of the Merge Join transformation) and any matching rows from the right side (which is from the Sales Territory source). Now select all the columns from the left list and the *Name*, *CountryRegionCode,* and *Group* columns from the right list. Rename the Name column as **TerritoryName** and the *Group* column as **TerritoryGroup** by writing the new names in the Output Alias column in the output list. Click OK to save the changes.

EXERCISE 2 Load the *dbo.Customers* Dimension Table into the Data Warehouse

In this exercise, you continue preparing the data for the *dbo.Customers* dimension as begun in the previous exercise and then load the data into the data warehouse.

1. You will retrieve additional information about the customer from the *stg.Customer-Information* table. To achieve this, you could use the Merge Join transformation again, but to test an alternative, this time you will use a Lookup task.

2. Drag a Lookup transformation from the SSIS Toolbox onto the data flow design surface. Rename the Lookup task **Get Customer Information**. Connect the output arrow of the Merge Join transformation to the Lookup transformation.

3. Double-click the Lookup transformation to display the Lookup Transformation Editor. Select Full Cache mode and OLE DB Connection Manager. In the Specify How To Handle Rows With No Matching Entries drop-down list, select Redirect Rows To No Match Output.

4. In the Lookup Transformation Editor, click the Connection tab and select TK463DW for the OLE DB connection manager. In the Use A Table Or View drop-down list, select the *stg.CustomerInformation* table.

5. In the Lookup Transformation Editor, click Columns tab. Link the *BusinessEntityID* column from the Available Input Column list to the *PersonID* column in the Available Lookup Columns list by dragging the *BusinessEntityID* column over the *PersonID* column. (Note that if you want to later change the mapping, you can right-click the link between the columns and choose Edit Mappings.) From the Available Lookup Columns list, select the check boxes for the *EnglishEducation*, *EnglishOccupation*, *Birth-Date*, *Gender*, *MaritalStatus*, and *EmailAddress* columns. Click OK to save the changes.

6. Drag a Derived Column transformation from the SSIS Toolbox onto the data flow area. Rename it **Set Default Values**. Connect the output arrow of the Get Customer Information Lookup transformation to the Derived Column transformation. When prompted with the Input Output Selection dialog box, choose Lookup No Match Output from the Input drop-down list, and then click OK.

7. Double-click the Derived Column transformation and, in the Derived Column Transformation Editor, add six new columns, as shown in Table 5-7, by specifying the column name in the Derived Column Name column and the appropriate SSIS expression in the Expression column.

TABLE 5-7 Derived Column Information

Derived column name	SSIS expression
EnglishEducation	"N/A"
EnglishOccupation	"N/A"
BirthDate	NULL(DT_DBDATE)
Gender	"N/A"
MaritalStatus	"N/A"
EmailAddress	"N/A"

8. Click OK to save the changes.

9. Drag a Union All transformation from the SSIS Toolbox to the data flow area. Connect the output arrow from the Get Customer Information Lookup transformation to the Union All transformation. Also connect the output arrow from the Derived Column transformation to the Union All transformation.

10. Double-click the Union All transformation and, in the Union All Transformation Editor, select the appropriate columns in the Union All Input 2 column. Create all mapping between columns from both sources. Map rows that have an *<ignore>* value by clicking them and selecting the appropriate value from the drop-down list.

11. Before inserting the data into the *dbo.Customers* table, you have to check whether the record already exists. Drag a Lookup transformation from the SSIS Toolbox to the data flow area. Rename it **Check Customer Exists**. Drag the output arrow from the Union All transformation to the new Lookup component.

12. Double-click the Lookup component and, in the Lookup Transformation Editor, specify to ignore failure in the Specify How To Handle Rows With No Matching Entries drop-down list. On the Connection tab, select TK463DW as an OLE DB connection manager, choose Use Results Of An SQL Query, and type the following query.

```
SELECT CustomerDwKey, CustomerKey FROM Customers;
```

13. On the Columns tab of the Lookup Transformation Editor, link the *BusinessEntityID* and *CustomerKey* columns. Choose to retrieve the *CustomerDwKey* column from the Available Lookup Columns list. Click OK to save the changes.

14. Drag a Derived Column transformation from the SSIS Toolbox and connect the output arrow from the Check Customer Exists Lookup transformation to the new Derived Column transformation. When prompted with the Input Output Selection dialog box, choose Lookup Match Output from the Input drop-down list, and then click OK. Rename the Derived Column transformation **Calc Columns**.

15. Edit the Derived Column transformation by adding a new derived column called **FullName** and typing the following SSIS Expression.

```
LastName + " " + FirstName
```

16. Click OK to save the changes.

17. Now you need to check whether the record exists in the target table. Drag a Conditional Split transformation onto the data flow design surface, and then connect the output arrow from the Derived Column transformation to the Conditional Split transformation.

18. Double-click the Conditional Split transformation to display the Conditional Split Transformation Editor dialog box. Create a new output by typing **New record** in the Output Name box for the first row of the output list. In the same row of the output list, type the following code in the Condition field.

```
ISNULL(CustomerDwKey)
```

19. Click OK to save your changes.

20. From the SSIS Toolbox, drag an OLE DB destination adapter to the data flow design surface, and then change its name to **Dim Customer**. Drag an output arrow from the Conditional Split transformation onto this new OLE DB destination adapter. When prompted in the Input Output Selection dialog box, select New Records from the Output drop-down list, and then click OK.

21. Double-click the Dim Customer destination adapter that you just created to display the OLE DB Destination Editor dialog box. Set TK463DW in the OLE DB connection manager drop-down list, set Table Or view—Fast Load for the Data Access Mode, and select the *dbo.Customer* table. Choose the Mappings tab, and set the mappings as displayed in Table 5-8.

TABLE 5-8 Column Mapping for the OLE DB Destination Adapter

Input column	Destination column
<ignore>	CustomerDwKey
BusinessEntityID	CustomerKey
FullName	FullName
EmailAddress	EmailAddress
BirthDate	BirthDate

Input column	Destination column
MaritalStatus	MaritalStatus
Gender	Gender
EnglishEducation	EnglishEducation
EnglishOccupation	EnglishOccupation
<ignore>	City
TerritoryName	StateProvince
CountryRegionCode	CountryRegion
<ignore>	Age
<ignore>	CurrentFlag

22. Click OK to save the changes.

23. Execute the DimCustomer.dtsx package. Observe the execution to confirm successful completion of this exercise.

> **NOTE CONTINUING WITH PRACTICES**
>
> Do not exit SSDT if you intend to continue immediately with the next practice.

Lesson Summary

- Remember which transformations are non-blocking, partly-blocking, and blocking.
- Use the Resolve References dialog box to solve mapping errors.
- Use Derived Column transformation to add new columns or replace the value in existing ones.

Lesson Review

Answer the following questions to test your knowledge of the information in this lesson. You can find the answers to these questions and explanations of why each answer choice is correct or incorrect in the "Answers" section at the end of this chapter.

1. Which transformation can you use if you would like to convert data from one data type to another? (Choose all that apply.)

   A. Audit

   B. Derived Column

   C. Data Conversion

   D. Script Component

2. Which transformations are fully blocking? (Choose all that apply.)

   A. Lookup transformation

   B. Sort transformation

   C. Merge Join transformation

   D. Aggregate transformation

3. Which transformations are new in SQL Server 2012 SSIS? (Choose all that apply.)

   A. CDC Splitter

   B. Pivot

   C. Fuzzy Lookup

   D. DQS Cleansing

Lesson 3: Determining Appropriate ETL Strategy and Tools

The volume of data that must be managed by data warehouses is growing every day, and data integration is becoming the biggest issue, with increasing demand for the implementation of different analytical solutions ranging from enterprise data warehouses to specific data marts needed for predictive analytics. Most of the cost and maintenance of complex data integration processing occurs in the bulk data movement space. ETL has experienced explosive growth in both frequency and size in the past 15 years. In the mid-1990s, pushing 30 gigabytes (GB) to 40 GB of data on a monthly basis was considered a large effort. However, some companies have requirements for moving a terabyte of data on a daily basis. In addition to standard flat file and relational data formats, data integration environments need to consider XML and unstructured data formats. With these new formats, along with the exponential growth of transactional data, the data integration process is just getting more complex and demanding.

This lesson looks at some of the ETL strategies and how you can get optimal performance from SSIS by taking advantage of the database layer by using SQL.

After this lesson, you will be able to:

- Define an ETL strategy.
- Use an appropriate mixture of SSIS transformations and SQL code.

Estimated lesson time: 80 minutes

ETL Strategy

ETL strategy is a very broad term. It is sometimes seen only as part of a data warehouse project; others include it as a subdiscipline of an enterprise integration framework. ETL strategy can cover the whole methodology from the analysis phase of a project, when you are mapping logical models to source systems; or it can encompass a more technical view of the engineering process, minimizing the potential risks of data integration. Because there are entire books written on just this subject, this book focuses on three technical areas:

- Defining the architecture for ETL
- Deciding what to do in the SSIS and what to push down to the database layer
- Managing the whole ETL process

The first and second areas will be explained with examples in this chapter. The last area involves efficient tracking and parameterization of the ETL process, which will be explained in later chapters.

ETL Architecture

Data integration reference architecture defines the processes and environments that support the capture, quality checking, processing, and movement of data, whether it is transactional or bulk, to one or many targets. A typical architecture layer for ETL consists of a process and a landing zone, which is usually inside the database. Each process follows a landing zone. A standard architecture would be:

- Extract the data (process)
- Initial Staging (landing zone)
- Data Quality (process)
- Clean Staging (landing zone)
- Transformation (process)
- Load-ready Publish (landing zone)
- Load Enterprise Data Warehouse (process)
- Enterprise Data Warehouse (landing zone)
- Load Data Marts (process)
- Data Marts (landing zone)

When you design your architecture, you must decide which landing zones you will materialize in terms of writing the data to the specific tables inside a schema or a database. Usually the Initial Staging is very beneficial after the Extract phase, which can be a 1:1 copy, a change data capture, or an incremental copy. If you are using multiple data sources, this is the first area where you unify everything in one database and can use common SQL language over all the extracted data. The next phase depends on the quality of the data. If it is bad, even more interaction with the business users and data stewards would be required, in which case this landing zone would be very beneficial. Transforming the data and loading it into a data warehouse is usually done inside the SSIS without explicitly staging the transformed data. Depending on the model of the data warehouse and its size, the ETL job for data marts can also become very complex (for example, consider a large industry model with more than 200 entities in third normal form (3NF) that now must be changed to a star schema model).

Based on this architecture, the ETL solution using SSIS should have multiple packages dedicated to each process. It is better to have multiple packages than to have too many data flows in one package. Another important thing to remember is team development, which can be managed if you create multiple packages. In SQL Server 2012, with the addition of data quality tools and a separated master data management service, the ETL architecture is getting more attention, and thanks to this multi-process/multilayer architecture, you can fit new possibilities into your ETL strategy.

Lookup Transformations

When inserting data into a data warehouse fact table, you need to get an appropriate data warehouse key (usually a surrogate key) from the dimension table. As you may remember from Chapter 2 that columns in a fact table include foreign keys and measures, and dimensions in your database define the foreign keys. The Lookup transformation is very useful in an ETL process for solving this problem, because it performs lookups by joining data in input columns with columns in a reference dataset.

Using a Lookup Transformation

You add a Lookup transformation by dragging the component from the SSIS Toolbox to the data flow design area. Using the Lookup Transformation Editor, you specify the reference dataset. This can be a cache file, an existing table or view, a new table, or the result of a SQL query. The Lookup transformation uses either an OLE DB connection manager or a Cache connection manager to connect to the reference dataset. In Figure 5-14, you can observe the configurations on the General tab.

You specify how the reference dataset will be stored in memory by selecting the appropriate cache mode:

- *Full cache* is the default mode. In this mode, the database is queried once during the pre-execute phase of the data flow, and the entire reference set is stored into memory. Lookup operations will be very fast during their execution, but you need to have enough memory to fit the needed dataset.

■ *Partial cache* means that the lookup cache is empty at the beginning of the data flow. When a new row comes in, the Lookup transformation checks its cache for the matching values. If no match is found, it queries the database. If the match is found at the database, the values are cached so they can be used the next time a matching row comes in. In SQL Server 2008 and SQL Server 2012, it is also possible to set up the Miss Cache feature, which allows you to allocate a certain percentage of your cache to remembering rows that had no match in the database.

■ The *no cache* mode will store only the last matched row, which means that the Lookup transformation will query the database for each row. This mode should be avoided in data warehouse scenarios when you are loading a fact table, because it will work too slowly.

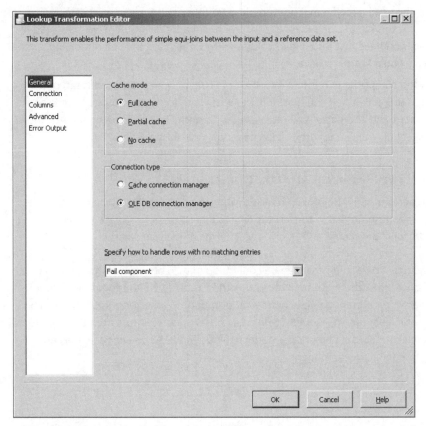

FIGURE 5-14 The General tab of the Lookup Transformation Editor, in which you can define the kind of cache mode to use.

On the Connection tab of this dialog box, you specify the referenced dataset. Based on the fact that Full Cache mode is the optimum choice, it is a best practice to write a SQL query that will return only the needed columns. For example, if you specify a table in the Use A Table Or A View option and this dimension table has 50 or more columns, all of them will be stored in memory. Usually you need just a couple of columns—those that are needed for joining, and the columns you would like to retrieve.

You specify the composite join (a join over multiple columns) on the Columns tab of the Lookup Transformation Editor. If you have to write a join with a range predicate—for example, between a start and end date—you must use the Custom Query option on the Advanced tab. In a case like that, you cannot use Full Cache mode, only Partial Cache.

IMPORTANT **LOOKUP TRANSFORMATION CASE SENSITIVITY**

The lookups performed by the Lookup transformation are case sensitive. Use either the Character Map transformation to convert the data to uppercase or lowercase and use appropriate SQL functions such as UPPER or LOWER for the referenced dataset.

Another important parameter that can be configured in the Lookup Transformation Editor is how to handle rows that have no matching entries. You can fail the component, ignore failure, or redirect rows either to a new "no match" output or to an error output. This can be specified on the General tab. In Figure 5-15, you can observe two outputs from the Lookup task, one for matching output and one for nonmatching output. As you can see, they are merged using the Union All component.

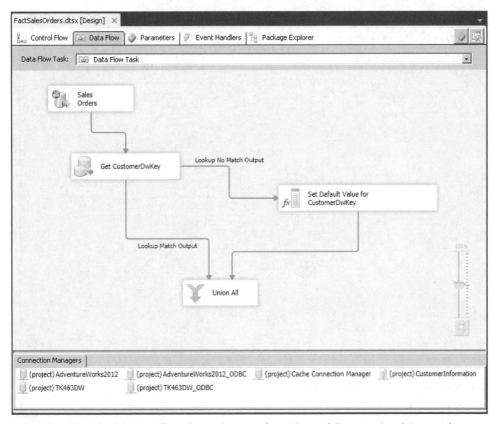

FIGURE 5-15 Using both outputs from the Lookup transformation and then merging them together.

This seems natural in terms of data flow—if a match is not found, some default value is applied for this row and then both outputs are merged into one to write the data to the destination adapter. But in terms of performance and best practices, it is better to apply a different approach. Figure 5-16 shows the alternative solution. Inside the Lookup Transformation Editor, the data flow was set up to ignore failure by setting the Specify How To Handle Rows With No Matching Entries to that choice. This means that the result will get matched values from the Lookup transformation and also rows with a NULL inside the lookup result columns. Then a Derived Column component is added and an SSIS Expression is written to replace an existing lookup result column by the following logical expression.

```
ISNULL(CustomerDwKey) ? 0 : CustomerDwKey
```

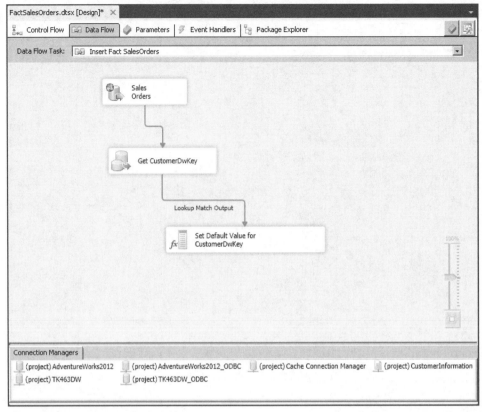

FIGURE 5-16 An alternative approach to the data flow shown in Figure 5-15, using the Ignore Failure option in the Lookup component.

The second approach is much faster and uses fewer resources. This is because the Union All transformation is partially blocked. As you will learn in Chapter 13, the buffers that store the data need to be copied, and this takes time and server resources.

 Quick Check

- What is the difference between the Lookup and Merge Join transformations?

Quick Check Answer

- The Lookup transformation does not need a sorted input; it is a non-blocking transformation, and in cases when more matching rows exist from the referenced dataset, only the first one will be retrieved. This means that the transformation will never retrieve more rows than exist in the input rows. With the Merge Join transformation more rows can be retrieved, because all matching data is retrieved.

Using the Cache Transform Transformation with the Lookup Transformation

The Cache Transform transformation writes data from a connected data source in the data flow to a Cache connection manager. The Cache connection manager provides an alternative to doing lookups against a database table with an OLE DB connection.

After a cache is created in an SSIS package, it will be kept in memory until the package has finished executing, if the Cache connection manager is set on the package level. If the Cache connection manager is set on a project level, it can be shared by other packages. With this approach, the cache can be reused across multiple packages and data flows, and shared between multiple lookups. It can also be persisted to disk.

Figure 5-17 shows that the cache must first be created in a separate data flow by using the Cache Transform so that it can be referenced in other data flow tasks.

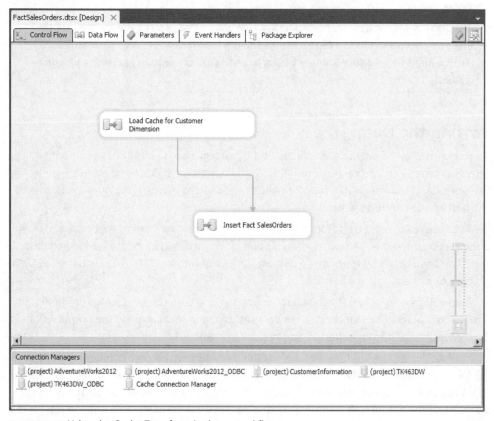

FIGURE 5-17 Using the Cache Transform in the control flow.

The following lists the benefits of using the Cache connection manager:

- It allows you to reuse the cache to reduce database load.
- It allows you to share the cache between lookups to reduce memory usage. For example, consider a role-playing dimension in data warehousing, where there is one physical table, but in the fact table there are multiple foreign key relationships for each of its roles (for the Date dimension, there could be InvoiceDateID, ShippingDateID, DocumentDateID, and so on).
- You can do lookups against other (non OLE-DB) sources.

In terms of cache modes and the best practices that surround them, using a Cache connection manager is equivalent to using Full Cache mode. Because the cache is essentially clear text, it is not recommended that sensitive data be stored in the cache.

EXAM TIP

A cache is created in a standard data flow, which means that you can use any data source that SSIS can connect to as a source for the Lookup transformation. With the Cache connection manager, you are no longer bound to an OLE DB connection to create a lookup dataset.

Sorting the Data

As you learned in the previous lesson, the Sort transformation is an expensive component in terms of memory and processor consumption, and it is also a full blocking transformation. On the other hand, the Merge Join transformation needs sorted input; so the question is, what is the best way to develop the package?

If you are reading the data from a database—either from the staging area or directly from a transactional system—you can put the burden of sorting the data on the underlying database. You achieve this by specifying a custom SQL query with an ORDER BY clause in the Data Source component.

Then you have to inform the data flow engine that the data source is sorted. In the Advanced Editor dialog box for the created data source component, expand the output columns on the Input And Output Properties tab, as show in Figure 5-18.

Now set the SortKeyPosition property for the columns that are part of the sorting key (1 for the first column, 2 for the second, and so on); the value 0 is the default value for all columns that are not part of the sort key. You must also specify that the whole output is sorted by selecting the output (this is the OLE DB Source Output node in Figure 5-18) and setting the IsSorted property to True.

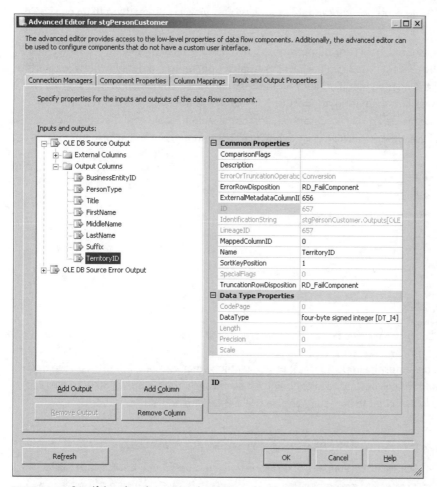

FIGURE 5-18 Specifying that the output data is sorted in the Advanced Editor.

Set-Based Updates

In a data warehouse environment, it is usually best to avoid using UPDATE and DELETE operations on the data and in the ETL strategy. This recommendation is focused mostly on large
fact tables, for which you will learn an efficient way to incrementally update data in Chapter 7.
Of course, you still have to do some updating of the data when it comes to dimension tables.

Currently the only way to perform an update in SSIS is to use an OLE DB Command transformation that executes a SQL statement by using columns from the current row as parameters. This operation is done for each row inside the data flow and, because of this, it is useful only in specific cases when the total number of executed SQL statements will be small. For example, consider an update of the *dbo.Customer* dimension table, which has more than 100,000 rows. Suppose that a Lookup transformation returns 30,000 matched rows that need to be updated. If you map the output to the OLE DB Command to update these rows, it will execute the SQL statement 30,000 times. As you can see, this will be very slow and something that you should avoid.

So the question is, how can you perform a batch update in SSIS? The native SSIS functionality currently prevents you from performing a batch update from a data flow task without first staging the needed modified data. Figure 5-19 shows the combination of first using a data flow task and then using an Execute SQL task inside the control flow. The data flow task writes the needed modified data to an additional staging table, and then the Execute SQL task will use either the UPDATE or the MERGE T-SQL statement to perform a set-based update.

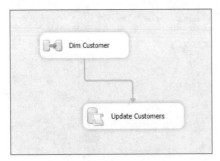

FIGURE 5-19 Combining the data flow task and the Execute SQL task.

This demonstrates the importance of understanding what you can do better on the database layer and what is best done in SSIS. With this approach, the update of 30,000 rows will take seconds, compared to an hour using an OLE DB Command transformation.

> ***NOTE*** **UPDATING DIMENSIONS USING THE T-SQL MERGE STATEMENT**
>
> Using the T-SQL MERGE statement, you can perform an "upsert" operation, which refers to any database statement or combination of statements that inserts a record to a table in a database if the record does not exist or, if the record already does exist, updates the existing record. If you want to perform such an operation directly in the data flow, then you can develop a custom transformation or use one from a third-party provider of custom data flow transformations.

Remember that even though the data flow engine is very fast, it is important to realize what can be done inside SSIS and what can be pushed to the database layer, so that you can find an optimum solution and design an effective ETL process.

REAL WORLD   EFFICIENTLY LOADING DATA

It makes sense to evaluate where operations take place in your data flow even when load-ing the data, and even if the data set is not large. For example, one client had about 10 million rows, but their T-SQL code for loading the data had about 40 UPDATE statements, joining different tables to get the information they needed. That process took about six hours. We changed the loading from the pure T-SQL procedures to SSIS and applied all rules in one data flow. The final result took only 10 minutes for loading the fact table data.

PRACTICE   Enhancing Data Flow Transformations

In this practice, you will apply some of the methods discussed in this topic. You will modify the ETL process created in the Lesson 2 exercise to see how things can sometimes be done more effectively.

If you encounter a problem completing an exercise, you can install the completed projects from the Solution folder that is provided with the companion content for this chapter and lesson.

EXERCISE 1   Join and Sort Tables in the Staging Area

In this exercise, you replace the Merge Join and Sort transformations by pushing the needed operation down to the database layer.

1. If necessary, start SSDT, open the TK 463 Chapter 5 project, right-click the DimCustomer package, and choose Copy. Right-click the SSIS Package folder in the Solution Explorer window, and select Paste. Rename the copied package **DimCustomerNew.dtsx**.

2. Click the Data Flow tab at the top of the SSIS Designer. Select the stgCustomer, stg-Person, Sort (sort step after stgPerson), Sort 1 (sort step after stgCustomer), Merge Join and Sort 3 (sort step after Merge Join) components, and press Delete on the keyboard. You will now replace the existing logic of sorting and merging data by doing this on the database layer.

3. In the SSIS Toolbox , drag an OLE DB Source adapter onto the data flow workspace. Rename the OLE DB Source adapter **StgPersonCustomer**. Edit the source adapter and set an OLE DB connection manager to TK463DW, set the Data Access Mode to SQL Command, and type the following SQL statement.

```
SELECT
    P.BusinessEntityID,
    P.PersonType,
    P.Title,
    P.FirstName,
```

```
        P.MiddleName,
        P.LastName,
        P.Suffix,
        C.TerritoryID
FROM stg.Person AS P
INNER JOIN stg.Customer AS C ON C.CustomerID = P.BusinessEntityID
ORDER BY C.TerritoryID;
```

4. Click OK to save changes.

5. Right-click the stgPersonCustomer object and select Show Advanced Editor. On the Input And Output Properties tab, click OLE DB Source Output in the Inputs And Outputs area. Under Common Properties, set the IsSorted property to True. This property provides a hint to the SSIS that the data coming from the OLE DB Source adapter is sorted.

6. Now you have to define the sorting columns by expanding the OLE DB Source Output in the Inputs And Outputs area. Expand the Output Columns and click *TerritoryID*. In Common Properties, set the SortKeyPosition property to 1, and click OK to close the Advanced Editor. This will indicate that *TerritoryID* is the first column for sorting and that it is sorted in ascending order. (For descending order, use –1.)

7. Connect the output arrow of the stgPersonCustomer object to the Merge Join 1 transformation. Open the Merge Join Transformation Editor for the Merge Join 1 transformation to observe the mappings between the left and right inputs. Click OK.

8. Execute the DimCustomerNew.dtsx package. Observe the execution to confirm successful completion of this exercise.

EXERCISE 2   Create Efficient Lookups

In this exercise, you replace the Union All transformation by not having multiple outputs from the Lookup transformation. This is usually very useful in data warehousing when you are loading fact tables and you need to perform multiple lookups to get the appropriate dimension surrogate key.

1. If necessary, start SSDT, open the TK 463 Chapter 5 project, and then open the DimCustomerNew.dtsx package from the previous exercise for editing.

2. On the Data Flow tab, open the Lookup Transformation Editor for the Get Customer Information Lookup task.

3. In the Specify How To Handle Rows With No Matching Entries drop-down list, select Ignore Failure. Click OK to save the changes.

4. Delete the Union All transformation and the Set Default Values Derived Column transformation.

5. Drag a Derived Column transformation from the SSIS Toolbox onto the data flow design area and rename it **Set default values**.

6. Connect the output arrow of the Get Customer Information Lookup component to the new Derived Column transformation.

7. Edit the Set Default Values Derived Column transformation. In the Derived Column Transformation Editor, replace six of the existing columns as shown in Table 5-9 by specifying them in the *Derived Column* column. Add the appropriate SSIS expression in the *Expression* column.

TABLE 5-9 Derived Column Information

Derived column	SSIS expression
Replace 'EnglishEducation'	**ISNULL(EnglishEducation) ? "N/A" : EnglishEducation**
Replace 'EnglishOccupation'	**ISNULL(EnglishOccupation) ? "N/A" : EnglishOccupation**
Replace 'BirthDate'	**ISNULL(BirthDate) ? NULL(DT_DBDATE) : BirthDate**
Replace 'Gender'	**ISNULL(Gender) ? "N/A" : Gender**
Replace 'MaritalStatus'	**ISNULL(MaritalStatus) ? "N/A" : MaritalStatus**
Replace 'EmailAddress'	**ISNULL(EmailAddress) ? "N/A" : EmailAddress**

8. Click OK to save the changes.

9. Connect the output arrow of the Set Default Values Derived Column component to the Check Customer Exists Lookup transformation.

10. Execute the DimCustomerNew.dtsx package. Observe the execution to confirm successful completion of this exercise.

EXERCISE 3   Update the *Customer* Dimension Table

In the Exercise 1 of Lesson 2, you only inserted new rows in the *Customer* table. You did not develop any mechanism for updating existing columns for the existing row. Usually you need to update the columns for which you do not want to keep a history of changes (Slowly Changing Dimension Type 1). For simplicity, in this exercise, you will update all the rows, not only those that have changed. You will implement this by having a set-based update instead of using the existing OLE DB Command transformation, because the latter is too slow in such a scenario.

1. Start SSMS and connect to your SQL Server instance. Open a new query window by clicking the New Query button. Select the TK463DW database in the database drop-down list. Use the following code to create the *dbo.UpdateCustomers* staging table based on a structure similar to that of the *dbo.Customers* dimension table (for example, you do not need computed columns and the surrogate key).

```
CREATE TABLE dbo.UpdateCustomers
(
CustomerKey    INT           NOT NULL,
FullName       NVARCHAR(150) NULL,
EmailAddress   NVARCHAR(50)  NULL,
BirthDate      DATE          NULL,
MaritalStatus  NCHAR(5)      NULL,
Gender         NCHAR(5)      NULL,
Education      NVARCHAR(40)  NULL,
Occupation     NVARCHAR(100) NULL,
City           NVARCHAR(30)  NULL,
StateProvince  NVARCHAR(50)  NULL,
CountryRegion  NVARCHAR(50)  NULL
);
```

2. If necessary, start SSDT, open the TK 463 Chapter 5 project, and then open the DimCustomerNew.dtsx package from the previous exercise for editing.

3. Click the Data Flow tab and drag an OLE DB Destination adapter from the SSIS Toolbox onto the data flow design area, under the existing Conditional Split transformation. Rename the component **Update Dim Customer**.

4. Connect the output arrow from the Conditional Split transformation to the new OLE DB Destination component.

5. Open the OLE DB Destination Editor for the Update Dim Customer component. Set an OLE DB connection manager to TK463DW, set the Data Access Mode to Table Or View—Fast Load, and select the *dbo.UpdateCustomers* table. On the Mappings tab, ensure that the columns are linked as shown in Table 5-10.

TABLE 5-10 Column Mapping for the OLE DB Destination Adapter

Input column	Destination column
BusinessEntityID	CustomerKey
FullName	FullName
EmailAddress	EmailAddress
BirthDate	BirthDate
MaritalStatus	MaritalStatus
Gender	Gender
EnglishEducation	Education
EnglishOccupation	Occupation
<ignore>	City
TerritoryName	StateProvince
CountryRegionCode	CountryRegion

6. Click OK to save the changes.

7. Now you will add a T-SQL UPDATE statement in the control flow area to update the *dbo.Customers* table. Click the Control Flow tab and drag the Execute SQL task onto the workspace. Rename it **Update Customers**.

8. Open the Execute SQL Task Editor and, under the Connection property, choose TK463DW. For the SQLStatement property, type the following SQL statement to update *dbo.Customers*.

```
UPDATE C
SET
  FullName = U.FullName,
  EmailAddress = U.EmailAddress,
  BirthDate = U.BirthDate,
  MaritalStatus = U.MaritalStatus,
  Gender = U.Gender,
  Education = U.Education,
  Occupation = U.Occupation,
  City = U.City,
  StateProvince = U.StateProvince,
  CountryRegion = U.CountryRegion
FROM dbo.Customers AS C
INNER JOIN dbo.UpdateCustomers AS U ON U.CustomerKey = C.CustomerKey;
-- truncate table
TRUNCATE TABLE dbo.UpdateCustomers;
```

9. Click OK to close the Execute SQL task. Connect the data flow task with the Execute SQL task.

10. Execute the DimCustomerNew.dtsx package. Observe the execution to confirm successful completion of this exercise.

Lesson Summary

- Use sorting on the database layer as much as possible.
- When joining large tables, consider doing so on the database layer.
- Insert the data that needs to be updated into a temporary table and then perform a set-based update using SQL.

Lesson Review

Answer the following questions to test your knowledge of the information in this lesson. You can find the answers to these questions and explanations of why each answer choice is correct or incorrect in the "Answers" section at the end of this chapter.

1. Which data flow transformation would you use if you had to join data from two different database tables that exist on two different servers? (Choose all that apply.)

    A. Merge Join transformation

    B. Union All transformation

    C. Merge transformation

    D. Lookup transformation

2. Suppose that you want to load the data from a flat file and write it into a SQL Server, Excel, and Raw File transformation inside one data flow task. How many Data Source adapters could you use? (Choose all that apply.)

    A. 0

    B. 1

    C. 2

    D. 3

3. Which sentence is true regarding Cache connection manager? (Choose all that apply.)

    A. Cache can be reused by multiple Lookup transformations.

    B. You cannot incrementally update the cache while the package is running.

    C. The Cache connection manager can be set on a project level.

    D. You can do lookups against other (non OLE-DB) sources.

Case Scenario

In the following case scenario, you apply what you've learned about designing and implementing a data flow. You can find the answers to these questions in the "Answers" section at the end of this chapter.

Case Scenario: New Source System

The marketing department has requested that you add the market share by product information into the data warehouse. They have purchased a yearly subscription for this information feed, and the data is available monthly on an FTP server. The data is in a flat file. It contains information about the product group in the first field, and the market share information is in 12 fields (a separate field for each month).

You need to integrate this new source to an existing DW. Answer the following questions:

1. How would you model the fact table to store market share results?

2. Which tasks and transformations in SSIS would you use to populate this fact table?

Suggested Practices

To help you successfully master the exam objectives presented in this chapter, complete the following tasks.

Create and Load Additional Tables

In order to experience the range of possibility of data flow transformations, prepare different packages for loading the data in the dimension and fact tables created in Chapter 1, "Data Warehouse Logical Design."

- **Practice 1**   Create a package for loading the *dbo.Products* table. Use the same source that you used in the SQL statements for populating the *dbo.Products* table in Chapter 2. First, stage all the needed tables.

- **Practice 2**   Create a new package for loading the *dbo.InternetSales* fact table. Use the same logic for source tables that you used in the SQL statement used for populating the *dbo.InternetSales* table in Chapter 2.

Answers

This section contains answers to the lesson review questions and solutions to the case scenarios in this chapter.

Lesson 1

1. **Correct Answers: A, C and D**

   A. **Correct:** ADO NET supports SQL Server.

   B. **Incorrect:** The Raw File source is used to read SSIS raw files.

   C. **Correct:** OLE DB supports SQL Server.

   D. **Correct:** With ODBC, you can connect to SQL Server.

2. **Correct Answers: B and C**

   A. **Incorrect:** The OLE DB destination is not used for flat files.

   B. **Correct:** This is the main destination adapter for flat files.

   C. **Correct:** The SSIS Raw File destination is used for staging data to the file system.

   D. **Incorrect:** The Recordset destination is used to store the data in memory.

3. **Correct Answers: A and D**

   A. **Correct:** You can change how source data is mapped to SSIS data types in the Advanced Editor.

   B. **Incorrect:** You can have multiple data source adapters within one data flow task.

   C. **Incorrect:** You can select specific columns to be extracted using the source adapter.

   D. **Correct:** You can use the XML source adapter to read the data from an XML file.

Lesson 2

1. **Correct Answers: B, C, and D**

   A. **Incorrect:** This adds additional columns to each row based on system package variables.

   B. **Correct:** Using the SSIS Expression language, you can use functions that enable you to convert data from one data type to another.

   C. **Correct:** This is the main purpose of the Data Conversion transformation.

   D. **Correct:** Using the Script component, you can use VB.NET or C# and convert the data from one data type to another.

2. **Correct Answers: B and D**

   A. **Incorrect:** A Lookup transformation is a non-blocking transformation.

   B. **Correct:** A Sort transformation has to wait for all the input rows before passing the rows onward.

   C. **Incorrect:** A Merge Join transformation is partly blocking.

   D. **Correct:** An Aggregate transformation is fully blocking, because all rows have to be read before an aggregation can be applied and rows passed onward.

3. **Correct Answers: A and D**

   A. **Correct:** CDC Splitter is a new transformation.

   B. **Incorrect:** The Pivot transformation was available in previous versions.

   C. **Incorrect:** The Fuzzy Lookup transformation was available in previous versions.

   D. **Correct:** DQS Cleansing is a new transformation.

Lesson 3

1. **Correct Answer: A and D**

   A. **Correct:** Using the Merge Join transformation, you can join two sources by applying an inner join, left outer join, or a full outer join.

   B. **Incorrect:** The Union All transformation does not join two data sources.

   C. **Incorrect:** The Merge transformation is similar to Union All and does not join two data sources.

   D. **Correct:** The Lookup transformation can associate data from two sources.

2. **Correct Answers: B, C and D**

   A. **Incorrect:** You need to have at least one data source adapter to read the flat file.

   B. **Correct:** One data source adapter is enough, because you can use the Multicast transformation to write data to three data destination adapters.

   C. **Correct:** You can map two data source adapters to three data destination adapters by using a Multicast transformation for one data source to write to two data destination adapters.

   D. **Correct:** You can map three data source adapters to three data destination adapters.

3. **Correct Answers: A, C, and D**

   A. **Correct:** You can use the same cache for multiple Lookup transformations.

   B. **Incorrect:** In SQL Server 2012 SSIS, it is possible to incrementally update the cache while the package is running.

C. **Correct:** You can set the Cache connection manager on the project level.

D. **Correct:** First you can load the data from various sources in to a Cache connection manager and then use it for the Lookup transformation.

Case Scenario

1. You would need to have three columns (two dimensions and one measure)—product group, reporting month, and a market share value. The fact table would be semi-additive (not additive over time).

2. First, you would use an FTP task to copy the file to the machine on which SSIS is installed. You can then import the file by using a data flow task configured with a Flat File source adapter. Then you would need to unpivot the columns for months to get a row for each month, and use the Lookup task to get appropriate surrogate keys from the existing dimension, and use the ODBC Destination adapter to write the data to the new fact table.

## PART III

Enhancing SSIS Packages

CHAPTER 6   Enhancing Control Flow   **239**

CHAPTER 7   Enhancing Data Flow   **283**

CHAPTER 8   Creating a Robust and Restartable Package   **327**

CHAPTER 9   Implementing Dynamic Packages   **353**

CHAPTER 10   Auditing and Logging   **381**

Enhancing Control Flow

Exam objectives in this chapter:

- Load Data
    - Design control flow.
    - Implement package logic by using SSIS variables and parameters.
    - Implement control flow.

Microsoft SQL Server Integration Services (SSIS) solutions are automated solutions—their operation requires no user interaction whatsoever; in fact, in all the activities surrounding SSIS solutions, the human presence is limited to development (obviously), deployment (for example, when solutions are initially set up in production or when new versions of the solutions are set up), and maintenance (for example, to reconfigure a solution, to analyze its operation, or to troubleshoot it).

This significant characteristic has a profound effect on SSIS development; every process and every operation—regardless of its complexity—must be planned and implemented in such a way that its execution can be automated. Not only does this mean the execution itself, but also error detection. The response to errors must also be automated, and, ideally, the same applies to recovery from them.

Determinism is what allows automation in the first place. As long as an operation can be described deterministically (and translated to a programming language), then the operation can be automated. Most data warehousing operations are automated; they are performed by machines instead of humans, allowing us humans to spend the predominant part of our workday doing what we do best—thinking, creating, and responding to challenges that no machine currently in existence is able to respond to.

Of course, not all data warehousing operations can be automated; not necessarily because they cannot be described deterministically, but because they cannot be described in a sufficient degree of determinism in advance. Some operations—troubleshooting activities, usually—cannot be predicted and therefore cannot be automated until they have been encountered at least once. From then on, every known set of circumstances identified during the "manual" troubleshooting operation can be defined deterministically; therefore, an appropriate automated response becomes a possibility.

Predictability is also highly significant to automation. It contributes to the foundations of solution development; it enables reusability. In a simple definition, *reusability* is achieved when a solution is designed once and then used many times. Reusability helps reduce the time needed to develop a solution, reduces the need for resources, and also simplifies solution deployment and maintenance.

Another significant characteristic essential for efficient automation is *adaptability*. In order for an automated solution to be capable of detecting problems, capable of responding to them without any user intervention, or even capable of preventing them from occurring in the first place, it needs to be adaptable. It needs to identify the state of its environment and adjust itself accordingly during execution.

High determinism, which is a characteristic of many data management processes, especially in data warehousing, allows these processes to be automated. The ability to determine at design time which data management operations will be required, under what conditions they will be performed at run time, and in what order, are the principal prerequisites of automation.

Nevertheless, "deterministic" does not mean "rigid"—although most circumstances can be predicted at design time, unfortunately some cannot. What cannot be predicted cannot be preset. Just consider the differences between the development and the production environments: any element of an automated solution that depends on the environment and that is not adjusted appropriately might render the deployed solution useless or even harmful, or could prevent its execution altogether.

To respond to this particular challenge, SSIS solutions can be parameterized; this allows the essence of any automated operation to remain unchanged while its properties, which might depend on the environment or other circumstances, can be modified accordingly. Typically, the administrator in charge of maintenance will use the parameters to control the behavior of the solution's execution by setting the exposed properties.

Not only does parameterization enable deployment in the first place, but it also improves the SSIS solution's reusability by allowing the same solution to be deployed multiple times, and to different environments.

A high degree of determinism might even allow some SSIS solution properties to be set automatically—either because they are based on parameterized settings (for example, if the root path pointing to the location of data files is parameterized and will eventually be controlled by the administrator, then the paths to folders below the root folder can be determined automatically), or because they are based on automatically discoverable properties (for example, the number of CPUs, the size of available system memory, or the amount of free disk space) and therefore do not even need to be set by the administrator.

> **IMPORTANT** **PARAMETERS**
>
> Always parameterize properties that cannot be determined any other way, except for being set by the administrator (such as file paths, server and database names, or entire connection strings).
>
> Avoid parameterizing properties that can also be determined automatically (such as the number of CPUs); furthermore, do not parameterize automatically determinable properties that, if set by the administrator, could cause the solution to fail (such as data source queries) or cause it to underperform (such as batch sizes).

Lessons in this chapter:

- Lesson 1: SSIS Variables
- Lesson 2: Connection Managers, Tasks, and Precedence Constraint Expressions
- Lesson 3: Using a Master Package for Advanced Control Flow

Before You Begin

To complete this chapter, you must have:

- Experience working with SQL Server Management Studio (SSMS).
- Experience working with Microsoft Visual Studio, SQL Server Business Intelligence Development Studio (BIDS), or SQL Server Data Tools (SSDT).
- A working knowledge of the Transact-SQL language.

Lesson 1: SSIS Variables

SSIS *variables* can be used to store values that are determined automatically at run time and that are to be used or reused in various elements of the solution. Some variables (such as the time the process started, the name of a dynamically created folder to be used for storing temporary files, or the number of CPUs) are set once—for example, at the beginning of the execution, or just before they are actually needed—and then can be used multiple times, where some variables (such as the name of the file being processed by the Foreach Loop container using the Foreach File Enumerator or values from the current row in a Foreach Loop container using a Foreach ADO Enumerator) are set iteratively and used until the next iteration.

Parameters and variables can be used in SSIS packages interchangeably, but there are a few differences that you should be aware of:

- Parameters are exposed to the caller, but variables are not. If a particular property needs to be set dynamically but should not be set by the administrator, use a variable; otherwise, use a parameter.

- Within an SSIS package, parameters are read-only. They can only be set by the caller, and after they are set, they cannot be changed.

After this lesson, you will be able to:

- Determine variables.
- Understand and use user variables.
- Understand variable scope and data type.
- Implement parameterization of properties by using variables.

Estimated lesson time: 45 minutes

System and User Variables

There are two types of SSIS variables:

- A fixed set of *system variables*, representing specific properties of various SSIS objects (packages, tasks, containers, components, and event handlers). System variables are read-only; their values are set by SSIS.

- *User-defined variables,* defined by the SSIS developer and used to store various pieces of information acquired or created during execution. By default, user-defined variables can be written to, but it is also possible to limit their usage to read-only.

Apart from the limitations mentioned here, there is no difference in behavior between system and user variables.

For a list of all available system variables, refer to the article entitled "System Variables" in Books Online for SQL Server 2012 at *http://msdn.microsoft.com/en-us/library/ms141788*.

Generally, variables are used to store scalar values, but they can also be used for storing *row sets*, such as row sets to be consumed by a Foreach Loop Container using the Foreach ADO Enumerator.

> **NOTE LARGE ROW SETS IN VARIABLES**
>
> You should avoid storing large row sets in variables, because they are kept in memory and could cause the system to run out of memory. Consider storing large data sets in staging tables (permanent or temporary tables) in a database, or in SSIS raw data files, instead of in variables.

SSIS variables can be used by control flow tasks and containers and by data flow components, and they are available to event handlers. Variables can be created using the Variables pane or via the Add Variable dialog box available in certain task and component editors. They can even be added programmatically.

Table 6-1 lists all available SSIS variable properties; some of these are discussed later in this chapter.

TABLE 6-1 SSIS Variable Properties

Property	Description
Name	The name of the variable. This must be supplied when you are creating user variables.
Scope	The scope of the variable, designating which SSIS objects will be able to access it. Variable scope is discussed in more detail later in this chapter.
Data type	The data type of the variable. Variable data types are discussed in more detail later in this chapter.
Value	The value of the variable. All user variables must be initialized by using a default value, except variables of Object or DBNull data types.
Namespace	For the two types of variables, there are two variable namespaces: system variables exist in the System namespace, and user variables exist in the User namespace.
RaiseChangeEvent	A Boolean value determining whether an event is raised when the value of the variable changes; can be very useful for logging and troubleshooting.
Description	An optional description of the variable, used mainly for documentation purposes.
Expression	An expression used to determine the value of the variable. This is useful for variables whose values are determined automatically based on other accessible system or user variables or parameters, by using expressions. Variable expressions are discussed in more detail later in this chapter.
EvaluateAsExpression	A Boolean value determining whether the value of the variable is provided by an expression or not. This property cannot be set in the Variables pane; however, it is available in the Properties pane, or when you are adding variables programmatically.
Read only	A Boolean value determining whether the variable can be modified or whether it is read-only. This property cannot be set in the Variables pane; however, it is available in the Add Variable dialog box and via the Properties pane, or when you are adding variables programmatically.
IncludeInDebugDump	A Boolean value determining whether the variable is included in debug dump files or not. By default, the value of the property is True for both system and user variables. However, the value is set to False automatically for expression-based variables and variables whose data type is changed to string. This property cannot be set in the Variables pane; however, it is available in the Properties pane or when you are adding variables programmatically.

To display system variables in the Variables pane, you can set the filter accordingly in the Variable Grid Options dialog box, shown in Figure 6-1. This dialog box is accessible from the Grid Options toolbar command.

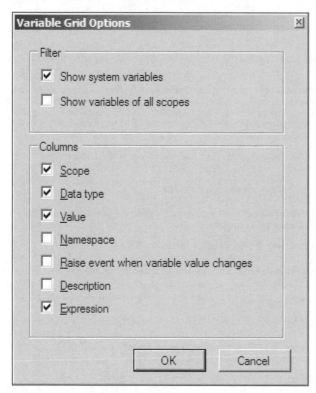

FIGURE 6-1 The Variable Grid Options dialog box.

System variables are only displayed in the grid when the Show System Variables option is checked.

Variable Data Types

The data types of SSIS variables are based on the Microsoft .Net Framework System.TypeCode enumeration, shown in Table 6-2.

At design time, variables are configured, validated (the value defined in the designer or the value set by the expression is validated against the defined data type, and a design-time error is raised in case of a type mismatch), and enlisted (made accessible to various SSIS object editors). Variables are not actually created until run time, when the SSIS package is compiled; at run time, during package validation, the variables are validated again, and a run-time error is raised in case of a type mismatch.

EXAM TIP

You should be familiar with the available SSIS variable data types, understand how and when to use them in your variables, and also understand their limitations very well (especially with respect to numeric data types and their decimal precision).

TABLE 6-2 SSIS Variable Data Types

Type name	Description
Empty	A null reference. This data type is part of the System.TypeCode enumeration but is not supported by SSDT.
Object	A general type representing any reference or value type not explicitly represented by another TypeCode. You can use this type for storing values of unsupported data types in SSIS variables. Before the value can be used, it needs to be explicitly converted to the appropriate destination data type; debugging values stored in Object type variables requires additional programming (such as using event handlers).
DBNull	A database null (column) value. Use this data type to explicitly pass a NULL value to the consuming task or component.
Boolean	A simple type representing Boolean values of True or False.
Char	An integral type representing unsigned 16-bit integers with values between 0 and 65,535. The set of possible values for the Char type corresponds to the Unicode character set.
SByte	An integral type representing signed 8-bit integers with values between –128 and 127.
Byte	An integral type representing unsigned 8-bit integers with values between 0 and 255.
Int16	An integral type representing signed 16-bit integers with values between –32,768 and 32,767.
UInt16	An integral type representing unsigned 16-bit integers with values between 0 and 65,535.
Int32	An integral type representing signed 32-bit integers with values between –2,147,483,648 and 2,147,483,647.
UInt32	An integral type representing unsigned 32-bit integers with values between 0 and 4,294,967,295.
Int64	An integral type representing signed 64-bit integers with values between –9,223,372,036,854,775,808 and 9,223,372,036,854,775,807.
UInt64	An integral type representing unsigned 64-bit integers with values between 0 and 18,446,744,073,709,551,615.
Single	A floating-point type representing values ranging from approximately 1.5×10^{-45} to 3.4×10^{38} with a precision of seven digits.
Double	A floating-point type representing values ranging from approximately 5.0×10^{-324} to 1.7×10^{308} with a precision of 15 or 16 digits.
Decimal	A simple type representing values ranging from 1.0×10^{-28} to approximately 7.9×10^{28} with 28 or 29 significant digits.
DateTime	A type representing a date and time value.
String	A sealed class type representing Unicode character strings.

In addition to the set of data types used by SSIS variables, two additional groups of data types exist in SSIS:

- Each data provider supports its own set of data types—these vary depending on the particular data provider (such as OLE DB, ADO.NET, or ODBC).

- The data flow buffer uses a special set of data types—these are provided by the SSIS engine and are used by the data flow components. These types are discussed in Chapter 5, "Designing and Implementing Data Flow."

Each of these three groups of data types serves a particular purpose, supporting a principal SSIS objective of providing a common environment for data integration when data originates in diverse and heterogeneous data stores. The predominant majority of cases in which an SSIS solution accesses data stored in various data stores should not suffer from any data type compatibility issues. However, you should always be aware of the fact that not every data type from one group of data types can be mapped to the most appropriate data type in another group. Some data types, for instance, are not even supported by some data type sets available in SSIS.

NOTE **HETEROGENEOUS DATA TYPES**

When integrating data from heterogeneous data sources, your best option is to identify a common-denominator set of data types and convert the data appropriately, ideally upon retrieval, or in the data flow task (for example, by using the Data Conversion component).

NOTE **UNSUPPORTED DATA TYPES**

When you find yourself in a situation when you are required to store a value of an unsupported type in an SSIS variable, you can resort to using the Object type for this particular variable. Object, being the base type from which all other types are derived, is implicitly convertible to any other data type, which still enables you to use unsupported data types and use variables to pass data between SSIS objects.

When variables are used to store row sets—that is, to store the result of a Transact-SQL query that produces one or more row sets, such as the result of an Execute SQL Task—two data types can be used:

- If the query produces a regular row set, you can store the result in a variable of the Object type.

  The Object type variable can then be used in a row set consumer (such as a Foreach Loop Container using the Foreach ADO Enumerator, or a Script Task or a Script Component with the appropriate programmatic logic to access the row set data).

- If the query produces an XML result, you can store it in a variable of the Object or the String type.

  The Object type variable containing an XML representation of an ADO.NET dataset can be used in an ADO.NET dataset consumer (such as a Foreach Loop Container using the Foreach ADO Enumerator, a Foreach Loop Container using the Foreach NodeList Enumerator, or a Script Task or a Script Component with custom programmatic logic to access data in the XML document).

  The String variable containing an XML representation of an ADO.NET dataset can be used in an XML data consumer (such as a Foreach Loop Container using the Foreach NodeList Enumerator, a Script Task or a Data Flow Script Component with the appropriate programmatic logic to access data in the XML document, or a Data Flow XML Source Component).

Variable Scope

The *scope* of a variable is determined through the SSIS object hierarchy; scope restricts the visibility and accessibility of a variable to a particular branch of the SSIS object hierarchy.

The package represents the root of the hierarchy; therefore, all variables defined at the package level can be accessed by any task, container, or component defined inside this package. *Package-scoped variables* can be considered global.

Variables defined at container level are only accessible to that particular container and to other objects it contains (containers can contain tasks and other containers). In the SSIS object hierarchy, objects have access to their own local variables as well as the variables of their respective ancestor objects.

Variables defined at task level are only accessible to that particular task, because tasks cannot contain other SSIS objects. The only exception to this rule is the data flow task—variables defined at the data flow task level can be used by the data flow components it contains; other than that, task-scoped variables cannot be reused elsewhere.

Figure 6-2 illustrates how the position of an object in the hierarchy affects the scope of a variable. The figure shows variables from different scopes; by default, only variables accessible to the SSIS object selected in the designer pane are shown in the Variable pane. To show variables of all scopes, open the Variable Grid Options dialog box, shown previously in Figure 6-1, and select the Show Variables Of All Scopes option.

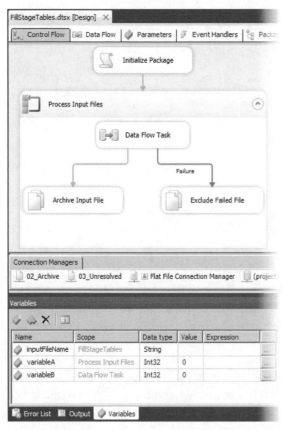

FIGURE 6-2 Variable scope.

Figure 6-2 shows three variables, each of them in its own scope:

- The *inputFileName* variable is package-scoped and therefore accessible to all SSIS objects: the Initialize Package task, the Process Input Files Foreach Loop container, the data flow task, the Archive Input File task, and the Exclude Failed File task.

- The *variableA* variable is *container-scoped* and therefore only accessible to the container and the tasks it contains. It is not accessible to the Initialize Package task.

- The *variableB* variable is *task-scoped* and therefore only accessible to the data flow task and the data flow components it contains. It is not accessible to the Archive Input File task, the Exclude Failed File task, the Process Input Files container, or the Initialize Package task.

By default, every newly created variable is package-scoped. You can change the scope of any variable by using the Move command from the Variables pane toolbar, which opens the Select New Scope pane, as shown in Figure 6-3.

FIGURE 6-3 The Select New Scope pane.

> **IMPORTANT** **CHANGING VARIABLE SCOPE**
>
> When you are changing variable scope, consider existing dependencies—if by changing its scope you cause a variable to become inaccessible to a dependent task or component, validation errors will be raised.

Variable scope provides another useful feature. Variable names must be unique, obviously, to prevent ambiguity, but only within a particular scope. Two or more variables can share a name, as long as they exist in separate scopes. In this case, ambiguity is resolved by proximity—the nearest accessible variable in the SSIS object hierarchy is used.

For instance, consider the example in Figure 6-2: you can add another variable named *variableA* in the scope of the data flow task. After that, the *variableA* variable defined in the scope of the Process Input Files container will no longer be accessible to the data flow task and the data flow components it contains, being effectively overridden by the *variableA* variable created in the scope that is nearest to the data flow task—its own scope.

Variables sharing a name, but not their scope, can even use different data types.

EXAM TIP

To understand variable behavior, you really need to understand variable scope—variable accessibility inside the SSIS object hierarchy.

Scope allows you to restrict variable accessibility to a specific branch of the package hierarchy, and it also allows you to effectively "override" variables when necessary.

Property Parameterization

Property parameterization, allowing specific SSIS object properties to be set dynamically, can be implemented in several ways:

- SSIS object properties associated with parameters can be set dynamically from the calling environment—even after deployment.
- Explicit assignment of property values from variables is available in some tasks and components to facilitate the most common use cases and to simplify development. For example, the Execute SQL task supports three methods of assigning a value to the SQLStatement property: direct input, in which the SQL statement is a predefined constant; file connection, in which the SQL statement is extracted from the contents of a file; and Variable, in which the SQL statement is supplied via an SSIS variable.
- Assignment through expressions is available for most SSIS object properties, allowing property values to be computed by using a combination of constants, variables, parameters, or by using expression functions.

Property parameterization using SSIS parameters is discussed in Lesson 3 of Chapter 3, "Creating SSIS Packages," and parameterization using expressions is discussed in Lesson 2 of this chapter. In the practice in this lesson, you will learn how to parameterize SSIS object properties using explicit assignment.

> ✔ **Quick Check**
>
>   1. Which SSIS objects can access container-scoped variables?
>   2. How many namespaces are available for SSIS variables?
>   3. How can you modify the value of a system variable?
>
> **Quick Check Answers**
>
>   1. Container-scoped variables are only accessible to the container and the SSIS objects it contains.
>   2. SSIS variables can exist in two namespaces: user variables in the User namespace, and system variables in the System namespace.
>   3. System variables are read-only; their values are determined by SSIS.

 PRACTICE **Creating a User Variable and Parameterizing a Task**

In this practice, you will create three variables, define their values, and then reconfigure three Execute SQL tasks to use the variables.

In Chapter 5, you created an SSIS package that implements three Execute SQL tasks with Transact-SQL statements. These statements were embedded inside their corresponding tasks, and as a result they could not be reused by any other task. By using variables instead of constants, you can assign the same Transact-SQL statement to more than one Execute SQL task.

EXERCISE 1   Prepare the Environment

1. Start SSMS. On the File menu, under Open, select File and then navigate to the C:\TK463\Chapter06\Code folder. Open the TK463Chapter06.sql Transact-SQL script.

2. After you have reviewed the script, execute it. The script creates the database and the objects you will be using throughout this chapter.

EXERCISE 2   Create User Variables

1. Start SSDT. On the Start page, select Open Project, navigate to the C:\TK463 \Chapter06\Lesson1\Starter folder, and open the TK 463 Chapter 6.sln solution.

2. Open the FillStageTables.dtsx package.

3. Open the Variables pane by selecting Variables from the SSIS menu, or by clicking the Variables icon at the top of the SSIS Designer window.

4. In the Variables pane, create three variables, using the information provided in Table 6-3.

    TABLE 6-3 Transact-SQL Statement Variables

Name	Data type	Value
truncateStgCustomer	String	TRUNCATE TABLE stg.Customer;
truncateStgCustomerInformation	String	TRUNCATE TABLE stg.CustomerInformation;
truncateStgPerson	String	TRUNCATE TABLE stg.Person;

5. Save the solution but keep it open, because you will need it in the following exercise.

EXERCISE 3   Parameterize Control Flow Tasks by Using Variables

1. Double-click the Truncate Table stgCustomer Execute SQL task, or right-click it and then select Edit from the shortcut menu, to open the Execute SQL Task Editor.

2. Change the SQLSourceType property to Variable and change the SourceVariable property to truncateStgCustomer. When done, confirm the change by clicking OK.

3. Repeat steps 1 and 2 for the Truncate Table stgCustomerInformation task, assigning the *truncateStgCustomerInformation* variable to its SourceVariable property, and for the Truncate Table stgPerson task, assigning the *truncateStgPerson* variable to its SourceVariable property.

4. Save the solution, and then execute it in debug mode. Observe the execution. When the execution completes successfully, close the solution.

Lesson Summary

- You can use variables in SSIS packages to determine certain values once, and then re-use them multiple times.
- Variable values can be assigned literally or by using expressions. SSIS implements a variety of data types to be used in SSIS variables.
- SSIS variables can be assigned dynamically as the package is executed—either once per execution or iteratively.
- Variable accessibility is determined by scope.
- SSIS variables can be used to parameterize SSIS object properties.

Lesson Review

Answer the following questions to test your knowledge of the information in this lesson. You can find the answers to these questions and explanations of why each answer choice is correct or incorrect in the "Answers" section at the end of this chapter.

1. In your SSIS package you need to retrieve a scalar value from a table in the destination database, to be used by multiple tasks. What is the most appropriate method to achieve this?

   A. Embed a subquery in every existing query used by the package, so that the database engine can prepare the most appropriate execution plan to retrieve it at run time.

   B. Create a variable and use an expression to retrieve the value from the database once, and then use it throughout the execution.

   C. Create a variable and use the Execute SQL task to retrieve the value once, and then use it throughout the execution.

   D. Create a variable and use the Expression task to retrieve the value from the database as many times as needed.

2. In your SSIS package, you created a package-scoped variable to hold a value that you want to reuse throughout the package. Later you discover that this value must be set differently in one container, but the original variable should not be affected. What can you do?

   A. Create a new package-scoped variable with a different name and reconfigure the tasks accordingly, to either use the new variable or the original one.

   B. Create a new container-scoped variable with a different name and reconfigure only the tasks that it contains to use the new variable.

   C. Create a new container-scoped variable with the same name, and leave the tasks unchanged.

   D. Use a package-scoped parameter, because this problem cannot be solved by using variables.

3. In your SSIS process, a specific property will be determined by the administrator in the production environment. The value supplied by the administrator will be used in multiple properties and will have to be overridden automatically if certain conditions are met at run time. What is the most appropriate method to achieve this in SSIS?

A. Create a parameter and use expressions to assign its value to the corresponding properties, but use an expression at the beginning of the execution to change the parameter value if needed.

B. Create a parameter, use an expression at the beginning of the execution to either assign its value to a variable or override the value if needed, and use expressions to assign the value of the variable to the properties.

C. Create a read/write variable, use expressions to assign its value to the appropriate properties, and assign the correct value to the variable via property paths at run time.

D. Create a parameter and use expressions to either assign its value to the property or override it if needed.

Lesson 2: Connection Managers, Tasks, and Precedence Constraint Expressions

As mentioned earlier in this chapter, there is a myriad of settings in an SSIS solution that can be parameterized or configured dynamically. Obviously, most of them will never need to be set dynamically, and never exposed to the caller environment via parameters, but there are settings in an SSIS solution that typically do need to be determined dynamically; some of them to allow appropriate adjustments of the solution to the target environment (such as settings that depend on available resources—batch sizes, maximum cache sizes, and similar), and some to enable deployment in the first place (such as settings reflecting the environment itself—connection strings, file paths, and similar).

Typically, in an SSIS solution, the following SSIS objects should be parameterized (by using one of the methods described in Lesson 1 of this chapter):

- **Connection managers** During development, the SSIS solution connects to data stores in the development or testing environment, but a deployed solution will connect to production data stores. Certain connection managers also have to be configured at run time iteratively—such as file connection managers used by a Foreach Loop Container using the Foreach File Enumerator, as demonstrated in Lesson 2 of Chapter 3.

- **Tasks and components** Depending on dynamically determined settings, if an operation depends on values determined by using additional programmatic logic (either at the beginning of the execution or per iteration of a Loop Container), you can use an Expression task or a Script task to compute the values and store them in an SSIS variable, which is then passed to the appropriate task or component. Examples include, an Execute SQL task or a source component using dynamically created queries with a varying set of parameters.

- **Data flow tasks** You can parameterize data flow tasks to allow them to work better with the current state of the environment. Large data movements are typically resource intensive; therefore, in order to prevent them from running out of resources, you could adjust their behavior in accordance with the actual availability of resources at run time by using appropriate programmatic logic (using an Expression task or a Script task)—for example, by setting the batch size and the maximum cache size for a data flow task based on the amount of available system memory and I/O resources.

After this lesson, you will be able to:

- Implement parameterization of properties by using variables.
- Refer to SSIS system variables.
- Use expressions.
- Use property expressions.
- Implement dynamic package behavior.

Estimated lesson time: 60 minutes

Expressions

An *expression* is a combination of constants, variables, parameters, column references, expression functions, and/or expression operators, allowing you to prescribe at design time how a specific value will be determined at run time. Expressions are used to determine values dynamically in an automated process, rather than having these values set manually and in advance using constants.

Expressions are written in a special expression language native to SSIS. This language uses syntax similar to that of the C++ and C# programming languages—it implements a predefined set of *operators*, shown in Table 6-4, and a predefined set of *functions*, shown in Tables 6-5 through 6-8.

TABLE 6-4 SSIS Expression Operators

Operator	Description
(type_spec) (Data type Cast)	Converts an expression from one data type to a different data type. A Data Flow Buffer data type is provided as the type_spec argument. Depending on the selected data type, additional arguments might be required. Data Flow Buffer data types are discussed in Chapter 5.
() (Parentheses)	Identifies the evaluation order of expressions.
+ (Add)	Adds two numeric expressions.
+ (Concatenate)	Concatenates two expressions.

Operator	Description
- (Subtract)	Subtracts the second numeric expression from the first one.
- (Negate)	Negates a numeric expression.
* (Multiply)	Multiplies two numeric expressions.
/ (Divide)	Divides the first numeric expression by the second one.
% (Modulo)	Provides the integer remainder after dividing the first numeric expression by the second one.
|| (Logical OR)	Performs a logical OR operation.
&& (Logical AND)	Performs a logical AND operation.
! (Logical Not)	Negates a Boolean operand.
| (Bitwise Inclusive OR)	Performs a bitwise OR operation of two integer values.
^ (Bitwise Exclusive OR)	Performs a bitwise exclusive OR operation of two integer values.
& (Bitwise AND)	Performs a bitwise AND operation of two integer values.
~ (Bitwise Not)	Performs a bitwise negation of an integer.
== (Equal)	Performs a comparison to determine if two expressions are equal.
!= (Unequal)	Performs a comparison to determine if two expressions are not equal.
> (Greater Than)	Performs a comparison to determine if the first expression is greater than the second one.
< (Less Than)	Performs a comparison to determine if the first expression is less than the second one.
>= (Greater Than or Equal To)	Performs a comparison to determine if the first expression is greater than or equal to the second one.
<= (Less Than or Equal To)	Performs a comparison to determine if the first expression is less than or equal to the second one.

The elementary computations can be performed by using operators: addition, subtraction, multiplication, and division for numerical data, and concatenation for strings. Value comparison is also supported by using operators; comparison expressions return a Boolean value. Some tasks and components (such as the Conditional Split component) use Boolean functions to determine their operation (for example, redirecting the rows in a data flow to different outputs based on the comparison test).

Boolean expressions can also be used in precedence constraints to extend the built-in functionality used in determining the control flow based solely on the success, failure, or completion of a preceding task. Precedence constraint expressions are discussed later in this lesson.

TABLE 6-5 SSIS Expression Mathematical Functions

Function	Description
ABS	Returns the absolute, positive value of a numeric expression.
EXP	Returns the exponent to base e of the specified expression.
CEILING	Returns the smallest integer that is greater than or equal to a numeric expression.
FLOOR	Returns the largest integer that is less than or equal to a numeric expression.
LN	Returns the natural logarithm of a numeric expression.
LOG	Returns the base-10 logarithm of a numeric expression.
POWER	Returns the result of raising a numeric expression to a power.
ROUND	Returns a numeric expression that is rounded to the specified length or precision.
SIGN	Returns the positive (+), negative (-), or zero (0) sign of a numeric expression.
SQUARE	Returns the square of a numeric expression.
SQRT	Returns the square root of a numeric expression.

Mathematical functions perform calculations against numerical values and return numerical results. Operators provide the essential computational methods, whereas mathematical functions provide computation that would be cumbersome or even impossible to implement by using operators alone.

TABLE 6-6 SSIS Expression String Functions

Function	Description
CODEPOINT	Returns the Unicode code value of the leftmost character of a character expression.
FINDSTRING	Returns the 1-based index of the specified occurrence of a character string within an expression.
HEX	Returns a string representing the hexadecimal value of an integer.
LEN	Returns the number of characters in a character expression.
LEFT	Returns the specified number of characters from the leftmost portion of the given character expression.
LOWER	Returns a character expression after converting uppercase characters to lowercase characters.
LTRIM	Returns a character expression after removing leading spaces.
REPLACE	Returns a character expression after replacing a string within the expression with either a different string or an empty string.
REPLICATE	Returns a character expression, replicated a specified number of times.
REVERSE	Returns a character expression in reverse order.

Function	Description
RIGHT	Returns the specified number of characters from the rightmost portion of the given character expression.
RTRIM	Returns a character expression after removing trailing spaces.
SUBSTRING	Returns a part of a character expression.
TRIM	Returns a character expression after removing leading and trailing spaces.
UPPER	Returns a character expression after converting lowercase characters to uppercase characters.

String functions perform operations against string and hexadecimal values and return string or numerical results. The typical string functions are available in the expression language; however, for more sophisticated string manipulation, you might have to resort to script tasks, script components, or even custom tasks or custom components, depending on the degree of complexity required in a particular case.

TABLE 6-7 SSIS Expression Date and Time Functions

Function	Description
DATEADD	Returns a new DT_DBTIMESTAMP value by adding a date or time interval to a specified date.
DATEDIFF	Returns the number of date and time boundaries crossed between two specified dates.
DATEPART	Returns an integer representing a part of a date.
DAY	Returns an integer that represents the day of the specified date.
GETDATE	Returns the current date of the system.
GETUTCDATE	Returns the current date of the system in UTC time (Universal Time Coordinate or Greenwich Mean Time).
MONTH	Returns an integer that represents the month of the specified date.
YEAR	Returns an integer that represents the year of the specified date.

Date and time functions perform operations against date and time values and return date and time, string, or numerical results. Date and time dimensions play an important part in data warehousing, and these functions can be used to simplify their maintenance.

TABLE 6-8 SSIS Expression Null Functions

Function	Description
ISNULL	Returns a Boolean result based on whether an expression is null.
NULL	Returns a null value of a requested data type.

Use these functions to test for null values or to pass them to a consumer (a task or a component). Although by default nulls are not associated with any type, the consumer might expect values to be passed in specific types, so the NULL function accepts one argument specifying the data type of the result.

Property Expressions

Property expressions are available to most SSIS objects and can either be set by using the object's editor or in the object's property pane. Although for most SSIS objects the use of property expressions is completely optional, there are components (such as the Derived Column Component) for which expressions are mandatory; otherwise, the component cannot even be configured.

Typically, expressions are used to determine specific SSIS properties that depend on data or conditions not known until run time. If a dependency between a particular property and one or more other properties, values, or settings can be described deterministically, then the dependent setting does not have to be guessed at design time but can be computed at run time.

If the result of an expression can be used to determine settings for more than one SSIS object, the Expression task can be used to compute the result once and store it in a variable, which can then be used multiple times avoiding the necessity of performing the same calculation more than once.

At design time, if expressions do not evaluate to expected values (because one or more values that the result of the expression depends on are not known, or have not been populated), the design time validation will return an error. To prevent this, you can either provide appropriate default values or delay validation until run time, when the expected values will be available.

> **NOTE** **DELAYED VALIDATION**
>
> Design time validation can be disabled for every individual SSIS object by setting the DelayValidation property to True.

Precedence Constraint Expressions

Precedence constraints are discussed in detail in Lesson 3 of Chapter 4, "Designing and Implementing Control Flow." In that chapter, the focus was on the elementary functionalities of precedence constraints—defining the conditions of control flow execution, based solely on the execution result of the preceding task or container.

Expressions provide a way of extending precedence constraints with additional conditions, thus reducing the possible rigidity of using just the three elementary options. Through this extension, the conditions of SSIS package execution can be made more strict (for example, by using the "Constraint and Expression" rule), or less strict (for example, by using the "Constraint or Expression" rule). Alternatively, the expression can even be used instead of the constraint, to completely eliminate the success (or failure) of the preceding task or container from the condition.

With precedence constraint expressions, the range of possibilities is extended significantly, as shown in Table 6-9.

TABLE 6-9 Precedence Constraint Expression Combinations

Evaluation operation	Constraint evaluates to	Expression evaluates to	Constrained executable runs
Constraint	True	N/A	True
Constraint	False	N/A	False
Expression	N/A	True	True
Expression	N/A	False	False
Constraint and Expression	True	True	True
Constraint and Expression	True	False	False
Constraint and Expression	False	True	False
Constraint and Expression	False	False	False
Constraint or Expression	True	True	True
Constraint or Expression	True	False	True
Constraint or Expression	False	True	True
Constraint or Expression	False	False	False

 Quick Check

1. Which .NET Framework programming language is used for SSIS expressions?

2. What are SSIS expressions typically used for?

Quick Check Answers

1. SSIS expressions use a special, proprietary expression language that is only available for SSIS development and is therefore not part of the .NET Framework.

2. SSIS expressions allow you to determine values needed in SSIS execution dynamically at run time, rather than having to assign constants to them at design time.

In this practice, you will create an SSIS variable and build an expression to determine its value automatically at run time, rather than using a constant provided at design time.

EXERCISE 1   Use an Expression to Assign a Variable

1. Start SSDT. On the Start page, select Open Project, navigate to the C:\TK463 \Chapter06\Lesson2\Starter folder, and open the TK 463 Chapter 6.sln solution.

2. Open the FillStageTables.dtsx package.

3. Using the Variables pane, create a new variable based on the information provided in Table 6-10.

TABLE 6-10 The *dayOfWeek* Variable

Name	Data type
dayOfWeek	*Byte*

Leave its value unchanged for now. (By default, the value of numeric variables is zero.)

4. On the right, next to the Expression column of the newly added variable, click the ellipsis (...) to open the Expression Builder dialog box, shown in Figure 6-4.

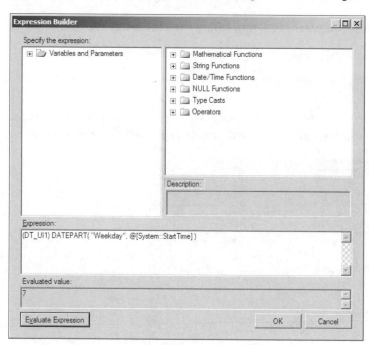

FIGURE 6-4 The Expression Builder.

5. Use the Expression Builder to build the expression shown in Listing 6-1.

   In the tree view on the left side of the dialog box, you can access existing system and user variables as well as parameters, to be used in expressions. In the tree view on the right are six groups of SSIS expression functions. Use the Expression text box to edit the expression; you do not have to actually type in an entire expression—simply drag any variable, parameter, or function from the tree views at the top of the dialog box into the Expression text box and edit any missing elements.

LISTING 6-1 Expression

(DT_UI1)DATEPART("Weekday", @[System::StartTime])

The expression shown in Listing 6-1, uses the *StartTime* system variable, holding the time when the execution of the package started, to calculate an Int32 (DT_I4) value of the day of the week, which is then cast to a Byte (DT_UI1) value, as required by the user variable you created earlier.

6. Click Evaluate Expression to test your expression; it should return the value for the current day of the week (between 1 for Monday and 7 for Sunday in most languages) in the Evaluated Value box at the bottom of the Expression Builder dialog box.

7. When you have finished preparing the expression, click OK to confirm the changes.

8. Save the solution, but keep it open, because you will need it in the following exercise.

EXERCISE 2 Use Expressions to Control Data Flow Behavior

1. Make sure that the FillStageTables.dtsx package is open in the SSIS Designer.

2. Right-click the Insert stgCustomer data flow task and select Properties from the shortcut menu.

   In the Property grid, find the Expressions property collection and click the ellipsis (...)" next to the value box to open the Property Expression Editor, shown in Figure 6-5.

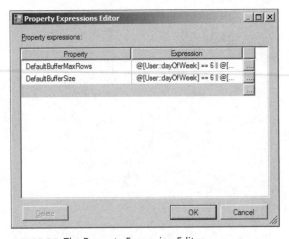

FIGURE 6-5 The Property Expression Editor.

3. In the Property column of the Property Expression Editor, select the DefaultBuffer-MaxRows property.

4. Click the ellipsis (...) next to the property's Expression column to open the Expression Builder, and use it to build the expression shown in Listing 6-2.

LISTING 6-2 The DefaultBufferMaxRows Property Expression

@[User::dayOfWeek] == 6 || @[User::dayOfWeek] == 7 ? 20000 : 10000

This expression uses a conditional operator to determine the value of the property based on the *dayOfWeek* variable: if the SSIS package is executed on a Saturday or on a Sunday, the default maximum number of rows is set to 20,000; otherwise it is set to 10,000, allowing the process to use more resources on a nonworking day.

5. Click Evaluate Expression to see the computed result based on the current day. When done, click OK to confirm the creation of the expression.

6. Repeat steps 2 through 4 for the DefaultBufferSize property, this time using the expression shown in Listing 6-3.

LISTING 6-3 The DefaultBufferSize Property Expression

@[User::dayOfWeek] == 6 || @[User::dayOfWeek] == 7 ? 20971520 : 10485760

Much like before, the expression calculates the default buffer size of the data flow task based on the value of the *dayOfWeek* variable, allowing the SSIS package to reserve twice as much memory on nonworking days as it is allowed to reserve on working days.

> *NOTE* **LANGUAGE SETTINGS AND DATE/TIME FORMATS**
> Depending on your environment, either Monday or Sunday is used as the first day of the week; by default, this is determined by the operating system regional settings.
> If Monday is used as the first day of the week (for instance, if the language used in your environment is British English) then Saturday and Sunday are represented by numbers 6 or 7, respectively. ON the other hand, if Sunday is used as the first day fo the week (for instance, if the language used in your environment is U.S. English) then Saturday and Sunday are represented by numbers 7 and 1, respectively.

7. Click Evaluate Expression to see the computed result based on the current day. When done, click OK to confirm the creation of the expression.

8. When you are finished configuring properties, click OK in the Property Expression Editor to confirm the configuration.

9. Save the solution, and then execute it in debug mode to test it. When you are done, close SSDT.

Lesson Summary

- The SSIS runtime provides information about the execution environment and other system information via SSIS system variables.
- Expressions can be used to compute the values of SSIS object properties at run time.
- Variables and expressions can also be used to extend the elementary functionality of precedence constraints based on information available at run time that usually is not available at design time.

Lesson Review

Answer the following questions to test your knowledge of the information in this lesson. You can find the answers to these questions and explanations of why each answer choice is correct or incorrect in the "Answers" section at the end of this chapter.

1. In your SSIS package, there are several data flow tasks, each importing data into the destination database. You need to log the number of rows that have been inserted or updated in each data flow. What options provided by SSIS can you use to accomplish this? (Choose all that apply.)

    A. You can use the Row Count task to count the rows passed through a data flow.

    B. You can use the Row Count component to count the rows passed through a data flow.

    C. You can store the values in variables before saving them to the log.

    D. You can use an expression to calculate the total number of processed rows.

2. In your SSIS package, you need to set the properties of several tasks based on the information available about the run time environment. Each of the properties you need to compute can be calculated by using a mathematical expression. What would be the most appropriate method?

    A. Use the Expression Builder to build and test the expression, and then copy it to all of the corresponding task definitions.

    B. Place an Expression Task into the control flow, preceding each task whose properties need to be determined dynamically.

    C. Use as many Expression tasks as necessary to compute as many variables as there are different calculations, and then use the variables to assign the values to the corresponding tasks.

    D. Use a single Expression task and store all required computed values in a row set (Object) variable to be used in property expressions to configure the corresponding tasks.

3. In the control flow of your SSIS package, you need to add a data maintenance task that will rebuild the indexes of your dimension tables after they have been populated successfully. You have implemented each dimension table load in an individual data flow.

The Execute SQL task containing the index rebuild script must be executed after the preceding data flow has completed successfully, but only on Saturdays. The name of the current day is stored in a variable. Is it possible to achieve this in SSIS control flow? If so, how?

A. No, this is not possible in the control flow because the conditional split transformation is only available in a data flow.

B. Yes, it is possible to achieve this in the control flow, but only by using a Script task.

C. Yes, this can be achieved by using a success precedence constraint leading from the data flow task to the Execute SQL task, with a precedence constraint expression checking whether the value of the variable is Saturday.

D. Yes, this can be achieved by using a regular success precedence constraint leading from the data flow task to the Execute SQL task.

Lesson 3: Using a Master Package for Advanced Control Flow

 The *master package* is not a special type of SSIS package; it is a concept, an approach to SSIS development, deployment, maintenance, and operation. The implementation of this concept, which takes advantage of the standard built-in SSIS functionalities, is based on the Execute Package task. Individual operations or processes can be distributed among multiple SSIS packages, but a single package—the master package—is used to provide a central control flow and the shared and centralized configuration of all individual packages.

Typically, a complete data warehousing solution contains a variety of operations, some of them quite diverse:

- **Data extraction** When you are working with large amounts of data, using a staging area reduces the impact of data movement operations on the source system, with data being transferred to the staging data store in simple data moves without any transformations.

- **Stage preparation** As the size of data grows, so do the resource needs of the staging data store. To reduce the impact of stage maintenance on other processes, or to even eliminate it altogether, you can arrange stage maintenance in a dedicated process, rather than as part of any other process.

- **Data transformations** The stage data store plays the role of the source data store in transformation processes, reducing the dependency of these transformations on data extraction processes. The stage data store can also serve as temporary storage for complex transformations that cannot be performed entirely in memory, and it can also serve as the temporary destination data store, before the data is moved to its final destination.

- **Data warehouse maintenance**   Index rebuilds and reorganizations, statistics updates, and purge operations represent typical data warehouse maintenance operations. Obviously, they do not have to be performed as part of any other process.

- **Data loads**   If the stage data store can provide temporary storage for transformed data, then the final transfer of data can be performed by using simple data movements, reducing the impact on the destination data store, and reducing if not eliminating the dependency of load processes on transformation processes.

   Not all data load operations are the same—fact loads differ from dimensional loads, and data is managed differently depending on the treatment of historical data (that is, Slowly Changing Dimensions); fact loads do not have to be developed, deployed, and maintained together with dimension loads, and different dimension loads do not have to be developed, deployed, and maintained together, even though they usually should be executed as a whole.

- **Multidimensional processing**   Before data can be moved into the multidimensional data store (such as a SQL Server Analysis Services [SSAS] database), it needs to be stable, meaning that any preceding processes (extract-transform-load) should be completed successfully and in their entirety before the move is executed. It is therefore quite natural that multidimensional processing does not have to be performed as part of any other process.

The master package concept supports the division of operations across several smaller SSIS packages, rather than keeping all of them inside a single large SSIS package. Using the master package concept, each individual package can be developed, tested, deployed, and maintained separately, which reduces total development time.

Operations that are different in their nature, purpose, and/or objective can be implemented in separate packages, and different developers on the team can be assigned to these separate work items, allowing them to focus on a few elements of the solution or even on just a single element, rather than on all of the elements, which is unavoidable when the solution is designed as a whole. By using the master package concept, individual developers—experts in particular domains—can complete their tasks in parallel, which not only reduces total development time, but also allows their manager to assign the most appropriate developer to each separate development task.

As individual parts of the solution are being developed independently, one team member can be assigned to design the complete control flow and to plan its deployment and maintenance. Using the master package concept allows the entire set of individual SSIS packages to be executed as if they were all parts of a single SSIS package, without interfering with their individual life cycles.

If operations (or processes) implemented in individual packages constitute what could, in business terms, be qualified as "atomic operations," another benefit of using master packages becomes apparent; namely, improved reusability. If the same operations can be used for different purposes, workloads, or objectives, or could be deployed to different environments, then these atomic packages could be shared among different master packages, rather than, for instance, copied to different SSIS projects or solutions.

Individual parts of the solution are deployed and maintained separately and independently from one another. Therefore, SQL Server security functionalities could be used to grant access to each individual package only to the persons in charge of its maintenance, improving the safety of the entire solution without having to prevent individual developers from accessing their own packages. You will learn more about SSIS project deployment in Chapter 11, "Installing SSIS and Deploying Packages."

> **After this lesson, you will be able to:**
>
> - Understand workloads.
> - Understand the purposes and objectives of data management operations.
> - Decide between one package or multiple packages.
> - Use the Execute Package task.
>
> **Estimated lesson time: 90 minutes**

Separating Workloads, Purposes, and Objectives

The individual elements of a typical data warehousing solution can be quite diverse—they have different purposes and different objectives, and they operate on different workloads. By separating them, and placing each in its own SSIS package, these elements can be developed, tested, deployed, and maintained separately, any corrections to them can also be applied independently, and they can be executed independently.

- **Extraction processes**   Simple data movements from the operational data store into the staging data store are less resource intensive and can be performed more quickly than complex data movements, which include data transformations, thus reducing the impact on the actual data store to a portion of time that is typically significantly shorter than the duration of the entire maintenance window.

- **Transformation processes**   When the data is available in the staging data store, any transformation operations, regardless of their complexity, have zero impact on the initial data store, or the operational system. Transformation processes can be executed independently of load processes. Based on their complexity, it could be beneficial to further separate simple transformations from complex ones, and maybe even isolate exceptionally complex transformations—for example, for a more optimal division of labor; to reduce mutual dependencies in testing, deployment, and maintenance; or to provide more possibilities for parallelism in execution.

- **Stage maintenance processes**   When transformations have been completed successfully, parts of the stage data store used in data loads can be purged, and parts used in consequent loads can now be optimized for data retrieval (index creation, rebuilds, and reorganization).

- **Load processes**   When the data has been transformed and prepared appropriately, and when the staging data store has been optimized for retrieval, data can finally be loaded into the destination data store by using simple data movements, thus reducing the impact on the destination data store to a portion of time significantly shorter than the duration of the entire maintenance window.

- **Multidimensional processing**   Only after the entire extract-transform-load (ETL) process has been completed successfully, and only if the data in the data warehouse has actually changed, is it appropriate to prepare the data for consumption.

Harmonizing Workflow and Configuration

While individual elements of the data warehousing solution are still being planned and developed, the skeleton of the master package can already be designed: by considering the relationships between the individual elements of a typical data warehouse solution as discussed just previously, the complete workflow can be designed in advance:

1. The process should start with initial configurations—parameterization that does not depend on values determined iteratively, during execution.

2. If any maintenance operations need to be performed in the staging data store, before the data extraction can begin, they should be performed next.

3. During data extraction, the impact on the source data store should be considered, with the focus on keeping the duration of the extraction short and keeping resource use as high as possible—taking advantage of parallelism and keeping the I/O system busy.

4. If any additional maintenance operations need to be performed in the staging data store to accommodate transformation processes, they should be performed right after the successful completion of the data extraction phase.

5. Data transformations are performed next. In this phase, you should also try to maximize resource use—taking advantage of parallelism by executing CPU-intensive operations with low to moderate I/O in parallel with I/O-intensive operations with low to moderate CPU use. If certain transformations need to be performed in sequence, the sequence must be preserved.

6. When data is loaded into the staging data store, and when transformations are performed that also include data movement, indexes on the staging tables are not needed. However, they could be useful in retrieval operations, especially for merges and updates. If indexes could be useful in the following phases. they should be created in this phase.

7. After the data has been prepared for loading, the load processes can begin. Again, most data movements should be simple, so by maximizing resource use you can reduce the duration of the process, minimizing the impact on the destination system. In SQL Server 2012 Enterprise edition with partitioned staging and destination tables, the final data movement could be simply a metadata operation (using partition switching, when both staging as well as destination tables exist in the same database).

8. After the data load has been completed successfully, the destination tables should be optimized for retrieval—index creation, rebuilds, and/or reorganization, as well as statistics updates, should be performed.

9. After destination data store maintenance has been completed, multidimensional processing should be performed—assuming that in previous operations data modifications have actually taken place.

The order of operations and the conditions of execution constitute the skeleton of the master package. However, for the master package concept to live up to its potential, another requirement must be met.

Individual SSIS packages typically contain enough configuration logic for successful deployment and maintenance, as well as execution. Though it is true that the packages will be deployed and maintained individually, their execution will actually be governed as a whole, centrally—through the master package. Therefore, in SSIS, the configuration of child packages can be controlled from the master package (through child package parameters).

The Execute Package Task

This task is used to execute other SSIS packages (referred to as *child packages*) from the current package (referred to as the *parent package*). The task can be used to invoke a child package belonging to the same project, a package located in the file system, or a package deployed to a SQL Server instance.

SQL Server 2012 introduces a new deployment model for SSIS solutions: the Project Deployment model, in addition to the existing Package Deployment model. You will learn more about SSIS deployment in Chapter 11. For now, you should know that the master package concept is compatible with either of the deployment models; however, the new Project Deployment model provides an improved development, deployment, and maintenance experience, especially for implementing the master package concept, when compared to the older Package Deployment model.

The Execute Package task provides two methods for the parameterization of child packages:

- **Package configurations** For every property that should be exposed to the caller (the parent package), a parent package variable configuration must be prepared in the child package. This configuration can reference a variable or an SSIS object property in the child package. The name of the parent package variable must match the name of the corresponding variable in the child package.

- **Parameters** Variables, project parameters, or package parameters of the parent package can be mapped to the parameters of the child package belonging to the same project as the master package. This method is only available in the Project Deployment model.

The Execute SQL Server Agent Job Task

This task is used to execute SQL Server Agent jobs—that is, operations or processes deployed to the SQL Server Agent Service (Transact-SQL scripts, ActiveX scripts, operating system scripts, Windows PowerShell scripts, replication tasks, SSAS commands, SSAS queries, and SSIS packages).

In essence, this task could also be used in a master package; however, it is significantly limited in functionality compared to the Execute Package task. This is mostly due to the nature of the SQL Server Agent Service—the task can be used to start jobs, but it does not provide a way to monitor their execution (that is, the Execute SQL Server Agent Job task does not provide a way to detect when a job has completed, let alone determine whether it was completed successfully or not).

Based on these shortcomings, the Execute SQL Server Agent Job task is not really suited for use in data warehousing master packages, where the order of operations as well as the conditions of execution are both vital to the workflow.

The Execute Process Task

This task is used to execute external processes (solutions that exist outside the SQL Server environment) as part of the SSIS process. If your SSIS solution depends on external processes, you can use the master package to configure and execute them.

EXAM TIP

Study all workflow tasks carefully in order to understand which of them can be used in a master package, which situations they are most suited for, and how they should be implemented in various business cases.

Individual workflow tasks are discussed in more detail in Chapter 4.

 Quick Check

1. What is the principal purpose of a master package?

2. Can child package properties be set from the master package?

Quick Check Answers

1. A master package provides centralized control flow and configuration to SSIS solutions using multiple SSIS packages.

2. Yes, master package parameters and variables can be used to set the child package parameters.

PRACTICE **Creating and Configuring a Master Package**

In this practice, you will implement a master package to provide control flow for the execution of individual, specialized packages. You will use the master package to configure the child packages, and you will use information provided by one child package to control the execution of another.

You are going to merge some of the processes and operations that you designed in preceding chapters into a single SSIS package for configuration and execution purposes, without restricting their independence as far as development, deployment, and maintenance are concerned.

EXERCISE 1 Prepare the Environment

1. Start SSMS. On the File menu, under Open, select File, navigate to the C:\TK463 \Chapter06\Code folder, and open the TK463Chapter06.sql Transact-SQL script.

2. Review the script, and then execute it. The script will recreate the objects you need to complete the exercises in this chapter.

3. Start SSDT. On the Start page, select Open Project, navigate to the C:\TK463 \Chapter06\Lesson3\Starter folder, and open the TK 463 Chapter 6.sln solution.

4. Open the DimCustomerNew.dtsx package and review it.

    The package contains one package-scoped parameter, named MasterPackageID. This parameter is used to identify the master package executing the selected package, if the package is in fact invoked by a master package. You will see exactly how this parameter is used later in this practice.

    The package also contains three package-scoped variables, shown in Table 6-11.

TABLE 6-11 Package Variables

Name	Description
newRecordCount	The number of rows added to the *Customer* dimension.
modifiedRecordCount	The number of modified rows in the *Customer* dimension.
computedPackageID	This variable uses an expression in determining the package identifier to be used for each execution. If a master package is used and the identifier is supplied via the MasterPackageID parameter, then the identifier of the master package is used to document the execution; otherwise, the package's own identifier is used, supplied via the *PackageID* system variable.

The number of newly added rows is determined in the New Record Count Row Count component of the Dim Customer data flow task.

The number of modified rows is determined with the Modified Record Count Execute SQL task.

Both values are saved to the *dbo.ETLHistory* table in the TK463DW database, together with the package identifier and a date/time value designating the time of the execution.

All of these variables and the parameter will be used by the master package to determine whether any rows have actually been changed in the *Customer* dimension, to optimize the execution.

EXERCISE 2 Create a Master Package

1. Add new SSIS package to the TK 463 Chapter 6.sln solution. Change its name to **Master.dtsx**.

2. Drag three Execute Package tasks from the SSIS Toolbox onto the SSIS Designer surface and configure two of them, using the information provided in Tables 6-12 and 6-13.

TABLE 6-12 The FillStageTables Execute Package Task

Tab	Property	Value
General	Name	FillStageTables
Package	ReferenceType	Project Reference
Package	PackageNameFromProjectReference	FillStageTables.dtsx

TABLE 6-13 The DimCustomerNew Execute Package Task

Tab	Property	Value
General	Name	DimCustomerNew
Package	ReferenceType	Project Reference
Package	PackageNameFromProjectReference	DimCustomerNew.dtsx

3. On the Parameter Bindings tab of the DimCustomerNew Execute Package task, click Add to add a new parameter mapping. In the Child Package Parameter list box, select the MasterPackageID parameter, and in the Binding Parameter Or Variable list box select the *System::PackageID* system variable.

When the child package is executed, the identifier of the master package will be passed to the child package as expected.

4. Configure the last task, using the information provided in Table 6-14.

TABLE 6-14 The ProcessSSAS Execute Package Task

Tab	Property	Value
General	Name	ProcessSSAS
Package	ReferenceType	Project Reference
Package	PackageNameFromProjectReference	ProcessSSAS.dtsx

The ProcessSSAS.dtsx package does not actually contain a control flow; it is used in this exercise to simulate a real-life situation in which the master package can be designed in advance, even though a part of the solution is not yet available.

5. In the Variables pane, create a new, project-scoped integer (Int32) variable named lastRecordCount.

6. Drag an Execute SQL task from the SSIS Toolbox onto the SSIS Designer surface, and configure it using the information provided in Table 6-15.

TABLE 6-15 The Get Last Record Count Execute SQL Task

Tab	Property	Value
General	Name	Get Last Record Count
General	ResultSet	Single row
General	ConnectionType	OLE DB
General	Connection	TK463DW
General	SQLSourceType	Direct input

For the SQLStatement property, use the Transact-SQL statement shown in Listing 6-4.

LISTING 6-4 The Get Last Record Count Transact-SQL Query

```
SELECT TOP(1)
  H.NewRecordCount + H.ModifiedRecordCount AS LastRecordCount
  FROM dbo.ETLHistory AS H
  WHERE H.PackageID = ?
  ORDER BY H.RunTime DESC;
```

7. On the Parameter Mapping tab of the Get Last Record Count Execute SQL task, click Add to add a new parameter, using the information provided in Table 6-16.

TABLE 6-16 The Get Last Record Count Parameter Mapping

Property	Value
Variable Name	*System::PackageID*
Direction	Input
Data Type	GUID
Parameter Name	@p1
Parameter Size	-1

8. On the Result Set tab of the Get Last Record Count Execute SQL task, click Add to configure the result set, using the information provided in Table 6-17.

TABLE 6-17 The Get Last Record Count Result Set

Property	Value
Result Name	0
Variable Name	User::lastRecordCount

The Get Last Record Count Execute SQL task is configured to process a single, one-row result set, and the Transact-SQL query used in the task, shown previously in Listing 6-4, only returns a single column containing the number of rows that have been affected by the last execution of the DimCustomerNew.dtsx package.

Therefore, the result returned by the task can be mapped to a single scalar variable.

9. When you are done configuring the Get Last Record Count Execute SQL task, click OK to confirm the settings.

10. Save the solution but keep it open, because you will need it in the following exercise.

EXERCISE 3 Configure the Master Package

1. Make sure that the Master.dtsx package is open in the SSIS Designer.

2. Define the order of execution for the package (using precedence constraints) so that the tasks are executed in the following order:

    A. The FillStageTables Execute Package task

    B. The DimCustomerNew Execute Package task

    C. The Get Last Record Count Execute SQL task

    D. The ProcessSSAS Execute Package task

3. Double-click the precedence constraint leading from the Get Last Record Count task to the ProcessSSAS task, or right-click it and select Edit from the shortcut menu, to open the Precedence Constraint Editor.

4. Change the Evaluation operation constraint option from Constraint to Expression and Constraint, leave Success as the evaluation value, then click the ellipsis (...) at the right of the Expression text box to open the Expression Builder dialog box, and build the expression shown in Listing 6-5.

LISTING 6-5 The Last Row Count Expression

```
@[User::lastRecordCount] > 0
```

5. When you are done, click OK to confirm the expression's creation.

The Precedence Constraint Editor dialog box should look like the one shown in Figure 6-6.

You have just extended the precedence constraint with an expression; now the ProcessSSAS child package will only be executed if all preceding tasks have completed successfully and at least one row has been added to or modified in the *Customer* dimension. If no changes have occurred in the data warehouse, there is no need to process any dependent multidimensional objects.

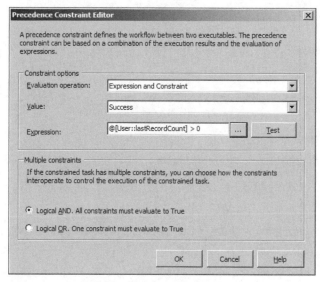

FIGURE 6-6 A precedence constraint that uses an expression.

6. When you have completed the configuration of the precedence constraint, click OK to confirm the configuration.

7. Save the master package, and then execute it in debug mode. Observe the execution. When it is run for the first time, all child packages will be executed.

8. Run the master package in debug mode again. Because no changes are made to the *Customer* dimension this time, the ProcessSSAS child package should not be executed.

9. When you are done, close SSDT.

Lesson Summary

- SSIS operations can be distributed across multiple SSIS packages by using the master package concept.
- The master package (also referred to as the parent package) can execute dependent packages (or child packages) by using the Execute Package task; this task can also be used to set child package parameters from the parent package at run time.

Lesson Review

Answer the following questions to test your knowledge of the information in this lesson. You can find the answers to these questions and explanations of why each answer choice is correct or incorrect in the "Answers" section at the end of this chapter.

1. What methods does SSIS provide for configuring child packages from the master package? (Choose all that apply.)

   A. Project parameters

   B. Global variables

   C. Package parameters

   D. Solution parameters

2. Expressions can be used in precedence constraints to... (one or more answers are correct)

   A. ...replace constraints.

   B. ...resolve conflicts between multiple constraints.

   C. ...add conditions to constraints.

   D. ...determine variables.

3. Which of the following statements about master packages are true? (Choose all that apply.)

   A. Master packages are used to configure child packages.

   B. Master packages are used to execute child packages.

   C. Master packages prevent child packages from being executed directly.

   D. Master packages are used to control the order in which child packages are executed.

Case Scenarios

In the following case scenarios, you apply what you've learned about enhancing control flow. You can find the answers to these questions in the "Answers" section at the end of this chapter.

Case Scenario 1: Complete Solutions

Your manager has asked you to develop a complete data warehousing solution—the ETL as well as multidimensional processing, and even report caching. He suggested using a single SSIS package for this particular solution.

The manager has used the following claims about his proposal:

- Using a single SSIS package simplifies deployment and maintenance.

- Placing all the elements into a single package will also allow any additional development activities to be performed more quickly.

- Using a single SSIS package is the only way of ensuring the correct order of execution for such a high number of operations.

- SSIS development does not require any division of labor; all developmental tasks can be performed by a single developer.

- Variables in one package are not accessible to other packages; therefore, using a single package ensures proper variable reusability.

How would you approach this proposal? Do you agree with the manager's claims?

Case Scenario 2: Data-Driven Execution

You have been tasked with consolidating existing data warehousing solutions that are currently implemented as individual SSIS packages performing data extraction, transformations, and loading. A part of the solution depends on two external services that provide the data from remote data stores, saving it to files on your local network.

All data processing should be performed during a nightly maintenance window. Your system communicates to the external services using special tools that are installed locally. The services are not completely reliable—occasionally one or both of them are unresponsive, but the data they provide is essential to your company. If any of the services fails to produce the expected files, you want the administrators at the remote locations to be notified so that they can remove any obstacles.

All available data should, of course, still be processed and loaded into the data warehouse; however, if external data is not available, or is not complete, the changes must not be propagated to the Analysis Services database used for reporting. The middle management in your company prefers the analytical data to be complete, rather than current and incomplete, and they are prepared to wait a day or two for it to be updated accordingly.

- What data warehousing concepts can you use to accomplish your task?

- What solutions, provided by the SSIS toolset, can you use?

- How can you prevent incomplete data from being loaded into the SSAS database?

Suggested Practices

To help you successfully master the exam objectives presented in this chapter, complete the following tasks.

Consider Using a Master Package

Consider your existing data warehousing solutions in light of the master package concept.

- **Practice 1**   How is your solution implemented? Are you already using master packages in your SSIS development?

- **Practice 2**   How many distinct processes constitute your solution? How are you determining and maintaining the correct order of their execution?

- **Practice 3**   Create a list of benefits and the drawbacks of using master packages in your business.

Answers

This section contains answers to the lesson review questions and solutions to the case scenarios in this chapter.

Lesson 1

1. **Correct Answer: C**
    - **A.** **Incorrect:** The variable needs to be retrieved from the destination database, and typically not all queries will read data from the destination database. Also, nothing has been said in the description to suggest that the value will be used in queries.
    - **B.** **Incorrect:** Expressions cannot be used to retrieve data from databases.
    - **C.** **Correct:** If multiple tasks are going to use the same value, it can be retrieved once, stored in a variable, and reused.
    - **D.** **Incorrect:** The Expression task cannot be used to retrieve data from databases.

2. **Correct Answer: C**
    - **A.** **Incorrect:** Although it is true that an additional package-scoped variable would solve the problem, it is really not needed.
    - **B.** **Incorrect:** Although it is true that an additional container-scoped variable would solve the problem, it is also not needed.   ·
    - **C.** **Correct:** Variable names must only be unique within a particular scope. For variables that share the name, but that exist in separate scopes, references are resolved based on proximity—the variable nearest to the consumer will be used.
    - **D.** **Incorrect:** This statement does not make any sense at all. The behavior of parameters and variables might be different, but they serve the same purpose.

3. **Correct answer: B**
    - **A.** **Incorrect:** Parameter values cannot be changed during run time.

B. Correct: A parameter will allow the administrator to set the value, but instead of mapping the parameter directly to the properties, the properties will be determined from a variable whose value will be assigned using a single expression.

C. Incorrect: Though it is possible to assign values to SSIS object properties at run time by using property paths, this option requires a perfect understanding of the internal structure of the package and is therefore not very practical.

D. Incorrect: If a parameter is used to assign values directly to multiple properties, and this must be performed by using expressions, multiple instances of the same expression would be required, which is not at all practical and might complicate package development and later modifications significantly.

Lesson 2

1. **Correct Answers: B, C, and D**

   A. Incorrect: A Row Count control flow task does not exist.

   B. Correct: The Row Count data flow component can be used to count the number of rows passed through the data flow.

   C. Correct: The principal purpose of variables is to store values.

   D. Correct: Expressions can be used for calculations.

2. **Correct Answer: C**

   A. Incorrect: Copying the expression to different tasks in the same package would mostly cause maintenance problems.

   B. Incorrect: Using multiple Expression tasks to calculate the same value is really not necessary.

   C. Correct: If a value can safely be calculated in advance, then there is no need to calculate it more than once.

   D. Incorrect: The Expression task cannot be used to compute multiple results.

3. **Correct answer: C**

   A. Incorrect: The conditional split transformation is used to redirect a subset of rows in the buffer to a different branch of the data flow and cannot be used to control the execution of tasks.

   B. Incorrect: Though it is true that a Script task could be used to perform operations conditionally, it is not the only available method.

   C. Correct: The success precedence constraint with a precedence constraint expression can be used in this case: it will allow the following task to execute if the preceding task has completed successfully and if the expression resolves to True.

   D. Incorrect: A simple success constraint will not be enough, because it will allow the following task to execute every day.

Lesson 3

1. **Correct Answers: A and C**

   A. **Correct:** Project-scoped parameters are accessible to all packages of the same project.

   B. **Incorrect:** Master package variables are not directly accessible to child packages, and child package variables cannot be accessed from the master package.

   C. **Correct:** The master package can be configured to access child package parameters.

   D. **Incorrect:** There is no such thing as a "solution parameter."

2. **Correct Answers: A and C**

   A. **Correct:** Constraints in a precedence constraint can be replaced by expressions.

   B. **Incorrect:** Potential conflicts between multiple precedence constraints leading to the same task or container cannot be resolved by expressions.

   C. **Correct:** A precedence constraint expression can be implemented as an additional execution condition.

   D. **Incorrect:** Precedence constraints cannot be used for variable assignment.

3. **Correct answers: A, B, and D**

   A. **Correct:** Child packages can be configured from the corresponding master package at run time.

   B. **Correct:** Master packages do execute child packages.

   C. **Incorrect:** Any SSIS package can be executed directly, even if it represents a logical part of a master package.

   D. **Correct:** Master packages determine the order in which the corresponding child packages are executed.

Case Scenario 1

When discussing the proposed plan with your manager, you could start by addressing the concerns (and some misconceptions) that he has regarding SSIS development.

- In previous versions of SQL Server, it might have been more difficult to deploy and maintain an SSIS solution distributed across multiple SSIS packages, but in SQL Server 2012, the Project Deployment model addresses many of these issues.

- With the introduction of project-scoped parameters and connection managers, it becomes possible for individual SSIS packages to share resources. New additions to the solution will allow you to leave existing elements unchanged.

- The Execute Package task has been available in previous versions, so this statement is completely unfounded.

- It is true that in the majority of cases a BI developer would be capable of developing the complete data warehousing solution on his or her own, but there really is no need for this. And furthermore, even if only one BI developer is available, he or she might still benefit from dividing conceptually different tasks into individual SSIS packages—both for improved manageability as well as improved reusability.

- This is true. Variables are not exposed outside of SSIS packages and cannot be accessed from other packages. This shortcoming is reduced with the introduction of parameters, which can be used to pass scalar values to child packages. On the other hand, variables never were the only method available for exchanging data between the elements of an SSIS solution. (Hint: consider files and staging tables.)

Case Scenario 2

- You could consolidate the solution by using a master package; all of the requirements suggest that this would be the right approach: there are multiple SSIS packages that need to be executed in a particular order; two external processes should also be integrated into the solution; and you also need to automate the communication between your local system and the two remote systems to respond to circumstances detected during execution.

- Obviously you will use the Execute Package and Execute Process tasks to control the execution of existing solutions, as well as the Send Mail task to notify the remote administrators of failure.

- To prevent incomplete data from being available to the consumers, you will need to detect issues with the data extraction, transformation, and data loading processes, and only invoke the propagation of data into the SSAS database if no errors were detected. You could use variables and precedence constraint expressions to guide the execution of the master package, based on available information about the state of the environment and the child processes.

## CHAPTER 7

Enhancing Data Flow

Exam objectives in this chapter:

- Extract and Transform Data
  - Design data flow.
  - Implement data flow.
- Load Data
  - Implement data load options.

In Chapter 5, "Designing and Implementing Data Flow," you learned about the data flow task, which is a crucial component in data warehouse projects when it comes to extracting, transforming, and loading data (ETL). Building on the foundation laid in that chapter, this chapter focuses on specific solutions for common data warehouse problems such as managing Slowly Changing Dimensions (SCD) and loading incremental data.

Lessons in this chapter:

- Lesson 1: Slowly Changing Dimensions
- Lesson 2: Preparing a Package for Incremental Load
- Lesson 3: Error Flow

Before You Begin

To complete this chapter, you must have:

- Basic knowledge of Microsoft SQL Server 2012 Integration Services (SSIS) control flow and data flow features and components.
- Experience working with SQL Server 2012 Management Studio (SSMS).
- A working knowledge of the Transact-SQL language.
- Experience working with SQL Server Data Tools (SSDT) or SQL Server Business Intelligence Development Studio (BIDS).
- An understanding of dimensional design.

Lesson 1: Slowly Changing Dimensions

In Chapter 1, "Data Warehouse Logical Design," you learned how to model dimensions in a data warehouse (DW). Because data changes over time, you need to choose the attributes on which you will maintain history. The management of this is usually known as the Slowly Changing Dimension (SCD) problem. In SQL Server Integration Services you can address this problem by using the predefined Slowly Changing Dimension data flow task, or you can create a custom solution by using existing control flow and data flow tasks.

After this lesson, you will be able to:

- Implement a Slowly Changing Dimension data flow task.
- Implement alternative solutions for the SCD problem.

Estimated lesson time: 60 minutes

Defining Attribute Types

When you are preparing to load dimension tables, you must first define for each attribute what should happen when new values are inserted. If you want to track history for at least one attribute, you usually add two additional columns showing the interval of validity for a value. The data type of the two columns should be Date or DateTime, and the columns should show the values Valid From and Valid To. For the current value, the Valid To column should be NULL. When you are in the process of modeling and mapping source data to your data warehouse, it is a good practice to divide attributes by different types:

- **Business Key**   An attribute of this type is part of the business key from the source data.
- **Fixed**   The value of an attribute of this type should never change in the data warehouse.
- **Type 1 SCD**   Attributes of Type 1 SCD overwrite the history for an attribute.
- **Type 2 SCD**   Attributes of Type 2 SCD keep the history for an attribute.

Based on this information, you can start implementing an SSIS package to update a dimension.

> *NOTE* **USING SURROGATE KEYS**
>
> In cases when you have to implement Type 2 SCD, you will need to have a new data warehouse key in the dimension. This key is called a surrogate key.

Inferred Dimension Members

In data warehouse scenarios, it is possible for fact records to arrive with a source business key that has not yet been loaded in the dimension table. This problem is known in DW jargon as *late-arriving dimensions* or *early-arriving facts*. When inserting records to a fact table that cannot be resolved to a dimension surrogate key, the typical solution is as follows:

1. Insert a row in the dimension table by using the source system key, and assign a surrogate key to this member. Mark this record to indicate that it was populated as an inferred member by adding a column to your dimension (for example, by adding an *InferredMember* column and setting its value to True).

2. Use the newly created surrogate key and assign it to the fact record.

3. Change the loading process for the dimension to check whether a record was populated as an inferred member. If this is the case, you must treat all the attributes as Type 1 SCD regardless of your specification, except for the surrogate key and the business key. If you do not, then all Type 2 SCD attributes will create a new row, because the inferred row has no value for this attribute. So the process is to update the row and set the value of the *InferredMember* column to False.

   If you do not need support for inferred members, it is still a good practice to have a process that assigns a default surrogate key in the dimension for non-matched rows (for example, –1). The aggregate values from the DW and the source systems will match, because all data was loaded in the fact table, but you will later have to either reload or update the data when a dimension has the appropriate dimension row.

Using the Slowly Changing Dimension Task

SSIS has a predefined Slowly Changing Dimension (SCD) transformation that guides you through multiple steps for creating the complete logic for inserting and updating data for a dimension table. Before you can use this transformation, you must have at least one data flow task present in your package and one data flow source adapter defined.

   The following steps show how to implement the SCD transformation:

1. In the SSIS Toolbox, drag the Slowly Changing Dimension task onto the data flow design surface.

2. Connect the existing data flow to the new Slowly Changing Dimension task. Figure 7-1 shows the data flow design area with the new task.

3. Double-click the Slowly Changing Dimension task to open the Slowly Changing Dimension Wizard.

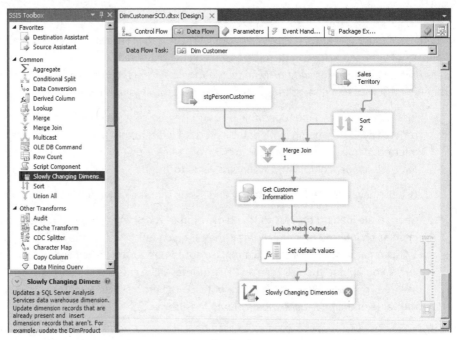

FIGURE 7-1 The data flow design area with a Slowly Changing Dimension task.

4. On the welcome page of the wizard, click Next.

5. Specify the connection manager and select the target dimension table.

6. Based on this information, the wizard lists all columns from the dimension table, as shown in Figure 7-2. You must now specify the mapping between the source data columns and the dimension columns. You do this by selecting the appropriate columns under Input Columns for each destination column. Then you must specify which column or columns are part of the source business key. You do this by setting the value of the Key Type column to Business Key.

7. On the next page, you specify a change type for the dimension columns. The choices are Fixed Attribute, Changing Attribute (Type 1 SCD), or Historical Attribute (Type 2 SCD). This can be done for the columns that were mapped to the source columns in the previous step.

8. On the next page, under Fixed And Changing Attribute Options, you can specify whether the transformation should fail if changes are detected in a fixed-type attribute and whether all matching records should be updated for Type 2 SCD attributes.

FIGURE 7-2 Selecting a dimension table and keys in the Slowly Changing Dimension Wizard.

9. If you set up at least one column as a Historical Attribute (Type 2 SCD) in step 7, on the next page you must specify how to track history in the dimension table. There are two options:

- **Use A Single Column To Show Current And Expired Records**   With this option, you specify one column in the dimension table to show which row is currently active. Also with this option, you must specify the current value and the expiration value (for example, True/False or Current/Expired).

- **Use Start And End Dates To Identify Current And Expired Records**   For this option, you specify two columns in the dimension table to reflect the validity of each record. You also specify the SSIS variable for setting the date value, as shown in Figure 7-3. The date information is used to set the Valid To value for the previous version of the row and the Valid From value for the current version of the row.

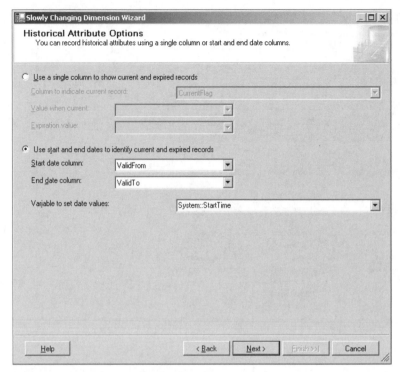

FIGURE 7-3 Setting historical attribute options.

10. On the next page of the Slowly Changing Dimension Wizard, you can set inferred dimension member support by selecting the Enable Inferred Member Support check box. Then you indicate how to show which rows should be updated because they were inserted when the fact table was loaded. The two options are to update when all attributes that you have specified as changing are NULL or to update based on an additional column in your dimension table that has a True/False value.

> **NOTE** **SUPPORTING EARLY-ARRIVING FACTS**
>
> The inferred member setup in the Slowly Changing Dimension Wizard only specifies how your dimension will be updated. To fully support the early-arriving facts, you must implement the necessary logic when loading your fact table.

11. On the last page, you can review the configuration. Then click Finish.

After you click Finish, the Slowly Changing Dimension Wizard builds the appropriate transformations in your data flow to support the desired logic for updating the dimension. It uses Derived Column, OLE DB Command, and Union All transformations and the Data Destination adapter, as shown in Figure 7-4.

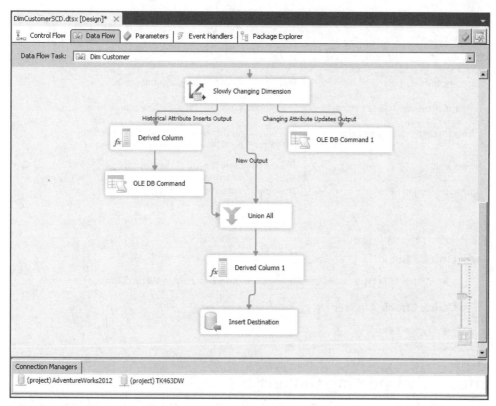

FIGURE 7-4 Transformations automatically created by the Slowly Changing Dimension Wizard.

EXAM TIP

Use the Slowly Changing Dimension Wizard to quickly build the ETL process for updating dimension tables with a small number of rows.

IMPORTANT **THE SLOWLY CHANGING DIMENSION WIZARD LIMITATION**

The Slowly Changing Dimension Wizard only supports connections to SQL Server.

The Slowly Changing Dimension transformation creates up to six outputs based on the update and insert requirements of the row. Table 7-1 lists all possible outputs.

TABLE 7-1 Slowly Changing Dimension Transformation Outputs

Output	Purpose
Changing Attributes Updates output	This output is used for Type 1 SCD attribute rows.
Fixed Attribute output	This output is used for fixed attribute rows.
Historical Attributes Inserts output	This output is used for Type 2 SCD attribute rows.
Inferred Member Updates output	This output consists of all rows that should update the rows in the dimension table's inferred members.
New output	This output consists of all of the new rows.
Unchanged output	This output is used for unchanged rows.

 Quick Check

- Which SCD types does the Slowly Changing Dimension Wizard support?

Quick Check Answer

- Types 1 and 2

Effectively Updating Dimensions

Although the Slowly Changing Dimension transformation is very easy to use and can quickly create the whole data flow process for updating dimensions, be aware that it does not work optimally in terms of performance, and thus it should only be used for small dimensions (no more than 10,000 rows).

If you look at the transformations used by the wizard, you can see that it uses an OLE DB Command transformation, which works on the row level and executes a T-SQL UPDATE statement for each change (either Type 1 or Type 2 SCD). This is very expensive in terms of performance and on larger dimensions (millions of rows) can be completely useless. Therefore, this section looks at an alternative approach to updating a dimension by using SSIS.

The algorithm for updating a dimension that has Type 1 and Type 2 SCD attributes is as follows:

1. Check whether the attributes from the source row have changed.

2. Mark rows for Type 1 or Type 2 SCD change depending on the attribute specification for the dimension.

3. Apply the required update logic to the dimension:

   - For Type 1 SCD, update the row.

   - For Type 2 SCD, update the current row's validity to indicate that it was valid until now, and insert the new row.

Checking Attribute Changes

When you start comparing changes between source and destination rows, you can first check to see whether the business key already exists in your dimension by using, for example, a Lookup transformation. All the new rows will then be part of the lookup "no match" output, and you can insert them into the dimension. More problematic is to effectively check the existing records to see whether their attributes have changed and what kind of change type should later be applied.

Using standard SSIS functionality, you could use the Conditional Split transformation to write an expression to check whether columns have changed. For example, suppose you have three columns: *FullName*, *City*, and *Occupation*. The expression should compare each source column to a destination column, as in *source.FullName <> destination.FullName || source.City <> destination.City || source.Occupation <> destination.Occupation* (the || operator is the logical OR). At the end, you would have two data outputs from the Conditional Split transformation, one passing only changed rows and one for the unchanged rows.

In real life, dimensions usually have many columns, and comparing all of them is not optimal. That is why in ETL processes a hash function is usually used to store information about all the needed attributes, so that the process can quickly check whether there has been a change. A *hash function* is any algorithm or subroutine that maps large data sets of variable length, called keys, to smaller data sets of a fixed length. The selected algorithm for hashing in this case must be deterministic (that is, the function must always return the same result any time it is called with a specific set of input values) and must have a very low possibility of mapping two or more keys to the same hash value. One of the most widely used algorithms is the *MD5 Message-Digest Algorithm* cryptographic hash function, which produces a 128-bit (16-byte) hash value.

To implement a hash function inside SSIS, you have a few options:

- Write a SELECT statement and add a calculated column using the T-SQL HASHBYTES function when reading the data.

- Use the Script Component transformation and use the Microsoft .NET Framework to calculate the needed hash value.

- Deploy a custom SSIS component that calculates the hash value based on different algorithms.

Of course, you must extend your dimension by adding an additional column or columns for storing the hash values. If you have a lot of columns and half of them should be treated as Type 2 SCD, you can also have two hash values—one for all columns, and one for only Type 2 SCD columns—so that you can efficiently check whether a row has been modified and also whether it needs a Type 2 SCD change.

> **MORE INFO   CUSTOM SSIS COMPONENTS**
>
> A good place to get custom SSIS components is at Microsoft CodePlex, an open source project community at *http://www.codeplex.com*.

Set-Based Update Logic

One of the key reasons why the Slowly Changing Dimension transformation is slow is because it performs row-level SQL updates. That is why it is important to implement set-based logic when you are designing SSIS processes that need to apply Type 1 or Type 2 SCD changes. You learned in Chapter 5 how to implement a set-based update in SSIS by using an additional table to store the needed rows in the data flow and then applying an Execute SQL task in the control flow.

This section uses an example to show the necessary steps for this approach. Table 7-2 lists the current data warehouse data for a customer dimension. The *City* column is a Type 2 SCD column, and the *FullName* and *Occupation* columns are Type 1 SCD.

TABLE 7-2 Current DW Data for a Customer Dimension

DWCID	CustomerID	FullName	City	Occupation	ValidFrom	ValidTo
289	17	Bostjan Strazar	Vienna	Professional	1.1.1900	NULL

To implement a Type 1 or Type 2 SCD change, you should store all rows that have changed in an additional temporary table in the data flow and add columns indicating whether the change is a Type 1 or Type 2 SCD change. Table 7-3 shows only the changed source data after the final step in the data flow.

TABLE 7-3 Changed Source Data Stored As an Additional Temporary Table

CustomerID	FullName	City	Occupation	Type1	Type2
17	Bostjan Strazar	Ljubljana	Teacher	True	True

Then, using the Execute SQL task in the control flow, you would execute SQL statements as described here:

1. Update the dimension rows that have Type 1 SCD changes (for which the *Type1* column has a value of True) based on the source business key, which in this example is thee *CustomerID* column. Table 7-4 shows the result in a data warehouse after this step.

TABLE 7-4 DW Data for a Customer Dimension After the Type 1 SCD Change Is Applied

DWCID	CustomerID	FullName	City	Occupation	ValidFrom	ValidTo
289	17	Bostjan Strazar	Vienna	Teacher	1.1.1900	NULL

2. Update the *ValidTo* column for the dimension rows that have Type 2 SCD changes (for which the *Type2* column has a value of True) with the current date (in this example, 1.1.2012). Table 7-5 shows the result in a data warehouse after this step.

TABLE 7-5 DW Data for a Customer Dimension with an Updated *ValidTo* Column

DWCID	CustomerID	FullName	City	Occupation	ValidFrom	ValidTo
289	17	Bostjan Strazar	Vienna	Teacher	1.1.1900	1.1.2012

3. Insert the new rows that have Type 2 SCD changes and set the *ValidTo* column to NULL. Table 7-6 shows the result in a data warehouse after this step.

TABLE 7-6 Final DW Data for a Customer Dimension

DWCID	CustomerID	FullName	City	Occupation	ValidFrom	ValidTo
289	17	Bostjan Strazar	Vienna	Teacher	1.1.1900	1.1.2012
943	17	Bostjan Strazar	Ljubljana	Teacher	1.1.2012	NULL

NOTE   **USING THE T-SQL MERGE STATEMENT**

In this example, which uses a combination of SQL UPDATE and INSERT statements in the Execute SQL task, you could apply the necessary logic even more efficiently by using a T-SQL MERGE statement.

REAL WORLD   **OPTIMIZING THE PROCESS TO LOAD A DIMENSION TABLE**

On a project for a financial institution, the company had more than 4 million customers and about 120 attributes in the customer dimension. They needed to track more than 40 attributes as Type 2 SCD changes. A solution that used hashing functions to quickly iden-tify what had changed, and set-based logic to manage Type 1 and Type 2 changes, opti-mized the update process for this dimension from a couple of hours to a couple of minutes by using a combination of SSIS and T-SQL!

PRACTICE   **Implementing Slowly Changing Dimension Logic**

In this practice, you will load data into your *Customer* dimension table. You will first use a Slowly Changing Dimension transformation and then modify the created transformations to include a set-based update. You will use an existing package, similar to the one you devel-oped in Chapter 3, "Creating SSIS Packages," that reads the source data for the *Customer* dimension.

If you encounter a problem completing an exercise, you can install the completed projects from the Solution folder that is provided with the companion content for this chapter and lesson.

EXERCISE 1   Load the Customer Dimension by Using a Slowly Changing Dimension Transformation

In this exercise, you implement the Slowly Changing Dimension transformation to load the *dbo.Customer* dimension table. Assume that you have a specification for the dimension table telling you that the Type 1 SCD columns are *EmailAddress* and *FullName*, and that the Type 2 SCD columns are *CountryRegion* and *MaritalStatus*.

1. Start SSMS and connect to your SQL Server instance. Open a new query window by clicking the New Query button.

2. If you are missing the database object from Chapter 5, execute the SQL code from that chapter to have all the stage and dimension tables available in the TK463DW database.

3. Alter the existing *dbo.Customers* table to include two additional columns for the validity of the rows for Type 2 SCD.

    ```
    ALTER TABLE dbo.Customers
    ADD
          ValidFrom DATE,
          ValidTo DATE;
    ```

4. Delete all rows in the *dbo.Customers* table.

    ```
    TRUNCATE TABLE dbo.Customers;
    ```

5. If necessary, start SQL Server Data Tools (SSDT), open the TK 463 Chapter 7 project in the Starter folder, and then execute the FillStageTables.dtsx package. This will populate the staging tables so that you can load the *dbo.Customer* dimension table.

6. Open the DimCustomerSCD package for editing.

7. Click the Data Flow tab at the top of the SSIS Designer. Notice the existing transformations that prepare the data for loading (similar to what you saw in Chapter 5).

8. In the SSIS Toolbox, drag a Slowly Changing Dimension transformation from the Common area onto the data flow workspace. Connect the output of the Set Default Values derived column item to the new Slowly Changing Dimension transformation by dragging the blue output arrow.

9. Right-click the Slowly Changing Dimension item and then click Edit to open the Slowly Changing Dimension Wizard.

10. On the welcome page, click Next.

11. Select TK463DW from the Connection Manager drop-down list, and select the *dbo.Customers* table from the Table Or View drop-down list.

12. Now map the Input Columns to the Dimension Columns as specified in Table 7-7.

TABLE 7-7 Dimension Table and Keys

Input columns	Dimension columns	Key type
BirthDate	BirthDate	Not a key column
CountryRegionCode	CountryRegion	Not a key column
BusinessEntityID	CustomerKey	Business key
EmailAddress	EmailAddress	Not a key column
FullName	FullName	Not a key column
Gender	Gender	Not a key column
MaritalStatus	MaritalStatus	Not a key column

13. Specify the Slowly Changing Dimension columns as shown in Table 7-8.

TABLE 7-8 Slowly Changing Dimension Columns

Dimension columns	Change type
BirthDate	Fixed attribute
EmailAddress	Changing attribute
FullName	Changing attribute
Gender	Fixed attribute
MaritalStatus	Historical attribute
CountryRegion	Historical attribute

14. Click Next. Leave the Fail The Transformation If Changes Are Detected In A Fixed Attribute check box selected, and click Next.

15. On the Historical Attribute Options page, select Use Start And End Dates To Identify Current And Expired Records. For the start date column, select *ValidFrom*, and for the end date column, select *ValidTo*. In the Variable To Set Date Values drop-down list, select *System::StartTime*. Click Next.

16. Disable inferred member support by clearing the Enable Inferred Member Support check box. Click Next. Review the output that the Slowly Changing Dimension Wizard will build, and click Next.

17. Observe the created transformations and execute the package. If you get an error, please change the data access mode on the destination adapter to *Table/View-fast load*. There is an issue, because we are using a sequencer to populate the surrogate keys and the SCD wizard sets the destination by default to an access mode that does not allow a trigger with a sequencer on the destination table.

18. In SSMS, open a new query window by clicking the New Query button.

19. Write a SELECT statement to observe some of the inserted rows.

```
SELECT
 CustomerDwKey,
 CustomerKey,
 FullName,
 MaritalStatus,
 Gender,
 CountryRegion,
 ValidFrom,
 ValidTo
FROM dbo.Customers
WHERE CustomerKey IN (15001, 14996, 14997);
```

20. Now modify some of the records in stage tables to simulate a change in the source data.

```
UPDATE stg.Customer
SET TerritoryID = 4
WHERE
 CustomerID  IN (15001, 14996, 14997);
```

21. Execute the DimCustomerSCD package and observe that three records were inserted because of a change in a Type 2 SCD column.

22. Execute the SQL statement provided in step 19 to observe the changes in the *dbo.Customers* dimension table.

EXERCISE 2   Modify the Package to Include a Set-Based Update Process

In this exercise, you modify the implemented Slowly Changing Dimension transformation to use a set-based update of attributes of Type 1 SCD. You will have to remove the OLE DB Command transformation and stage the data into a temporary table and then use an Execute SQL task in the control flow.

1. Start SSMS, if necessary, and connect to your SQL Server instance. Open a new query window by clicking the New Query button.

2. Use the following code to create a table to store rows needed for the update.

```
CREATE TABLE dbo.UpdateCustomers
(
CustomerKey  INT       NOT NULL,
FullName     NVARCHAR(150) NULL,
EmailAddress NVARCHAR(50)  NULL
);
```

3. If necessary, start SQL Server Data Tools (SSDT), open the TK 463 Chapter 7 project in the Starter folder, and open the DimCustomerSCD package that was created in the previous exercise.

4. In the Dim Customer data flow, find the OLE DB Command transformation that was used to update Type 1 SCD attributes (it has "Changing Attribute Updates Output" written on the data path) and delete it.

5. Drag an OLE DB destination adapter from the SSIS Toolbox to the location of the deleted OLE DB Command transformation. Connect the Slowly Changing Dimension transformation to the added OLE DB destination adapter. In the Input Output Selection dialog box, under Output, select Changing Attribute Updates Output value. Rename the adapter **UpdatedRows**.

6. Open the OLE DB Destination Editor for UpdatedRows and select the TK463DW For OLE DB connection manager. Select the *dbo.UpdateCustomers* table in the Name Of The Table Or The View drop-down list.

7. Select the Mappings tab and connect the *BusinessEntityID* column to the *CustomerKey* column. Click OK.

8. In the control flow, add an Execute SQL task to the design surface. Connect the Dim Customer data flow task to the added Execute SQL task.

9. Open the Execute SQL Task Editor and set the Connection property to TK463DW. For the SQLStatement property, enter the following T-SQL update statement.

```
UPDATE C
SET
  FullName = U.FullName,
  EmailAddress = U.EmailAddress
FROM dbo.Customers AS C
INNER JOIN dbo.UpdateCustomers AS U ON U.CustomerKey = C.CustomerKey;
```

10. Click OK to save the changes, and rename the Execute SQL task **Update Dim Customer**.

11. Add another Execute SQL task before the Dim Customer data flow task.

12. In the Execute SQL Task Editor, set the Connection property to TK463DW and, for the SQLStatement property, enter the following T-SQL statement to truncate the *dbo.UpdateCustomer* table.

```
TRUNCATE TABLE dbo.UpdateCustomers;
```

13. Click OK to save the changes, and rename the Execute SQL task **Truncate UpdateCustomers**.

14. Save the package and execute it.

> **NOTE** **MODIFYING THE SLOWLY CHANGING DIMENSION TRANSFORMATION**
>
> If you would like to change the properties of the Slowly Changing Dimension transformation, you can open the wizard again by right-clicking the existing transformation and selecting Edit. Go through the required steps and the tasks will be regenerated.

Lesson Summary

- Define each attribute's SCD type in the data modeling phase of the data warehouse project.
- Use the Slowly Changing Dimension Wizard for dimensions with a small number of rows.
- Use an alternative solution to the Slowly Changing Dimension Wizard for larger dimensions to solve the problem of updating the Type 1 and Type 2 SCD attributes of a dimension.

Lesson Review

Answer the following questions to test your knowledge of the information in this lesson. You can find the answers to these questions and explanations of why each answer choice is correct or incorrect in the "Answers" section at the end of this chapter.

1. Which functionality does the Slowly Changing Dimension transformation support? (Choose all that apply.)

   A. Type 1 SCD

   B. Type 2 SCD

   C. Type 3 SCD

   D. Inferred members

2. Which transformations can you use to determine whether the values of specific columns have changed between the source data and the destination table? (Choose all that apply.)

   A. Data Conversion

   B. Derived Column

   C. Conditional Split

   D. Multicast

3. Which statement is true regarding the Slowly Changing Dimension transformation? (Choose all that apply.)

   A. The Slowly Changing Dimension transformation supports set-based updates.

   B. The Slowly Changing Dimension transformation supports inferred members.

   C. You can have multiple Slowly Changing Dimension transformations in one data flow.

   D. The Slowly Changing Dimension Wizard supports only connections with a SQL Server database.

Lesson 2: Preparing a Package for Incremental Load

In the data warehouse design process, one of the tasks is to analyze the source data that will be used to load fact tables and decide how to incrementally load this data. This is very important, because loading fact data usually takes the most time, and the time frame for ETL is limited.

For each fact table, you must define an increment window. The best way to do so depends on your source data. The following are some common scenarios:

- Load only the new data from the source based on the specific value of the column.
- Load data in a sliding, overlapping window (for example, one that reads data for the previous and current month each day).
- The source system does not have any information about how to get only new data.

Based on this range of possibility, it is important to know how to use the different approaches provided by SSIS, such as the new change data capture (CDC) functionality, to prepare your packages for incremental load.

> **After this lesson, you will be able to:**
> - Use dynamic SQL to read data from the source adapters.
> - Implement the new change data capture (CDC) functionality by using SSIS.
> - Use appropriate ETL strategy to incrementally load fact tables.
>
> **Estimated lesson time: 90 minutes**

Using Dynamic SQL to Read Data

Assume that you have a source table that has a column that can be used to filter rows for a specific incremental window. For example, suppose that the source table has the *OrderDate* column of type Date, and in your SSIS package you would like to read only those rows that have an order date later than a particular value stored in an SSIS variable called *@IncrementalDate*.

There are different approaches to creating and passing the dynamic SQL to the source adapter based on the type of data source adapter you will use in SSIS.

Using the OLE DB Source Adapter

With the OLE DB Source adapter, you have two options for creating and using dynamic SQL:

- **Writing an SQL command with a parameter** You can supply a parameter to an SQL statement by setting the data access mode to SQL Command in the OLE DB Source Editor, as shown in Figure 7-5. In your SQL command, you use the ? character to set the placeholder for a parameter. You can have multiple parameter placeholders.

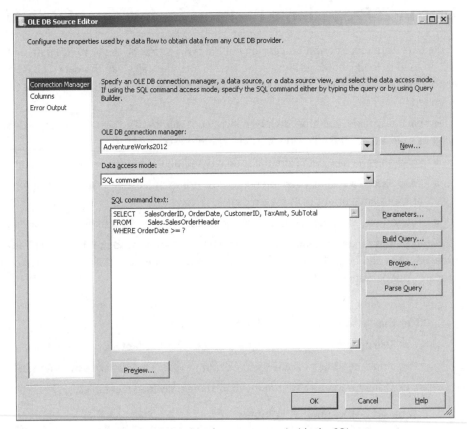

FIGURE 7-5 Using ? to create a placeholder for a parameter inside the SQL statement.

When you click the Parameters button in the OLE DB Source Editor, a Set Query Parameters dialog box opens. Here you can map the SQL parameter placeholders to SSIS variables or parameters, as shown in Figure 7-6.

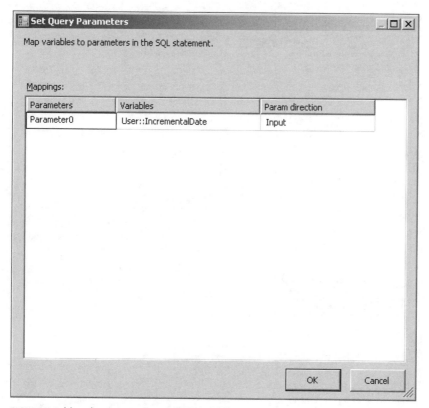

FIGURE 7-6 Mapping parameters to SSIS variables.

- **Using an SQL command from a variable**   In this case, you have to store the complete SQL query in a variable. First you must define a variable of type String—for example, *@SQLQuery*—and set the value to a fixed SQL query statement so that you can read the metadata when using the variable as a SQL command inside the OLE DB Source Editor. Using the previous example, the value for the variable should look like this.

```
SELECT SalesOrderID, OrderDate, CustomerID, TaxAmt, SubTotal
FROM Sales.SalesOrderHeader;
```

Then you must set the value of the variable to be dynamically set up each time you run the package. This can be done either inside the control flow by using the new Expression task, as shown in Figure 7-7, or by specifying an expression in the Variables window to set up the value at run time.

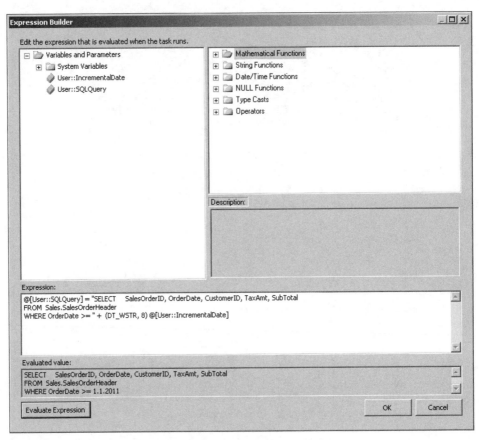

FIGURE 7-7 Writing dynamic SQL by using an SSIS expression.

When you have defined a variable, you can then specify the data access mode as SQL Command from the variable in the OLE DB Source Editor.

EXAM TIP

In SQL Server 2012, you can also use parameters in SSIS to store information that you would like to change at run time.

Using the ODBC or ADO Net Source Adapter

When using an ADO Net source adapter or the new ODBC source adapter, you can parameterize an SQL query only outside the data flow task, by using the Expressions property. The Expressions property of the SSIS task enables you to set different properties dynamically to be evaluated at run time. You can set some of the general properties for the data flow task and also some of the properties of specific data flow transformations that you have added into your data flow. When you add an ODBC or ADO Net source adapter, its properties are visible inside the Property Expressions Editor, as shown in Figure 7-8. As before, you can set an expression for the SqlCommand property, and at run time, SSIS will send an SQL query based on this expression.

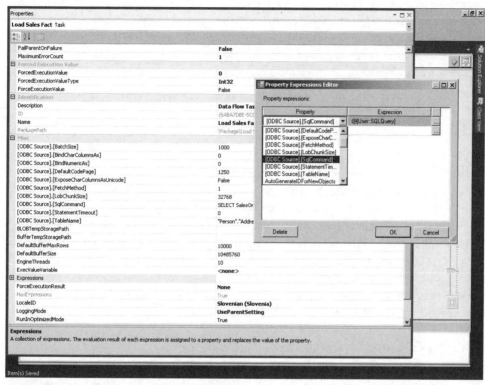

FIGURE 7-8 Setting properties by using expressions.

 In SQL Server 2012, it is also possible to use SSIS parameters to modify the SqlCommand property for the data flow task. *SSIS parameters* allow you to assign values to properties within packages at the time of package execution. You can create project parameters at the project level and package parameters at the package level. Project parameters are used to supply any external input the project receives to one or more packages in the project. Package parameters allow you to modify package execution without having to edit and redeploy the package. Parameters are explained in detail in Chapter 9, "Implementing Dynamic Packages." If you right-click the data flow task and select Parameterize, a Parameterize dialog box opens. Here you can map a specific property to a specific parameter. It is important to remember that if you set up a parameter here for a specific property, it will also be visible under the Expressions property, as in the previous case.

 EXAM TIP

The value of a parameter cannot change within the execution instance of a package. This means that you cannot change its value inside the package, because its value must remain the same for the entire execution of the package.

The question now is whether it is better to use a variable with an expression or a parameter to set up a dynamic query. If you need to filter the data based on information that you get while your package is running, then you must use a variable, because you will change the SQL based on some information that is not known when you run the package. On the other hand, if you know at the time of package execution that you would like to, for example, filter all rows that have an *OrderDate* column value higher than 1.1.2012, then you can supply this information as an InputDate parameter to a package and use an expression inside SSIS, like this.

```
"SELECT SalesOrderID, OrderDate, CustomerID, TaxAmt, SubTotal
FROM Sales.SalesOrderHeader
WHERE OrderDate > " +  @[$Package::InputDate]
```

Implementing CDC by Using SSIS

The example in the previous topic had a column you could use to incrementally load data from the source system. When such a possibility does not exist, you have two options: read the whole set of data each time or implement some kind of change data capture (CDC) solution that will enable you to read only the changed rows from the source system. Of course, in a perfect DW scenario, you would always want to receive only changed data from source systems, but first the source system must support some kind of CDC functionality—and don't forget that such a solution would also add overhead to the source system, so always check the impact of such solution.

Enabling CDC on the Database

With SQL Server 2008, Microsoft added a new functionality called *change data capture (CDC)*. CDC provides an easy way to capture changes to data in a set of database tables so that these changes can be transferred to a second system, such as a data warehouse. If you want to enable CDC functionality, you must enable it for each table in which you would like to track changes, but first you must enable the database itself to support CDC. Here is a sample of the T-SQL code that enables CDC on the TK463DW database and for the *stg.CDCSalesOrderHeader* table.

```
USE TK463DW;
-- Enable database for CDC
EXEC sys.sp_cdc_enable_db;
-- Add a custom role for CDC
CREATE ROLE cdc_role;
-- Enable table for CDC
-- Ensure that the SQL Server Agent is running
EXEC sys.sp_cdc_enable_table
    @source_schema = N'stg',
    @source_name = N'CDCSalesOrderHeader',
    @role_name = N'cdc_role',
    @supports_net_changes = 1;
```

It is also mandatory that the SQL Server Agent be running when you apply CDC. When enabling CDC, the server will generate a new *cdc* schema, several system tables, and two jobs inside the SQL Server Agent. The tables are:

- **cdc.captured_columns**   A list of captured columns.
- **cdc.change_tables**   All the tables that are enabled for CDC.
- **cdc.ddl_history**   History of all of the data definition (DDL) changes since CDC enablement.
- **cdc.index_columns**   Indexes associated with CDC tables.
- **cdc.lsn_time_mapping**   Used to map between log sequence number (LSN) commit values and the time the transaction was committed.
- **cdc.stg_CDCSalesOrderHeader_CT**   Each table that is enabled for CDC has a "copy" where all the changes are stored with additional columns describing, for example, the type of change.

> *MORE INFO*   **CHANGE DATA CAPTURE**
>
> For more information on change data capture, see "Tuning the Performance of Change Data Capture in SQL Server 2008" at *http://msdn.microsoft.com/en-us/library/ dd266396(v=sql.100).aspx.*

SSIS CDC Components

SQL Server 2012 introduces new components that make it easier to do change data capture (CDC) using SSIS:

- **CDC Control task**   Used to control the life cycle of CDC packages. This task handles CDC package synchronization with the initial load package and oversees the management of the *log sequence number (LSN)* ranges that are processed in the run of a CDC package (every record in the SQL Server transaction log is uniquely identified by an LSN). In addition, the CDC Control task deals with error scenarios and recovery and is part of the control flow in SSIS.
- **CDC source adapter**   Reads a range of change data from CDC change tables and delivers the changes downstream to other SSIS components. The CDC source adapter is one of the data flow source adapters.
- **CDC splitter**   Splits a single flow of change rows from a CDC source component into different data flows for insertion, update, and deletion operations. The splitter is essentially a preconfigured Conditional Split transformation that automatically handles the standard values of the __$operation column of a table that holds the changed data.

The CDC Control task maintains the state of the CDC package in an SSIS package variable, and it can also persist an SSIS package variable in a database table so that the state is maintained across package activations and between multiple packages that together perform a common CDC process (for example, one task might be responsible for the initial loading and the other for the incremental updates). This variable must be a String data type. It will be loaded, initialized, and updated by the CDC Control task, and it will be used by the CDC source data flow component to determine the current processing range for change records. You set the processing range by specifying the CDC Control Operation value in the CDC Control Task Editor, as shown in Figure 7-9.

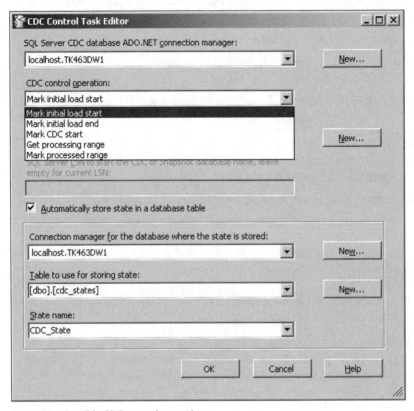

FIGURE 7-9 Possible CDC control operations.

The CDC source offers five different ways to retrieve change data. The format you receive the data in is determined by the CDC processing mode you select in the CDC Source Editor dialog box. The five possible options are as follows:

- **All** In this process mode, a row will be returned for each change applied to the source table. If three UPDATE statements were applied to the same row, you will get back three records. The rows will be ordered by LSN (that is, in the order in which they were applied). This mode is useful in ETL processes that require detailed auditing, but it does complicate the ETL process, because you will need to merge the changes yourself to get the latest change for a specific record.

- **All with old values** This processing mode is similar to All, except that you get two rows for each UPDATE statement—one with the Before Update values, and one containing the After Update values. There is an additional __*$operation* column to distinguish between different updates.

- **Net**   In this mode, the CDC server will apply all changes that were done for a specific row and will return only one row for each unique record. If an INSERT statement added a row and then two UPDATE statements ware applied, you will only get back one row containing all changes. This mode is very suitable for typical DW ETL scenarios.

- **Net with update mask**   This mode is similar to Net except that this mode includes an additional Boolean column for each source column, indicating whether a column value changed. This might be useful when you need to provide additional processing logic when changes are made to a specific field.

- **Net with merge**   Similar to Net mode, but the UPDATE and INSERT rows are grouped together with the same operation value. This option is designed to improve query performance when it is sufficient to indicate that the operation needed to apply the change data is either an insert or an update, but when it is not necessary to explicitly distinguish between the two. You can then process the changes with the T-SQL MERGE statement.

> **NOTE   INITIAL AND INCREMENTAL LOADS**
>
> When using CDC functionality in SSIS, you usually have separate packages for the initial and incremental loads. Remember also that it is possible to set the value of the TaskOperation property of the CDC Control task dynamically by using expressions, which means that with some additional logic you can have a single package for both initial and incremental load when you are using CDC functionality.

 Quick Check

- Which are the new data flow components in SQL Server 2012 for implementing CDC functionality?

Quick Check Answer

- The CDC source, for reading the changed rows, and the CDC splitter, for splitting the input rows into different outputs.

ETL Strategy for Incrementally Loading Fact Tables

ETL strategy for loading fact tables should always start with analysis of the source data to specify how you can incrementally load the data. Also always check with business owners to determine what possible exceptions might happen. For instance, in some countries it is possible to post account ledger entries for a couple of months back from the current date. In such cases, you need to have a more flexible sliding window of a few months, not just the latest data.

The next important thing to consider is how to manage delete and update operations. In most cases, both of these operations should be avoided when it comes to data warehousing, because of their impact on performance.

The following lists some general guidelines for loading fact tables:

- Partition your fact tables.
- Incremental data should be on one partition, so that you can easily remove this data without a delete operation by using partition switching.
- Use this loading strategy:
  - **A.** Load incremental data to a table that has the same structure as the destination fact table, without compression or indexes.
  - **B.** Apply the necessary indexes and compression.
  - **C.** Switch the loaded table with the partition in the destination fact table.
- Use fully cached lookups to get appropriate surrogate keys.

All these topics were explained in Chapter 2, "Implementing a Data Warehouse," and Chapter 5, but from an SSIS perspective, it means that when you are loading incremental data, you will have to use a combination of the Execute SQL task to manage partitions and a data flow task to load all the needed data. This loading strategy is also important for the new column store index that was also explained in Chapter 2, because it is a read-only index and you must use the logic of partition switching to efficiently load data.

PRACTICE Implementing Change Data Capture (CDC) by Using SSIS

In this practice, you will incrementally load data into a stage table by using the new CDC functionality in SSIS. First you will create a package for initial loading and then one for incremental loading. You will also create a sample table based on the AdventureWorks2012 database and enable CDC on the database and table level. Then you will simulate some changes and observe how your package loads the data.

If you encounter a problem completing an exercise, you can install the completed projects from the Solution folder that is provided with the companion content for this chapter and lesson.

EXERCISE 1 Create an Initial Loading Package

In the first exercise, you create a sample table that will be the source for the stage table and, you enable it for CDC. Then you build a package for initial load using the CDC functionality in SSIS. This package will only be run once.

1. If necessary, start SSMS and connect to your SQL Server instance. Open a new query window by clicking the New Query button.

2. Use the following code to create two tables, one to simulate the source table for CDC based on data from the *Sales.SalesOrderHeader* table in the AdventureWorks2012 database, and one to act as a stage table for this source data.

```sql
USE TK463DW;
-- Create needed tables
IF OBJECT_ID('stg.SalesOrderHeader','U') IS NOT NULL
  DROP TABLE stg.SalesOrderHeader;
GO
IF OBJECT_ID('stg.CDCSalesOrderHeader','U') IS NOT NULL
  DROP TABLE stg.CDCSalesOrderHeader;
GO
CREATE TABLE stg.SalesOrderHeader
(
  SalesOrderID      INT NULL,
  OrderDate                   DATETIME NULL,
  SalesOrderNumber  NVARCHAR(50),
  CustomerID              INT NULL,
  SalesPersonID           INT NULL,
  TerritoryID             INT NULL,
  SubTotal                DECIMAL(16,6) NULL,
  TaxAmt                  DECIMAL(16,6) NULL,
  Freight                 DECIMAL(16,6) NULL
);
GO
CREATE TABLE stg.CDCSalesOrderHeader
(
  SalesOrderID      INT NOT NULL PRIMARY KEY,
  OrderDate                   DATETIME NULL,
  SalesOrderNumber  NVARCHAR(50),
  CustomerID              INT NULL,
  SalesPersonID           INT NULL,
  TerritoryID             INT NULL,
  SubTotal                DECIMAL(16,6) NULL,
  TaxAmt                  DECIMAL(16,6) NULL,
  Freight                 DECIMAL(16,6) NULL
);
GO
-- Populate a sample table stg.CDCSalesOrderHeader from AdventureWorks2012 DB
INSERT INTO stg.CDCSalesOrderHeader (
  SalesOrderID, OrderDate, SalesOrderNumber, CustomerID,
  SalesPersonID, TerritoryID, SubTotal, TaxAmt, Freight
)
SELECT
  SalesOrderID, OrderDate, SalesOrderNumber, CustomerID,
  SalesPersonID, TerritoryID, SubTotal, TaxAmt, Freight
FROM AdventureWorks2012.Sales.SalesOrderHeader;
```

3. Enable the TK463DW database for CDC.

```sql
EXEC sys.sp_cdc_enable_db;
```

4. Create a cdc_role database role to use it for change data capture. Enable CDC functionality for the *stg.CDCSalesOrderHeader* table.

```
-- Add a custom role for CDC
CREATE ROLE cdc_role;
-- Enable table for CDC
-- Ensure that the SQL Server Agent is running
EXEC sys.sp_cdc_enable_table
  @source_schema = N'stg',
  @source_name = N'CDCSalesOrderHeader',
  @role_name = N'cdc_role',
  @supports_net_changes = 1;
```

5. Ensure that the SQL Server Agent is running.

6. If necessary, start SQL Server Data Tools (SSDT), open the TK 463 Chapter 7 project, and then add a new package and rename it **InitLoadStgSalesHeader**.

7. Drag a CDC Control task from the SSIS Toolbox onto the control flow workspace. Rename the CDC Control task **CDC Start** and double-click the new CDC Control task to open the editor.

8. Add a new ADO.NET connection by clicking New next to the SQL Server CDC Database ADO.NET Connection Manager drop-down list.

9. In the Configure ADO.NET Connection Manager dialog box, select New and create the connection to the TK463DW database.

10. Select the new ADO.NET connection in the CDC Control Task Editor.

11. Set CDC Control Operation to Mark Initial Load Start.

12. Create a new package variable by clicking New next to the Variable Containing The CDC State drop-down list. Name the variable **CDC_State**. This variable will hold the CDC state information.

13. Set the connection manager for the database where the state is stored to the connection you created in step 8.

14. Create a table for storing the state data by clicking New next to the Table To Use For Storing State drop-down list. A dialog box with the CREATE statement will open. Click Run to create a table called *dbo.cdc_states*. This table will be used to track the CDC load information so that you will only pick up new changes each time the incremental load package is run.

15. Set the state name to **CDC_State**. This value acts as a key for the CDC state information. Packages that are accessing the same CDC data should be using a common CDC state name. Figure 7-10 shows what your configuration should look like. Click OK to close the CDC Control Task Editor.

16. Add a data flow task and connect it to the CDC Control task. Rename the data flow task **Init Load SalesHeader**.

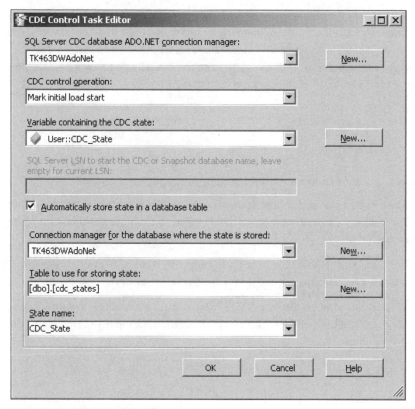

FIGURE 7-10 CDC Control Task final configuration.

17. In the Data Flow area, add an OLE DB source adapter. Open the OLE DB Source Editor, set the OLE DB connection manager to TK463DW, and select the *stg.CDCSalesOrderHeader* table.

18. Drag an OLE DB Destination adapter to the data flow workspace and connect the OLE DB source adapter to the new OLE DB destination adapter. Rename the OLE DB source item **stgCDCSalesOrderHeader** and the OLE DB Destination adapter **stgSalesOrderHeader**.

19. Open the stgSalesOrderHeader destination adapter, set the connection manager to TK463DW, and select the *stg.SalesOrderHeader* table. Click the Mappings tab and then click OK.

20. On the control flow, add another CDC Control task and rename it **CDC End**. Connect the Init Load SalesHeader data flow task to the new CDC Control task.

21. Configure the CDC Control task with the same settings as the first one, but set the CDC Control Operation to Mark Initial Load End.

22. Execute the package.

23. When you run the package, all of the data in the *stg.CDCSalesOrderHeader* table will be transferred to the *stg.SalesOrderHeader* table, and the initial CDC state markers will be created. If you write a SELECT statement against the *dbo.cdc_states* table, you will see one row with the stored CDC state from the initial load. You will use this information to build an incremental package in the next exercise.

```
SELECT
  name,
  state
FROM dbo.cdc_states;
```

EXERCISE 2   Create an Incremental Loading Package

In this exercise, you implement an incremental package for the table used in the previous exercise. This package can then be executed every time you want to get the latest changes from the source table.

1. If necessary, start SQL Server Data Tools, open the TK 463 Chapter 7 project, and then add a new package and rename it **IncLoadStgSalesHeader**.

2. Drag a CDC Control task from the SSIS Toolbox onto the control flow workspace. Rename the CDC Control Task **CDC Start** and double-click the new CDC Control Task to open the editor.

3. Add a new ADO.NET connection to the TK463DW database.

4. Select the new ADO.NET connection in the CDC Control Task Editor.

5. Set CDC Control Operation to Get Processing Range.

6. Create a new package variable by clicking New next to the Variable Containing The CDC State drop-down list. Name the variable **CDC_State**. It will hold the CDC state information.

7. Set the connection manager for the database in which to store the state to the new connection from step 3.

8. Set Table To Use For Storing State to the *dbo.cdc_states* table created in the previous exercise.

9. Set CDC_State as the state name. Click OK to close the CDC Control Task Editor.

10. Add a data flow task and connect it to the CDC Control task. Rename the data flow task **Inc Load SalesHeader**.

11. In the data flow area, add a CDC source adapter. Open the CDC Source Editor and set the ADO.NET connection manager to the one created in step 3 (TK463DW database).

12. Select the *stg.CDCSalesOrderHeader* table in the CDC Enabled Table drop-down list.

13. Set the CDC processing mode to Net, and select the *CDC_State* variable to contain the CDC state.

14. Click the Columns tab and observe that you have three additional columns for CDC processing logic. Click OK to close the editor.

15. Drag a CDC Splitter transformation to the data flow workspace and connect the CDC source adapter to the new CDC Splitter transformation. The CDC Splitter has multiple outputs based on the type of modification.

16. First you will store the new rows from the source table by adding an OLE DB destination adapter to the data flow area. Connect the CDC Splitter and the new OLE DB destination adapter. In the Input Output Selection dialog box, select InsertOutput in the Output drop-down list.

17. Open the OLE DB Destination Editor and set the connection manager to use TK463DW. Select *stg.SalesOrderHeader* as the target table. Select the Mappings tab to check whether every column is mapped correctly, and then click OK. Rename the OLE DB destination adapter **Insert new rows**.

For the rows that should be updated or deleted, you will use two additional tables to store these intermediate results so that you can later apply a set-based operation using T-SQL.

18. Open the SSMS and create two additional tables with a structure that is the same as the *stg.SalesOderHeader* table.

```
CREATE TABLE stg.tmpUpdateSalesOrderHeader
(
  SalesOrderID      INT NULL,
  OrderDate                       DATETIME NULL,
  SalesOrderNumber  NVARCHAR(50) NULL,
  CustomerID              INT NULL,
  SalesPersonID           INT NULL,
  TerritoryID             INT NULL,
  SubTotal                DECIMAL(16,6) NULL,
  TaxAmt                  DECIMAL(16,6) NULL,
  Freight                 DECIMAL(16,6) NULL
);
GO
CREATE TABLE stg.tmpDeleteSalesOrderHeader
(
  SalesOrderID      INT NULL,
  OrderDate                       DATETIME NULL,
  SalesOrderNumber  NVARCHAR(50)NULL,
  CustomerID              INT NULL,
  SalesPersonID           INT NULL,
  TerritoryID             INT NULL,
  SubTotal                DECIMAL(16,6) NULL,
  TaxAmt                  DECIMAL(16,6) NULL,
  Freight                 DECIMAL(16,6) NULL
);
```

19. Inside the IncLoadStgSalesHeader package, add an OLE DB destination adapter. Connect the CDC Splitter transformation with the new OLE DB destination adapter and, in the Input Output Selection dialog box, select UpdateOutput in the Output drop-down list.

20. Configure the OLE DB destination adapter to use the TK463DW connection manager, and select the *stg.tmpUpdateSalesOrderHeader* table. Click the Mappings tab and then click OK. Rename the OLE DB Destination adapter **Updated rows**.

21. Inside the IncLoadStgSalesHeader package, add another OLE DB destination adapter. Connect the CDC Splitter transformation with the new OLE DB destination adapter.

22. Configure the OLE DB destination adapter to use the TK463DW connection manager, and select the *stg.tmpDeleteSalesOrderHeader* table. Click the Mappings tab and then click OK. Rename the OLE DB Destination adapter **Deleted rows**.

23. On the Control Flow tab, drag an Execute SQL task to the control flow area and connect the existing data flow task with the new task.

24. Open the Execute SQL Task Editor, set the Connection property to TK463DW, and in the SQLStatement property, write a SQL statement to update the *stg.SalesOrderHeader* table.

```
UPDATE S
SET
OrderDate = U.OrderDate,
 SalesOrderNumber = U.SalesOrderNumber,
 CustomerID = U.CustomerID,
 SalesPersonID = U.SalesPersonID,
 TerritoryID = U.TerritoryID,
 SubTotal = U.SubTotal,
 TaxAmt = U.TaxAmt,
 Freight = U.Freight
FROM stg.SalesOrderHeader AS S
INNER JOIN stg.tmpUpdateSalesOrderHeader AS U ON S.SalesOrderID = U.SalesOrderID;
```

25. Click OK to close the editor, and rename the Execute SQL task **Update data**.

26. Add another Execute SQL task to the control flow and connect the existing Update Data Execute SQL task to the newly added task.

27. Open the Execute SQL Task Editor, set the Connection property to TK463DW, and in the SQLStatement property write a SQL statement to delete the data from the *stg.SalesOrderHeader* table based on the *stg.tmpDeleteSalesOrderHeader* table.

```
DELETE stg.SalesOrderHeader
WHERE SalesOrderID IN
 (SELECT SalesOrderID FROM stg.tmpDeleteSalesOrderHeader);
```

28. Click OK to close the editor, and rename the Execute SQL task **Delete data**.

29. In the control flow, add another CDC Control task and rename it **CDC End**. Connect the Delete Data Execute SQL task to the new CDC Control task.

30. Configure the CDC Control task with the same settings as the first one (CDC Start), but this time set the CDC Control Operation to Mark Processed Range. Your package should look like the one in Figure 7-11.

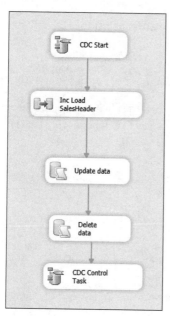

FIGURE 7-11 The final control flow for incremental CDC package.

31. Execute the package. The package should run successfully but with no changes, because there are no changes to the source table.

32. Modify the *stg.CDCSalesOrderHeader* table by executing the following UPDATE statement.

```
UPDATE stg.CDCSalesOrderHeader
SET TerritoryID = 6
WHERE SalesOrderID = 43659;
```

33. Execute the package and observe the data flow to notice one row being inserted into the *stg.tmpUpdateSalesOrderHeader* table.

34. Notice that there is a missing step to delete the data in stg.tmpDeleteSalesOrderHeader and stg.tmpUpdateSalesOrderHeader tables since each time you will run the package, additional data will be inserted in to these two tables. Drag an Execute SQL task from the SSIS Toolbox onto the control flow area. Rename the task "Truncate tables" and double-click the new task to open the editor.

35. Change the Connection property to use the TK463DW connection. In the SQL State-ment property of the Execute SQL Task Editor dialog box, type the following code

    TRUNCATE TABLE stg.tmpUpdateSalesOrderHeader;
    TRUNCATE TABLE stg.tmpDeleteSalesOrderHeader;

36. Set the Truncate tables Execute SQL task as the first task in the control flow by con-necting it with the CDC Start CDC Control Task.

37. Write different INSERT, UPDATE, and DELETE statements against the *stg.CDCSales-OrderHeader* table and test your package.

> **NOTE** **USING SSIS CDC FUNCTIONALITY ON AN ORACLE DATABASE**
>
> One of the new features introduced in SQL Server 2012 is the ability to use SQL Server CDC for tracking changes on an Oracle table. Also the new CDC functionality in SSIS supports an Oracle database.

Lesson Summary

- You can use expressions to dynamically set properties for tasks and transformations inside the data flow task.
- Use CDC when you cannot define an exact rule for changed data and when your source systems support this functionality.
- Use partitions for your fact tables and apply partition switching instead of deleting data.

Lesson Review

Answer the following questions to test your knowledge of the information in this lesson. You can find the answers to these questions and explanations of why each answer choice is correct or incorrect in the "Answers" section at the end of this chapter.

1. Which process modes in a CDC Source can be used directly to load data without ap-plying the additional ETL process of getting the current value of the row? (Choose all that apply.)

    A. Net

    B. All

    C. All with old value

    D. Net with merge

2. Which method can you use to dynamically set SQL inside SSIS at run time if you are using an OLE DB source adapter? (Choose all that apply.)

    A. Use a stored procedure as a source.

B. Use parameters inside the SQL statement.

C. Use expressions.

D. Use an SQL command from a variable.

3. Which guidelines are good to follow when you are applying an ETL strategy for incremental loading? (Choose all that apply.)

A. Use partitioning on fact tables.

B. Avoid fully cached lookups.

C. If you have an overlapping window with source data, first use the DELETE statement to remove overlapping rows in the fact table.

D. Load incremental data to a table that has the same structure as the destination fact table.

Lesson 3: Error Flow

Making ETL packages robust is an important task. This is difficult, because in the real world no data source is perfect. The problem is usually that you cannot predict that data coming from source systems will always be structured as you thought at design time. This means that you might be sent some data that would make your existing ETL package fail. It is important to capture such rows of data, route them to additional transformations, and notify either the administrators for ETL or data stewards. In this lesson, you look at using *error paths* to route failed rows to different subsets of components.

> **After this lesson, you will be able to:**
> - Implement error flows.
>
> **Estimated lesson time: 30 minutes**

Using Error Flows

SSIS includes the capability of routing "bad rows" away from the data flow and handling the data problem without affecting the good rows. As you learned in Chapter 5, data flow paths handle rows of data. In addition to the data paths, however, there are also error paths. You can see these in the data flow area as red connectors between data flow components. They contain data rows that fail in a component when the error rows are set to be redirected.

Not all components in the data flow use error paths. For example, the Multicast component only copies the data; it does not perform any operation on the data itself, so there is no possible point of failure, and there are no error paths. Components that use error paths include all source adapters, destination adapters, Lookup transformations, Conditional Split transformations, and so on.

To use error paths, you need to configure the error output. There are three options for handling errors in the data flow components:

- Setting the error output to Fail Transformation causes the data flow to fail if an error is encountered.

- Using the Ignore Failure option allows the row to continue out the normal green data path, but the value that resulted in the error is changed to NULL in the output.

- Setting the error output to Redirect Rows sends the error row out the red error path; this is the only way to handle errors with separate components.

These error-handling options are available for the entire row as well as for the operation for each column within the row. This does not mean that a single column gets redirected, but rather that some columns can be set to ignore failures, while errors in other columns cause redirects. Figure 7-12 shows the Configure Error Output dialog box, which you use to set the properties. To navigate to this dialog box, you can either double-click to edit the component and then select Configure Error Output, or you can simply drag the red error path output arrow onto the next component, which opens the same dialog box.

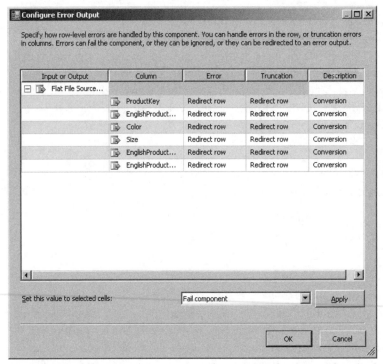

FIGURE 7-12 The Configure Error Output dialog box, in which you can set what happens when an error occurs.

Common reasons for using error path output are for text file source data that does not match the data type specified in the data flow or a Lookup transformation that does not find a match. Sometimes a destination runs into an error row if a constraint is violated when the inserts are performed. In addition, the error rows can be handled differently depending on whether you need to send them to a temporary table for review or whether you need to clean up the data and bring the rows back into the data flow through a Union All transformation.

 Quick Check

- Can you add an error flow path to the OLE DB destination adapter to store all rows that could not be loaded into a destination table?

Quick Check Answer

- Yes, this is a very useful feature when you are designing a robust ETL process.

PRACTICE **Using Error Flow**

In this practice, you will add an error flow path to a source adapter to capture all rows that do not match the data type specified in the data flow.

If you encounter a problem completing an exercise, you can install the completed projects from the Solution folder that is provided with the companion content for this chapter and lesson.

EXERCISE **Add Error Flow Paths**

In this exercise, you first create a package to read the product information from a flat file. You encounter an error when running the package because of a possible truncation of source data. This is a common error when data types do not match in the data flow. You then add an error flow path to capture these rows.

1. Start SSMS and connect to your SQL Server instance. Open a new query window by clicking the New Query button.

2. Create a dimension table named *dbo.Products*.

   ```
   USE TK463DW;
   CREATE TABLE dbo.Products
   (
   ProductKey    INT      NOT NULL,
   ProductName   NVARCHAR(50) NULL,
   Color         NVARCHAR(15) NULL,
   Size          NVARCHAR(50) NULL,
   SubcategoryName NVARCHAR(50) NULL,
   CategoryName   NVARCHAR(50) NULL,
   CONSTRAINT PK_Products PRIMARY KEY (ProductKey)
   );
   ```

3. If necessary, start SQL Server Data Tools, open the TK 463 Chapter 7 project, and then add a new package and rename it **DimProduct**.

4. Drag a data flow task from the SSIS Toolbox onto the control flow workspace. Rename the data flow task **Load Products**.

5. In the Data Flow area, add a Flat File source adapter. Right-click the Flat File source adapter and select Edit.

6. In the Flat File Source Editor dialog box, create a new connection manager by selecting New.

7. In Flat File Connection Manager Editor, change the name to **Products** and click Browse near the File Name text box. In the Open dialog box, find and select the Products.txt file in the Chapter07\Code directory. Select the Unicode check box.

8. Click the Advanced tab in the Flat File Connection Manager Editor and select Suggest Types. In the Suggest Column Types dialog box, leave the default values and click OK. This will create the preferred data types for your source columns.

9. Click OK to close the Flat File Connection Manager Editor and, in the Flat File Source Editor, select the newly created connection manager. Click the Columns tab and then click OK. Rename the Flat File Source adapter **Products**.

10. From the SSIS Toolbox, drag an OLE DB destination adapter and connect the Products Flat File source adapter to the new OLE DB destination adapter.

11. Open the OLE DB destination adapter, and under OLE DB Connection Manager, select TK463DW. Select the *dbo.Products* table and click the Mappings tab to make sure that everything is connected on the column level. Map the *EnglishProductName* column to *ProductName*, the *EnglishProductSubcategoryName* column to *SubcategoryName*, and the *EnglishProductCategoryName* column to the *CategoryName* column.

12. Rename the OLE DB destination **Dim Products** and execute the package.

13. The package fails. Select the Progress tab and read the data conversion error status text—Text Was Truncated Or One Or More Characters Had No Match In The Target Code Page.

14. Drag a Flat File destination adapter from the SSIS Toolbox. Connect the error data path from the Product Flat File source adapter to the new Flat File destination adapter. This will open a Configure Error Output dialog box. Set the value to Redirect Row for each row in the Error and Truncation columns.

15. Open the Flat File destination adapter and, in the Flat File Destination Editor dialog box, create a new Flat File connection manager by select New.

16. In the Flat File Format dialog box, select Delimited and click OK. In the Flat File Connection Manager Editor, set the name **ErrorRows** and under the File Name text box click Browse.

17. In the Open dialog box, browse to the Chapter07\Lesson3\Starter folder and, in the File Name text box, enter **ErrorRows**. Then click Open. Select the Unicode check box and click OK. This will create a new file called ErrorRows.txt at run time to store all source rows with an error.

18. In the Flat File Destination Editor, select the ErrorRows For Flat File connection manager and click the Mappings tab to observe how columns will be mapped. Click OK. Rename the Flat File destination **Error Products Rows**.

19. Execute the package. Notice that fifteen rows were transferred through the error path, and the package ran successfully.

Lesson Summary

- Error flow is a very powerful method for making your data flow task robust when you are loading data into a data warehouse.

- Use error flows to capture problematic rows and store them in a table or file for business users to inspect.

Lesson Review

Answer the following questions to test your knowledge of the information in this lesson. You can find the answers to these questions and explanations of why each answer choice is correct or incorrect in the "Answers" section at the end of this chapter.

1. Which data flow elements have an error flow? (Choose all that apply.)

   A. The OLE DB Source adapter

   B. The Union All transformation

   C. The Merge transformation

   D. The Lookup transformation

2. Which options are available for handling errors on the row level? (Choose all that apply.)

   A. Ignore failure

   B. Fail component

   C. Redirect row

   D. Delete row

3. Which data source adapters have an error flow? (Choose all that apply.)

   A. OLE DB source

   B. Raw File source

   C. ODBC source

   D. Excel source

Case Scenario

In the following case scenario, you apply what you've learned about enhancing data flow. You can find the answers to these questions in the "Answers" section at the end of this chapter.

Case Scenario: Loading Large Dimension and Fact Tables

You work for a telecommunication provider and you have to load the customer dimension and the call detail records (CDR) fact table. Your company has 2 million subscribers and you receive 5 million rows daily regarding CDR data.

You need to integrate this new source to an existing DW. Answer the following questions:

1. How would you load the Customer dimension table—should you use Slowly Changing Dimension task?

2. How would you create your fact table to store CDRs? How would you implement your daily loading of CDRs?

Suggested Practices

To help you successfully master the exam objectives presented in this chapter, complete the following tasks.

Load Additional Dimensions

In order to practice loading dimension tables and implementing change data capture functionality, prepare the following different packages.

- **Practice 1** Create a package to load the *dbo.Products* table by using a Slowly Changing Dimension task. Choose some attributes as Type 1 and some as Type 2 SCD.

- **Practice 2** Create a package to load the *dbo.Products* table by using CDC functionality and custom SCD logic to mimic the solution you came up with for Practice 1.

- **Practice 3** Create a fact table to store data from the *stg.SalesOrderHeader* table and implement the capability of passing a variable or a parameter to dynamically filter rows on the *OrderDate* column. Apply the necessary transformations and tasks to remove existing data based on this parameter and populate the fact table with new data.

Answers

This section contains answers to the lesson review questions and solutions to the case scenarios in this chapter.

Lesson 1

1. **Correct Answers: A, B, and D**

    A. **Correct:** Type 1 SCD is supported.

    B. **Correct:** Type 2 SCD is supported.

    C. **Incorrect:** Type 3 SCD is unsupported because Type 3 should add new columns.

    D. **Correct:** Support for inferred members is possible.

2. **Correct Answers: B and C**

    A. **Incorrect:** Data conversion is used for converting the data, not for comparing columns.

    B. **Correct:** You can write an expression comparing two or more columns in a Derived Column transformation.

    C. **Correct:** Conditional Split accepts expressions. You write different outputs based on column comparison.

    D. **Incorrect:** Multicast creates a logical copy of data. You cannot use it to compare columns.

3. **Correct Answers: B, C, and D**

    A. **Incorrect:** The Slowly Changing Dimension transformation uses the OLE DB Command transformation to update SCD Type 1 rows; this transformation is executed for each row.

    B. **Correct:** The Slowly Changing Dimension transformation supports inferred members.

    C. **Correct:** You can have more than one Slowly Changing Dimension transformation in one data flow.

    D. **Correct:** The Slowly Changing Dimension Wizard only supports connections with SQL Server databases.

Lesson 2

1. **Correct Answers: A and D**

   A. **Correct:** The Net option returns only the current value of the row.

   B. **Incorrect:** The All option returns all changes, and additional steps in ETL must be developed to get the latest value.

   C. **Incorrect:** This option has the same issue as the All option.

   D. **Correct:** The Net with merge option is similar to the Net option, but it returns UPDATE and INSERT operations as one.

2. **Correct Answers: A, B, and D**

   A. **Correct:** You can have a parameterized stored procedure and execute it with a parameter inside the OLE DB source adapter.

   B. **Correct:** The OLE DB source adapter supports parameters in an SQL statement.

   C. **Incorrect:** Expressions in the data flow do not allow you to set the query value at run time for the OLE DB source adapter.

   D. **Correct:** You can populate a variable with an SQL statement in SSIS and then use it as an SQL command inside the OLE DB source adapter.

3. **Correct Answers: A and D**

   A. **Correct:** Partitioning fact tables is a good strategy for incremental loading.

   B. **Incorrect:** Try to use fully cached lookups when loading fact tables to get the needed surrogate keys from dimension tables.

   C. **Incorrect:** Try to completely avoid the DELETE statement when loading the fact tables. Instead, use partition switching methods to control which rows need to be removed based on the overlapping window.

   D. **Correct:** When you are loading fact tables, it is a good practice to load incremental data to a table that has the same structure as the destination table and then use partition switching to replace the data.

Lesson 3

1. **Correct Answers: A and D**

   A. **Correct:** The OLE DB source adapter has an error flow.

   B. **Incorrect:** The Union All transformation does not have an error flow.

   C. **Incorrect:** The Merge transformation does not have an error flow.

   D. **Correct:** The Lookup transformation can route unmatched data to an error flow.

2. **Correct Answers: A, B, and C**

   A. **Correct:** Ignore failure is an available option.

   B. **Correct:** Fail component is an available option.

   C. **Correct:** Redirect row is an available option.

   D. **Incorrect:** Delete row is not a possible option.

3. **Correct Answers: A, C, and D**

   A. **Correct:** OLE DB source has an error flow.

   B. **Incorrect:** Raw File source does not have an error flow.

   C. **Correct:** ODBC source has an error flow.

   D. **Correct:** Excel source has an error flow.

Case Scenario

1. Based on the size of the data, you should not use the Slowly Changing Dimension task. It would be wise to implement some sort of CDC on the source data to get only changed rows from the source system. If this is impossible, then you should add an additional column in your dimension to store the hash value of the columns to allow you to compare what has changed without comparing each column. Based on the size of the data, also adding a MERGE statement using an Execute SQL task to apply the necessary INSERT and UPDATE operations to the dimension would be beneficial.

2. Create a fact table with multiple partitions—probably on a daily basis would be most useful if you have to reload the data for a specific day. Apply compression or, if using SQL Server 2012, use the column store index, because on a monthly basis you will get around 150 million rows and on a yearly basis 1.8 billion. The loading process should load the data into a heap table and then, by switching partitions and applying either compression or a column store index, include the new partition in the existing fact table.

## CHAPTER 8

Creating a Robust and Restartable Package

Exam objectives in this chapter:

- Extract and Transform Data
  - Manage SSIS package execution.
- Load Data
  - Design control flow.
  - Implement control flow.
- Configure and Deploy SSIS Solutions
  - Implement auditing, logging, and event handling.

Package development and implementation goes beyond just using transformations to apply the necessary logic to transfer data from sources to destinations. You must also implement error handling, and you must test and troubleshoot your packages as you develop them. As you learned in previous chapters, Microsoft SQL Server 2012 Integration Services (SSIS) provides several ways to handle errors at different levels of the SSIS architecture. For example, at the control flow level, you can add a failure constraint that redirects the workflow to a specified alternative task if an error occurs. Similarly, in the data flow, if a row causes an error in the transformation, you can send the row out an error path.

In this chapter, you will first look at capabilities in SSIS for making your packages more robust by configuring transactions and checkpoints. Then you will learn how to include event-handling capabilities that let you trap different events, such as the OnWarning and OnError events, and apply additional tasks in your package when such events occur.

Lessons in this chapter:

- Lesson 1: Package Transactions
- Lesson 2: Checkpoints
- Lesson 3: Event Handlers

Before You Begin

To complete this chapter, you must have:

- Basic knowledge of SISS control flow and data flow features and components.
- Experience working with SQL Server 2012 Management Studio (SSMS).
- Experience working with SQL Server Data Tools (SSDT) or SQL Server Business Intelligence Development Studio (BIDS).
- Practice working in the control flow and data flow.

Lesson 1: Package Transactions

Most relational databases such as SQL Server perform operations in atomic units. This means that a single statement or series of statements is either successful and affects data or is not successful and the system returns the data to the state it was in before the attempted statement execution. The unit of work that needs to be completed successfully in order for the data changes to be applied is called a *transaction*.

Transaction support is built into SSIS. Transaction support can be set at various package levels, and you can coordinate transactions through package restart ability. You can configure packages to allow initiation of a single transaction or multiple transactions, and you can set transaction inheritance so that a child package can inherit its parent package's transaction.

> **After this lesson, you will be able to:**
>
> - Understand different transaction possibilities in SSIS.
> - Enable and implement transactions in SSIS.
>
> **Estimated lesson time: 30 minutes**

Defining Package and Task Transaction Settings

You can set package transactions at the entire package level or at any control flow container level or task level. Transactions in SSIS use the *Microsoft Distributed Transaction Coordinator (MSDTC)*; the MSDTC service needs to be started on the computer for transactions to work. Any service or program that is enabled to work with the MSDTC can be part of a transaction in SSIS. This also means that the MSDTC allows you to perform distributed transactions—for example, updating a SQL Server database and an Oracle database in the same transaction.

To enable a transaction within a package, you need to set the TransactionOption property of the task or container to Required. The TransactionOption property exists at the package level and at the container level, as well as for almost any control flow task.

It can be set to one of the following:

- **Required**   If a transaction already exists, join it; if not, start a new transaction.
- **Supported**   If a transaction exists, join it (this is the default setting).
- **NotSupported**   The package, container, or task should not join an existing transaction.

Figure 8-1 shows the property values for a sequence container in the control flow area. Note that in this case the TransactionOption property value is set to Required.

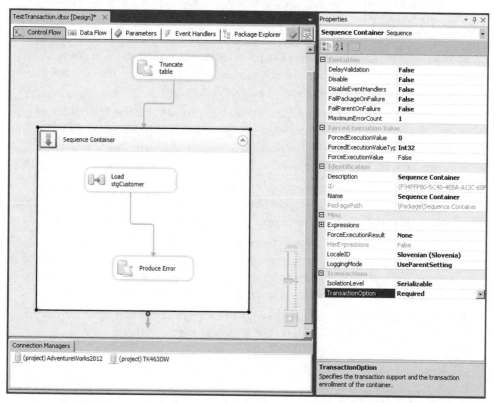

FIGURE 8-1 The TransactionOption property set to Required, enabling transactions in SSIS.

When deciding whether and how to implement a transaction, follow these guidelines:

- To enable transactions in SSIS, you must start the MSDTC service, and the tasks that you want to include as part of the transaction must work with MSDTC services natively.
- If a series of tasks must be completed as a single unit in which either all the tasks are successful and committed or an error occurs and none of the tasks are committed, place the tasks within a sequence container and set the TransactionOption property of the container to Required.

- A task can inherit the transaction setting of its parent when the TransactionOption property is set to Supported, which is the default setting for task or container creation.

- If you want to exclude a specific task from participating in a transaction, set the TransactionOption property to NotSupported.

- If you set the TransactionOption property of a Foreach Loop container or For Loop container to Required, a new transaction will be created for each loop of the container.

- Transactions work on the control flow level and not within a data flow. Therefore, you can turn on a transaction for a data flow task, but you cannot turn it on separately for selected components within the data flow; either the entire data process will be successful or it will be rolled back.

- Running your tasks in transactions requires additional overhead in terms of SSIS and has an impact on the performance of your packages, so use them only in cases when it is mandatory to execute your task as a single unit.

- Configuring the MSDTC to communicate across hosts and machine boundaries is usually a complex task (mixing a Windows environment with one that is not based on Windows). You must observe the possible timeouts and unexpected termination of connections on long-running queries.

- To enlist a data flow in a transaction, the underlying data provider used by your connection manager must also support MSDTC transactions. Microsoft providers typically support the MSDTC, but the same might not be true for third-party providers.

- By just observing your package in the control flow, you cannot distinguish between containers or tasks that actually support transactions or are configured to be part of transactions and those that are not. You must take an explicit look at the TransactionOption property for each of them to get the needed information.

- Not every task is able to roll back its work when a transaction fails. Tasks such as the XML task and the File System task do not support the transactions.

EXAM TIP

At times, you might want to enable a transaction for a container but exclude some of the tasks within the container. For example, if you have a couple of Execute SQL tasks that are used for auditing purposes in a container and the TransactionOption property for the container is set to Required, the logging tasks will also be rolled back if an error occurs. To prevent the auditing tasks from rolling back, set the TransactionOption property for those tasks to Not Supported. This will still let the other tasks in the container be in the transaction, but it will not include the auditing tasks as part of the transaction.

Transaction Isolation Levels

Transaction isolation levels control the degree of locking that occurs when data is being selected. Setting the transaction isolation level for a container or a task inside SSIS allows you to specify how strictly the transaction should be isolated from other transactions. In terms of the database, transaction isolation levels specify what data is visible to statements within a transaction. These levels directly affect the level of concurrent access by defining what interaction is possible between transactions against the same target data source.

You set the needed transaction isolation level in SSIS by specifying the IsolationLevel property of a task or container. The following isolation levels are supported:

- **Unspecified** A different isolation level than the one specified is being used, but the level cannot be determined. Set this value to an entire package to override the isolation levels inside the package and then use specific levels for containers or tasks inside the package.

- **ReadUncommitted** Does not lock the records being read. This means that an uncommitted change can be read and then rolled back by another client, resulting in a local copy of a record that is not consistent with what is stored in the database. This is called a *dirty read* because the data is inconsistent.

- **Chaos** Behaves the same way as ReadUncommitted, but checks the isolation level of other pending transactions during a write operation so that transactions with more restrictive isolation levels are not overwritten. Furthermore, it is not supported on the SQL Server platform, is not an ANSI standard Isolation level, and cannot be rolled back.

- **ReadCommitted** Locks the records being read and immediately frees the lock as soon as the records have been read. This prevents any changes from being read before they are committed, but it does not prevent records from being added, deleted, or changed by other clients during the transaction.

- **RepeatableRead** Locks the records being read and keeps the lock until the transaction completes. This ensures that the data being read does not change during the transaction.

- **Serializable** Locks the entire data set being read and keeps the lock until the transaction completes. This ensures that the data and its order within the database do not change during the transaction. This is the default value in SSIS.

- **Snapshot** The data read within a transaction will not reflect changes made by other simultaneous transactions. The transaction uses the data row versions that exist when the transaction begins. No locks are placed on the data when it is read. The Snapshot value of the IsolationLevel property is incompatible with package transactions. Therefore, you cannot use the IsolationLevel property to set the isolation level of package transactions to Shapshot. Instead, use an SQL query to set package transactions to Snapshot.

Quick Check

- Suppose you have a package to which you add a sequence container that contains several tasks, one that calls a command on a legacy system and another that is a data flow task that imports data into SQL Server. Both tasks have the Transaction-Option property set to Required. Even with the MSDTC service started and transactions turned on, your sequence container fails before tasks even run. What is the problem?

Quick Check Answer

- The transactions featured in SSIS use the MSDTC service. However, not all systems support the MSDTC, and a transaction cannot be forced on a noncompliant system, so the container will fail. You should remove the legacy task from the sequence container or set the TransactionOption property to NotSupported.

Manually Handling Transactions

In addition to the built-in functionality of transaction handling, it is also possible to manage transactions yourself. You do this by explicitly opening a transaction on the database layer, using the Execute SQL task and then executing an SQL statement to open a transaction. Figure 8-2 shows an example that uses a SQL Server database. This example first uses a SQL statement.

```
BEGIN TRAN;
```

Then it applies the necessary business logic using the data flow task, and finally it commits the transaction by using an additional Execute SQL task to run the statement.

```
COMMIT TRAN;
```

To manage transactions within multiple SSIS tasks, you must enable a behavior that allows you to retain a connection through the tasks. This can be done by setting the connection manager's RetainSameConnection property to True. When this is set up, the connection manager will attempt to reuse an existing connection when a task asks for one (instead of creating a new connection each time). By default, most SQL Server providers allow this property setting, but remember that the RetainSameConnection property is determined by the underlying provider; you will have to check to ensure that the provider supports this functionality.

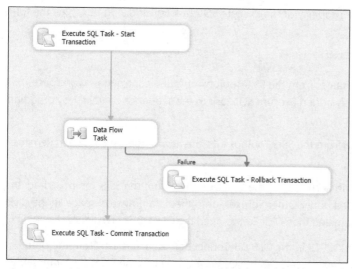

FIGURE 8-2 Adding manual transactional handling by adding multiple Execute SQL tasks.

Implementing Transactions

In this practice, you will test how transactions work in SSIS. You will first create a package to load a table. Then you will enable transactions and simulate an error by writing a custom SQL statement. You will put both tasks in a container to see whether the tasks are rolled back.

If you encounter a problem completing an exercise, you can install the completed projects from the Solution folder that is provided with the companion content for this chapter and lesson.

EXERCISE   Enable Transactions and Observe a Transaction Rollback

In this exercise, you use a data flow task to populate the *stg.Customer* table and then turn on transactions at the container level. Then you simulate an error and observe the result.

1. If you are missing the database objects from Chapter 5, "Designing and Implementing Data Flow," execute the needed SQL code from that chapter to have all the stage and dimension tables available in the TK463DW database.

2. Start SQL Server Data Tools (SSDT), open the TK 463 Chapter 8 project in the Starter folder, and then create a new package and rename it **TestTransactions**.

3. Drag an Execute SQL task from the SSIS Toolbox onto the control flow workspace. Rename the task **Truncate table** and double-click the new task to open the editor.

4. Change the Connection property to use the TK463DW connection.

5. In the SQL Statement property of the Execute SQL Task Editor dialog box, type the following code.

```
TRUNCATE TABLE stg.Customer;
```

6. Drag a sequence container from the SSIS Toolbox onto the control flow workspace. Connect the previously added Execute SQL task to the sequence container by dragging the green output arrow.

7. Drag a data flow task from the SSIS Toolbox into the new sequence container. Rename it **Load stgCustomer**.

8. Click the Data Flow tab at the top of the SSIS Designer. From the SSIS Toolbox, drag an OLE DB source, located under Other Sources, onto the data flow workspace. Right-click the OLE DB source item and then click Edit to open the OLE DB Source Editor dialog box.

9. Select AdventureWorks2012 in the OLE DB Connection Manager list. From the Data Access Mode drop-down list, select Table Or View, and select the *Sales.Customer* table in the Name Of The Table Or The View drop-down list. Click OK. Rename it **Person**.

10. From the SSIS Toolbox, drag an OLE DB destination object onto the data flow design surface. Connect the output of the OLE DB source named Person to the new OLE DB destination object by dragging the blue output arrow from the OLE DB source onto the OLE DB destination adapter.

11. Double-click the OLE DB destination adapter to display the OLE DB Destination Editor dialog box. Set the OLE DB connection manager to TK463DW and, from the Data Access Mode drop-down list, select Table Or View – Fast Load. Select the *stg.Customer* table.

12. On the Mapping tab of the OLE DB Destination Editor, check to make sure that all destination columns are mapped to input columns. Click OK.

13. In the control flow area, drag an Execute SQL task into the sequence container. Double-click the new task to open the editor.

14. Change the Connection property to use the TK463DW connection.

15. In the SQL Statement property of the Execute SQL Task Editor dialog box, type the following code.

```
UPDATE stg.Customer
SET CustomerID = 'ASD';
```

16. Click OK and rename the Execute SQL task **Produce Error**. Connect the data flow task to the new Execute SQL task.

17. Execute the package.

You will get an error in the last step—in the Produce Error task.

18. In SSMS, connect to TK463DW and write a SELECT statement against the populated table *stg.Customer*.

```
SELECT
    CustomerID, PersonId, StoreID, TerritoryID, AccountNumber, ModifiedDate
FROM stg.Customer;
```

You can see the loaded rows. This means that although you got an error in the last task in the package, the data flow task executed successfully. Now you will process the sequence container in a transaction so that if an error occurs in the last task, the loaded data will be rolled back.

19. On the control flow design surface, right-click the sequence container object and select Properties.

20. Set the TransactionOption property to Required by using the drop-down list.

21. Save the package by clicking the Save button on the toolbar. Check if the MSDTS is running by looking at windows services if Distributed Transaction Coordinator service is running.

22. Execute the package. Again an error occurs in the last task.

23. Go back to SSMS and execute the same SELECT statement as in step 18.

The table is empty because the transaction was rolled back in SSIS.

Lesson Summary

- You can enlist a container or a task to be part of a transaction.
- It is important to understand different transaction isolation levels.

Lesson Review

Answer the following questions to test your knowledge of the information in this lesson. You can find the answers to these questions and explanations of why each answer choice is correct or incorrect in the "Answers" section at the end of this chapter.

1. Which task in the control flow supports transactions? (Choose all that apply.)

   A. Data flow task

   B. Execute SQL task

   C. File System task

   D. XML task

2. Which transaction isolation level does not lock the records being read? (Choose all that apply.)

   A. Serializable

   B. Snapshot

   C. Chaos

   D. ReadUncommitted

3. Which T-SQL statements can you use to manually handle a transaction? (Choose all that apply.)

   A. BEGIN TRAN

   B. ROLLBACK TRAN

   C. END TRAN

   D. COMMIT TRAN

Lesson 2: Checkpoints

You can configure a package to start from the point of failure or from an earlier step when the package is rerun. In SSIS, this configuration process is called adding *checkpoints*. Checkpoints work together with transactions to enable package restartability.

> **After this lesson, you will be able to:**
>
> ■ Use checkpoints to restart your package from point of failure.
>
> **Estimated lesson time: 25 minutes**

Implementing Restartability Checkpoints

Sometimes you need to be able to restart a package if it fails, starting it at the point of failure, especially if you are working with complicated or long-running packages. In other words, you might not want successfully completed tasks to run again if you have to restart the package. You can accomplish this restartability by enabling checkpoints in the package.

To enable restartability within a package, you first must enable the package to use checkpoints and then set the specific tasks and containers to write checkpoints. To turn on checkpoints within a package, follow these steps:

1. Within the package, open the Properties window if necessary, and then click the Control Flow tab of the SSIS Designer, which will reveal the package properties.

2. Set the SaveCheckpoints property at the package level to True. This allows SSIS to save checkpoints during package execution.

3. For the CheckpointFileName property, provide a valid path and file name to the checkpoint file. Packages use files to maintain their state information, so if a package fails and is then restarted, the package can read the checkpoint file to determine where it left off and to track the state information at the last successful task.

4. Set the CheckpointUsage property to IfExists, which causes the package to run from the beginning if the checkpoint file is not present or to run from the identified point if the file exists. Figure 8-3 shows the package properties set in steps 1 through 4.

5. After you enable checkpoints in a package, the final step is to set checkpoints at the various tasks within your package. To do this, set the FailPackageOnFailure property at each task or container to True.

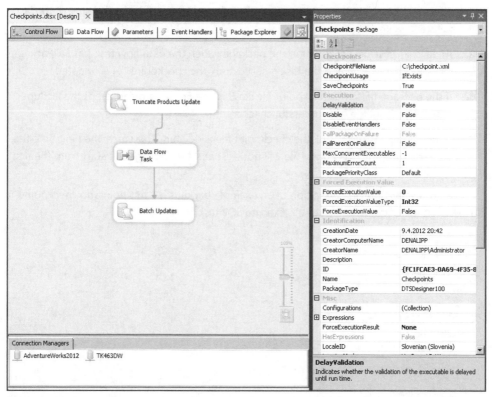

FIGURE 8-3 The CheckpointFileName, CheckpointUsage, and SaveCheckpoints properties set on the package level to enable checkpoints.

After you have performed the steps to set up checkpoints for your package, including the control flow objects, your packages are set up to restart in case of failure. Here is what happens when you run a package that has checkpoints enabled:

1. The package checks to see whether the checkpoint file exists. If the checkpoint file does not exist, the package begins at the first task (or parallel tasks) in the control flow. If the checkpoint file does exist, the package reads the file to find out where to start (and how to update the values of the variables and connections at the time of the last failure).

2. At each successful checkpoint in the package (when the data flow task has FailPackageOnFailure set to True and the task is successful), the checkpoint file is updated.

3. If the package fails, the checkpoint file stays in the file system and keeps the last update it had from the last successful checkpoint.

4. If the package is successful, the checkpoint file is deleted. Therefore, the next time the package runs, the checkpoint file will not exist and the package will start from the first task or tasks.

Figure 8-4 shows the first execution of an example package. At this point, no checkpoint file exists, so the package begins at the Execute SQL task.

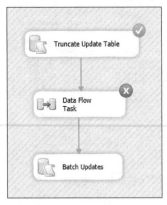

FIGURE 8-4 A package failing at the data flow task.

During the execution of the control flow shown in Figure 8-4, the Truncate Update Table task succeeds, and SSIS writes a checkpoint to the checkpoint file. However, the data flow task fails, which does not update the checkpoint file, so the package stops.

At this point, the failure is corrected in the data flow task, and the package is rerun. Figure 8-5 shows the control flow of the rerun package. As you can see, this failed at step 2 on the first run. After the problem was corrected, the second execution of the package started at step 2 and continued to completion.

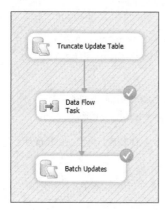

FIGURE 8-5 The second execution, in which the data flow task is the first task to run.

After completion of the last step, which is called Batch Updates in Figure 8-5, the checkpoint file was deleted.

EXAM TIP

If you set the CheckpointUsage property to Always, the checkpoint file must be present or the package will not start. In addition, using checkpoints is not allowed if you have set the TransactionOption of the package to Required.

By enabling checkpoints, you can save a lot of time on large and complex packages during subsequent execution by skipping the tasks that executed successfully in the last run and starting from the task that failed. Remember that you can enable a data flow task to participate in a checkpoint, but this does not apply inside the data flow task. This means that if you have three transformations inside the data flow task and execution fails on the third transformation, on subsequent execution the execution will start from the data flow task, and the first two transformations will run again before coming to the third one.

Setting and Observing Checkpoints in a Package

In this practice, you will set checkpoints in your package and observe how the package executes when you run it multiple times.

If you encounter a problem completing an exercise, you can install the completed projects from the Solution folder that is provided with the companion content for this chapter and lesson.

EXERCISE   Observe Checkpoints

In this exercise, you first enable checkpoints on the sequence container in the previously created package. Then you enable checkpoints on each specific task and run the package to observe how checkpoints work.

1.   Start SQL Server Data Tools, open the TK 463 Chapter 8 project under C:\TK463\ Chapter08\Lesson2\Starter\, and open the TestCheckpoints.tdsx package.

2.   Execute the package and notice that you get an error in the last task. If you restart the package, it will start from the first task.

3.   Now enable checkpoints by opening the Properties window on the Control Flow tab and changing the following package-level properties:

    A.   Set CheckPointFileName to C:\TK463\Chapter08\Lesson2\Starter\checkpoint.xml.

    B.   Set CheckPointUsage to IfExists.

    C.   Set SaveCheckpoints to True.

4.   Select the sequence container and, in the Properties window, set the FailPackageOn-Failure property to True.

5.   Execute the package. Stop the package in the debugger, and then check C:\TK463 \Chapter08\Lesson2\Starter\ in Windows Explorer for the existence of the check-point.xml file. This file contains the state information that was current when the package failed.

6.   Restart the package and notice that the execution starts from the sequence container. Now you will set checkpoints on both tasks inside the sequence container so that you can run the package only from the failed task onwards.

7.   Select the sequence container and, in the Properties window, set the FailPackageOn-Failure property to False.

8.   Select both tasks inside the sequence container and, in the Properties window, set the FailPackageOnFailure property to True.

9.   If you did not finish the previous exercise, please check if the checkpoint.xml file exists and delete it (in Windows Explorer, delete the checkpoint.xml file under C:\TK463\ Chapter08\Lesson2\Starter\).

10. Execute the package and then execute it again. Notice that it executed from the last task that has an error.

11. Modify the SQL statement in the Produce Error task by opening the Execute SQL Task Editor and changing the SQLStatement property to the following.

```
UPDATE stg.Customer
SET CustomerID = 1
WHERE PersonID = 1;
```

12. Click OK to close the SQL Task Editor, and rerun the package. Notice that only the last task was run, because you are using checkpoints. Check if the checkpoint.xml file was automatically deleted and rerun the package.

Lesson Summary

- Enable checkpoints to restart your package from the last successful step.
- Enable checkpoints on the package level and then for each task inside the control flow.

Lesson Review

Answer the following questions to test your knowledge of the information in this lesson. You can find the answers to these questions and explanations of why each answer choice is correct or incorrect in the "Answers" section at the end of this chapter.

1. Which properties do you need to set on the package level to enable checkpoints? (Choose all that apply.)
   A. CheckpointFileName
   B. CheckpointUsage
   C. SaveCheckpoints
   D. FailPackageOnFailure

2. On which SSIS objects can you set checkpoints to be active? (Choose all that apply.)
   A. Data flow task
   B. Control flow tasks
   C. Sequence container
   D. Sort transformation

3. Which statements are correct regarding SSIS checkpoints? (Choose all that apply.)
   A. You can have multiple checkpoint files per package.
   B. If the data flow task fails, you can store rows with errors in the checkpoint file.
   C. If the package is successful, the checkpoint file is deleted.
   D. If you set the CheckpointUsage property to Always, the checkpoint file must be present or the package will not start.

Lesson 3: Event Handlers

Packages, containers, and control flow tasks raise events at run time. SSIS provides the capability to listen for execution events and perform other operations when an event happens. This SSIS capability is called *event handling*. You can create custom event handlers to extend package functionality and make packages easier to manage at run time. Event handlers can perform tasks such as cleaning up temporary data storage when a package or task finishes running, or retrieving system information to assess resource availability before a package runs. You can also implement custom logging and auditing solutions for your ETL by using event handlers.

> **After this lesson, you will be able to:**
> - Implement event handlers.
>
> **Estimated lesson time: 30 minutes**

Using Event Handlers

Event handlers use the control flow paradigm for workflow processing, which includes all the same control flow tasks and containers that are in the SSIS Toolbox in the control flow design area. You can define any number of event handlers for a package. To add an event handler to a package, follow these steps:

1. Click the Event Handlers tab in the SSIS Designer.

2. Select the executable component for an event handler from the Executable drop-down list, as shown in Figure 8-6.

3. Select an event from the Event Handler drop-down list.

4. Using the SSIS Toolbox, drag the tasks to be executed based on selected scope and event.

The executable component is the task, container, or even a package itself that triggers the event. The event handler is the actual event that causes the event workflow to execute. Table 8-1 explains different event handler types.

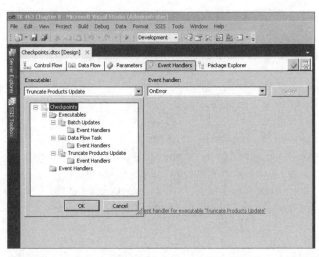

FIGURE 8-6 Defining event handlers on the Event Handlers tab of the SSIS Designer.

TABLE 8-1 Event Handler Types

Event handler	Description
OnError	Runs when an executable component reports an error
OnExecStatusChanged	Runs for all tasks and containers when the execution status changes to In Process, Success, or Failed
OnInformation	Runs when SSIS displays information messages during the validation and execution of a task or container
OnPostExecute	Runs after a container or task successfully completes
OnPostValidate	Executes after the task or container has been successfully validated
OnPreExecute	Runs before an executable component is executed
OnPreValidate	Runs before a component is validated by the engine
OnProgress	Executed when a progress message is sent by the SSIS engine, indicating tangible advancement of the task or container
OnQueryCancel	Invoked when an Execute SQL task is canceled through manual intervention, such as stopping the package
OnTaskFailed	Similar to OnError, but runs when a task fails rather than each time an error occurs
OnVariableValueChanged	Runs when the value changes in a variable for which the RaiseChangeEvent property is set to True
OnWarning	Runs when a task returns a warning event such as a column not being used in a data flow

In addition, event handlers assigned to an executable scope propagate down to child events when the event fires. If an event is assigned to a container, the child executable files include the tasks and containers that are embedded within the parent container. This means that if you assign an OnError event to the package and an OnError event occurs at the task level, the event handler fires both for the task and the package (and for any containers between).

> *NOTE* **DEVELOPING A CUSTOM AUDITING AND LOGGING PROCESS**
>
> You can use event handlers to develop a custom auditing and logging process. Each package contains a set of system variables that are updated for the various levels in the package during package execution. With event handlers, you can capture these variables and values, which provide contextual information such as the ErrorCode, ErrorDescription, and SourceName (the task), when the event fires.

PRACTICE **Implementing Event Handlers**

In this practice, you will add additional steps to the package created in the first lesson to use event handlers. These event handlers will clean the target table if an error occurs inside the sequence container and write data to a text file if an error occurs in the last Execute SQL task.

If you encounter a problem completing an exercise, you can install the completed projects from the Solution folder that is provided with the companion content for this chapter and lesson.

EXERCISE Use Event Handlers

In this exercise, you first create an event handler process for an OnError event for a sequence container. Next you add an additional step in the Execute SQL task that is in the sequence container to write data to a flat file in case of an error.

1. If necessary, start SQL Server Data Tools (SSDT), open the TK 463 Chapter 8 project, and then open the EventHandlers package.

2. Notice that this is the same package as in the exercise in Lesson 1, without enabled transactions. Execute the package.

3. In SSMS, connect to TK463DW and write a SELECT statement against the populated *stg.Customer* table.

```
SELECT
  CustomerID, PersonId, StoreID, TerritoryID, AccountNumber, ModifiedDate
FROM stg.Customer;
```

4. You can see the loaded rows. This means that although you got an error in the last task in the package, the data flow task executed successfully.

   Now you will add a process that truncates the target table if an error occurs in any task inside the sequence container.

5. Click the Event Handlers tab.

6. In the Executable drop-down list, select Sequence Container, and in the Event Handler drop-down list, select OnError. Click in the design area to create this event handler.

7. Drag an Execute SQL task from the SSIS Toolbox onto the control flow workspace. Rename the task **Truncate table** and double-click the new task to open the editor.

8. Change the Connection property to use the TK463DW connection.

9. In the SQL Statement property of the Execute SQL Task Editor dialog box, type the following code.

```
TRUNCATE TABLE stg.Customer;
```

10. Execute the package. In SSMS, execute the same SELECT statement as in step 3 and notice that the table is empty. Because you received an error in the sequence container, the OnError event handler was executed and truncated the table.

11. Add another event handler by selecting the Event Handlers tab. In the Executable drop-down list, select the Produce Error task, and in the Event Handler drop-down list, select OnError. Click in the design area to create this event handler.

12. Drag a data flow task from the SSIS Toolbox onto the Event Handler design area.

13. Double-click the data flow task. From the SSIS Toolbox, drag an OLE DB source adapter onto the data flow workspace. Right-click the OLE DB source item and then click Edit to open the OLE DB Source Editor dialog box.

14. Select TK463DW in the OLE DB Connection Manager list. From the Data Access Mode drop-down list, select Table Or View, and select the *stg.Customer* table in the Name Of The Table Or The View drop-down list.

15. From the SSIS Toolbox, drag a Flat File destination adapter onto the data flow workspace. Connect the OLE DB source and the new Flat File destination adapter. Right-click the Flat File destination adapter and then click Edit to open the editor.

16. In the Flat File Destination Editor dialog box, click New to define a new flat file connection manager. In the File Format dialog box, select Delimited.

17. In the Flat File Connection Manager Editor, click Browse near the File Name text box and, in the Open dialog box, enter **C:\TK463\Chapter08\Code\stgCustomerError.txt** and click OK to return to the editor. Set the code page to 1252 (ANSI – Latin I) and select the Column Names In The First Data Row check box.

18. Select the Columns tab and set the Column delimiter to Semicolon. Click OK to close the Flat File Connection Manager Editor.

19. Inside the Flat File Destination Editor, select the new flat file connection manager and click the Mappings tab. Check that everything is correctly mapped. Click OK.

20. Execute the package.

21. Using SSMS, check that the *stg.Customer* table is empty and that you created a file named C:\TK463\Chapter08\Code\stgCustomerError.txt.

EXAM TIP

You can turn off event handlers for any task or container by setting the DisableEvent-Handlers property of the task or container to True. So if you have an event handler defined but you do not want it to be invoked for a specific task, you can turn off event handlers for that task only.

Lesson Summary

- Event handlers enable you to have more control over the execution of a package.
- You can use all the control flow tasks and containers when creating event handlers.
- Use event handlers if you need to integrate the execution information of SSIS packages into a central logging database.

Lesson Review

Answer the following questions to test your knowledge of the information in this lesson. You can find the answers to these questions and explanations of why each answer choice is correct or incorrect in the "Answers" section at the end of this chapter.

1. Which components in SSIS can act as executable components that trigger an event? (Choose all that apply.)

   A. Sequence container

   B. Package

   C. Data flow task

   D. Data flow transformation

2. Which event handler types can you use if you want to log all the package errors? (Choose all that apply.)

   A. OnPostExecute

   B. OnError

   C. OnWarning

   D. OnTaskFailed

3. Which event handler types can you use if you want to log information before the task starts in the package? (Choose all that apply.)

   A. OnTaskFailed

   B. OnProgress

   C. OnPreExecute

   D. OnWarning

Case Scenario

In the following case scenario, you apply what you've learned about creating a robust and restartable package. You can find the answers to these questions in the "Answers" section at the end of this chapter.

Case Scenario: Auditing and Notifications in SSIS Packages

You are creating a set of SSIS packages to move data from a data warehouse to data mart tables. You need to ensure that your database is in a consistent state and not in an intermediate state when an error occurs. In addition, you need to prepare an audit trail of information and build alerts into your package design.

How would you handle the following requirements?

1. Each destination table in you data mart must have its inserts and updates fully complete and committed; otherwise you need to roll back the changes so that the table is in a consistent state. You also need a way to restart the packages from the point of failure.

2. You need to capture the count of rows that are inserted into the destination tables.

3. When a package fails, you must immediately send email messages that identify the task that failed and describe the error.

Suggested Practices

To help you successfully master the exam objectives presented in this chapter, complete the following tasks.

Use Transactions and Event Handlers

In order to practice what you have learned in this chapter, you will modify the packages created in this chapter to include custom transaction handling and a simple audit solution.

- **Practice 1** Take the package created in the exercise in Lesson 1 and implement custom transaction handling on the database layer by using an Execute SQL task.

- **Practice 2** Take the package created in the exercise in Lesson 1 and add an event handler that will store the number of rows processed by the data flow task on successful execution of the task. Also create the necessary audit table.

Answers

This section contains answers to the lesson review questions and solutions to the case scenario in this chapter.

Lesson 1

1. **Correct Answers: A and B**

    A. **Correct:** Data flow supports transactions.

    B. **Correct:** The Execute SQL task supports transactions.

    C. **Incorrect:** The File System task does not provide a rollback mechanism, so it cannot support transactions.

    D. **Incorrect:** The XML task does not provide a rollback mechanism, so it cannot support transactions.

2. **Correct Answers: B, C, and D**

    A. **Incorrect:** Serializable is the strictest isolation level.

    B. **Correct:** Snapshot isolation does not lock the data.

    C. **Correct:** Chaos is similar to ReadUncommitted, but it checks the isolation level of other pending transactions during a write operation.

    D. **Correct:** ReadUncommitted is the least restrictive isolation level because it ignores locks placed by other transactions.

3. **Correct Answers: A, B, and D**

    A. **Correct:** You start the transaction by executing the BEGIN TRAN statement.

    B. **Correct:** You can roll back the transaction by executing the ROLLBACK TRAN statement.

    C. **Incorrect:** END TRAN is not a valid T-SQL statement.

    D. **Correct:** You can commit the transaction by executing the COMMIT TRAN statement.

Lesson 2

1. **Correct Answers: A, B, and C**

    A. **Correct:** CheckpointFileName defines a file for checkpoints.

    B. **Correct:** CheckpointUsage sets the usage for checkpoints.

    C. **Correct:** SaveCheckpoints saves the checkpoint states.

    D. **Incorrect:** The FailPackageOnFailure property is used for tasks that should be part of checkpoint checks. It is not set on the package level.

2. **Correct Answers: A, B, and C**

   A. **Correct:** All control flow tasks can be used.

   B. **Correct:** All control flow tasks can be used.

   C. **Correct:** All control flow containers can be used.

   D. **Incorrect:** You cannot put a checkpoint on any data flow transformation.

3. **Correct Answers: C and D**

   A. **Incorrect:** You can only have one checkpoint file per package.

   B. **Incorrect:** No data-level information can be stored in the checkpoint file.

   C. **Correct:** If the package runs successfully, the checkpoint file is deleted.

   D. **Correct:** You must have the checkpoint file created.

Lesson 3

1. **Correct Answer: A, B, and C**

   A. **Correct:** The sequence container can act as an executable component for an event.

   B. **Correct:** The package level also can set up event handlers.

   C. **Correct:** The data flow task is part of control flow tasks, so you can enable it for event handling.

   D. **Incorrect:** You cannot put an event handler in a specific data transformation.

2. **Correct Answer: B and D**

   A. **Incorrect:** The OnPostExecute event triggers after the execution and not only when an error occurs.

   B. **Correct:** The OnError event captures all errors.

   C. **Incorrect:** Warnings are not the same as errors; the package will not fail.

   D. **Correct:** If task fails, this event is triggered.

3. **Correct Answer: C**

   A. **Incorrect:** The OnTaskFailed event triggers after the task has failed.

   B. **Incorrect:** The OnProgress event triggers when a progress message is sent by the SSIS engine.

   C. **Correct:** You can use the OnPreExecute event trigger to log information before the task starts.

   D. **Incorrect:** The OnWarning event triggers when a task returns a warning event.

Case Scenario

1. Because the commit level is configured on a table-by-table basis, all the data flow and control flow tasks that operate on a single task need to be grouped together in a container, and the TransactionOption property must be set to Required for each container. You should also implement checkpoints on the containers, which will let you restart the packages at the point of failure after you have resolved the problems. You can simplify this implementation by creating a master package that has checkpoints turned on and that uses the Execute Package task to call child packages for each destination table that has transactions enabled.

2. To capture the destination row count, you add several Row Count transformations to your package. Place a Row Count transformation in the pipeline before each destination and store the number of rows inside a variable. To capture the variable values, set the RaiseChangeEvent property to True and add the OnVariableValueChange event handler. This event will fire each time the variable value has changed, and you can then use an SQL statement to store the number of rows to a tracking table.

3. Using an OnError event, you can create a new event handler on the package level. You can then add a Send Mail task to the event handler and configure it to send an email message when any tasks fail. You can use the *SourceName* and *ErrorDescription* system variables to identify which task failed and to get the error description.

## CHAPTER 9

Implementing Dynamic Packages

Exam objectives in this chapter:

- Extract and Transform Data
  - Define connection managers.
- Load Data
  - Implement package logic by using SSIS variables and parameters.

When you are developing Microsoft SQL Server Integration Services (SSIS) packages, it is a good practice to make each task or transformation as dynamic as possible. This enables you to move your packages from one environment to another (for example, from development to a test environment, and then to a production environment) without opening and changing the package. You can also configure your packages to set different properties at run time.

To do this, you can use the new features in SQL Server 2012, such as parameters and project-level connection managers, or you can use the package configurations that were first made available in the package deployment model in earlier versions of SQL Server. This chapter discusses both possibilities for designing and configuring your package to dynamically set values at run time. Using dynamic packages eliminates the need to make changes as you move from one environment to the other or to open the project when you want to run your packages using different property or variable values.

Lessons in this chapter:

- Lesson 1: Package-Level and Project-Level Connection Managers and Parameters
- Lesson 2: Package Configurations

Before You Begin

To complete this chapter, you must have:

- Basic knowledge of SQL Server 2012 SISS control flow and data flow features and components.

- Experience working with SQL Server 2012 Management Studio (SSMS).

- Experience working with SQL Server Data Tools (SSDT) or SQL Server Business Intelligence Development Studio (BIDS).

- An understanding of the basics of file copying and security.

- Knowledge of system environment variables.

Lesson 1: Package-Level and Project-Level Connection Managers and Parameters

In SQL Server 2012, SSIS introduces parameters and project-level connection managers. Parameters enable you to assign values to properties within packages at the time of package execution. Project-level connection managers allow you to define the data source connection once and use it in all packages that are part of the project. Both features are available only to projects developed for the project deployment model. This means that SSIS packages created with prior versions of SQL Server have to be upgraded to the new project deployment model if you want to use these new features.

 Both functionalities are a replacement for the package configurations used in previous versions of SQL Server. In SQL Server 2012, SSIS also takes advantage of *build configurations* from Microsoft Visual Studio, which enable you to define multiple configurations and set the values of your parameters per configuration. This makes it easier to debug and deploy packages in SQL Server Data Tools against different SSIS servers.

> **After this lesson, you will be able to:**
>
> - Understand the difference between package-level and project-level connection managers.
>
> - Implement parameters.
>
> - Use property expressions to make your packages dynamic.
>
> **Estimated lesson time: 30 minutes**

Using Project-Level Connection Managers

Project-level connection managers allow you to set up a connection manager on the project level. This means that you can define a connection for the whole project and use it in all packages that are part of the project. In prior versions of SQL Server, the connections were always contained within each package.

To create a project-level connection, define a new connection manager by right-clicking Connection Managers in Solution Explorer under your project and selecting the New Connection Manager option. An alternative method is to convert an existing package-level connection to a project-level connection. You can do this by opening the package, right-clicking the connection you want to convert in the Connection Managers window, and selecting Convert To Project Connection, as shown in Figure 9-1.

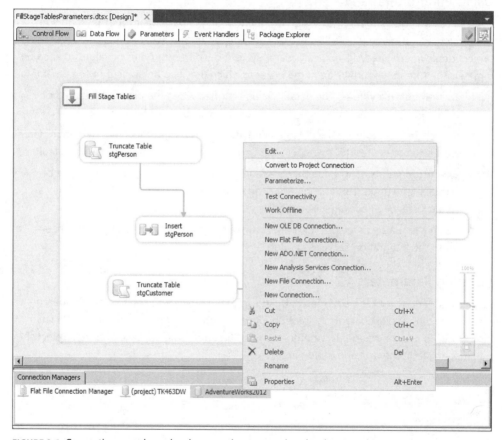

FIGURE 9-1 Converting a package-level connection to a project-level connection.

Project-level connections are a very useful new feature when it comes to developing and maintaining your packages. Note that in cases when you need to have a connection available only for the specific package, you can still create a connection at the package scope.

Parameters

In SQL Server 2012, SSIS introduces parameters. Parameters allow you to assign values to properties within packages at the time of package execution. They can also be used in SSIS expressions—for example, to use an Expression task to set a variable value based on the specific value of the parameter. There are two types of parameters: project parameters, which are created on the project level, and package parameters, which are created at the package level. You can use and set parameters only in projects developed for the project deployment model. When you are using the project deployment model, projects are deployed to the *Integration Services catalog*. Details regarding deployment possibilities are explained later in Chapter 11, "Installing SSIS and Deploying Packages."

Using Parameters

You can use a single parameter to assign a value to multiple package properties, and you can use a parameter in multiple SSIS expressions. Depending on where the project is in the project deployment life cycle, you can assign up to three different types of values to each parameter. The three types are listed in the order in which they can be applied to the parameter:

- **Design default value** The default value assigned when the project is created or edited in SQL Server Data Tools (SSDT). This value persists with the project.

- **Server default value** The default value assigned during project deployment or later, while the project resides in the SSIS catalog. This value overrides the design default.

- **Execution value** The value that is assigned in reference to a specific instance of package execution. This assignment overrides all other values but applies to only a single instance of package execution.

Note that the last two types of values become relevant after the SSIS project has been deployed to the Integration Services catalog.

Defining Parameters

You add project or package parameters by using SSDT. Usually you create a project parameter by selecting Project.params in Solution Explorer under your project name, as shown in Figure 9-2. To add a package parameter, you must first open the package and then select the parameters tab in the package design area.

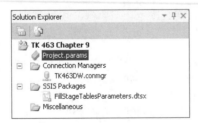

FIGURE 9-2 Solution Explorer with Project.params selected.

When you open the package or project parameters window, you can define a new parameter by clicking the Add Parameter icon (the first icon on the left; it looks like a blue cube). Figure 9-3 shows a parameter window with one parameter called pTK463DWConnectionString.

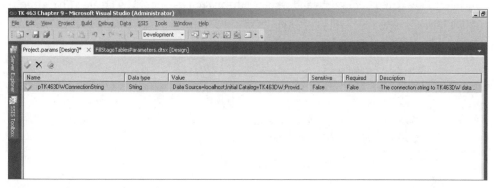

FIGURE 9-3 The parameters window.

When you create a parameter in SSDT, there are several properties to specify:

- **Name** The name of the parameter. The first character of the name must be a letter or an underscore.

- **Data type** The data type of the parameter.

- **Value** The default value for the parameter assigned at design time. This is also known as the design default.

- **Sensitive** If the value of this property is True, parameter values are encrypted in the catalog and appear as NULL when viewed with Transact-SQL or SQL Server Management Studio.

- **Required** Requires that a value other than the design default be specified before the package can be executed.

- **Description** For maintainability, the description of the parameter. In SSDT, set the parameter description in the Visual Studio Properties window when the parameter is selected in the applicable parameters window.

EXAM TIP

Parameter design values are stored in the project file.

You can edit parameters in the list in the parameter window, or you can use the Properties window to modify the values of parameter properties. You can delete a parameter by using the Delete Parameter toolbar button. By using the Add Parameters To Configurations toolbar button (the last button on the right), you can specify a value for a parameter for a specific build configuration that is used only when you execute the package in SQL Server Data Tools. Build configurations are explained in the next topic.

Another approach to creating a parameter is to do so implicitly by right-clicking a control flow task or a connection manager and selecting the Parameterize option. A Parameterize dialog box opens, as shown in Figure 9-4. Here you can specify which property should be dynamically evaluated at run time and whether the parameter should be created (the latter is specified by selecting the Create New Parameter option).

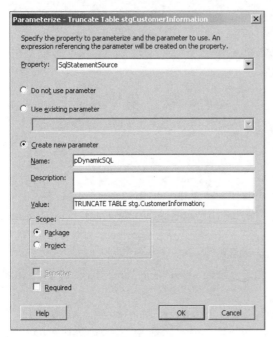

FIGURE 9-4 The Parameterize dialog box.

EXAM TIP

You cannot change the value of a parameter while a package is running.

Build Configurations in SQL Server 2012 Integration Services

Build configurations in Visual Studio provide a way to store multiple versions of solution and project properties. The active configuration can be quickly accessed and changed, allowing you to easily build multiple configurations of the same project. Two levels of build configurations can be defined in Visual Studio: solution configurations and project configurations.

The new project deployment model in SQL Server 2012 takes advantage of more possibilities for build configurations from Visual Studio than earlier versions did. You can now set project and package parameters to get values from build configurations. Also, some of the project-level properties can be set via build configurations (for example, deployment server name and server project path).

Creating Build Configurations

A project can have a set of defined project properties for every unique combination of a configuration and platform. You can create an additional project or solution configuration by using the Configuration Manager:

1. Select the Configuration Manager option from the Configurations drop-down list on the Standard toolbar to open the Configuration Manager dialog box. Alternatively, you can first open the project's Property Pages dialog box (right-click the project name in Solution Explorer and select Properties), as shown in Figure 9-5, and click the Configuration Manager button.

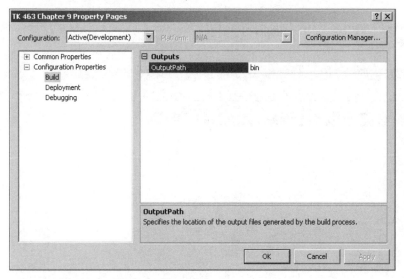

FIGURE 9-5 The project Property Pages dialog box.

2. In the Active Solution Configuration drop-down list, select New.

3. In the New Solution Configuration dialog box, enter the name of the solution configuration you would like to create. Select the Create New Project Configurations check box to also create the project configuration.

You can now change the active configuration directly from the Solution Configurations drop-down list on the Standard toolbar or from the Configuration Manager dialog box.

Using Build Configurations

You can bind parameter values to build configurations by using the parameter window:

1. Open the project or package parameters window.

2. In the parameters window, select the last toolbar button on the left (Add Parameters To Configurations).

3. In the Manage Parameter Values dialog box that appears, you can add values for each parameter for each configuration. Click the Add button to add a parameter to the configuration.

4. In the Add Parameters window, select parameters and click OK.

5. Set the appropriate values of parameters for your configurations, as shown in Figure 9-6.

Figure 9-6 shows that the pNoOfRows parameter will have a value of 10,000 when the package is executed using the Production configuration and 100 when using the Development configuration. This means that if you have multiple parameters and need to change the value of the parameters at design time when you are developing or debugging the SSIS project, you just need to switch between build configurations to have all parameter values changed at once.

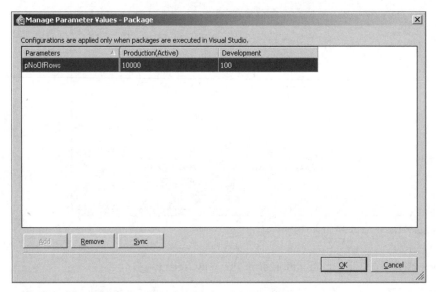

FIGURE 9-6 Managing parameter values.

You can also use build configurations to set build, deployment, and debugging configuration properties for a project. To assign different project properties based on configuration, right-click the project in Solution Explorer and select Properties. Figure 9-7 shows the deployment properties inside the project's Property Pages dialog box. If you have to deploy your project to multiple servers, you can set different values for the Server Name and Server Project Path properties for each configuration, so that you can quickly switch between deployment environments at design time by using configurations.

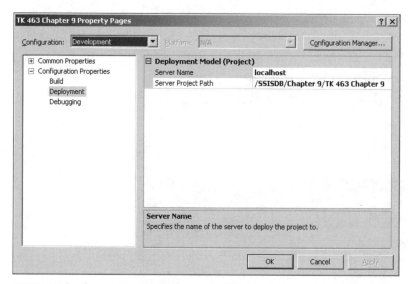

FIGURE 9-7 Deployment properties in a project's Property Pages dialog box.

Property Expressions

In previous chapters, you saw some examples of setting connection managers or control flow task properties at run time. The SSIS expressions used to update properties of the control flow during package execution are called *property expressions*. You can apply a property expression in two ways. First, you can set the property as an expression through the properties window by clicking the ellipsis (...) button of the Expressions property. This will open the Property Expression Editor, as shown in Figure 9-8. In this dialog box, you can select a property from the drop-down list and then type an expression.

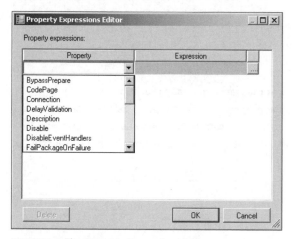

FIGURE 9-8 The Property Expressions Editor.

The second way to set property expressions is to use the task or container editors, which offer one or more ways to set properties through expressions. Figure 9-9 shows the Execute SQL Task Editor. On the Expressions tab, you can specify property expressions.

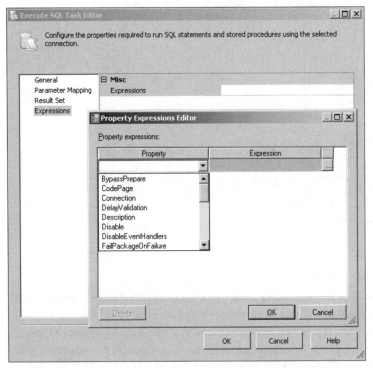

FIGURE 9-9 The Property Expressions Editor opened from the Expressions tab.

 Quick Check

- When are property expressions evaluated as a package is running?

Quick Check Answer

- Unlike parameters that are read at the start of package execution, property expressions are updated when the property is accessed by the package during package execution. A property expression can change the value of a property in the middle of package execution, so that the new value is read when the property is needed by the package.

EXAM TIP

You can also update the value of connection properties while a package is running. This capability is especially useful when you have a Foreach Loop that is iterating over files. You can use a variable to indicate that the full path is being captured and update the connection for the file with a property expression. Remember that you cannot use a parameter in this case to store the full file path, because parameter values cannot change while a package is running.

PRACTICE **Implementing Parameters**

In this practice, you will use parameters to make your packages dynamic. In the first exercise you will parameterize the connection string, and in the second exercise you will use a parameter value to filter the source query in the data flow task. The third exercise focuses on setting up an additional build configuration to test project execution against another database.

If you encounter a problem completing an exercise, you can install the completed projects from the Solution folder that is provided with the companion content for this chapter and lesson.

EXERCISE 1   Set a Parameter for a Connection String

In this exercise, you parameterize a connection string by using a project parameter.

1. If you are missing the database objects from Chapter 5, "Designing and Implementing Data Flow," execute the needed SQL code from that chapter to have all the stage and dimension tables available in the TK463DW database.

2. Start SQL Server Data Tools, open the TK 463 Chapter 9 project in the Starter folder, and then open the FillStageTablesParameters.dtsx package.

   Notice that this package is using two connections, AdventureWorks2012 and TK463DW.

3. In the Connection Managers window, right-click the TK463DW connection and select Convert To Project Connection. You have changed the connection from the package level to the project level and can now see this connection in the Solution Explorer window in the Connection Managers folder. The TK463DW connection can now be used by any other package within the same SSIS project.

4. Right-click Project.params in Solution Explorer, and then click Open or double-click Project.params to open it.

5. Click the Add Parameter button on the toolbar.

6. Name the parameter by setting the Name property to **pTK463DWConnString** and set the Data Type property to String. In the Value property field, type **Data Source=localhost;Initial Catalog=TK463DW;Provider=SQLNCLI11.1;Integrated Security=SSPI;**.

7. Close the Project.params window.

8. Inside the FillStageTablesParameters package, right-click the (project) TK463DW connection in the Connection Managers window and select Parameterize.

9. In the Parameterize dialog box, select the Use Existing Parameter check box and select the pTK463DWConnString parameter in the drop-down list. Notice that the project parameter name starts with $Project::. Click OK to close the Parameterize dialog box.

10. Look at the (project) TK463DW connection in the Connection Managers window and notice a small icon next to it reflecting that this connection is parameterized.

EXERCISE 2   Use a Parameter in the Data Flow Task

In this exercise, you create a package-level parameter that will be used to filter source data. You will use this parameter in the data flow task to filter only rows from the source for which the year of the modified date is equal to or greater than the parameter value.

1. If necessary, start SQL Server Data Tools, open the TK 463 Chapter 9 project, and then open the FillStageTablesParameters.dtsx package from the previous exercise for editing.

2. Select the Parameters tab and click the Add Parameter button on the toolbar.

3. Name the parameter by setting the Name property to **pYear** and set the Data Type property to Int16. For the Value property, enter **2002**.

4. Click the Data Flow tab and open the Person OLE DB Source adapter.

5. In the OLE DB Source Editor, change the data access mode to SQL Command and enter the following SELECT statement to retrieve the necessary rows and use a parameter placeholder inside the query.

```
SELECT
  BusinessEntityID,
  PersonType,
  NameStyle,
  Title,
  FirstName,
  MiddleName,
  LastName,
  Suffix,
  EmailPromotion,
  AdditionalContactInfo,
  Demographics,
  rowguid,
    ModifiedDate
FROM
  Person.Person
WHERE
  YEAR(ModifiedDate) >= ?
```

6. Click the Parameters button to open the Set Query Parameters dialog box.

7. For the Variables property, select the $Package::pYear parameter as the source for the query parameter. Click OK twice to close the window and the OLE DB Source Editor.

8. Execute the package and observe the number of rows displayed in the data flow area.

9. Change the parameter value to **2008** and execute the package. Notice that fewer rows are read from the OLE DB Source adapter in the data flow area.

EXERCISE 3   Use Build Configurations

In this exercise, you create an additional database, TK463DWProd, and then create a new build configuration in Visual Studio to use this database when running the SSIS package build from the previous exercise.

1. Start SSMS and connect to your SQL Server instance. Open a new query window by clicking the New Query button.

2. You will create a new database and the *stg.Person* table so that you can execute the SSIS package created in the previous exercise. Execute the provided T-SQL code to create the database and the table.

```
USE master;
IF DB_ID('TK463DWProd') IS NOT NULL
  DROP DATABASE TK463DWProd;
GO
CREATE DATABASE TK463DWProd
 ON PRIMARY
 (NAME = N'TK463DWProd', FILENAME = N'C:\TK463\TK463DWProd.mdf',
  SIZE = 307200KB , FILEGROWTH = 10240KB )
 LOG ON
 (NAME = N'TK463DWProd_log', FILENAME = N'C:\TK463\TK463DWProd_log.ldf',
  SIZE = 51200KB , FILEGROWTH = 10%);
GO
ALTER DATABASE TK463DWProd SET RECOVERY SIMPLE WITH NO_WAIT;
GO
USE TK463DWProd;
GO
CREATE SCHEMA stg AUTHORIZATION dbo;
GO
CREATE TABLE stg.Person
(
 BusinessEntityID INT         NULL,
 PersonType       NCHAR(2)    NULL,
 Title            NVARCHAR(8) NULL,
 FirstName        NVARCHAR(50) NULL,
 MiddleName       NVARCHAR(50) NULL,
 LastName         NVARCHAR(50) NULL,
 Suffix           NVARCHAR(10) NULL,
 ModifiedDate     DATETIME    NULL
);
```

3. If necessary, start SQL Server Data Tools, open the TK 463 Chapter 9 project, and then open the FillStageTablesParameters.dtsx package from the previous exercise for editing.

4. Select the Configuration Manager option in the Solution Configurations drop-down list.

5. In the Configuration Manager dialog box, select the New option in the Active Solution Configuration drop-down list.

6. In the New Solution Configuration dialog box, enter **Production** as the name of the configuration and click OK. Close the Configuration Manager dialog box.

7. Right-click Project.params in Solution Explorer, and then click Open (or double-click Project.params).

8. Click the Add Parameter To Configurations button on the toolbar.

9. In the Manage Parameter Values dialog box, click Add. Select the pTK463DWConnString parameter and click OK. Notice that the value of the parameter was copied to both configurations.

10. Change the Production configuration to use the newly created database, TK463DWProd. The value should look like this—**Data Source=localhost;Initial Catalog=TK463DWProd;Provider=SQLNCLI11.1;Integrated Security=SSPI;**.

11. Click OK and save the SSIS project to store the values for the configurations.

12. Execute the package first under the Development configuration and then under the Production configuration by selecting the different values in the Solution Configurations drop-down list. Look at the *stg.Person* table in the TK463DWProd database to see if it contains data.

> **NOTE CONTINUING WITH PRACTICES**
>
> Do not exit SSMS or SSDT if you intend to continue immediately with the next practice.

Lesson Summary

- Use parameters to set up connection properties at run time.
- Parameters and project-level connection mangers can only be used with the new project deployment model introduced with SSIS in SQL Server 2012.
- Use property expressions to change the control flow properties at run time.

Lesson Review

Answer the following questions to test your knowledge of the information in this lesson. You can find the answers to these questions and explanations of why each answer choice is correct or incorrect in the "Answers" section at the end of this chapter.

1. Which parameter types are available in SSIS in SQL Server 2012? (Choose all that apply.)

   A. Project-level parameters

   B. Solution-level parameters

   C. Control flow–level parameters

   D. Package parameters

2. Which properties can be set by using build configurations? (Choose all that apply.)

   A. Parameter values

   B. Variable values

   C. Control flow task properties

   D. The Deployment Server Name property

3. Which properties can be set by using property expressions? (Choose all that apply.)

   A. SQL statement for the Execute SQL task

   B. Variable values

   C. Data flow task properties

   D. The Lookup transformation SqlCommand property

Lesson 2: Package Configurations

In versions of SSIS before SQL Server 2012, you had to use package configurations to update properties, variable values, and connections at run time. You could have the package look to an external source for configuration information that changed the settings within the package when it executed. Package configurations are optional, but in real-life scenarios they are almost mandatory, because they provide a way for you to update package settings without having to open each package in Business Intelligence Development Studio (BIDS) or SSDT. For example, by using package configurations, you can maintain connection strings and variable settings for all of your packages in a single location.

> **After this lesson, you will be able to:**
>
> ■ Implement package configurations.
>
> **Estimated lesson time: 40 minutes**

Implementing Package Configurations

When you are executing a package in a package deployment model, the first action the package takes is to look at its configurations and overwrite the package's current settings with the new settings from the configurations. Common elements that are configured by using package configurations are:

- **Connection properties** These include properties that set the connection string, the server name, the user name, and the password.

- **Package variable properties** You can set variable values, variable descriptions, and the Raise Change Event property.

- **Package properties** These include any property on the package level, such as checkpoint and security settings.

Before you can enable package configuration, you must convert your SSIS project to the package deployment model. By default, a new package in the SQL Server 2012 version of SSIS is set up for the project deployment model. You can change this by selecting Convert To Package Deployment Model under the project's name on the main toolbar. Note that you can convert only projects that do not have any parameters or project-level connection managers defined.

By default, each package has its package configuration turned off. To enable and set up configurations, you use the Package Configuration Organizer, with which you can perform the following tasks:

- Enable or disable a package's package configurations
- Add or remove configurations assigned to the package
- Define the order in which the configurations are applied

To open the Package Configurations Organizer, open the package for which you want to turn on configurations, and then choose SSIS Configurations from the SSIS menu. To enable configurations, select the Enable Package Configurations check box at the top of the dialog box. Figure 9-10 shows the Package Configurations Organizer dialog box with package configurations enabled.

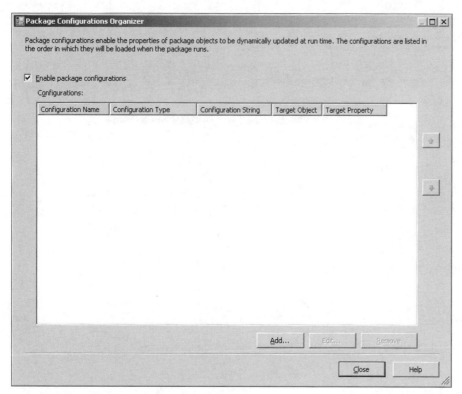

FIGURE 9-10 The Package Configurations Organizer.

Creating a Configuration

To create a new configuration, click the Add button in the Package Configurations Organizer dialog box to start the Package Configuration Wizard. First you must specify the configuration type by selecting the appropriate value from the drop-down list, as shown in Figure 9-11. SSIS supports different package configuration types; Table 9-1 describes the configuration types you can use.

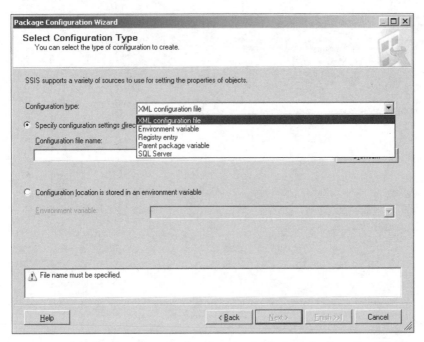

FIGURE 9-11 Selecting a configuration type by using the Package Configuration Wizard.

TABLE 9-1 Package Configuration Types

Type	Description
XML Configuration File	Stores configuration settings in an XML file in the file system. Use this option if you are comfortable working with configuration files and your project requirements let you store configuration information in a file system file. Note that you can store multiple configurations in a single XML file.
Environment Variable	Saves the configuration information inside the system's global variables collection, which is called an *environment variable*. Only one property can be stored in each Environment Variable configuration.
Registry Entry	Lets you save package properties and settings in your computer's registry.
Parent Package Variable	Provides a way for your package to inherit the value of a variable from a parent package. When a package is executed from another SSIS package by using the Execute Package task, the values of its variables are available to the child package through the Parent Package Variable configuration. With this configuration type, you can choose only one package property setting at a time.
SQL Server	Stores configuration settings in a SQL Server table. You can store multiple configurations in a single table.

EXAM TIP

In a package deployment model, you can pass a variable value from one package to another only by using package configurations and selecting the Parent Package Variable package configuration type.

Choose the most appropriate configuration for your environment and your project requirements. Ensure that you consider how the package will be supported in a production environment and how other technologies are supported and configured. Take care to evaluate any security and compliance requirements when you are storing connection information such as server name, user name, or password information.

IMPORTANT   **PARAMETERS OR PACKAGE CONFIGURATIONS?**

If you are using SQL Server 2012, use the new project deployment model with parameters and project-level connection managers to support moving your solution from one environment to another. These new features provide better package management and flexibility in package development compared to package configurations. These new features are positioned as an evolution of Integration Services deployment and administration in SQL Server.

The most commonly used configuration types are the XML Configuration File and SQL Server configurations. The next section looks more closely at each of these types.

Creating an XML File Configuration

When you choose the XML Configuration File type, you can specify the location for your configuration file. There are two ways to specify the location of the XML file:

- Enter the location of the file directly in the Configuration File Name text box. Use this when you intend to always use the same location and name for your configuration file.

- Use an environment variable that contains the location and name of the configuration file. To use this approach, you must create a system variable in your computer's system properties. The value of the variable must contain the full path, name, and extension of the file.

    Using an environment variable for the file location pointer is called the *indirect file location approach* and is very valuable if your XML file location or file name might change in the future or already changes between environments. If you choose to use the environment variable, be sure to add it to the servers on which the package will run.

EXAM TIP

Indirect configurations are useful when the location of the file changes between the development and the production server. To use the indirect configuration, you first need to create the file by using the wizard and then go back and edit the configuration to assign the environment variable.

As with all of the configuration types, more than one package can use the same XML Configuration File. If you have several packages that have common properties, such as connection strings, you might want to have all of them use one XML file for configuration.

After you have defined the location and name of the file, you define the server settings and properties that the XML Configuration File should contain. Because these are common among all configuration types, this chapter reviews the SQL Configuration setup before describing the server settings and property definitions.

Creating a SQL Server Configuration

To store your package configurations in a SQL Server table, select SQL Server from the Configuration Type drop-down list in the Package Configuration Wizard. Using SQL Server as the storage mechanism for your configurations requires a different group of settings than those used by the other configuration types, such as XML Configuration File. Figure 9-12 shows the SQL Server configuration options available for setting up configurations.

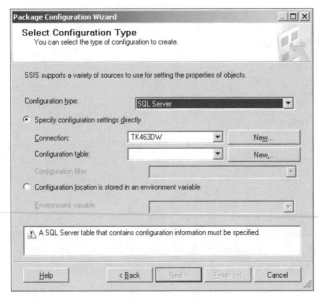

FIGURE 9-12 The Package Configuration Wizard for a SQL Server table configuration.

Just as with the XML Configuration File type, you can specify an environment variable as the location of your configuration (for example, the data source name for the SQL Server configuration), or you can specify configuration settings directly. There are three settings that define the table location details:

- **Connection** This must be a SQL Server–based connection that sets the server and database in which your configurations will be stored and read. If you did not define the connection you need, you can click New next to Connection to open the Configure OLE DB Connection Manager dialog box.

- **Configuration Table** This is the name of the table in which the configurations will reside. This table has predefined column name and data type definitions that cannot be changed. To create the table, you click New next to the Configuration Table text box to open the Create Table dialog box, in which you can change the name of the table and execute the table creation statement for the connection that you specified in the previous setting.

- **Configuration Filter** Multiple SQL Server configurations can share the same table, and you can specify the configuration you want by using the Configuration Filter drop-down list. You can enter a new filter or use an existing one. The name you select or enter for this property is used as a value in the Configuration Filter column in the underlying table.

Adding Properties to Your Configuration

No matter which SSIS configuration type you are using, you can select Properties To Export on the next page of the wizard to select the SSIS package and object properties that are to be used in the configuration. After you define the configuration type properties in the Package Configuration Wizard, click Next.

At this point, SSIS prompts you to verify whether configuration entries already exist for the configuration type you selected. If they do, SSIS prompts you to either reuse the configuration entries or overwrite them. If you see this dialog box, you will probably want to share the existing configurations between packages. If you do, click the Reuse Existing button. If you want to clear the existing entries and create new ones, click Overwrite.

If configuration entries do not already exist in this configuration, or if you clicked Overwrite, you will see the Select Properties To Export page, as shown in Figure 9-13.

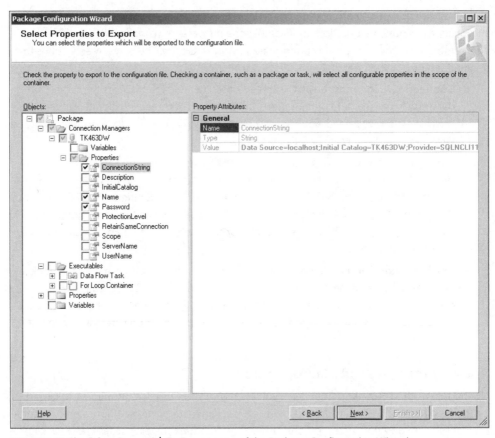

FIGURE 9-13 The Select Properties To Export page of the Package Configuration Wizard.

The Select Properties To Export page uses a tree view structure of your package properties, allowing you to select the properties for the SSIS configuration you have selected. Properties are grouped within the following folders:

- **Variables** Lists all of the package variables you can select for configuration entries, along with their properties.

- **Connection Managers** Lists all of the package connections, from which you can choose the specific properties for your connections.

- **Log Providers** Lets you dynamically set the log configuration.

- **Properties** Displays a list of all package-level properties that you can use to configure your package.

- **Executables** Contains the tree structure of your tasks and containers. By navigating through this tree, you can configure the specific properties of your tasks and containers.

If you are using an XML Configuration File, SQL Server, or Registry Entry configuration, you can set multiple configuration properties at one time by selecting multiple property check boxes.

Sharing, Ordering, and Editing Your Configurations

If you have several configurations in your list, you can define the order in which configurations are applied in a package. The configurations are called in the order in which they are listed in the Package Configuration Organizer. This is an important consideration if you have multiple configurations that will update the same property or if you have configurations that have a dependency on prior configurations. For example, you might have a configuration that updates a connection string, which is then used as the location of the configuration entries in a second configuration. Note that the last-applied property update will be the value that is used in the package.

A common approach is to share configurations between packages. If you do this, you might have configuration entries that apply to one package and not another. This does not affect package execution, but you will receive a warning to indicate that a configuration property does not exist in the package.

As a final note, you can modify all SSIS configuration entries you have made by simply editing the file, SQL Server, registry, or environment variable value. Look for the Configured Value property and change it as necessary.

> **REAL WORLD** **MULTIPLE CONFIGURATIONS**
>
> In previous versions of SQL Server, the use of configurations was almost mandatory for moving from a development to a test environment and then to a production environment. Because user names and passwords for connection strings should not be stored as clear text in an XML file, most of the clients store configuration properties in SQL Server. To have the flexibility to move from one environment to another, you also need to put the information about the SQL Server instance used for storing configurations in a configuration setup. A common solution is to first use an XML configuration that contains the location of the file stored as an environment variable and that includes only the connection string property for the SQL Server configuration that will hold other configuration values. Then you create a second configuration that is a SQL Server configuration, and you use that configuration for all configuration values.

PRACTICE Using Package Configurations

In this practice, you will create an XML Configuration File and share it between two packages.

If you encounter a problem completing an exercise, you can install the completed projects from the Solution folder that is provided with the companion content for this chapter and lesson.

EXERCISE Create an XML Configuration

In this exercise, you use SSIS configurations to create an SSIS XML Configuration File that contains the connection string property of the AdventureWorks2012 and TK463 databases. You then share this configuration with another package.

1. Start SQL Server Data Tools, open the TK 463 Chapter 9 project, and open the FillStageTables_1.dtsx package.

2. Now you need to convert the project to a package deployment model. Click Project on the toolbar and select Convert To Project Deployment Model. Click OK in the dialog box.

3. In the Convert To Package Deployment Model dialog box, every step should show the Result value as Passed. Click OK to convert the project to a package deployment model.

4. Choose Package Configurations from the SSIS menu.

5. Select the Enable Package Configurations check box in the Package Configurations Organizer dialog box.

6. Click Add to create a new configuration.

7. Click Next on the Welcome To The Package Configuration Wizard page.

8. In the Configuration Type drop-down list, select XML Configuration File.

9. Click the Browse button next to the Configuration File Name box, browse to the \Chapter09\Lesson2\Starter\ installed files folder, and then type **SSIS_Conn.dtsConfig**. Click Save to save the file name and path.

10. Click Next in the Package Configuration Wizard to go to the Select Properties To Export page.

11. Under Objects, expand the Connection Managers folder, expand the Properties folder for the AdventureWorks2012 connection, and select the check box next to the ConnectionString property. Repeat the process for the TK463DW connection. Click Next.

12. Name the configuration **MainXMLConfiguration** and close the Configuration Organizer dialog box.

13. Save and close the FillStageTables_1.dtsx package.

14. Open the FillStageTables_2.dtsx package and repeat steps 4 through 9. Select the file you created in step 9, and click Next. You will be prompted to overwrite the existing file or reuse the configuration that it contains. Click the Reuse Existing button.

15. Name the configuration **MainXMLConfiguration** and close the Configuration Organizer dialog box.

16. Save and close the FillStageTables_2.dtsx package.

17. Execute the packages and try to change the XML file so that the connection string points to the TK463DWProd database created in the previous lesson, and execute the packages again.

Lesson Summary

- Package configurations are available in the package deployment model.
- Use package configurations if you are using previous versions of SSIS to set connection properties at run time.
- Use a combination of XML and SQL Server configurations to provide additional portability for your packages.

Lesson Review

Answer the following questions to test your knowledge of the information in this lesson. You can find the answers to these questions and explanations of why each answer choice is correct or incorrect in the "Answers" section at the end of this chapter.

1. Which configuration types can you use to store configuration values? (Choose all that apply.)

    A. XML Configuration File

    B. SQL Server

    C. Any relational database system

    D. Registry entry

2. On which objects can you set dynamic properties by using package configurations? (Choose all that apply.)

    A. Parameters

    B. Variables

    C. Data flow transformations

    D. The Sequence Container task

3. Which SSIS elements can be configured by using a package configuration? (Choose all that apply.)

    A. Connection properties

    B. Package variable properties

    C. Parameter properties

    D. Package properties

Case Scenario

In the following case scenarios, you apply what you've learned about implementing dynamic packages. You can find the answers to these questions in the "Answers" section at the end of this chapter.

Case Scenario: Making SSIS Packages Dynamic

You are creating a set of SSIS packages to move data from flat files and different databases to a data warehouse. Because of strict development, test, and production procedures, your SSIS project must support these possibilities:

1. You need to test different deployment options for your SSIS packages in the development phase by using SSDT.

2. You have a development, test, and production environment and would like to minimize any changes to packages when they are ready for the test phase.

3. You need to parameterize the location of the flat files but still be able to dynamically set the correct file name when using the Foreach Loop container to read all the files inside the specified folder.

How would you address these issues? What would your solution look like?

Suggested Practices

To help you successfully master the exam objectives presented in this chapter, complete the following tasks.

Use a Parameter to Incrementally Load a Fact Table

In order to practice what you have learned in this chapter, you will create a package to load a fact table that will store Internet sales data based on the AdventureWorks2012 database.

- **Practice 1**   Create the necessary package to load the fact table. At each execution of the package, do the full load and truncate the table at the beginning.

- **Practice 2**   Add a project parameter that will accept the incremental date and use it to load only data that is newer than the supplied value. Replace the TRUNCATE T-SQL statement at the beginning with the DELETE T-SQL statement.

- **Practice 3**   Parameterize all connection strings.

Answers

This section contains answers to the lesson review questions and solutions to the case scenario in this chapter.

Lesson 1

1. **Correct Answers: A and D**

    A. **Correct:** Project-level parameters are available.

    B. **Incorrect:** Solution-level parameters are not available.

    C. **Incorrect:** Parameters can be defined on the project or package level.

    D. **Correct:** SSIS supports package-level parameters.

2. **Correct Answers: A and D**

    A. **Correct:** Parameter values can be bound to build configurations.

    B. **Incorrect:** Variables cannot be bound to build configurations.

    C. **Incorrect:** Control flow task properties cannot be bound to build configurations.

    D. **Correct:** Project-level properties can be set for each build configuration.

3. **Correct Answers: A and C**

    A. **Correct:** You can set the SQL statement of the Execute SQL task at run time by using property expressions.

    B. **Incorrect:** Variable properties cannot be set by using property expressions.

    C. **Correct:** General data flow task properties can be set by using property expressions.

    D. **Incorrect:** You can only change the SQL command of the Lookup task when you are using property expressions for the data flow task that has a Lookup task inside it.

Lesson 2

1. **Correct Answers: A, B, and D**

    A. **Correct:** You can use XML as a configuration file.

    B. **Correct:** You can store the configuration values in a SQL Server database.

    C. **Incorrect:** You can only use a SQL Server database.

    D. **Correct:** You can use registry entries to store configuration values.

2. **Correct Answers: B and D**

   A. **Incorrect:** Parameters can be used in the project deployment model.

   B. **Correct:** You can set variable properties.

   C. **Incorrect:** You can only set data flow task properties, and not for a specific transformation.

   D. **Correct:** You can dynamically set properties for a Sequence Container task by using configurations.

3. **Correct Answers: A, B, and D**

   A. **Correct:** Connection properties can be set by using package configurations.

   B. **Correct:** You can set variable properties.

   C. **Incorrect:** You cannot use parameters when using package configurations.

   D. **Correct:** You can dynamically set properties for the package by using package configurations.

Case Scenario

1. Add parameters for the connection strings. Create development, test, and production build configurations and bind parameters to each of them with different data source values. This will allow you to execute the package from SSDT against different configurations without manually changing the value of parameters.

2. Add parameters and parameterize all needed connection managers.

3. Create a parameter that will hold the value of the file location folder. Create a new variable to store the current file name. Using SSIS expression language, set the new variable value to combine the value from the parameter with the value you get from the Foreach Loop container. Use the new variable as the property expression for the Foreach Loop to dynamically change the fully qualified file name while the package is running.

## CHAPTER 10

Auditing and Logging

Exam objectives in this chapter:

- Extract and Transform Data
  - Design data flow.
- Load Data
  - Design control flow.
  - Implement control flow.
- Configure and Deploy SSIS Solutions
  - Troubleshoot data integration issues.
  - Implement auditing, logging, and event handling.

Even in automated data management solutions, errors can and eventually do occur. Not every potential problem can be predicted, and not every contingency can be prepared for in advance. It is therefore impossible to prevent failure altogether, but there is a lot you can do to significantly reduce the probability of failure.

As long as it is possible to anticipate a problem and either prevent it from occurring in the first place (for example, by checking for the existence of a resource before attempting to use it) or prepare a way to respond to it automatically (for example, by redirecting Microsoft SQL Server Integration Services (SSIS) package execution to a contingency branch, by stopping it altogether before failure occurs, or by implementing automated restarts), failure can be avoided.

Nonetheless, being informed of the fact that unforeseen or exceptional circumstances actually have occurred, even if they were successfully avoided, could be beneficial; when you know that a particular problem has in fact occurred, you can take steps to prevent it from occurring again.

In the majority of cases, a notification of the plain fact that an issue has been detected (for instance, that an error has occurred) could be enough to prepare an appropriate response. On the other hand, there are cases for which being aware of the event might not be sufficient on its own—perhaps because the error message was too vague or too generic to serve as a reliable reason for a particular action. In these (mostly rare) cases, additional information describing a wider context of the situation might be required.

SSIS provides two methods of detecting exceptions and capturing additional contextual information about them natively:

- **Integration Services Logging**   This method allows you to configure an SSIS package to automatically log information about each execution. With this method, you can identify a variety of *events* that take place during package execution, including exceptions (such as validation and execution errors and failures).

  The amount of available information as well as the structure of each log entry depend on the actual event—some events are quite verbose, while others are less so. Also note that some events that can be traced don't originate in SSIS; they can originate from any one of the components participating in an SSIS process (such as data providers, database management systems, and operating systems).

- **Integration Services Auditing**   Provided by a dedicated data flow transformation component, auditing provides additional capabilities that can be used to extend the collection of information accompanying the captured events with additional information about the state of the SSIS process, among other things.

  The Audit component can be used to add *system variables* to the data flow, providing contextual information about the SSIS process in which a particular row of data was prepared. Auditing information can be stored with the data being processed or separately.

SSIS event handlers, which are used to respond to a variety of SSIS events, can be used for logging as well. SSIS event handlers are discussed in Lesson 3 of Chapter 8, "Creating a Robust and Restartable Package."

Precedence constraints can also be used to detect errors or to respond to certain states of the SSIS package or the environment and redirect the execution accordingly. See Chapter 3, "Creating SSIS Packages," for examples of how precedence constraints can be used to respond to various situations.

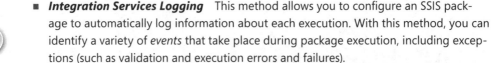

Most data flow components also provide *error output*, which can be used to respond to potential problems because it allows erroneous data passing through a data flow at run time to be captured and either stored to be analyzed later or redirected to a dedicated branch of the data flow for further processing. The error flow is discussed in Chapter 7, "Enhancing Data Flow."

Lessons in this chapter:

- Lesson 1: Logging Packages
- Lesson 2: Implementing Auditing and Lineage
- Lesson 3: Preparing Package Templates

Before You Begin

To complete this chapter, you must have:

- Experience working with SQL Server Management Studio (SSMS).
- Elementary experience working with Microsoft Visual Studio or SQL Server Data Tools (SSDT).
- A working knowledge of the Transact-SQL language.

Lesson 1: Logging Packages

As a process is executed, the SSIS engine allows the progress to be monitored in the calling environment; it does so by reporting certain states or milestones that are reached as a result of the invocation, the continuation, and the completion of operations.

The states and milestones are reported to the calling environment by SSIS events. These events can be captured and processed further (for instance, by SSIS event handlers) or consumed (for instance, by SSIS *log providers*). By themselves, SSIS events report a predefined set of information about the state or the milestone that generated them; however, it is possible to extend this set of information with additional data, either through event handlers or by associating individual log entries with data provided by SSIS auditing.

You will learn more about SSIS auditing in Lesson 2 of this chapter.

> **After this lesson, you will be able to:**
>
> - Determine how much information you need to log from a package.
> - Demonstrate awareness of the new SSIS logging infrastructure (that is, the information available through the catalog views).
> - Use log providers.
> - Log an SSIS execution.
> - Implement custom logging.
>
> **Estimated lesson time: 60 minutes**

Log Providers

There are five distinct log providers available in SSIS that can consume information from captured events; they are listed in Table 10-1. SSIS logging can target one or more log providers (and destinations) simultaneously; therefore, logging does not have to depend on a single log provider. Multiple logging targets make this particular SSIS feature significantly more robust—after all, the log providers themselves, or the destinations to which log information is written, could eventually also fail. For SSIS logging to serve its purpose completely, at least one of the active log providers should be available throughout the execution.

TABLE 10-1 Log Providers

Log provider	Operation
Text file	Writes log entries as comma-separated strings (ASCII) to a text file, using an appropriate File connection manager
SQL Server Profiler	Writes log entries as traces that can later be consumed by the SQL Server Profiler, using a File connection manager
SQL Server	Writes log entries to the sysssislog system table in a SQL Server database, using an OLE DB connection manager
Windows Event Log	Writes log entries to the operating system Application log that can be viewed by using the Windows Event Viewer
XML file	Writes log entries to an XML file, using an appropriate File connection manager

> **NOTE** **SQL SERVER PROFILER LOG PROVIDER**
>
> The SQL Server Profiler log provider cannot be used when the SSIS package is running in 64-bit mode.

Log providers can be configured at design time by using the SSIS Designer or programmatically at run time.

Selecting a Log Provider

To help you select the most appropriate log provider (one or more) to be used in a particular SSIS solution, consider the following guidelines:

- **How will the log be used?** The first thing to consider is log usage—how sophisticated or complex the expected consumption of the log data will be. If the log will be used solely to identify failures or execution errors (that is, events that will occur infrequently at best, or even not occur at all), resulting in a low number of records, then perhaps there is no need to store these entries in a SQL Server database—the operating system's Application log would probably be enough.

  If, on the other hand, the expected number of log entries could be quite high—for instance, if events indicating normal (successful) execution need to be captured so that they can be analyzed later (perhaps to monitor the size of data, to analyze task durations, or to measure SSIS performance)—then either a table in a database or a SQL Server Profiler trace file would be the more appropriate option. In fact, when measuring SSIS performance, a SQL Server Profiler trace would likely be the most appropriate option, considering the fact that Profiler trace data can easily be aligned with performance data provided by the operating system's Reliability And Performance Monitor.

Log data stored in a file (a comma-separated values file or an XML file) would probably have to be loaded into an application or a database before it could be used. On the other hand, file logs are independent of the operating system and independent of the database management system being used as the data source or the destination; furthermore, files are transport-friendly—they can be copied or sent to their final destination via FTP, with minimal or no overhead.

- **Who will use the log information?** It is also crucial to know who the intended audience for the SSIS logs is. Based on the typical organizational schema in most companies, the audience will probably consist of database administrators and SSIS developers.

  Both of these audiences would first want to know whether SSIS processes have been executed at all and then whether the executions were successful. Finally, both audiences would be interested in investigating the characteristics of an SSIS execution more thoroughly, especially after it has become apparent that potential performance or data corruption problems exist.

  All three levels of interest could be covered by two logs: one with entries indicating execution boundaries at the package level (the beginning and the end of package executions, and package-scoped errors or failures, if any), and another more detailed one perhaps even at the task level (the beginning and the end of task executions, with task-scoped errors). In other words, the administrator and the developers could be satisfied with log entries in the Application log and a Profiler trace (or a table log, if the environment prohibits the use of the SQL Server Profiler log provider).

- **What is the probability of a particular log provider failing along with another element of the SSIS solution?** Obviously, logging is used to document at least the most important aspects of an SSIS execution—the problems with the execution, manifesting themselves as errors or failures.

  An efficient and robust logging solution should not fail even if most elements of an SSIS solution have failed. In other words, SSIS logging should never depend on a single log provider but should implement at least one log provider that is only likely to fail when the operating system or server hardware fails. This will allow you to identify the actual cause of the problem with a sufficient degree of certainty to be able to avoid investigating causes of SSIS failure outside your control.

EXAM TIP

Study the differences in the operation of the available log providers and how the information in each corresponding log type can be used later. Some log types provide better integration with the operating system, whereas others provide better integration with the data in a database. Not every log type is best suited for every intended use.

Configuring Logging

The purpose of log configuration is to prepare log definitions that are aligned with the expectations of the target audience. This means:

- **Determining which events need to be captured**   The events that can be captured in SSIS logs are the same events that can be used for binding event handlers. These are discussed in more detail in Lesson 3 of Chapter 8.

  From the perspective of SSIS logging, SSIS events can be divided into three distinct groups: *execution boundary events* (OnPreValidate, OnPreExecute, OnPostExecute, and OnPostValidate), *execution progress events* (OnExecStatusChanged, OnProgress, OnVariableValueChanged, PipelineComponentTime, and Diagnostic), and *execution exception events* (OnInformation, OnWarning, OnQueryCancel, OnError, and OnTaskFailed).

  Execution boundary and execution exception events are essential for top-level logs because they provide an overview of SSIS processes—when they start and when they finish—with the addition of information about any exceptions during execution.

  Logs used in measuring performance of SSIS processes benefit from the addition of execution progress events to the execution boundary events. Execution progress events document not only when an execution had started and finished, but also additional information about the progress of each operation. When these logs are aligned with Reliability And Performance Monitor traces, you can see what actually goes on during execution, allowing you to improve your understanding of the actual resource requirements of a particular SSIS solution.

- **Determining which event properties need to be captured**   Possible event properties that can be captured are shown in Table 10-2.

TABLE 10-2 Event Properties

Property	Operation
Computer	The name of the computer on which the log event occurred. SSIS processes can be executed at different servers; therefore, knowing where a particular execution occurred is essential, especially for troubleshooting.
Operator	The identity of the user who launched the SSIS package. Different users might have different permissions and privileges; therefore, knowing who started an SSIS process is essential when you are trying to solve permission-related problems. Also, if a particular SSIS solution is meant to be executed automatically, knowing that it was actually invoked manually could be important.
SourceName	The name of the container or task in which the log event occurred. When you are measuring performance or detecting errors, the granularity of information should be at the task level; otherwise, it can prove quite difficult to identify the operations in which suboptimal performance occurred.
SourceID	The unique identifier of the SSIS package; the For Loop, Foreach Loop, or sequence container; or the task in which the log event occurred. You can use this identifier to associate each log entry with corresponding auditing data, where additional information about each task would be stored.

Property	Operation	
ExecutionID	The GUID of the package execution instance. You can use this identifier to associate a particular execution instance with corresponding auditing data that includes additional information about each execution instance.	
MessageText	A message associated with the log entry. This property exposes the description of the event and might contain information essential to the interpretation of an event. More often than not, this information is also vital to troubleshooting.	
DataBytes	A byte array specific to the log entry. The meaning of this property varies by log entry.	
StartTime	The time at which the container or task starts to run.	Execution boundary events would be completely useless without temporal information.
EndTime	The time at which the container or task stops running.	
DataCode	An optional integer value that typically contains a value from the DTSExecResult enumeration that indicates the result of running the container or task: 0 – Success 1 – Failure 2 – Completed 3 – Canceled Knowing the outcome of an operation is essential for the analysis of SSIS execution data in troubleshooting. Also, when you are analyzing performance issues, failed tasks might not be crucial to identifying performance issues (other than indicating that a lack of resources had led to failure).	

> **NOTE CONFIGURABLE EVENT PROPERTIES**
>
> The StartTime, EndTime, and DataCode event properties are always captured and are therefore not listed among the customizable event properties in the SSIS Designer.

Inheritance of Log Settings

Logging can be configured at different levels in the SSIS object hierarchy—at the package level, the container level, and the task level. When determining which event properties should be captured by which SSIS object, you should keep in mind that SSIS object hierarchy supports inheritance: tasks can either use proprietary logging settings or they can inherit them from the parent object (container or package). If a particular branch of the SSIS object hierarchy should be configured to log the same events and the same set of properties, you can place the whole branch in a container to avoid having to configure every single SSIS object; after logging has been configured at the container, the other objects it contains will use the same settings, as long as inheritance is enabled.

When the LoggingMode property for a particular SSIS object is set to UseParentSetting (which it is by default), the logging settings will be inherited from the parent in the SSIS hierarchy (the container if the object is placed in a container, or the package itself if the object exists in the scope of the package). Of course, the parent must be configured for logging, either directly or via inheritance.

On the other hand, to configure logging for a particular task differently from its parent, you must set the LoggingMode property to Enabled and configure the task separately.

To prevent a task from logging its events, set the LoggingMode property to Disabled.

Log Configuration Templates

You can save logging configurations as files so that you can reuse them as SSIS *log configuration templates* in other SSIS objects, or even in other SSIS projects. With log configuration templates, a logging strategy can be implemented harmoniously across an SSIS solution and beyond (in other solutions or in other departments of the organization, for example).

Log configuration templates are stored as XML files, which means that they can be copied to other projects and also edited manually.

 Quick Check

1. How are SSIS events propagated to the environment?
2. Which SSIS object can be configured for logging?
3. Can SSIS variables create log entries?

Quick Check Answers

1. SSIS events can be consumed by log providers, which send them to destinations in the environment (such as tables in a database, files in the file system, or operating system event handlers).
2. Any SSIS package executable (control flow container or task) can be configured for logging, including the package itself.
3. Variables can be configured to trigger an event when their values change, and this event can then be propagated to a log provider.

PRACTICE   **Configuring SSIS Logging**

In this practice, you will configure an SSIS container for logging. You will learn how to select a log provider, how to select events that are going to be captured, and which event properties will be written to the log.

After configuring one container, you will learn how to use a log configuration template to apply the same log settings on another container.

If you encounter a problem completing an exercise, you can install the completed projects from the Solution folder that is provided with the companion content for this chapter and lesson.

EXERCISE 1   Prepare the Environment

1. Start SSMS and on the File menu, under Open, select File. Then navigate to the C:\TK463\Chapter10\Code folder and open the TK463Chapter10.sql Transact-SQL script.

2. After you have reviewed the script, execute only the part of the script for the Lesson 1 practice. The script creates the database and the objects you will be using in this lesson.

EXERCISE 2   Configure an SSIS Container for Event Logging

1. Start SSDT. On the Start page, select Open Project, navigate to the C:\TK463 \Chapter10\Lesson1\Starter folder, and open the TK 463 Chapter 10.sln solution.

2. Open the FillStageTables.dtsx package.

3. Right-click the SSIS package designer surface or, on the SSIS menu, select Logging, to open the Configure SSIS Logs editor, shown in Figure 10-1.

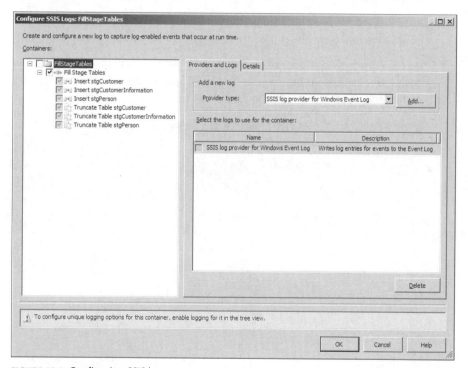

FIGURE 10-1 Configuring SSIS logs.

4. On the left, in the Containers tree view, expand all levels of the SSIS object hierarchy to display all SSIS objects in this package.

5. The root of the tree represents the SSIS package itself; select it but leave the check box cleared. Instead of configuring the entire SSIS package for logging, you are just going to configure logging for specific SSIS objects.

6. On the right, on the Providers And Logs tab, add a new SSIS log provider to the package by selecting SSIS Log Provider For Windows Event Log in the Provider Type list box and clicking Add.

   Log providers are assigned to the SSIS package, but that by itself does not mean that the SSIS package is configured for using them; it just means that the assigned log providers can be used for logging.

7. In the Containers tree view, make sure that the check box next to the Fill Stage Tables container is selected. This will enable logging on the container.

   A cleared check box next to the object node indicates that logging is disabled on the corresponding object, and a check box with a gray background indicates that the logging settings will be inherited from the object's parent in the SSIS object hierarchy.

8. After logging has been enabled on the Fill Stage Tables container, select the container node in the tree view. The rest of the settings can now be configured.

9. On the Providers And Logs tab, as shown in Figure 10-2, SSIS Log Provider For Windows Event Log should be available for the Fill Stage Tables container. Select this particular log provider by selecting the check box on its left.

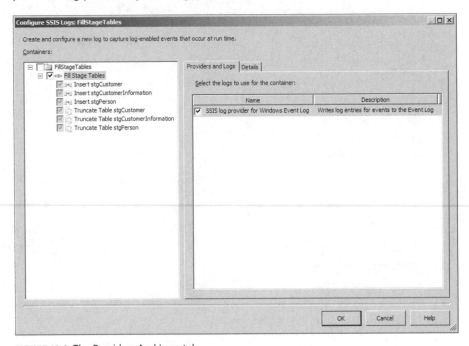

FIGURE 10-2 The Providers And Logs tab.

This means that the Fill Stage Tables container will be able to log its events to the Windows Event Log.

10. On the Details tab of the Configure SSIS Logs editor, shown in Figure 10-3, you can select individual SSIS events to be captured and sent to the selected log providers. Select the following SSIS events to be logged:

- OnError

- OnPostExecute

- OnPreExecute

- OnTaskFailed

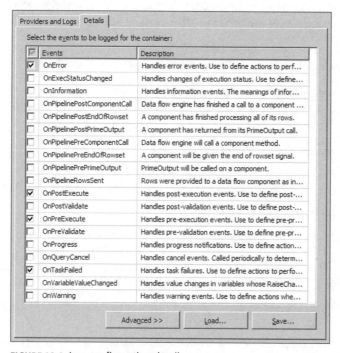

FIGURE 10-3 Log configuration details.

11. Click Advanced to switch the Details tab to the advanced mode to select the individual properties of the selected events to be logged. By default, all properties are selected; deselect the DataBytes property for all selected events to exclude it from being logged.

12. After you have configured the logging properties of the Fill Stage Tables container, click OK to confirm the settings.

13. Save the SSIS project but leave it open; you will need it in the following exercise.

EXERCISE 3 Create a Log Configuration Template

1. Make sure that the FillStageTables.dtsx SSIS package of the TK 463 Chapter 10.sln solution is open in SSDT.

2. On the SSIS menu, select Logging, or right-click the SSIS Designer surface and in the shortcut menu select Logging, to open the Configure SSIS Logs editor.

3. In the Containers tree view on the left, select the Fill Stage Tables container node.

4. Open the Details tab for the selected SSIS object and, at the bottom of the tab, click Save to export the logging configuration to an XML file.

5. In the Save As dialog box, navigate to the C:\TK463\Chapter10\Lesson1\Starter folder and type **LogTaskBoundaries.xml** into the File name text box.

6. Click Save to save the file, and then in the Configure SSIS Logs editor, click Cancel to close it. No other changes to the configuration are necessary.

7. Open the DimCustomer.dtsx SSIS package and open the Configure SSIS Logs editor, either by selecting Logging from the SSIS menu or by accessing the SSIS Designer's shortcut menu.

8. Assign the SSIS log provider for Windows Event Log to the DimCustomer.dtsx SSIS package.

9. Enable logging for the Process Customer Dimension container, and while its node is selected in the Containers tree view, open the Details tab.

10. At the bottom of the tab, click Load to import the logging configuration from a template.

11. In the Open dialog box, navigate to the folder you used in step 5 of this exercise.

12. Select the XML file you created in step 5 of this exercise, and click Open to apply the template.

    The Process Customer Dimension container of the DimCustomer.dtsx SSIS package should now be configured for logging the same way you configured the Fill Stage Tables container of the FillStageTables.dtsx SSIS package in Exercise 2.

13. After applying the template, click OK to confirm the settings.

14. Save the FillStageTables.dtsx SSIS package and execute it in debug mode.

15. After the execution has completed successfully, on the Windows Start menu, locate Control Panel, and then under Administrative Tools, select Event Viewer to access the Windows logs.

Navigate to the Application log and view the entries. The last 10 or so entries in the application log should be information-level log entries passed from SSDT documenting the execution of the FillStageTables.dtsx SSIS package in debug mode, as shown in Figure 10-4.

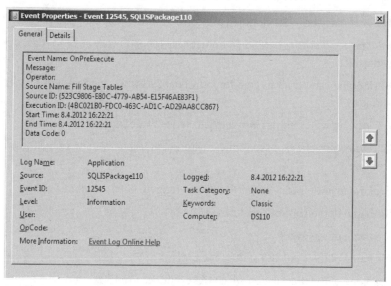

FIGURE 10-4 Event details.

16. Return to SSDT, open the Master.dtsx SSIS package, and execute it in debug mode.

17. After the execution has completed successfully, return to the Event Viewer and refresh the Application log. The list should now display log entries from events of both the FillStageTables.dtsx and the DimCustomer.dtsx SSIS packages.

18. After you are done testing the solution and inspecting the Windows Application log, close SSDT.

Lesson Summary

- Before enabling SSIS package logging, you should determine how much information you actually need to log and choose the appropriate log providers.
- Depending on the selected log provider, log information is written to the Windows logs, to a SQL Server Profiler trace, to a database, or to files in the file system.

Lesson Review

Answer the following questions to test your knowledge of the information in this lesson. You can find the answers to these questions and explanations of why each answer choice is correct or incorrect in the "Answers" section at the end of this chapter.

1. Which statements about SSIS logging are correct? (Choose all that apply.)

    A. Every task and every operation automatically reports every error to the output file by default.

    B. SSIS logging can be configured for individual SSIS tasks or containers or at the package level.

    C. SSIS logging writes entries into the SQL Server Error Log.

    D. SSIS log entries are exposed to the environment using a variety of built-in log providers.

2. Which of the following SSIS properties can be logged? (Choose all that apply.)

    A. The name of the control flow task

    B. The name of the event

    C. The name of the user who started the process

    D. The name of the machine on which the event occurred

3. Which feature allows you to configure logging once on a particular task or container, and then reuse the same settings on other tasks and/or containers?

    A. A log template

    B. A log configuration template

    C. A log settings template

    D. A package configuration template

Lesson 2: Implementing Auditing and Lineage

 In data management, the term *auditing* is used to describe a collection of activities and processes used in determining when, how, and possibly why data being managed or consumed in a data management solution has been added, modified, or removed and by whom or through which automated process.

The relationship between auditing and logging is complementary:

- Logging captures information about *how* a process is being executed (the events, as they occur), whereas auditing provides an overview of *what* is being processed (the data itself, or aggregated values based on it). Procedural information about the events that have been captured in the log is given a material context by the corresponding audits.

- Audits describe the individual states of data, without any notion of the process needed to get from one state to the other, whereas a log describes the transitions between states, without showing either the preceding or the following state of data. Logs and audits together describe pretty much the same thing, but from different perspectives, by providing different pieces of the same puzzle.

There is no need for any overlap in the information acquired by an audit and the information acquired by an event log. Each of the two functionalities serves a particular purpose, and the purposes are independent of one another, but when they are correlated, they serve additional purposes—a log entry is complemented by context, and the results of an audit can be complemented with a reference to a real-world event.

After this lesson, you will be able to:

- Determine auditing needs.
- Audit package execution by using system variables.

Estimated lesson time: 60 minutes

Auditing Techniques

Depending on their objectives, purposes, and intended usage, auditing techniques can be divided into two major groups:

- ***Elementary auditing*** Provides very basic (elementary) information about the state of an individual unit of information (such as a business entity or an attribute). Typically, an elementary audit captures changes in data, the type of the change (an addition, a modification, or a removal [optional]), and the time when the change was made and a reference to the origin of the change, which could either be a person or an automated process. Elementary audits are usually implemented in a row (as additional properties of an entity or an attribute) and only rarely in a separate auditing store (such as an audit table). After all, the relationship between the unit of data being audited and the corresponding audit record is one to one.

- ***Complete auditing*** Extends the elementary audit information, both in terms of quantity and quality. Typically, complete audits go as deep as to capture every single atomic activity against the data—not only the changes to the data (additions, modifications, and removals), but also its usage (the fact that the data has been retrieved from the data store). Complete auditing is usually implemented by using a dedicated table—the relationship between primary data and audit data could be one to many (for instance, an update can be audited as two separate states: the state before the change and the state after the change). However, complete audits are typically implemented externally (that is, they are performed independently of the primary data management application, with audit data stored outside the data store where primary data is kept); this eliminates possible dependencies of the auditing solution on the target of the audit.

Either of the two auditing techniques just described can capture information at various levels, ranging from top-level audits (for example, at the process level) that gather data about the process as a whole, intermediary-level audits (for example, at the entity level) that gather data about principal business entities, or low-level audits (for example, at the table row level) that gather data about individual rows in one or more tables of the database.

Although complete auditing is often found in operational applications and data stores, and only rarely in data warehouses, elementary auditing is found in both types of data stores.

In data warehousing, the purpose of auditing is to provide information about when the data was changed, using what operation, and by whom. Determining why a particular change occurred would rarely be done in a data warehouse—documenting the reasons for data to change is typical for operational applications, not analytical ones. In the data warehouse, historical versions of business entities would be stored, but in most cases without any additional information as to why a certain entity was added, modified, or removed.

Data warehouse audits are performed at various levels, gathering level-dependent information. For instance, at the process level, information relevant to execution performance would be acquired; at the entity level, the focus of data gathering would be on providing a distinction between added, modified, and removed entities; but at row level, the audit requirements would mostly depend on the type of the table (fact tables versus dimension tables) and the method used in modifications (Slowly Changing Dimension types).

Based on its purpose and on the level, a data audit would be implemented using one or more of the following methods to store execution data:

- Audit data that documents a particular business entity or one or more of the entity's properties is known as *row-level audit data*. This type of audit data is generally not logged and therefore needs to be provided separately.

  As far as its storage is concerned, row-level audit data can be stored in the same table with the primary data, as long as the elementary auditing technique is used—the relationship between primary data and audit data must be one to one.

  An example of a table schema used for storing primary as well as audit data in the same row is shown in Table 10-3.

TABLE 10-3 Same-Table Row-Level Audits (with Audit Data Columns in Italics)

Column name	Column description
Id	The identifier of the entity
Name	The name of the entity
Description	A description of the entity
CreatedOn	An audit date/time value indicating when the row was added
CreatedBy	An audit value indicating the person who added the row

Column name	Column description
LastChangeType	An audit value indicating the type of the change, such as Added for new rows, Modified for changed rows, and Removed for inactive, historical rows
ChangedOn	An audit date/time value indicating when the row was changed
ChangedBy	An audit value indicating the person who implemented the change

On the other hand, if the granularity, quantity, and/or quality of audit data exceed the capabilities of the elementary auditing technique, a separate table, or even a separate data store, would be required to store audit data; with increased granularity, the relationship between primary data and audit data becomes one to many.

An example of a table schema in which audit data is stored separately from primary data is shown in Tables 10-4 and 10-5.

TABLE 10-4 Primary Table Schema

Column name	Column description
ID	The identifier of the entity
Name	The name of the entity
Description	A description of the entity

TABLE 10-5 External Audit Table Schema

Column name	Column description
ID	The identifier of the entity, referencing the primary table shown in Table 10-4.
Name	All updatable columns of the primary data table are repeated in the audit table, storing historical data. The number of rows designating an individual operation is governed by change types: updates require two rows, one to store the previous value and one to hold the new value; inserts require one row to store the newly added value; and deletions also require a single row to store the value as it was before the row was removed.
Description	
LastChangeType	An audit value indicating the type of the change; such as Added for new rows, Modified for changed rows, and Removed for inactive, historical rows.
ChangedOn	An audit date/time value indicating when the row was changed.
ChangedBy	An audit value indicating the person who implemented the change.

- Audit data that documents a particular execution instance can be limited to the number of rows and the size of data affected by a particular execution, as long as execution boundary and execution exception events are properly logged. In other words, package-level audit data could be aggregated from row-level audits—that is, of course, if row-level audits are available. Alternatively, package-level aggregates could be determined during execution (for example, by using the Row Count or Aggregate data flow transformation).

An example of a table schema used to store package-level audit data of a specific execution instance is shown in Table 10-6.

TABLE 10-6 Package-Level Audit Table Schema

Column name	Column description
PackageID	The SSIS package identifier, referencing package metadata
TaskID	The SSIS task identifier, referencing task metadata
ExecutionID	The identifier of the execution instance, used to correlate audit data with package-level log entries
RowsAdded	An audit data value indicating the total number of rows inserted during an execution
RowsModified	An audit data value indicating the total number of rows updated during an execution
RowsRemoved	An audit data value indicating the total number of rows deleted during an execution
DataSizeAdded	An audit data value indicating the total size of data (in bytes) inserted during an execution
DataSizeModified	An audit data value indicating the total size of data (in bytes) updated during an execution
DataSizeRemoved	An audit data value indicating the total size of data (in bytes) deleted during an execution

- Audit data that documents a particular data management process (an SSIS solution or an SSIS project) as a whole can be aggregated from package-level audits. As long as SSIS process metadata is stored in the database, the audit data at the process level can be computed from corresponding execution data by using a view or a SQL Server Analysis Services (SSAS) multidimensional model.

EXAM TIP

In order to use auditing and logging appropriately, you should understand the differences between them very well.

Rather than trying to gather as much information as possible using just one or the other of the functionalities, you should focus on using each for the specific features it provides, and balance their capabilities to achieve a common objective.

In previous versions of SQL Server, SSIS audit data storage and maintenance had to be provided by using a proprietary solution; SQL Server 2012 introduces native auditing capabilities in the form of the SSISDB catalog, which already provides storage for SSIS package metadata, as well as appropriate maintenance functionalities. If, for some reason, you need to extend the SSISDB catalog, you are allowed do so by creating custom objects in the SSISDB database.

The SSISDB catalog is discussed in more detail in Chapter 11, "Installing SSIS and Deploying Packages," and Chapter 12, "Executing and Securing Packages."

Row Count Data Flow Transformation Component

The Row Count transformation, also mentioned in Lesson 2 of Chapter 5, "Designing and Implementing Data Flow," is a data flow transformation component used to count the number of rows that have passed through the data path that the component is connected to.

The Row Count transformation must be associated with an SSIS variable. After the last row has passed through the component, the total row count is stored in this variable.

The Row Count component is used in Exercise 1 of Lesson 3 in Chapter 6, "Enhancing Control Flow."

Aggregate Data Flow Transformation Component

The Aggregate transformation, also mentioned in Lesson 2 of Chapter 5, is a data flow transformation component used to aggregate data in the data flow. Typical aggregation functions are available, as shown in Table 10-7.

TABLE 10-7 Aggregate Transformation Operations

Operation	Description
Group by	Divides datasets into groups; if grouping is not specified, all rows are included in aggregations. Columns of any data type can be used for grouping.
Sum	Sums the values in a column. Only columns with numeric data types can be summed.
Average	Returns the average of the column values in a column. Only columns with numeric data types can be averaged.
Count	Returns the number of items in a group.
Count distinct	Returns the number of unique non-null values in a group.
Minimum	Returns the minimum value in a group. This operation can only be used with numeric, date, and time data types.
Maximum	Returns the maximum value in a group. This operation can only be used with numeric, date, and time data types.

The Multicast transformation, also mentioned in Lesson 2 of Chapter 5, allows aggregated data to be redirected to a different destination in a data flow, effectively separating data aggregations from principal data movements. This way, the Aggregate transformation can be used to gather audit data at a level above row-level audits.

Audit Data Flow Transformation Component

The Audit transformation is used to add auditing information to the data flow; this is achieved by adding columns to the data flow buffer. Several system variables are available to the Audit transformation, as shown in Table 10-8.

TABLE 10-8 Audit Transformation System Variables

Name	Description
Execution instance GUID	The GUID that uniquely identifies the execution instance of the SSIS package
Package ID	The GUID that uniquely identifies the SSIS package
Package name	The SSIS package name
Version ID	The GUID that uniquely identifies the version of the SSIS package
Execution start time	The time at which SSIS package execution started
Machine name	The name of the computer on which the SSIS package was launched
User name	The login name of the user who launched the SSIS package
Task name	The name of the data flow task that contains the Audit transformation
Task ID	The GUID that uniquely identifies the data flow task with which the Audit transformation is associated

The Audit transformation can be used to implement the elementary auditing technique; audit information can be stored in the same table with the primary data or in a separate table (for instance, if audit data is redirected to a separate destination by a Multicast transformation). The Audit component is one of the few data flow transformations without an error output.

Additional audit information not available via the Audit transformation can be added to the data flow buffer by using the Derived Column transformation, discussed in Chapters 5 and 7.

Correlating Audit Data with SSIS Logs

As mentioned earlier in this lesson, audit data and SSIS logs represent two individual, yet complementary, sets of information about the execution of an SSIS process. In the operational sense, both sets are individual, each being acquired independently of the other. Although both sets could also be consumed individually (for example, log analysis without the material context or data evolution analysis without the procedural context), significantly more value can be generated from them being used together.

What is needed is a way to correlate audit data with the log entries that represent the operations in which this audit data was created.

In SSIS, multiple properties are shared between logs and audits: package identifiers (Package Name and PackageID), container identifiers (Container Name and ContainerID), task identifiers (Task Name and TaskID), and the execution instance identifier (ExecutionID).

Depending on the data model used for storing audit and log data, at least two properties (for example, TaskID and ExecutionID) would be required to uniquely identify audit rows associated with the log entry representing the operation responsible for the creation of the audit data.

Retention

Considering the amount of data—whether it is log data or audit data—that could be generated during a single execution (even just using the elementary auditing technique), it should be quite obvious that it probably would not take long for the combined size of logs and audits to outgrow the size of the primary data.

In most cases, the usability of logs and audits is limited to a specific time period. If any performance or quality issues are detected, they would probably be corrected as soon as possible. After the log and audit data has been consumed for troubleshooting purposes, resulting in the upgrading of the solution, these particular logs and audits would no longer be of much use, other than to prove that it once was necessary to have resources assigned to problem resolution.

In addition to that, especially when you are troubleshooting performance issues, the operational characteristics of an SSIS solution could change significantly after corrections are applied, so the consequent comparison of logs and audits that were generated before the correction to logs and audits generated after the correction would be of little use.

To prevent log and audit data from overwhelming a data management system, consider automating log and audit data removal. The criteria used in identifying log and/or audit data to be removed from the production environment could be based on various measurable properties of the data (such as the size of the data, the number of rows, or patterns identified by using data mining); however, usually the most appropriate method is to define a purely time-based *retention period* designating the maximum age of log and audit data.

When log and/or audit data rows reach the age defined by the retention period, they are removed from the data store. Optionally, a two-phase approach could also be used, with one retention period used for marking rows as "ready to be removed" and a second (shorter) one used for actually removing previously marked rows.

 Quick Check

1. Does the OnError event generated by a data flow task contain enough information to identify the erroneous rows?

2. Is it possible to correlate log entries generated by SSIS events with data generated by SSIS auditing?

Quick Check Answers

1. The quantity and quality of information available in an event depend on its origin (for example, SSIS run time, data providers, or database management systems).

2. Yes, both logging as well as auditing can be configured to generate information that can be used to correlate log entries generated by an SSIS executable with the corresponding audit entries.

PRACTICE Implementing Elementary Auditing

In this practice, you will implement row-level auditing in an existing data flow, using the Audit data flow transformation component.

You will configure the data flow task to write additional information about the execution that you can use later to identify which rows were added by which execution instance.

If you encounter a problem completing an exercise, you can install the completed projects from the Solution folder that is provided with the companion content for this chapter and lesson.

EXERCISE 1 Prepare the Environment

1. Start SSMS and, from the File menu, under Open, select File. Then navigate to the C:\TK463\Chapter10\Code folder and open the TK463Chapter10.sql Transact-SQL script.

2. After you have reviewed the script, execute only the part of the script for the Lesson 2 practice. The script creates the database and the objects you will be using in this lesson.

EXERCISE 2 Implement Row-Level Auditing Using the Audit Transformation

1. Start SSDT. On the Start page, select Open Project, navigate to the C:\TK463 \Chapter10\Lesson2\Starter folder, and open the TK 463 Chapter 10.sln solution.

2. Open the DimCustomer.dtsx SSIS package and double-click the Dim Customer data flow task, or right-click it and select Edit from the shortcut menu, to open the Data Flow Editor.

3. Delete the data path leading from the Calc Columns Derived Column transformation to the Conditional Split transformation.

4. Drag an Audit transformation component from the SSIS Toolbox onto the Data Flow design surface.

5. Connect the output of the Calc Columns transformation to the input of the newly added transformation.

6. Double-click the Audit transformation, or right-click it and then select Edit from the shortcut menu, to open the Audit Transformation Editor.

7. Configure the Audit transformation by using the information provided in Table 10-9.

TABLE 10-9 Audit Transformation Columns

Output column name	Audit type
ExecutionID	Execution instance GUID
PackageID	Package ID
PackageName	Package name
VersionID	Version ID
ExecutionStartTime	Execution start time
MachineName	Machine name
UserName	User name
TaskName	Task name
TaskID	Task ID

The completed editor is shown in Figure 10-5.

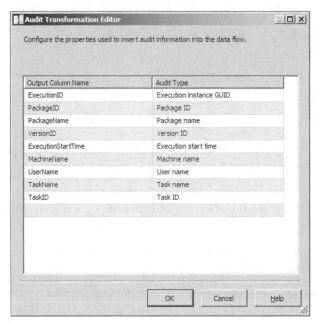

FIGURE 10-5 The Audit Transformation Editor.

8. When you have configured the transformation, click OK to confirm the settings.

   You have now added nine new columns to the data flow buffer.

9. Connect the output of the Audit transformation to the input of the Conditional Split transformation.

   If there are warnings on the Dim Customer and Update Dim Customer destinations, edit each of them and correct them by mapping the newly added data flow buffer columns to the corresponding destination table columns.

10. After you have configured the Dim Customer data flow task, save the project.

11. Open the Master.dtsx SSIS package and run it in debug mode. After the execution has completed successfully, inspect the *dbo.Customers* table in the TK463DW database, using the query in Listing 10-1.

LISTING 10-1 Select All Rows from *dbo.Customers*

```
SELECT *
  FROM dbo.Customers
```

The query should return all rows from the *dbo.Customers* table with additional columns holding audit data. Verify that all the audit data is present.

Lesson Summary

- SSIS auditing complements SSIS logging by providing additional information about how the data in the database was affected by the SSIS process.
- The SSIS run time provides information about the current execution instance, which you can include in your audits.

Lesson Review

Answer the following questions to test your knowledge of the information in this lesson. You can find the answers to these questions and explanations of why each answer choice is correct or incorrect in the "Answers" section at the end of this chapter.

1. What information can be added to the data flow buffer by using the Audit transformation? (Choose all that apply.)

   A. The name of the event

   B. The identifier of the event

   C. The identifier of the task

   D. The name of the machine

2. How can the Audit transformation be configured to provide additional system variables or user variables to the data flow?

   A. The set of properties provided by the Audit transformation is fixed and cannot be extended.

   B. The Audit transformation itself cannot be extended, but by using the Expression task, you can assign any value to an appropriate system variable used by the Audit transformation.

   C. The Audit transformation can be edited by using the Advanced Editor, which provides unlimited access to system and user variables, as well as the rest of the data flow columns.

   D. The set of properties provided by the Audit transformation can be extended at design time by switching to advanced mode.

3. Which of the following pieces of information represent typical examples of audit data? (Choose all that apply.)

   A. The date and time that the row was added to the table

   B. The date and time that the row was last modified

   C. A value designating the success or failure of an SSIS process

   D. The name of the SSIS task in which an error has occurred

Lesson 3: Preparing Package Templates

In every SSIS development project, there are certain tasks and activities that have to be completed every time, and in most cases they would just be performed the same way, producing pretty much exact same results; unless, of course, it was somehow possible to complete many of these tasks in advance.

So far, this book has covered almost every aspect of SSIS development: control flows, data flows, connection managers, parameterization, configuration, extensibility, reusability, automated recovery, event handling, logging, and auditing—all of these features together effectively constitute SSIS development. This also means that all of the activities required in establishing these features have to be repeated for every new SSIS solution.

 However, the reality is not quite as grim; like many other development tools, SSIS supports templates—*package templates*, to be exact. You can spend time creating and configuring all aspects of an SSIS package once, and then use the resulting SSIS package as a template for your consecutive SSIS development work.

As you discover new techniques and gain more experience, be sure to update your templates accordingly, or create new ones that reflect what you have learned.

> *NOTE* **SSIS PACKAGE TEMPLATES IN PRACTICE**
>
> If you are part of an SSIS development team, make sure your manager is aware of the benefits of using SSIS package templates; also ask him or her to periodically dedicate some time for training to allow the team members to share their experience in developing SSIS solutions. The combined knowledge of all team members is one of the principal assets of any team. Allow your teammates to learn from you, and learn as much as you can from them in return.

> **After this lesson, you will be able to:**
> - Create package templates.
>
> **Estimated lesson time: 20 minutes**

SSIS Package Templates

SSIS package templates are implemented as regular SSIS package files and are stored at a specific location in the file system; there is no special format that has to be applied to an SSIS package file in order for it to be used as a template.

By default, SSIS package templates are located in the C:\Program Files (x86)\Microsoft Visual Studio 10.0\Common7\IDE\PrivateAssemblies\ProjectItems\DataTransformationProject \DataTransformationItems folder.

When you use the Add New Item command to add a new SSIS package based on a template to a project, SSDT creates a copy of the template and places the new package into the project folder automatically. This process is automated only for templates located in the default folder. Alternatively, templates can be stored elsewhere and then added to SSIS projects by using the Add Existing Item command; in this case, SSDT also creates a copy of the file and places it into the project folder.

> **IMPORTANT   SOURCE CONTROL**
>
> You should keep your SSIS templates under source control, just as you would do for other development files.

Creating an SSIS Package Template

To create an SSIS package template, the first thing you need to decide is which SSIS objects to place into it and have them preconfigured. The essential SSIS objects should be quite easy to select: connection managers (parameterized appropriately, unless a project-scoped connection manager would be used instead), event handlers (if they are generic enough, such as one used to report failures by using a preconfigured Send Mail task), log providers, and any generic task that is used frequently enough in your business to belong in the template (such as an Execute SQL task used to truncate tables in the staging data store).

Additional objects to be considered for the SSIS package template are a typical data flow task (for example, with one source, one Audit transformation, and one destination), a preconfigured Foreach Loop container that uses the Foreach File Enumerator, and a set of Execute SQL tasks used to insert audit data to your proprietary auditing data store.

> **NOTE   TEMPLATE CONTENTS**
>
> You can place as many different objects into your template as you want, and configure them as needed, regardless of whether they will ultimately be needed in a particular project or not. When you create a package from a template, simply remove any objects that you do not need.

After you have configured the SSIS package, save a copy of it to the default location mentioned previously. The SSIS package can now be used as a template.

Using an SSIS Package Template

To use an existing SSIS package template to create a new package in a newly created project or an existing one, add a new item to the project, and instead of using the default blank template, select your own template from the list.

After the package has been created from a user-defined template, the value of its ID property will be the same as the one in the template. Because this could make it difficult to distinguish between different packages created from the same template in log entries and audits, you should change the identifier before deploying the package, at best right after creating it. The procedure of regenerating the package identifier with SSDT is explained in Exercise 2 later in this lesson.

 Quick Check

1. What is an SSIS package template?
2. Can log configurations be copied from one SSIS object to another?

Quick Check Answers

1. An SSIS package template is a regular SSIS package that has been stored in a specific location and can be used by SSDT when a developer adds new items to an SSIS project.

2. Yes. Log configurations can be exported to files and reapplied.

PRACTICE **Creating and Using an SSIS Package Template**

In this practice you will create and use an SSIS package template.

In Exercise 1, you will create a new SSIS package with a sequence container, which you will then configure for logging by using a log configuration template. You will save a copy of this package as a template.

In Exercise 2, you will create a new SSIS package, using the SSIS package template created in Exercise 1.

If you encounter a problem completing an exercise, you can install the completed projects from the Solution folder that is provided with the companion content for this chapter and lesson.

EXERCISE 1 Create an SSIS Package Template

1. Start SSDT, select New Project on the Start page, and create a new Integration Services project named TK 463 Chapter 10 in the C:\TK463\Chapter10\Lesson3\Starter\ folder.

2. The newly created project should contain one SSIS package, named Package.dtsx. Rename the package **ManuallyConfiguredPackage.dtsx**.

3. Drag a sequence container from the SSIS Toolbox onto the SSIS Designer surface.

4. Either from the SSIS menu or the SSIS Designer's shortcut menu, select Logging to open the Configure SSIS Logging editor.

5. Assign the SSIS log provider for Windows Event Log to the ManuallyConfigured-Package.dtsx SSIS package.

6. Enable logging for the sequence container, and while its node is selected in the Containers tree view, open the Details tab.

7. At the bottom of the tab, click Load to import the logging configuration from the template you created earlier in Lesson 1.

   The log configuration template, which is named LogTaskBoundaries.xml, should be located in the C:\TK463\Chapter10\Lesson1\Starter folder.

8. Open the template to apply the log configuration, and then click OK to confirm the settings.

   Optionally, you can add additional objects to the SSIS package. Depending on your own experience developing SSIS projects, these objects should be available in an SSIS package template.

9. After you are done adding objects and configuring the ManuallyConfiguredPackage.dtsx SSIS package, save it.

10. On the File menu, select Save Copy Of ManuallyConfiguredPackage.dtsx As to create a copy of the SSIS package.

11. In the Save Copy Of ManuallyConfiguredPackage.dtsx As dialog box, navigate to the C:\Program Files (x86)\Microsoft Visual Studio 10.0\Common7\IDE\PrivateAssemblies \ProjectItems\DataTransformationProject\DataTransformationItems folder.

12. In the Save dialog box, change the file name to **SequenceContainerWithLogging.dtsx** and, when you are done, click Save to save the newly created SSIS package template.

13. Leave the project open because you will need it in the following exercise.

EXERCISE 2   **Create a New SSIS Package by Using an SSIS Package Template**

1. Make sure the TK 463 Chapter 10.sln solution you created in Exercise 1 of this lesson is open in SSDT.

2. On the Project menu, select Add New Item, or press Ctrl+Shift+A on the keyboard to add a new item to the project.

3. In the Add New Item dialog box, select the SSIS package template named Sequence-ContainerWithLogging.dtsx, which you created in Lesson 1.

4. Change the default name of the new SSIS package from SequenceContainerWith-Logging1.dtsx to **PreConfiguredPackage.dtsx**, and then click Add.

   A new SSIS package should appear under SSIS Packages in the Solution Explorer pane.

5. Open the newly added SSIS package and view its contents. Also check the new package's logging settings.

6. To create a new package identifier, open the properties for PreConfiguredPackage.dtsx and find the ID property in the property grid.

7. Open the ID property's list box, and select <Generate New ID>.

   The ID of the SSIS package should now be changed to a new value.

8. After you are done configuring the packages, save the project and close SSDT.

Lesson Summary

- You can prepare SSIS package templates to simplify SSIS package development.
- When you share SSIS package templates with your colleagues, your team can implement common SSIS development practices.

Lesson Review

Answer the following questions to test your knowledge of the information in this lesson. You can find the answers to these questions and explanations of why each answer choice is correct or incorrect in the "Answers" section at the end of this chapter.

1. What are SSIS package templates used for? (Choose all that apply.)

   A. They can be used to develop new SSIS projects.

   B. They can be used to preconfigure SSIS packages.

   C. They can be used to apply log configurations for SSIS objects.

   D. They can be used to create SSIS packages.

2. What type is used for SSIS package template files?

   A. The .dotx file type

   B. The .dotsx file type

   C. The .dtsx file type

   D. The .xml file type

3. Which of the following statements about package templates are true? (Choose all that apply.)

A. SSIS package templates can be used to reapply log settings to SSIS tasks and/or containers.

B. SSIS package templates can be used to reduce the time needed to develop an SSIS package.

C. SSIS package templates can be used to preconfigure SSIS operations.

D. SSIS package templates can speed up SSIS process execution.

Case Scenarios

In the following case scenario, you apply what you've learned about auditing and logging. You can find the answers to these questions in the "Answers" section at the end of this chapter.

Case Scenario 1: Implementing SSIS Logging at Multiple Levels of the SSIS Object Hierarchy

You have been tasked with configuring logging in an existing SSIS project. The project implements a single master SSIS package, controlling the execution of multiple child packages.

The members of the development team and the administrators, tasked with the maintenance of deployed SSIS solutions, have sent you the following list of requirements:

- The start and the end of the execution for each package must be logged to the Windows Application Log.

- The start and the end of the execution of each control flow task must be logged to a comma-separated text file that will be copied, after all child packages have completed, from the server at which the SSIS project will be deployed to a secondary location where the files will be loaded into the process management and analysis database.

- Warnings and errors must be logged to the Windows Application Log and to the text files.

- In Foreach Loop containers using Foreach File Enumerators, the values of the variables holding file names must be logged at each iteration to the text files.

Case Scenario 2: Implementing SSIS Auditing at Different Levels of the SSIS Object Hierarchy

You have been tasked with adding appropriate auditing to an existing SSIS project. The project implements a single master SSIS package controlling the execution of multiple child packages.

The members of the development team and the analysts, tasked with analyzing the execution characteristics of deployed SSIS solutions, have prepared the following list of requirements for you:

- At the project, package, and task level, audit the duration of the execution with millisecond accuracy; the numbers of rows inserted, updated, and deleted; and the size of inserted, updated, and deleted data in bytes.

- At the row level, each row must contain reference information allowing the row to be associated with corresponding audit data at higher levels and with the corresponding log entries.

Suggested Practices

To help you successfully master the exam objectives presented in this chapter, complete the following tasks.

Add Auditing to an Update Operation in an Existing Execute SQL Task

In Exercise 2 of Lesson 2, earlier in this chapter, you configured a data flow to include audit properties in the destination rows. During the exercise, you added row-level auditing information to two data flow destinations, but only one of them was used as the final destination. To complete the solution, you need to further modify the SSIS package.

Newly added data is being sent to the destination table with all the audit properties, and the same goes for data that needs to be updated, yet the update operation has not been configured appropriately and might fail.

- **Practice 1** Identify the task in the DimCustomer.dtsx SSIS package that is used for updating the *dbo.Customers* destination table.

- **Practice 2** Change the Transact-SQL statement used by the update task and add all missing columns.

- **Practice 3** Change the update task so that the audit values will be passed to the Transact-SQL statement when the task is executed.

Create an SSIS Package Template in Your Own Environment

Consider all existing SSIS solutions in your working environment. Inspect them, and identify as many of the characteristics that they have in common as you can.

- **Practice 1** What elements are present in every SSIS project? Which SSIS objects can be found in any of the SSIS packages?

- **Practice 2** Create a list of objects that are common to all your SSIS solutions. Think about which of them are typically used together, in the same SSIS project, or even in the same SSIS package.

- **Practice 3** Based on your list, create one or more SSIS package templates.

Answers

This section contains answers to the lesson review questions and solutions to the case scenarios in this chapter.

Lesson 1

1. **Correct answers: B and D**

    A. **Incorrect:** Logging needs to be configured explicitly and there is no "default output file" used for logging.

    B. **Correct:** Logging can be configured at any level in the SSIS object hierarchy.

    C. **Incorrect:** No SSIS log provider uses the SQL Server Error Log as the destination.

    D. **Correct:** SSIS events are captured internally by the SSIS run time and are consumed by log providers, which expose them to the environment by storing log entries in files, tables, or the Windows Application Log.

2. **Correct answers: A, B, C, and D**

    A. **Correct:** The name of the task that generated the event is written to the log.

    B. **Correct:** The name of the event is written to the Windows Application log.

    C. **Correct:** The name of the user who started the process can be written to the log.

    D. **Correct:** The name of the machine on which the event occurred can be written to the log.

3. **Correct answer: B**

    A. **Incorrect:** There is no such thing as a log template in SSIS.

    B. **Correct:** Logging settings for a particular SSIS task or container can be saved to a file that is referred to as a log configuration template. This file can be used to apply the same logging settings to a different SSIS task or container.

    C. **Incorrect:** Log settings are stored in a log configuration template.

    D. **Incorrect:** There is no such thing as a package configuration template in SSIS.

Lesson 2

1. **Correct answers: C and D**

   A. **Incorrect:** The Audit transformation does not capture events; therefore, event names are not available to it.

   B. **Incorrect:** The Audit transformation does not capture events; therefore, event identifiers are not available to it.

   C. **Correct:** The identifier of the data flow task that contains the Audit transformation is available for auditing.

   D. **Correct:** The name of the machine on which the SSIS process is running is available to the Audit transformation.

2. **Correct answer: A**

   A. **Correct:** The set of properties available to the Audit transformation cannot be extended.

   B. **Incorrect:** System variables are read-only and cannot be modified by using the Expression task, only by the SSIS engine.

   C. **Incorrect:** The set of properties available to the Audit transformation cannot be extended even by configuring it using the Advanced Editor.

   D. **Incorrect:** There is no "advanced mode" for the Audit transformation.

3. **Correct answers: A and B**

   A. **Correct:** The date and time that a row was added to the table is a typical example of audit data. It documents the first time a particular row was added to the table.

   B. **Correct:** The date and time that a row was last modified is a typical example of audit data. It documents the last time the values of a particular row were changed.

   C. **Incorrect:** A value designating the success or failure of an SSIS process is typically written to the log, not to a data audit.

   D. **Incorrect:** The name of the SSIS task that has failed can be (and typically is) written to an SSIS log but is not typically found in a data audit. In fact, usually when failure occurs, no data is actually written to the destination table.

Lesson 3

1. **Correct answers: B and D**

   A. **Incorrect:** Package templates are not project templates.

   B. **Correct:** SSIS package templates are generally used to configure SSIS objects once in advance; you can reuse them many times later.

   C. **Incorrect:** SSIS package templates cannot be used to apply log configurations on SSIS objects.

   D. **Correct:** SSIS package templates are used to create SSIS packages.

2. **Correct answer: C**

   A. **Incorrect:** The .dotx file type is used for Microsoft Word templates.

   B. **Incorrect:** Even if the .dotsx file type actually exists, it is not used for SSIS package templates.

   C. **Correct:** The .dtsx file type is used for SSIS package files as well as SSIS package template files.

   D. **Incorrect:** Even though the SSIS packages and SSIS package templates are implemented as XML files, the .xml file type is not used for their files.

3. **Correct answers: B and C**

   A. **Incorrect:** To reuse SSIS logging settings, you can use log configuration templates. SSIS package templates can contain log configuration settings, but they cannot be used to reapply these settings to other SSIS tasks and/or containers.

   B. **Correct:** An SSIS package template can contain common SSIS tasks, containers, and data flow components that can already be partially configured in advance. The total time needed to design an SSIS package built from a template can be reduced to completing the configuration of existing SSIS objects, rather than having to create and configure them from scratch.

   C. **Correct:** Common SSIS operations can be designed and configured once and then placed in an SSIS template, so that they can later be reused in many different SSIS packages.

   D. **Incorrect:** Although SSIS package templates can reduce total development time of new SSIS packages, they cannot directly affect the performance of their execution.

Case Scenario 1

- An SSIS log provider for Windows Event Log and an SSIS log provider for text files must be assigned to all packages and enabled at the package level exclusively.

  To prevent duplicates in the log, every Execute Package task in the master package should have logging disabled.

  Package level logs must capture OnPreExecute, OnPostExecute, OnWarning, and OnError events.

- In every child package, the SSIS log provider for text files must be enabled at the task level and not enabled at package or container levels.

  Task-level logs must capture OnPreExecute, OnPostExecute, OnWarning, and OnError events.

  To reduce development time, you can configure one task and save its settings to a file, and then you can apply it to all other tasks.

- The SSIS log provider for text files should be enabled at every Foreach Loop container using the Foreach File Enumerator.

  Container-level logs must capture the OnVariableValueChanged event, and the variables used to hold the file names should have the RaiseChangedEvent property enabled (set to True). However, note that as a side effect, all other container-scoped variables of the Foreach Loop container with this property enabled will have their changes logged as well.

Case Scenario 2

- At the task level, row counts and data sizes must be collected for deleted data during execution; for instance, by using the Row Count and Aggregate transformations.

  At the package level, values can be aggregated from task-level data, and at the project level, values can be aggregated from package-level data.

- At the row level, all insert and all update operations must save data into the database—either in the same table with primary data or in separate tables.

  Row numbers and data sizes can then be computed at the row level and aggregated to higher levels.

## PART IV

Managing and Maintaining SSIS Packages

CHAPTER 11   Installing SSIS and Deploying Packages   **421**

CHAPTER 12   Executing and Securing Packages   **455**

CHAPTER 13   Troubleshooting and Performance Tuning   **497**

Installing SSIS and Deploying Packages

Exam objectives in this chapter:

- Configure and Deploy SSIS Solutions
    - Install and maintain SSIS components.
    - Deploy SSIS solutions.

During development, a Microsoft SQL Server Integration Services (SSIS) solution (much like any other solution) passes through many different phases on its way to becoming the finished product that responds to the real-world problem it needs to solve. What might start out as just an idea for how a particular problem can be solved sooner or later matures into one or more prototypes, either proving that the initial idea was correct or proving beyond a doubt that it was not, until finally it evolves into the most appropriate solution for solving the problem that started it all.

When the development of the solution is complete, it would be misleading to think that there is no more work to be done, because a very important development phase is about to begin. The deployment of a solution into production should not be considered an independent development phase, and certainly not a completely new or isolated process. The deployment of the finished solution into the real-world environment, where it is going to be used, is strongly related to many of the preceding development phases, and some aspects of these relationships can even go as far back as the original idea they are based on.

One such relationship between deployment and planning is the question of the destination environment. Will the solution be deployed to SQL Server? SSIS solutions can only be hosted in production environments built on the SQL Server platform. They do not depend on SQL Server as far as storage is concerned—SSIS packages can be stored in the file system. They do, however, depend on SQL Server for execution.

 SSIS processes are hosted in a specific element of the SQL Server platform, Integration Services, which at a minimum provides the *execution engine*, referred to as the *SSIS runtime*. The SSIS runtime is used to start, perform, and (if needed) stop the execution of SSIS processes.

Of course, the runtime is not the only component of Integration Services; SSIS solutions provide automated data management operations, access to various data sources and destinations, and collections of information at varying levels of quantity, quality, and sensitivity. Depending on its purpose, an SSIS solution could also be very potent in terms of the type of operations that it performs against data, data stores, and environments. Therefore, another component provided by Integration Services is the security model. After an SSIS solution has been deployed to production, the administrators of the target environment must have complete control of how the solutions are going to be executed, when, under what conditions, and by whom.

As far as resource requirements are concerned, or in terms of how SSIS executions affect the environment, Integration Services also provides capabilities to be used in analysis of completed processes, an overview of those currently running, and other functionalities used in troubleshooting and performance tuning.

Before SSIS solutions can be deployed, the destination environment should be prepared appropriately. SSIS projects can pretty much be stored anywhere—in a dedicated SQL Server database, or even in the file system—so storage is not really a principal concern. The principal concern is, or at least should be, the execution: in order for SSIS solutions to be executed in the destination environment, Integration Services must be installed there.

In this chapter, you will learn how to install SQL Server Integration Services (either on a new server or by upgrading an older version of the product), how to prepare SSIS project storage in a special SQL Server database, and how to deploy SSIS projects to the destination environment.

You will start by identifying the environment and selecting the appropriate components to be installed. You will learn about the SSIS production toolset and how to find your way around a typical SQL Server 2012 instance that hosts Integration Services and SSIS solutions.

Lessons in this chapter:

- Lesson 1: Installing SSIS Components
- Lesson 2: Deploying SSIS Packages

Before You Begin

To complete this chapter, you must have:

- Experience working with SQL Server Management Studio (SSMS).
- Experience working with Microsoft Visual Studio or SQL Server Data Tools (SSDT).
- A working knowledge of the Transact-SQL language.

Lesson 1: Installing SSIS Components

SQL Server Integration Services (SSIS) is an optional element of the SQL Server platform and can either be installed as part of the initial SQL Server installation or added to an existing SQL Server installation later. SSIS does not depend on any other element of the SQL Server platform; it can, however, use the Database Engine to provide secure storage for SSIS solutions.

In previous versions of SQL Server, the pivotal element of SSIS was the SSIS Service, which was used primarily to allow access to deployed SSIS packages (regardless of whether they were stored in a database or in the file system) and to host the SSIS execution (either on demand or through an automated process, such as the SQL Server Agent). Starting with SQL Server 2012, the SSIS Service is no longer needed—neither to manage SSIS packages nor to execute them. Nonetheless, the service, now referred to as the *SSIS Legacy Service*, is still available and can be used to manage, execute, and monitor the execution of SSIS packages with the familiar toolset from previous versions of SQL Server.

The functionalities that were once provided by the SSIS Service have been replaced in SQL Server 2012 by the *SSIS server*—an instance of SQL Server hosting the *SSISDB catalog*. SQL Server 2012 uses this new, special, database to store SSIS solutions (projects, packages, and parameters), together with the complete operational history. The SSISDB catalog is also used in managing SSIS security (assignment of permissions on the SSIS objects stored inside the SSISDB catalog).

In SQL Server 2012, SSIS manageability is integrated with SQL Server Management Studio (SSMS), providing every aspect of SSIS management—deployment, configuration, execution, and monitoring. Alternatively, SSIS management can be supported through a managed application programming interface (API). All SSIS management, execution, and monitoring capabilities are also accessible with Transact-SQL (with system catalog views providing access to data, and with stored procedures providing complete maintenance functionalities).

> **After this lesson, you will be able to:**
>
> - Install the software (SSIS and management tools).
> - Install the development workstation and server.
> - Install specifics for remote package execution.
> - Plan for installation (32-bit vs. 64-bit).
> - Upgrade an existing version of SQL Server.
> - Provision the accounts.
>
> **Estimated lesson time: 60 minutes**

Preparing an SSIS Installation

When you are planning the installation of SQL Server, an important decision that you need to make is which elements and/or features of the platform should be installed at a particular server. The general rule that applies in this situation is to minimize the installation footprint—to only install features that are actually going to be used. This rule might sound straightforward enough, but when you try to apply it to a particular real-world situation, it will not take long before you realize just how vague the rule really is.

The choice of features to be installed on a particular server very much depends on what the server is going to be used for. Only if you are certain that the server in question is going to require all SQL Server 2012 features should you install all of them. However, the more sensible approach would be to start by installing the Database Engine first and install additional features later, as it becomes clear that they will be needed.

The same rule applies to SSIS installations: start by installing the Database Engine and Integration Services as the minimum. This will allow you to deploy, maintain, and execute SSIS solutions. You can always install any additional features later (such as SSMS and SSDT).

Development vs. Production

SSIS installation also depends on the type of environment the server (or the workstation) in question belongs to—whether it is going to be used for SSIS development, or SSIS operations.

On a *production server*, where SSIS projects will be deployed, maintained, and executed, SSIS installation can be limited to features that provide SSIS storage and execution; there is no need to also install the management tools. As long as remote connections to the server are possible from SQL Server tools (such as SSMS or the deployment wizards and utilities) installed on a separate machine, no user components are needed on the production server.

In a *development environment*, the situation may be similar to the one mentioned previously—a dedicated development and testing server used for maintaining data in the test environment in the same way that it is maintained in production would not require any SQL Server management tools. On the other hand, SSDT and the SSIS Software Development Kit (SSIS SDK) represent the bare minimum for SSIS development, even without the need for any other SSIS server components.

EXAM TIP

You should understand SSIS installation requirements very well, especially from the perspective of the target environments. Typically, a production environment is governed by a set of very strict rules and principles determining the security and the collection of features to be deployed. On the other hand, in a development environment, some features would not be required at all.

The differences in SSIS installation requirements between production and development environments are shown in Table 11-1.

TABLE 11-1 SSIS Installation and Environments

Feature or component	Environment	
	Development	Production
SQL Server Database Engine	Optional; used to host development and testing data stores	Recommended; used to host the SSIS package store (SSIS server or the msdb database)
SQL Server Agent	Not needed	Recommended; used to automate and schedule SSIS execution
Integration Services	Not needed	Required
SQL Server Data Tools	Required; used for SSIS development and execution	Not needed
Management Tools – Complete	Recommended; used for SSIS management	Optional; used for SSIS management
Client Tools SDK	Required	Not needed
SSIS server	Not needed	Recommended; used as the SSIS package store

The SSIS server is configured separately, after the SSIS installation has been completed successfully. The SSIS server and the SSISDB catalog are discussed in more detail in Lesson 2, later in this chapter.

> **NOTE DATABASE ENGINE SERVICES**
>
> Database Engine Services, installed as part of the SQL Server Database Engine, provide only limited SSIS functionality: the SQL Server Import And Export Wizard, and support for SQL Server Maintenance Plans (development, deployment, maintenance, and execution).
>
> Complete SSIS deployment, maintenance, and execution functionalities are not available unless SSIS is installed.

Hardware and Software Requirements

SSIS hardware and software requirements are consistent with the general SQL Server hardware and software requirements, as described in Books Online for SQL Server 2012, in the article entitled "Hardware and Software Requirements for Installing SQL Server 2012" (http://msdn.microsoft.com/en-us/library/ms143506(SQL.110).aspx).

There are no additional considerations regarding SSIS installation except for hard disk space requirements: SSIS component files require approximately 600 megabytes (MB) of disk space.

Security Considerations

SSIS is used for specific purposes (for example, for data integration, data movements, data transformation, and automated maintenance), and the majority of these purposes do not require the same operating system privileges and SQL Server permissions that are required by other elements of the SQL Server platform (such as the Database Engine).

 SQL Server security is based on the *minimal rights principle*, in which operating system principals (in this case a Windows user or a service account) are granted only the privileges needed to perform their work.

Based on the server roles and the type of operating system used at the server where SSIS is going to be installed, the following accounts are recommended for SQL Server services:

- When SSIS is installed on a stand-alone server or a domain controller running Windows 7 or Windows Server 2008 R2, a dedicated virtual account should be used; however, if SSIS requires access to external resources, a managed service account (MSA) is required.

- When SSIS is installed on a SQL Server failover cluster instance on Windows 2008 R2, a dedicated virtual account should be used.

 Virtual accounts are special accounts available in Windows 7 and Windows Server 2008 R2 that have reduced administrative requirements (no password management). Virtual Accounts can access the network by using the computer identity in a domain environment.

 Managed service accounts (MSAs) are special accounts available in Windows 7 and Windows Server 2008 R2 that have reduced administrative requirements (automated password management and simplified service principal name management for Kerberos authentication). Managed service accounts are functionally equivalent to other domain accounts, even though they only exist on the local server.

Alternatively, a dedicated *domain account* (a domain user account) can also be used for the SSIS Service, which is the recommended choice when SSIS is installed on a server running Windows Vista or Windows Server 2008.

> **MORE INFO** **VIRTUAL ACCOUNTS AND MANAGED SERVICE ACCOUNTS**
>
> More information about virtual accounts and managed service accounts is available at MSDN or Microsoft TechNet:
>
> - Service Accounts Step-by-Step Guide (*http://technet.microsoft.com/en-us /library/dd548356(WS.10).aspx*).
> - Managed Service Accounts Frequently Asked Questions (FAQ) (*http://technet.microsoft.com/en-us/library/ff641729(WS.10).aspx*).

The appropriate accounts should be created with minimal operating system privileges before the installation of SQL Server 2012. During installation, all accounts will be assigned additional operating system privileges and SQL Server permissions automatically by the installation procedure.

If service accounts used for SQL Server services need to be changed later (after installation), the change should be made exclusively through the SQL Server Configuration Manager, which will automatically assign all appropriate permissions to the new account. Although service accounts can also be changed by using other operating system tools, these tools should not be used because they have not been programmed to assign all the necessary privileges required by SQL Server to the new accounts.

> **MORE INFO** **SQL SERVER SERVICE ACCOUNTS**
>
> More information on service accounts used for various elements of the SQL Server platform can be found in Books Online for SQL Server 2012, in the article entitled "Configure Windows Service Accounts and Permissions" (*http://msdn.microsoft.com/en-us/library /ms143504(SQL.110).aspx*).

64-Bit Environments vs. 32-Bit Environments

SQL Server 2012 is available in 32-bit as well as 64-bit editions; SSIS is included in both, but some SSIS features are available only in 32-bit editions, some features have limited functionality in 64-bit systems, and some are not supported on Itanium-based operating systems.

When you are installing SSIS on a 64-bit computer, all available 64-bit features and tools are installed, including SQL Server Integration Services Execute Package Utilities, SQL Server Integration Services Package Utility, and the SQL Server Import And Export Wizard.

Development tools (SSDT) are available only as 32-bit applications, and SSDT is not supported on Itanium-based operating systems and therefore cannot be installed on Itanium servers.

To run packages in 32-bit mode in a 64-bit environment, you must install the 32-bit runtime and tools. They will be installed if the SQL Server Data Tools and/or Management Tools – Complete options are selected during installation. Typically, SSIS packages that use 32-bit-only components (such as some data providers) have to be executed using the 32-bit runtime.

When SSIS packages are executed manually in a 64-bit environment with the 32-bit runtime and tools installed, the 32-bit edition of the SQL Server Integration Services Execute Package Utility will be invoked by default. This is because of the structure of the program files directory paths in the *PATH* environment variable: the directory path to the 32-bit program files (%ProgramFiles(x86)%) is listed before the directory path to the 64-bit program files (%ProgramFiles%). To correct this, edit the PATH environment variable and place the path to the 64-bit tools directory before the path to the 32-bit tools directory. Alternatively, you can always navigate to the appropriate folder in order to execute each SSIS package manually, using the appropriate runtime.

At design time, only 32-bit data providers are visible in SSDT; to configure a connection manager at design time that should use a 64-bit data provider at run time, you must first install the 32-bit edition of the data provider on the development machine. Connection managers and data providers are discussed in more detail in Chapter 4, "Designing and Implementing Control Flow."

EXAM TIP

Remember that SSDT is a 32-bit-only application; although it can be used in a 64-bit environment, all the data providers it uses are 32 bit. To enable the SSIS packages to be used in 64-bit environments, you must have the appropriate editions of the data providers; if you don't, they will have to be executed using the 32-bit run time.

The SQL Server Agent does not use the *PATH* environment variable when executing SSIS packages; therefore, automated SSIS execution is not affected on 64-bit servers with the 32-bit runtime and tools installed. You will learn how to specify the runtime to be used when executing SSIS packages through SQL Server Agent jobs, in Chapter 12, "Executing and Securing Packages."

MORE INFO   **64-BIT CONSIDERATIONS FOR INTEGRATION SERVICES**

Additional information on installing SSIS in 64-bit environments can be found in Books Online for SQL Server 2012, in the article entitled "Install Integration Services," in the section entitled "Installing Integration Services on 64-bit Computers" (*http://msdn.microsoft.com /en-us/library/ms143731(SQL.110).aspx*).

Installing SSIS

SSIS installation is performed by using the SQL Server Installation Center; by default, the tool is available on the Start menu, at All Programs/Microsoft SQL Server 2012/Configuration Tools.

The SQL Server Installation Center can be used to install additional instances of SQL Server, to add features to the existing installation, to perform advanced configuration, and more. It cannot be used to remove or change the installed features. Because SQL Server installation is integrated with the Windows operating system, removal of and changes to the installed components can be performed through the Windows Control Panel.

The following SSIS installation paths are supported:

- In a fresh installation, SSIS is installed as part of the installation of an instance of SQL Server 2012 or added to an existing SQL Server 2012 installation.

- In a side-by-side upgrade, SSIS is installed on a server with an existing instance of SQL Server 2005 or SQL Server 2008 Integration Services.

- In an in-place upgrade, an existing instance of SQL Server 2005 or SQL Server 2008 Integration Services is upgraded to SQL Server 2012. Upgrading SSIS is discussed later in this chapter, in the "Upgrading SSIS" section.

By default, the Integration Services service is configured to manage SSIS packages stored in the msdb database of the Database Engine that is installed in the same installation procedure.

If an instance of the Database Engine is not installed at the same time, the Integration Services service is configured to manage packages that are stored in the msdb database of the local, default instance of the Database Engine.

To manage packages that are stored in a named instance or a remote instance of the Database Engine, or in multiple instances of the Database Engine, you must modify the SSIS configuration file manually.

> **NOTE** **LEGACY SSIS SERVICE**
>
> More information about the manual configuration of the SSIS Service is available in Books Online for SQL Server 2012, in the article entitled "Configuring the Integration Services Service (SSIS Service)" (*http://msdn.microsoft.com/en-us/library/ms137789(SQL.110).aspx*).

The SSIS service is not instance-aware; it is not installed as part of a specific instance of SQL Server but is shared between all installed instances.

In contrast to previous versions, in SQL Server 2012 the SSIS service is secure by default. This means that right after it has been installed, the service is not accessible to any user until the users have been granted appropriate access permissions by the administrator.

Upgrading SSIS

The supported upgrade methods, the side-by-side upgrade and the in-place upgrade, have been mentioned previously; the supported upgrade paths are from SQL Server 2005 or SQL Server 2008. Before attempting an upgrade, you should run the SQL Server 2012 Upgrade Advisor on the upgrade target to identify potential issues with the upgrade of any existing SSIS packages. The SQL Server 2012 Upgrade Advisor is available on the SQL Server 2012 installation media and in the SQL Server Installation Center.

The upgrade cannot be used to reconfigure an existing SSIS installation, nor can it be used to migrate a 32-bit installation to 64-bit or vice versa, and it cannot be used to migrate from one localized version of SQL Server to another localized version. In all of these cases, the existing SSIS installation should first be removed and then installed using a different configuration, a different edition of the runtime, or a different localization.

EXAM TIP

Before attempting to upgrade an existing installation of SQL Server, you should be familiar with the limitations regarding versions and editions of SQL Server, as well as whether the target environment is a 32-bit or 64-bit environment.

SSIS and the Database Engine can be upgraded together or independently from one another; however, functionalities available in the newer version of the feature will not be available in the older version. For instance, if you upgrade just the Database Engine, the existing version of SSIS will remain functional, albeit without the functionalities available in the new version. Or if you upgrade just the SSIS, the new version of SSIS will be able to access data in the old version of the Database Engine, but it will not be able to use the SSISDB catalog, which is not available in previous versions of the Database Engine.

> **MORE INFO** **SQL SERVER AND SSIS UPGRADES**
>
> More information about the possibilities of upgrading to SQL Server 2012 Integration Services is available in Books Online for SQL Server 2012, in the article entitled "Upgrade Integration Services" (*http://msdn.microsoft.com/en-us/library/cc879336(SQL.110).aspx*).

SSIS Tools

The following stand-alone tools are available as part of SQL Server 2012 Integration Services:

- **SQL Server Import And Export Wizard**   Used to copy data between supported data stores; the wizard is discussed in detail in Chapter 3, "Creating SSIS Packages."

- **SQL Server Integration Services Deployment Wizard**   Used to deploy SSIS projects to an instance of SQL Server; you will learn how to use this tool in Lesson 2, later in this chapter.

- **SQL Server Integration Services Project Conversion Wizard**   Used to generate a project deployment file from a set of SSIS package files and accompanying configuration files.

  The resulting project deployment file is a compiled SSIS 2012 project file consisting of packages and parameters and can be deployed to an instance of SQL Server 2012 by using the Integration Services Deployment Wizard. The Project Conversion Wizard does not convert or upgrade SSIS package files.

- **SQL Server Integration Services Package Upgrade Wizard**   Used to upgrade SSIS packages created in previous versions of SQL Server to SQL Server 2012.

- **SQL Server Integration Services Package Installation Utility**   Used to deploy SSIS packages to an instance of SQL Server using the deployment manifest.

  This utility is provided for legacy reasons, to allow you to deploy SSIS packages created in previous versions of SQL Server to a SQL Server 2012 instance without creating an SSIS project deployment file.

- **SQL Server Integration Services Package Utility**   Used to manage SSIS packages (for example, to copy, move, or delete them, or to verify their existence) from the command line.

- **SQL Server Integration Services Execute Package Utilities**   Two utilities used to execute SSIS packages, either from the command line or from a user interface.

EXAM TIP

Become familiar with relevant SSIS tools, and understand what they are used for. If you have worked with SSIS in previous versions of SQL Server, remember that some tools are only provided for legacy reasons.

The following tools are available in the 32-bit version as well as the 64-bit version:

- SQL Server Import And Export Wizard
- SQL Server Integration Services Package Utility
- The command-line SQL Server Integration Services Execute Package Utility

✓ **Quick Check**

1. What are SQL Server Integration Services (SSIS)?

2. How can SSIS be installed?

Quick Check Answers

1. SSIS is a feature of SQL Server that hosts SSIS deployment, maintenance, execution, and monitoring.

2. SSIS can be installed together with other SQL Server features, added to an existing SQL Server installation, or used to upgrade an earlier version of SSIS.

PRACTICE **Installing SSIS**

In this practice, you will install SQL Server Integration Services (SSIS) to an existing installation of SQL Server 2012.

In Lesson 2, later in this chapter, you will add the SSISDB system catalog to the instance of SQL Server 2012, effectively turning it into an SSIS server. You will need this server to deploy and execute your SSIS projects.

To comply with security best practices, prepare a virtual account, a managed service account, or another dedicated account to be used by the SSIS service; you will need this account during SSIS installation. Alternatively, you can also use the default built-in network service account (NT AUTHORITY\NETWORK SERVICE) for this particular exercise. To choose the most appropriate SSIS service account to be used in a real-world production environment, refer to the "Security Considerations" section earlier in this lesson.

EXERCISE 1 Install SSIS to an Existing Instance of SQL Server

1. Start the SQL Server 2012 Installation Center and, under Installation, select New SQL Server Stand-Alone Installation Or Add Features To An Existing Installation.

   By default, the shortcut to the SQL Server 2012 Installation Center is located on the Start menu, under All Programs | Microsoft SQL Server 2012 | Configuration Tools.

2. Wait until the setup support rules are applied to verify whether the installation can be performed. If the operation completes without errors, click OK to proceed.

   If you encounter any errors at this point, consult the error messages, correct whatever might be wrong, and then restart the installation.

3. After the check for any relevant updates is completed, click Next.

4. Further setup rules will be checked. After the operation is completed without any errors, click Next to proceed.

   If you encounter any errors at this point, consult the error messages, correct whatever might be wrong, and then restart the installation.

5. On the Installation Type screen, similar to the one shown in Figure 11-1, select Add Features To An Existing Instance Of SQL Server 2012, and then select the MSSQLSERVER instance from the list box. Click Next to proceed.

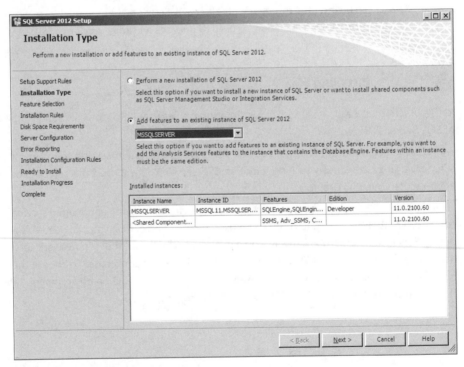

FIGURE 11-1 The Installation Type screen.

6. On the Feature Selection screen, shown in Figure 11-2, select the following features:

- Integration Services
- Client Tools SDK

Unless they are already installed, also select the following development features:

- SQL Server Data Tools
- Client Tools Connectivity
- Management Tools – Complete

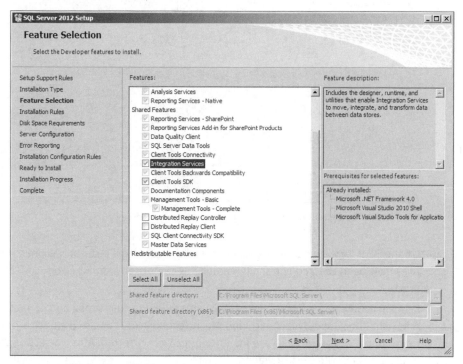

FIGURE 11-2 The Feature Selection screen.

When ready, click Next to continue.

7. On the Disk Space Requirements screen, verify that enough disk space is available, and then click Next to proceed.

8. On the Server Configuration screen, shown in Figure 11-3, enter the credentials of the account that will be used by the SSIS service.

9. If you created an account as suggested in the introduction to this practice, use that one; otherwise, use the default. Set the startup type of the SSIS service to Automatic. When ready, click Next to proceed.

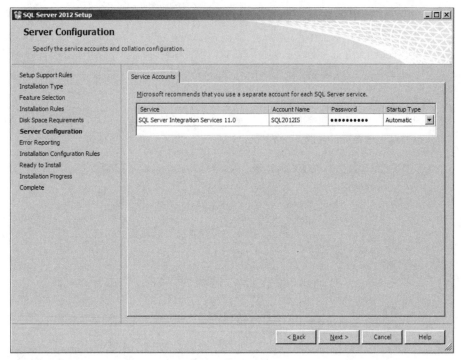

FIGURE 11-3 The Server Configuration screen.

10. On the Error Reporting screen, click Next, and then after the installation configuration rules have been checked and the operation has completed without errors, click Next to proceed.

   If you encounter any errors at this point, consult the error messages, and correct whatever might be wrong by reconfiguring the installation. You can use the Back button to return to previous screens where the settings can be corrected. After correcting the errors, proceed with the installation.

11. On the Ready To Install screen, you can verify which features are going to be installed. When ready, click Install to start the installation.

12. After the installation has completed without errors, click Close on the Complete screen to finish the installation wizard.

13. Close the SQL Server 2012 Installation Center.

EXERCISE 2   Verify the SSIS Installation

1. Start the SQL Server Configuration Manager. By default, its shortcut is located on the Start menu, under All Programs | Microsoft SQL Server 2012 | Configuration Tools.

2. On the left, in the browser pane, select the SQL Server Services node.

   On the right side of the window, you can observe all the SQL Server services currently installed.

3. Locate the SQL Server Integration Services 11.0 service and inspect its properties.

If you completed all installation steps as described in Exercise 1 earlier in this practice, the properties should match those listed in Table 11-2.

TABLE 11-2 SSIS Service Properties

Property	Value
State	Running
Start Mode	Automatic
Log On As	Either the dedicated service account you prepared before the practice or the NT AUTHORITY\NETWORK SERVICE default account.

4. Double-click the SQL Server Integration Services 11.0 service, or right-click it and select Properties from the shortcut menu, to open the service properties, as shown in Figure 11-4.

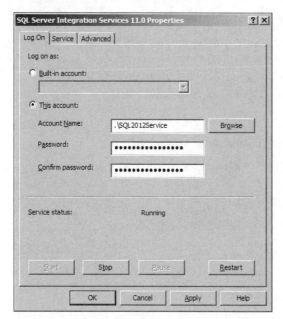

FIGURE 11-4 SQL Server Integration Services 11.0 properties.

If you ever need to modify the SSIS service account, you should do so using the SQL Server Configuration Manager, via the dialog box shown in Figure 11-4.

The SQL Server Configuration Manager will correctly assign all the appropriate operating system privileges and SQL Server permissions to this account, whereas other tools that can also be used to configure Windows services do not assign these permissions automatically.

5. When ready, click Cancel to close the dialog box, abandoning any changes you might have made, because no changes are needed at this time.

6. Close the SQL Server Configuration Manager.

Lesson Summary

- Before attempting the installation of SSIS, you need to know whether the target environment is going to be used in development and testing or in production, whether the environment is a 32-bit or 64-bit environment, and whether SQL Server has already been installed on the target server.
- Service accounts demand special consideration for security and manageability reasons.

Lesson Review

Answer the following questions to test your knowledge of the information in this lesson. You can find the answers to these questions and explanations of why each answer choice is correct or incorrect in the "Answers" section at the end of this chapter.

1. What kind of Windows account is the most appropriate for the SSIS service in a typical production environment where servers exist in a Windows domain, data needs to be accessed at different servers, and strict security policies must be followed?

   A. A local user account on the server hosting SSIS

   B. A virtual account on the server hosting SSIS

   C. A managed service account on the server hosting SSIS

   D. The Administrator account or another account with maximum operating system privileges

2. Which of the following features are required on a production server where SSIS processes will be executed?

   A. SQL Server Data Tools (SSDT)

   B. SQL Server Management Studio (SSMS)

   C. SQL Server Integration Services (SSIS)

   D. SSIS server

3. Which of the following tools can and should be used to change or modify the SSIS service account?

   A. SQL Server Management Studio (SSMS)

   B. The Windows Server Computer Management snap-in

   C. SQL Server Configuration Manager

   D. The Windows Server Services snap-in

Lesson 2: Deploying SSIS Packages

As is true for most development projects, SSIS solutions are developed in dedicated development and testing environments, isolated from production environments. This serves two very distinct objectives:

- Development activities must never interfere with principal business processes. Solution development is done in phases; completeness is achieved gradually, and during these phases, some parts of the evolving solution are not available, might not perform optimally, might cause errors, or might even lead to system failure. In contrast, the production environment assumes that every deployed solution is complete—either that it does not have any missing parts or that it implements contingencies to recover from failures due to a part of the solution not being available.

  After all, it is the uninterrupted flow of principal business processes that provides financing to the development, not the other way around. Allowing any development efforts to cause failure of business processes clearly is the cause of its own undoing—an organization that does not produce will not be able to develop.

- Production environments usually implement very strict security and maintenance rules and policies focused at maximizing stability and predictability. In a development environment, such strict rules and policies could present obstacles or even impede development, especially if the objective is to find new methods or techniques that could require the boundaries that facilitate stability and predictability to be pushed back, when ideas are validated through experimentation.

The separation of development and production environments is therefore essential, and the process in which a solution is transferred from the former into the latter therefore also deserves special care and attention.

In SQL Server 2012, solution deployment is integrated into the principal development tool, SSDT, and is even available in the principal management tool, SSMS. The new project deployment model implements a concept that significantly simplifies the move from development to production, because it allows the preparation for deployment to be present from the very start of development. A project encapsulates every aspect of an SSIS solution: all packages that constitute a specific unit of work, all connection managers used in a specific process, and all parameters that will eventually allow the solution to be configured as a single unit of work. When an SSIS solution is deployed as a whole, it conforms to the expectations and policies of the production environment regarding completeness, without having to be bound by these same rules during development.

SQL Server 2012 also introduces a new approach to SSIS solution storage, maintenance, execution, and monitoring in the form of the SSIS server with the SSISDB catalog. This new functionality provides storage for SSIS projects and includes standard built-in monitoring and logging capabilities aimed at improving SSIS process analysis, maintenance, and troubleshooting. In terms of optimization and security, the SSIS server with the SSISDB catalog represent a significant improvement over earlier versions of SQL Server.

SSISDB Catalog

The new SSIS server concept does not depend on the msdb system database, which is used primarily by SQL Server Agent, but also by SSMS, SQL Server Service Broker, and Database Mail. Instead, the SSIS server implements a new, specialized database dedicated to SSIS. The SSISDB catalog serves as the SSIS project and package repository and is the recommended deployment target for SQL Server 2012 SSIS solutions.

The SSISDB catalog stores SSIS metadata and definitions: projects, packages, parameters, and environment properties. When SSIS packages are executed, they are loaded from the SSISDB catalog, together with the corresponding configurations (parameters and connection managers).

The SSISDB catalog also stores information gathered from SSIS executions, to provide an overview of the operational history. The execution auditing and monitoring provided by the SSISDB catalog are discussed in more detail in Chapter 12.

> *IMPORTANT* **SSISDB ENCRYPTION**
>
> Data in the SSISDB catalog is encrypted. You can find more information about SQL Server cryptographic capabilities in Books Online for SQL Server 2012. Unless you are already familiar with SQL Server cryptography, start with the article entitled "SQL Server Encryption" (*http://msdn.microsoft.com/en-us/library/bb510663(SQL.110).aspx*).

Configuring SSISDB

The behavior of the SSISDB catalog is determined by the configuration of the catalog: the method used in data encryption, the criteria controlling automated SSISDB maintenance, and the default level of detail acquired in execution monitoring.

The available settings, shown in Table 11-3, can be set through SSMS or by using Transact-SQL (via the catalog.configure_catalog system stored procedure).

TABLE 11-3 SSISDB Catalog Properties

Property name	Description
Encryption Algorithm Name	The type of encryption algorithm that is used to encrypt sensitive data. The supported values include DES, TRIPLE_DES, TRIPLE_DES_3KEY, DESX, AES_128, AES_192, and AES_256 (default).
Clean Logs Periodically	When the value is True (default), operation details and operation messages older than the number of days specified by the Retention Period property are deleted from the catalog. When the value is False, all operation details and operation messages remain stored.
Retention Period (days)	The number of days (365 by default) that operation details and operation messages are stored in the catalog. When the value is -1, the retention window is infinite.
Server-wide Default Logging Level	The default logging level for the Integration Services server. You will learn more about SSISDB logging levels in Chapter 12.
Maximum Number of Versions per Project	The number of new project versions that will be retained for a single project. When version cleanup is enabled (by default), older versions beyond this count will be deleted.
Periodically Remove Old Versions	When the value is True (default), only the number of project versions specified by the Maximum Number of Versions per Project property are stored in the catalog. All other project versions are deleted. When the value is False, all project versions remain stored.
Validation Timeout	Validations will be stopped if they do not complete in the number of seconds specified by this property.

SSISDB configuration settings are accessible through the catalog.catalog_properties catalog view.

> *NOTE* **CHANGING SSISDB ENCRYPTION**
>
> The encryption method of the SSISDB catalog can only be changed if the database is in single-user mode.
>
> Also note that (depending on the number of existing SSISDB objects) changing the encryption method might be a highly time-consuming operation, because each object needs to first be decrypted and then be re-encrypted using the new method.

> *NOTE* **SSISDB CLEANUP**
>
> SSISDB operation cleanup is performed automatically by a special SQL Server Agent job, which is scheduled to run daily by default.

SSISDB Objects

SSISDB objects represent SSIS projects and packages (organized in folders) that have been deployed to the SSIS server, including SSIS project-scoped and package-scoped parameters and environment settings used in various SSIS configurations.

EXAM TIP

Become familiar with the internal layout and organization of the SSISDB database. Understand the purposes of folders, projects, packages, parameters, environments, and operations, as well as how they interact when SSIS projects are deployed, maintained, and executed.

The discussion of the SSISDB catalog in this chapter is limited to SSISDB metadata; operational data, concerning the validation and execution of projects and packages, is discussed in Chapter 12.

MORE INFO   **THE SSISDB CATALOG**

More information about the SSISDB catalog and SSISDB objects can be found in Books Online for SQL Server 2012, in the article entitled "SSISDB Catalog" (*http://msdn.microsoft .com/en-us/library/hh479588(SQL.110).aspx*).

Folders

When SSIS projects are deployed to the SSISDB catalog, they are placed in folders. The principal purpose of the folders is to provide a way of organizing one or more projects and the corresponding environments within a common security context.

Folders provide a way to store projects and packages that belong to different SSIS solutions separately and serve as entry points for deployment, maintenance, and execution of SSIS solutions on the SSIS server.

Folder metadata is accessible through the catalog.folders catalog view.

Projects and Packages

The project deployment model allows each SSIS project to be treated as a single unit, to be configured and deployed as a whole. A project can contain one or more packages, one or more parameters, and one or more connection managers. Under the project deployment model, all of these are deployed to the destination SSIS server as a single unit.

Of course, this deployment model does not imply that all packages in a common project should also be executed as a whole—individual maintenance, configuration, and execution are in no way impeded by the deployment model.

Project and package metadata is accessible through the catalog.projects, catalog.packages, and catalog.object_versions catalog views.

Parameters

Project and package parameters are exposed to the environment—or, more specifically, to the SSISDB. Through this mechanism, the SSIS server can facilitate dynamic configuration of projects and packages at run time.

The parameters can either be set once for each environment in which the corresponding projects and packages are going to be used, or they can be set at each execution.

In the SSISDB catalog, parameters, regardless of their scope, are accessible *directly* (they can be set by using system stored procedures or SSMS) or *indirectly* (they can be set through their association with environment variables).

Parameter metadata is accessible through the catalog.object_parameters and catalog.execution_parameter_values catalog views.

Server Environments, Server Variables, and Server Environment References

Parameter values can be assigned directly, but they can also be controlled through environment variables (also referred to as server variables) that are defined and stored in the SSISDB catalog.

Rather than relying on package configurations being maintained through user intervention ("manually," by using SSMS, stored procedures, or Transact-SQL scripts), you can bind parameter values to certain settings or values accessible in the environment to which the projects and the packages have been deployed. When parameters are associated with environment variables, even project and package configurations can be automated, in addition to their execution.

Environment references represent the association of server variables with project and package parameters.

Information about server environments, server variables, and environment references can be accessed through the catalog.environments, catalog.environment_variables, and catalog.environment_references catalog views.

Operations

Operations represent actions performed against the SSISDB catalog (deployments and catalog-level configurations) and against SSISDB projects and packages (validations and executions).

Operations are created when an SSIS process is prepared for execution; you will learn more about execution in Chapter 12. The nature of an operation is determined by its operation type, as shown in Table 11-4.

TABLE 11-4 SSISDB Operation Types

Operation type	Description
Integration Services initialization	Marks the initialization of SSIS after a restart
Retention window	Marks the execution of the SQL Server Agent job used in execution history cleanup
MaxProjectVersion	Marks the execution of the SQL Server Agent job used in project version cleanup
deploy_project	Marks the deployment of an SSIS project
restore_project	Marks the restoration of an SSIS project
create_execution	Marks the initialization of an execution
start_execution	Marks the start of an execution
stop_operation	Marks the stopping of an operation
validate_project	Marks the validation of a deployed project
validate_package	Marks the validation of a deployed package
configure_catalog	Marks a change to the SSISDB catalog properties

As operations are created, information about their creation is written to the SSISDB catalog and is accessible through the catalog.operations catalog view.

Project Deployment

As mentioned earlier in this chapter, SSIS project deployment is the process of moving an SSIS project from the development environment into the production environment. In SQL Server 2012, SSIS project deployment is integrated with the development tools (SSDT) and maintenance tools (SSMS).

Both of these solutions use the SQL Server Integration Services Deployment Wizard to perform the deployment. The deployment wizard can also be used explicitly—during SSIS installation, Integration Services project deployment files (denoted by the .ispac file name extension) are registered in the operating system and associated with the Integration Services Deployment Wizard.

The recommended practice is to use SSDT or SSMS for project deployments; however, if neither of these tools is available at the destination server, the Integration Services Deployment Wizard can be used.

An SSIS package created in an earlier version of SQL Server cannot be deployed directly to the SSIS server; it first needs to be processed by the SQL Server Integration Services Project Conversion Wizard to compile it into a deployment file, which can then be deployed to the SSISDB catalog.

Alternatively, SSIS packages created in earlier versions of SQL Server, or packages created in SSDT and converted to the package deployment model, can be deployed to the msdb system database or to the file system and then maintained and executed using the SSIS Legacy Service.

The recommended practice moving forward, however, is to use the new functionalities available in SQL Server 2012 Integration Services, because they provide superior security, maintenance, execution, and monitoring capabilities when compared to other available alternatives (msdb or the file system).

 Quick Check

   1. What is SSISDB?

   2. What is SSIS server?

   3. How can SSIS projects be deployed?

Quick Check Answers

   1. SSISDB is a special database provided by SQL Server 2012 to be used as the principal SSIS solution repository.

   2. SSIS server is a name used to refer to an instance of SQL Server hosting the SSISDB catalog. Any instance of SQL Server 2012 can be used as the SSIS server, except SQL Server Express.

   3. Under the project deployment model, SSIS project deployment is integrated into SQL Server Data Tools (SSDT), as well as SQL Server Management Studio (SSMS).

You will start this practice by creating and configuring the SSISDB catalog, effectively transforming an instance of SQL Server into the SSIS server, which you will use later as the destination in SSIS project deployments.

After the SSIS server is up and running, you will deploy two SSIS projects to it, using two different deployment methods.

You will complete this practice by exploring the SSIS project metadata in the SSISDB catalog.

If you encounter a problem completing an exercise, you can install the completed projects from the Solution folder that is provided with the companion content for this chapter and lesson.

EXERCISE 1 Create and Configure SSISDB

1. Start SSMS and connect the Object Browser to the SQL Server 2012 instance you have been using in the exercises throughout this book.

2. In the Object Explorer, under the node of the SQL Server instance that you are connected to, find the Integration Services Catalogs node. Right-click it and select Create Catalog from the shortcut menu to start the creation and configuration of the SSISDB catalog.

3. Use the Create Catalog dialog box to configure the SSISDB catalog. Configuration data is provided in Table 11-5.

TABLE 11-5 SSISDB Catalog Configuration

Property	Value	Description
Enable CLR Integration	Checked	SQL-CLR must be enabled on the SQL Server instance to create and use the SSISDB catalog. CLR stands for common language runtime.
Enable Automatic Execution Of Integration Services Stored Procedure At SQL Server Startup	Unchecked	When this check box is selected, a system stored procedure will be executed in the SSISDB database to perform cleanup operations every time SQL Server is started.
		When this check box is cleared, cleanup will only be performed at regular intervals, based on the SSISDB properties governing data retention.
Name Of The Catalog Database	SSISDB	The SSISDB catalog cannot be renamed.
Password	(Provide your own strong password.)	Create a strong password to be used to create the database master key, which will be used to protect the encryption key used in protecting SSISDB content. Keep the password in a secure location.

The completed dialog box should look like the one shown in Figure 11-5.

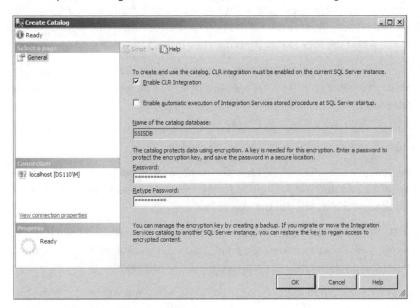

FIGURE 11-5 The Create Catalog dialog box.

IMPORTANT CLR INTEGRATION

CLR integration allows a SQL Server instance to use user assemblies, such as user-defined SQL CLR types, user-defined SQL CLR functions, SQL CLR procedures, or triggers. CLR integration is disabled by default.

Once enabled, the feature is available throughout the SQL Server instance and can be used in any database.

Learn more about SQL Server CLR integration in Books Online for SQL Server 2012, in the article entitled "Common Language Runtime (CLR) Integration Programming Concepts" (*http://msdn.microsoft.com/en-us/library/ms131102(SQL.110).aspx*).

4. When you have finished configuring the SSISDB catalog, click OK to proceed.

   The SSISDB catalog is created from a database backup file created during SSIS installation.

   You have now created an SSISDB catalog, and the SQL Server instance that you have selected for this practice now hosts the SSIS server.

5. In SSMS, in the Object Explorer, the SSISDB catalog should now be visible under the Integration Services Catalogs node. If the newly created catalog is not visible, refresh the Object Browser. Right-click the SSISDB node and select Properties from the shortcut menu to access the SSISDB catalog properties. Inspect the default SSISDB properties.

6. When done, click Cancel to close the Catalog Properties dialog box, abandoning any changes that you might have made. At this time, no changes to the SSISDB properties are needed.

7. Right-click the SSISDB node again, and this time select Create Folder from the shortcut menu to create a new folder in the SSISDB catalog.

8. In the Create Folder dialog box, enter the name for the new folder; use **TK 463 Chapter 11** and supply a description for the folder if you want. When done, click OK to confirm the creation of the new folder.

9. In the Object Explorer, expand the node of the newly created folder and inspect its contents. Newly created folders are empty, but you can observe from the Object Browser that a folder can contain projects and environments.

10. After you have finished this exercise, leave SSMS open. You will need it in the following exercises.

EXERCISE 2 Prepare the Environment

1. Start SSMS if necessary. On the File menu, under Open, select File, then navigate to the C:\TK463\Chapter11\Code folder and open the TK463Chapter11.sql Transact-SQL script.

2. After you have reviewed the script, execute only the part of the script for the Lesson 2 practice. The script creates the database and the objects you will be using in this lesson.

EXERCISE 3 Deploy an SSIS Project by Using the Deployment Wizard in SSDT

1. Start SSDT. On the Start page, select Open Project, navigate to the C:\TK463\Chapter11 \Lesson2\Solution folder, and open the TK 463 Chapter 11.sln solution.

2. The solution contains two SSIS projects that you have created in the exercises in Chapter 8, "Creating a Robust and Restartable Package," and Chapter 10, "Auditing and Logging."

3. In Solution Explorer, select the TK 463 Chapter 8 project, and on the Project menu select Deploy, or right-click the project and select Deploy from the shortcut menu, to start the Integration Services Deployment Wizard.

4. On the Introduction page of the wizard, review the deployment steps, and then click Next to proceed.

5. On the Select Destination screen, you will select the SSIS server, and the folder, to which the project will be deployed. Next to the Server Name text box, click Browse, and from the list of available servers select the SSIS server you created in Exercise 1.

6. Next to the Path text box, click Browse, and from the list of available folders select the one you created in Exercise 1. The wizard page should look similar to the one shown in Figure 11-6.

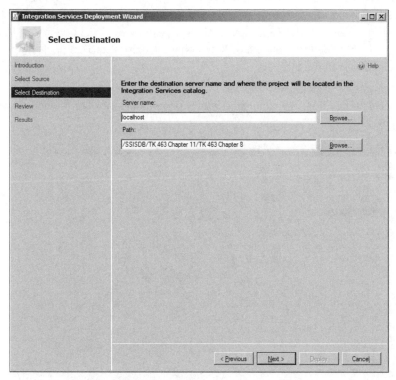

FIGURE 11-6 The Select Destination wizard page.

When you have selected the destination server and folder, click Next to proceed.

7. On the Review page, review the settings. If you need to make any changes, click Previous to go to a previous page. When you are done, click Deploy to start the deployment.

8. On the Results page, you can observe the progress of the deployment. When the process has completed successfully, click Close to finish the wizard.

EXERCISE 4 Deploy an SSIS Project by Using SQL Server Management Studio

1. In SSMS, in the Object Explorer, expand the Integration Services Catalogs node. Expand the folder you created in Exercise 1, right-click the Projects node, and select Deploy Project from the shortcut menu to start the Integration Services Deployment Wizard.

2. On the Introduction page of the wizard, review the deployment steps, and then click Next to proceed.

3. On the Select Source page, make sure that the Project Deployment File option is selected, and then click Browse on the right of the Path text box. Using the Open dialog box, navigate to the C:\TK463\Chapter11\Lesson2\Solution\TK 463 Chapter 10\bin \Development folder and select the TK 463 Chapter 10.ispac project deployment file. Click Open to load the file.

   In the preceding exercise, this step was skipped, because the source project was already selected in SSDT. The completed wizard page should look like the one shown in Figure 11-7.

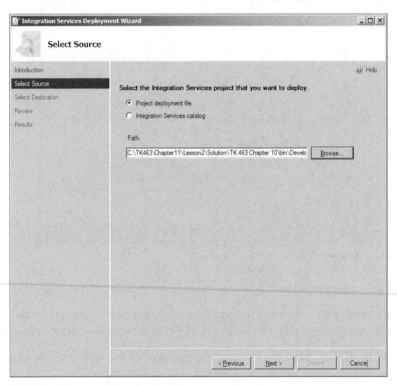

FIGURE 11-7 The Select Source wizard page.

4. When ready, click Next to proceed.

5. On the Select Destination page, select the destination SSIS server and folder, as you did in steps 4 and 5 of Exercise 3.

6. On the Review page, review the settings. If you need to make any changes, click Previous to go to a previous page.

7. When you are done, click Deploy to start the deployment, and observe the progress on the Results page. When the process has completed successfully, close the wizard.

EXERCISE 5 Inspect SSIS Package Metadata in the SSISDB Catalog

1. In SSMS, use the Object Explorer to inspect the contents of the SSISDB catalog.

   If you do not see both deployed projects, refresh the Object Browser.

2. Inspect the Databases node of the current SQL Server instance; the SSISDB database should be listed among the databases.

   Use the Object Explorer to inspect the database objects.

3. After you are done, on the File menu, select Open | File, or press Ctrl+O on the keyboard, to open a Transact-SQL script file.

4. Using the Open dialog box, navigate to the C:\TK463\Chapter11\Code folder and select the TK463Chapter11_Lesson2.sql Transact-SQL query file. Make sure SSISDB is selected as the current database.

> **NOTE SENSITIVE INFORMATION STORED IN SSIS PROJECTS**
>
> When sensitive information is stored inside an SSIS project, it is encrypted by default using a user key based on the credientials of the user who created the project. As a result, other users might not be able to decrypt this information when viewing or editing the project or when they create a project deployment file; this way any sensitive data will remain protected. BIDS and other tools of the SSIS toolset might issue warnings about not being able to encrypt or decrypt sensitive data even if the project definitions do not actually contain any encrypted data, when used on projects created by another user

During the creation of the project development file, or when performing other exercises in this training kit, you might receive such warnings; however, because no encrypted data is actually present in the project definitions, you can safely ignore them.

5. Review the script and execute each SELECT query to inspect the metadata of the SSISDB objects that you deployed in preceding exercises.

6. When done, close SSMS and SSDT.

Lesson Summary

- In SQL Server 2012, deployed SSIS projects are stored in the SSISDB catalog.
- The SSISDB catalog is used to store SSIS project and package definitions, as well as other SSIS metadata.

Lesson Review

Answer the following questions to test your knowledge of the information in this lesson. You can find the answers to these questions and explanations of why each answer choice is correct or incorrect in the "Answers" section at the end of this chapter.

1. Which of the following destinations are compatible with the project deployment model? (Choose all that apply.)

   A. The SSISDB catalog

   B. The msdb system database

   C. The SSIS server

   D. The file system

2. Where in the SSISDB catalog can SSIS projects be stored?

   A. In SSISDB folders

   B. At the SSISDB root

   C. In SSISDB server references

   D. In SSISDB environments

3. In your SSISDB catalog, you have enabled the Periodically Remove Old Versions setting and set the value of the Maximum Number Of Versions Per Project setting to 10. How do these settings affect the operation of the SSISDB catalog?

   A. After you deploy 10 versions of an SSIS project, you will no longer be able to deploy new versions.

   B. Deployed versions of your SSIS projects will be removed automatically when new versions are deployed, leaving only the 10 most recent versions.

   C. Deployed versions of your SSIS projects will be removed periodically when new versions are deployed, leaving only the 10 oldest versions.

   D. All versions of the SSIS projects older than version 10 will be removed automatically on the next run of the cleanup job.

Case Scenarios

In the following case scenarios, you apply what you've learned about installing SSIS and deploying packages. You can find the answers to these questions in the "Answers" section at the end of this chapter.

Case Scenario 1: Using Strictly Structured Deployments

In your organization, SSIS development and SSIS operations are strictly separated; not only is development restricted to its own dedicated environment with copies of production data stores, the production environment cannot be accessed by any member of the development team. As a consequence, SSIS deployment can only be performed by production administrators.

- How can you use your development tools to deploy SSIS solutions despite these restrictions?
- What tools will be required in the production environment to facilitate SSIS deployments?

Case Scenario 2: Installing an SSIS Server

You have been tasked with installing SQL Server 2012 on a new server, to be used as the SSIS server.

- Which SQL Server features will you have to install? How would you configure the instance of SQL Server to serve as the SSIS server?
- What other features could you also install, without turning the server into a development machine?

Suggested Practices

To help you successfully master the exam objectives presented in this chapter, complete the following tasks.

Upgrade Existing SSIS Solutions

Migrating SSIS development from SQL Server 2005 or SQL Server 2008 Integration Services to SQL Server 2012 is not a trivial task. The migration will eventually have to be done in the development environment as well as the production environment.

- **Practice 1** Think about how your existing SSIS projects can be upgraded. What tools will you use for this? What issues could you expect? For instance, have you used any non-standard or custom tasks or components?
- **Practice 2** Think about how the upgrade or migration will be performed in the production environment. What tools can you use to plan the migration? How will you determine if an upgrade is possible? Will you be able to take advantage of the SSISDB catalog immediately, or only for later work?
- **Practice 3** Think about the tasks that would need to be performed in your environments, based on what you have learned in this chapter. Create one checklist for the development environment and another for the production environment.

Answers

This section contains answers to the lesson review questions and solutions to the case scenarios in this chapter.

Lesson 1

1. **Correct answer: C**

   A. **Incorrect:** Local users cannot access network resources in a domain.

   B. **Incorrect:** Even though a virtual account can access network resources in the domain, it does so by using the identity of the machine. Assigning permissions to this identity could represent a security threat, because other services could also use this identity to gain access to domain resources.

   C. **Correct:** Although the managed service account is local to a particular server, it can access network resources in a domain and can have privileges assigned to it explicitly, without compromising overall security.

   D. **Incorrect:** Administrator accounts or other accounts with elevated privileges should only be used to perform administrative operations in a secure environment and should not be used for running services, because this represents a very serious security threat. If, for instance, security was breached at the service level, the culprit could now have complete and uninhibited access to the domain.

2. **Correct answer: C**

   A. **Incorrect:** SSDT is not needed in the production environment. SSIS development can be performed on any workstation and should not be allowed in production environments.

   B. **Incorrect:** Installing SSMS in a production environment is optional and not needed at all, as long as the production environment can be accessed remotely.

   C. **Correct:** SSIS must be installed, because otherwise SSIS execution is not possible.

   D. **Incorrect:** The SSIS server is not required, because SSIS packages can also be deployed to the file system.

3. **Correct answer: C**

   A. **Incorrect:** SSMS cannot be used to modify service accounts.

   B. **Incorrect:** Although you can access any service via the Computer Management snap-in, this tool should not be used to modify any SQL Server service account, because it is unable to assign the appropriate SQL Server permissions or operating system privileges to the service account.

C. **Correct:** SQL Server Configuration Manager is the only tool you should use to make changes to any of the SQL Server services, including the SSIS service.

D. **Incorrect:** Although you can access any service via the Services snap-in, this tool should not be used to modify any SQL Server service account, because it is unable to assign the appropriate SQL Server permissions or operating system privileges to the service account.

Lesson 2

1. **Correct answers: A and C**

   A. **Correct:** Project deployments target the SSISDB catalog.

   B. **Incorrect:** The msdb system database is not compatible with the project deployment model.

   C. **Correct:** The SSIS server hosts the SSISDB catalog.

   D. **Incorrect:** File system deployments are not supported by the project deployment model.

2. **Correct answer: A**

   A. **Correct:** SSIS projects can only be stored in SSISDB folders.

   B. **Incorrect:** SSIS projects cannot be saved to the SSISDB root.

   C. **Incorrect:** SSISDB server references cannot contain SSIS projects.

   D. **Incorrect:** SSISDB environments cannot contain SSIS projects.

3. **Correct answer: B**

   A. **Incorrect:** SSIS project deployment is not blocked when the maximum number of versions is reached.

   B. **Correct:** When the periodic removal of old versions is enabled, the maximum number of versions per project determines the number of most recent versions to remain in the SSISDB catalog. The cleanup job runs once per day, making it possible to have more than the maximum number of versions stored in SSISDB on a given day.

   C. **Incorrect:** The most recent versions are retained; the older versions are removed.

   D. **Incorrect:** The maximum number of versions refers to the total count of versions, not the version numbers.

Case Scenario 1

Typically, developers are not locked out completely from production environments; however, there are cases in which production data stores, even if used exclusively to host SSIS processes, are off limits to members of development teams.

Even under circumstances such as these, SSIS deployment is still possible:

- The development team will have to configure SSDT to place the project deployment files in a location in the file system that is accessible to the production administrators.

  This must be set for each project, in the project properties, under Configuration Properties. In the Build section of the properties, you can locate the OutputPath property and replace the default value, bin, with the path to the common location.

  When the projects are ready for deployment, you will have to notify the administrators to proceed with the deployment.

- The administrators will either use SSMS or the Integration Services Deployment Wizard to perform the deployment.

  Even if they have not installed SSMS to the production server, they can connect to it remotely; however, the Integration Services Deployment Wizard will also be available at the destination server.

Case Scenario 2

- To install an SSIS server, you must install the SQL Server 2012 Database Engine and Integration Services on the destination server and also create and configure an SSISDB catalog on the newly installed instance of SQL Server. To provide automated SSIS execution, you must also install SQL Server Agent.
- You could also install the Management Tools, and the Client Tools Connectivity feature. Without SQL Server Data Tools, the server cannot be used for SSIS development, so you would not install SSDT.

## CHAPTER 12

Executing and Securing Packages

Exam objectives in this chapter:

- Extract and Transform Data
  - Manage SSIS package execution.
- Load Data
  - Design control flow.
- Configure and Deploy SSIS Solutions
  - Configure SSIS security settings.

After a Microsoft SQL Server Integration Services (SSIS) solution has been successfully deployed to its intended environment, it can be integrated into existing production processes. Usually, the execution of SSIS processes is automated. In most cases, this means that the processes will be executed by SQL Server Agent, an integral element of the SQL Server platform, or by another, similar solution. Alternatively, the execution of SSIS processes could also be integrated into an organization's existing proprietary solutions, allowing them to be executed programmatically or through user interaction ("manually").

Regardless of the method used, SSIS solutions should also be secured appropriately. This means determining which users or processes will be allowed to execute the solutions or even be aware of their existence. First of all, SSIS solutions are sensitive in terms of the data management operations that they provide—not every person or process should be allowed to perform those. And second, SSIS solutions might contain sensitive information about the environment itself that needs to be protected (such as locations of data and user credentials).

In this chapter, you will learn about the methods and techniques that can be used to execute SSIS solutions, to monitor the executions, and to examine and analyze the history of executions. You will learn how to automate SSIS execution by using SQL Server Agent or by integrating SSIS operations with your existing solutions. You will also learn about SSISDB security, including how to control which users and/or processes can deploy, maintain, execute, and monitor SSIS solutions. Finally, you will see how SSISDB configurations together with SSISDB security can be used to improve the reusability of SSIS solutions after they have been deployed.

Lessons in this chapter:

- Lesson 1: Executing SSIS Packages
- Lesson 2: Securing SSIS Packages

Before You Begin

To complete this chapter, you must have:

- Experience working with SQL Server Management Studio (SSMS).
- Experience working with Microsoft Visual Studio or SQL Server Data Tools (SSDT).
- A working knowledge of the Transact-SQL language.

> **IMPORTANT** **COMPLETE CHAPTER 11 EXERCISES FIRST**
>
> To complete the exercises in this chapter, you first need to complete the exercises in Chapter 11, "Installing SSIS and Deploying Packages."

Lesson 1: Executing SSIS Packages

To allow maximum integration of SSIS solutions into existing environments and at the same time maximize integration of SSIS solutions into the SQL Server platform itself, several methods and techniques are available for the execution of SSIS solutions. They can be divided into two groups:

- On-demand execution allows SSIS processes to be initiated from various existing systems—programmatically, in which they are invoked from user applications, as well as through user intervention, in which they are executed by human operators directly and interactively.
- Automated execution allows SSIS processes to be initiated automatically, without user interaction and even without the need for proprietary applications.

Either way, SSIS execution is performed by using the SSIS runtime, discussed in Chapter 11, which is part of the SQL Server 2012 Integration Services installation and must be present in the production environment, because SSIS execution cannot be performed any other way.

On-Demand SSIS Execution

After they have been deployed (and configured), SSIS processes can be executed through user interaction (by using SSMS) or programmatically (by using the DTExec utility, Transact-SQL, Windows PowerShell, or the SSIS managed API).

Typically, on-demand execution is used when SSIS processes cannot be started automatically. This might be because the SSIS processes depend on other processes for which it cannot be automatically determined when their execution completed or whether it completed with the appropriate result. In cases like these, only a human operator will have the insight to determine whether a dependent SSIS process needs to be executed or not.

On-demand execution is also used if an SSIS process cannot be started automatically simply because it is not used on a regular basis. An example is a process used in migrating production data into a development and testing data store. Though it might be beneficial to have up-to-date production data available in the testing environment, sometimes the testing data store contains special data samples that were created artificially and should not be overwritten.

However, most SSIS processes, especially in data warehousing systems, are automated.

SQL Server Management Studio

SSMS supports the execution of packages stored on the SSIS server as well as packages that are accessible through the older SSIS service (that is, packages stored in the msdb system database or in the managed file system).

Packages stored in the SSISDB catalog can be started by using the Execute Package dialog box. This dialog box also provides access to parameters, connection managers, and package properties, so that these can be set before each execution.

The dialog box can also be used to script the execution; instead of executing the package immediately, you can configure, script, and execute the package later. The script can be reused and modified to use different parameter values, connection managers, or other properties.

DTExecUI

The DTExecUI utility can be used to execute SSIS packages that are accessible through the older SSIS service (stored in the msdb system database or in the managed file system). In the initial release of SQL Server 2012, DTExecUI cannot be used to execute packages stored in the SSISDB catalog, nor can it be used to execute SSIS packages that were created by using SQL Server 2012. In fact, this utility is only provided for compatibility with older versions—to execute SSIS packages created in previous versions of SQL Server.

The DTExecUI executable is located at %ProgramFiles(x86)%\Microsoft SQL Server\110\Tools\Binn\ManagementStudio; only a 32-bit edition of this tool exists. To execute an SSIS package by using the 64-bit SSIS runtime, you must use another tool (such as the 64-bit edition of the DTExec command-line utility).

Transact-SQL, Windows PowerShell, the SSIS Managed API, and DTExec

In addition to being executed by user interaction, SSIS packages can be executed programmatically, by using Transact-SQL, Windows PowerShell, the SSIS managed application programming interface (API), or the DTExec command-line utility.

Programmatic execution using Transact-SQL, Windows PowerShell, or the SSIS managed API is performed in two or more steps:

1. First, a new execution operation is created. The creation references a particular package and can include a reference to an environment that provides package configuration information.

2. Next, execution properties can be set. For instance, this might be done if no configuration was provided at creation, if certain parameters are not set by the configuration, or if certain configuration properties need to be overridden.

3. Finally, the execution is started. The invocation can be asynchronous (which it is by default), meaning that the package is started and then the control is returned to the caller immediately; or it can be invoked synchronously, meaning that the invocation procedure will keep running until the execution has completed.

Listing 12-1 shows an example of SSIS package execution using Transact-SQL. The execution is performed by using SSISDB system stored procedures.

LISTING 12-1 Executing a Package by Using Transact-SQL

```
DECLARE @execution_id     BIGINT;
DECLARE @use32bitruntime  BIT       = CAST(0 AS BIT);
DECLARE @logging_level    INT       = 1;

EXEC catalog.create_execution
    @folder_name = N'TK 463 Chapter 11',
    @project_name = N'TK 463 Chapter 10',
    @package_name = N'Master.dtsx',
    @use32bitruntime = @use32bitruntime,
    @reference_id = NULL,
    @execution_id = @execution_id OUTPUT;

EXEC catalog.set_execution_parameter_value
    @execution_id,
    @object_type = 50,
    @parameter_name = N'LOGGING_LEVEL',
    @parameter_value = @logging_level;

EXEC catalog.start_execution
    @execution_id;
GO
```

In Listing 12-1, you can observe all three execution steps:

1. A package named Master.dtsx, which is part of the TK 463 Chapter 10 project and is located in the TK 463 Chapter 11 folder of the SSISDB catalog, is selected for execution, and the execution is created by using the 64-bit runtime without an environment reference.

2. The LOGGING_LEVEL execution property is set.

3. The execution is started asynchronously.

MORE INFO **SSISDB CATALOG SYSTEM STORED PROCEDURES**

More information about the SSISDB catalog system stored procedures can be found in Books Online for SQL Server 2012, starting with the article entitled "Stored Procedures (Integration Services Catalog)" (*http://msdn.microsoft.com/en-us/library/ff878099(SQL.110).aspx*).

Windows PowerShell can also be used to access objects on the SSIS server and can therefore also be used to validate and execute SSIS projects and/or packages.

Before SSIS packages can be executed by using Windows PowerShell, the SSIS management assembly must be loaded. Then the operation is prepared and executed, as described earlier in this section. An example is shown in Listing 12-2.

LISTING 12-2 Executing a Package by Using Windows PowerShell

```
# Assign SSIS namespace to variable
$ssisNamespace = "Microsoft.SqlServer.Management.IntegrationServices"

# Load the SSIS Management Assembly
$assemblyLoad = [Reflection.Assembly]::Load($ssisNamespace + ", Version=11.0.0.0,
Culture=neutral, PublicKeyToken=89845dcd8080cc91")

# Create a connection to a SQL Server instance
$connectionString = "Data Source=localhost;Initial Catalog=master;Integrated
Security=SSPI; "
$connection = New-Object System.Data.SqlClient.SqlConnection $connectionString

# Instantiate the SSIS object
$ssis = New-Object $ssisNamespace".IntegrationServices" $connection

# Instantiate the SSIS package
$catalog = $ssis.Catalogs["SSISDB"]
$folder = $catalog.Folders["TK 463 Chapter 11"]
$project = $folder.Projects["TK 463 Chapter 10"]
$package = $project.Packages["Master.dtsx"]

# Set package parameter(s)
$package.Parameters["somePackageParameter"].Set
( [Microsoft.SqlServer.Management.IntegrationServices.ParameterInfo+ParameterValueType]:
:Literal, "parameter value")
$package.Alter()

# Execute SSIS package ($environment is not assigned)
$executionId = $package.Execute("false", $environment)
```

Currently, no SSIS Windows PowerShell cmdlets are available; however, the entire SSIS object model is accessible via the SSIS management assembly ("Microsoft.SqlServer.Management. IntegrationServices, Version=11.0.0.0, Culture=neutral, PublicKeyToken=89845dcd8080cc91").

> **MORE INFO** **SQL SERVER AND WINDOWS POWERSHELL**
>
> More information about Windows PowerShell and its use in SQL Server can be found in Books Online for SQL Server 2012, starting with the article entitled "SQL Server PowerShell Overview" (*http://msdn.microsoft.com/en-us/library/cc281954(SQL.110).aspx*).

SSIS objects can be accessed through the SSIS managed API. They are exposed through the Microsoft.SqlServer.Management.IntegrationServices namespace in the Microsoft .NET

Framework. In Listing 12-3, you can see an example of SSIS package execution via the SSIS managed API, written in Microsoft Visual C#.

LISTING 12-3 Executing a Package by Using SQL Server Management Objects

```
using System;
using Microsoft.SqlServer.Management.IntegrationServices;
using SMO = Microsoft.SqlServer.Management.Smo;
...
// Create a connection to a SQL Server instance
SMO.Server ssisServer = new SMO.Server("localhost");
Console.WriteLine("Connected to:\t\t" + ssisServer.Name);

// Instantiate the SSIS object
IntegrationServices ssis = new IntegrationServices(ssisServer);

// Instantiate the SSIS package
Catalog catalog = ssis.Catalogs["SSISDB"];
CatalogFolder folder = catalog.Folders["TK 463 Chapter 11"];
ProjectInfo project = folder.Projects["TK 463 Chapter 10"];
PackageInfo package = project.Packages["Master.dtsx"];
Console.WriteLine("Selected package:\t" + System.IO.Path.Combine(catalog.Name, folder.
Name, project.Name, package.Name));

// Set package parameter(s)
package.Parameters["someParameter"].Set
    (
    ParameterInfo.ParameterValueType.Literal, "parameter value"
    );
package.Alter();
catalog.ServerLoggingLevel = Catalog.LoggingLevelType.None;

// Execute SSIS package
package.Execute(false, null);
```

To access a SQL Server instance for administrative purposes, consider using Server Management Objects (SMO), as shown in Listing 12-3 (Microsoft.SqlServer.Management.Smo).

> **MORE INFO** **THE INTEGRATION SERVICES CATALOG MANAGED API**
>
> More information about the SSISDB catalog managed API can be found in Books Online for SQL Server 2012, starting with the article entitled "Microsoft.SqlServer.Management.IntegrationServices Namespace" (*http://msdn.microsoft.com/en-us/library/microsoft.sqlserver* *.management.integrationservices(SQL.110).aspx*).

The DTExec command-line utility can be used to execute packages stored in the SSISDB catalog, as well as those accessible through the older SSIS service (that is, those that are stored in the msdb system database or in the managed file system). DTExecUI cannot be used to execute packages stored in the SSISDB catalog.

Listing 12-4 shows an example of the use of the DTExec command-line utility to invoke the execution of an SSIS package stored in the SSISDB catalog.

LISTING 12-4 Executing a Package by Using DTExec

```
DTExec /Server localhost /ISServer "\SSISDB\TK 463 Chapter 11\TK 463 Chapter 10\Master.
dtsx" /Par $ServerOption::LOGGING_LEVEL(Int32);1
```

> **MORE INFO** **THE DTEXEC COMMAND-LINE UTILITY**
>
> More information about the DTExec command-line utility can be found in Books Online for SQL Server 2012, in the article entitled "dtexec Utility" (*http://msdn.microsoft.com/en-us /library/hh231187.aspx*).

> **REAL WORLD** **SSIS EXECUTION AND DATA WAREHOUSING**
>
> Typically, in data warehousing solutions, execution of SSIS processes is fully automated. In most cases, on-demand SSIS package execution outside of predefined maintenance windows should be prevented altogether.

Automated SSIS Execution

Obviously, the ability to execute SSIS processes on demand has merit. However, in the majority of cases, SSIS process execution is automated. This is especially true for data warehousing solutions: after a data warehousing process has been developed and deployed, it will be scheduled for automatic execution during maintenance windows.

Typically, data warehouse maintenance operations are performed at times when systems are not being used by the end users (for instance, at night).

Alternatively, data warehouse maintenance could also be performed on standby servers, and after it has completed, the live servers can be taken offline and the standby servers brought online to replace them.

In both cases, the entire process can and should be automated: in the former case, because most likely no administrator would be available during the night to execute the process manually, and in the latter case, because no human operator could ever perform all the steps of such a complex process as quickly and as reliably as a machine can.

SQL Server Agent

SQL Server Agent is a component of the SQL Server platform; its principal purpose is to facilitate automatic execution of processes in the SQL Server environment on a predefined schedule or in response to predefined environment conditions.

In SQL Server 2012, SQL Server Agent supports the execution of SSIS packages stored on an SSIS server, as well as packages accessible through the older SSIS service (located in the msdb system database or in the managed file system).

JOBS AND JOB STEPS

The principal unit of work in SQL Server Agent processes is a *job*. A SQL Server Agent job does not actually represent any specific operations; it serves as a container for *job steps*, which represent the actual operations.

A SQL Server job step can invoke executable programs and operating system commands, Transact-SQL statements, Windows PowerShell scripts, ActiveX scripts, SQL Server Replication tasks, SQL Server Analysis Services tasks, and SSIS packages.

A job must contain at least one step in order to perform any operations; multiple steps are executed in the order specified when the job is created. Each step can be configured to log information about its execution to the job step log in the msdb system database (some operation types can even log their execution to a file). Steps can also be configured to respond to failures (such as execution errors) by using notifications, alerts, or operators.

The principal execution mode in SQL Server Agent is to execute a job as a whole; however, execution of individual steps is also supported. When a job is executed as a whole, all steps are executed in the specified order, starting with step number one. However, if a specific step is chosen to start the execution, after the selected step has completed, the execution will advance to any following job step, and the rest of the steps will be performed in the specified order.

SCHEDULES

SQL Server Agent jobs can be scheduled to run whenever SQL Server Agent is started, when the server CPU is idle (that is, when CPU utilization falls below a certain level), or on a specified date and time.

To execute a job when the CPU is idle, the CPU utilization condition must first be set for the server. CPU idle time is measured as a percentage of utilization below a specified level for a specified time. Whenever this occurs, all jobs scheduled to run at CPU idle time will be started automatically.

Jobs can be scheduled to run at a specified date and time—once or repeatedly. When jobs are executed repeatedly, the following schedule types can be used:

- **Overall recurrence frequency**   For jobs executed once per a specified period (once per day, week, month, or year)
- **Daily frequency**   For jobs executed continuously during the day
- **Specific duration**   For jobs executed after a specified period of time has passed

Every schedule has a start time, denoting when the schedule was created or modified. The end time can also be set, indicating that the schedule will cease to be used after the end time has passed. If the end time is not set, the schedule is used indefinitely.

SQL SERVER AGENT JOBS VS. THE MASTER PACKAGE CONCEPT

There are several similarities between SQL Server Agent jobs and the master package concept, discussed in Chapter 6, "Enhancing Control Flow":

- Both can be used to configure individual operations.
- Both can execute operations in sequence.
- Both can respond to execution errors.

However, there are also a few significant differences between jobs and master packages:

- Only a single instance of any SQL Server job can be started at any particular time, whereas multiple instances of a master package can be executed concurrently, practically without any limitations.

  Any attempt to start a job with an instance of it already running will be prevented, and an exception will be raised. This is useful in cases when multiple instances should not be allowed to run concurrently—for instance, because they access the same resources in ways that could cause resource contention or, more critically, lead to conflicts between them, in which one instance modifies or removes data used by another instance.

- Master packages can be configured to execute multiple operations in parallel; in contrast, jobs only support linear execution (only one step can be executed at a time).

- In jobs, the options to respond to execution errors or failures are fairly limited, whereas in master packages they are virtually limitless.

  In a job, if an error is detected during the execution of a step, the execution can continue with the next step, with a warning being reported to the job step log. To respond to an error, the execution can also be stopped. Alternatively, each step can be configured to be retried a specified number of times before the execution proceeds to the following step or is stopped.

  After the execution has been stopped, notifications can be sent or alerts can be triggered, or both—regardless of the success of the execution. An alert can either send notifications or execute other jobs.

- In master packages, the order and the conditions of execution can be set at design time, whereas in jobs they can only be set after deployment.

> **MORE INFO** **SQL SERVER AGENT**
>
> More information about SQL Server Agent, jobs, steps, schedules, alerts, notifications, and other related subjects can be found in Books Online for SQL Server 2012. Unless you are already familiar with SQL Server Agent, you should start with the Books Online article entitled "SQL Server Agent" (*http://msdn.microsoft.com/en-us/library/ms189237(SQL.110).aspx*).

Monitoring SSIS Execution

SSIS execution monitoring provides information about SSIS processes as they are being executed, allowing you to track their progress and status. More importantly, information about each execution is written to the database and is available for analysis even after the processing has completed.

Typically, SSIS execution monitoring serves two purposes:

- It provides an overview of how SSIS solutions are used, how they use available resources, and whether they are completed successfully or not. At this level, the information about SSIS executions is useful for resource planning and problem detection.

- It supports SSIS troubleshooting activities when problems with SSIS execution have been detected. Troubleshooting usually requires more detailed information about SSIS execution than that used for a more general overview. Additional information that might not have been captured by SSIS logging or auditing might also be required, especially when you are troubleshooting performance issues or problems that originate outside the SSIS or the SQL Server platform.

SSIS logging and auditing were discussed in Chapter 10, "Auditing and Logging," and you will learn more about troubleshooting in Chapter 13, "Troubleshooting and Performance Tuning."

In the discussion of SSISDB objects in Chapter 11, it was mentioned that not only is SSIS object metadata stored in the SSISDB catalog, but also operational data—information about SSIS executions—is stored there.

Operations

Operations represent actions performed against SSISDB objects and the SSISDB catalog itself. Operations were discussed in more detail in Chapter 11; however, they need to be mentioned again in this chapter because of their specific role in SSISDB package execution.

Every action performed against the SSISDB catalog, or against an SSISDB object, is represented by an operation in the SSISDB catalog—a new row reported by the catalog.operations catalog view. In this way, every action against the SSISDB catalog is recorded, regardless of its type—whether it represents a deployment, maintenance, or execution operation.

Operation data is accessible through the catalog.operations catalog view. Additional data about operations is accessible through the catalog.extended_operation_info and catalog.operation_messages catalog views; both of these might contain multiple rows related to a single operation.

As the execution of an operation progresses and certain milestones are reached, the status of the operation is reflected in the catalog.operations catalog view. Possible operation status values are presented in Table 12-1.

TABLE 12-1 Operation Status

Status	Description
Created	The operation has been created and is not currently running.
Running	The operation has been started and is currently running.
Canceled	The operation has been canceled.
Failed	The operation has failed and has stopped running.
Pending	The operation has been suspended or is waiting for the resolution of a condition.
Ended unexpectedly	The operation has ended unexpectedly, but it cannot be determined whether it has succeeded or failed.
Succeeded	The operation has completed successfully.
Stopping	The operation has been ordered to stop and is performing cleanup. After it has been stopped, it will be marked as Canceled.
Completed	The operation has completed.

Validations

Validations are used to check SSISDB projects or packages for common problems, especially in project or package configurations.

Validations can be initiated at any time after a project has been deployed to the SSISDB catalog; typically, projects and packages are validated after deployment or maintenance operations (for example, after environment references have been added). To prevent problems during execution, projects and packages should be validated explicitly before being executed for the first time after they have been deployed or after they have been configured or reconfigured.

When package execution is started, the project to which the package belongs is validated automatically, before the package is run.

The following checks are performed during *project validations*:

- Parameters marked as required must have default values set.
- Parameter values must have the expected data types.
- Environments referenced by the project must exist.
- Validation of each package in the project must be successful.

The following checks are performed during *package validations*:

- The definition of every component in the package must correspond to the metadata of any external resources referenced by that component. Components with the Validate-ExternalMetadata property disabled (set to False) are not validated.
- If a package uses custom components, they must be installed on the server.

- If a script task or a script component references an assembly, that assembly must be installed on the server and registered in the global assembly cache.

- Environment references must be available and of the expected data types. The following validation modes can be used for *environment reference validation*:

  - **All environment references**   An environment variable must be available in all environments referenced by the project and must be of the correct data type.

  - **A single environment reference**   An environment variable must be available in the specified environment and must be of the correct data type.

  - **No environment references**   All default parameter values must be supplied by using literal values.

All packages are validated when the project they belong to is validated.

Depending on the complexity of an SSISDB project or package, validations can take a long time to complete. To prevent validations from running too long and using too many system resources, you can use the Validation Timeout property of the SSISDB catalog to ensure that validations will be stopped automatically when they reach the specified limit.

When executed manually, validation is performed asynchronously. As the validation progresses, results are written to SSISDB. Validation data is accessible through the catalog.validations catalog view.

You will learn how to validate SSISDB projects and packages by using SSMS in the practice exercises at the end of this lesson.

Executions

As mentioned earlier in this lesson, the execution of an SSISDB package begins with the creation of a new *execution instance*; the principal purpose of the execution instance is to provide a reference between a package being prepared for execution and its corresponding configuration. Another purpose is to document (log) the execution itself.

Packages stored in the SSISDB catalog are *abstract entities*. When an execution instance is created and a configuration is assigned to it, a *concrete instance* of the package is created, containing all of the information that is required for its execution. The abstract entity of a package *can* be executed in as many different ways as there are possible configurations, but a concrete instance of the package *is* executed by using a specific configuration.

When the execution instance is created, an environment containing configuration information expected by the package can be assigned to it. Only a single environment reference can be assigned to a particular execution instance.

After the execution instance has been created, additional configurations can be assigned to it. These direct assignments can target the properties of the instance, as well as the parameters and/or properties of the package being executed. For instance, direct assignments can be used to supply values to properties and parameters that are not supplied by the environment, or to override the values supplied by the environment.

After the execution instance has been configured, it can be started. The action of starting an execution instance begins with the validation of the package; if the validation is successful, the processing begins.

Though all this may sound complicated, it guarantees that the process will be configured and performed correctly.

You will learn how to execute SSISDB packages by using SSMS in the practice later in this lesson.

Logging Levels

SSISDB supports several execution logging modes, as shown in Table 12-2. These modes differ in the amount of information they provide about the execution.

TABLE 12-2 Logging Levels

Logging level	Description
None	Logging is turned off. Only the package execution status is logged; errors and warnings are not logged.
Basic	All events are logged except custom and diagnostic events. This is the default logging level.
Performance	Only performance statistics, errors, and warnings are logged. This logging level should be used for benchmarking or performance tuning, because it provides execution data relevant for just these purposes.
	Compared to the Basic level, Performance level logs fewer messages but captures more events, which are needed to analyze the performance of the data flow components. You should avoid using this level for normal operation. You will learn more about SSIS troubleshooting and performance tuning in Chapter 13.
Verbose	All events are logged, including custom and diagnostic events. Custom events are events logged by Integration Services tasks in addition to general events, which were discussed in Chapter 10.

EXAM TIP

You should understand the differences between individual SSISDB logging levels in order to be able to choose the most appropriate one for a particular purpose. For instance, by turning logging off, you could slightly improve execution performance at the cost of losing all ability to detect execution errors. On the other hand, using verbose logging will provide a lot of information about the execution but will lead to less-than-optimal performance.

SSIS Monitoring in SQL Server Management Studio

SSMS provides essential SSIS monitoring functionalities, most of which are implemented by using reports and some by using built-in viewers.

Active operations can be monitored by using the Active Operations dialog box, which is accessible via the Object Browser in SSMS.

When an operation, such as a validation or an execution, is started by using SSMS, you are prompted to open the corresponding report, which provides an overview of the active operation.

All available reports can be accessed through the Object Browser, via the shortcut menu of each node (catalog, project, package, or environment). The standard reports are listed in Table 12-3.

TABLE 12-3 Standard Validation Reports

Level	Title	Description
Catalog	Integration Services Dashboard	Information about all operations performed in the past 24 hours
Catalog, folder, project, package	All Executions	Information about all executions that have been performed
Catalog, folder, project, package	All Validations	Information about all validations that have been performed
Catalog	All Operations	An overview of all operations that have been performed
Catalog	All Connections	The connection context of execution errors that have occurred

The amount of information presented in the standard reports is filtered based on the selected level; for instance, the All Executions report retrieved at the Catalog level displays information about all executions on the SSIS server, whereas the same report retrieved at the Project level displays only information about package executions for that particular project.

Additional custom reports can also be added to SSMS to extend the existing capabilities.

The amount of information available in the SSISDB catalog depends on the Retention Period and Clean Logs Periodically catalog properties; if Clean Logs Periodically is enabled, entries older than the number of days specified by Retention Period are removed from the catalog automatically by the SSIS Server Maintenance job, scheduled by default to run every day at midnight.

 Quick Check

1. Is it possible to execute a deployed SSIS package manually?
2. How can SSIS packages be executed programmatically?
3. Is it possible to monitor SSIS executions?

Quick Check Answers

1. Yes. After deployment, SSIS packages can be executed on demand by using SSMS or by using the DTExec command-line utility.
2. Programmatic access to deployed SSIS packages is possible through Transact-SQL, Windows PowerShell, and the SSIS managed API.
3. Yes. The execution of SSIS processes can be monitored by using the Active Operations viewer in SSMS, as well as by using a variety of standard built-in reports. Additionally, custom reports can be developed, and integrated with SSMS.

PRACTICE **Starting and Monitoring SSIS Processes**

In this practice, you will execute SSIS packages by using various methods, monitor their execution, and become familiar with the standard SSIS reports available in SSMS for the SSISDB catalog.

You will start by validating SSISDB projects and packages, after which you will execute and monitor packages by using SSMS and use SQL Server Agent jobs to execute SSIS packages.

EXERCISE 1   Validate SSIS Projects and Packages by Using SSMS

1. Start SSMS and connect to the instance of SQL Server 2012 that you set up as the SSIS server in Lesson 2 of Chapter 11. Connect the Object Explorer to the same instance, unless it is already connected.

2. In the Object Explorer, under Integration Services Catalogs, expand the SSISDB catalog node to display all deployed projects.

3. Right-click the TK 463 Chapter 10 project, and on the shortcut menu, select Validate to start project validation.

4. In the Validate Project dialog box, shown in Figure 12-1, you can configure the validation criteria before initiating validation.

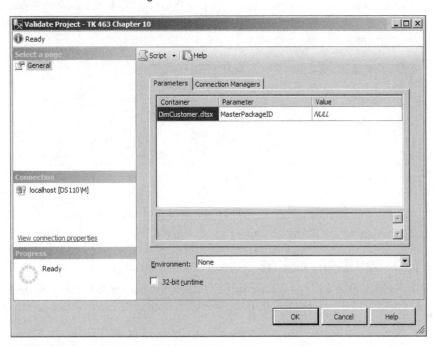

FIGURE 12-1 The Validate Project dialog box.

On the right side of the window, on the Parameters tab, you can set parameter values, and on the Connection Managers tab, you can configure the connection managers to be used in the validation. This way, you can verify whether certain parameter or connection manager settings can be used in the execution of affected packages.

Below the tabs, in the Environment list box, you can set the criteria for environment-based validation. You will learn more about this option in the practice in Lesson 2.

The check box at the bottom of the Validate Project dialog box can be used to specify that the 32-bit runtime be used for the validation.

Do not make any changes, because the default settings should be used for this validation.

> **IMPORTANT** **VALIDATION LIMITATIONS**
>
> SSISDB validation only checks project or package configurations. Do not rely on SSISDB validation alone to predict successful completion of SSIS processes.

5. When ready, click OK to start the validation.

    After the validation is started, you will be prompted by SSMS, as shown in Figure 12-2, to indicate whether to open the built-in Validation Overview report to observe the validation process and the results.

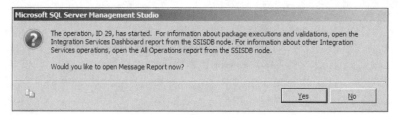

FIGURE 12-2 The Validation Report prompt.

6. Click Yes. A project validation report will be generated, listing the validation activities and their results. While the validation is running, the Status property in the header of the report will display Running, and after the validation has completed, it will display Succeeded if the validation was successful or Failed if it was not.

    The validation should complete in just a few seconds. Refresh the report, if needed, to see the final validation result. Browse through the report to see what was checked and to see the validation results.

7. In the Object Explorer, expand the TK 463 Chapter 10 project node to display all the packages it contains.

8. Right-click the Master.dtsx package, and on the shortcut menu, select Validate to start package validation.

    As you can see, the Validate Package dialog box has the same structure and functionalities as the Validate Project dialog box.

9. Click OK to validate the package, and in the prompt that appears after validation has started, click Yes to generate the package validation report.

10. Browse through the report and compare it to the one generated earlier.

11. When done, leave SSMS open, because you will need it in the following exercise.

EXERCISE 2   Execute and Monitor an SSIS Package by Using SSMS

1. In SSMS, in the Object Explorer, right-click the Master.dtsx package again, and this time select Execute from the shortcut menu to initiate the execution.

    The Execute Package dialog box, shown in Figure 12-3, is similar to the Validate dialog boxes but has an Advanced tab.

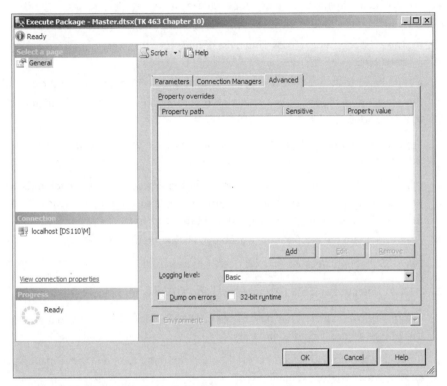

FIGURE 12-3 The Execute Package dialog box.

The Parameters and Connection Managers tabs can be used to set parameter values and configure the connection managers for the execution, as in the Validation dialog boxes.

The Advanced tab provides a few additional options: the Property Overrides grid can be used to set any additional package properties; you do so by providing the full path to a property and the value for it.

Below the grid, in the Logging Level list box, you can select the logging mode for the execution. For this execution, leave the Basic logging level selected.

The Dump On Errors check box, when selected, instructs the SSIS runtime to create a memory dump in case errors are encountered during execution.

2. When ready, click OK to start the execution.

3. When prompted whether to generate the execution report, click Yes. An Overview report will be generated.

    While the package is being executed, the Status property in the header of the report will display Running, and after the execution has completed, it will display Succeeded if the validation was successful or Failed if it was not.

4. Three distinct reports are created for each execution:

    - The Overview report, displaying the general information about the execution

    - The Messages report, providing a list of messages that were generated during execution

    - The Performance report, displaying performance information about the execution

    Browse all three reports to see what kind of information about the execution each of them provides.

5. Repeat steps 1 through 3 to execute the same package once more, but this time, on the Advanced tab of the Execute Package dialog box, select the Verbose logging mode.

6. Allow SSMS time to generate the report. After the execution has completed (which you will know if you refresh the report after a couple of minutes), compare the newly generated execution report with the one created earlier.

    Again, compare the information available in all three report types.

7. Leave SSMS open, because you will need it in Exercise 5.

EXERCISE 3   Execute an SSIS Package by Using DTExec

1. Using Windows Explorer, navigate to the C:\TK463\Chapter12\Code folder and locate the DTExec_Example.cmd command file.

2. Right-click the file and select Edit on the shortcut menu to open the file in Notepad or another appropriate text editing tool.

    Inspect the DTExec command line and the arguments.

3. When you are done reviewing the command line, close the editing tool and return to Windows Explorer.

4. Double-click the DTExec_Example.cmd command file to execute it, and observe the execution progress in the Overview report that you used in Exercise 2.

EXERCISE 4   Execute an SSIS Package by Using Windows PowerShell

1. Using Windows Explorer, navigate to the C:\TK463\Chapter12\Code folder and locate the PowerShell_Example.ps1 Windows PowerShell script file.

2. Right-click the file and select Edit on the shortcut menu to open the file either in Notepad or in the Windows PowerShell Integrated Scripting Environment (ISE).

    Inspect the script, following the comments inside it.

3. When you are done reviewing the script, close the editing tool and return to Windows Explorer.

4. Right-click the PowerShell_Example.ps1 Windows PowerShell script again, and select Run with PowerShell on the shortcut menu to execute it.

NOTE WINDOWS POWERSHELL EXECUTION

Depending on the environment in which you perform this exercise, you might or might not be allowed to execute Windows PowerShell scripts. By default, the execution of Windows PowerShell scripts is restricted; this means that you can only execute individual commands, entered at the Windows PowerShell prompt, but you are not allowed to execute Windows PowerShell scripts.

In order to execute the script, you can change the default execution policy by using the Set-ExecutionPolicy Windows PowerShell command. By default, this setting affects all users of the local machine, but you can limit its scope to your Windows user account or the current process.

The subject of Windows PowerShell execution policies is very much outside the scope of this book, so please consult Windows PowerShell documentation for more details. The documentation is available online, at *http://msdn.microsoft.com/en-us/library/windows/desktop/ms714469.aspx*, and can also be downloaded from *http://www.microsoft.com/en-us/download/details.aspx?id=30002.*.

Observe the execution progress in the Overview report that you used in the preceding exercises.

EXERCISE 5 Create, Schedule, and Execute an SSIS Package by Using SQL Server Agent

1. In SSMS, in the Object Explorer, under the SQL Server Agent node, expand Jobs.
   At least one SQL Server job should be listed: SSIS Server Maintenance Job. This job was created when you created the SSISDB catalog in Lesson 2 of Chapter 11.

2. Right-click Jobs, and on the shortcut menu, select New Job to start the creation of a new SQL Server Agent job.

3. Use the New Job editor to configure a new job. On the General page, provide a name for the job (**TK 463 Chapter 10 Master Package**) and a description if you want, as shown in Figure 12-4.

FIGURE 12-4 The General page of the New Job dialog box.

4. On the Steps page, click New to open the New Job Step editor.

5. Create a job step and configure it to execute an SSIS package by using the information provided in Table 12-4.

TABLE 12-4 New Step Configuration

Page	Property	Value
General	Step name	Master Package
General	Type	SQL Server Integration Services Package
General	Run as	SQL Server Agent Service Account
General (Package tab)	Package source	SSIS Catalog
General (Package tab)	Server	localhost

The dialog box should look similar to the one shown in Figure 12-5.

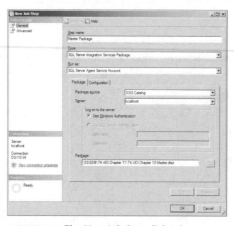

FIGURE 12-5 The New Job Step dialog box.

6. To select the package, on the Package tab, click the ellipsis (...) on the right side of the Package text box and use the Select An SSIS Package dialog box to navigate in the SSISDB catalog to the TK 463 Chapter 11 folder. In the TK 463 Chapter 10 project, select the Master.dtsx package. Click OK to confirm the selection.

   On the Configuration tab, you can adjust the configuration settings for the package: you can assign parameter values, configure connection managers, and adjust advanced settings, such as assigning values to package properties, enabling memory dumps in case errors are encountered, or setting the package to be executed using the 32-bit runtime. In this exercise, you will not need any additional configuration settings.

   > **NOTE** SQL SERVER AGENT JOBS AND REMOTE SSIS SERVER
   >
   > SQL Server Agent job steps can reference SSIS packages that are stored on remote servers. However, SSIS packages stored in an SSISDB catalog are always executed on the SQL Server instance where the SSISDB catalog is located. To scale SSIS execution to additional servers, an SSISDB catalog containing the appropriate SSIS projects and/or packages must be available at each one of them.

7. On the Advanced page of the New Job Step dialog box, you can set additional settings for this job step, such as how to respond to success or failure, and you can adjust SQL Server Agent logging settings. In this exercise, you will not need to adjust any advanced job step configuration settings, so just review them and leave them unchanged.

8. When you are ready, click OK to confirm the creation of a new job step.

   The job should now contain a single step named Master Package, configured to execute the Master.dtsx package of the TK 463 Chapter 10 project.

9. In the New Job editor, on the Schedules page, click New to open the New Job Schedule editor.

10. Configure the schedule by using the information provided in Table 12-5.

TABLE 12-5 New Job Schedule Configuration

Property	Value
Name	Continuous
Schedule type	Recurring
Enabled	(Selected)
Occurs	Daily
Recurs every	1 day(s)
Occurs every	3 minute(s)

The completed dialog box should look similar to the one shown in Figure 12-6.

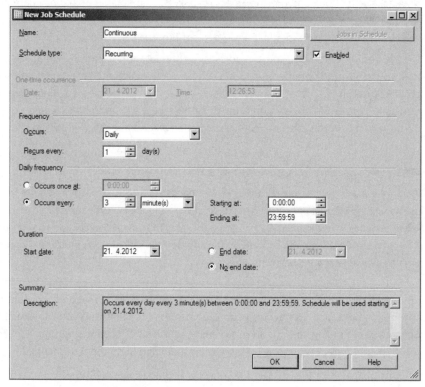

FIGURE 12-6 The New Job Schedule dialog box.

11. When you are done, click OK to complete the creation of a new schedule.

12. In the New Job editor, click OK to complete the creation of the new job.

13. In SSMS, in the Object Browser, double-click the Job Activity Monitor node, or right-click it and select View Job Activity from the shortcut menu, to open the Job Activity Monitor.

The job you just created should be executed automatically every three minutes; refresh the Job Activity Monitor to capture its execution.

14. Right-click the TK 463 Chapter 10 Master Package job in the Job Activity Monitor, and select View History from the shortcut menu to open the Log File Viewer. Observe the SQL Server Agent log entries for the job you just created. When you're done, close the Log File Viewer and return to the Job Activity Monitor.

> **IMPORTANT** **JOB SCHEDULING**
>
> Use SQL Server Agent job schedules to distribute operations throughout the day (or other appropriate periods), and try to maximize resource utilization. Avoid scheduling jobs that might end up competing for the same resources for concurrent execution.

15. Right-click the TK 463 Chapter 10 Master Package, and on the shortcut menu, select Disable Job. This will prevent the job from running automatically. When you are done, close the Job Activity Monitor.

16. Close SSMS.

Lesson Summary

- SSIS packages can be executed manually (for instance, by using SSMS or the DTExec utility) or programmatically (for instance, by using Windows PowerShell or proprietary applications). SSIS execution can even be automated—for instance, by using SQL Server Agent jobs.

- You are free to determine the most appropriate methods to execute SSIS processes in your environment.

- SSIS execution monitoring is available in SSMS through standard built-in reports, but you can also implement your own custom reports if needed.

Lesson Review

Answer the following questions to test your knowledge of the information in this lesson. You can find the answers to these questions and explanations of why each answer choice is correct or incorrect in the "Answers" section at the end of this chapter.

1. Which of the following methods and techniques can be used to execute SSIS packages deployed to the SSISDB catalog? (Choose all that apply.)

   A. Transact-SQL Data Definition Language (DDL) statements

   B. SSIS managed API

   C. Windows PowerShell

   D. The DTExecUI utility

2. Which of the following methods are available for monitoring SSIS executions? (Choose all that apply.)

   A. SSIS Performance Monitor

   B. SSIS Profiler

   C. SSMS built-in reports

   D. SSMS custom reports

3. Which of the following statements about SSIS project and package validation are true? (Choose all that apply.)

   A. Project validation cannot succeed if default values are not set for all required parameters.

   B. Successful validation guarantees successful execution of a package.

   C. Package validation cannot succeed if the metadata of an external resource does not match the metadata in the definition of the component using that external resource.

   D. Project validation is successful if at least one package in the project is validated successfully.

Lesson 2: Securing SSIS Packages

Whether SSIS solutions are deployed to an SSIS server (that is, to the SSISDB catalog) or to the older SSIS package store (that is, to the msdb system database or to the managed file system), they can be secured appropriately by restricting access to them only to certain users or processes.

The SSISDB catalog serves as the dedicated storage facility for SSIS solutions, providing not only a safe location for storing SSIS projects, packages, and configurations, but also SSIS solution maintenance, monitoring, and troubleshooting. In contrast to the older SSIS package store, SSISDB is not shared with any other part of the SQL Server platform (which is the case with the msdb system database) and does not depend on any external features that are not part of SQL Server (which is the case with the file system). Therefore, for your future work, you should plan on exclusively using the SSISDB catalog as the deployment target for all your SSIS solutions.

The SSISDB security model is based on the general SQL Server security model, allowing explicit as well as implicit assignment of permissions on all relevant objects as soon as they have been deployed to the SSIS server. In SQL Server 2012, no user has access to any SSIS solution unless he or she is permitted by the administrator. In addition, all data in SSISDB is encrypted to improve the protection of deployed SSIS solutions, even in the unlikely event that SSISDB database files are stolen.

The combination of the ability to associate multiple configurations with SSIS solutions that are deployed to the SSISDB catalog and the ability to assign permissions on these configurations independently from one another can also be used to improve the reusability of SSIS solutions. This combined ability allows different users (or processes) to use the same SSIS packages to perform data management operations against different data sources or data destinations, and it allows data transformations to be configured differently for different purposes.

> **After this lesson, you will be able to:**
>
> - Determine security needs.
> - Understand SSIS catalog database roles.
> - Understand package protection levels.
> - Secure Integration Services parameters and configurations.
>
> **Estimated lesson time: 60 minutes**

SSISDB Security

The SSISDB security model is implemented as relationships between SSISDB *principals* (SSISDB catalog users) and SSISDB *securables* (SSISDB folders, projects, and/or operations). SSISDB *permissions* define which SSISDB principals can perform which SSISDB operations on which SSISDB securables.

By default, after the SSISDB catalog has been created, no users are granted access to it. An administrator has to grant access permissions to the users explicitly before the SSISDB catalog can actually be used.

EXAM TIP

You should understand the principles of the general SQL Server security model before learning about the specifics of the SSIS security model. Although both of them have a lot in common, there are significant differences between them that you should understand well—particularly with respect to securables and permission granularity.

Principals

SSISDB principals are implemented the same way as in any other SQL Server 2012 database. A SQL Server user who has been granted access to the SSISDB catalog, also referred to as an *SSISDB user*, can query any public catalog view and execute any public stored procedures, except for the following administrative stored procedures: catalog.configure_catalog, catalog.grant_permission, and catalog.revoke_permission.

There is one database role in the SSISDB catalog named ssis_admin. The members of this role can perform administrative tasks on the SSIS server; they can view and modify any SSISDB securable.

The db_owner database role is a default member of the ssis_admin role; therefore, the person who creates the SSISDB catalog automatically becomes a member of the ssis_admin role.

Securables

In addition to tables, views, functions, procedures, and other objects found in any SQL Server 2012 database, the following SSISDB objects represent SSISDB securables:

- **Folders**   These represent the topmost securables in the SSISDB object hierarchy; they contain all other objects.

- **Projects**   These represent child securables of the folders they belong to; they contain packages and environment references.

- **Environments**   These represent child securables of the folders they belong to; they contain environment variables.

Permissions

SSISDB permission assignment is similar to that implemented in the regular SQL Server database security model; the permissions shown in Table 12-6 can be *granted*, *denied*, or *revoked*, by using system stored procedures.

TABLE 12-6 SSISDB Permissions

Permission name	Permission description	Applicable object types
READ	Allows the principal to read object properties. Does not allow the principal to enumerate or read the contents of other objects contained within the object.	Folder, Project, Environment, Operation
MODIFY	Allows the principal to modify object properties. Does not allow the principal to modify other objects contained within the object.	Folder, Project, Environment, Operation
EXECUTE	Allows the principal to execute all packages in the project.	Project
MANAGE_PERMISSIONS	Allows the principal to assign permissions to the objects.	Folder, Project, Environment, Operation
CREATE_OBJECTS	Allows the principal to create objects in the folder.	Folder
READ_OBJECTS	Allows the principal to read all objects in the folder.	Folder
MODIFY_OBJECTS	Allows the principal to modify all objects in the folder.	Folder
EXECUTE_OBJECTS	Allows the principal to execute all packages from all projects in the folder.	Folder
MANAGE_OBJECT_PERMISSIONS	Allows the principal to manage permissions on all objects in the folder.	Folder

SSISDB securables are stored in SSISDB in a manner similar to how SQL Server data is stored in tables—each SSISDB object is represented by a row in the corresponding table. Therefore, the SSISDB security model needs to extend the *regular* SQL Server security model, in which permissions are assigned on tables (and optionally on columns) by implementing *row-level security*, in which permissions are assigned on individual rows in the table, thus allowing a lower level of permission granularity, which is required by the specific needs of the SSISDB catalog.

The implementation of SSISDB row-level security is provided internally by Integration Services, not by the database engine.

SSISDB permission management is integrated into SSMS; alternatively, permissions can be managed by using Transact-SQL (using system stored procedures) or programmatically through the SSISDB application programming interface (API).

PERMISSION INHERITANCE

The structure of the SSIS object model is hierarchical: some objects also serve as containers for other objects—objects contained in another object are children of that object in the SSISDB object hierarchy. These hierarchical relationships between SSISDB objects allow permissions to be *inherited* from the ancestral object. The following objects cannot have permissions assigned directly, only through inheritance:

- Packages and environment references inherit permissions from the containing project.
- Environment variables inherit permissions from the containing environment.

Though inheritance does simplify permission assignment, it makes determining permissions slightly less transparent when SSISDB data is accessed. Therefore, the actual permissions are computed from explicitly assigned and inherited permissions every time an SSISDB object is accessed.

DEFAULT PERMISSIONS

By default, any SSISDB user is permitted to deploy projects to the SSIS server; any other permissions must be granted explicitly. However, the following implicit permissions are granted automatically to SSISDB users who create SSISDB objects:

- Any user who deploys a project is automatically granted permissions to read (enumerate), modify, and execute that project.
- Any user who creates an environment is automatically granted permissions to read and modify that environment.
- Any user who creates an operation is automatically granted permissions to read and modify that operation.

All permissions granted by default to the individual SSISDB users are at the same time automatically granted to the members of the ssis_admin role.

Default permissions cannot be revoked from the members of the ssis_admin role.

> **IMPORTANT** **SSISDB FOLDERS**
>
> Only members of the ssis_admin role are permitted to create folders in the SSISDB catalog. SSISDB users must be granted the Read and Create Objects permissions on at least one existing SSISDB folder in order to be able to deploy projects to the SSISDB catalog.

 Quick Check

1. Who can access SSISDB objects after they have been deployed?
2. How can permissions on various SSISDB objects be controlled?

Quick Check Answers

1. By default, access to SSISDB objects is limited to the users who created them and the members of the ssis_admin database role. Of course, for any user other than the SSISDB database owner to be able to create SSISDB objects, the administrator must first allow that user access to the SSISDB catalog.

2. Permissions can be controlled explicitly on folders, projects, and environments, but not on packages, environment references, or variables. Permissions on the latter are inherited from the containing object (the project or the environment to which the object belongs).

PRACTICE **Managing SSISDB Permissions**

In this practice, you will simulate a production environment with multiple server and database principals accessing the SSIS server to perform their work.

You will create multiple environments to be used by different users when configuring SSIS processes. You will use SSMS to control permissions inside the SSISDB catalog, and you will practice using environments in combination with SSISDB security features to improve the reusability of SSIS solutions.

EXERCISE 1 **Create SSISDB Users**

1. Start SSMS and connect to the instance of SQL Server 2012 that you set up as the SSIS server in Lesson 2 of Chapter 11. Connect the Object Explorer to the same instance, unless it is already connected.

2. On the File menu, select Open/File, or press Ctrl+O on the keyboard, to open a Transact-SQL script file.

3. Using the Open dialog box, navigate to the C:\TK463\Chapter12\Code folder and select the TK463Chapter12_Lesson2.sql Transact-SQL query file. Make sure SSISDB is selected as the current database.

4. Review and execute the part of the script marked Exercise 1 to create three SQL Server logins and three corresponding SSISDB users.

5. Leave SSMS open, because you will need it in the following exercises.

EXERCISE 2   Create and Secure SSISDB Environments

1. In the Object Explorer, under Integration Services Catalogs/SSISDB, expand TK 463 Chapter 11 so that the Environments node is visible.

2. Right-click the Environments node and select Create Environment from the shortcut menu to create a new environment that you will use for SSISDB project configuration.

3. In the Create Environment editor, provide a name for the configuration (**Production1**) and an optional description, as shown in Figure 12-7.

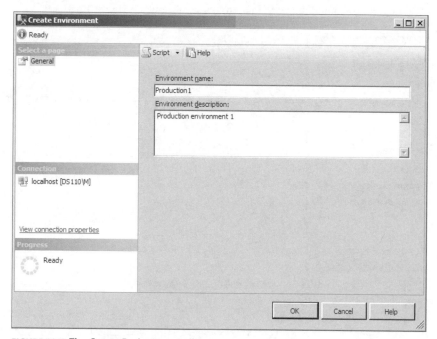

FIGURE 12-7 The Create Environment editor.

When done, click OK to confirm the creation of a new environment.

4. Repeat step 3 to create two additional environments named **Production2** and **Production3**.

5. In the Object Explorer, double-click the Production1 environment, or right-click it and then select Properties from the shortcut menu, to open the Environment Properties dialog box.

6. On the Variables page of the Environment Properties dialog box, create a new environment variable by using the information provided in Table 12-7.

TABLE 12-7 Environment Variable

Property	Value
Name	TK463DW_CS
Type	String
Value	Data Source=localhost; Initial Catalog=TK463DW; Provider=SQLNCLI11.1; Integrated Security=SSPI; Auto Translate=False;
Sensitive	(Cleared)

The dialog box should appear similar to the one shown in Figure 12-8.

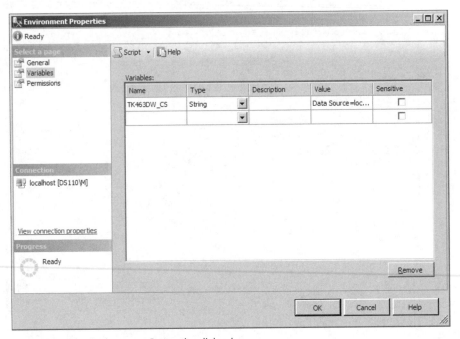

FIGURE 12-8 The Environment Properties dialog box.

7. On the Permissions page, click Browse, and from the list of database principals, select Dejan and then click OK to confirm the selection.

8. Make sure Dejan is selected in the Logins Or Roles list box, and then in the Permissions For Dejan grid, select the Grant check box for the Read permission. When you are done, click OK to confirm variable creation and permission assignment.

9. Repeat steps 5 through 8 to create the same environment variable in the Production2 and Production3 environments, assigning read permissions on them to Grega and Matija, respectively.

   In the end, you should have three environments, each one assigned to a single SSISDB user, so that each user could execute SSIS packages using the appropriate environment and effectively execute his own "version" of the SSIS solution.

   Of course, in a real-world environment, all three users would have their specific environments configured differently, accessing different servers, but this exercise assumes that only one server is available.

EXERCISE 3   Configure an SSISDB Project

1. In the Object Explorer, right-click the TK 463 Chapter 10 project, and from the shortcut menu, select Configure, to configure the project.

2. On the References page of the Configure dialog box, click Add, and in Browse Environments, select the Production1 environment. When you are ready, click OK to confirm the selection.

3. Repeat step 2 to add the Production2 and Production3 environments to the projects as well. The dialog box should look like the one shown in Figure 12-9.

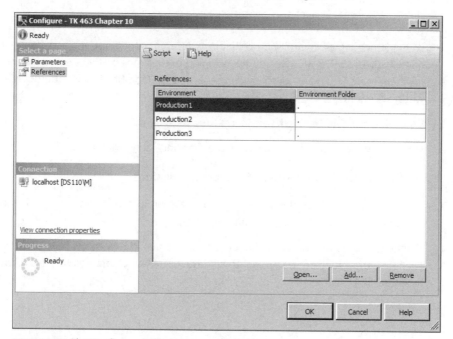

FIGURE 12-9 The Configure dialog box.

4. On the Parameters page, select the Connection Managers tab.

5. Select connection manager named TK463DW, and in the Properties grid, click the ellipsis (...) next to the ConnectionString property.

6. In the Set Parameter Value dialog box, configure the ConnectionString property to use the TK463DW_CS environment variable, as shown in Figure 12-10.

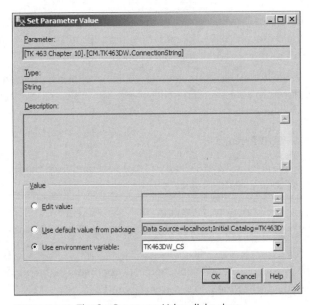

FIGURE 12-10 The Set Parameter Value dialog box.

By implementing an environment variable in different configurations, associating it by name with an SSISDB project, and by assigning permissions on these environments to different users, you have now allowed the same project to be used in different real-world environments.

7. When you are done, click OK to confirm the assignment.

8. In the Configure dialog box, click OK to confirm the configuration.

EXERCISE 4   Manage and Verify SSIS Project Permissions

1. In the Object Explorer, right-click the TK 463 Chapter 10 project, and on the shortcut menu, select Properties to access the project's properties.

2. On the Permissions page of the Project Properties dialog box, grant Read and Execute permissions on the project to all three users you created earlier, as shown in Figure 12-11.

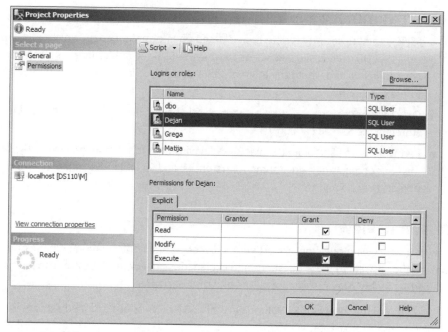

FIGURE 12-11 Granting project permissions.

3. When you are done, click OK to confirm permission assignment.

   All three users are now allowed to execute any package in the TK 463 Chapter 10 project. Before that, as the owner of the database, you were the only user allowed to execute this project.

4. Return to the script that you opened in Exercise 1.

5. Review and execute individual steps in the part of the script marked Exercise 5 to verify that each SSISDB user is allowed to execute packages of the TK 463 Chapter 10 project, and that each of them can access the environments assigned to them.

> **IMPORTANT EXECUTE AS**
>
> The EXECUTE AS Transact-SQL statement allows you to test the permission assignments for a particular user, in order to ensure that the SSISDB objects have been secured appropriately. Of course, to be able to use the statement accordingly, you yourself need permission to impersonate the user in question.

6. When you are done, close SSMS.

Lesson Summary

- SSISDB catalog security is determined based on information about which SSISDB principal (SSISDB user) is allowed access to which SSISDB securables (folders, projects, and environments) and what the nature of this access is (to view, to execute, to modify, or to remove them).
- Only members of the ssis_admin database role have full access to any of the objects stored in the SSISDB catalog.
- Permissions on SSIS folders, projects, and environments are managed explicitly; permissions on packages, environment references, and variables, are inherited from the objects they belong to.

Lesson Review

Answer the following questions to test your knowledge of the information in this lesson. You can find the answers to these questions and explanations of why each answer choice is correct or incorrect in the "Answers" section at the end of this chapter.

1. Which of the following SSISDB objects can have permissions assigned explicitly? (Choose all that apply.)

   A. Folders

   B. Packages

   C. Environment variables

   D. Projects

2. Which permissions must be granted to SQL Server logins in order to allow them to deploy SSIS projects to the SSISDB catalog?

   A. They must be granted the Deploy Project permission.

   B. They must be members of the ssis_admin role.

   C. They must be members of the sysadmin fixed server role.

   D. They must be SSISDB database users.

3. Which of the following permissions are granted by default to any SSISDB user? (Choose all that apply.)

   A. Permission to create folders in the SSISDB catalog

   B. Permission to deploy SSIS projects to the SSISDB catalog

   C. Permission to modify SSIS projects that they themselves have deployed

   D. Permission to create environments

Case Scenarios

In the following case scenarios, you apply what you've learned about executing and securing packages. You can find the answers to these questions in the "Answers" section at the end of this chapter.

Case Scenario 1: Deploying SSIS Packages to Multiple Environments

You have been asked by your manager to prepare a deployment plan for an SSIS data warehousing solution. The plan is to allow the solution to be executed on six different servers, each of them targeting the same environment but processing only a specific subset of source data.

Of course, your boss also expects you to find a way to minimize the maintenance, and possibly centralize monitoring and troubleshooting of the solution.

- Can this be achieved at all? If so, how?
- Which SQL Server 2012 features could you use to distribute SSIS processing to meet the requirements? What would you still have to develop yourself?

Case Scenario 2: Remote Executions

Your organization would like to minimize total cost of ownership, and so SQL Server Integration Services will only be installed on a single production server. This server will host the SSISDB catalog where all the company's SSIS solutions will be stored, maintained, and executed.

The data managed by your organization should be available in a distributed environment, where subsets of data are managed at different servers and in different applications. Some subsets of data need to be downloaded to remote locations and occasionally uploaded from them to the central location.

It has been decided that all data movement operations will be implemented as SSIS packages.

- Is it possible to execute SSIS packages remotely? If so, how?
- What features of the SQL Server platform could you use to enable remote SSIS execution?

Suggested Practices

To help you successfully master the exam objectives presented in this chapter, complete the following tasks.

Improve the Reusability of an SSIS Solution

In the production environment in your organization, you probably have a situation for which you either had to deploy the same SSIS solution to different environments or have had to distribute SSIS processing to multiple servers for performance reasons.

- **Practice 1** Think about the methods that you used to achieve this. Were you able to actually reuse the same SSIS packages for different purposes simply by associating them with different configurations, or did you deploy the same package multiple times to different destination servers?

- **Practice 2** Consider what you have learned so far about the SSISDB catalog, and think about how you could use its configuration and security features to improve the reusability of your existing SSIS solutions.

- **Practice 3** Create a checklist of proprietary features you had to develop for this purpose that could be replaced by the functionalities available in the SSISDB catalog.

Answers

This section contains answers to the lesson review questions and solutions to the case scenarios in this chapter.

Lesson 1

1. **Correct Answers: B and C**

   A. **Incorrect:** No Transact-SQL DDL statements are available to control SSIS execution.

   B. **Correct:** The SSIS managed API provides functionalities for executing SSIS processes programmatically from .NET applications.

   C. **Correct:** Windows PowerShell scripts can be used to execute SSIS processes.

   D. **Incorrect:** The DTExecUI utility is not compatible with the SSISDB catalog.

2. **Correct Answers: C and D**

   A. **Incorrect:** There is no such thing as an SSIS Performance Monitor.

   B. **Incorrect:** There is no such thing as an SSIS Profiler.

   C. **Correct:** The SSMS standard built-in reports can be used to view SSIS execution history.

   D. **Correct:** Custom reports can be added to SSMS to view SSIS execution history.

3. **Correct Answers: A and C**

   A. **Correct:** All project parameters marked as required must have their default values set in order for SSIS project validation to succeed.

   B. **Incorrect:** Validation only checks the metadata and the configuration of SSIS packages, projects, and environment references; no other circumstances that could affect the result of SSIS package execution are checked.

   C. **Correct:** The metadata of external resources used by SSIS components must match the metadata in the definition of these components.

   D. **Incorrect:** The validation of an SSIS project cannot succeed unless all of the packages it contains are validated successfully.

Lesson 2

1. **Correct Answers: A and D**

   A. **Correct:** Permissions can be assigned explicitly on SSISDB folders.

   B. **Incorrect:** Permissions on SSISDB packages are inherited from the containing project.

   C. **Incorrect:** Permissions on SSISDB environment variables are inherited from the containing environment.

   D. **Correct:** Permissions can be assigned explicitly on SSISDB projects.

2. **Correct Answer: D**

   A. **Incorrect:** There is no Deploy Project permission.

   B. **Incorrect:** Although members of the ssis_admin database role have the permission to deploy projects to the SSISDB catalog, membership in this role is not required to deploy projects.

   C. **Incorrect:** Although members of the sysadmin fixed server role have the permission to deploy projects to the SSISDB catalog, membership in this role is not required to deploy projects.

   D. **Correct:** Any user who has been granted access to the SSISDB database is permitted to deploy projects to the SSISDB catalog, unless, of course, the CREATE_OBJECTS permission has been denied to that user on specific folders.

3. **Correct Answers: B and C**

   A. **Incorrect:** Only members of the ssis_admin role are permitted to create folders in the SSISDB catalog.

   B. **Correct:** Any SSISDB user is permitted to deploy SSIS projects to the SSISDB catalog.

   C. **Correct:** Any SSISDB user is permitted to modify SSIS projects that they have created.

   D. **Incorrect:** To create an environment, an SSISDB user must be granted the Create_Objects permission in the corresponding folder.

Case Scenario 1

- To allow the same SSIS solution to be executed at different servers, it would have to be deployed multiple times.

  You would start by parameterizing individual SSIS packages so that the queries used for data extraction would use parameters or would be created dynamically, so that only a well-defined subset of data could be extracted when the package is executed.

  You could then associate these parameters with environment variables and prepare six different environments for six servers.

- You would create an SSISDB catalog at each server and deploy the solution multiple times.

  SQL Server Integration Services would also have to be installed at each of the six servers. You would have to create a SQL Server Agent job at each of the six servers, and configure the relevant job steps, executing SSIS packages, to use the corresponding environment created earlier.

  To centralize SSIS execution monitoring you would have to consolidate information from six SSIS servers in a single location, for instance, by implementing partitioned views.

Case Scenario 2

- Remote SSIS execution is supported. You could execute SSIS packages by using Transact-SQL, execute SQL Server Agent jobs by using Transact-SQL, or even go as far as designing your own service (a Windows service or a web service) to invoke SSIS processes on the central server.

- As long as all machines used in this distributed environment belong to the same domain or appropriate authentication can be used to access the SSIS server, you would not have to design any part of this solution yourself. In a heterogeneous environment, you would have to resort to a custom service, deployed to the same domain as the SSIS server but also accessible from outside the domain.

## CHAPTER 13

Troubleshooting and Performance Tuning

Exam objectives in this chapter:

- Extract and Transform Data
  - Design data flow.
  - Implement data flow.
- Load Data
  - Implement control flow.
- Configure and Deploy SSIS Solutions
  - Troubleshoot data integration issues.

This chapter first looks at the various capabilities in Microsoft SQL Server Integration Services (SSIS) for debugging packages during development and how to troubleshoot errors during production execution. The second lesson focuses on good package design as a foundation for good performance of your packages. To make the right performance design decisions, you need to understand the performance architecture of SSIS and the techniques that enable you to maximize the utilization of system resources such as memory and the CPU.

Lessons in this chapter:

- Lesson 1: Troubleshooting Package Execution
- Lesson 2: Performance Tuning

Before You Begin

To complete this chapter, you must have:

- Knowledge of SQL Server 2012 SSIS control flow and data flow features and components.
- Experience working with SQL Server 2012 Management Studio (SSMS).
- Experience working with SQL Server Data Tools (SSDT) or SQL Server Business Intelligence Development Studio (BIDS).
- Practice working in the control flow and data flow.

Lesson 1: Troubleshooting Package Execution

With SSIS, you can troubleshoot package execution in the development phase and later in the production phase. The availability of different options for debugging your packages in the development environment is crucial in the test phase for quickly identifying logical errors in the control flow and data flow. In SQL Server 2012, SSIS also provides a lot of new features when it comes to troubleshooting package execution at run time in the production environment.

> **After this lesson, you will be able to:**
>
> - Understand control flow and data flow troubleshooting possibilities.
> - Debug a control flow by using breakpoints.
> - Enable and use data viewers in a data flow.
> - Use the new SSISDB execution reports and data taps.
>
> **Estimated lesson time: 60 minutes**

Design-Time Troubleshooting

The first way to troubleshoot your package is to observe the execution at design time. While a package is running in the debug environment (when you run it in SSDT), you can see the status of both control flow and data flow components. SSDT adds new icons in the upper-right corner of each task to help you see what is happening in the package:

- Objects that do not have an icon in the upper-right corner when the package is running have not yet started. In versions before SQL Server 2012, objects that have not yet started are not highlighted.

- Objects that have a yellow circle icon showing some sort of progress are in progress. In previous versions of SQL Server, this object is highlighted in yellow. In the data flow, you can also see the number of rows that have gone through the source, transformation, and destination components.

- Objects that have an icon with a red circle and a white cross have failed. In previous versions of SQL Server, the object is highlighted in red. Even after an error has occurred, other components in the package might still be executing.

- When the control flow task or container is complete or all the available rows have gone through the components successfully, then the object will have an icon with a green circle.

> **IMPORTANT   ALLOWING MULTIPLE ERRORS IN PACKAGE EXECUTION**
>
> The MaximumErrorCount control flow property allows a package to continue to run to completion even after errors have occurred. This property specifies the number of errors that can occur before the package will stop executing and report failure.

If you are using a For Loop container or a Foreach Loop container, the embedded tasks might change the various status icons at different times as the loops are performed. Even when all the tasks in a package have been completed, the package will remain in debug mode until the package has been stopped. This behavior lets you easily see the final status of tasks and the row counts in the data flow.

In addition to the visual display of the execution of the package, you can also read the execution details on the Progress tab in the SSIS Designer when in debug mode. When you stop the package, this tab changes its name to Execution Results, where you can still read the latest details of execution of the package.

Figure 13-1 shows the Progress tab as it appears while the package is executing. Note that the figure shows only some of the possible results, which can include error descriptions (with red icons), warning descriptions (with yellow triangle icons), execution times, final destination row counts, and other execution information, such as validation steps and configuration usage.

Notice that the listed results consist of the same information that can be captured by using the SSIS built-in logging features, which are discussed in Chapter 10, "Auditing and Logging."

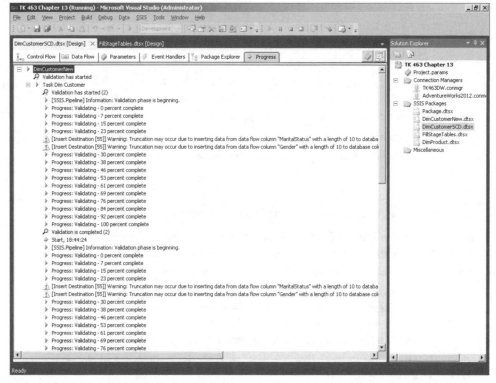

FIGURE 13-1 The Progress tab in the SSIS Designer.

Debugging the Control Flow with Breakpoints

Sometimes you want to know what is going on during package execution so that you can troubleshoot or validate processing logic. This can be achieved in the control flow area by setting *breakpoints* in the package, which will pause the control flow execution so that you can observe the execution state. SSIS takes advantage of the breakpoint functionality that comes with Microsoft Visual Studio, which means that you can view execution information about a package when you execute it in the SSIS Designer. Remember that breakpoints work only in the control flow.

To set a breakpoint, right-click the task or container you want to observe, and select Edit Breakpoints to open the Set Breakpoints dialog box. In the Set Breakpoints dialog box, you can enable breakpoints on the listed conditions, which are similar to the ones used by event handlers (discussed in Chapter 8, "Creating a Robust and Restartable Package"). This means that when a task or container receives the specified event (for example, OnError or OnVariableValueChanged), the breakpoint will be triggered. Figure 13-2 shows all of the possible break conditions on a specific event for a selected task.

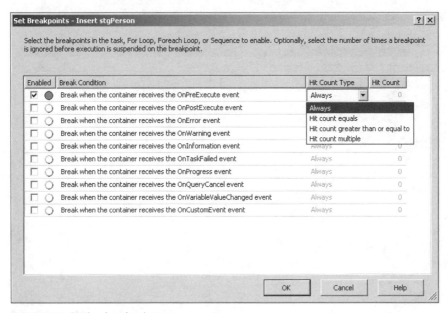

FIGURE 13-2 Setting breakpoints.

By using the Set Breakpoints dialog box, you can add additional flexibility and power to a breakpoint by specifying two properties:

- The Hit Count, or the maximum number of times that a break condition must occur before the execution is suspended.

- The Hit Count Type, or the rule that specifies when the break condition triggers the breakpoint. For example, if the type is Hit Count Equals, then Visual Studio checks the Hit Count value and suspends execution when the number of occurrences equals the Hit Count value. Changing the Hit Count Type from the default value of Always is usually useful when you are debugging the For Loop container or Foreach Loop container.

Alternatively, if you want to set a breakpoint on the OnPreExecute event, you can just select the task or container you want and press F9 or, on the Debug menu, choose Toggle Breakpoint. You can set multiple breakpoints in a package, and you can embed a breakpoint within a script task at the line of code. A task that has a breakpoint set will appear with a red dot; when the package is executed, the icon will change to include a yellow arrow, indicating which task the package is currently waiting for. Figure 13-3 shows a package that is running with an execution paused at the breakpoint.

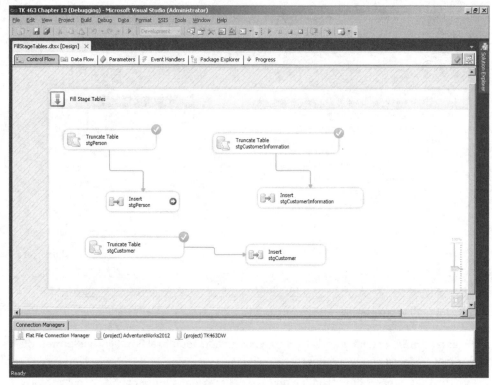

FIGURE 13-3 Execution paused at the breakpoint.

When you are paused in the debug environment, you can do the following things to help troubleshoot your package:

- You can open the Locals windows to see all the variable values and the package status. To open this window, on the Debug menu, select Windows | Locals. If you have several variables in a package that you can actively use to control logic and precedence, you can use a breakpoint to pause the execution, which lets you troubleshoot variable value handling before the package execution completes. You can view the values of all system and user variables from the Locals window. You can also add variables to the other watch windows by right-clicking the variables you want in the Locals window and choosing Add Watch.

- You can change the value of variables on the fly. In the watch window, select and expand the variable information, right-click the Value property, and click Edit Value.

- When the package is paused on a task, you can continue running the package to completion or to the next breakpoint by clicking the Continue button on the Debug toolbar or by pressing F5.

- You can open the Call Stack debugging window to show a list of the tasks that have executed up to the breakpoint. This can be very useful when you are trying to figure out a very complex workflow.

- You can stop the package during execution, whether the package is paused at a breakpoint or not, by pressing the Stop button on the toolbar or by pressing Shift+F5.

In SQL Server 2012, you can now debug the script component by setting breakpoints and running the package in SSDT. When the package execution enters the script component, the Visual Studio Tools for Applications (VSTA) IDE reopens and displays your code in read-only mode. When execution reaches your breakpoint, you can examine variable values and step through the remaining code. The breakpoints that you set in script tasks are integrated with the breakpoints that you set on packages and the tasks and containers in the package, enabling seamless debugging of all package elements.

Using Data Viewers in the Data Flow

Troubleshooting data issues can be frustrating, especially when you are not able to easily identify the problem row or issues. Therefore, SSIS includes a very important capability that allows you to watch rows in the data flow as they pass through the pipeline. This capability is implemented through *data viewers*, a feature you can use when you are running packages in SSDT during development. For any path in the data flow, you can add a data viewer that pauses the execution of the data flow and displays the data in the data viewer in one of four formats.

You add a data viewer by right-clicking the path and then clicking Enable Data Viewers or by opening the Data Flow Path Editor, selecting the Data Viewer tab, and selecting the Enable Data Viewer check box. As shown in Figure 13-4, the Data Flow Path Editor allows you to select the columns that should be visible in the data viewer (by default, all columns are selected).

In SQL Server 2012, the only available type of data viewer is the grid display. In prior versions of SSIS, the data viewer could also be in the form of a histogram, a scatter plot, or a column chart. The grid display is a logical choice for the new version of the product; it is the one mostly commonly used, because it shows the actual rows of data. When you execute the package in SSDT, the data viewer displays a set of rows at a time. Figure 13-5 shows the Data Viewer dialog box as a package is executing.

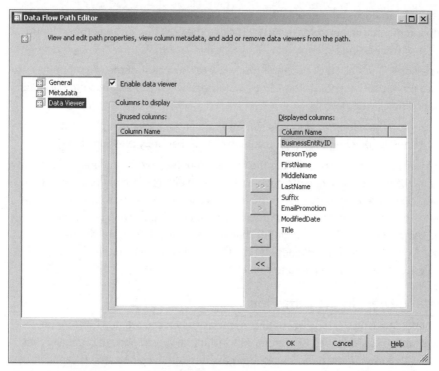

FIGURE 13-4 Enabling a data viewer in the Data Flow Path Editor.

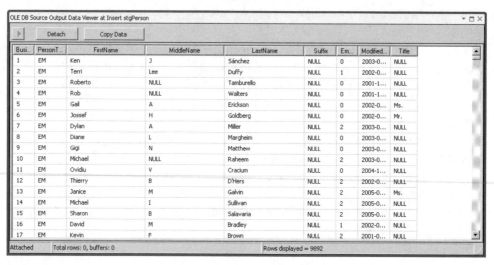

FIGURE 13-5 Data Viewer

After reviewing the rows, you can choose to allow the data to move on until completion by clicking Detach in the Data Viewer window, or you can return the next batch of rows by clicking the Play button. If you use a data viewer on an error path, you can add the Error and Error Code columns to the outputs to identify the column in the row that caused the row to fail a component.

As you add more and more data viewers, you might want to eventually remove them to speed up your development execution. You can remove them by right-clicking the path and clicking Disable Data Viewer. You can also delete all the data viewers and breakpoints at one time by selecting Delete All Breakpoints on the Debug menu.

Using Other Methods for Debugging

When you are troubleshooting your package at design time, you can also use some existing tasks and transformations to accomplish some troubleshooting tasks.

- **Use error outputs.** Chapter 7, "Enhancing Data Flow," explains how to create an error flow in the data flow to redirect rows that have errors. This possibility is also useful when you are debugging source and destination adapters; it allows you to see all of the rows that, for example, will generate a conversion or a truncation error. You use a flat file destination adapter to store rows with errors.

- **Interrupt the execution of a package by using a pop-up message window.** You can also monitor the execution of the control flow or the data flow by using the script component or script task. You interrupt the execution of a package by using the MessageBox.Show method in the System.Windows.Forms namespace to display a modal message.

- **Test with only a subset of data.** If you want to troubleshoot the data flow in a package by using only a sample of the dataset, you can include a Percentage Sampling or Row Sampling transformation to create an inline data sample at run time.

- **Capture the count of rows processed.** One of the basic automated tests you can develop in SSIS is one that compares the number of rows coming from a source component or components to the number of rows written in a destination adapter or adapters (this is only useful, of course, for data flows in which the numbers should be equal). This can be achieved by adding a Row Count transformation to the data flow to capture the start row count and final row count in multiple variables (depending on the number of source and destination adapters). You usually add this test logic by using event handlers in the package and applying different tasks when rows do not match (such as raising an error, logging the information, or sending an email message).

Production-Time Troubleshooting

To troubleshoot package execution in the production environment, you can use the various logging capabilities of SSIS to analyze how SSIS packages are performing. Continuous monitoring not only focuses on capturing errors and their details, but it also enables you to prevent possible errors and make your projects and packages perform predictively. In SQL Server 2012, SSIS offers new options for monitoring the execution of packages: you can use predefined reports in the SSISDB Integration Services catalog, and you can also query the SSISDB database directly through catalog views, by using T-SQL to get the needed information. This helps you to more efficiently troubleshoot your packages in the production environment.

Troubleshooting Packages by Using the SSISDB Catalog

Chapter 10 discussed the logging possibilities in SSIS. One of the new features of SQL Server 2012 is the SSISDB catalog, which acts as a central storage and administration point for SSIS projects, packages, parameters, and environments. This new catalog and its underlying database comes with a set of capabilities that offer much better logging and monitoring capabilities for package execution when compared to previous versions.

The SSISDB catalog has a couple of predefined reports available for monitoring the execution of your packages, and the SSISDB database has multiple catalog views that you can query directly to get information about package execution. You access the SSISDB catalog via SSMS by connecting to the SQL Server Database Engine and then expanding the Integration Services Catalogs node in the Object Explorer.

By default, the logging level of the SSISDB catalog is set to Basic. When you need to troubleshoot your packages, you can set this property to Verbose to track more details when you are executing packages. To change the logging level, right-click the SSISDB catalog in SSMS and select Properties. In the Catalog Properties window, change the Server-Wide Default Logging Level property to Verbose.

There are five main reports on the SSISDB catalog level to troubleshoot your packages:

- The Integration Services Dashboard shows information about all operations (this can be from multiple projects) that have run in the last 24 hours. Multiple hyperlinks are provided in the report to allow you to access other predefined reports.
- The All Executions report shows all package executions.
- The All Validations report displays all package validations.
- The All Operations report shows an overview of all Integration Services operations that have been performed.
- The All Connections report displays the connection context of execution errors.

On the package level, more detailed reports are available to display all messages and execution performance information for your package. You can access all predefined reports by right-clicking the SSISDB catalog or right-clicking a project or package and selecting Reports. The Standard Reports list contains the available reports.

Using Data Taps

Data taps are a new feature in SQL Server 2012 for troubleshooting package execution. With *data taps*, you can capture a copy of the data from a specific data path in your data flow task in a comma-delimited file at run time. Much like data viewers are used to monitor the data in the data flow at design time, data taps enable you to analyze data in a production environment for specific execution of the package.

To be able to use data taps, you must first use T-SQL to execute the provided stored procedures inside the SSISDB database. You start by creating an execution instance for the package by executing the catalog.create_execution stored procedure, then you add the data tap or taps by running catalog.add_data_tap, and finally you run the package by using the catalog.start_execution procedure. To be able to execute the catalog.add_data_tap stored procedure, you must pass the needed parameter values:

■ **@execution_id**   The execution ID for the execution that contains the package.

■ **@task_package_path**   The package path for the data flow task. This can be read from the PackagePath property of the selected data flow task in SSDT.

■ **@dataflow_path_id_string**   The identification string for the data flow path. In SQL Server Data Tools, the IdentificationString property for the data flow path specifies the string, as shown in Figure 13-6.

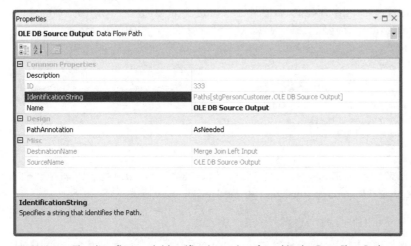

FIGURE 13-6 The data flow path identification string, found in the Data Flow Path properties.

- **@data_filename** The name of the file that will store the tapped data.
- **@max_rows** The number of rows to be captured during the data tap. If this value is not specified, all rows will be captured.

You can return the ID of the data tap by using the @data_tap_id argument. The output file will be stored in the \Microsoft SQL Server\110\DTS\DataDumps folder. A sample implementation is provided in the practice for this lesson.

EXAM TIP

Data taps cannot be defined at design time.

PRACTICE   **Troubleshooting Packages**

In this practice, you will first analyze a package error and correct the issue. In the second exercise, you will implement one data tap for your package.

If you encounter a problem completing an exercise, you can install the completed projects from the Solution folder that is provided with the companion content for this chapter and lesson.

EXERCISE 1   Fix a Truncation Error

In this exercise, you observe an error when executing a package and apply needed corrections to successfully execute the package.

1. If you are missing the database objects from Chapter 5, "Designing and Implementing Data Flow," execute the needed SQL code from that chapter to have all the stage and dimension tables available in the TK463DW database. Execute also the FillStageTables package to load the needed stage tables with sample data. Start SSMS and connect to your SQL Server instance. Open a new query window by clicking the New Query button. Select the TK463DW database in the database drop-down list. Create the stg. SalesTerritory staging table by executing the following SQL statement.

   ```
   CREATE TABLE stg.SalesTerritory
   (
   TerritoryID INT NULL,
   Name NVARCHAR(50) NULL,
   CountryRegionCode NVARCHAR(10) NULL,
   [Group] NVARCHAR(50) NULL,
   ModifiedDate DATETIME NULL
   );
   ```

2. Start SQL Server Data Tools (SSDT), open the TK 463 Chapter 13 project in the Starter folder, and then open the DimCustomerNew.dtsx package.

3. Execute the package. You will get an error.

4. Look in the data flow to see that the error occurred at the derived column transformation called Set Default Values.

5. Look on the Progress tab while in debug mode and find the first error message:

```
[Set default values [197]] Error: The "Set default values" failed because
truncation occurred, and the truncation row disposition on "Set default values.
Inputs[Derived Column Input].Columns[Gender]" specifies failure on truncation. A
truncation error occurred on the specified object of the specified component.
```

> **NOTE READING ERROR MESSAGES**
>
> Sometimes you cannot read the full error message on the Progress tab. One way to address this is to right-click the message, select Copy Message Text, and paste the information to some other program, such as Notepad, so that you can read the full error message.

6. Open the Set Default Value derived column transformation and, in the Derived Column Transformation Editor, notice that the Gender Expression will return the value N/A if the value is NULL. On the other hand, the *Length* column has the value 1 for this column. You cannot change the size of this column here, but you can do so at the transformation or adapter that produced this column.

7. Close debug mode and open the Advanced Editor for the Get Customer Information lookup transformation.

8. In the Advanced Editor for Get Customer Information, select the Input And Output Properties tab. Under Lookup Match Output, expand Output Columns and select the *Gender* column. Set the Length property from a value of 1 to a value of *5*. Click OK. This will change the initial size for this column to five characters so that it is the same size as the destination column in the database.

9. Execute the package. Notice that it runs successfully.

EXERCISE 2 Add a Data Tap

In this exercise, you deploy the package to the Integration Services server and add a data tap to store the data from one data path to a file.

1. If necessary, start SQL Server Data Tools (SSDT), open the TK 463 Chapter 13 project, and open the DimCustomerNew.dtsx package.

2. In the Solution Explorer window, right-click TK 463 Project 13 and click Deploy.

3. In the Integration Services Deployment Wizard, click Next, and in the Server Name text box enter the name of your SQL Server instance with SSISDB.

4. Under the Path text box, click Browse. Select SSISDB, click the New Folder button, and create a new folder called *TK463*. Select this new folder and click OK. Click Next, and on the next page, click Deploy.

5. When the process completes, click Close.

6. Open the Properties For Dim Customer data flow task and make a note of the value of the *PackagePath* property (\Package\Dim Customer).

7. In the Dim Customer data flow, right-click the data path between the *stgPerson-Customer* OLE DB Source adapter and the Merge Join transformation, and then click Properties.

8. In the Data Flow Path Properties window, note the value of the *IdentificationString* property (*Paths[stgPersonCustomer.OLE DB Source Output]*).

9. Open the SQL Server Management Studio (SSMS) and connect to the SQL Server instance where you deployed your SSIS project.

10. Open the new query window and connect to the SSISDB database. Then execute the following stored procedure to create an execution instance.

```
DECLARE  @execution_id bigint;
EXEC catalog.create_execution
  @folder_name = N'TK463',
  @project_name = N'TK 463 Chapter 13',
  @package_name = N'DimCustomerNew.dtsx',
  @execution_id = @execution_id OUTPUT;
```

11. Add a data tap by executing the catalog.add_data_tap stored procedure.

```
EXEC catalog.add_data_tap
  @execution_id = @execution_id,
  @task_package_path = N'\Package\Dim Customer',
  @dataflow_path_id_string = N'Paths[stgPersonCustomer.OLE DB Source Output]',
  @data_filename = N'stgPersonCustomerDataTap.csv';
```

12. Execute the package by using the catalog.start_execution stored procedure.

```
EXEC catalog.start_execution @execution_id;
```

13. Using Windows Explorer, navigate to the \Microsoft SQL Server\110\DTS\DataDumps folder and open the stgPersonCustomerDataTap.csv file to see what was captured using the data tap.

Lesson Summary

- Use breakpoints when debugging packages at design time.
- SQL Server 2012 provides new ways to efficiently monitor and troubleshoot packages in a production environment.

Lesson Review

Answer the following questions to test your knowledge of the information in this lesson. You can find the answers to these questions and explanations of why each answer choice is correct or incorrect in the "Answers" section at the end of this chapter.

1. On which components can you set breakpoints? (Choose all that apply.)

   A. Data flow task

   B. Sequence container

   C. Script component

   D. Script task

2. Which troubleshooting techniques can you apply at design time? (Choose all that apply.)

   A. Observing the package execution

   B. Using breakpoints

   C. Using data taps

   D. Using data viewers

3. Which logging levels are available on the SSISDB catalog? (Choose all that apply.)

   A. Full

   B. None

   C. Simple

   D. Verbose

Lesson 2: Performance Tuning

Most of the performance issues in SSIS can be solved with a good package design. This lesson focuses on giving you an overview of the data flow engine and what to watch for when designing your package to get the best performance. Because performance can change over time, it is mandatory to monitor the execution of packages and apply different techniques to prevent degradation of performance.

After this lesson, you will be able to:

- Gain a better understanding of the SSIS data flow engine and different transformation types.
- Improve the design of your packages.
- Troubleshoot performance issues.

Estimated lesson time: 60 minutes

SSIS Data Flow Engine

You can achieve a solid understanding of the performance-tuning capabilities of the data flow by first understanding several data flow concepts, which will give you a better perspective on what is going on when a package is being executed. Also, when you have learned the basics of data flow architecture, you will be able to create your own efficient design patterns for data integration with SSIS. The main concepts that will be covered in this section are:

- Data buffer architecture
- Transformation types
- Execution trees
- Backpressure mechanism

Data Buffer Architecture

The data flow manages data in groups called buffers. A buffer is an area of memory that is used to store rows of data on which transformations are applied. Recall from Chapter 5 that rows of data are extracted from sources by using data flow source adapters, and each column data type is mapped to a specific SSIS data type. Based on this information, the SSIS engine knows how large each row should be in terms of memory, and it will preallocate memory buffers (the exact size and number of needed buffers will also be calculated based on the transformations involved, so you cannot assume that the row will consist only of columns coming from the source adapter, but it is a good estimation). Buffer size is dynamically determined according to package and server properties. You will learn later in this section how to change the default settings.

The amount of data or the number of rows that each buffer can store depends on the row size that is calculated from each column. For example, there can be 10,000 rows in a buffer if the row consists of only a couple of columns with integer data type. On the other hand, there might be only 2,000 rows if the row has multiple columns with larger character data types. Although it might seem that the buffers would be passed down from transformation to transformation in the data flow because a data flow is an in-memory pipeline, this is not always true. There are times when buffers need to be copied between transformations and when buffers are held up in cache by transformations. Understanding how memory buffers are managed requires some knowledge of the different types of data flow transformations and adapters.

Transformation Types

Transformations and adapters can be classified by their characteristics into different categories. The first difference, as you may recall from Chapter 5, is how and when data is handed off from one transformation to another. This was described as types of blocking (non-blocking transformations, partial-blocking transformations, and blocking transformations). The other difference is how the transformations are communicated: synchronously or asynchronously.

As you will see, both of these classifications are related. Transformations can be divided into three groups:

- Non-blocking or row-based (synchronous) transformations
- Partial-blocking (asynchronous) transformations
- Blocking (asynchronous) transformations

Non-blocking transformations logically work row by row; in this case, the buffer is re-used and no memory is copied. Partial-blocking transformations work with groups of rows; memory is copied, and the structure of the buffer can change (for example, in a Union All transformation, a new buffer is created). Blocking transformations store all rows from all buffers before producing any output rows. For example, a Sort transformation must get all rows before sorting and block any data buffers from being passed down the pipeline until the output is generated.

It's important to remember that a synchronous component reuses buffers and therefore is generally faster than an asynchronous component, which needs a new buffer, performs the most work, and can have the greatest impact on available resources. The tables in Chapter 5 provide more detailed information about each type of transformation in the data flow.

Execution Trees

An execution tree is a logical group of transformations that starts at either a source adapter or an asynchronous transformation and ends at the first asynchronous transformation or at a destination adapter. This means that the groupings are divided by asynchronous transformation output. Execution trees specify how buffers and threads are allocated in a package. Each tree creates a new buffer and might execute on a different thread. Note that the scope of a buffer is an execution tree.

At run time, the SSIS engine creates execution trees for each data flow task. If there is a partial-blocking or blocking transformation, a new buffer will be created and added to the pipeline; this means that additional memory will be required to handle the data transformation. It is important to note that each new tree might also require an additional worker thread.

Execution trees are very important in understanding buffer usage. You can display execution tree information by turning on package logging (as described in Chapter 10); enable logging for the data flow task, and then select the PipelineExecutionTrees event related to the pipeline. When you execute the package, the execution trees appear in the Log Events window in SSDT, as shown in Figure 13-7.

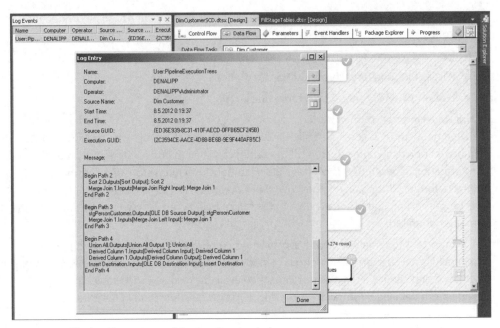

FIGURE 13-7 The Log Entry screen of the Log Events window.

Note that the number of execution trees in this figure is five (Path 0 is the first one). There is also an additional event for monitoring the execution trees called PipelineExecutionPlan.

Backpressure Mechanism

One of the mechanisms that the SSIS data flow engine uses to achieve high performance is *backpressure*. If a source or an asynchronous transformation is too fast (compared to the next transformation or destination farther down the path), the source is suspended when its execution tree creates too many buffers (currently the limit is fixed at five buffers). If the source is slow (that is, if transformations and destinations can process data faster than sources generate it), the backpressure mechanism does not get involved and sources can run at full speed. Because of the backpressure mechanism, you can process fast sources without worrying about opening too many buffers and eventually running out of memory.

Data Flow Tuning Options

Data flow tuning options can be divided in two categories: one type involves setting different properties inside the data flow, and the other type involves data flow design. Remember that design is much more important when it comes to optimizing the data flow.

Buffer Optimization

At execution time, before the data is read from the sources, SSIS automatically tunes buffer sizes to achieve maximum memory utilization based on a series of input parameters. SSIS applies the size of the buffers based on these input parameters:

- **Estimated Row Size** This is not a specific data flow property but is something that SSIS calculates based on the metadata that it collects about your source data at design time. You can shrink the row size by identifying the smallest possible data types for all of your columns as early in the data flow as possible and selecting only needed columns. This is especially important for flat file data sources, because each column is automatically read into SSIS as a string data type unless you configure the column's data type explicitly.

- **DefaultMaxBufferRows** This setting of the data flow task is automatically set at 10,000 records. SSIS multiplies Estimated Row Size by DefaultMaxBufferRows to get a rough sense of your dataset size per 10,000 records.

- **DefaultMaxBufferSize** This is also a setting of the data flow task. It is set to 10 MB by default. As you configure this setting, keep in mind that its upper bound is constrained by an internal SSIS parameter called MaxBufferSize, which is set to 100 MB and cannot be changed.

- **MinBufferSize** This is not configurable, but it is still important to know about because SSIS uses this internal parameter to gauge whether you have set the DefaultMaxBufferSize too low. MinBufferSize is defined by the granularity of your operating system's virtual memory allocation functionality. Typically, this is set to 65,536 bytes, but it differs from machine to machine.

You can configure the DefaultMaxBufferRows and DefaultMaxBufferSize properties and, depending on your configured values, SSIS will tune buffer sizes at execution time by using one of the following scenarios:

- When Estimated Row Size * DefaultMaxBufferRows exceeds MaxBufferSize, SSIS reduces the number of rows that will be stored in a buffer to manage the memory footprint.

- When Estimated Row Size * DefaultMaxBufferRows is less than MinBufferSize, SSIS increases the number of rows that will be stored in a buffer to maximize memory utilization.

- When Estimated Row Size * DefaultMaxBufferRows is between MinBufferSize and DefaultMaxBufferSize, then SSIS attempts to size the buffer as closely as possible to the result of Estimated Row Size * DefaultMaxBufferRows by using a multiple of the MinBufferSize to increase memory utilization.

Data Flow Tips for Performance

In previous chapters and in this chapter, you have read a lot about different best practices regarding data flow design. The following list summarizes the general best practices when it comes to optimizing your data flow task:

- Try to keep everything in memory, so that no swapping to disk occurs. Disk-swapping has a major impact on performance.

- Understand each transformation by its type and use a combination of SSIS and the underlying database to get optimal performance. For example, if you need sorted input, try to push the sorting to the database layer, because the Sort transformation is a blocking transformation and will fill as many buffers as needed before pushing the data onward.

- Design has a major impact on performance when compared to setting buffer optimization properties, so be careful about changing the buffer values.

- Before you start data flow optimization, you can realize significant gains by making sure that your system is in good shape. The things to consider are CPU, memory, disk I/O, and network connection. Remember that memory is extremely important in SSIS.

- Always use only the columns you need when reading data from source components or inside lookup queries.

- Use the right data types; try to be as narrow as possible, because this will produce less memory allocation. Avoid binary large object (BLOB) types because these get swapped to disk (this includes the VARCHAR(MAX) columns).

- Avoid the OLE DB transformation when you are doing multiple updates or deletions. Instead, stage the data and apply a set-based operation by using T-SQL in the next task inside the control flow.

- Try to always use full-cache lookups. If you need to run multiple lookups against the same query, use the Cache connection manager to reuse the cache. When you need a solution for range lookups, try to use the Script transformation instead.

- For source adapter optimization, consider the capabilities of different providers if you are working with databases other than SQL Server.

- Always use the Fast Load option on the destination adapter.

Parallel Execution in SSIS

Parallel execution improves performance on computers that have multiple physical or logical processors. The SSIS run time engine is a highly parallel engine that coordinates the execution of tasks or units of work within SSIS and manages the engine threads that carry out those tasks. You can influence SSIS parallel execution inside the control flow and the design flow either by changing properties or by changing the design of your package. Inside the control flow is the MaxConcurrentExecutables property of the package. It defines the number of tasks (executables) that can run simultaneously. This property has a default value of −1, which is translated to the number of logical processors plus 2. To be able to execute multiple tasks simultaneously in a package, those tasks must not be connected with precedence constraints. For example, if you have a master package that executes 10 packages to load dimensions and then 4 packages to load fact tables in your data warehouse, you will probably not connect them with precedence constraints but rather put all of the Execute Package tasks that are used for dimension loading inside one sequence container and all the Execute Package tasks for fact tables in another sequence container. With this approach, all of the Execute Package tasks for dimension loading will be executed in parallel—how many of them depends on the value of the MaxConcurrentExecutables property (or your hardware configuration, if the property uses the default value).

For the data flow, there is an EngineThreads property that determines how many work threads the scheduler will create and run in parallel. This property's default value is 5. Remember also that this property value governs both source threads (for source components) and work threads (for transformation and destination components). Source threads and work threads are both engine threads created by the data flow's scheduler. So the default value of 5 allows up to 5 source threads and 5 work threads. Note that if the number of threads exceeds the number of available processors, you might end up hurting throughput due to an excessive amount of context switches, so be cautious with this property.

Troubleshooting and Benchmarking Performance

A good practice when troubleshooting poor performance is to isolate the execution of various parts of your package to find the operations that should be optimized first. To isolate SSIS operations, consider the following steps:

1. Establish the overall package execution speed by executing the package using DTEXEC. (The debug mode of SSDT adds execution time and will not give you an accurate result.) Define the overall execution speed as the sum of source speed (time to read the data from source adapters), transformation speed (time that data rows need to pass through all transformations), and destination speed (time to write the data to the destination adapters).

2. Create a copy of your original package, because you will isolate the steps to find the main cause for performance issues.

3. Isolate the source and transformation speeds to find out how fast SSIS is reading from a source and performing transformations. You do this by removing the destination associated with the source. If you have more than one destination, isolate one at a time. Replace the destination with a RowCount transformation and measure the execution performance from source through transformations to RowCount.

4. Remove the transformations and measure the source speed of your data flow.

5. Calculate the destination speed and the transformation speed from the previous two results.

6. If necessary, isolate individual transformations to identify the performance of a specific transformation for further troubleshooting.

When you get all of the necessary measures, you can focus on the part that will bring the most benefit in terms of performance.

Using the SSISDB Catalog to Benchmark Package Performance

Another possibility for troubleshooting performance is to benchmark your packages by using the SSISDB catalog views and predefined reports when your packages are deployed to the Integration Services server. To enable detailed tracking of performance metrics, you have to first set the appropriate logging level of the SSISDB catalog to gather the appropriate level of detail during package execution.

You do so by using SQL Server Management Studio (SSMS) to log on to the SQL Server instance where you have the SSISDB catalog, right-clicking SSISDB in the Integration Services Catalogs folder, and clicking Properties. In the Operations Log area, find Server-Wide Default Logging Level and change the property value to **Performance**. Now when you run your packages, you will have more detailed information about duration for each subcomponent in your package.

To open the Execution Performance report, follow these steps:

1. Using SSMS, right-click the package under the selected project in Integration Services Catalogs and click Reports | Standard Reports | All Executions.

2. An All Executions report opens, listing all executions of the package. To display the performance information, click Execution Performance for the specific execution ID.

3. In the Execution Performance report, you can observe information about the most recent executions of your package and the three-month average duration and standard deviation of duration information. For detailed performance information about each data flow component, look under Data Flow Components Information; each subcomponent has an Active Time (Sec) column that displays the execution time, as shown in Figure 13-8.

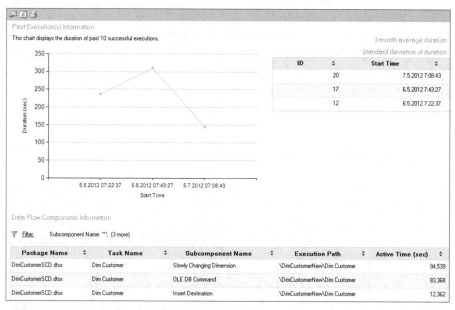

FIGURE 13-8 A predefined report in the SSISDB catalog.

You can also obtain the same performance information by writing a query against the catalog.execution_component_phases SSISDB catalog view. An example is provided in the practice for this lesson.

Monitoring SSIS Performance with Performance Counters

To better analyze hardware consumption by SSIS, you can use the Windows operating system tool called Performance Monitor, which is available to local administrators in a computer's Administrative Tools. When SSIS is installed on a computer, a set of counters is added that allows the tracking of the data flow's performance.

These counters include buffer-related counters, which are most interesting because the whole data flow operates by using buffers. The Buffer Memory and Buffers In Use counters provide totals for the server, both memory use and total buffer count. The Buffer Memory counter is very useful because it shows the total memory being used by SSIS and can be compared with the total amount of available system memory, so that you can tell if SSIS processing is limited by the available physical memory. The Buffers Spooled counter shows whether your data flow has started swapping to disk storage. When this counter is greater than zero, you should first try to optimize your package; if that does not help, increase the server memory.

The counters can be analyzed in the Performance Monitor in real time or captured at a recurring interval for later evaluation.

 Quick Check

- Which performance counters display information that the data flow has started swapping to disk storage?

Quick Check Answer

- The Buffers Spooled counter

PRACTICE **Observing Package Execution**

In this practice, you will view a package execution tree, deploy the project to the SSIS server, run the package, and monitor the detailed execution information.

If you encounter a problem completing an exercise, you can install the completed projects from the Solution folder that is provided with the companion content for this chapter and lesson.

EXERCISE 1 Display the Execution Tree

In this exercise, you open a package you created in Chapter 7 and display the execution tree.

1. If necessary, start SQL Server Data Tools (SSDT), open the TK 463 Chapter 13 project, and open the DimCustomerNew.dtsx package.

2. Open the Dim Customer data flow and observe all the transformations and adapters. How many execution trees should this data flow have?

3. To see if you answered correctly, define the log provider by selecting SSIS from the main menu and clicking Logging.

4. In the Configure SSIS Logs dialog box, select the check box next to the Dim Customer data flow to explicitly enable it.

5. With the Dim Customer data flow selected on the left side, select the Details tab on the right side. Enable the PipelineExecutionTrees event by selecting the check box next to it. Click OK to save and close the logging dialog box.

6. Show the Log Events window by selecting SSIS from the main menu and clicking Log Events.

7. Execute the package and observe the Log Events window.

8. In the Log Events window, double-click the created entry (User:PipelineExecutionTrees) to display a Log Entry window.

9. Read the message in the Log Entry window and notice that the largest path number (Begin Path) statement has the number 3. Because the path numbering starts with zero, this means that this package has four execution trees.

EXERCISE 2   Monitor Execution of the Package

In this exercise, you first deploy the project to the SSIS server, then execute the package and observe the performance results.

1. If you completed Exercise 2 in Lesson 1 of this chapter, skip steps 1 through 6 and go directly to step 7.

2. If necessary, start SQL Server Data Tools (SSDT), open the TK 463 Chapter 13 project, and open the DimCustomerNew.dtsx package.

3. In the Solution Explorer window, right-click TK 463 Project 13 and click Deploy.

4. In the Integration Services Deployment Wizard, click Next. In the Server Name text box, enter the name of your SQL Server instance with SSISDB.

5. Under the Path text box, click Browse. Select SSISDB and click New Folder. Create a new folder called **TK463**. Select this folder and click OK. Click Next and, on the next page, click Deploy.

6. When everything is done, click Close.

7. Open SQL Server Management Studio (SSMS) and connect to the SQL Server instance where you have deployed your SSIS project.

8. In the Integration Services Catalogs folder, expand SSISDB, TK463, and Projects. You should now see your deployed project. By expanding it you can see the Dim-CustomerNew.dtsx package in the Packages folder.

9. Set the logging level for additional information regarding performance by right-clicking SSISDB and selecting Properties.

10. In the Catalog Properties window, change the Server-Wide Default Logging Level property to Performance. Click OK to save the changes.

11. Execute the DimCustomerNew.dtsx package in SSMS.

12. Right-click the DimCustomerNew.dtsx package and select Reports | Standard Reports | All Executions. A new tab will open in SSMS showing an All Executions report.

13. Click Execution Performance inside the report.

14. In the Execution Performance report, observe the detailed information about the data flow components.

15. To get the same information by using the SSISDB catalog views, create a new query in SSMS and select the SSISDB database. Write the following T-SQL query to display the detailed steps of executed packages.

```
SELECT
  MIN(start_time) AS start_time,
  execution_id,
  package_name,
  task_name,
  subcomponent_name,
  SUM(DATEDIFF(ms, start_time, end_time)) AS active_time,
  DATEDIFF(ms, MIN(start_time), MAX(end_time)) AS total_time
FROM
  catalog.execution_component_phases
GROUP BY execution_id, package_name, task_name, subcomponent_name, execution_path
ORDER BY execution_id, package_name, task_name, subcomponent_name, execution_path;
```

16. Save the query and close SSMS.

Lesson Summary

- Package design is crucial for good performance.
- Monitor package execution with the new functionality of SSISDB catalog views.

Lesson Review

Answer the following questions to test your knowledge of the information in this lesson. You can find the answers to these questions and explanations of why each answer choice is correct or incorrect in the "Answers" section at the end of this chapter.

1. Which transformation types are asynchronous? (Choose all that apply.)

   A. Lookup

   B. Union All

   C. Sort

   D. Aggregate

2. Which properties can you set to influence SSIS buffer management? (Choose all that apply.)

   A. DefaultMaxBufferRows

   B. MinBufferSize

   C. DefaultMaxBufferSize

   D. Estimated Row Size

3. Which statements are true when you are using the SSISDB catalog to benchmark the performance of SSIS projects? (Choose all that apply.)

   A. If you want to monitor the execution process in detail, you must set the Server-Wide Default Logging Level property value to Basic.

   B. There is a predefined All Executions report that you can use to analyze the performance of each execution of a package or project.

   C. You can obtain performance information by writing a query against the catalog.execution_component_phases SSISDB catalog view.

   D. You can also analyze packages by using predefined SSISDB catalog reports that use the package deployment model.

Case Scenario

In the following case scenario, you apply what you've learned about troubleshooting and performance tuning. You can find the answers to these questions in the "Answers" section at the end of this chapter.

Case Scenario: Tuning an SSIS Package

You have been tasked with optimizing a package created by one of your colleagues. When you open the package, you notice that it is very large and complex—it has multiple data flow transformations, merging data from multiple sources and writing the data to your SQL Server instance.

1. How would you approach the optimization?

2. What would be your preferences when redesigning the package?

Suggested Practice

To help you successfully master the exam objectives presented in this chapter, complete the following task.

Get Familiar with SSISDB Catalog Views

The SSISDB database has a lot of predefined views available for displaying information about the execution of packages. Write queries to get more knowledge about this new functionality. Do not forget to set the logging level to Verbose and also execute a couple of packages that produce errors and use parameters to get data from most of the predefined views.

Answers

This section contains answers to the lesson review questions and solutions to the case scenario in this chapter.

Lesson 1

1. **Correct answers: A, B, and D**

   A. **Correct:** You can set a breakpoint on any control task.

   B. **Correct:** You can set a breakpoint on any container in the control flow.

   C. **Incorrect:** You cannot set the breakpoint on a data flow transformation.

   D. **Correct:** You can set the breakpoint on the script task or even at the code of the script task.

2. **Correct answers: A, B, and D**

   A. **Correct:** Just by looking at the execution of the package, you can see at which steps an error occurs.

   B. **Correct:** Breakpoints are a powerful design-time troubleshooting option.

   C. **Incorrect:** Data taps are only available when you are executing a package deployed to the SSISDB catalog.

   D. **Correct:** Data viewers enable you to monitor data passing through the pipeline at design time.

3. **Correct answers: B and D**

   A. **Incorrect:** There is no Full level logging.

   B. **Correct:** To disable logging, set the value to None.

   C. **Incorrect:** There is no Simple level logging.

   D. **Correct:** The Verbose level is a valid logging level for the SSISDB catalog.

Lesson 2

1. **Correct answers: B, C, and D**

   A. **Incorrect:** Lookup is a synchronous transformation.

   B. **Correct:** Union All is a partial-blocking transformation and is also asynchronous.

   C. **Correct:** The Sort transformation is asynchronous.

   D. **Correct:** The Aggregate transformation is asynchronous.

2. **Correct answers: A and C**

   A. **Correct:** You can change the DefaultMaxBufferRows property.

   B. **Incorrect:** MinBufferSize is defined by SSIS.

   C. **Correct:** The default value of MaxBufferSize can be changed, but it cannot be larger than 100 MB.

   D. **Incorrect:** Estimated Row Size is calculated by SSIS.

3. **Correct answers: B and C**

   A. **Incorrect:** You must set the Server-Wide Default Logging Level property value to Performance.

   B. **Correct:** There is a predefined All Executions report.

   C. **Correct:** You can write a query directly against the SSISDB catalog view to gather performance information.

   D. **Incorrect:** You can only analyze packages that use the new project deployment model.

Case Scenario

1. First you should measure the package's memory consumption to see if all the operations are kept in the memory and no disk swapping occurs. Then you should measure each task execution to evaluate which task takes most of the time. Then start decomposing the task. If it is a data flow task, you should measure the execution time for reading the data (to determine how fast the source adapters are), for applying transformations, and for writing data to the destination. With this information, you can then focus on applying different optimization techniques for transformations or looking at the possible enhancements at the source or the destination.

2. Because the package contains multiple data flows, consider splitting multiple data flows to multiple packages and analyzing each data flow in terms of transformations used. Observe whether some row-by-row operations are done against the database and, if possible, push down some processing logic (such as sorting or joining data) to the underlying database. Check whether the Lookup transformation is fully cached and that the query contains only the needed columns. The last step is to optimize the buffer settings of the data flow.

## PART V

Building Data Quality Solutions

CHAPTER 14 Installing and Maintaining Data Quality Services **529**

CHAPTER 15 Implementing Master Data Services **565**

CHAPTER 16 Managing Master Data **605**

CHAPTER 17 Creating a Data Quality Project to Clean Data **637**

Installing and Maintaining Data Quality Services

Exam objectives in this chapter:

- Build Data Quality Solutions
    - Install and maintain Data Quality Services.
    - Create a data quality project to clean data.

It is hard to find a company that does not have any data quality issues. Even if a line of business (LOB) application uses a proper relational model with all constraints, there is still no guarantee that data would always be accurate. Database models and constraints enforce data integrity. *Data integrity* means that data complies with business rules. *Data quality* is a much stricter term; even if data complies with business rules, it can still be wrong. For example, consider a business rule that says that a column that contains integers representing a discount percentage can take values from a domain of integers between 0 and 100. If the column contains a value of 45 instead of 54, it complies with business rules, but the data is still not accurate.

Data quality deals with questions such as accuracy and similar issues: Is the data complete? Do you trust it? Is data available in a timely fashion? All of these are data quality problems. You can solve data quality problems in a reactive way, by constantly profiling and correcting the data. You can also solve data quality problems in a proactive way. This can be done by defining the most important data—the *master data*—and then implementing a *master data management* (MDM) solution. The MDM solution database is then an authoritative source of master data.

Part V of this book deals with two features in the Microsoft SQL Server 2012 suite: Microsoft SQL Server 2012 *Data Quality Services (DQS)* and Microsoft SQL Server 2012 *Master Data Services (MDS)*. DQS helps you profile and correct data, and MDS is a master data management solution.

This chapter starts with a theoretical introduction to data quality. Then it describes how to install and secure DQS. Chapter 15, "Implementing Master Data Services," is similarly organized. It starts with a theoretical introduction to master data management, and then it deals with MDS installation. In the last part of Chapter 15, you will build your first MDM solution.

Chapter 16, "Managing Master Data," expands on the introduction to MDS from Chapter 15. It explains how to import data to the MDS database and export it to different applications. It also shows the new MDS Microsoft Excel add-in. Chapter 17, "Creating a Data Quality Project to Clean Data," teaches you how to create a DQS knowledge base and then a cleansing project. After reading the four chapters in this part of the book, you will be able to maintain a high quality of data in your databases.

Lessons in this chapter:

- Lesson 1: Data Quality Problems and Roles
- Lesson 2: Installing Data Quality Services
- Lesson 3: Maintaining and Securing Data Quality Services

Before You Begin

To complete this chapter, you must have:

- Experience working with SQL Server 2012 setup.
- SQL Server 2012 Database Engine Services without Data Quality Services and complete management tools installed.
- An understanding of relational and dimensional data.

Lesson 1: Data Quality Problems and Roles

Data quality is indivisibly interleaved with master data management (MDM). The most important goal of an MDM solution is to raise the quality of master data. Data quality issues must be addressed in any MDM project. However, data quality activities, such as data profiling, finding the root cause of poor data, and improvements of quality can be independent of an MDM project as well. It is possible for an enterprise to define data quality policies and processes through existing applications, but a specialized MDM solution can mitigate implementation of those policies a great deal. You will learn more about master data and about SQL Server 2012 Master Data Services in Chapters 15 and 16.

Before you define your data quality activities, you must decide for which aspects you will measure and improve the quality of your data. *Data quality dimensions* capture a specific aspect of general data quality. Measuring data quality, also known as *data profiling*, should be an integral part of the implementation of an MDM solution. You should always get a thorough comprehension of source data before you start merging it. You should also measure improvements of data quality over time to understand and explain the impact of the MDM solution. This lesson starts by describing data quality dimensions, explaining the various aspects of data quality that can be measured and how best to measure them. Then it deals with data quality activities and the people who execute those activities. You will learn about specific data quality and master data management *roles*.

Data Quality Dimensions

Data quality dimensions can refer to data values or to their schema. Evaluating the quality of a relational or dimensional model cannot be done with Data Quality Services. This chapter focuses on pure data quality dimensions and Data Quality Services, although for the sake of completeness, schema quality dimensions are described in this lesson as well.

There is no consensus on which data quality dimensions should be inspected. Different tools and different books list different sets of dimensions. Nevertheless, some dimensions are analyzed more frequently than others. This lesson focuses on those most frequently analyzed.

You can measure some data quality dimensions with tools such as Transact-SQL queries. Measurable dimensions are called *hard dimensions*. In contrast, some dimensions depend on the perception of the users of the data; these are called *soft dimensions*. You cannot measure soft dimensions directly; you can measure them indirectly through interviews with data users or through any other kind of communication with users. Note that this communication can unfortunately include unpleasant events, such as customer complaints—the events you want to prevent. This lesson describes hard dimensions in detail and takes only a quick overview of soft and schema dimensions.

Completeness

Completeness is one of the easiest dimensions to measure. You can start measuring it on a population level. In a closed-world assumption, you can state that no other values except the values actually present in a relational table represent facts in the real world. If the relation does not have unknown values (NULLs), the relation is complete from the population perspective. In an open-world assumption, you cannot state the population completeness, even if your relation does not contain unknown values. In order to evaluate the completeness of a relation in the open-world assumption, you need to get a reference relation that contains the entire population. When you have a reference relation, you can define the completeness as the proportion of the number of tuples presented in the relation and the number of tuples in the reference relation. Because of privacy and law constraints, it is commonly not possible to acquire the reference relation. However, usually you can get at least the number of tuples in a reference relation. For example, you can easily get the number of citizens of a country. From a technical point of view, it is very easy to measure the completeness of a relation when you have the number of tuples in a reference relation.

In a closed-world assumption in a relational database, the presence of NULLs is what defines the completeness. You could measure *attribute completeness* (the number of NULLs in a specific attribute), *tuple completeness* (the number of unknown values of the attributes in a tuple), and *relation completeness* (the number of tuples with unknown attribute values in the relation). Finally, you could also measure *value completeness*, which makes sense for complex, semi-structured columns such as XML data type columns. In an XML instance, a complete element or attribute can be missing. In addition, XML standards also define a special xsi:nil attribute as a placeholder for missing values; this is similar to the relational NULL.

Accuracy

Accuracy is a complicated dimension. First, you have to determine what is inaccurate. Accuracy is stricter than just conforming to business rules; the latter should be enforced with data integrity. For data that should be unique, duplicate values are inaccurate. Finding duplicate values might be quite easily accomplished with simple queries, or it might be very difficult, if you have to find duplicates across different systems. Finding other inaccurate data might involve some manual work. With various algorithms, you can extract data that is only *potentially* inaccurate.

We can offer some advice on how to isolate inaccurate data. For discrete data values, you can use frequency distribution of values. A value with very low frequency is probably incorrect. For strings, you can search for string length distribution. A string with a very atypical length is potentially incorrect. For strings, you can also try to find patterns and then create pattern distribution. Patterns with low frequency probably denote wrong values. For continuous attributes, you can use descriptive statistics. Just by looking at minimal and maximal values, you can easily spot potentially problematic data. No matter how you find inaccurate data, you can flag it and then measure the level of accuracy. You can measure this for columns and tables.

Information

Another measurable dimension is information. Information Theory, an applied mathematics branch, defines entropy as the quantification of information in a system. You can measure entropy on a column and table level. The more dispersed the values you have are and the more the frequency distribution of a discrete column is equally spread among the values, the more information you have in the column. Information is not a direct data quality dimension; however, it can tell you whether your data is suitable for analysis or not.

Consistency

Consistency measures the equivalence of information stored in various databases. You can find a lot of inconsistent data by comparing values with a predefined set of possible values; you can find some inconsistencies by comparing data among systems. You can find some inconsistencies manually. No matter how you find inconsistencies, you can flag them and then measure the level of inconsistency on the column or table level.

EXAM TIP

Analyzing both hard and soft data quality dimension is considered a best practice.

Data Quality Soft Dimensions

You can measure soft dimension indirectly, through interaction with users. Questionnaires, quick polls, user complaints, or any other communication with data users are your tools for measuring the quality of soft data dimensions. The following list includes some typical soft dimensions:

- **Timeliness** This tells you the degree to which data is current and available when needed. There is always some delay between change in the real world and the moment when this change is entered into a system. Although stale data can appear in any system, this dimension is especially important for web applications and sites. A common problem on the web is that owners do not update sites in a timely manner; you can find a lot of obsolete information on the web.

- **Ease of use** This is a very typical dimension that relies on user perception. Ease of use depends on the application or on the user interface. In addition, users of data can also perceive usage as complex because they are undereducated.

- **Intention** Is the data the right data for its intended use? Sometimes you do not have the exact data you need; however, you can substitute the data needed with data that has similar information. For example, you can use phone area codes instead of ZIP codes to locate customers approximately. Although phone numbers were not intended for analyses, they can give you reasonable results. An example of unhelpful unintended usage is the use of a column in a table for storing unrelated information, such as using the product name column to store product taxonomy. This is an unintended usage of the schema, which leads to many problems with data cleansing and integration.

- **Trust** You have to ask users whether they trust the data. This is a very important dimension. If users do not trust data in operational systems, they will create their own little, probably unstructured, databases. Integration of master data from unstructured sources is very challenging. If users do not trust data from analytical applications, they will simply stop using them.

- **Presentation quality** This is another dimension that depends on user perception. When an application presents data, format and appearance should support the appropriate use of the information. In operational systems, this dimension is closely related to the ease of use dimension and depends a lot on the user interface. For example, an application can force users to enter dates manually or guide them through a calendar control. In analytical systems, presentation is probably even more important. Do you show data in graphs or in tables? How much interactivity should you put in your reports? Questions like this and answers to these questions can have a big influence on the success or failure of analytical systems.

Data Quality Schema Dimensions

A common perception is that schema quality cannot be measured automatically. Well, this is true for some dimensions; you cannot measure them without digging into a business problem. Nevertheless, it is possible to find algorithms and create procedures that help measure some part of schema quality. The following lists the most important schema quality dimensions with brief descriptions of how to measure them, when applicable.

- **Schema completeness**   This tells you to the extent to which the schema covers the business problem. You cannot measure this dimension without in-depth analysis of the business problem and its needs.

- **Schema correctness**   The correctness of a model is concerned with the correct representation of real-world objects in the schema and the correct representation of requirements. For example, a first name could be modeled as an entity with a one-to-one relationship to the Customers entity or as an attribute of the Customers entity. Of course, the latter is correct. The first name cannot be uniquely identified and is therefore not an entity. This is the problem with attempts to correctly represent real-world objects. An example of incorrectness that has to do with requirements is the following model of departments and managers. If a requirement says that a manager can manage a single department and that each department has a single manager, then the relationship between managers and departments should be one to one. Modeling this relationship as many to many would be an incorrect schema. You can measure this dimension manually, by investigating business requirements and object definitions and their representation in the schema.

- **Documentation**   This tells you whether the schema is properly documented. Schema diagrams, such as entity-relationship diagrams, should always be part of the documentation. In addition, all business rules that cannot be represented in a diagram should be documented in text format. In short, you should have complete documentation of a conceptual schema. You can check the quality of this dimension manually, with a schema documentation overview.

- **Compliance with theoretical models**   Is the database schema for transactional applications in a properly normalized and specialized relational schema, and does the schema for a data warehouse consist of star schemas? This dimension must be partially measured manually, with an overview of the data model. However, you can find some problematic areas in the schema procedurally. For example, you can check the correlations between non-key attributes; attributes with very high correlation in a table can indicate that the schema is not normalized, or at least that it is not in third normal form. In addition, many NULLs can indicate that there is not enough specialization—that is, subtypes in the schema. This is especially true if some values of an attribute always lead to NULLs in another attribute. You can measure this with database queries.

- **Minimalization**   Abstraction is a very important modeling technique. It means that you should have only objects in a model that are important for the business problems that you are solving. The number of schema entities should be minimal and should not include objects that are not pertinent to the problem the schema is solving. Again, you can measure this dimension with a manual overview and comparison to business requirements.

 Quick Check

- Is trust a hard data quality dimension?

Quick Check Answer

- No, trust is a typical soft data quality dimension.

Data Quality Activities and Roles

Data quality projects are very intensive in terms of resources needed. In order to execute a project successfully, you have to show possible benefits to key stakeholders. First, you need to understand the business needs. You can use interviews, overviews of organizational charts, analyses of existing practices in an enterprise, and other such information sources. You must *prioritize the business issues* and make a clear project plan. For a project to be successful, it is important to start either with a business area that is very painful for the stakeholders or with a business problem that is quite simple to solve. You should always implement data quality projects step by step.

Before you start any data quality or MDM project, you have to understand the sources and destinations of problematic data. Therefore, data quality activities must include overviews. You must make an extensive overview of all of the schemas of the databases that pertain to the problem data. You should interview domain experts and users of data. This is especially important for gaining a comprehension of the quality of the schema dimensions. In addition, after this step, you should also have a clear understanding of the technology that the enterprise is using. If necessary, you might need to plan to include appropriate technology experts in the project. During the overview of the data, you should also focus on the data life cycle so that you can understand retention periods and similar.

The next step is the data quality assessment. You can assess hard dimensions with procedural analysis of the data, also known as data profiling. There are many different tools for data profiling. You should exploit all knowledge you have and all tools available for this task. You should measure soft data quality dimensions in this step as well. You can get a lot of insight on the state of the company by comparing hard and soft dimensions. If your evaluation of the hard dimensions is bad, but you get good evaluations for the soft dimensions, then the company does not realize that they have problems with data. In such a case, additional assessment of the potential damage caused by the bad data can help key stakeholders understand the data quality problems. If both soft and hard dimensions are evaluated low, then the company is ready for a data quality and/or MDM project. If hard dimensions get good evaluations, whereas soft dimensions get bad evaluations, this means that for some reason domain experts and users do not trust the data. Usually this situation is because of a previous system, a previous version of the system, or lack of education. If both hard and soft dimensions get good evaluations, the company does not need a special data quality project; however, the company could still decide to initiate an MDM project in order to minimize expenses with master data maintenance.

After finishing with the data assessment, you can re-assess the business impact of low-quality data. You should meet again with key stakeholders in order to review the priorities and elaborate on the improvements part of the project plan in detail.

Before you can start improving the data quality, you need to find the root causes for the bad data. Finding root causes can substantially narrow down the amount of work required for data quality improvements. For finding root causes, you can use the "five whys" method introduced by Sakichi Toyoda and used first at the Toyota Motor Corporation. With this method, you simply ask "why" five times. For example, suppose the problem is with duplicate records for customers. Applying the "five whys" approach to find the root cause would look like this:

- You can ask why there are duplicate records. An answer might be because operators frequently insert new customer records instead of using existing ones.

- You should ask the second why: why are operators creating new records for existing customers? The answer might be because operators do not search for the existing records of a customer.

- You then ask the third why: why don't they search? The answer might be because the search would take too long.

- The next why is, of course, why does it take so long? The answer might be because it is very awkward to search for existing customers.

- Now you ask the final, fifth why: why is searching so awkward? The answer might be because the operator can search only for exact values, not for approximate strings, and the operator does not have an exact name, address, or phone number of a customer in memory. You have found the root cause of the duplication for this example, the problem is with the application—specifically with the user interface. Now you know where to put effort in order to lower the number of duplicates.

Of course, the "five whys" method is not the only technique for finding root causes. You can also just track a piece of information through its life cycle. By tracking it, you can easily spot the moment when it becomes inaccurate. You can find root causes for some problems procedurally as well. For example, you can find that NULLs are in the system because of a lack of subtypes with queries. No matter how you find root causes, you have to use this information to prepare a detailed improvements plan.

An improvement plan should include two parts: *correcting* existing data and, even more important, *preventing* future errors. If you focus on correcting existing data only, you will have to repeat the correction part of the data quality activities regularly. Of course, you do need to spend some time correcting existing data; however, you should not forget the prevention part. When you have both parts of the improvement plan, you can start implementing it.

Implementation of corrective measures involves automatic and manual cleansing methods. Automatic cleansing methods can include your own procedures and queries. If you have known logic for correcting the data, you should use it. You can solve consistency problems by defining a single way to represent the data in all systems, and then replace inconsistent representations with the newly defined ones. For example, if gender is represented in some system with the numbers 1 and 2 but you have decided that it should be represented with the letters F and M, you can replace numbers with letters in a single update statement. For de-duplication and merging from different sources, you can use string-matching algorithms. For correcting addresses, you can use validating and cleansing tools that already exist in the market and use some registries of valid addresses. However, you should always prepare for the fact that part of the data cleansing must be done manually.

Preventing new inserts of inaccurate data involves different techniques as well. The most important one is to implement an MDM solution. For an MDM solution, you need an MDM application. SQL Server Master Data Services is an example of the tool you could use.

In addition to enabling central storage for master data and its metadata, the MDM application has to support explicit data stewardship, versioning, auditing, and *data governance* workflows. Data governance refers to the activities performed to improve and maintain data quality; *data stewards* are the people responsible for these activities. For a data quality and/or master data management project to be successful, explicit *data stewardship* roles must be defined. In addition to the data quality or MDM solution, you should also focus on source systems. It is very unlikely that your solution will ever cover all possible master entities with all of their attributes. Therefore, part of the data is still going to be maintained in source, operational applications. You have to enforce proper data models, constraints, and good user interfaces wherever possible.

After you have implemented the data quality corrective and preventive solutions, you should measure how they perform. Even better, you should prepare the improvement infrastructure in advance, before starting to implement your solutions. By measuring the improvements, you can easily show the value of the solutions to key stakeholders. In addition, this approach allows you some measure of control over your work, in case your improvements fail and lead to even worse data quality problems. You can measure soft dimensions by conducting ongoing interviews with end users and domain experts. You can store the results of the interviews in a special data quality data warehouse to track the data quality over time. For hard dimensions, you can measure these automatically on a predefined schedule, and again store the results in the data quality data warehouse. Figure 14-1 shows a potential schema for a data quality data warehouse for measuring completeness and accuracy.

Although this was not mentioned as an explicit data quality activity step, it is very important to *communicate actions and results* throughout the project. The more communication you have, the better. Domain experts can always help you with their knowledge. IT professionals and end users put much more effort into helping a project achieve success if they are involved, if they feel that the project is their project. Key stakeholders should always know how the project progresses and must be involved in all decision milestones.

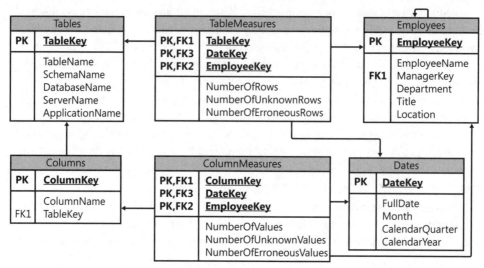

FIGURE 14-1 A potential schema for a data quality data warehouse.

Checking for Data Quality Issues

In this practice, you analyze part of the AdventureWorksDW2012 sample database and a production system you are familiar with for potential data quality issues.

EXERCISE 1 Check for Data Quality Issues in AdventureWorksDW2012

In this theoretical exercise, you check for potential data quality issues in the AdventureWorks-DW2012 sample database.

1. Start SSMS and connect to your SQL Server instance. Expand the Databases folder and then the AdventureWorksDW2012 database.

2. Expand the Tables folder. Expand the Columns folder for the following tables:
   - *DimCustomer*
   - *FactInternetSales*
   - *DimDate*
   - *DimSalesReason*
   - *DimProduct*
   - *DimProductCategory*
   - *DimEmployee*
   - *FactResellerSales*

3. Identify which of the columns you have expanded could have problems with completeness.

4. After you have finished with the review of the AdventureWorksDW2012 tables, close SSMS.

EXERCISE 2 Review Potential Data Quality Issues in a Production System

Now that you have analyzed the AdventureWorksDW2012 database, you use a production system with which you are familiar for a similar analysis.

- Think of a production system from your company or from a company you know. Try to answer the following questions:
  - Can you think of any data quality issues?
  - Are there any duplicate customers?
  - On which entities should you focus for data profiling?
  - Is an explicit data stewardship role present in the company?
  - Does the company have a website? Is the data on the site stale?
  - Do employees trust the data?
  - What should be changed in order to improve the data quality?

Lesson Summary

- Data quality issues can be categorized into data quality dimensions.
- Data governance is the activity of taking care of data quality, and data stewards are people responsible for the quality of particular data.

Lesson Review

Answer the following questions to test your knowledge of the information in this lesson. You can find the answers to these questions and explanations of why each answer choice is correct or incorrect in the "Answers" section at the end of this chapter.

1. Which of the following are hard data quality dimensions? (Choose all that apply.)

   A. Trust

   B. Documentation

   C. Accuracy

   D. Presentation quality

   E. Consistency

2. Which data model you should use for LOB applications?

   A. A dimensional model

   B. An XML schema

   C. A relational model

   D. No specific model; a model will arise over time, with eventual consistency

3. Which of the following is a data quality role?

   A. Data modeling

   B. Data stewardship

   C. Data profiling

   D. Data improving

Lesson 2: Installing Data Quality Services

SQL Server 2012 Data Quality Services (DQS) is a knowledge-driven data quality solution. This means that it requires you to maintain one or more *knowledge bases* (KBs). In a KB, you maintain all knowledge related to a specific portion of data—for example, customer data. In DQS projects, you perform cleansing, profiling, and matching activities. You can also use an intermediate staging database to which to copy your source data and export DQS project results. DQS includes server and client components. In order to use DQS, you must start by installing the DQS components.

> **After this lesson, you will be able to:**
> - Understand DQS architecture.
> - Install DQS components.
>
> **Estimated lesson time: 45 minutes**

DQS Architecture

With DQS, data quality is now available to a broader audience than was the case with previous SQL Server tools. DQS was designed for ease of use. Through a simple and intuitive interface, DQS empowers business users and DBAs to engage more directly in data quality activities. With this functionality, you can realize data quality improvements in a very short time. As mentioned earlier, DQS includes server and client components. Figure 14-2 shows a quick overview of DQS architecture.

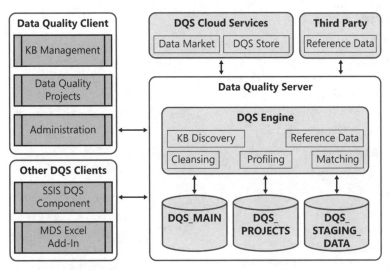

FIGURE 14-2 DQS architecture.

The Data Quality Server component includes three databases:

- DQS_MAIN, which includes DQS stored procedures. The DQS stored procedures make up the actual DQS engine. In addition, DQS_MAIN includes published knowledge bases. A published KB is a KB that has been prepared to be used in cleansing projects.

- DQS_PROJECTS, which includes data for knowledge base management and data needed during cleansing and matching projects.

- DQS_STAGING_DATA, which provides an intermediate storage area where you can copy source data for cleansing and where you can export cleansing results.

You can prepare your own knowledge bases locally, including reference data. However, you can also use reference data from the cloud. You can use Windows Azure MarketPlace DataMarket to connect to reference data providers. Of course, you can also use a direct connection to a third-party reference data provider through a predefined interface.

EXAM TIP

Remember what is stored in each of the three Data Quality Server databases.

With the Data Quality Client application, you can manage knowledge bases; execute cleansing, profiling, and matching projects; and administer Data Quality Services. SQL Server 2012 includes two new tools to assist with these tasks. You can use the SSIS DQS Cleansing transformation to perform cleansing inside a data flow of your SSIS package. This allows you to perform batch cleansing without the need for interactivity required by Data Quality Client. With the free Master Data Services (MDS) Microsoft Excel add-in, you can perform matching of master data in an Excel worksheet. The DQS components must be installed together with MDS in order to enable DQS/MDS integration. Additional clients, including third-party applications, will very likely be forthcoming in the future.

DQS Installation

Before installing DQS, you should determine whether your system meets the prerequisites. For Data Quality Server, you need to have SQL Server 2012 Database Engine Services installed. In addition, in order to administer DQS databases, you need to have the SQL Server Management Tools installed as well. Figure 14-3 shows the Feature Selection page of SQL Server 2012 Setup. The features selected in this figure are the minimum that must be selected to meet the Data Quality Server prerequisites.

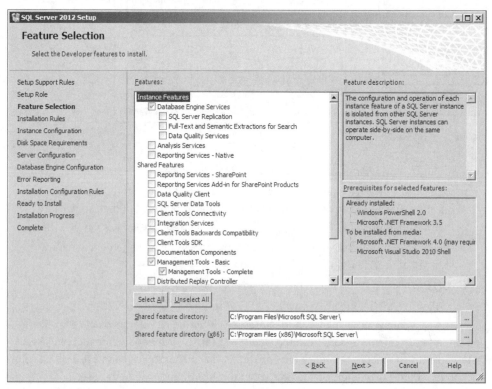

FIGURE 14-3 SQL Server features needed for Data Quality Server.

For Data Quality Client, you need the Microsoft .NET Framework 4. If you don't have it installed on your computer, it will automatically be installed during the Data Quality Client installation. In addition, you need at least Windows Internet Explorer 6 SP1.

You install the DQS components by using SQL Server 2012 Setup. You will need to select the following features:

- Data Quality Services under Database Engine Services to install Data Quality Server.
- Data Quality Client to install Data Quality Client.

SQL Server Setup installs an additional installer file, DQSInstaller.exe, when you select the Data Quality Services check box. This file is copied into the SQL Server instance folder on your computer. In addition, you will need to add the current user (yourself) to the sysadmin fixed server role during installation, so that you can run the DQSInstaller later to finish the installation.

✔ **Quick Check**

1. What are the prerequisites for installing Data Quality Server?

2. What are the prerequisites for installing Data Quality Client?

Quick Check Answers

1. SQL Server 2012 Database Engine Services are needed for Data Quality Server. In addition, it is highly recommended that you install Management Tools as well.

2. For Data Quality Client, you need to have the .NET Framework 4 and at least Internet Explorer 6 SP1 installed on your computer. The .NET Framework 4 is installed automatically during Data Quality Client setup if it was not already installed on the machine.

After SQL Server Setup finishes installation, you will need to perform some post-installation tasks. First, you must run the DQSInstaller application. This application does the following:

- It creates the DQS_MAIN, DQS_PROJECTS, and DQS_STAGING_DATA databases.

- It creates two logins needed by Data Quality Server: ##MS_dqs_db_owner_login## and ##MS_dqs_service_login##.

- It creates three roles in the DQS_MAIN database: dqs_administrator, dqs_kb_editor, and dqs_kb_operator.

- In the master database, it creates the DQInitDQS_MAIN stored procedure.

- It logs the installation in the DQS_install.log file. This file is typically created in the C:\Program Files\Microsoft SQL Server\MSSQL11.<*instance_name*>\MSSQL\Log folder.

- For MDS integration, if an MDS database is installed in the same SQL Server instance as Data Quality Server, the DQSInstaller application creates a user mapped to the MDS login. It also adds this user to the dqs_administrator role in the DQS_MAIN database.

Users must be members of any of the three DQS roles in the DQS_MAIN database in order to be able to connect to Data Quality Server. Members of the sysadmin fixed server roles can connect to Data Quality Server by default. You will learn more about security in Lesson 3, "Maintaining and Securing Data Quality Services," later in this chapter.

The SSIS DQS Cleansing transformation is installed during SSIS installation. The MDS Excel add-in is a separate download. You will install it in Chapter 15.

If you install Data Quality Client on a different computer from the one Data Quality Server is installed on, you must enable the TCP/IP protocol for the SQL Server instance where Data Quality Server is installed. Use the SQL Server Configuration Manager to perform this task.

PRACTICE Installing Data Quality Services

In the following exercises, you will install Data Quality Server and Data Quality Client. This practice assumes that your computer meets the prerequisites for this installation.

EXERCISE 1 Run SQL Server Setup

In the first exercise, you use SQL Server Setup to install DQS components.

1. Start SQL Server 2012 Setup.

2. In the SQL Server Installation Center, select the Installation tab (second from the top on the left side).

3. Select the New SQL Server Stand-Alone Installation Or Add Features To Existing Installation link.

4. Wait until the Setup Support Rules have been checked. When the operation is finished, click OK.

5. In the Product Updates window, click Next.

6. Wait while the setup files are installed. The Setup Support Rules page of SQL Server 2012 Setup should appear. Correct any errors and check any warnings. If there are no errors, click Next.

7. On the Installation Type page, select the Add Features To An Existing Instance Of SQL Server 2012 option. Select the instance on which you want to host the DQS databases from the drop-down list of installed instances on your computer. Click Next.

8. On the Feature Selection page, select the check boxes for the Data Quality Services and Data Quality Client options, as shown in Figure 14-4. Then click Next.

9. Wait while the installation rules are checked.

10. On the Disk Space Requirements page, click Next.

11. On the Error Reporting page, clear the only check box and click Next.

12. On the Installation Configuration Rules page, click Next.

13. On the Ready To Install page, click Install.

14. Wait until installation is finished.

15. On the Complete page, click Close.

16. Close the SQL Server Installation window.

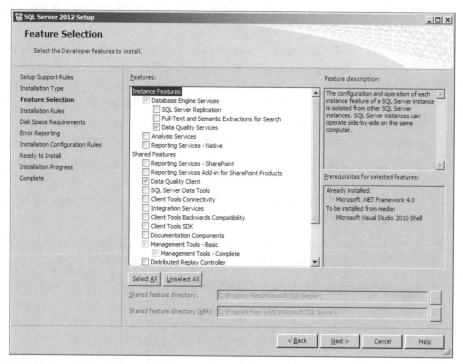

FIGURE 14-4 DQS features selection.

EXERCISE 2   Perform DQS Post-Installation Tasks

After you complete the part of the installation that involves SQL Server 2012 Setup, you have to finish the post-installation tasks as well. In this exercise, you use the installer application, DQSInstaller.exe, to complete the Data Quality Server installation.

1. Start DQSInstaller. You can start it from the Start menu. On the taskbar, click Start, point to All Programs, and click Microsoft SQL Server 2012. In the Microsoft SQL Server 2012 folder, click Data Quality Services, and then click Data Quality Server Installer.

   You can also start DQSInstaller from Windows Explorer. If you used default installation folders for the default instance, then the application is located in the C:\Program Files \Microsoft SQL Server\MSSQL11.MSSQLSERVER\MSSQL\Binn folder.

   In addition, you can run DQSInstaller from the command prompt as well. Refer to Books Online for SQL Server 2012 for details about command-line parameters.

2. You are prompted for a password for the database master key. This key is used to encrypt reference data service provider keys if you set up reference data providers. The keys are stored in the DQS_MAIN database. The password must be at least eight characters long and must contain an English uppercase letter (A, B, C, ... Z), an English lowercase letter (a, b, c, ... z), and a numeral (0, 1, 2, ... 9). Provide a password, confirm it, and press Enter.

3. Wait until DQSInstaller finishes. Press any key in the command prompt window to finish. If there are any errors, check the error log. DQSInstaller creates an installation log file named DQS_install.log, which is located in the C:\Program Files\Microsoft SQL Server\MSSQL11.MSSQLSERVER\MSSQL\Log folder for the default instance.

   You should grant DQS roles to users to authorize them to perform DQS activities. However, you will do this during the practice in Lesson 3 of this chapter.

4. Check to see whether you can connect from Data Quality Client to your Data Quality Server. On the taskbar, click Start, point to All Programs, and click Microsoft SQL Server 2012. In the Microsoft SQL Server 2012 folder, click Data Quality Services, and then click Data Quality Client.

5. In the Connect To Server window that appears, select the server on which you installed your Data Quality Server, as shown in Figure 14-5. Click Connect.

FIGURE 14-5 From Data Quality Client, connect to your Data Quality Server.

6. After Data Quality Client connects to the server, the main screen of Data Quality Client should appear, as shown in Figure 14-6.

7. With SSMS Object Explorer, check also to see whether the three DQS databases were successfully installed. If they were, they should appear in Object Explorer as shown in Figure 14-7.

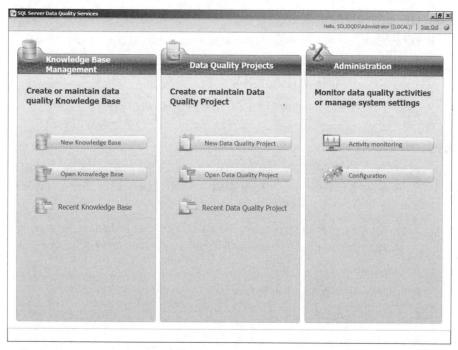

FIGURE 14-6 The Data Quality Client main screen.

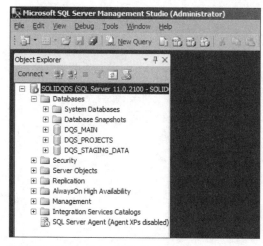

FIGURE 14-7 The three DQS databases.

NOTE **CONTINUING WITH PRACTICES**

Do not exit Data Quality Client if you intend to continue immediately with the next practice

Lesson Summary

- Data Quality Services consists of Data Quality Server and Data Quality Client.
- There are some prerequisites for installing both components.
- You start installation with SQL Server Setup.
- You finish the installation with the DQSInstaller.exe application.

Lesson Review

Answer the following questions to test your knowledge of the information in this lesson. You can find the answers to these questions and explanations of why each answer choice is correct or incorrect in the "Answers" section at the end of this chapter.

1. After SQL Server Setup finishes with Data Quality Server and Client installation, which application do you need to run in order to finish the Data Quality Server installation?

    A. SQLCMD

    B. SQL Server Management Studio

    C. Windows Update

    D. DQSInstaller

2. Which DQS client tools are available with SQL Server 2012? (Choose all that apply.)

    A. MDS Excel Add-in

    B. Data Quality Client

    C. SSIS DQS Cleansing Transformation

    D. SQL Server Data Tools

    E. DQS Microsoft Visio Add-in

3. Which of the following is not a Data Quality Server database?

    A. DQS_KNOWLEDGE_BASE

    B. DQS_STAGING_DATA

    C. DQS_MAIN

    D. DQS_PROJECTS

Lesson 3: Maintaining and Securing Data Quality Services

Administering Data Quality Services includes maintaining security, backing up DQS databases, setting configuration settings, monitoring DQS activities and logging, and configuring threshold values for cleansing and matching.

> **After this lesson, you will be able to:**
>
> - Monitor DQS activities.
> - Configure threshold values and enable profile notifications.
> - Back up and restore DQS databases.
> - Manage DQS log files.
> - Set up DQS security.
>
> **Estimated lesson time: 35 minutes**

Performing Administrative Activities with Data Quality Client

You can perform most of the administrative activities for Data Quality Services with the Data Quality Client application. With Data Quality Client, you can:

- Monitor DQS activities.
- Configure reference data service settings.
- Configure threshold values for the cleansing and matching.
- Enable or disable notifications.
- Configure logging.

You will learn about monitoring DQS activities in the practice at the end of this lesson. Therefore, this section begins with a discussion of configuring reference data services. Note that this section explains only how to start configuring reference data services, because these are not available in all markets yet. For the practice for this lesson, you will use built-in reference data. The procedure for setting up reference data services is:

1. Open the Data Quality Client application and connect to your Data Quality Server.

2. Click the Configuration button in the Administration area of the screen (on the right). The Reference Data tab is selected by default.

3. If you already have a DataMarket account ID, enter it in the first text box, as shown in Figure 14-8. If you don't have one, you can create one by clicking the Create A Data-Market Account ID link.

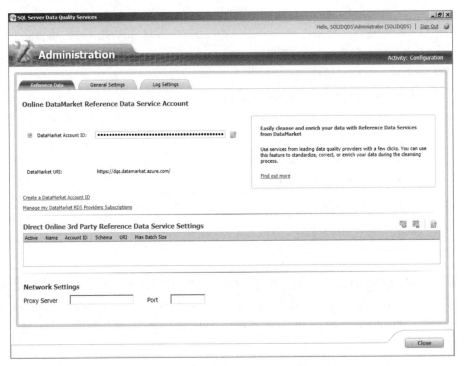

FIGURE 14-8 Setting up reference data.

4. Use the Manage My DataMarket RDS Providers Subscriptions link to set up your Data-Market subscriptions.

Note that DataMarket reference data is not available for all markets yet. The number of markets for which reference data is available is growing continuously, so you might want to check frequently to see whether there is something available for your country or region. Figure 14-9 shows an example of a screen showing that reference data is not available in a particular market yet.

See Books Online for SQL Server 2012 for more information about using reference data.

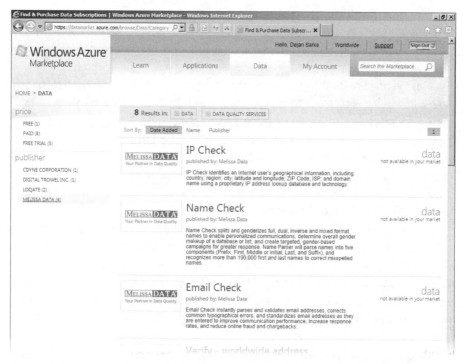

FIGURE 14-9 A screen showing that reference data is not available for a specified market.

You can use the General Settings tab on the Administration screen of Data Quality Client to configure the threshold values for cleansing and matching. You can configure the following values:

- **Min Score For Suggestions**   This is the confidence level that DQS uses for suggesting replacements for a value during cleansing. The default value is 0.7. The value must be between 0 and 1. A higher value means fewer suggestions, and thus fewer replacements. You should run tests to determine the most appropriate value by cleansing a sample of your data. This value should be less than or equal to the value for Min Score For Auto Corrections.

- **Min Score For Auto Corrections**   This is the confidence level for automatically correcting a value during cleansing. As with Min Score For Suggestions, you should run tests to determine the most appropriate value for your data.

- **Min Record Score**   This is the threshold value for the matching policy. It denotes the minimum score for a record to be considered as a match for another record. The default value is 80 percent.

- **Enable Notifications** Data profiling is integrated into DQS. Data profiling gives you basic information about the quality and completeness of your data. A DQS notification can point you quickly to a potential problem. A notification is indicated by a tooltip with an exclamation point on the Profiling tab of a data quality project, as you will see in the practice for this lesson. Because there is no performance impact if you use notifications, it is recommended that you leave this check box selected.

DQS log files help you diagnose and troubleshoot issues with Data Quality Server, Data Quality Client, and the DQS Cleansing component in Integration Services. The Data Quality Server log file is called DQServerLog.DQS_MAIN.log. If you use the default instance installation, this log file is located in the C:\Program Files\Microsoft SQL Server \MSSQL11.MSSQLSERVER\MSSQL\Log folder. This is a rolling file; you can delete old log files manually from Windows Explorer.

The Data Quality Client log file, DQLog.Client.xml, is located in the %APPDATA%\SSDQS \Log folder. You can find the location to which your %APPDATA% operating system variable is pointing by using the ECHO %APPDATA% command prompt command. For example, if you are logged on as an administrator, this file would be in the C:\Users\Administrator\AppData \Roaming\SSDQS\Log folder. This is a rolling file as well. The DQS Cleansing component in Integration Services logs activities to the DQSSSISLog.log file, which is also located in the %APPDATA%\SSDQS\Log folder.

You can use the Log Settings tab in the Data Quality Client's configuration settings screen to configure severity levels for the logging of different DQS activities. You can configure the following log settings:

- Domain Management
- KnowledgeDiscovery
- Cleansing Project (except Reference Data Services)
- Matching Policy And Matching Project
- Reference Data Services (RDS)

You can set each of these activities to the following logging levels:

- **Fatal** This setting will log critical runtime errors.
- **Error** This setting will log other runtime errors.
- **Warn** This setting will log warnings about events that might result in an error.
- **Info** This setting will log information about general events.
- **Debug** This setting will log detailed (verbose) information about events.

Figure 14-10 shows how the various logging settings can be modified.

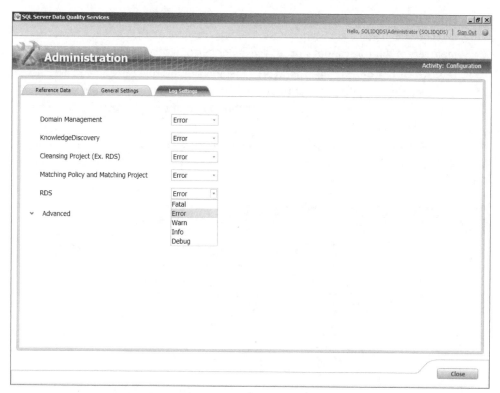

FIGURE 14-10 Setting the DQS logging level.

The Advanced section on the Log Settings tab enables you to configure log severity settings at a modular level. Modules are DQS system assemblies that implement various functionalities within a feature in DQS. You will generally not have a need to use these advanced log settings. You will use them only to trace problems with a specific module.

Performing Administrative Activities with Other Tools

Data Quality Services must be partially administered in SQL Server Management Studio (SSMS) or with Transact-SQL commands. With these tools, you can manage DQS security and backup and restore DQS databases.

DQS security uses the SQL Server infrastructure. There are three predefined DQS roles in the DQS_MAIN database. You administer DQS security by adding users to these three roles. The roles are:

- **DQS Administrator (dqs_admininstrator)**   Members of this role can do everything in the scope of Data Quality Services. They can create or edit a knowledge base, create and execute a DQS project, terminate a running project or other activity, stop a process, and change the Reference Data Services and other settings.

- **DQS KB Editor (dqs_kb_editor)** Members of this role can edit and execute a project and create and edit a knowledge base. They can monitor all DQS activity; however, members of this role cannot stop an activity or perform other administrative tasks.

- **DQS KB Operator (dqs_kb_operator)** Members of this role can edit and execute a project. However, they cannot create or change a knowledge base. They can monitor all DQS activity; however, members of this role cannot stop an activity or perform other administrative tasks.

Permissions for the roles are cumulative. The dqs_kb_editor and dqs_administrator roles are members of the dqs_kb_operator role, as you can see in Figure 14-11. The dqs_administrator role is also a member of the dqs_kb_editor role.

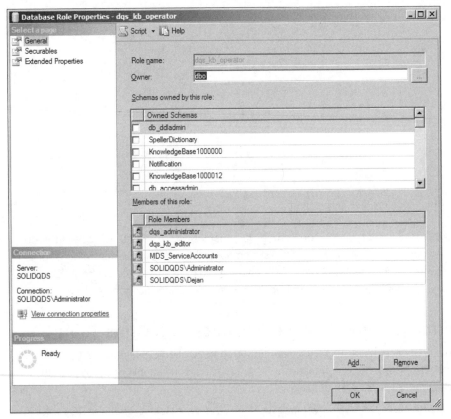

FIGURE 14-11 Cumulative permissions of the DQS roles.

You manage DQS security by adding users to appropriate DQS roles.

You back up and restore DQS databases with the regular SQL Server backup and restore functionalities. However, you must synchronize the backups of the two primary DQS databases, DQS_MAIN and DQS_PROJECTS. The third DQS database, the DQS_STAGING_DATA database, is less important, because you use it for staging data only. You might even decide to not use it for staging data and operate in the context of other user databases.

Data cleansing with DQS is usually an occasional, not an ongoing, activity. Therefore, you might decide to back up full databases only, and never back up the transactional logs. If you decide on full database backups only, you should change the recovery model of all three DQS databases to Simple.

 Quick Check

- How can you delete old DQS log files?

Quick Check Answer

- You have to use Windows Explorer to delete old log files. There is no user interface for this task in Data Quality Client or SQL Server Management Studio.

PRACTICE **Monitoring DQS Activity**

In the following exercises, you learn how to monitor DQS activity with Data Quality Client. In order to monitor the activity, you create your first DQS project.

EXERCISE 1 Create Your First DQS Project

You start with creating your first DQS project. You use the knowledge base that comes with the Data Quality Services installation out of the box.

1. If you closed Data Quality Client, start it and connect to your SQL Server instance that includes the DQS databases.

2. On the opening screen of the client, in the Data Quality Projects section, click the New Data Quality Project button. Name the project **AWLastNames**.

3. Check that the DQS Data knowledge base is selected. In the Knowledge Base Details—DQS Data area, select the US – Last Name domain.

4. Check at the bottom of the page to make sure that the Cleansing activity is selected. Your New Data Quality Project page should look like the one in Figure 14-12.

5. Click Next.

6. On the Map page, select SQL Server as the data source, AdventureWorksDW2012 as the database, and *DimCustomer* as the table.

7. In the Mappings table, map the *LastName* source column from the *DimCustomer* table to the US – Last Name domain. You should have the same settings as shown in Figure 14-13.

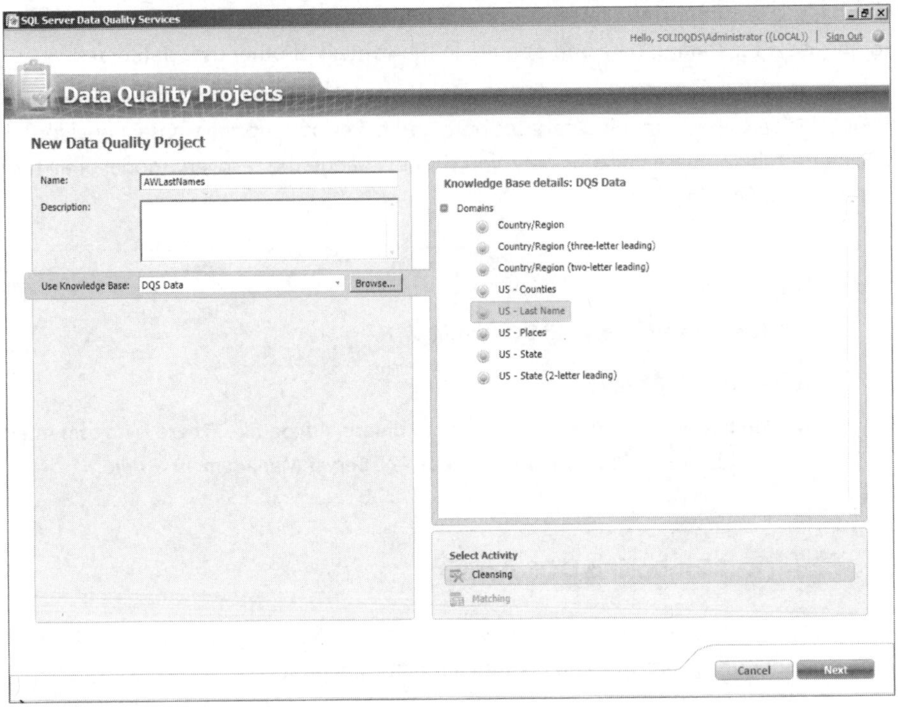

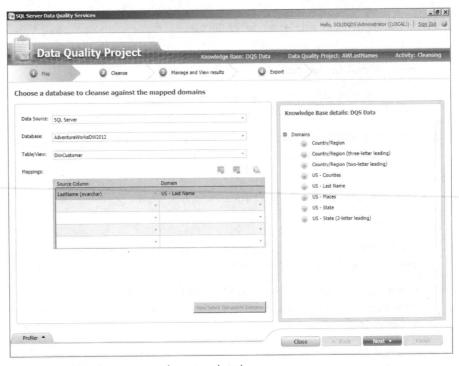

FIGURE 14-12 New data quality project settings.

FIGURE 14-13 Mapping a source column to a domain.

8. Click Next. On the Cleanse page, click the Start button.

9. When the cleansing is finished, review the profiling results in the Profiler area. Also check the notifications, which will appear as tooltips. Your page should look like the one shown in Figure 14-14.

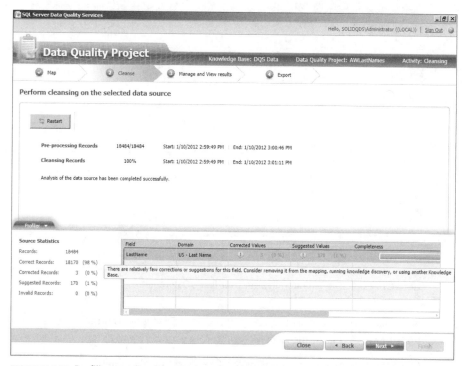

FIGURE 14-14 Profiling results after the cleansing is finished.

10. Click Next.

11. On the Manage And View Results page, check the Suggested, New, and Corrected values. After you are done checking, click Next.

12. On the Export page, click Finish (you will not export the results for this project).

EXERCISE 2   Monitor DQS Activity

1. If you closed Data Quality Client, start it and connect to the SQL Server instance where you created your first DQS project in the previous exercise.

2. In the main Data Quality Client window, in the Administration pane, click the Activity Monitoring button.

3. In the upper window, click the AWLastNames project. Details of the project should appear in the lower window. Check the Activity Steps information and the Profiler information. Figure 14-15 shows the Activity Monitoring window.

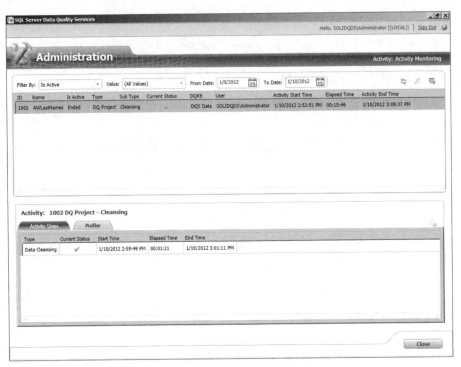

FIGURE 14-15 Activity monitoring after your first DQS project.

4. Note that you can export the selected activity to Excel by using the button in the upper-right corner of the Activity Monitoring window.

5. Close the Activity Monitoring window. Close Data Quality Client.

Lesson Summary

- DQS administration involves setting up reference data sources, configuring general and log settings, monitoring activity, managing security, and backing up and restoring DQS databases.
- You perform all of these tasks except for security management and backup and restoration with Data Quality Client.
- You manage security and backup and restoration of DQS databases with SQL Server Management Studio or with Transact-SQL commands.

Lesson Review

Answer the following questions to test your knowledge of the information in this lesson. You can find the answers to these questions and explanations of why each answer choice is correct or incorrect in the "Answers" section at the end of this chapter.

1. Which of the following activities cannot be performed with Data Quality Client?

    A. Setting up reference data sources

    B. Managing security

    C. Monitoring DQS activity

    D. Changing log settings

2. Which is not a predefined DQS role?

    A. dqs_user

    B. dqs_kb_editor

    C. dqs_administrator

    D. dqs_kb_operator

3. Members of which predefined DQS role can create and edit a knowledge base? (Choose all that apply.)

    A. dqs_user

    B. dqs_kb_editor

    C. dqs_administrator

    D. dqs_kb_operator

Case Scenario

In the following case scenario, you apply what you've learned about installing and maintaining Data Quality Services. You can find the answers to these questions in the "Answers" section at the end of this chapter.

Case Scenario: Data Warehouse Not Used

You are in a conversation with a DBA of a company you know. The DBA has told you that the company has already implemented a data warehouse and an analytical system based on the data from the data warehouse. However, the DBA complains that end users do not use this analytical system. Although it is a much more complex process, the end users prefer to create their own analyses in Excel from LOB database data. Answer the following questions:

1. What do you think went wrong with the data warehouse?

2. How could you help this company?

Suggested Practices

To help you successfully master the exam objectives presented in this chapter, complete the following tasks.

Analyze the AdventureWorksDW2012 Database

To understand the problems that might arise with data quality, study the AdventureWorks-DW2012 sample database.

- **Practice 1** In the *DimProduct* dimension, check for all nullable columns.
- **Practice 2** Are there any relationships between NULLs in these columns? Does an unknown value in one column lead to NULL in another column? This would mean that there might be some functional dependency between columns.
- **Practice 3** Analyze relationships between NULLs and known values in the *DimProduct* table. Does a known, specific value in one column lead to NULL in another column? This would mean that there might be a need for introducing subtypes.

Review Data Profiling Tools

Use your company or a company that you know as an example.

- **Practice 1** Which tools currently present in the company could be used for data profiling?
- **Practice 2** Is the company using these tools?

Answers

This section contains answers to the lesson review questions and solutions to the case scenario in this chapter.

Lesson 1

1. **Correct answers: C and E**

    A. **Incorrect:** Trust is a soft data quality dimension.

    B. **Incorrect:** Documentation is a schema quality dimension.

    C. **Correct:** Accuracy is a hard data quality dimension.

    D. **Incorrect:** Presentation quality is a soft data quality dimension.

    E. **Correct:** Consistency is a hard data quality dimension.

2. **Correct answer: C**

    A. **Incorrect:** You should use a dimensional model for your data warehouse.

    B. **Incorrect:** You should use an XML schema for XML documents only. If XML documents are stored in an LOB database directly, then you should validate them against an XML schema. However, XML data can be just part of an LOB database; in general, an LOB database should use a relational schema.

    C. **Correct:** The relational model is the most appropriate for LOB databases. It enforces data integrity more than any other data model.

    D. **Incorrect:** Eventual consistency is typically not allowed for LOB applications. Consistency has to be enforced at any time.

3. **Correct answer: B**

    A. **Incorrect:** Data modeling is an activity in the database development phase, not a data quality role.

    B. **Correct:** Data stewardship is a role that is responsible for data quality.

    C. **Incorrect:** Data profiling is a data quality activity, not a role.

    D. **Incorrect:** Data improvement is the goal of data quality activities, it is not a role.

Lesson 2

1. **Correct answer: D**

    A. **Incorrect:** You do not finish DQS setup with SQLCMD.

    B. **Incorrect:** You do not finish DQS setup with SSMS.

    C. **Incorrect:** You do not use Windows Update during DQS installation.

    D. **Correct:** In order to finish DQS Server installation, you need to run DQSInstaller.

2. **Correct answers: A, B, and C**

    A. **Correct:** Although it is a separate download, the MDS Excel add-in is one of the client tools available with SQL Server 2012.

    B. **Correct:** Data Quality Client is the most important DQS client tool.

    C. **Correct:** Although installed during SSIS installation, SSIS DQS Cleansing transformation is one of the client tools available with SQL Server 2012.

    D. **Incorrect:** SQL Server Data Tools is not a DQS client.

    E. **Incorrect:** There is no DQS Add-in for Visio.

3. **Correct answer: A**

    A. **Correct:** DQS_KNOWLEDGE_BASE is not a Data Quality Server database.

    B. **Incorrect:** DQS_STAGING_DATA is a Data Quality Server database.

    C. **Incorrect:** DQS_MAIN is a Data Quality Server database.

    D. **Incorrect:** DQS_PROJECTS is a Data Quality Server database.

Lesson 3

1. **Correct answer: B**

    A. **Incorrect:** You set up reference data sources with Data Quality Client.

    B. **Correct:** You manage DQS security with SSMS or with T-SQL commands.

    C. **Incorrect:** You monitor DQS activity with Data Quality Client.

    D. **Incorrect:** You change log settings with Data Quality Client.

2. **Correct answer: A**

    A. **Correct:** dqs_user is not a predefined DQS role.

    B. **Incorrect:** dqs_kb_editor is a predefined DQS role.

    C. **Incorrect:** dqs_ administrator is a predefined DQS role.

    D. **Incorrect:** dqs_kb_operator is a predefined DQS role.

3. **Correct answers: B and C**

    A. **Incorrect:** dqs_user is not a predefined DQS role.

    B. **Correct:** Members of the dqs_kb_editor role can create and edit a knowledge base.

    C. **Correct:** Members of the dqs_administrator role can create and edit a knowledge base.

    D. **Incorrect:** Members of the dqs_kb_operator role cannot create and edit a knowledge base.

Case Scenario

1. End users probably do not trust the data warehouse (DW) data.

2. You should suggest that the DBA do data profiling of the DW data in order to assess the quality of its data. If the quality is good, then the DBA should educate end users and prove to them they can rely on the DW data. If the quality is not good, then the DBA should suggest to managers that they implement a data quality solution and define explicit data stewardship roles in the company.

## CHAPTER 15

Implementing Master Data Services

Exam objectives in this chapter:

- Build Data Quality Solutions
  - Implement master data management solutions.

M aster data management (MDM), the process of creating and maintaining master data, is one of the most challenging IT tasks for an enterprise. In this chapter, you will learn what exactly the term "master data" means and what the most important challenges are, including data quality problems and ways to solve them. You will install Microsoft SQL Server 2012 Master Data Services (MDS) and create your first MDS model.

Lessons in this chapter:

- Lesson 1: Defining Master Data
- Lesson 2: Installing Master Data Services
- Lesson 3: Creating a Master Data Services Model

Before You Begin

To complete this chapter, you must have:

- Basic knowledge of Windows management tools.
- Experience working with SQL Server 2012 Setup.
- An understanding of relational and dimensional data.
- SQL Server 2012 and Microsoft Excel 2010 installed.
- The AdventureWorks2012 demo database installed.

Lesson 1: Defining Master Data

In an average company, many types of data are encountered. These types include:

- **Metadata** This is data about data. Metadata includes database schemas for transactional and analytical applications, XML document schemas, report definitions, additional database table and column descriptions stored with extended properties or custom tables provided by SQL Server, application configuration data, and more.

- **Transactional data** This is data maintained by line of business (LOB) online transaction processing (OLTP) applications. In this context, the term "transactional" refers to business transactions, not database management system transactions. This data includes, for example, customer orders, invoices, insurance claims, and data about manufacturing stages, deliveries, and monetary transactions. In short, this is OLTP data about events.

- **Hierarchical data** This type of data typically appears in analytical applications. Relationships between data are represented in hierarchies. Some hierarchies represent an intrinsic structure of the data—they are natural for the data. An example is product taxonomy. Products have subcategories, which are in categories. There can be multiple levels of hierarchies. Such hierarchies are especially useful for drilling down from a general to a detailed level in order to find reasons, patterns, and problems. This is a very common way of analyzing data in online analytical processing (OLAP) applications.

- **Semi-structured data** This type of data is typically in XML form. XML data can appear in stand-alone files or as part of a database (as a column in a table). Semi-structured data is useful when metadata (the schema) changes frequently, or when you do not have a need for a detailed relational schema. In addition, XML is widely used for data exchange.

- **Unstructured data** This involves all kinds of documents with instructions, company portals, magazine articles, email messages, and similar items. This data can appear in a database, in a file, or even in printed material.

- **Master data** The final type of data is master data, which is defined in the first section in this lesson.

After this lesson, you will be able to:

- Understand what master data is.
- Determine the goals of master data management.
- Understand the most common master data management challenges.

Estimated lesson time: 40 minutes

What Is Master Data?

Everybody has some intuitive idea as to what kind of data constitutes master data. However, this lesson starts with some more precise definitions and examples.

In the relational model, a table represents a predicate, and a row represents a proposition about a subject, object, or event from the real world. You start building a relational database by describing the business problems in sentences. Nouns in the sentences describe real-world entities that are of interest for the business, such as customers, products, and employees. Verbs in the sentences describe relationships between nouns—more precisely, the roles that the nouns play in the relationships. Nouns define the *master data*. Verbs lead to transactional data. From a description of a relational database, you can easily find the nouns. These critical nouns typically define one of the following:

- **People**   Including customers, suppliers, employees, and sales representatives
- **Things**   Including products, equipment, assets, and stores
- **Concepts**   Including contracts, licenses, and bills of material
- **Places**   Including company locations and customer geographic divisions

Any of these entity sets can be further divided into specialized subsets. For example, a company can segment its customers based on previous sales into premier and other customers, based on customer type, or based on whether the customer is a person or a company.

For analytical applications, data is often organized into a dimensional model. A popular name for the dimensional model is the Star schema (although, to be precise, a dimensionally modeled database can include multiple Star and Snowflake schemas). This is because it has a central fact table and surrounding dimensional tables, usually just referred to as "dimensions." Fact tables hold measures (data that is being measured). Dimension attributes are used for pivoting fact data; they give these measures some meaning. Essentially, it can be said that dimensions give context to measures. Fact tables are populated from transactional data, and dimensions are populated from entities that represent nouns in a relational database description. Therefore, in a dimensional model, dimensions are the master data.

As already mentioned, OLAP analyses typically involve drilling down into hierarchies. Dimensions can include multiple hierarchies.

Master data appears in probably every single application in an enterprise. Enterprise resource planning (ERP) applications include data about products, bills of material, customers, suppliers, contracts, and similar entities. Customer Relationship Management (CRM) applications deal, of course, with customers. Human Resources Management (HRM) applications are about employees. Analytical applications often include all of an enterprise's master data. You can easily see why master data is a very important part of data. It is crucial that this master data be known and correct.

Data quality issues are mostly about master data. You can easily imagine that having the same master data in multiple sources can immediately lead to problems with the same definitions, the same identifications, and duplication. Master data typically changes at a much slower rate than transactional data. Customers, for example, do not frequently change addresses; however, they interact with your company through orders, services, or even complaints, probably on a daily basis. Nevertheless, although it is less volatile than transactional data, master data has a life cycle that is still a classical *CRUD* cycle: create, read, update, and delete. The question that then arises is whether any data about people, things, places, or concepts is really master data for any company.

If a company sells only five different products, product data is not master data for that company. Although technically it is master data, the company does not need any specific management of this data. It is very likely that every single attribute of these five products has a correct value in the system, and it is unlikely that an inaccurate value will appear. Therefore, for this company, product data is not considered master data. Cardinality has an influence on whether specific data is considered master data or not.

If a company collects only a few attributes for product categories—for example, if the categories entity has only two attributes, category ID and category name—that company probably does not consider this master data. Complexity of data is another criterion that helps you decide which data needs special treatment and is master data.

Another factor to consider when defining master data is volatility. It was already mentioned that master data tends to change less frequently than transactional data. Now imagine that some data does not change at all. Consider, for example, geographic locations. Data about geographic locations changes quite infrequently; in some systems, you can even consider this data to be static. As soon as you have cleansed this data, it does not need any further treatment, and therefore you do not consider this to be master data.

Some data needs to have a history maintained for it. In transactional applications, you need to know how the data came to be in its current state. Government or other authorities prescribe a formal auditing process for some business areas. In analytical applications, analysis often is performed over time; for example, you might compare this year's sales with sales from the previous year in a geographic region. In order to make proper analyses, you need to take into account the possible movements of customers from region to region; therefore, you need to maintain history again. Data that needs versioning, auditing, or any other kind of maintenance of history is typically master data.

Finally, you give more attention to data that you reuse repeatedly. Reusage increases the value of data. The value of the data can increase because of other factors as well. For example, in a pharmacy, an error in a bill of materials can lead to huge damage. Therefore, the more valuable the data is for you, the more likely it is that you will define it as master data.

Master Data Management

Data that does not need special treatment is not master data. Clearly, you can conclude that
master data needs some special treatment, and this treatment is called master data management. In a more formal definition, master data management (MDM) is a set of coordinated
processes, policies, tools, and technologies used to create and maintain accurate master data.

Even the formal definition of MDM is still very broad. There is no single tool that can address all MDM concerns. You can consider anything used to improve the quality of master
data as an MDM tool. Any formal, scheduled or repeated, ad-hoc activity that improves master data quality is an MDM process. Any technology such as a relational database management system (RDBMS) that enforces data integrity is a part of MDM technology. However,
depending on the approach you use to maintain master data, you might consider using a
specialized tool that clearly defines the process for managing master data.

Some of the most important goals of MDM include:

- Unifying or at least harmonizing master data between different transactional or
  operational systems.
- Maintaining multiple versions of master data for different needs in different op-
  erational systems.
- Integrating master data for analytical and CRM systems.
- Maintaining history for analytical systems.
- Capturing information about hierarchies in master data, which is especially useful for
  analytical applications.
- Supporting compliance with government prescriptions (such as the Sarbanes-Oxley
  Act) through auditing and versioning.
- Maintaining a clear CRUD process through a prescribed workflow.
- Maximizing return on investment (ROI) through reusage of master data.

Note the last bullet point; master data management can be quite costly and very intensive
in terms of resources used, including work hours. For a small company with a single operational system, probably no specific MDM tool is needed. Such a company can maintain master data in its operational system. The more you reuse master data (for example, in multiple
operational, CRM, and analytical applications), the bigger the ROI.

RDBMSs and applications can and should enforce data integrity. Data integrity means that the data conforms to business rules. Business rules can be quite simple, such as requiring that order numbers must be unique, that there should be no order without a known customer, and that the quantity ordered must be greater than zero. Business rules can also be more complicated. For example, a company can define that no customer should order in a single web order a product in a quantity that is more than half of the quantity of the product in stock. If the database and the application do not enforce data integrity, you can expect dirty data.

 Even if the database and the application do enforce data integrity, you still should not take *data accuracy* for granted. How can you prevent typos? For example, an operator could enter "42 Hudson Avenue" instead of "24 Hudson Avenue"; both addresses are valid from a data integrity perspective. Another issue arises if you have multiple systems. Do all operators enter data in a consistent way? Some operators could write the correct address, but in a slightly different form, as in "24 Hudson Ave."

You could resolve data quality issues with occasional data cleansing. With cleansing, data quality rises; however, over time, the quality falls again. This is a reactive approach. A proactive approach, which prevents the entry of low-quality data in the first place, is even better. What is needed for this approach is explicit data governance. You must know who is responsible for the data, and you must have clearly defined the process of maintaining the data. Data governance sets the policies for master data. Data governance rules can prescribe data requirements, such as which information is required, how values are derived, and what the data retention periods are. Data governance can also prescribe security policies, such as which master data needs to be encrypted and which part of the master data has to be audited. It can prescribe versioning and workflows. It defines how to address data inconsistencies between different source systems; for example, it can define the authoritative source. Data governance policies should also define how to bring new systems online without breaking existing master data processes and compromising quality. Finally, data governance can define the need for explicit roles in an enterprise—the roles responsible for maintaining master data and implementing data governance.

In MDM terminology, you have to define the data stewards, the people responsible for their part of the master data. Data stewards are the governors. They should work independently of any specific source or destination system for master data, in an objective way. Data stewards must have deep knowledge about the data they govern. In a common scenario, one data steward covers one business area of the master data; you have one steward for customers, one for products, and so on. Data stewardship roles should be defined and data stewards designated early in the process of implementing an MDM solution.

From what you have seen so far, you can conclude that there are different approaches to master data management. Here is a list of possible approaches:

- **No central MDM** In this situation, the systems do not communicate at all. When any kind of cross-system interaction is required, such as performing analysis on data from multiple systems, ad-hoc merging and cleansing is performed. This approach is very inexpensive at the beginning; however, it turns out to be the most expensive over time. You should not treat this approach as a real MDM approach.

- **Central metadata storage** With this approach, there are at least unified, centrally maintained definitions for master data. All of the systems should follow and implement these central definitions. Ad-hoc merging and cleansing becomes somewhat simpler. This scenario typically does not use a specialized solution for the central metadata storage. The central storage of metadata is probably in an unstructured form—in the form of documents, worksheets, or even just on paper.

- **Central metadata storage with identity mapping** In addition to maintaining unified, centrally maintained definitions for master data, this approach also stores keys that map tables in the MDM solution. Data integration applications can be developed much more quickly and easily. Although this solution seems quite appealing, it has many problems with regard to maintaining master data over time. The system only has keys from the systems in the MDM database; it does not have any other attributes. All attributes in source systems change over time, and there is no versioning or auditing in place to follow the changes. Therefore, this approach is viable for a limited time only. It is useful, for example, during upgrading, testing, and the initial usage of a new ERP system to provide mapping back to the old ERP system.

- **Central metadata storage and central data that is continuously merged** This approach stores metadata as well as master data in a dedicated MDM system. However, master data is not inserted or updated in the MDM system; the merging (and cleansing) of master data from source systems occurs continuously, on a daily basis. There are multiple issues with this approach, and continuous merging can become expensive. The only viable use for this approach is for finding out what has changed in source systems from the last merge, enabling you to merge only the delta—only the new and updated data. This approach is frequently used for analytical systems. A data warehouse (DW) is prepared as central storage for analytical data (which includes transactional and master data). The DW is populated overnight, and during population, data is merged and cleansing issues are resolved. Although you typically do not create the DW with MDM as the main goal, you can treat the DW as an authoritative source of master data.

- **Central MDM, single copy** This approach involves a specialized MDM application, where master data, together with its metadata, is maintained in a central location. All existing applications are consumers of this master data. This approach seems preferable at first glimpse. However, it has its own drawbacks. You have to upgrade all existing applications to consume master data from central storage instead of maintaining their own copies. This can be quite costly, and maybe even impossible with some older systems. In addition, central master metadata should union all metadata from all source systems. Finally, the process of creating and updating master data could simply be too slow. It could happen, for example, that a new customer would have to wait for a couple of days before submitting his or her first order, because the process of inserting customer data with all of the possible attributes involves contacting all source systems and simply takes too long.

- **Central MDM, multiple copies** This approach also uses central storage of master data and its metadata. However, the metadata here includes only an intersection of common metadata from source systems. Each source system maintains its own copy of master data, with additional attributes that pertain to that system only. After master data is inserted into the central MDM system, it is replicated (preferably automatically) to source systems, where the source-specific attributes are updated. This approach is a good compromise between cost, data quality, and the effectiveness of the CRUD process. Still, as with every other MDM solution, this solution has its drawbacks. Because different systems can also update the common data, you can have update conflicts. Therefore, this approach involves continuous merges as well. However, because at least part of the data is updated centrally, this approach requires less work than the approaches that involve central metadata storage and central data that is continuously merged.

The last two approaches require a special MDM application. A specialized MDM solution could also be useful for the approach that uses central metadata storage with identity mapping and the one that uses central metadata storage and central data that is continuously merged. SQL Server 2012 Master Data Services (MDS) is a specialized MDM application. You could also write your own application. Other SQL Server tools, such as SQL Server Integration Services (SSIS) and SQL Server Analysis Services (SSAS), are helpful in the MDM process as well. However, for the last two approaches to MDM, MDS is the most efficient solution.

MDM Challenges

For an MDM project to be successful, you have to tackle all of the challenges you meet. These challenges include:

- **Different definitions of master metadata in source systems** You can have different coding schemes, data types, collations, and more. You must unify the metadata definitions.

- **Data quality issues** This is something you always have to expect. In short, if you do not have data quality issues, then you probably do not need a specialized MDM solution anyway. You have to improve the data quality; otherwise, the MDM project fails to accomplish its most important goal.

- **Authority** Who is responsible for master data? Every department wants to be authoritative for its part of the master data, and the authority for master data can overlap in an enterprise. You have to define policies for master data, with an explicit data stewardship process. You also must define data ownership as part of authority issue resolution.

- **Data conflicts** When you prepare the central master data database, you have to merge data from your sources. You must resolve data conflicts during the project and, depending on the MDM approach, replicate the resolved data back to the source systems.

- **Domain knowledge** You should include domain experts in an MDM project.
- **Documentation** Be sure to properly document your master data and metadata.

No matter which approach is taken, MDM projects are always challenging. However, tools such as MDS can efficiently help resolve possible issues.

 Quick Check

1. Are constraints in a relational database enough to enforce data accuracy?

2. Do fact tables in a data warehouse contain master data?

Quick Check Answers

1. No, constraints enforce data integrity; they cannot enforce data accuracy as well.

2. No, fact tables in a data warehouse typically contain transactional data, which is usually not considered to be master data.

PRACTICE **Defining Master Data**

In this theoretical practice, you define master data for the AdventureWorksDW2012 sample database and for a production system you know.

EXERCISE 1 Identify AdventureWorksDW2012 Master Data

In the first exercise, you identify master data in the AdventureWorksDW2012 sample database.

1. Start SSMS and connect to your SQL Server instance. Expand the Databases folder and then the AdventureWorksDW2012 database.

2. Expand the Tables folder. Read table names thoroughly.

3. Using the criteria explained in this lesson, try to figure out which of the following tables could be defined as master data tables:

- *DimCustomer*
- *FactInternetSales*
- *DimDate*
- *DimSalesReason*
- *DimProduct*
- *DimProductCategory*
- *DimEmployee*
- *FactResellerSales*

4. If you cannot determine which tables contain master data from the table names, try to figure this out from the table content.

5. After you have finished with the review of the AdventureWorksDW2012 tables, close SSMS.

EXERCISE 2   Define Master Data in a Custom Production System

In this exercise, you define master data for a production system you know.

- Think of a production system from your company or from a company you know. Try to answer the following questions:
  - Can you find any master data in the system?
  - Is there any data that needs to be audited or versioned?
  - Which data is reused the most?
  - Are there multiple sources of some of the master data?
  - Are there any data quality issues with the data?
  - Has the company defined explicit data stewardship roles?
  - What should be changed in order to improve the data quality?

Lesson Summary

- Master data management is a set of coordinated processes, policies, tools, and technologies used to create and maintain accurate master data.
- Master data management has to deal with many challenges.
- Master data typically needs auditing, versioning, or some other kind of maintenance of history.
- Reusage increases the value of master data.
- If you use a data warehouse, you should map your master data to dimensions in the data warehouse.
- SQL Server 2012 Master Data Services (MDS) is a specialized master data management application.

Lesson Review

Answer the following questions to test your knowledge of the information in this lesson. You can find the answers to these questions and explanations of why each answer choice is correct or incorrect in the "Answers" section at the end of this chapter.

1. What are some of the goals of master data management? (Choose all that apply.)

   A. Data reuse

   B. Versioning

   C. Improving the performance of queries

   D. Data quality

   E. Data integrity

2. What are some of the challenges of master data management? (Choose all that apply.)

   A. Relationships between entities

   B. Database schema normalization

   C. Authority

   D. Data conflicts

3. What sets the policies for master data?

   A. Data stewardship

   B. Data governance

   C. Data integrity rules

   D. Data quality prescriptions

Lesson 2: Installing Master Data Services

Master Data Services (MDS) is a master data management application included with SQL Server. In order to use it, you have to understand the application architecture. Of course, you also need to install it.

> **After this lesson, you will be able to:**
> - Describe MDS architecture.
> - Install MDS.
>
> **Estimated lesson time: 50 minutes**

Master Data Services Architecture

 There are four main parts of the Master Data Services application. In the *MDS database*, the master data is stored along with MDS system objects. MDS system objects include system tables and many programmatic objects such as system stored procedures and functions. The *MDS service* performs the business logic and data access for the MDS solution. *Master Data Manager* is a web application for MDS users and administrators. In addition, advanced users can use the Master Data Services add-in for Microsoft Excel. Figure 15-1 shows the MDS architecture.

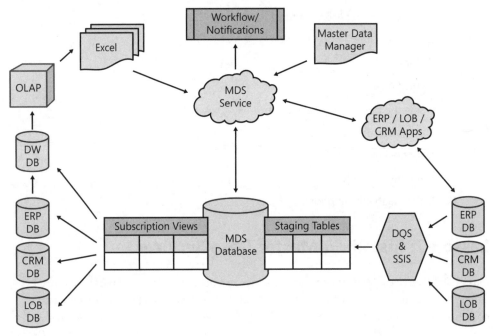

FIGURE 15-1 MDS architecture.

You can insert master data into your MDS database manually through Master Data Manager or through Excel with the help of the MDS add-in for Excel. In addition, you can import master data from existing databases through staging tables. The staging tables are a part of the MDS database. During the import process, you can cleanse your data with the help of SQL Server 2012 Data Quality Services, and integrate it from multiple sources with the help of SQL Server Integration Services. You can also export MDS data to other transactional databases and data warehouses. You can do the exporting through subscription views you create in the MDS database.

You can also integrate your applications with Master Data Services. You perform the integration through the Master Data Manager web service. In addition, you can create master data workflows and notifications. MDS uses SQL Server Database Mail for notifications. For workflows, you can either create a custom solution through the web service or use Microsoft SharePoint workflows. You define workflows and notifications through business rules.

As you can see, the MDS architecture enables you to achieve one of the most important master data management goals—the data reuse goal—in many ways.

MDS Installation

MDS installation involves quite a few steps. These steps are divided into three main groups:

- Pre-installation tasks
- Installation operations
- Post-installation tasks

During the pre-installation tasks, you verify the installation requirements. You can create an MDS database with the SQL Server 2012 Enterprise edition, SQL Server 2012 Business Intelligence edition, or SQL Server 2012 Developer edition. Note that MDS supports 64-bit editions only.

During the installation operations, you use the MDS Configuration Manager application. With the MDS Configuration Manager, you have to connect to your SQL Server instance with a user account that has sysadmin privileges. One of the pre-installation tasks is to create such an account. In addition, when you create an MDS database, you must specify a domain user account to be the Master Data Services system administrator. You should create this domain user account during the pre-installation tasks.

The Master Data Manager web application is hosted by Internet Information Services (IIS). Windows Internet Explorer version 7, 8, or 9 must be used as a client tool. Older versions of Internet Explorer are not supported. In addition, Master Data Manager needs Microsoft Silverlight 5. If Silverlight 5 is not installed on your computer, you will be prompted to install it when you navigate to a page in Master Data Manager where Silverlight 5 is needed for the first time. The Master Data Services web application needs the following Windows Web Server roles and role services:

- Common HTTP Features
  - Static Content
  - Default Document
  - Directory Browsing
  - HTTP Errors
- Application Development
  - ASP.NET
  - .NET Extensibility
  - ISAPI Extensions
  - ISAPI Filters
- Health and Diagnostics
  - HTTP Logging
  - Request Monitor

- Security
  - Windows Authentication
  - Request Filtering
- Performance
  - Static Content Compression
- Management Tools
  - IIS Management Console.

In addition, the Master Data Manager application requires that you have the following Windows features enabled:

- .NET Framework 3.0 or 3.5 Features
  - WCF Activation
  - HTTP Activation
  - Non-HTTP Activation
- Windows Process Activation Service
  - Process Model
  - .NET Environment
  - Configuration APIs

In the Windows Server 2008 or Windows Server 2008 R2 operating system, you use the Server Manager administrative tool to install the appropriate roles and features. In Windows Vista or Windows 7, you use Programs And Features from Control Panel to install the necessary roles and features.

EXAM TIP

Remember that the Master Data Services web application requires specific Windows Web Server roles and role services, and you must have specific Windows features enabled. It is not enough to use only SQL Server Setup to install the MDS web application.

The installation operations are quite simple. You use SQL Server Setup to install MDS. MDS is available on the Feature Selection page of SQL Server Setup, under Shared Features. SQL Server Setup installs MDS folders and files in the location you specify for shared features. It also registers MDS assemblies in the global assembly cache (GAC) of your computer. Finally, it installs the Master Data Services Configuration Manager, a tool you use during the post-installation tasks.

For the post-installation tasks, you have to run the MDS Configuration Manager. When you run it for the first time, it creates a Windows group called MDS_ServiceAccounts. This group contains MDS service accounts for IIS application pools. The MDS Configuration Manager then creates the MDSTempDir folder in your MDS installation path and assigns appropriate permissions for MDS_ServiceAccounts. This folder is used by the Master Data Manager application for temporary compilation files. Finally, during the first run, the MDS Configuration Manager configures the tempDirectory attribute in the MDS Web.config file to point to the MDSTempDir folder.

You use the MDS Configuration Manager to create the MDS database on your SQL Server instance. Then you create the Master Data Manager web application. Next you must associate the MDS database you created with your Master Data Manager web application. If you install MDS on a Windows Server 2008 or Windows Server 2008 R2 operating system, you might have to configure Internet Explorer Enhanced Security to allow scripting for the Master Data Manager site. Otherwise, you might have problems when browsing to the Master Data Manager site.

The MDS add-in for Excel is a separate download from the Microsoft Download Center. You have to download either the 32-bit or the 64-bit version of the .msi package, depending on the version of Microsoft Office you are using. Then you install it by simply double-clicking the .msi package in Windows Explorer and following the setup wizard.

You can integrate Master Data Services with Data Quality Services. In order to integrate both products, you have to install Data Quality Services and Data Quality Client on the same SQL Server instance where you installed your MDS database.

 Quick Check

- How can you export data from your MDS database?

Quick Check Answer

- You can query the subscription views you create, or you can integrate your application directly to Master Data Services through the Master Data Manager web service.

PRACTICE **Installing Master Data Services**

In this practice, you will install Master Data Services.

EXERCISE 1 Perform MDS Pre-Installation Tasks

In the first exercise, you prepare your computer to host Master Data Services. This exercise assumes you are using Windows Server 2008 or Windows Server 2008 R2. If you are using Windows Vista or Windows 7, use Control Panel | Programs And Features and the Turn Windows Features on or off instead of Server Manager.

1. Open Administrative Tools|Server Manager. When the console opens, click Roles in the left pane.

2. In the right pane, click the Add Roles link. In the Add Roles Wizard, click Next.

3. On the Select Server Roles page, select the check box next to the Web Server (IIS) role. Click Next.

4. On the next page, the Web Server (IIS) page, read the information provided and click Next.

5. On the Select Role Services page, select all of the role services needed:

   - Common HTTP Features
     - Static Content
     - Default Document
     - Directory Browsing
     - HTTP Errors
   - Application Development
     - ASP.NET
     - .NET Extensibility
     - ISAPI Extensions
     - ISAPI Filters
   - Health and Diagnostics
     - HTTP Logging
     - Request Monitor
   - Security
     - Windows Authentication
     - Request Filtering
   - Performance
     - Static Content Compression
   - Management Tools
     - IIS Management Console

6. When you select the check box next to the ASP.NET role service, an additional window appears. It tells you that you have to install additional role services required for Microsoft ASP.NET. Confirm the addition by clicking the Add Required Role Services button. When you are back on the Select Role Services page and have selected all of the required role services, click Next.

7. On the Confirm Installation Selections page, review your selections and read the informational messages. Then click Install.

8. Watch the installation progress. When it is finished, click the Close button on the Installation Results page.

9. In the left pane of the Server Manager console, click Features.

10. In the right pane, click the Add Features link.

11. On the Select Features page, select the check box for .NET Framework 3.5.1 Features. In the additional window that appears, confirm the addition of the features required for the Microsoft .NET Framework 3.5.1 by clicking the Add Required Features button.

12. Check to ensure that the following features are selected, and click Next:

   - NET Framework 3.0 or 3.5 Features
     - WCF Activation
     - HTTP Activation
     - Non-HTTP Activation
   - Windows Process Activation Service
     - Process Model
     - .NET Environment
     - Configuration APIs.

13. On the Confirm Installation Selections page, review your selections and read the informational messages. Then click Install.

14. Watch the installation progress. When it is finished, click the Close button on the Installation Results page.

15. Close Server Manager.

EXERCISE 2 Perform MDS Installation Operations

In this exercise, you use SQL Server Setup to install the Master Data Services components.

1. Run SQL Server 2012 Setup.

2. In the SQL Server Installation Center, click the Installation link in the left pane.

3. Select the New SQL Server Stand-Alone Installation Or Add Features To Existing Installation link.

4. Wait until the Setup Support Rules are checked. When the operation completes, click OK.

5. On the Product Updates page, click Next.

6. Wait until the setup files are installed. Then the Setup Support Rules page should appear. Check any warnings. If there are no errors, click Next.

7. On the Installation Type page, check the Add Features To An Existing Instance Of SQL Server 2012 option. Select the instance where you want to host Master Data Services from the drop-down list of installed instances on your computer. Click Next.

8. On the Feature Selection page, select the check box next to the Master Data Services option. Then click Next.

9. Wait while the Installation Rules are checked, then on the Disk Space Requirements page, click Next.

10. On the Error Reporting page, clear the only check box, and click Next.

11. On the Installation Configuration Rules page, click Next.

12. On the Ready To Install page, click Install.

13. Wait until installation is finished, and then on the Complete page, click Close.

14. Close the SQL Server Installation window.

EXERCISE 3 Perform MDS Post-Installation Tasks

You are now ready to perform the MDS post-installation tasks.

1. Make sure that you are logged on to your operating system with an account that is a member of the sysadmin SQL Server server role.

2. Open the Master Data Services Configuration Manager console. You can find it in All Programs | Microsoft SQL Server 2012 | Master Data Services.

3. When the Master Data Services Configuration Manager opens, click the Database Configuration option in the left pane.

4. In the Database Configuration window in the right pane, click the Create Database button.

5. When the Create Database Wizard opens, read the information and click Next.

6. Provide connection information for the SQL Server instance where you want to create the MDS database, and click Next.

7. Choose the database name. You can use **MDSTK463**, as shown in Figure 15-2. Use SQL Server default collation for the database collation. Click Next.

8. On the next page, define the Windows account that will have full access to all MDS models. If you are following this practice for your own education, then this should probably be your account. For a real-life scenario, this should be the account of the user who will be the MDS administrator. Click Next.

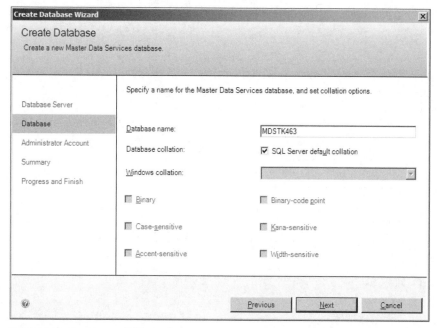

FIGURE 15-2 Creating an MDS database.

9. On the Summary page, read the information, and click Next.

10. When the database has been created, click Finish.

11. In the MDS Configuration Manager, click the Web Configuration option in the left pane.

12. In the Website drop-down list, select the Create New Website option.

13. When the Create Website window appears, change the port used by the MDS application to 8080. Under Application Pool at the bottom of the window, enter the user name and password (and retype the password) for the Windows user name used for the application pool for the MDS web application. The Create Website window should look similar to the one shown in Figure 15-3. When you have entered all the information, click OK.

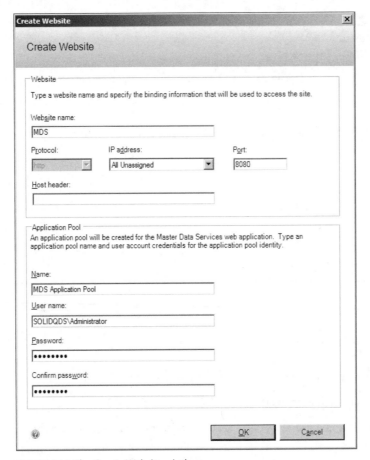

FIGURE 15-3 The Create Website window.

14. In the HTTP Binding Information window, read the information provided and click OK.

15. Now you have to associate the web application with the database you just created. In the MDS Configuration Manager, click the Select button in the middle of the right pane.

16. In the Connect To Database window, click the Connect button. Connect to your SQL Server instance and select the MDS database you created in this exercise. Click OK.

17. Click the Apply button. Click OK in the Configuration Complete window. Wait until Internet Explorer opens. Then switch to the MDS Configuration Manager and click the Exit button.

18. Switch to Internet Explorer. The Getting Started With Microsoft SQL Server 2012 Master Data Services page should be open. If you have problems with security settings in Internet Explorer, add your Master Data Manager site to the trusted sites. Read the information on this page and then click the Open The Master Data Manager Home Page link.

    Alternatively, you can open the Master Data Manager home page directly from Internet Explorer: Open Internet Explorer and go to the Master Data Manager site. If you followed the steps in this practice, the link should be as follows:

    http://<yourcomputername>:8080/

    If you have problems with security settings in Internet Explorer, add your Master Data Manager site to the trusted sites.

19. When the Master Data Manager application opens, provide the requested login information. Log on with the user credentials that allow full access to MDS as you specified in step 8 of this exercise.

20. When you are logged on, wait until the Master Data Manager home page opens. Figure 15-4 shows the home page. Then click the Explorer link.

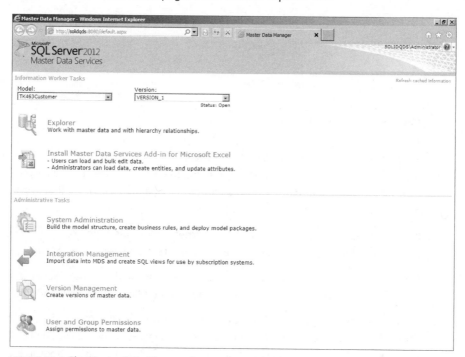

FIGURE 15-4 The Master Data Manager home page.

21. If you do not have Silverlight 5 installed, you should see a link for installing it, as shown in Figure 15-5 (for Internet Explorer 9). If this is the case, click the Click Now To Install button. Run the Silverlight.exe installation application.

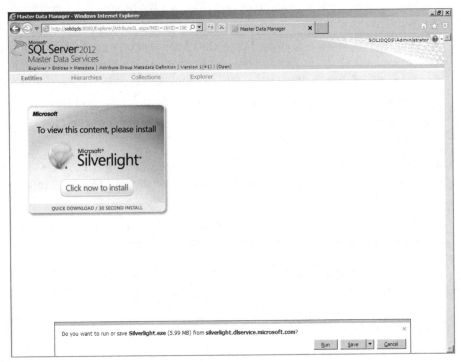

FIGURE 15-5 Installing Silverlight.

22. Follow the instructions in the Silverlight installation wizard. When it is finished, refresh the page. You might get a message telling you that you need to install a newer version of Silverlight. If this happens, just install Silverlight again; this time it should be the latest version.

23. If you needed to install Silverlight, close Internet Explorer and then reopen it. Reconnect to your Master Data Manager site and provide login information again.

24. On the Master Data Manager home page, click the Install Master Data Services Add-In For Microsoft Excel link. You will be redirected to the Microsoft Download Center.

25. In the new Internet Explorer window that opens, download the appropriate (32-bit or 64-bit) version of the add-in. When it has been downloaded, double-click the Master-DataServicesExcelAddin.msi file to start installation. Follow the instructions in the installation wizard.

Lesson Summary

- During the pre-installation tasks, you have to prepare your system for the MDS database and the web application.
- During the installation operations, you use SQL Server Setup to install MDS.
- During the post-installation tasks, you configure the MDS database, the Master Data Manager web application, and the MDS add-in for Excel.

Lesson Review

Answer the following questions to test your knowledge of the information in this lesson. You can find the answers to these questions and explanations of why each answer choice is correct or incorrect in the "Answers" section at the end of this chapter.

1. Which of the following roles is needed for the Master Data Manager web application?

    A. Application Server

    B. Remote Desktop Services

    C. Web Server (IIS)

    D. DNS Server

2. How can you enter data into your MDS database? (Choose all that apply.)

    A. With the Master Data Manager web application

    B. Through staging tables in the MDS database

    C. By using Microsoft Word 2010

    D. By using Microsoft Excel 2010 with the MDS add-in

    E. By integrating the Master Data Manager web service in your application

3. Which part of the Master Data Services application performs the business logic and data access for the MDS solution?

    A. The MDS database

    B. The MDS add-in for Excel

    C. Master Data Manager

    D. The MDS service

Lesson 3: Creating a Master Data Services Model

A *Master Data Services model* is a container for all master data objects. One model typically covers one master data business area. When you create an MDS model, you should create all of the objects needed for a specific business area. For example, when you create a model for products, you should include in the model all related data, as well as product subcategories and product categories. In this lesson, you will learn about the MDS objects in an MDS model.

> **After this lesson, you will be able to:**
>
> - Create an MDS model.
> - Create entities, attributes, hierarchies, and collections.
> - Create business rules.
>
> **Estimated lesson time: 50 minutes**

MDS Models and Objects in Models

MDS models organize master data into logical groups for a specific business area. As mentioned earlier, master data is typically organized into four types: people, things, concepts, and places. A model contains the following objects:

- Entities
- Attributes and attribute groups
- Explicit and derived hierarchies
- Collections

Figure 15-6 is an example of an MDS model showing the relationships among the MDS model and its MDS objects.

A model contains entities. In Figure 15-6, the Product model contains two entities: Product and Subcategory. Entities contain attributes. For example, the Product entity contains the attributes Code, Name, Weight, and more. Some attributes are domain-based. This means that their value comes from a domain of possible values defined by another entity. In a classical relational model, this second entity would be a lookup table. For example, one Code attribute in Figure 15-6 connects the Product and Subcategory entities. This code is the key for the subcategories.

You might wonder why the name "Code" is used twice in Figure 15-6, once to identify products and once to identify subcategories. This is because in MDS, every entity must have two attributes with defined names: Code and Name.

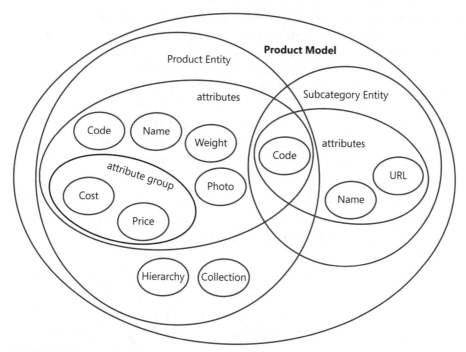

FIGURE 15-6 An example MDS model and objects.

Attributes can be further organized into attribute groups. Also, entities can have hierarchies. Some hierarchies are natural and stem from domain-based attributes. For example, a product belongs to a subcategory, which further belongs to a category. In addition to the natural hierarchies, you can also define explicit hierarchies in which you organize data according to your business needs. For example, you can organize countries, regions, and cities for your sales representatives in a way that optimizes travel expenses rather than using the natural hierarchy of country/region/city. Furthermore, you can define arbitrary collections of entities.

MDS Objects

The basic MDS object is the *entity*. An entity represents a thing or a concept from the real world that you can identify and that is of business interest. In a relational model, a *relation* is a set of entities that are related, or in other words, are similar. A relation represents an *entity set*. If an entity is of business interest, then it should have some *attributes* that describe interesting properties of that entity. In a relational model, you represent entity sets with tables and attributes with columns. You can think of an MDS entity as a table, and MDS attributes as columns in that table.

In an MDS model, one entity is central for the model, and other entities relate to this central entity. For example, the Product entity in Figure 15-6 is the central entity, and the Subcategory entity relates to this entity. The central entity in a model is typically also a starting point in navigation for end users. An entity that you use as a starting point in a user interface for Master Data Manager is called a *base entity*. You can define any entity in a model as the base entity.

Entities have attributes. Each entity must have at least two attributes, the Name and Code attributes. These two attributes are created automatically and cannot be removed. Values for the Code attribute must be unique within an entity. You can think of the Code attribute as the key of an entity. There are three types of attributes:

- *Free-form attributes*, which allow free-form input for strings, numbers, dates, and links.
- *Domain-based attributes*, for which the domain of possible values exists in a related entity. You can think of domain-based attributes as similar to the foreign keys in a relational model.
- *File attributes*, which you use to store documents such as descriptions and images of an entity. You can limit the file extensions that are allowed for a file attribute.

Numeric free-form attributes are limited to the .NET SqlDouble data type. This means that they represent floating-point numbers. You should be aware of the following limitations when working with floating-point numbers:

- Two floating-point numbers that appear as equal to you might not compare as equal. This is because you only see a particular level of precision; however, the numbers might differ in some less significant digits.
- Some mathematical or comparison operations that use floating-point numbers might give you unexpected results—that is, different results than you would get if you were using decimal numbers. This is because the floating-point number might not exactly equal the decimal number.
- Sometimes a floating-point value is cast to a decimal and then back to a floating-point number. This might lead to the so-called "roundtrip problem": when you cast a value back to a floating point number, the value differs from the original value. The roundtrip problem can arise because some less significant digits are lost in the conversion.

Domain-based attributes form natural hierarchies, which in MDS terminology are known as *derived hierarchies*. Therefore, for a derived hierarchy, relationships between entities must already exist in a model. You can think of a hierarchy as an inverted tree. At the lowest level are the leaf-level members. Members from a lookup entity define the grouping for members of a base entity; members of the base entity are thus leaf-level members of this derived hierarchy.

Derived hierarchies can be recursive. A hierarchy is *recursive* when a recursive relationship exists; this happens when an entity has a domain-based attribute based on the entity itself. Consider, for example, an Employee entity that has a Manager attribute. The Manager attribute is domain based, and domain values come from the Employee entity itself. If the

Manager attribute has no value—that is, if it is NULL—then this member is on the top of the hierarchy. Recursive hierarchies have the following limitations:

- You can have only one recursive relationship in a derived hierarchy.

- In a recursive hierarchy, you cannot assign member permissions. You can think of member permissions as row-level security in a table.

- You cannot have circular relationships.

In an *explicit hierarchy*, entity members can be organized in any way. The hierarchy structure can be ragged, which means that the hierarchy can end at different levels. You create *consolidated members* for the purpose of grouping other members. A consolidated member belongs to a single explicit hierarchy. The leaf-level members can be under a single level or under multiple levels of consolidated members; however, you can include each leaf member in an explicit hierarchy only once. A consolidated member might not even have any leaf members. In order to use explicit hierarchies, you must enable them on an entity. An explicit hierarchy can be mandatory, in which all leaf-level members must be part of the hierarchy, or non-mandatory, where some leaf-level members are not part of the hierarchy. The leaf-level members that do not belong to a consolidated member remain in a special system-created node (consolidated member) called Unused.

You can also organize members into *collections*. A collection can include leaf-level and consolidated members of a single entity. A collection is not a hierarchical structure; it is, rather, a flat list of members. You can use collections when you do not need a complete hierarchy or when you want to create a completely custom group of members from any level.

EXAM TIP

Make sure you understand the difference between derived hierarchies, explicit hierarchies, and collections.

An entity can have many attributes. You can organize the attributes into *attribute groups*. Attribute groups help organize the user interface of the Master Data Manager application. Attribute groups are displayed as tabs in the user interface when a user manages data in the Explorer functional area of Master Data Manager. Each attribute group includes the Name and Code attributes. Any other attribute can belong to one or more attribute groups. There is a predefined attribute group, All Attributes, which, as you can conclude from its name, includes all attributes.

MDS can generate values for attributes automatically. You can generate sequential numbers for the Code attribute. You define an initial value, and MDS increases each subsequent Code value by one. End users can still insert a value of their choice, as long as it is unique. You can generate values for other attributes automatically as well, through MDS business rules. You can think of generating Code values automatically as similar to using the IDENTITY property in a SQL Server table, and you can think of generating other attribute values as similar to using an advanced DEFAULT constraint.

MDS business rules ensure data integrity. You can use business rules to find erroneous data, to automatically generate or update data, to send email messages, or to start a workflow. You express business rules as If/Then statements. If an attribute value meets a specific condition, then MDS takes an action. You can specify a condition to be a specific attribute value, or to be whenever an attribute value changes. In order to use business rules, you have to publish them after you create them. You can apply business rules to complete data or to just a subset of data, and you can apply them to a specific version of data. You will learn more about versioning master data in the next chapter of this book. Business rules are applied in a defined order, based on the action they take:

1. Generating a default value

2. Changing an existing value

3. Validation

4. External action, such as starting a workflow

You can define multiple business rules for any action and also define priority for the business rules. Then MDS will apply the business rules in the priority order you have specified within an action group.

 Quick Check

- You want to improve the quality of your master data. You want to prevent the insertion of inaccurate values into an attribute, and furthermore, you want to notify a data steward responsible for this attribute when an inaccurate value is inserted. How can you achieve these two tasks?

Quick Check Answer

- You can create one or more change value and/or validation business rules to prevent the insertion of inaccurate values or to correct inaccurate values automatically. You can create a business rule for an external action such as sending an email message in order to notify the data steward responsible for the attribute.

PRACTICE **Creating an MDS Model**

Suppose that you have been tasked with managing master data about customers. In this practice, you will create an MDS model with the objects needed.

EXERCISE 1 **Create a Model and Basic Objects**

In this exercise, you create a model with the entities, attributes, and hierarchies you need for the customers entity set.

1. If you closed the Master Data Manager application, reopen Internet Explorer, navigate to your Master Data Manager site, and log on. Navigate to the home page.

2. Click the System Administration link.

3. In the Model View, click the Manage tab, and then select the Models option.

4. In the Model Maintenance area, click the green plus (+) sign to add a model.

5. Name the model **TK463Customer**. Make sure that the check boxes for creating an entity with the same name and for creating an explicit hierarchy with the same name as the model name are selected, and that the check box for making the explicit hierarchy mandatory is cleared, as shown in Figure 15-7. Click the Save button in the upper-left corner.

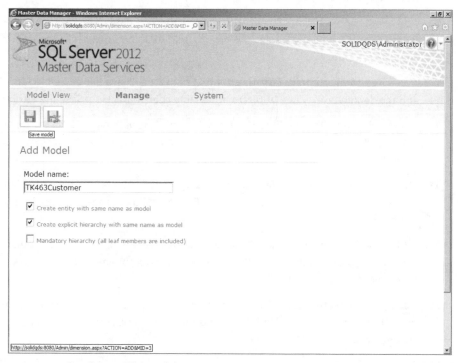

FIGURE 15-7 Creating an MDS model.

6. In the Model View, click the Manage tab again, and then select the Entities option. In the Model drop-down list, select the TK463Customer model. Click the TK463Customer entity to enable the Entity Maintenance buttons.

7. In the Entity Maintenance button list, click the Add Entity button, the button with the green plus (+) sign, to add an entity. Name the entity **StateProvince**. Select the Create Code Values Automatically check box. Do not enable explicit hierarchies and collections. Click the Save button.

8. Create another entity, **CountryRegion**, with the same settings as for the StateProvince entity, and save it.

9. Click the StateProvince entity in the list of entities. In the Entity Maintenance button group, click the Edit Selected Entity button (second from the left).

10. At the bottom of the page, click the Add Leaf Attribute button. Name the attribute **CountryRegion**. Make the new attribute domain based and use the CountryRegion entity for the domain values. Do not change the display pixel width or enable change tracking. Save the attribute and then save the entity.

11. Start editing the TK463Customer entity. Add a domain-based leaf-level attribute, **StateProvince**. Use the StateProvince entity for the domain of possible values. Do not enable change tracking. Save the attribute.

12. Add a free-form attribute, **StreetAddress**. Use the Text data type. Leave the default length (100). Change the display pixel width to 200. Do not enable change tracking. Save the attribute.

13. Add a free-form attribute, **City**. Use the Text data type. Leave the default length (100) and the default pixel width (100). Do not enable change tracking. Save the attribute.

14. Add a free-form attribute, **EmailAddress**. Use the Text data type. Leave the default length (100) and the default pixel width (100). Do not enable change tracking. Save the attribute.

15. Add a free-form attribute, **MaritalStatus**. Use the Text data type. Change the length to **1**. Change the display pixel width to **20**. Do not enable change tracking. Save the attribute.

16. Add a free-form attribute, **BirthDate**. Use the DateTime data type. Use the default pixel width (100). Use the yyyy/MM/dd input mask. Do not enable change tracking. Save the attribute.

17. Add a free-form attribute, **YearlyIncome**. Use the Number data type with two decimals. Use the default pixel width (100). Use the -#### input mask. Do not enable change tracking. Save the attribute.

18. Save the TK463Customer entity.

19. In the Model View, click the Manage tab, and then select the Attribute Groups option. In the Model drop-down list, select the TK463Customer model. In the Entity drop-down list, select the TK463Customer entity. Click the LeafGroups text to enable the Attribute Group Maintenance buttons.

20. Click the Add Attribute Group button. Name the group **Demography** and save it.

21. On the Attribute Group Maintenance page, click the small plus (+) sign near the Demography group under Leaf Groups to expand the folder. Click the Attributes name to enable the edit button, as shown in Figure 15-8. Click the Edit Selected Item button.

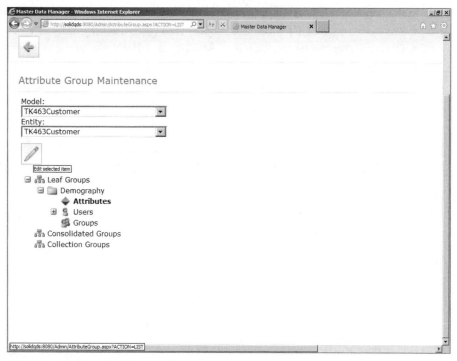

FIGURE 15-8 Editing a leaf-level attribute group.

22. Add MaritalStatus, BirthDate, and YearlyIncome to the group and save it.

23. In the Model View, click the Manage tab, and then select the Derived Hierarchies option. In the Model drop-down list, select the TK463Customer model.

24. Click the Add Derived Hierarchy button. Name the hierarchy **Geography** and save it.

25. On the Edit Derived Hierarchy: Geography page, drag the TK463Customer entity from the Available Entities And Hierarchies area on the left side to Current Levels on the right side. Also drag the StateProvince and CountryRegion entities to form the hierarchy. Click the Back To Model View button in the upper-left corner, the button with the green arrow.

26. In the Model View, click the Manage tab, and then select the Business Rules option. In the Model drop-down list, select the TK463Customer model. In the Entity drop-down list, select the TK463Customer entity. In the Member Type drop-down list, select the Leaf member type. In the Attribute drop-down list, select the EmailAddress attribute. Click the Add Business Rule button.

27. Double-click in the Name field in the table with the new business rule. Name the rule **EmailAt** and click outside the Name field to stop editing the field.

28. Make sure that your EmailAt rule is selected, and then click the Edit Selected Rule button.

29. In the Edit Business Rule: EmailAt window, click the small plus (+) sign near Actions in the Components area. Drag the Must Contain The Pattern action from the Validation area of the components and drop it on Actions in the THEN part in the lower-right section of the screen.

30. Drag the EmailAddress attribute onto the Select Attribute text in the Edit Action group under the THEN group in the lower-right of the screen. The text should change to EmailAddress and the Attribute Value text box should appear. Enter the at sign (@) in the text box, as shown in Figure 15-9.

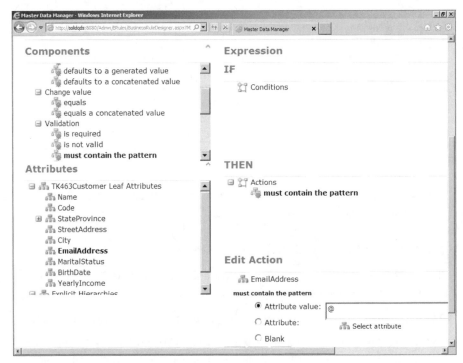

FIGURE 15-9 Editing a business rule.

31. Save the rule and then click the Back button.

32. On the Business Rule Maintenance page, click the Publish Business Rules button. In the window that appears, click OK. Click the Home button (the Microsoft SQL Server 2012 Master Data Services logo in the upper-left corner) to go to the Master Data Manager home page.

EXERCISE 2 Populate the Entities

In the final exercise of this chapter, you populate the entities and check your business rule.

1. If you closed the Master Data Manager application, reopen Internet Explorer, navigate to your Master Data Manager site, and log on. Navigate to the home page.

2. In the Model drop-down list, select the TK463Customer model. Click the Explorer link. The editor for the TK463Customer entity opens. However, you have to populate other entities first.

3. On the Entities tab, select the CountryRegion entity. In the editor, click the Add Member button.

4. In the Details window, enter **Australia** for the value of the Name field. Note that the value for the Code field is assigned automatically. Click OK.

5. Add another member with the value **United States** for the Name field.

6. On the Entities tab, select the StateProvince entity. In the editor, click the Add Member button.

7. In the Details window, enter **Queensland** for the value of the Name field. Note that the value for the Code field is assigned automatically. In the CountryRegion drop-down list, select the value 1. Click OK.

8. Add another member with the value **Washington** for the Name field. Click the button to the right of the CountryRegion drop-down list to open another window with a list of members of the CountryRegion entity. Check the code for the United States member. Go back to the window where you are editing the StateProvince entity and insert the appropriate CountryRegion code. Click OK. Your StateProvince entity should look like the one shown in Figure 15-10.

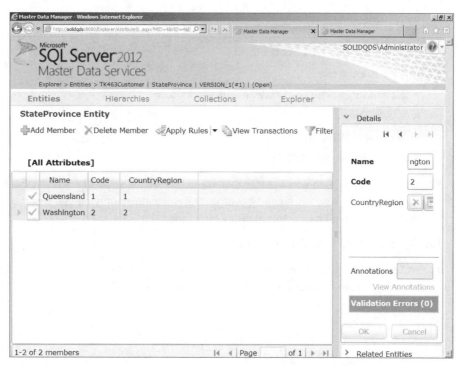

FIGURE 15-10 The members of the StateProvince entity.

9. On the Entities tab, select the TK463Customer entity. Note that there are two views—one with the attributes from the Demography attribute group only and one with all attributes. Click the [All Attributes] tab to see all of the attributes. You are going to add two members with data based on the customers data from the *dbo.DimCustomer* table in the AdventureWorksDW2012 sample database. In the editor, click the Add Member button.

10. Insert the following information and then click OK:

   - Name: **Jon Yang**
   - Code: **1**
   - StateProvince: **1**
   - StreetAddress: **3761 N. 14th St**
   - City: **Rockhampton**
   - EmailAddress: **jon24@adventure-works.com**
   - MaritalStatus: **M**
   - BirthDate: **1970/04/08**
   - YearlyIncome: **90,000.00**

11. Add another customer with the following information:

   - Name: **Lauren Walker**
   - Code: **2**
   - StateProvince: **2**
   - StreetAddress: **4785 Scott Street**
   - City: **Bremerton**
   - EmailAddress: **lauren41#adventure-works.com**
   - MaritalStatus: **M**
   - BirthDate: **1970/01/18**
   - YearlyIncome: **100,000.00**

12. Before clicking OK to save the member, try to change the value of the MaritalStatus field to UNKNOWN. You should get an error immediately notifying you that the length of this field cannot be greater than 1. Correct the value back to M.

13. Try to insert the birth date in a different format.

14. Note that the EmailAddress field contains the # character instead of the @ character. Click OK to save the member anyway.

15. Note that in the grid showing all customers, there is a red exclamation point near the Lauren Walker entry. Point to it and read the message. Note also the message about validation errors in the Details pane on the right, as shown in Figure 15-11.

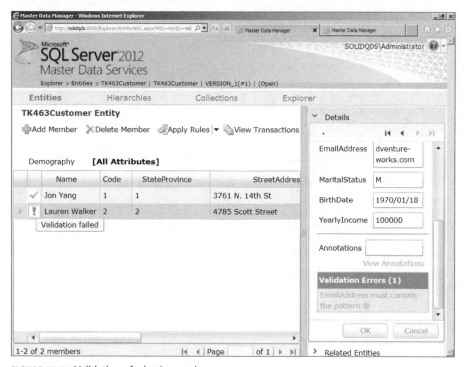

FIGURE 15-11 Validation of a business rule.

16. In the Details pane, correct the value in the EmailAddress field and click OK. Now the validation should succeed.

17. Close all Internet Explorer windows.

Lesson Summary

- In MDS, models are containers for other objects.
- Entities have attributes, derived and explicit hierarchies, collections, and attribute groups.
- Attributes can be free-form, file, or domain based.
- You can define several business rules for each attribute.

Lesson Review

Answer the following questions to test your knowledge of the information in this lesson. You can find the answers to these questions and explanations of why each answer choice is correct or incorrect in the "Answers" section at the end of this chapter.

1. Why would you create a consolidated member?

    A. To serve as the root for derived hierarchies

    B. To enable advanced attribute data types

    C. To enable attribute groups

    D. To group other members in an explicit hierarchy

2. In which order, based on the actions they take, are business rules applied?

    A. Default value – change value – validation – external action

    B. Change value – default value – validation – external action

    C. Default value – change value – external action – validation

    D. Default value – validation – change value – external action

3. What types of attributes of an entity are supported in MDS? (Choose all that apply.)

    A. Free-form

    B. Unnamed

    C. File

    D. Domain-based

Case Scenarios

In the following case scenarios, you apply what you've learned about implementing Master Data Services. You can find the answers to these questions in the "Answers" section at the end of this chapter.

Case Scenario 1: Introducing an MDM Solution

A company you know complains about data quality. The company acquired three smaller companies in the past, and now they have four different LOB systems. They have big problems with inaccurate and duplicate customer data. In addition, they would like to implement a data warehouse. You need to help this company. Answer the following questions:

1. Is this company a candidate for a master data management solution?

2. What data would you immediately define as master data?

3. Would an MDM solution provide a reasonable ROI for this company?

Case Scenario 2: Extending the POC Project

Assume that you have implemented Master Data Services for the company in Case Scenario 1. However, your customer was still not satisfied. When interviewing department managers, you discovered some points of dissatisfaction.

Interviews

Here's a list of company personnel who expressed some dissatisfaction during their interviews, along with their statements:

- **Sales Manager** "Information about marketing campaign discounts for specific customers frequently comes from the Marketing department after the sales are already done."

- **Marketing Manager** "In the Sales department, they want to update data about discounts, whereas our department clearly owns this data."

You need to solve these issues.

Questions

1. What do you think is missing in the MDM solution you implemented?

2. Would you suggest any specific role for customer and campaign data?

Suggested Practices

To help you successfully master the exam objectives presented in this chapter, complete the following tasks.

Analyze the AdventureWorks2012 Database

To understand exactly how to define master data, examine the AdventureWorks2012 OLTP sample database thoroughly.

- **Practice 1** Find tables that are candidates for master data tables.
- **Practice 2** Find all tables with transactional data.

Expand the MDS Model

In addition to practices in this module, you can expand your MDS model.

- **Practice 1** Add more entities and attributes. Add address information to the TK463Customer entity.
- **Practice 2** Define rules for address patterns.
- **Practice 3** Define additional attribute collections.

Answers

This section contains answers to the lesson review questions and solutions to the case scenarios in this chapter.

Lesson 1

1. **Correct answers: A, B, and D**

   A. **Correct:** When you implement an MDM solution, one of the most important goals is to reuse the master data as much as possible.

   B. **Correct:** If you need versioning, then versioning should be a goal of master data management.

   C. **Incorrect:** Although performance tuning of queries could be an important issue for a company, it is not one of the MDM goals.

   D. **Correct:** One of the most important goals of MDM is improving data quality.

   E. **Incorrect:** Your data model, database, and application constraints should take care of data integrity. MDM cares about a more complex problem—data quality.

2. **Correct answers: C and D**

   A. **Incorrect:** You should take care of the relationships between entities in your data model.

   B. **Incorrect:** Database normalization is part of relational database modeling, not part of master data management.

   C. **Correct:** Data authority could be an important challenge when introducing an MDM solution.

   D. **Correct:** Whenever there are multiple sources of master data in a company, you can expect data conflicts.

3. **Correct answer: B**

   A. **Incorrect:** Data stewardship is the role that implements the master data policies.

   B. **Correct:** Data governance sets the policies for master data.

   C. **Incorrect:** Data integrity rules define how data conforms to business rules.

   D. **Incorrect:** Data quality prescriptions deal with data completeness, accuracy, and similar characteristics.

Lesson 2

1. **Correct answer: C**

   A. **Incorrect:** The Application Server role is not needed for MDS.

   B. **Incorrect:** The Remote Desktop Services role is not needed for MDS.

   C. **Correct:** The Web Server (IIS) role is needed for MDS.

   D. **Incorrect:** The DNS Server role is not needed for MDS.

2. **Correct answers: A, B, D, and E**

   A. **Correct:** You can use the Master Data Manger web application to enter data.

   B. **Correct:** You can import data through staging tables in the MDS database.

   C. **Incorrect:** You cannot use Word 2010 to enter data in your MDS database.

   D. **Correct:** Advanced users can use the MDS add-in for Excel to enter data into the MDS database.

   E. **Correct:** You can integrate MDS to your application with the help of the Master Data Manager web service and then enter the data from your application.

3. **Correct answer: D**

   A. **Incorrect:** The MDS database stores the master data along with MDS system objects.

   B. **Incorrect:** Excel with the MDS add-in for Excel is a rich MDS client application for advanced users.

   C. **Incorrect:** Master Data Manager is a web application for MDS users and administrators.

   D. **Correct:** The MDS service performs the business logic and data access for the MDS solution.

Lesson 3

1. **Correct answer: D**

   A. **Incorrect:** A derived hierarchy has its own root member.

   B. **Incorrect:** Attribute data types are fixed; you cannot add them.

   C. **Incorrect:** Attribute groups are always enabled.

   D. **Correct:** You create consolidated members to group other members in an explicit hierarchy.

2. **Correct answer: A**

   A. **Correct:** The order in which MDS applies business rules by the action they take is default value – change value – validation – external action.

   B. **Incorrect:** The order in which MDS applies business rules by the action they take is default value – change value – validation – external action.

   C. **Incorrect:** The order in which MDS applies business rules by the action they take is default value – change value – validation – external action.

   D. **Incorrect:** The order in which MDS applies business rules by the action they take is default value – change value – validation – external action.

3. **Correct answers: A, C, and D**

   A. **Correct:** MDS supports free-form types of attributes.

   B. **Incorrect:** Every attribute must have a name in MDS.

   C. **Correct:** MDS supports file types of attributes.

   D. **Correct:** MDS supports domain-based types of attributes.

Case Scenario 1

1. Yes, this company is prepared for an MDM solution.

2. Customer data is definitely part of master data.

3. An MDM solution would give a reasonable ROI to this company. With an MDM solution, you would resolve data conflicts. Data is reused in many places and will be reused even more with a data warehouse implemented.

Case Scenario 2

1. You didn't resolve authority problems. In addition, you didn't define workflow properly.

2. You should suggest to your customer that they define an explicit data stewardship role. Currently each department is responsible for its own part of the master data; data stewards should be responsible for the complete master data.

## CHAPTER 16

Managing Master Data

Exam objectives in this chapter:

- Build Data Quality Solutions
  - Implement master data management solutions.

U sing a master data management (MDM) solution that does not exchange data with other databases and applications makes no sense. You should use Microsoft SQL Server 2012 Master Data Services (MDS) as an authoritative source of master data for as many applications in the enterprise as possible. When you use MDS for the first time, you probably already have some master data. In this chapter, you will learn how to import master data to MDS and export it to other applications.

For times when you want to edit a batch of master data entities, such as customers from one region, but find the Master Data Manager application too slow, you will learn how to use Microsoft Excel 2010 with Master Data Services Add-in for Excel as an advanced MDS client.

Master data must be secured. You will also learn how to define MDS security.

Lessons in this chapter:

- Lesson 1: Importing and Exporting Master Data
- Lesson 2: Defining Master Data Security
- Lesson 3: Using Master Data Services Add-in for Excel

Before You Begin

To complete this chapter, you must have:

- SQL Server 2012 Master Data Services installed.
- Excel 2010 with MDS Add-in for Excel installed.
- An understanding of Windows security.
- An understanding of SQL Server security.
- Basic Excel skills.

Lesson 1: Importing and Exporting Master Data

Importing and exporting data might involve dealing with metadata as well. Sometimes you will have to transfer the complete MDS model to another server. You perform such transfers by creating MDS *model deployment packages* and deploying the packages on other servers. MDS packages include metadata and, if needed, data as well. You can import batches of data from existing systems through MDS staging tables. You can export data to other systems through MDS subscription views.

> **After this lesson, you will be able to:**
> - Create and deploy MDS model deployment packages.
> - Import batches of data through staging tables.
> - Export MDS data through subscription views.
>
> **Estimated lesson time: 75 minutes**

Creating and Deploying MDS Packages

An MDS model deployment package is an XML file that contains MDS metadata and some-times data as well. You can use MDS packages to transfer MDS models from one MDS instance to another.

MDS packages have the default file extension .pkg. These files include the following meta-data from MDS models:

- Entities
- Attributes
- Attribute groups
- Hierarchies
- Collections
- Business rules
- Version flags
- Subscription views

Note that permissions are not included. After you deploy a model to a new MDS instance, you have to assign appropriate permissions to users. You will learn more about security in the next lesson of this chapter.

You can create and deploy MDS packages by using two different tools:

- The Model Deployment Wizard, which is accessible from the Master Data Manager application
- The MDSModelDeploy command prompt utility

If you create a package with the Model Deployment Wizard, you can only include meta-data. If you want to include data in your model deployment package, you have to use the MDSModelDeploy utility. This utility is located in the MDS Configuration folder. If you used the default installation path, this folder is in C:\Program Files\Microsoft SQL Server\110 \Master Data Services\Configuration. You run this utility from the command prompt, from its installation folder. Following are some examples of how to use this utility. By running just the command, as shown in the following example, you get a list of all possible commands for this utility.

```
MDSModelDeploy
```

You can get help for a specific command, such as the listmodels command that lists all of the models from an MDS instance, with the following command.

```
MDSModelDeploy help listmodels
```

Finally, here is an example of how to create a deployment package from an MDS model with data included.

```
MDSModelDeploy createpackage -model TK463Customer -version VERSION_1
 -package C:\TK463\Chapter16\TK463CustomerData.pkg -includedata
```

Importing Batches of Data

Importing batches of data is a very straightforward process. First you load the data to staging tables. Then you use a *staging process* to load the data from the staging tables to MDS models. You can use the staging process to:

- Create, update, deactivate, and delete leaf and consolidated members.
- Update attribute values.
- Designate relationships in explicit hierarchies.

The first step in uploading data is to populate the staging tables. Each entity in your model can have three associated staging tables in the *stg* schema:

- **stg.entityname_Leaf**   The staging table where you insert leaf-level members for an entity with the name entityname. The columns of this table will be described in detail later in this lesson.

- **stg.entityname_Consolidated**   The staging table you populate with consolidated members.

- **stg.entityname_Relationship**   You can use this table to move batches of members in an explicit hierarchy.

After you populate the staging tables, you initiate the staging process from the Master Data Manager application or by calling staging stored procedures. Each staging table has an associated staging procedure. The names of the staging procedures follow conventions similar to those for staging table names—*stg.upd_entityname_Leaf, stg.upd_entityname_Consolidated,* and *stg.upd_entityname_Relationship.*

The staging process can take some time, depending on the amount of data you are importing. MDS starts the staging process asynchronously after you initiate it from the Master Data Manager application. The staging process starts at intervals that are determined by the Staging Batch Interval setting for the MDS database. By default, this interval is set to 60 seconds. You can change it with Master Data Services Configuration Manager.

If you start the staging process with staging procedures, you can also log transactions. If you start the process from the Master Data Manager application, transactions are not logged.

After you import data, you have to validate it against business rules. You can initiate validation from the Master Data Manager application or by calling the validation stored procedure mdm.udpValidateModel.

The *stg.entityname_Leaf* table has the following columns:

- **ID**   This is an automatically assigned integer. You should not provide it when you are inserting data into this table.

- **ImportType**   The value in this column determines what to do if data you inserted in the staging table already exists in the model. This is a required column of type TINYINT. Some of the most important codes for this column include:

    - 0: Use this when you want to create new members and replace existing data with the staging data, but only if the staging data is not NULL.

    - 1: Use this when you want to create new members only.

    - 2: Use this when you want to create new members and replace existing data with the staging data, even if the staging data is NULL.

- **ImportStatus_ID**   This is the status of the import process. You have to specify a value of 0 here. After the staging process finishes, this value is updated to either 1, meaning a successful import of a record, or 2, if the import of the record failed.

- **Batch_ID**   The value for this column is assigned automatically by the staging process.

- **BatchTag**   You have to provide a unique name for the batch, up to 50 characters.

- **ErrorCode**   The value of this column is populated automatically by the staging process if the import of the record failed. You can use Books Online for SQL Server 2012 to find details about each error code.

- **Code**   This is a unique member code. You have to provide this value if you do not use automatically generated codes.

- **Name**   This is the name of the member.

- **NewCode**   This is the new code of a member. Use this only if you want to change the existing code of a member. Note that changing member codes, like changing primary keys in relational tables, is a bad practice.

- **<Attribute name>**   There is one column for each attribute of an entity. Note that for domain-based attributes, you need to find the appropriate value of the Code attribute of the entity that serves as the domain of possible values.

 Quick Check

- Can you deploy an existing MDS model to another MDS instance with data included?

Quick Check Answer

- Yes. You have to extract the package with the MDSModelDeploy command.

Exporting Data

 As you already know, data reusage is one of the most important goals of master data management. Master Data Services allows you to use data in other applications in two ways: through methods exposed by the *MDS web service* and through subscription views. You can use web methods from any Microsoft .NET application. *Subscription views* are regular SQL Server views created in an MDS database. You can export master data by using T-SQL queries on subscription views. You can expose the following data through subscription views:

- All leaf members and their attributes

- All consolidated members and their attributes

- All collections and their attributes

- The members explicitly added to a collection

- The members in a derived hierarchy, in either a parent/child or level format

- The members in all explicit hierarchies for an entity, in either a parent/child or level format

You can create subscription views with the Master Data Manager web application, in the Integration Management area, on the Create Views tab. On that tab, you can create a new view and check existing views in a grid. Subscription views can become outdated when schemas of underlying entities changes. Schema changes are not propagated automatically to subscription views. In the grid on the Create Views page, there is a column called Changed. When this column shows a value of True, you should regenerate the subscription view. You regenerate a view when you edit it and save it. You will become familiar with this part of the Master Data Manager application in the practice exercises for this lesson.

In this practice, you will create a model package, delete a model, and then deploy the package to get an empty MDS model. Then you will populate the model by using the staging process. During the staging process, you will need subscription views to get the code values of the members of entities that serve as domains of possible values for attributes of other entities.

If you encounter a problem completing an exercise, you can install the completed projects from the Solution folder that is provided with the companion content for this chapter and lesson.

EXERCISE 1   Create a Model Deployment Package and Deploy the Package

In the first exercise, you create a model deployment package, delete your model, and then re-create the model by deploying the package.

1. Open the Master Data Manager application and log on to your MDS instance.

2. Click the System Administration link.

3. Point to the System tab and select Deployment. The Model Deployment Wizard should start, as shown in Figure 16-1.

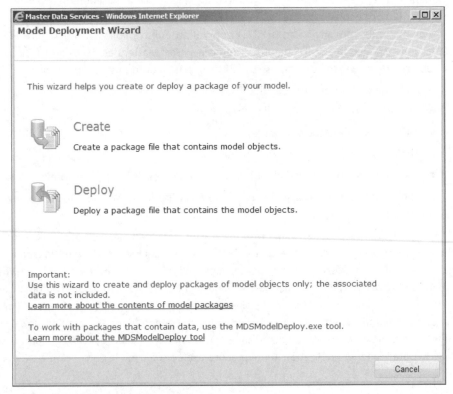

FIGURE 16-1 The Model Deployment Wizard.

4. Click the Create link.

5. On the Create Package page, select the TK463Customer model and click Next. Note that you need to have the TK463Customer model created. This model was created in the practice for Lesson 3 of Chapter 15, "Implementing Master Data Services."

6. Wait while the package is created. When the message on the Create Package page says that the package was created successfully, click the Download button.

7. Save the package as a file with the name **TK463Customer.pkg** in the Solution folder for this practice. Click the Close button.

8. When the Model Deployment Wizard closes, you should be back in the System Administration area of the Master Data Manager application. Point to the Manage tab and select Models from the pop-up list.

9. On the Model Maintenance page, select the TK463Customer model. Click the Delete button (the icon with the red cross). Click OK in the first message box.

10. Note the message in the second message box. It informs you that you are going to delete all data from the model. Click OK.

11. Navigate to the Master Data Manager System Administration area.

12. Point to the System tab, and select Deployment.

13. Click the Deploy link.

14. On the Deploy Package page, click the Browse button.

15. In the Choose File To Upload window, navigate to the package you just saved. Note that if you did not do the practices in the previous chapter and you do not have a package in the Solution folder, you can upload the package provided in the Starter folder for this lesson.

16. Select the TK463Customer.pkg file and click Open. The Choose File To Upload window should close.

17. On the Deploy Package page, click Next.

18. When you see the message informing you that the package was loaded successfully on the Deploy Package page, click Next.

19. Wait until the package is deployed. Then click Finish.

20. Use the Explorer functional area of the Master Data Manager application to check whether all entities from the TK463Customer model were recreated. Note that all entities are empty.

EXERCISE 2   Import Data and Create Subscription Views

In the second exercise, you upload data in batches. You also create subscription views to get codes of members of entities used for domains of possible values for attributes of other entities.

1. Open SQL Server Management Studio (SSMS) and connect to your SQL Server instance with the MDS database. Open a new query window. Change the context to the MDSTK463 database.

2. In the Object Explorer, try to find the staging tables for your model.

3. You should have the following staging tables—*stg.CountryRegion_Leaf, stg.StateProvince_Leaf, stg.TK463Customer_Leaf, stg.TK463Customer_Consolidated,* and *stg.TK463Customer_Relationship.*

4. Use the following query to populate the *stg.CountryRegion_Leaf* table.

```
INSERT INTO stg.CountryRegion_Leaf
  (ImportType, ImportStatus_ID, BatchTag, Name)
SELECT DISTINCT 1, 0, N'CountryRegionLeaf_Batch00001',
  G.EnglishCountryRegionName
FROM AdventureWorksDW2012.dbo.DimCustomer AS C
  INNER JOIN AdventureWorksDW2012.dbo.DimGeography AS G
    ON C.GeographyKey = G.GeographyKey;
```

5. In the Master Data Manager application, on the home page, click the Integration Management link.

6. On the Import Data page, make sure that the TK463Customer model is selected in the upper-left drop-down list.

7. Click the Start Batches button to start the staging process, as shown in Figure 16-2.

8. In the Run Selected Batches pop-up window, make sure that the VERSION_1 version is selected, and click OK.

9. Note that the status of the batch is QueuedToRun. Wait for about a minute and then refresh the web page. The status should change to Completed.

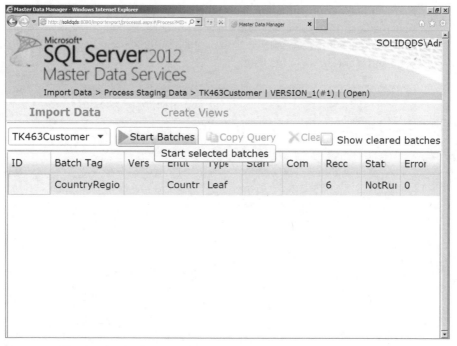

FIGURE 16-2 Starting the staging process.

10. Use the Explorer functionality of the Master Data Manager application to check the data that was imported for the six countries. Note the automatically assigned codes. Note also that members have not been validated yet.

11. In the Apply Rules drop-down list, select the Apply To All option. Click OK in the Apply To All pop-up window.

12. Refresh the page. All members should be successfully validated.

13. Before importing data into the StateProvince entity, you need to have the Country-Region generated codes available. You need to create a subscription view for the CountryRegion entity. Navigate to the Integration Management area. Click the Create Views tab.

14. In the Subscription Views window, click the Add Subscription View button.

15. Name the view **CountryRegion**. Select the TK463Customer model, the VERSION_1 version, the CountryRegion entity, and the Leaf members format, as shown in Figure 16-3. Note that the Format drop-down list is on the right side of the Create Subscription View page and is not shown in the figure.

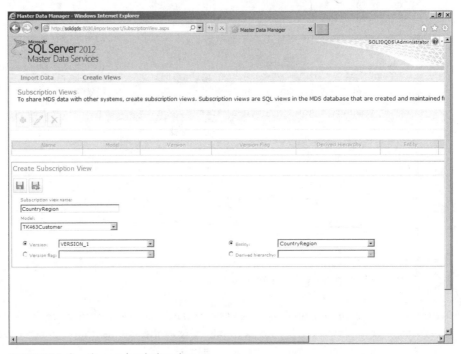

FIGURE 16-3 Creating a subscription view.

16. Click the Save button.

17. Use the following query to populate the *stg.StateProvince_Leaf* table.

```
INSERT INTO stg.StateProvince_Leaf
 (ImportType, ImportStatus_ID, BatchTag,
  Name, CountryRegion)
SELECT DISTINCT 1, 0, N'StateProvinceLeaf_Batch00001',
 G.StateProvinceName, CR.Code
FROM AdventureWorksDW2012.dbo.DimCustomer AS C
 INNER JOIN AdventureWorksDW2012.dbo.DimGeography AS G
  ON C.GeographyKey = G.GeographyKey
 INNER JOIN mdm.CountryRegion AS CR
  ON G.EnglishCountryRegionName = CR.Name;
```

18. Start the staging process for populating the StateProvince entity. When it is finished, validate all members of this entity.

19. Create a subscription view for the StateProvince entity. Name it **StateProvince**; use the same settings for other options as you used for the CountryRegion subscription view.

20. Use the following query to populate the *stg.TK463Customer_Leaf* staging table.

```
INSERT INTO stg.TK463Customer_Leaf
 (ImportType, ImportStatus_ID, BatchTag,
  Code, Name, StateProvince, StreetAddress,
  City, EmailAddress, MaritalStatus,
  BirthDate, YearlyIncome)
SELECT 1, 0, N'TK463Customer_Batch00001',
 C.CustomerKey,
 C.FirstName + ' ' + c.LastName AS Name,
 SP.Code, C.AddressLine1 AS StreetAddress,
 G.City, C.EmailAddress, C.MaritalStatus,
 C.BirthDate, C.YearlyIncome
FROM AdventureWorksDW2012.dbo.DimCustomer AS C
 INNER JOIN AdventureWorksDW2012.dbo.DimGeography AS G
  ON C.GeographyKey = G.GeographyKey
 INNER JOIN mdm.StateProvince AS SP
  ON G.StateProvinceName = SP.Name
WHERE C.CustomerKey % 10 = 0;
```

Note that the query selects each tenth customer only in order to speed up the process. Also note that this time the original customer key is used for the *Code* column value. For this entity, MDS does not generate the code values automatically.

21. Start the staging process for populating the TK463Customer entity. When it is finished, validate all members of this entity.

> **NOTE   CONTINUING WITH PRACTICES**
>
> Do not exit SSMS if you intend to continue immediately with the next practice.

Lesson Summary

- You can use model deployment packages to export and import metadata, and in some cases data as well.
- You can use the staging process for importing batches of data.
- Applications can use the MDS web service and subscription views to get master data from an MDS instance.

Lesson Review

Answer the following questions to test your knowledge of the information in this lesson. You can find the answers to these questions and explanations of why each answer choice is correct or incorrect in the "Answers" section at the end of this chapter.

1. After you insert data to staging tables, how can you initiate the staging process? (Choose all that apply.)

   A. By executing the staging procedures

   B. By starting the InitiateStaging SQL Server Agent job created when you installed MDS

   C. By using the Master Data Manager application

   D. By using the MDSModelDeploy command prompt utility

2. How can you export model data and metadata together?

   A. By using the Model Deployment Wizard

   B. By creating subscription views

   C. By using the staging process

   D. By using the MDSModelDeploy command prompt utility

3. What can you do with the staging process? (Choose all that apply.)

   A. Create hierarchies.

   B. Create, update, deactivate, and delete leaf and consolidated members.

   C. Update attribute values.

   D. Designate relationships in explicit hierarchies.

   E. Change the attribute data type.

Lesson 2: Defining Master Data Security

Master data is the most important part of data in an enterprise. Of course, because of its importance, you have to take special care about security. Master Data Services supports very detailed security settings.

> **After this lesson, you will be able to:**
> - Describe MDS security.
> - Define MDS security.
>
> **Estimated lesson time: 30 minutes**

Users and Permissions

MDS security is based on Windows local users and groups and Active Directory users and groups. You enable access to an MDS application to a Windows user or group. Inside MDS, users are separated into two distinct groups: *Administrators* and regular *users*. To give an MDS user permission to use MDS, you have to assign:

- **Functional area access**   This determines which of the functional areas of the Master Data Manager application a user can access.

- **Model object permissions**   This determines which objects in a model a user can access.

- **Hierarchy member permissions**   This determines which members of a hierarchy a user can access.

The use of hierarchy member permissions is an advanced option that limits permissions on specific subtrees or members in a hierarchy. An end user needs at least functional area access and model object permissions in order to use Master Data Services. Permissions can also overlap and become quite complicated. You will learn more about overlapping permissions later in this lesson.

REAL WORLD   **COMPLEX SECURITY SETTINGS**

Keep security settings as simple as possible. In real projects, whenever security is too complicated, the system is actually not secure. This is true for all applications and databases, not only for MDS.

There are two levels of administrators in MDS: the *MDS System Administrator* and *Model Administrators*. The MDS System Administrator is only one user. You specify the MDS System Administrator by defining the Administrator Account when you create the MDS database in the MDS Configuration Manager tool. The MDS System Administrator has access to all functional areas of Master Data Manager, including the Explorer area, and to all models. Thus, the MDS System Administrator can update data in any model of the MDS instance.

Sometimes you need to change the MDS System Administrator. There is no user interface for this task within current MDS tools. An MDS instance stores all users, including users with administrative permissions, in its database, in the *mdm.tblUser* table. In order to change the MDS System Administrator, you need to have permissions to view this table, and to execute the mdm.udpSecuritySetAdministrator MDS system stored procedure. In order to change the System Administrator, you need to:

1. Use SSMS to query the *mdm.tblUser* table. You need to find the user who will be the new administrator and copy the value in the *SID* column for this user.

2. Use the following piece of code (replace *DOMAIN\user_name* with the new administrator's user name, and replace *SID* with the value you got in the previous step).

   ```
   EXEC mdm.udpSecuritySetAdministrator @UserName='DOMAIN\user_name', @SID = 'SID', @
   PromoteNonAdmin = 1
   ```

Model Administrators are the users who have Update permissions on the complete model—that is, on the top-level object—and no other assigned permissions on lower levels, such as the entity level. However, Model Administrators still need functional area access in order to do anything with the Master Data Manager application. If you need to have multiple Model Administrators for a model, consider grouping the users as early as possible, into Windows groups. If you define Windows groups appropriately, after you set up MDS security you can maintain the MDS security simply by maintaining Windows group membership.

Regular users access MDS through Windows users and groups. A regular user must have some permission on model objects and Explorer functional area access to start using MDS. You should use Windows groups as much as possible in order to simplify administration. However, note that even if you give access to a Windows group only, a Windows user who is a member of that group is added automatically to MDS users when the user logs on to MDS for the first time. In addition, if you delete the group from MDS, the user is not automatically deleted. Of course, the user does not retain any group permissions and cannot use MDS unless you assigned some permission to the user directly.

Functional area access includes access to five functional areas of the Master Data Management application:

- Explorer
- Version Management
- Integration Management
- System Administration
- User and Group Permissions

Model object permissions determine access to objects in an MDS model. You can define permissions up to the attribute level of granularity. You can assign Read-Only, Update, or Deny permissions. The Deny permission denies any access to the object and overrides other permissions. You can use this permission to make sure a user can't access some model objects even if the group of which the user is a member has Update or Read-Only permission on the same object.

You start assigning model object permissions by granting the Update permission on the model. Permissions are inherited. If you don't specify permissions on a lower level of granularity, then the user is a Model Administrator. For regular users, you override the inherited permissions by assigning permissions on objects inside the model.

Model permissions apply to all entities, derived hierarchies, explicit hierarchies, and collections of that model. *Entity permissions* apply to all attributes, including Name and Code, for leaf and consolidated members, all collections, and all explicit hierarchies and relationships. *Leaf permissions* apply to attribute values of leaf-level members of an entity. For entities without explicit hierarchies, assigning leaf permissions is the same as assigning entity permissions. *Consolidated permissions* apply to the attribute values for consolidated members of entities that have explicit hierarchies enabled. *Collection permissions* apply to all collections for an entity; you can't assign permissions for individual collections.

MDS has also an implicit permission, *Navigational Access*. This permission is granted automatically to a user for higher levels of model objects than objects for which a user has some permissions assigned. For example, if a user has permission to update an attribute, the user automatically has the Navigational Access permission for the model and entity where the attribute is defined. This enables the user to navigate to the level where he or she has assigned permissions.

If you want a user to have limited access to specific members, you can use the *hierarchy member* permissions. You can assign permissions to any node of any hierarchy. Hierarchy member permissions are not applied immediately; they are applied asynchronously, in regular intervals. If you need to apply hierarchy member permissions immediately, you have to use the mdm.udpSecurityMemberProcessRebuildModel MDS system stored procedure.

EXAM TIP

Be sure you have a thorough understanding of how MDS determines effective permissions for a user.

Overlapping Permissions

In order to keep the security settings as simple as possible, you should use model object permissions only. If you assign *the same* (Read-Only or Update) hierarchy member permissions as well, then MDS resolves the *effective permissions* as an intersection of object and member permissions.

If permissions on objects and members differ, then MDS determines permissions for each individual attribute value. This situation is known as *overlapping model and member permissions*. In such a case, the effective permissions are determined to be the most restrictive ones:

- Deny overrides all other permissions.
- Read-Only overrides Update.

A user can belong to multiple groups. You can assign permissions to multiple groups and to the user directly. If each group and the user have assigned permissions to different objects and members, then the effective permissions are the union of all permissions. If you assign different permissions to groups and to a user for the same object, then you have *overlapping user and group permissions*. In this case, MDS determines effective permissions by using the following logic:

- Deny overrides all other permissions.
- Update overrides Read-Only.

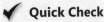

> ### ✔ Quick Check
>
> - A user is a member of two groups. You give Read-Only permission for an object to the first group, Update permission for the same object to the second group, and Read-Only permission for the same object to the user. What effective permission does the user have for that object?
>
> ### Quick Check Answer
>
> - The user has the Update effective permission for that object.

PRACTICE **Defining MDS Security**

In this practice, you will implement and test MDS security.

EXERCISE 1 Assign Permissions

In the first exercise, you create a Windows user and then assign permissions to the user. The user should become a Model Administrator for your TK463Customer model.

1. Use Server Manager or the Active Directory Users And Computers console to create a user named **TK463MDSAdmin**. Assign the password **Pa$$w0rd** to the user. Clear the User Must Change Password At Next Login check box in the New User dialog box, as shown in Figure 16-4.

FIGURE 16-4 Creating a Windows user.

2. If you closed Master Data Manager, open it. On the Home page, navigate to the User And Group Permissions area.

3. On the Manage Users page, click the Add Users button.

4. On the Add Users page, enter **domain\TK463MDSAdmin** in the User Names text box, where *domain* is either the domain in which you created the users and group or the name of your stand-alone server, if you are using a stand-alone server.

5. Click the Check Name icon (the small icon below the lower-right corner of the User Names text box), as Figure 16-5 shows. Then click OK.

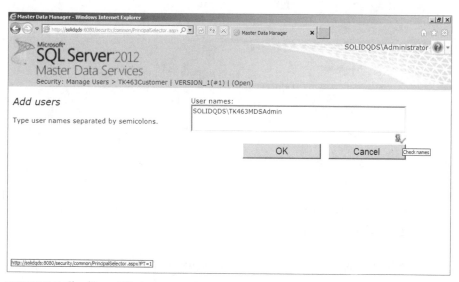

FIGURE 16-5 Checking a Windows user name.

6. In the Users grid, select the TK463MDSAdmin user. Click the Edit Selected User icon.

7. Read the information on the General tab.

8. Click the Functions tab. Click the Edit button.

9. In the Available Functions list box, click Explorer, and then click the single right arrow to add Explorer to the Assigned Functions list box. Note that if you click the icon with two right arrows, all functional areas are added to the Assigned Functions list box.

10. Repeat the same process for the Integration Management functional area. Then click the Save button.

11. Click the Models tab. In the Model drop-down list, select the TK463Customer model. Click the Edit button.

12. In the Model Permissions tree, right-click the TK463Customer model and select the Update permission, as Figure 16-6 shows. Click the Save button.

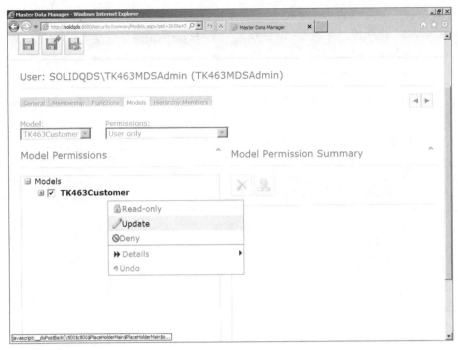

FIGURE 16-6 Assigning model permission to a user.

The TK463MDSAdmin user is now a Model Administrator for your model.

13. Explore permissions on lower-level objects. Check the Hierarchy Members tab as well.

14. When you are done exploring, click the back button (the button with the green left-pointing arrow, in the upper-left corner of the page).

> **NOTE CONTINUING WITH PRACTICES**
>
> Leave Master Data Manager open if you intend to continue with the practice for the next lesson.

EXERCISE 2 Test Permissions

You are ready to test the permissions of the TK463MDSAdmin user.

1. Run Internet Explorer in the context of the *domain*\TK463MDSAdmin user. In Windows Server 2008 R2, you can do this by holding the Shift button while right-clicking the Internet Explorer link from the Start | All Programs menu and then selecting the Run As Different User option.

2. Enter the *domain*\TK463MDSAdmin user credentials in the Windows Security pop-up window.

3. In Internet Explorer, navigate to the Master Data Manager home page.

4. Another login window should appear, this time for you to log on to your MDS instance. Again, enter the *domain*\TK463MDSAdmin user credentials.

If you connected successfully, you should see Master Data Manager with only the Explorer (including a link for installing MDS Add-in for Excel) and Integration Management functional areas available.

5. Click in the Model drop-down list. Only the TK463Customer model should be available, as Figure 16-7 shows.

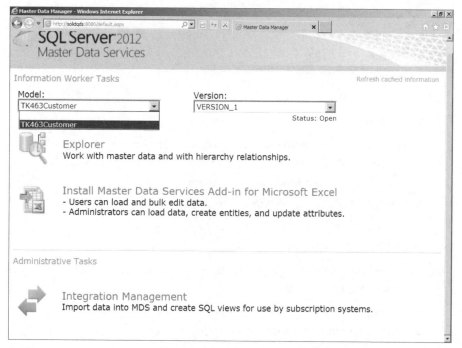

FIGURE 16-7 Limited options in Master Data Manager for the TK463MDSAdmin user.

6. Close this Master Data Manager instance.

7. If you need to clean up, delete the TK463MDSAdmin user from MDS and from Windows.

Lesson Summary

- Keep security settings simple.
- An end user must have at least Explorer functional area access and permissions on at least one object from a model in order to get access to the model.
- Overlapping permissions make security more complicated.

Lesson Review

Answer the following questions to test your knowledge of the information in this lesson. You can find the answers to these questions and explanations of why each answer choice is correct or incorrect in the "Answers" section at the end of this chapter.

1. Which of the following are entity permissions in MDS? (Choose all that apply.)
   - **A.** Read-Only
   - **B.** Insert
   - **C.** Deny
   - **D.** Read-Write
   - **E.** Update

2. A user needs to have permissions to update any member and any attribute of an entity. Which permissions should you assign to the user? (Choose all that apply.)
   - **A.** Hierarchy member Read-Only permission
   - **B.** System Administration functional area
   - **C.** Explorer functional area
   - **D.** Entity Update permission

3. When you have overlapping model and member permissions, which of the following is true? (Choose all that apply.)
   - **A.** Deny overrides all other permissions.
   - **B.** Member permissions override model permissions.
   - **C.** Model permissions override member permissions.
   - **D.** Read-Only overrides Update.

Lesson 3: Using Master Data Services Add-in for Excel

Master Data Services Add-in for Excel puts a lot of power into the hands of advanced users. Instead of updating MDS data row by row, entity by entity, users who are familiar with Excel 2010 can use it with all of its capabilities to edit batches of data. When the edit is finished, they can publish the batch to the MDS database. Of course, all security is maintained inside Excel as well; users can load and publish only data for which they have permissions granted.

Editing MDS Data in Excel

The first thing you need to do in Excel to take advantage of this capability is to establish a connection to your MDS service. The connection string is just the URL to your MDS instance; for example, *http://localhost:8080*, if the instance is on your local computer and listens on port 8080. If you have MDS Add-in for Excel installed, a new Master Data tab will appear in Excel. On this tab, in the upper-left corner, in the Connect And Load group, you can find the Connect button. There you can select a saved connection or, through the Manage Connections dialog box, create a new one. Figure 16-8 shows the Connect drop-down list.

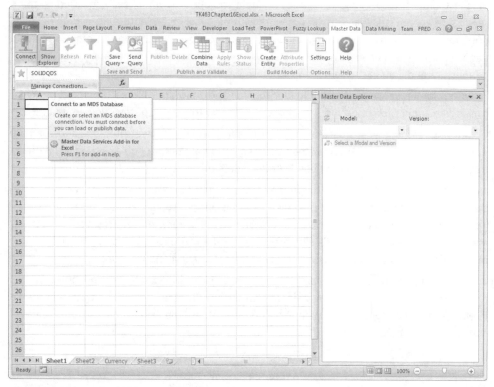

FIGURE 16-8 Managing MDS connections in Excel.

If you click the Show Explorer button, the Model Data Explorer pane will be displayed on the right side of the worksheet. After you connect, you can select the model and version you want to edit. In the list box below the model is a list of entities. There you can select an entity. If you double-click an entity, you automatically select all members for loading into Excel.

You probably don't want to load an entity with millions of members into a worksheet. Instead of double-clicking an entity in the Model Data Explorer, just select it there and click the Filter button in the Connect And Load group of the Master Data ribbon tab. Then you can select only the attributes you need and filter rows on values of attributes. While you are filtering your entity data, you can also reorder columns for display in Excel.

When you select an entity, filter data, and organize columns, you are actually creating a query. You can name and save this query for reuse. A query is saved in a text file in XML format. You can even send a query to your colleagues in an email message immediately. You manage queries with two buttons, Save Query and Send Query, both of which are in the Save And Send group of the Master Data tab.

After you have finished editing the data, you can publish it to your MDS model. You do this by using the Publish button in the Publish And Validate group. A problem might arise if multiple users publish updates to the same data at the same time. MDS resolves this problem on a first come/first serve basis. If part of the data you updated was already changed on the server side, that means that you did not work with the most recent data. Out-of-date data is not published. Multiple users should filter entities to non-overlapping groups of rows to avoid this problem. Note that you could also use security methods to define hierarchy member permissions and limit each user to a group of rows only.

Each published change is a transaction. You can add annotations to each transaction. You can add an annotation to each row that has changed or to a batch of rows you are publishing.

Before publishing, you can even combine data from two worksheets into one and compare it. Then you can further edit and correct the combined data before publishing. You can use the Combine Data button in the Publish And Validate group to do so.

One of the most powerful options in the MDS Add-in for Excel is the ability to de-duplicate data by using Data Quality Services. You can use this option if your Data Quality Services instance is installed on the same SQL Server instance as Master Data Services. You use the Match Data button in the Data Quality group for this task. You will learn more about identity mapping and de-duplication in Chapter 20, "Identity Mapping and De-Duplicating."

When you publish data, the published data is automatically validated against business rules. You can see the status of the validation when you click the Show Status button in the Publish And Validate group. In the same group, you can use the Apply Rules button to validate in advance, before publishing.

Creating MDS Objects in Excel

With MDS Add-in for Excel, you can even edit the model itself. You can create an entity and change an attribute property. This is possible with the Create Entities and Attribute Properties buttons in the Build Model group of the Master Data ribbon tab. Of course, this option should be reserved for the most advanced users only.

Note that the add-in fully supports MDS security. In order to edit and publish data, you must have the Update MDS permission on the affected objects, and you must have Explorer functional area access. In order to create an entity, you must be a Model Administrator and have access to the System Administration and Explorer functional areas.

To create an entity with Excel, follow this procedure:

1. In the Excel worksheet, select the cells you want to load into the new entity. The cells should have a header row. Note that you can import data into Excel from an existing database as well.

2. On the Master Data tab, in the Build Model group, click Create Entity. The Create Entity dialog box appears.

3. If you are not connected to your MDS instance yet, you will see a prompt to connect at this time.

4. In the Create Entity dialog box, leave the default range or change it so that it applies to the data you want to load.

5. Do not clear the My Data Has Headers check box.

6. In the Model list, select the model in which you want to create the new entity.

7. In the Version list, select a version.

8. In the New Entity Name box, type a name for the entity.

9. In the Code list, select the column that contains unique values for identification of each entity or select the option to have codes generated automatically.

10. In the Name list, select a column that contains names for each member. Figure 16-9 shows an example of creating an entity named Currency. The data for this entity comes from the *dbo.DimCurrency* table in the AdventureWorksDW2012 database.

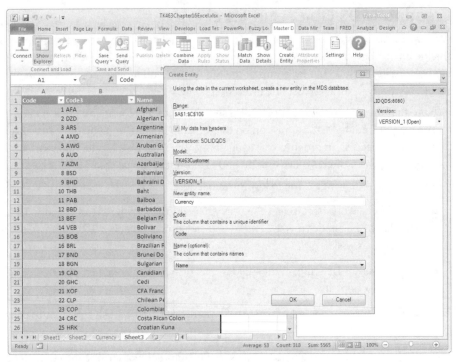

FIGURE 16-9 Creating an entity from Excel.

11. Click OK. When the entity has been created successfully, Excel displays a new header row and updates the sheet name with the same name as the entity name.

You can also check the new entity in the Master Data Manager application.

 Quick Check

■ How can you update batches of MDS data without using the staging process?

Quick Check Answer

■ Use Excel 2010 with MDS Add-in for Excel to update batches of data in an MDS model.

In this practice, you will use Excel with MDS Add-in for Excel.

EXERCISE 1 Load MDS Data in Excel

You will use Excel to connect to your MDS service and load data into Excel.

1. Open Excel 2010 with MDS Add-in for Excel installed. Navigate to the Master Data ribbon tab.

2. In the Connect button list, click Manage Connections.

3. In the Manage Connections dialog box, click New.

4. Enter a description for this connection; for example, **TK463MDS**. For the MDS server address, enter the URL to your MDS instance, such as ***http://localhost:8080***. Click OK.

5. Click the Test button to test the connection. Wait while Excel connects to MDS. Then click OK in the confirmation window.

6. In the Manage Connections window, click Close.

7. If the Master Data Explorer pane does not appear on the right of your worksheet, click the Show Explorer button.

8. In Master Data Explorer, select the TK463Customer model, version VERSION_1. Click the TK463Customer entity to select it. Note—do not double-click it; this would load all of the members.

9. Click the Filter button.

10. In the Filter dialog box, select the Leaf attribute type. Select the following attributes: Name, Code, EmailAddress, StreetAddress, and City.

11. Use the up and down arrows near the field list to organize the order as follows: Name, Code, EmailAddress, StreetAddress, and City.

12. Under the Rows grid, click the Add button to add a filter for the rows. Select the City attribute and the Is Equal To operator, and enter the value **Salem**. Your filter should look like the one shown in Figure 16-10.

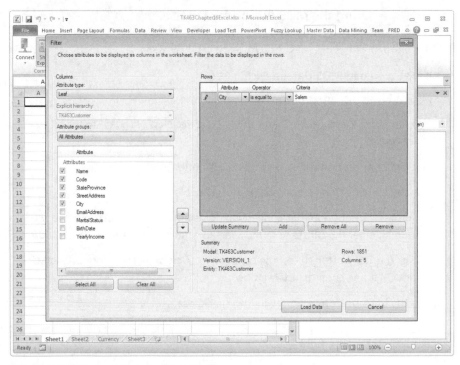

FIGURE 16-10 Filtering data to load into Excel.

13. Click Load Data.

EXERCISE 2   Modify MDS Data in Excel

In this exercise, you edit the data you loaded in Excel and then publish it.

1. After the data is loaded, change the email address for Melissa Sanchez (in the first row) from melissa40@adventure-works.com to **melissa40#adventure-works.com**. Note that the background color changed for the updated field.

2. Click Publish.

3. In the Publish And Annotate dialog box, select Use Same Annotation For All Changes, and then in the text box below this option, enter **TK463 testing MDS Excel Add-in**. Then click Publish.

4. When you publish data, MDS validates it. You should see two additional columns on the left side of your columns, showing the validation status. If you do not see the validation status, click the Show Status button.

5. Validation for the first row, for Melissa Sanchez, should fail. Point to the validation status cell for Melissa Sanchez and read the error message.

6. Correct the email address of Melissa Sanchez back to the following:

   melissa40@adventure-works.com

7. Click Publish.

8. In the Publish And Annotate dialog box, select Use Same Annotation For All Changes, and then in the text box below this option, enter **TK463 cleaning up**. Then click Publish.

9. Switch to Master Data Manager. Navigate to the home page. Select the TK463Customer model and the VERSION_1 version. Click the Explorer link. If the TK463Customer entity is not shown by default, select it from the Entities list.

10. Use the Filter button to filter the data the same way you filtered it in Excel—with the attribute of City, the operator Is Equal To, and the value **Salem**. Click Apply. Figure 16-11 shows what the screen should look like.

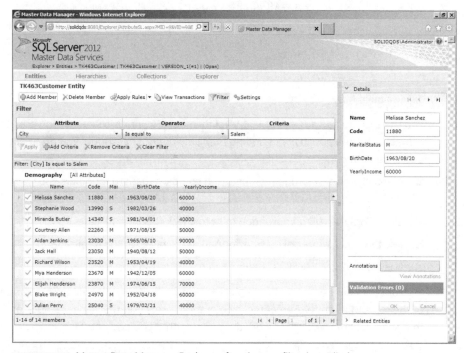

FIGURE 16-11 Master Data Manager Explorer after the row filter is applied.

11. Click the Melissa Sanchez row to select it.

12. Click the View Transactions button. Review the transactions and annotations.

13. Save the Excel file to the Solution folder for this lesson. Name it as follows:

    TK463Chapter16Excel.xlsx

14. Close Master Data Manager and Excel.

Lesson Summary

- With MDS Add-in for Excel, you can edit MDS data in batches by using all Excel capabilities.
- Advanced users can even create new entities and manage attributes from Excel.
- MDS maintains security and validation for Excel data the same way it does for data updated with Master Data Manager.

Lesson Review

Answer the following questions to test your knowledge of the information in this lesson. You can find the answers to these questions and explanations of why each answer choice is correct or incorrect in the "Answers" section at the end of this chapter.

1. What can you do with MDS Add-in for Excel? (Choose all that apply.)

   A. Edit batches of MDS data.

   B. Create a new MDS entity.

   C. Create a new MDS model.

   D. Maintain MDS security.

2. You use Excel to add a batch of leaf-level members to your MDS entity. You are concerned about the possibility of adding duplicate data. What should you do to find the duplicates in the most efficient way?

   A. Manually review existing members and compare them to members you want to add from Excel.

   B. Use a DQS matching knowledge base to check for the duplicates.

   C. Use the SSIS Fuzzy Lookup transformation to check for the duplicates.

   D. Use the T-SQL SOUNDEX() function to check for the duplicates.

3. In your company, several users use MDS Add-in for Excel to edit batches of members of the same MDS entity. Sometimes two or more users edit the same member, and thus there is some redundant work done. How could you prevent this?

   A. Create a separate SSIS package for each user to import data in Excel.

   B. Advise the users to filter the data when importing it into Excel with the MDS Add-in for Excel.

   C. Teach users how to write the T-SQL SELECT command, especially the WHERE clause.

   D. Use MDS security to define row-level security for the users.

Case Scenario

In the following case scenario, you apply what you've learned about managing master data. You can find the answers to these questions in the "Answers" section at the end of this chapter.

Case Scenario: Editing Batches of MDS Data

A company that uses MDS has to update data for 4,000 customers in four different countries. They have dedicated four people to this task. However, they have realized that using the Master Data Manager application is not the most effective way for such mass updates. In addition, they have realized that two of their users actually occasionally updated the same members, and thus they spent some wasted effort. The company has asked you for a better solution. Answer the following questions:

1. How can you help them speed up the editing process?

2. How would you prevent users from updating the same members?

Suggested Practices

To help you successfully master the exam objective presented in this chapter, complete the following tasks.

Analyze the Staging Tables

To understand all options for batch imports of data, study staging tables.

- **Practice 1**   Read details about staging tables in Books Online for SQL Server 2012. You can find details about the leaf member staging table at *http://msdn.microsoft.com /en-us/library/ee633854.aspx*, about the consolidated member staging table at *http://msdn.microsoft.com/en-us/library/ee633772.aspx*, and about the relationship staging table at *http://msdn.microsoft.com/en-us/library/ee633902.aspx*.

- **Practice 2**   Examine the structure of staging tables.

Test Security

In addition to the practices in this chapter, you should test other MDS security possibilities in order to understand them thoroughly.

- **Practice 1**   Give permissions to a Windows group.

- **Practice 2**   Log on to MDS with a Windows user that is a member of the group to which you gave permissions.

- **Practice 3**   Test how permissions work in this case.

Answers

This section contains answers to the lesson review questions and solutions to the case scenario in this chapter.

Lesson 1

1. **Correct Answers: A and C**

   A. **Correct:** You can initiate the staging process with staging procedures.

   B. **Incorrect:** There is no InitiateStaging SQL Server Agent job created when you install MDS.

   C. **Correct:** You can use the Import Data page in the Integration Management area of the master Data Manager application to initiate the staging process.

   D. **Incorrect:** You use the MDSModelDeploy command prompt utility to create and deploy MDS packages that can contain data and metadata.

2. **Correct Answer: D**

   A. **Incorrect:** With the Model Deployment Wizard, you can extract model metadata only.

   B. **Incorrect:** You use subscription views to export data.

   C. **Incorrect:** You use the staging process to import data.

   D. **Correct:** You use the MDSModelDeploy command prompt utility to create and deploy MDS packages that can contain data and metadata.

3. **Correct Answers: B, C, and D**

   A. **Incorrect:** You cannot create hierarchies with the staging process.

   B. **Correct:** You can create, update, deactivate, and delete leaf and consolidated members with the staging process.

   C. **Correct:** You can update attribute values with the staging process.

   D. **Correct:** You can designate relationships in explicit hierarchies with the staging process.

   E. **Incorrect:** You cannot change an attribute data type with the staging process.

Lesson 2

1. **Correct Answers: A, C, and E**

   A. **Correct:** Read-Only is an entity permission.

   B. **Incorrect:** There is no Insert permission in MDS.

   C. **Correct:** Deny is an entity permission.

   D. **Incorrect:** There is no Read-Write permission in MDS.

   E. **Correct:** Update is an entity permission.

2. **Correct Answers: C and D**

   A. **Incorrect:** Because the user needs Update permission, you cannot assign Read-Only permission. In addition, the user needs permissions on all members; therefore, you do not need to assign hierarchy member permissions.

   B. **Incorrect:** A user does not have to be the MDS System Administrator to update MDS data.

   C. **Correct:** A user needs the Update object permission and Explorer functional area access to update data.

   D. **Correct:** A user needs the Update object permission and Explorer functional area access to update data.

3. **Correct Answers: A and D**

   A. **Correct:** When model and member permissions are overlapping, the Deny permission overrides all other permissions.

   B. **Incorrect:** Member permissions do not override model permissions.

   C. **Incorrect:** Model permissions do not override member permissions.

   D. **Correct:** When model and member permissions are overlapping, the Read-Only permission overrides the Update permission.

Lesson 3

1. **Correct Answers: A and B**

   A. **Correct:** With Excel, you can edit batches of MDS data.

   B. **Correct:** With Excel, you can create new entities.

   C. **Incorrect:** You cannot create a new MDS model with Excel.

   D. **Incorrect:** You cannot maintain MDS security with Excel.

2. **Correct Answer: B**

   A. **Incorrect:** Although you could manually check for the duplicates, this would not be an efficient solution.

   B. **Correct:** You can use a DQS matching knowledge base directly from Excel with the MDS Add-in for Excel.

   C. **Incorrect:** Although the SSIS Fuzzy Lookup transformation is extremely powerful, using a DQS matching knowledge base directly from Excel is more efficient.

   D. **Incorrect:** The T-SQL SOUNDEX() function is too simple to give you good matching results. In addition, using a DQS matching knowledge base directly from Excel is more efficient.

3. **Correct Answer: D**

   A. **Incorrect:** Creating a separate SSIS package for each user would not guarantee that somebody could not change a package and load the same data as some other user. In addition, this would be an inefficient solution.

   B. **Incorrect:** Filtering data works; however, this does not guarantee that a user would not create a wrong filter and import to Excel the same data as another user.

   C. **Incorrect:** End users typically do not write T-SQL queries.

   D. **Correct:** You should use MDS security to define row-level security and create non-overlapping groups of members for different users.

Case Scenario

1. You should introduce Excel 2010 with MDS Add-in for Excel.

2. You should use hierarchy member permissions to limit each user to members of a single country.

## CHAPTER 17

Creating a Data Quality Project to Clean Data

Exam objectives in this chapter:

- Build Data Quality Solutions
  - Create a data quality project to clean data.

In Chapter 14, "Installing and Maintaining Data Quality Services," you learned about data quality problems. You also learned how to install and maintain Microsoft SQL Server 2012 Data Quality Services (DQS). It is time to start using DQS to improve the quality of your data.

DQS is a knowledge-driven solution. Therefore, you need to learn how to prepare a knowledge base (KB). Then you use this KB to cleanse data by using data quality projects. In the last lesson of this chapter, you will learn how to profile data with tools other than DQS, such as the SQL Server Information Services (SSIS) Data Profiling task and T-SQL queries.

Lessons in this chapter:

- Lesson 1: Creating and Maintaining a Knowledge Base
- Lesson 2: Creating a Data Quality Project
- Lesson 3: Profiling Data and Improving Data Quality

Before You Begin

To complete this chapter, you must have:

- SQL Server 2012 Database Services, Integration Services, and Data Quality Services installed.
- An understanding of data quality problems.
- Intermediate Transact-SQL skills.

Lesson 1: Creating and Maintaining a Knowledge Base

In order to successfully clean your data with DQS, you need to have a good knowledge base. You can create a KB interactively or with automatic knowledge discovery from existing trustworthy data. Then you can use this knowledge to cleanse your data by using a DQS project. During cleansing, you gain new knowledge; you can integrate this new knowledge into your knowledge base. A knowledge base consists of *domains* that are mapped to data source fields. You can create composite domains for advanced rules that span multiple fields. In this lesson, you will learn how to create and maintain a DQS knowledge base and domains.

> **After this lesson, you will be able to:**
> - Create a DQS knowledge base.
> - Discover knowledge in existing trustworthy data.
> - Create and manage KB domains.
>
> **Estimated lesson time: 35 minutes**

Building a DQS Knowledge Base

Typically, you start building a knowledge base with a computer-guided process called knowledge discovery. The DQS knowledge discovery process has a lot of built-in heuristics. You feed the process with sample data that you trust. The process analyzes the data for data inconsistencies and syntax errors, and it proposes corrections.

To initiate knowledge discovery, you as a data steward link a DQS KB domain to a field of an existing table that has data similar to the data you need to cleanse. You do not need to use the data you need to cleanse for the knowledge discovery activity. A DQS KB is extensible; after initial knowledge discovery, you can edit the KB manually. You can also re-run the knowledge discovery process.

Building a DQS KB involves the following processes:

- ***Knowledge discovery*** A computer-guided process that uses a data sample
- ***Domain management*** An interactive process in which you manually verify and extend domains in a KB
- ***Reference data services*** A process in which you validate domain data against external data maintained and guaranteed by an external provider
- ***Matching policy*** A process in which you define rules to identify duplicates

DQS is case-insensitive. It does not distinguish values by case when you perform knowledge discovery, prepare a matching policy, or manage a domain. However, you can control the case when you export cleansing results.

A matching policy includes matching rules that you create to help DQS identify duplicate rows for a single entity. To do so, you must define which columns DQS should use to compare the rows and calculate the probability of a match. You will learn more about identity mapping and de-duplicating with DQS and other SQL Server tools in Chapter 20, "Identity Mapping and De-Duplicating."

DQS includes some default knowledge out of the box. This knowledge is stored in the DQS Data knowledge base. You can use this KB to start a cleansing project quickly. You should treat this KB as read-only. It is not attached to a reference data provider. You can use this default KB to create your own read-write KB, which you can then edit. The DQS Data KB includes three Country/Region domains (one with full-name leading values, one with three-letter abbreviation leading values, and one with two-letter abbreviation leading values), two US State domains (one with full-name leading values and one with two-letter abbreviation leading values), US Counties, US Last Name, and US Places domains. A *leading value* in a domain is the value to which you want DQS to correct the data.

You can export or import a domain, an entire knowledge base, or all knowledge bases from a DQS instance. You have the following options:

- Import and export all knowledge bases from an instance with the DQSInstaller.exe command prompt utility. When you export all KBs, you create a DQS backup (.dqsb) file.
- Import or export (to a .dqs file) an entire knowledge base from Data Quality Client.
- Import or export (to a .dqs file) a domain with Data Quality Client.
- Import values from a Microsoft Excel file to a domain with Data Quality Client.
- Import domains from an Excel file with the knowledge discovery activity in Data Quality Client.
- Import new values from a finished DQS cleansing project with Data Quality Client.

Domain Management

A domain contains a semantic representation of a specific field (column of a table) in your data source. You can define the following properties for a domain:

- **Data type**   The data type of a domain can be string, date, integer, or decimal.
- **Use leading values**   This property defines whether to replace all synonyms of a value with the leading value you define.
- **Normalize**   With this property, you can normalize strings to remove special characters and thus improve the likelihood of matches.
- **Format output**   You can use this property to format strings to uppercase, lowercase, or capitalized for each word.
- **Speller**   With this property, you can enable the spelling checker on a string domain.
- **Syntax algorithms**   You can use this property to disable checking strings for syntax errors. This is useful for names and addresses, for which you probably don't want DQS to automatically correct the syntax of strings for international values.

Besides creating a domain manually, creating one with knowledge discovery, or importing one, you can also create a domain as a copy of an existing domain. In addition, you can also create a *linked domain*. Linked domains are useful for mapping two data source fields to the same domain. You cannot map two fields to a single domain directly; instead, you can create a linked domain and link one field to the original domain and one field to the linked domain.

You can change the domain values after you populate the domain values through the knowledge discovery process, manually, or by importing the values. You can change the type of the value, designate synonyms, and define the value to correct to a selected value. The type of a value can be correct, invalid (meaning that the value does not conform to the rules for the domain and is thus out of scope for the domain), or error (meaning that the value is in the scope of the domain but is erroneous). If you change the type to invalid or error, you should provide the corrected value. When you select a set of values as synonyms, you should also select the leading value. DQS uses the leading value as a replacement for its synonyms.

If you use the spelling checker and the value is underscored with a red squiggly line, you can select a correction if the spelling checker proposes any. The value will remain erroneous, and the correction is added as the corrected value.

 Besides defining correct, invalid, erroneous, and corrected values for a domain, you can also define domain rules. A *domain rule* is a condition that DQS uses to validate, standardize, and/or correct domain values. You can define rules such that the value must be greater than a selected value, must begin with a value, must comply with a pattern or a regular expression, must contain a value, must be in a list of values you specify, and more. A single rule can have multiple conditions connected with logical AND or logical OR operators.

 In addition to synonyms, you can create term-based relations. You use a *term-based relation* to correct a term that is part of a domain value and not the complete domain value. You define a term-based relation once, and DQS uses it for all values in a domain. For example, you could define that the string Inc. should always be expanded to Incorporated.

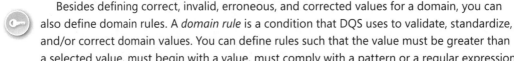

EXAM TIP

Understand the difference between synonyms and term-based relations.

Sometimes a single domain does not represent real data satisfactorily. For example, a complete address can consist of street address, postal code, city, and country, and you need the complete address for de-duplicating. For cases like this, you can define a composite domain that consists of two or more single domains. A composite domain can have a *cross-domain rule*, a rule that tests the relationships between two or more single domains. For example, you can check that a specific city is always in a specific country. In Data Quality Client, you can check the number of occurrences of value combinations of a composite domain in order to mitigate the process of creating the cross-domain rules. If you need to change the values of a composite domain, you change them in each of the single domains that the composite domain consists of. You will use composite domains in Chapter 20.

After you finish with knowledge base editing, you have to publish the KB. If it is not published, it is locked. You can only unlock your own knowledge bases.

 Quick Check

- You want to use a knowledge base that exists in one DQS instance in another DQS instance. Should you re-create the knowledge base on the second DQS instance manually?

Quick Check Answer

- No, you should export the knowledge base from the first DQS instance and import it into the other.

PRACTICE **Creating a Knowledge Base**

In this practice, you will create a DQS knowledge base.

If you encounter a problem completing an exercise, you can import the completed knowledge base from the Solution folder that is provided with the companion content for this chapter and lesson.

EXERCISE 1 Use Knowledge Discovery

In this exercise, you use knowledge discovery as the starting point for building a knowledge base.

1. You begin this exercise by preparing a view with all possible valid cities, states or provinces, and countries or regions for your customers. Start SQL Server Management Studio (SSMS), connect to your SQL Server instance that includes DQS databases, open a new query window, and change the context to the DQS_STAGING_DATA database.

2. Create a view named **TK463CitiesStatesCountries** that selects all distinct cities, states or provinces, and countries or regions from the *dbo.Dimgeography* table in the Adventure-WorksDW2012 demo database. You can use the following code.

```
CREATE VIEW dbo.TK463CitiesStatesCountries
AS
SELECT DISTINCT
 City, StateProvinceName AS StateProvince,
 EnglishCountryRegionName AS CountryRegion
FROM AdventureWorksDW2012.dbo.DimGeography;
```

3. Open the Data Quality Client application and connect to your DQS instance.

4. In the Knowledge Base Management group, click the New Knowledge Base button.

5. Name the database **TK463Customers**. If you want, write a description. Make sure that the None option is selected in the Create Knowledge Base From drop-down list. Select the Knowledge Discovery option in the Select Activity list in the lower-right corner of the screen. Click Next.

6. On the Map tab of the Knowledge Base Management screen, select SQL Server as your data source. Select the DQS_STAGING_DATA database and the dbo.TK463CitiesStates-Countries view.

7. In the Mappings section, click the Create A Domain button (third from the left in the buttons group above the Mappings grid; it looks like a circle with a yellow star) to create a domain.

8. In the dialog box that appears, name the domain **City**, using the String data type. Make sure that the Use Leading Values, Normalize String, and Disable Syntax Error Algorithms check boxes are selected, and that the Enable Speller check box is cleared. Make sure that Format Output is set to None and that the language selected is English, as Figure 17-1 shows. Click OK.

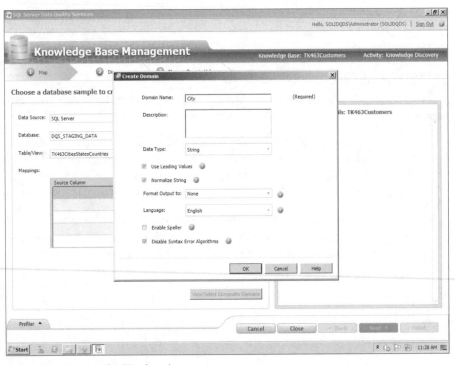

FIGURE 17-1 Creating the City domain.

9. Create two additional domains called **State** and **Country** with the same settings you used for the City domain.

10. In the Mappings grid, select the *City* column from the source in the left column of the first row and map it to the City domain in the right column of the first row of the grid.

11. Repeat step 10 twice to add mappings from the *StateProvince* source column to the State domain and the *CountryRegion* source column to the Country domain. Then click Next.

12. On the Discover tab, click the Start button to start the knowledge discovery. Wait until the process is finished, and then read all of the information in the Profiler section. This section gives you a quick profile of your data. When you are finished reading the profiler information, click Next.

13. In the Manage Domain Values tab, make sure that the City domain is selected in the left pane. Then click the Add New Domain Value button (the button with a small green plus sign on a grid) in the right pane above the grid with extracted domain values.

14. In the Value cell, enter **Munich**. Change the type to Error (a red cross). Enter **München** in the Correct To cell. Click outside the cell and note how data is rearranged alphabetically.

15. Click the other two domains in the left pane to check the extracted values. Then click Finish. Select No in the pop-up window. You are not ready to publish the KB yet. In the next exercise, you will edit the domains. Do not close Data Quality Client.

EXERCISE 2   Edit Domains

Now that you have created a KB with the help of the knowledge discovery process, in this exercise you edit the domains manually.

1. Click the Open Knowledge Base button in the Knowledge Base Management group on the Data Quality Client main screen.

2. In the grid in the left pane, select the TK463Customers KB. Make sure that the Domain Management activity is selected. Click Next.

3. In the Domain Management window, make sure that the City domain is selected in the left pane. Click the Domain Values tab in the right pane. Then click the Add New Domain Value button in the right pane above the grid with the extracted domain values.

4. In the Value cell, enter **Muenchen**. Change the type to Error (a red cross). Enter **München** in the Correct To cell. Click outside the cell and note how data is rearranged alphabetically.

5. Find the München value in the grid. Note that this is now the leading value for two additional synonyms, Munich and Muenchen.

6. In the left pane, click the Create A Domain button. Name the domain **StreetAddress**. Use the data type String. Make sure that the Use Leading Values, Normalize String, and Disable Syntax Error Algorithms check boxes are selected, and that the Enable Speller check box is cleared. Also make sure that Format Output is set to None and that the language selected is English. Click OK.

7. Click the Term-Based Relations tab for the StreetAddress domain. You will add a term-based relation to correct all occurrences of a term in domain values.

8. Click the Add New Relation button. Enter **Ct.** in the value cell and **Court** in the Correct To cell. Press Enter. The Apply Changes button should be unavailable, because you do not have any domain values yet. (Note that even if it is available, you can click it without any effect, because you are not making any changes.)

9. Add a new domain called **BirthDate**. Select the data type Date. Use leading values and no formatting of output. However, check the formatting options. Then click OK.

10. Click the Domain Rules tab for the BirthDate domain. In the right pane, click the Add A New Domain Rule button.

11. In the rules grid, enter **MinBirthDate** in the Name cell.

12. In the Build A Rule: MinBirthDate section, make sure that the Value Is Greater Than option is selected in the drop-down list for conditions. Then enter **1/1/1900** in the text box and press Enter. Check whether this was successfully changed to Monday, January 01, 1900.

13. Add a new domain, **Occupation**. Use the String data type. Make sure that the Use Leading Values and Normalize String check boxes are selected. However, this time enable the speller and do not disable syntax error algorithms. Do not format the output, and use the English language. Click OK.

14. Add a new domain, **EmailAddress**. Use the String data type. Make sure that the Use Leading Values, Normalize String, and Disable Syntax Error Algorithms check boxes are selected, and that the Enable Speller check box is cleared. Set Format Output to None, and set Language to English. Click OK.

15. Click the Domain Rules tab for the EmailAddress domain. Add a new rule called **EmailRegEx**.

16. Select the Value Matches Regular Expression option in the Build A Rule: EmailRegEx Conditions drop-down list. Enter the string **\p{L}+\d\d@ADVENTURE-WORKS\.COM** as the expression. Then click outside the text box.

17. Click the Add A New Condition To The Selected Clause button (the leftmost button in the upper-right part of the Build A Rule area).

18. Select the OR operator to connect the conditions. Select the Value Matches Regular Expression option for the second condition from the drop-down list in the Build A Rule: EmailRegEx Conditions drop-down list. Then enter the following string as the expression: **\p{L}+\d@ADVENTURE -WORKS \.COM**. Click outside the text box.

> ***NOTE*** **FINDING STRING PATTERNS AS REGULAR EXPRESSIONS**
>
> You will extract regular expressions for the email addresses with the help of the SSIS Data Profiling task in the practice for the third lesson of this chapter.

19. Click Finish to finish the domain management activity. Then click the Publish button in the pop-up window. Finally, click OK in the next pop-up window. Your knowledge base is prepared to use.

> **NOTE CONTINUING WITH PRACTICES**
>
> Do not exit Data Quality Client or SSMS if you intend to continue immediately with the next practice.

Lesson Summary

- You can start building a knowledge base with knowledge discovery.
- You can manually edit domains after the discovery process is finished.
- You can import and export knowledge bases and domains.

Lesson Review

Answer the following questions to test your knowledge of the information in this lesson. You can find the answers to these questions and explanations of why each answer choice is correct or incorrect in the "Answers" section at the end of this chapter.

1. How can you get the domain values for a domain? (Choose all that apply.)

    A. By knowledge discovery

    B. With manual editing

    C. By using the SSIS Data Profiling task

    D. By importing the values from an Excel file

2. What process do you use to define a KB for de-duplication?

    A. Use reference data services.

    B. Define matching policy for a KB.

    C. Use knowledge discovery.

    D. Manually insert matching data.

3. What kind of knowledge would you build into your knowledge base if you needed to correct automatically all appearances of the string "St." to "Street"?

    A. Term-based relation

    B. Synonyms

    C. Cross-domain rule

    D. Matching policy

Lesson 2: Creating a Data Quality Project

After you have a knowledge base, you can use DQS projects to validate and cleanse your data. You do not modify the data directly on the source; instead, you export the results of a DQS project to SQL Server tables or Excel files and then use queries to cleanse the source data. In this lesson, you will learn how to use DQS knowledge bases for DQS projects.

> **After this lesson, you will be able to:**
>
> - Create a DQS project.
> - Validate data against a DQS KB.
> - Export the corrected and validated data.
>
> **Estimated lesson time: 30 minutes**

DQS Projects

You can create a *cleansing* or a *matching* DQS project. You will learn more about matching projects in Chapter 20. Creating a DQS project is a quite simple task; a wizard guides you through individual steps. During the cleansing and matching, you can also see the profiling results for your data. DQS profiling provides you with two data quality dimensions: *completeness* and *accuracy*. Based on data profiling information and defined notifications, you can also get warnings when a threshold is met.

You can use the SSIS DQS Cleansing component to cleanse batches of data. It is a best practice to cleanse data before you perform de-duplication. You will use the DQS Cleansing component in Chapter 20. You can open an SSIS cleansing project to review the results in the DQS Data Quality Client application as well.

EXAM TIP

Use the DQS Cleansing transformation for batch cleaning during your extract-transform-load (ETL) process.

Sometimes you need to perform some management activities on an existing project. These management activities can include:

- Opening an existing data quality project. You use the Open Data Quality Project button of the Data Quality Client tool to display a grid of existing DQS projects.
- Unlocking a DQS project. You use the Open Data Quality Project button of the Data Quality Client tool to display a grid of existing DQS projects. Then you right-click a project in the grid and select the Unlock option. A project is locked when someone edited it without finishing the edit.

- Renaming a DQS project. You can right-click a project and rename it.

- Deleting a DQS project. Again in the displayed list of existing projects, you select a project and right-click it to display the Delete option.

Note that you cannot open, unlock, rename, or delete a data quality project that was created by another user. You can unlock only those projects created by you. Also, you cannot delete a locked project; you first have to unlock it.

Data Cleansing

DQS uses knowledge bases for automatic, computer-assisted data cleansing. After the automatic process is done, you can manually review and additionally edit the processed data. When you finish with editing, you can export the cleansed data. In addition, you can use the results of a DQS project to improve a knowledge base—for example, by adding new correct or corrected values to existing domain values in the knowledge base. Figure 17-2 shows the complete life cycle of DQS activities.

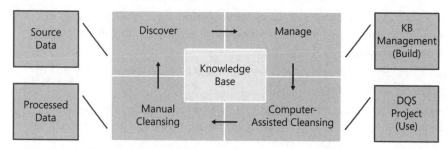

FIGURE 17-2 The life cycle of DQS activities.

You can use SQL Server or Excel data sources. If the source data is in an Excel file, then Excel must be installed on the same computer as Data Quality Client. The Excel files can have the extension .xlsx, .xls, or .csv. However, if you are using a 64-bit version of Excel, .xlsx files (from Excel 2007 and Excel 2010) are not supported. Save the Excel files you want to use as source data in .xls or .csv format. Note that 32-bit .xlsx files are supported. For more details, see the MSDN article "Cleanse Data Using DQS (Internal) Knowledge" at *http://msdn.microsoft.com/en-us/library/hh213061.aspx*.

A DQS knowledge base must exist before you can start a DQS cleansing or matching project. Of course, the knowledge base must contain the knowledge about the type of data you are going to cleanse. For example, if you are cleansing company names, the knowledge base you use should have high-quality data about company names. In addition, a KB used for cleansing company names could have synonyms and term-based relations defined. A DQS project uses a single KB; multiple projects can use the same KB.

A cleansing project has the following stages:

1. **Mapping**   In this stage, you map source columns to KB domains.

2. **Computer-assisted cleansing**   In this stage, DQS uses the KB with built-in algorithms and heuristics to find the best match of an instance of data you are cleansing to known data domain values.

3. **Interactive cleansing**   In this stage, you review the results of the computer-assisted cleansing and additionally correct data. You see the changes that DQS proposes and decide whether to approve or reject the changes.

4. **Export**   In this stage, you export the cleansed data. You can export the data to SQL Server tables or Excel files (.xlsx, .xls, and .csv). You can also standardize output if you defined standardized output in the appropriate domain of the knowledge base used. You can decide to export data only, or data and cleansing information. The data cleansing information includes source value, output value, reason for correction, confidence for correction, and the status of the operation performed on the data.

You can see and modify the status of the operation performed on the data during the interactive cleansing stage. Based on the confidence level and thresholds defined, the status can be one of the following:

- **Invalid**   This status denotes values that DQS found as invalid because they do not comply with domain rules.

- **Corrected**   This status denotes values that DQS corrected during the computer-assisted cleansing because the confidence for the correction was above the minimal score for the auto-corrections threshold.

- **Suggested**   The values have a confidence level higher than the auto-suggestions threshold and lower level than the threshold for auto-corrections.

- **Correct**   The values were found as correct. For example, a value matched a domain value in the knowledge base used for the project.

- **New**   The value cannot be mapped to another status. However, the value complies with the domain rules. This means that this value is either a correct new value or a potentially incorrect value for which DQS does not have enough information to map it to another status, or that the confidence level is too low for mapping the value to corrected or suggested values. If you approve a new value, DQS moves it to the corrected values; if you reject it, DQS moves it to the invalid values.

 Quick Check

- Which are the two cleansing phases of a DQS project?

Quick Check Answer

- The two cleansing phases of a DQS project are computer-assisted cleansing and interactive cleansing.

In this practice, you will create a DQS cleansing project.

If you encounter a problem completing an exercise, you can import the completed knowledge base and T_SQL code from the Solution folder that is provided with the companion content for this chapter and lesson.

EXERCISE 1   Create a View to be Cleaned

In this exercise, you create a view with partially dirty data.

1. If necessary, start SQL Server Management Studio (SSMS) and connect to your SQL Server instance that includes DQS databases. Open a new query window and change the context to the DQS_STAGING_DATA database.

2. Create a view named **TK463CustomersDirty** that selects every tenth customer from the *dbo.Dimcustomer* table, joined to the *dbo.Dimgeography* table in the Adventure-WorksDW2012 demo database. Add two rows with incorrect data. Use the following query, in which the comments point to where the dirty data was added.

```
CREATE VIEW dbo.TK463CustomersDirty
AS
SELECT C.CustomerKey,
  C.FirstName + ' ' + c.LastName AS FullName,
  C.AddressLine1 AS StreetAddress,
  G.City, G.StateProvinceName AS StateProvince,
  G.EnglishCountryRegionName AS CountryRegion,
  C.EmailAddress,
  C.BirthDate,
  C.EnglishOccupation AS Occupation
FROM AdventureWorksDW2012.dbo.DimCustomer AS C
  INNER JOIN AdventureWorksDW2012.dbo.DimGeography AS G
   ON C.GeographyKey = G.GeographyKey
WHERE C.CustomerKey % 10 = 0
UNION
SELECT -11000,
  N'Jon Yang',
  N'3761 N. 14th St',
  N'Munich',                    -- wrong city
  N'Kingsland',                 -- wrong state
  N'Austria',                   -- wrong country
  N'jon24#adventure-works.com', -- wrong email
  '18900224',                   -- wrong birth date
  'Profesional'                 -- wrong occupation
UNION
SELECT -11100,
  N'Jacquelyn Suarez',
  N'7800 Corrinne Ct.',         -- wrong term
  N'Muenchen',                  -- another wrong city
  N'Queensland',
  N'Australia',
  N'jacquelyn20@adventure-works.com',
  '19680206',
  'Professional';
```

EXERCISE 2   Cleanse Data with a DQS Project

In this exercise, you create a DQS cleansing project to cleanse the data from the view you created in the previous exercise.

1. Open the Data Quality Client application if necessary, and connect to your DQS instance.

2. In the Data Quality Projects group, click the New Data Quality Project button.

3. Name the project **TK463CustomersCleansing**. Use the TK463Customers knowledge base you created in the practice for the previous lesson. Make sure that the Cleansing activity is selected. Click Next.

4. The Data Quality Project window opens with the first tab, the Map tab, active. Select SQL Server as the data source, the DQS_STAGING_DATA database, and the TK463-CustomersDirty view in the Table/View drop-down list.

5. In the Mappings area, click twice on the Add A Column Mapping button (the button with the small green plus sign, above the mappings grid) to add two rows to the mappings grid. You need seven mappings, and five are provided by default.

6. Use the drop-down lists in the Source Column and Domain cells to map the following columns and domains:

    A. The *BirthDate* column to the BirthDate domain

    B. The *StreetAddress* column to the StreetAddress domain

    C. The *City* column to the City domain

    D. The *StateProvince* column to the State domain

    E. The *CountryRegion* column to the Country domain

    F. The *EmailAddress* column to the EmailAddress domain

    G. The *Occupation* column to the Occupation domain.

7. Your mappings should look like the ones shown in Figure 17-3. Click Next.

8. On the Cleanse tab, click the Start button. Wait until the computer-assisted cleansing is finished, and then review the profiling results. Then click Next.

9. On the Manage And View Results tab, check the results domain by domain. Start with the BirthDate domain. There should be one invalid value. Make sure that the BirthDate domain is selected in the left pane, and click the Invalid tab in the right pane. Note the invalid value that was detected. You could write a correct value now in the Correct To cell of the grid with invalid values. Note that all correct values were suggested as new. You can accept all values in a grid by clicking the Approve All Terms button.

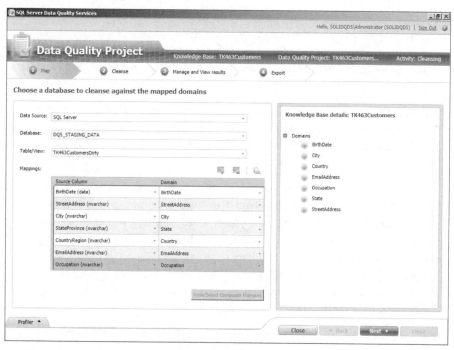

FIGURE 17-3 Mappings between columns and domains in the cleansing project.

10. Select the StreetAddress domain in the left pane. One value should be corrected. However, because only the term-based relation was corrected, not the whole value, it does not appear between corrected values. It should appear between the new values. Click the New tab in the right pane. Search for the value 7800 Corrinne Ct. and note that it was corrected with 100 percent confidence to 7800 Corrinne Court.

11. Select the State domain in the left pane. Click the New tab in the right pane. Note that one value (Kingsland) was found as new. The similarity threshold to the original value (Queensland) was too low for DQS to suggest or even correct the value automatically. You could correct this value manually.

12. Select the City domain in the left pane. Two values should be corrected. Click the Corrected tab in the right pane. Note the corrections of the synonyms for München to the leading value (München). Note also that the confidence for these two corrections is 100 percent. All other values already existed in the KB, and therefore DQS marked them as correct.

13. Select the Country domain in the left pane. One value should be suggested. Click the Suggested tab in the right pane. Note that DQS suggests replacing Austria with Australia with 70 percent confidence. You can approve a single value by checking the Approve option in the grid. However, don't approve it, because you will export results together with DQS information later. Note that DQS found other countries as correct.

14. Select the EmailAddress domain in the left pane. One value should be invalid. Click the Invalid tab in the right pane. DQS tells you that the jon24#adventure-works.com address does not comply with the EmailRegEx rule. Note that all other values are marked as new.

15. Select the Occupation domain in the left pane. Note that all values are new. Click the New tab in the right pane. Note that the value Profesional is underlined with a red squiggly line. This is because you enabled spelling checker for the Occupation domain. Enter **Professional** in the Correct To field for the incorrect row. Note that because you corrected the value manually, the confidence is set to 100 percent. Select the Approve check box for this row. The row should disappear and appear between the corrected values. Click the Corrected tab. Note the corrected value along with the reason. Click Next.

16. On the Export tab, look at the output data preview on the left side of the window.

17. Select the SQL Server destination type in the Export Cleansing Results pane on the right side of the screen. Select the DQS_STAGING_DATA database. Name the table **TK463CustomersCleansingResult**. Do not add a schema to the table name; DQS will put the results in the *dbo* schema. Make sure that the Standardize Output check box is selected and that the Data And Cleansing Info option is selected. Click Export.

18. When the export is complete, click the OK button in the pop-up window. Then click Finish.

19. Switch back to SSMS. Enter the following query to review the results.

```
SELECT *
FROM dbo.TK463CustomersCleansingResult
ORDER BY CustomerKey_Output;
```

> *NOTE* **CONTINUING WITH PRACTICES**
>
> You can close Data Quality Client, but do not exit SSMS if you intend to continue immediately with the next practice.

Lesson Summary

- A DQS project has four stages: mapping, computer-assisted cleansing, interactive cleansing, and export.
- You can cleanse data that comes from SQL Server or from Excel.
- You never modify the source data directly; you can export the data with the cleansing info as the result of your cleansing project.

Lesson Review

Answer the following questions to test your knowledge of the information in this lesson. You can find the answers to these questions and explanations of why each answer choice is correct or incorrect in the "Answers" section at the end of this chapter.

1. Which of the following is not a DQS cleansing project stage?
   - **A.** Knowledge discovery
   - **B.** Mapping
   - **C.** Computer-assisted cleansing
   - **D.** Interactive cleansing
   - **E.** Export

2. When would you find a value among the suggested values?
   - **A.** When the value does not comply with the domain rules.
   - **B.** When DQS can correct the value automatically because the confidence is above the auto-correction threshold.
   - **C.** When a value is correct—DQS puts it between suggested values because DQS suggests that the value is correct.
   - **D.** When a value has a confidence level higher than the auto-suggestions threshold and lower than the threshold for auto-corrections.

3. What kind of DQS projects can you create? (Choose all that apply.)
   - **A.** Knowledge discovery
   - **B.** Matching
   - **C.** Validating
   - **D.** Cleansing

Lesson 3: Profiling Data and Improving Data Quality

In addition to Data Quality Services, you can use many other tools from the SQL Server suite to profile data and thus improve data quality. For example, you can use Transact-SQL queries, and in SQL Server Integration Services, you can use the Data Profiling task. You will learn about this task and about some useful T-SQL queries for data profiling in this lesson.

> **After this lesson, you will be able to:**
> - Use the SSIS Data Profiling task.
> - Use T-SQL queries to profile data.
>
> **Estimated lesson time: 35 minutes**

Using Queries to Profile Data

Transact-SQL is a very powerful language. You can use it to find incomplete and inaccurate data.

In a relational database, the presence of NULLs is what defines completeness. NULLs are standard placeholders for unknown values. You can measure attribute completeness (that is, the number of NULLs in a specific attribute), tuple completeness (the number of unknown values of the attributes in a tuple), and relation completeness (the number of tuples with unknown attribute values in the relation).

You can start investigating the completeness of a relation by finding all attributes that allow NULLs. You can use the INFORMATION_SCHEMA ANSI standard and catalog SQL Server views for this task. For example, the following query finds which columns are nullable and which columns do not allow NULLs in the *dbo.DimCustomer* table of the AdventureWorks-DW2012 demo database.

```
USE AdventureWorksDW2012;
SELECT COLUMN_NAME, IS_NULLABLE
FROM INFORMATION_SCHEMA.COLUMNS
WHERE TABLE_SCHEMA = N'dbo'
 AND TABLE_NAME = N'DimCustomer';
```

From the results of this query, you can see that the *MiddleName* column is one of the nullable columns. You could then use the following query to find the number of NULLs in this column and the percentage of NULLs in all rows.

```
WITH CountNULLsCTE AS
(
SELECT COUNT(*) AS cnt
FROM dbo.DimCustomer
 WHERE MiddleName IS NULL
)
SELECT cnt AS NumberOfNulls,
```

```
100.0 * cnt / (SELECT COUNT(*) FROM dbo.DimCustomer)
  AS PercentageOfNulls
FROM CountNULLsCTE;
```

You can find that there are 7,830 NULLs in the *MiddleName* column, which is approximately 42.36 percent of all rows.

You can use many different queries to find inaccurate values as well. For finding potentially inaccurate dates, the MIN and MAX T-SQL aggregate functions are very useful. You can find, for example, the oldest and the youngest customer and check their ages.

With a couple of standard T-SQL aggregate functions, you can easily get an idea of the distribution of values of continuous numeric variables. You can use the MIN, MAX, AVG, and STDEV T-SQL aggregate functions to get basic information about the distribution. Then you can compare minimal and maximal values with the average. In addition, the standard deviation tells you about the spread of the distribution in general. The smaller the spread, the more likely it is that the outliers are inaccurate.

With a slightly more advanced query, you can get the distribution of discrete values, even with a graphical histogram. The following query shows this for the *Occupation* column of the dbo.TK463CustomersDirty view in the DQS_STAGING_DATA database created in the previous practice.

```
USE DQS_STAGING_DATA;
WITH freqCTE AS
(
SELECT Occupation,
 ROW_NUMBER() OVER(PARTITION BY Occupation
  ORDER BY Occupation, CustomerKey) AS Rn_AbsFreq,
 ROW_NUMBER() OVER(
  ORDER BY Occupation, CustomerKey) AS Rn_CumFreq,
 ROUND(100 * PERCENT_RANK()
  OVER(ORDER BY Occupation), 0) AS Pr_AbsPerc,
 ROUND(100 * CUME_DIST()
  OVER(ORDER BY Occupation, CustomerKey), 0) AS Cd_CumPerc
FROM dbo.TK463CustomersDirty
)
SELECT Occupation,
 MAX(Rn_AbsFreq) AS AbsFreq,
 MAX(Rn_CumFreq) AS CumFreq,
 MAX(Cd_CumPerc) - MAX(Pr_Absperc) AS AbsPerc,
 MAX(Cd_CumPerc) AS CumPerc,
 CAST(REPLICATE('*',MAX(Cd_CumPerc) - MAX(Pr_Absperc)) AS varchar(100)) AS Histogram
FROM freqCTE
GROUP BY Occupation
ORDER BY Occupation;
```

Table 17-1 shows the results. You can easily spot the suspicious value, the inaccurately spelled value Profesional.

You can develop many additional useful T-SQL queries for data profiling.

TABLE 17-1 Distribution of Values for the *Occupation* Column

Occupation	AbsFreq	CumFreq	AbsPerc	CumPerc	Histogram
Clerical	282	282	15	15	***************
Management	309	591	17	32	*****************
Manual	240	831	13	45	*************
Profesional	1	832	0	45	
Professional	552	1384	30	75	******************************
Skilled Manual	467	1851	25	100	*************************

REAL WORLD   **DATA PROFILING WITH SSAS**

You should use sample data for profiling if you have a large database. Profiling queries scan whole tables and are thus quite slow. Using SQL Server Analysis Services Tabular or Dimensional databases is preferred in real life to T-SQL queries for gathering the frequency distributions. With Count aggregates, you can easily get the distribution of any column. You can also easily get graphical presentations with client tools such as Excel. In addition, you work on a copy of the data, so you do not slow down the production SQL Server. In most of our real-life projects, we start data profiling with SSAS cubes.

SSIS Data Profiling Task

With the SSIS Data Profiling task, data profiling is very simple but also limited. The Data Profiling task saves the result in XML form, which cannot be used directly in an SSIS package. You can write custom code in the SSIS Script task in order to consume the results in the same package. For an overview of the result, an application called Data Profile Viewer is included within the SQL Server suite. You will learn how to read the results of the Data Profiling task inside your SSIS package in Chapter 19, "Implementing Custom Code in SSIS Packages."

EXAM TIP

You need to use custom code inside an SSIS package to use the results of the Data Profiling task in the same package.

You can use the SSIS Data Profiling task for profiling the following:

- **Column Length Distribution**   This helps you find strings of unexpected length.
- **Column Null Ratio**   Use this to find the percentage of NULLs in a column.
- **Column Pattern**   This is a very powerful profile that expresses patterns in strings as regular expressions and then calculates the distribution of these regular expressions.

- **Column Statistics** This gives you the minimum, maximum, average, and standard deviation for numeric columns, and the minimum and maximum for datetime columns.

- **Column Value Distribution** This gives you the distribution of values for discrete columns.

- **Candidate Key** This profile gives you the percentage of unique values in columns, thus helping you identify columns that are candidates for keys.

- **Functional Dependency** This profile reports how much the values in a dependent column depend on the values in a set of determinant columns.

- **Value Inclusion** This profile finds the extent to which column values from one table have corresponding values in a set of column values of another table, thus helping you find potential foreign keys.

 Quick Check

- Can you use the SSIS Data Profiling task to cleanse your data?

Quick Check Answer

- No, with the SSIS Data Profiling task you can only profile your data.

PRACTICE   Using the SSIS Data Profiling Task

In this practice, you will use the SSIS Data Profiling task.

If you encounter a problem completing an exercise, you can install the completed projects from the Solution folder that is provided with the companion content for this chapter and lesson.

EXERCISE 1   Profile the TK463CustomersDirty View

In this exercise, you use the Data Profiling task to find inaccurate data in the dbo.TK463-CustomersDirty view you created in the practice for the previous lesson, in the DQS_STAGING_DATA database.

1. Open SQL Server Data Tools (SSDT). Create a new SSIS project and solution named **TK 463 Chapter 17** in the Starter folder for this lesson. Do not create a directory for the solution.

2. Rename the default package to **ProfilingCustomers**.

3. Drag the Data Profiling task from the SSIS Toolbox (it should be in the Common Tasks group) to the control flow working area. Right-click it and select Edit.

4. On the General tab, use the Destination Property drop-down list to select New File Connection.

5. In the File Connection Manager Editor window, change the usage type to Create File. In the File text box, type the file name **ProfilingCustomers.xml**.

6. When you are back in the Data Profiling Task Editor, on the General tab, change the OverwriteDestination property to True to make it possible to re-execute the package multiple times (otherwise you will get an error saying that the destination file already exists when the package next executes).

7. In the lower-right corner of the Data Profiling Task Editor, on the General tab, click the Quick Profile button.

8. In the Simple Table Quick Profiling Form dialog box, click the New button to create a new ADO.NET connection. The Data Profiling task accepts only ADO.NET connections.

9. Connect to your SQL Server instance by using Windows authentication, and select the DQS_STAGING_DATA database. Click OK to return to the Simple Table Quick Profiling Form dialog box.

10. Select the dbo.TK463CustomersDirty view in the Table Or View drop-down list. Leave the first four check boxes selected, as they are by default. Clear the Candidate Key Profile check box, and select the Column Pattern Profile check box. The dialog box should look like the one shown in Figure 17-4. Click OK.

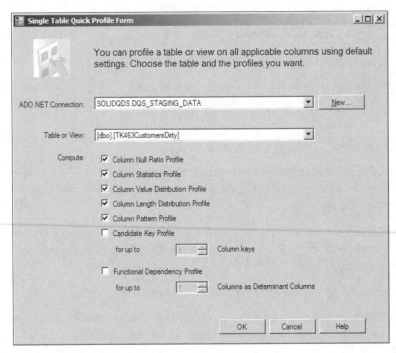

FIGURE 17-4 Selecting quick profiles.

11. In the Data Profiling Task Editor window, in the Profile Type list on the right, select different profiles and check their settings. Change the Column property for the Column Value Distribution Profile Request from (*) to Occupation (you are going to profile this column only). Change the ValueDistributionOption property for this request to All-Values. In addition, change the value for the Column property of the Column Pattern Profile Request from (*) to EmailAddress. Click OK.

12. Save the project. Right-click the Data Profiling task and select the Execute Task option. Wait until the execution finishes.

13. On the Debug menu, select the Stop Debugging option. Check whether the XML file appeared in the Starter folder for this lesson.

EXERCISE 2   View the Profiling Results

In this exercise, you use the Data Profile Viewer application to check the results of the Data Profiling task you used in the previous exercise.

1. On the Start menu, select All Programs | Microsoft SQL Server 2012 | Integration Services | Data Profile Viewer to start the Data Profile Viewer application.

2. Click the Open button. Navigate to the ProfilingCustomers.xml file and open it. Now you can start harvesting the results.

3. On the left, in the Profiles pane, select, for example, the Column Value Distribution Profiles. In the upper-right pane, select the *Occupation* column. In the middle-right window, you should see the distribution for the Occupation attribute. Click the value that has very low frequency (the Profesional value). Find the drill-down button in the upper-right corner of the middle-right window. Click it, and in the lower-right pane, check the row with this suspicious value.

4. Check the Column Pattern Profiles. Note that for the *EmailAddress* column, the Data Profiling task shows you the regular expression patterns for this column. Note that these two regular expressions are the regular expressions you used when you prepared a DQS knowledge base in the practice for Lesson 1 of this chapter.

5. Also check the other profiles. When you are done checking, close the Data Profile Viewer, SSMS, and SSDT.

Lesson Summary

- In addition to DQS, you can use many other tools from the SQL Server suite to improve the quality of your data.
- The SSIS Data Profiling task is easy to use for quick profiling of your data.

Lesson Review

Answer the following questions to test your knowledge of the information in this lesson. You can find the answers to these questions and explanations of why each answer choice is correct or incorrect in the "Answers" section at the end of this chapter.

1. How can you extract patterns in strings and express them in terms of regular expressions?

    A. With DQS knowledge discovery

    B. With T-SQL queries

    C. With the SSIS Data Profiling task

    D. With Master Data Manager

2. How could you find suspicious values in a string column? (Choose all that apply.)

    A. Check the distribution of the values.

    B. Check the distribution of the lengths of the values.

    C. Find the average value.

    D. Check the standard deviation of the values.

3. Which of the following cannot be profiled with the Data Profiling task?

    A. Column Null Ratio

    B. Column Pattern

    C. Value Inclusion

    D. Term-based relation

Case Scenario

In the following case scenario, you apply what you've learned about creating a data quality project to clean data. You can find the answers to these questions in the "Answers" section at the end of this chapter.

Case Scenario: Improving Data Quality

A company that you are consulting for complains that their customer data quality is low. Addresses in particular are often wrong and inconsistent. However, they have heard that there is a third-party provider that provides accurate addresses for all of the countries in which your client's customers reside. Answer the following questions:

1. What tool would you suggest the client use to solve this problem?

2. How can you use the third-party data?

Suggested Practices

To help you successfully master the exam objective presented in this chapter, complete the following tasks.

Create an Additional Knowledge Base and Project

To get used to DQS knowledge bases and projects, you should practice creating them.

- **Practice 1**   Create a knowledge base for *dbo.DimProduct* from the AdventureWorks-DW2012 demo database. Create at least a domain for product names.

- **Practice 2**   Change some product names. Create a DQS project and try to find the incorrect data.

Answers

This section contains answers to the lesson review questions and solutions to the case scenario in this chapter.

Lesson 1

1. **Correct Answers: A, B, and D**

   A. **Correct:** You can get domain values with the knowledge discovery process.

   B. **Correct:** You can edit domain values manually.

   C. **Incorrect:** With the SSIS Data Profiling task, you can profile data quickly. However, you cannot use this task to insert domain values into a DQS KB.

   D. **Correct:** You can import domain values from an Excel file.

2. **Correct Answer: B**

   A. **Incorrect:** You cannot use reference data services for creating a KB for de-duplicating.

   B. **Correct:** You have to define the matching policy in order to prepare a KB for de-duplicating.

   C. **Incorrect:** You cannot use knowledge discovery for defining the de-duplicating matching policy.

   D. **Incorrect:** You don't insert data manually for a matching policy.

3. **Correct Answer: A**

   A. **Correct:** You use a term-based relation in order to automatically correct all appearances of a string.

   B. **Incorrect:** You use synonyms to change one value to another.

   C. **Incorrect:** You use a cross-domain rule for a composite domain.

   D. **Incorrect:** You define a matching policy for identity mapping and de-duplication.

Lesson 2

1. **Correct Answer: A**

   A. **Correct:** Knowledge discovery is part of knowledge base management.

   B. **Incorrect:** Mapping is a DQS cleansing project stage.

   C. **Incorrect:** Computer-assisted cleansing is a DQS cleansing project stage.

   D. **Incorrect:** Interactive cleansing is a DQS cleansing project stage.

   E. **Incorrect:** Export is a DQS cleansing project stage.

2. **Correct Answer: D**

   A. **Incorrect:** If a value does not comply with the domain rules, DQS puts it in the invalid values.

   B. **Incorrect:** Automatically corrected values appear among the corrected values.

   C. **Incorrect:** If a value is correct, it appears among correct values.

   D. **Correct:** DQS puts a value among suggested values when a value has a confidence level higher than the auto-suggestions threshold and lower than the threshold for auto-corrections.

3. **Correct Answers: B and D**

   A. **Incorrect:** Knowledge discovery is part of domain management.

   B. **Correct:** You can create a cleansing or a matching DQS project.

   C. **Incorrect:** In a DQS project, you do not just validate your data; you cleanse it.

   D. **Correct:** You can create a cleansing or a matching DQS project.

Lesson 3

1. **Correct Answer: C**

   A. **Incorrect:** You cannot extract patterns from strings with DQS knowledge discovery.

   B. **Incorrect:** Although this is theoretically possible, you would need to create extremely complex T-SQL queries to extract patterns as regular expressions from strings.

   C. **Correct:** It is easy to extract patterns from strings with the SSIS Data Profiling task.

   D. **Incorrect:** Master Data Manager is not a data profiling application.

2. **Correct Answers: A and B**

   A. **Correct:** For discrete string columns, you can check the distribution of values to find values with low frequency.

   B. **Correct:** Lengths with low frequency can point to suspicious values.

   C. **Incorrect:** You cannot calculate an average value of strings.

   D. **Incorrect:** You cannot calculate standard deviation for strings.

3. **Correct Answer: D**

   A. **Incorrect:** Column Null Ratio is a profile of the Data Profiling task.

   B. **Incorrect:** Column Pattern is a profile of the Data Profiling task.

   C. **Incorrect:** Value Inclusion is a profile of the Data Profiling task.

   D. **Correct:** Term-based relation is a part of a DQS knowledge base; you cannot use this in the SSIS Data Profiling task.

Case Scenario

1. You should recommend that the company use Data Quality Services.

2. When creating a knowledge base, you can specify a reference data provider for the address domains.

## PART VI

Advanced SSIS and Data Quality Topics

CHAPTER 18   SSIS and Data Mining   **667**

CHAPTER 19   Implementing Custom Code in SSIS Packages   **699**

CHAPTER 20   Identity Mapping and De-Duplicating   **735**

SSIS and Data Mining

Exam objectives in this chapter:
- Extract and Transform Data
  - Design data flow.

Data mining is the most advanced part of a BI solution. Data mining should actually stand for the "I" in "BI." With data mining algorithms, you can automatically discover previously unknown patterns and rules in your data. Microsoft SQL Server Integration Services (SSIS) can use predictive models through the Data Mining Query task and transformation in the control flow or data flow of a package. You can add predictions from the mining model to your data. In addition, SSIS implements text mining through the Term Extraction and Term Lookup transformations.

In order to create a good mining model, you need to work on data preparation. You can use SSIS as an extract-transform-load (ETL) tool to help with this task as well. In this chapter, you will learn the basics of data mining, how to use mining models, how to create a text mining solution, and how to prepare data for data mining.

Lessons in this chapter:
- Lesson 1: Data Mining Task and Transformation
- Lesson 2: Text Mining
- Lesson 3: Preparing Data for Data Mining

Before You Begin

To complete this chapter, you must have:

- SQL Server 2012 Database Services, Integration Services, and Data Quality Services installed.
- SQL Server 2012 Analysis Services (SSAS) installed in Multidimensional and Data Mining mode.
- Intermediate Transact-SQL skills.
- The AdventureWorks2012 and AdventureWorksDW2012 sample databases installed.

Lesson 1: Data Mining Task and Transformation

Data mining is data-driven analysis. When you create a data mining (DM) model, you do not anticipate results in advance. You examine data with advanced mathematical methods or data mining algorithms, and then you examine the patterns and rules that your algorithms find. The SQL Server Analysis Services (SSAS) data mining engine runs the algorithms automatically after you set up all of the parameters you need, and therefore you can check millions of different pivoting options in a very limited time. In this section, you will learn how to perform data mining analyses with SQL Server 2012 Analysis Services and use it in an SSIS package.

> **After this lesson, you will be able to:**
> - Understand data mining.
> - Create a predictive mining model.
> - Use a predictive mining model in an SSIS package.
>
> **Estimated lesson time: 70 minutes**

What Is Data Mining?

What does the term *data mining* mean? In short, by using data mining (DM) you can deduce hidden knowledge by examining, or *training*, the data with data mining algorithms. Algorithms express knowledge found in patterns and rules. Data mining algorithms are based mainly on statistics, although some are based on artificial intelligence and other branches of mathematics and information technology as well. Nevertheless, the terminology comes mainly from statistics. What you are examining is called a *case*, which can be interpreted as one appearance of an entity or a row in a table. The attributes of a case are called *variables*. After you find patterns and rules, you can use them to perform predictions. In SSAS, the DM model is stored in the SSAS database as a kind of a table. It is not a table in a relational sense, because it can include nested tables in columns. The model stores the information about the variables, algorithms used, and the parameters of the algorithms. Of course, after the training, the extracted knowledge is stored in the model as well. The data used for training is not part of the model; however, you can enable drillthrough on a model and use drillthrough queries to browse the source data.

DM techniques are divided in two main classes: directed algorithms and undirected algorithms. In the directed approach, you have a target variable that is used to supervise the training; this target variable is the focus of the mining activities, and the trained model is used to explain the values of it with selected input variables. Then the directed algorithms apply gleaned information to unknown examples to predict the value of the target variable. In the undirected approach, you are trying to discover new patterns inside the data set as a whole, without any specific target variable. For example, you use a directed approach to find the reasons for purchases of an article, and an undirected approach to find out which articles are commonly purchased together. There are many business questions you can answer with data mining. A few of the thousands of uses for data mining are listed here:

- A bank might ask what the credit risk of a customer is.
- A Customer Relationship Management (CRM) application can ask whether there are any interesting groups of customers based on similarity of values of their attributes.
- A retail store might be interested in which products appear in the same market basket.
- A business might be interested in forecasting sales.
- If you maintain a website, you might be interested in usage patterns.
- Credit card issuers would like to find fraudulent transactions.
- Advanced email spam filters use data mining.

There are four distinct steps in a typical data mining project:

1. Identifying the business problem
2. Using DM techniques to transform the data into actionable information
3. Acting on the information
4. Measuring the result

These four steps are also shown in Figure 18-1.

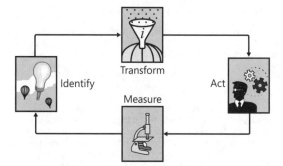

FIGURE 18-1 The four steps of a data mining project.

In the first step, you need to contact business subject matter experts in order to identify business problems. The second, the transform step, is where you use the SQL Server Business Intelligence suite to prepare the data and train the models on the data. This chapter is focused on the transform step. Acting means using patterns and rules learned in production. You can use data mining models as dimensions for SQL Server Analysis Services cubes, you can use them for advanced SQL Server Integration Services transformations, you can use them in your applications to implement constraints and warnings, you can create SQL Server Reporting Services reports based on mining models and predictions, and more. After deployment of the data mining model in production, you have to measure the improvements to your business. You can use UDM cubes with mining model dimensions as a very useful measurement tool. As you can see from Figure 18-1, the project does not have to finish here; you can continue it or open a new project, identifying new business problems.

The second step, the transform step, has its own internal cycle. You need to understand your data, making an overview of it. Then you have to prepare the data for data mining, and then you train your models. If your models do not give you the desired results, you have to return to the data overview phase and learn more about your data, or to the data preparation phase and prepare the data differently. You will learn more about data preparation for data mining in Lesson 3 of this chapter.

SSAS Data Mining Algorithms

SQL Services 2012 Analysis Services, when installed in Multidimensional and Data Mining mode, supports all of the most popular data mining algorithms. In fact, if you want to use data mining, your SSAS instance must be installed in the Multidimensional mode; SSAS in tabular mode does not support data mining. In addition, SSIS includes two text mining transformations. Table 18-1 summarizes the SSAS algorithms and their usage.

TABLE 18-1 SSAS Data Mining Algorithms

Algorithm	Usage
Association Rules	The Association Rules algorithm is the one used for market basket analysis. It defines an itemset as a combination of items in a single transaction; then it scans the data and counts the number of times the itemsets appear together in transactions. Market basket analysis is useful for detecting cross-selling opportunities.
Clustering	The Clustering algorithm groups cases from a dataset into clusters containing similar characteristics. You can use the Clustering method to group your customers for your CRM application to find distinguishable groups of customers. In addition, you can use it for finding anomalies in your data. If a case does not fit well into any cluster, it is kind of an exception. For example, an anomalous case might be a fraudulent transaction.
Decision Trees	The Decision Trees algorithm is the most popular DM algorithm. It is used to predict discrete and continuous variables. The algorithm uses discrete input variables to split the tree into nodes in such a way that each node is more pure in terms of target variable—that is, each split leads to nodes where a single state of a target variable is represented better than other states. For continuous predictable variables, you get a piecewise multiple linear regression formula with a separate formula in each node of a tree. A tree that predicts continuous variables is a Regression Tree.
Linear Regression	Linear Regression predicts continuous variables by using a single multiple linear regression formula. The input variables must be continuous as well. Linear Regression is a simple case of a Regression Tree, a tree with no splits.
Logistic Regression	As Linear Regression is a simple Regression Tree, a Logistic Regression is a Neural Network without any hidden layers.
Naïve Bayes	The Naïve Bayes algorithm calculates probabilities for each possible state of the input attribute for every single state of a predictable variable. Those probabilities are used to predict the target attribute based on the known input attributes of new cases. The Naïve Bayes algorithm is quite simple; it builds the models quickly. Therefore, it is very suitable as a starting point in your prediction project. The Naïve Bayes algorithm does not support continuous attributes.

Algorithm	Usage
Neural Network	The Neural Network algorithm is the one that comes from artificial intelligence. You can use this algorithm for predictions as well. Neural networks search for nonlinear functional dependencies by performing nonlinear transformations on the data in layers, from the input layer through hidden layers to the output layer. Because of the multiple nonlinear transformations, neural networks are harder to interpret as compared to Decision Trees.
Sequence Clustering	Sequence Clustering searches for clusters based on a model, and not on the similarity of cases as Clustering does. The models are defined on sequences of events by using Markov Chains. Typical usage of the Sequence Clustering algorithm would be an analysis of your company's website usage, although you can use this algorithm on any sequential data.
Time Series	You can use the Time Series algorithm to forecast continuous variables. Internally, Time Series uses two different algorithms. For short-term forecasting, the Auto-Regression Trees (ART) algorithm is used. For long-term prediction, the Auto-Regressive Integrated Moving Average (ARIMA) algorithm is used. You can mix the blend of algorithms used by using the mining model parameters.

EXAM TIP

Only SSAS installed in Multidimensional mode supports data mining.

Using Data Mining Predictions in SSIS

SSIS is connected to data mining in many ways. You can use SSIS packages to prepare data for data mining. You will learn about preparing data for data mining in Lesson 3 of this chapter. Text mining is incorporated in SSIS packages through the two text mining transformations, the Term Extraction and Term Lookup transformations. You will learn more about text mining in Lesson 2 of this chapter. You can use SSIS packages to process (or "train," in data mining jargon) data mining models, the same way you use them to process other SSAS objects. You learned about the Analysis Services Processing task in Chapter 4, "Designing and Implementing Control Flow." Finally, you can use data mining results in an SSIS package for creating an advanced control or data flow. You can use a predictive data mining model to add predictions to existing data in an SSIS package.

For example, you can have a Decision Trees mining model that tries to explain the reason for customers' decisions to buy bikes. You learn these patterns from your existing data. SSAS learns these patterns when you train the model. SSAS stores these patterns in the model, which is a table in an SSAS database. However, this table doesn't look like a SQL Server table; it is a table that allows *nested tables,* columns that are tables by themselves. You can use this model to predict who is going to buy a bike on a new dataset with prospective buyers. You can filter prospective buyers and select probable bike buyers, buyers who are likely to buy a bike. You can select a subset of prospective buyers and thus lower the expenses of marketing campaigns. However, you cannot use Transact-SQL to query SSAS mining models, because of the nested tables and other data mining specifics.

In order to add the predicted values of a mining model to existing SSIS data, you have to use a Data Mining Extensions (DMX) query that joins a mining model with your data with a special DMX prediction join. Learning DMX is out of the scope of this book. Fortunately, you can create DMX queries with the help of a DMX Query Editor built into the Data Mining Query task and Data Mining Query transformation. In the practice for this lesson, you will learn how to prepare and train a data mining model and then use predictions in your data flow.

 Quick Check

- How do you perform a prediction by using a data mining model?

Quick Check Answer

- You need to create a DMX prediction query that joins patterns stored in an SSAS mining model with your data.

PRACTICE **Using Data Mining Predictions in SSIS**

In this practice, you will create a predictive SSAS mining model. Then you will use this model in an SSIS package data flow.

If you encounter a problem completing an exercise, you can install the completed projects from the Solution folder that is provided with the companion content for this chapter and lesson.

EXERCISE 1 Create a Decision Trees Model

In this exercise, you create a Decision Trees prediction model and deploy it to your SSAS instance installed in the Multidimensional and Data Mining mode.

1. Open SQL Server Data Tools. Create a new solution named **TK 463 Chapter 18** and a new project in this solution named **TK 463 Chapter 18 SSAS**. For the project, use the Analysis Services Multidimensional and Data Mining Project template.

2. In Solution Explorer, right-click the Data Sources folder and select the New Data Source option.

3. On the Welcome page of the Data Source Wizard, click Next.

4. On the Select How To Define The Connection page, click New.

5. In the Connection Manager window, connect to your SQL Server instance and to the AdventureWorksDW2012 demo database. Use the Native OLE DB\SQL Server Native Client 11.0 provider. Click OK.

6. On the Select How To Define The Connection page, click Next.

7. In the Impersonation Information window, select the Use A Specific User Name And Password option. Here you define how SSAS connects to SQL Server. You can define a specific account for this data source, use the service account, or use the current user account. Using a specific Windows account is recommended as a best practice. The Inherit option means that SSAS will use the service account for processing and the current user account for prediction queries. Enter your Windows user name and password into the appropriate text boxes. Your Windows account should, of course, have permissions to read and write in the AdventureWorksDW2012 database. Click Next.

8. In the Completing The Wizard window, leave the default name (Adventure Works DW2012) and click Finish.

9. In Solution Explorer, right-click the Data Source Views folder and select the New Data Source View option.

10. On the Welcome page, click Next.

11. On the Select A Data Source page, make sure that the data source you just created is selected, and click Next.

12. In the Select Tables And Views pane, select only the vTargetMail view. Click Next.

13. In the Completing The Wizard window, leave the default name (Adventure Works DW2012) and click Finish.

14. In Solution Explorer, right-click the Mining Structures folder and select New Mining Structure.

15. On the Welcome page, click Next.

16. On the Select The Definition Method page, use the existing relational database or data warehouse (leave the first option selected). Click Next.

17. In the Create The Data Mining Structure window, in the Which Data Mining Technique Do You Want To Use drop-down list under the Create Mining Structure With A Mining Model option, select the Decision Trees algorithm from the drop-down list (the default). Click Next.

18. Use the Adventure Works DW2012 data source view on the Select Data Source View page, and click Next.

19. In Specify Table Types, select vTargetMail as a case table by selecting the Case check box for this table. Click Next.

20. By selecting the appropriate check boxes on the Specify The Training Data page, define *CustomerKey* as a key column (selected by default), *BikeBuyer* as predictable column, and *CommuteDistance, EnglishEducation, EnglishOccupation, Gender, HouseOwnerFlag, MaritalStatus, NumberCarsOwned, NumberChildrenAtHome, Region*, and *TotalChildren* as input columns. Click Next.

21. On the Specify Columns' Content And Data Type page, click the Detect button. The wizard should detect that all columns except the *CustomerKey* column have discrete content. The *CustomerKey* column content should be Key, as Figure 18-2 shows. If any of the content differs from Figure 18-2, change it appropriately. Then click Next.

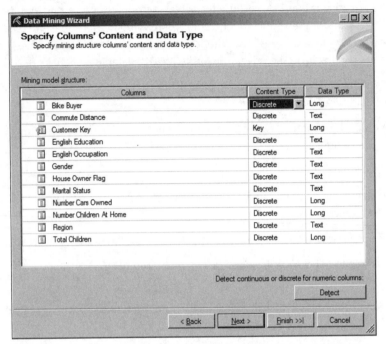

FIGURE 18-2 Column content and data type for a Decision Trees mining model.

22. On the Create Testing Set page, you can specify the percentage of the data or number of cases for the testing set—that is, the holdout data. Use 0 percent of data as the test set. You will learn more about data preparation in Lesson 3 of this chapter. Click Next.

23. Enter **TM** as the name of the mining structure and **TMDT** as the name of the model on the Completing The Wizard page. Click Finish. Save the solution.

24. In Solution Explorer, right-click the TK 463 Chapter 18 SSAS project and select Deploy. Note that if you want to deploy the solution to an SSAS instance other than the default localhost instance, you should change the project properties.

25. When the deployment is finished, close the Deployment Progress window.

26. In Data Mining Designer, click the Mining Model Viewer tab.

27. In the Background drop-down list, select a value of 1 for the Bike Buyer to check the potential buyers only. You are not interested in groups of customers who are not going to buy a bike. Note the color of the nodes: the darker the color is, the more bike buyers appear in the node. For example, you can see that the color of the node

that groups people for whom the Number Cars Owned attribute is equal to 0 and the Region is Pacific is quite dark. Therefore, the potential bike buyers are in that node. In the Mining Legend window, you can see the detail information: more than 91 percent of people in this node have bought a bike in the past. You can see this information in Figure 18-3.

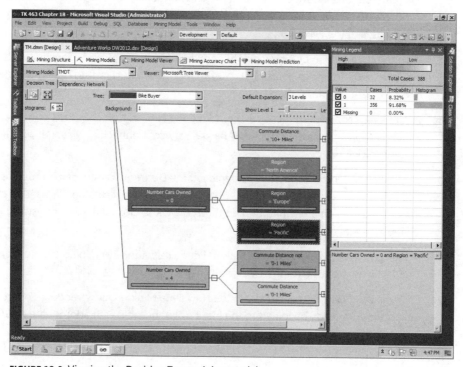

FIGURE 18-3 Viewing the Decision Trees mining model.

28. Close all open designers. Do not exit SSDT.

EXERCISE 2 Use a Mining Model in the SSIS Data Flow

In the second exercise of this practice, you use the Decision Trees mining model you created in the first exercise inside an SSIS package.

1. If you closed SSDT, open it and open the TK 463 Chapter 18 solution.

2. On the File menu, select Add, and then New Project. Select the Integration Services Project template. Name the project **TK 463 Chapter 18 SSIS** and click OK.

3. Rename the default package **ProbableBuyers**.

4. From the SSIS Toolbox, drag the data flow task to the Control Flow working area. Rename the task **ProbableBuyers**. Click the Data Flow tab.

5. Drag the OLE DB Source to the Data Flow working area. Rename the source **ProspectiveBuyer**. Open the OLE DB Source Editor.

6. Create a new connection manager to connect to your SQL Server instance and to the AdventureWorksDW2012 demo database. In the Data Access Mode drop-down list, use the Table Or View Mode. In the Name Of The Table Or The View drop-down list, select the *dbo.ProspectiveBuyer* table. Click the Columns tab to define the column mappings, and then click OK.

7. Drag the Data Mining Query transformation below the source and connect it with the gray arrow to the source. Rename it to **JoinTMDT**. Double-click it to open the Data Mining Query Transformation Editor.

8. Create a new connection manager by clicking the New button near the Connection Manager drop-down list. In the Add Analysis Services Connection Manager pop-up window, click Edit.

9. Select the SSAS instance where you deployed the Decision Trees mining model. Use integrated security. Select the TK 463 Chapter 18 SSAS initial catalog. Click OK to close the Connection Manager window, and then click OK to close the Add Analysis Services Connection Manager window.

10. In the Data Mining Query Transformation Editor, select the TM mining structure and TMDT mining model. Click the Query tab.

11. Click the Build New Query button. In the New Data Mining Query window, your mining model should already be joined to the Input Columns table with appropriate column names. In the grid at the bottom of the window, you just need to select additional columns for your data flow. These additional columns come from the mining model.

12. In the Source column, in the first row of the grid, select the TMDT mining model. Make sure that the Bike Buyer field is selected. In the Alias column, enter **BikeBuyer**. This is the name for this column later in your data flow. The content of this column will be the predicted value (1 for buyers, 0 for non-buyers). The predicted value comes from the knowledge stored in the mining model.

13. In the Source column, in the second row of the grid, select Prediction Function. In the Field column, select the PredictProbability function. In the Alias column, enter **PredictProbability**. In the Criteria/Argument column of the grid, enter **[TMDT].[Bike Buyer]**. This is the argument for the DMX PredictProbability function. This function will return the probability for the prediction in the *BikeBuyer* column. Your DMX query builder should look like the one in Figure 18-4. Click OK.

14. In the Data Mining Query Transformation Editor, check the DMX query created by the DMX query builder. Note the FLATTENED DMX keyword right after the DMX SELECT. This keyword flattens all nested tables so that the result is acceptable for SSIS. Click OK.

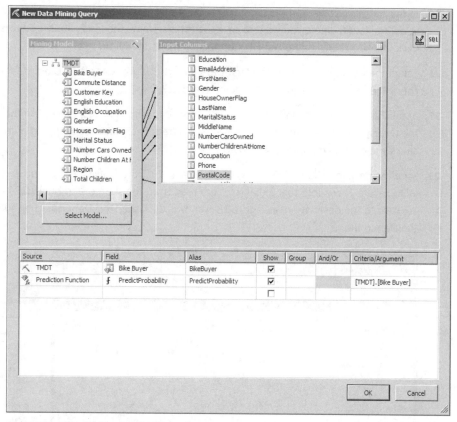

FIGURE 18-4 The DMX query builder.

15. Drag the Conditional Split transformation below the Data Mining Query transformation. Connect the two transformations with the grey arrow. Double-click the Conditional Split transformation to open the editor.

16. Add an output called **ProbableBuyers**. Use the following expression for the condition:

    `[BikeBuyer] == 1 && [PredictProbability] > 0.52`

17. Click OK to close the Conditional Split Transformation Editor.

18. Drag a Flat File Destination below the Conditional Split transformation. Rename it **ProbableBuyers**. Connect it to the Conditional Split transformation with the gray arrow. In the Input Output Selection pop-up window, select the ProbableBuyers output. Click OK. Double-click the destination to open the Flat File Destination Editor.

19. Click the New button on the right of the Flat File Connection Manager drop-down list. Select the Delimited format and click OK in the Flat File Format pop-up window.

20. In the Flat File Connection Manager Editor, on the General tab, use the Browse button to select the folder where you want to save the results. Name the file **ProbableBuyers.csv**. Click Open to return to the Flat File Connection Manager Editor.

21. Select the Column Names In The First Data Row check box. Click the Columns tab to check the default row and column delimiters. Click OK.

22. In the Flat File Destination Editor, on the Connection Manager tab, make sure that the Overwrite Data In The File check box is selected. Then click the Mappings tab and check the column mappings. Click OK.

23. Save the package. Right-click in an empty area in the Data Flow working area and select Execute Task. Note that 2,059 rows are read from the source, and only 1,104 rows are sent to the destination, as Figure 18-5 shows. Click the Stop Debugging option in the Debug menu.

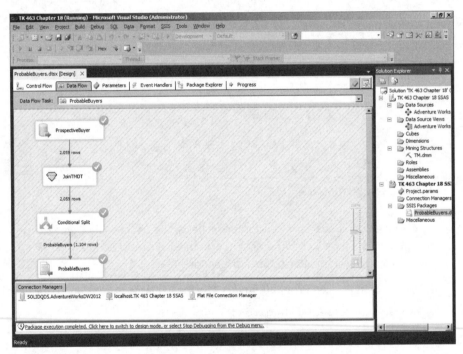

FIGURE 18-5 Data flow after executing the data flow task.

24. Open the .csv file with Microsoft Excel or, if that is not possible, with Notepad. Check the content.

Lesson Summary

- You create data mining models with SSDT by using the Analysis Services Multidimensional and Data Mining Project template.
- You can use mining model predictions in SSIS packages.

Lesson Review

Answer the following questions to test your knowledge of the information in this lesson. You can find the answers to these questions and explanations of why each answer choice is correct or incorrect in the "Answers" section at the end of this chapter.

1. Which SSAS mining algorithm is useful for forecasting?
   - **A.** Decision Trees
   - **B.** Time Series
   - **C.** Association Rules
   - **D.** Naïve Bayes

2. Which language do you use for data mining prediction queries?
   - **A.** MDX
   - **B.** T-SQL
   - **C.** DAX
   - **D.** DMX

3. Which SSAS mining algorithm is useful for market basket analysis?
   - **A.** Decision Trees
   - **B.** Time Series
   - **C.** Association Rules
   - **D.** Naïve Bayes

Lesson 2: Text Mining

Text mining is about using an application to automatically gain an understanding of specific text blocks. In SQL Server 2012, you can use two SSIS transformations for this task: the Term Extraction and Term Lookup transformations. These two transformations do not give you the understanding directly; instead, they form the infrastructure that enables you to better understand the content of the text you are analyzing. With this understanding, you can group text blocks into different categories. You can even perform further analyses on the results to form the groupings automatically.

> **After this lesson, you will be able to:**
> - Use the Term Extraction transformation.
> - Use the Term Lookup transformation.
>
> **Estimated lesson time: 30 minutes**

Term Extraction

With the Term Extraction transformation, you can retrieve the key terms from a Unicode string or text column. The transformation has built-in knowledge about the grammar and syntax of the English language. Therefore, you should use this transformation for English text only. If you use it for other languages, the results might be worse than you expect. The transformation does the following for English text:

- It identifies words by using different word separators in the English language. It preserves words connected by hyphens or underscores. It understands and keeps acronyms intact, even if they include periods. It can split words on special characters such as the slash (for example, it can split the expression "date/time" into the words "date" and "time"). It also recognizes that some special characters, such as apostrophes, do not split words. However, it can identify tokens by splitting time expressions (for example, the date January 31, 2004 is separated into the three tokens: January, 31, and 2004), monetary expressions, and email and postal addresses.

- It tags words in different forms: a noun in the singular or plural form; a proper noun in the singular or plural form; an adjective, a comparative adjective, and a superlative adjective; a number. You can extract nouns and noun phrases. A noun phrase has to include at least one noun.

- It stems words to their internal dictionary form.

- It normalizes words. For example, if words are capitalized only because of their position in a sentence, it uses their non-capitalized form instead. It can also perform case-sensitive normalization. You can configure it to consider lowercase and uppercase words as either distinct terms or as different variants of the same term.

- It also finds sentence boundaries by using standard English sentence separators.

 You can also define *exclusion terms*, which are terms you do not want to extract. For example, if you are analyzing text segments about SQL Server, you might not want to extract the term "SQL Server," because it probably appears in any single text block you are analyzing and by extracting it you would not gain any insight. You can store exclusion terms in any table available through an OLE DB connection, in a single column.

The Term Extraction transformation returns only two columns in the output: *Term* and *Score*. You can rename the columns if you want. The term is a noun or a noun phrase. The score is either the absolute *term frequency (TF)* or a special coefficient called *Term Frequency/ Inverse Document Frequency (TFIDF)*. The TFIDF score is defined as:

*TFIDF = (Term Frequency) * LOG((number of rows in input) / (number of rows having the term))*

The TFIDF score deemphasizes terms that appear in many documents and gives more importance to terms that appear multiple times in a small number of documents, thus characterizing the documents more than terms that appear in many documents.

You can also configure the following properties of the Term Extraction transformation:

- **Frequency threshold**   With this property, you specify the number of times a word or phrase must occur before the transformation extracts it. The default value is 2.
- **Maximum length of term**   This is the maximum number of words in a phrase. The default value is 12.
- **Use case-sensitive term extraction**   The default is False.

Term Lookup

The Term Lookup transformation uses a dictionary of terms that is stored in a column in a SQL Server table and applies this dictionary to an input data set that contains documents stored as a Unicode string or text column. The transformation counts how many times a term appears in a document. It extracts words from a document in an input column by using the same knowledge about the English language as the Term Extraction transformation, including:

- Breaking text into sentences
- Breaking sentences into words
- Normalizing words

The Term Lookup transformation uses the following rules for the lookup:

- Use a case-sensitive match. This is a configurable property.
- If a plural form of the noun or noun phrase exists in the reference table, the lookup matches only the plural form. A singular form is matched separately.
- If only the singular form exists in the reference table, then the transformation matches both the singular and the plural forms of the word or phrase to the singular form.
- If the text in the input column is a lemmatized noun phrase, then the transformation normalizes only the last word in the noun phrase. For example, the lemmatized version of "employees duties" is "employees duty."

The Term Lookup transformation adds two columns to the transformation output. These columns are named *Term* and *Frequency* by default. This information can give you insight into documents—for example, you can use it to classify the documents. You can store the results in a SQL Server table and then analyze the table with T-SQL queries. You can even use this table as input for data mining models and exploit SSAS data mining capabilities to gain more understanding about the documents you are analyzing.

EXAM TIP

Any table with a column with key terms can be used as the reference dictionary for the Term Lookup transformation. Although it is quite convenient to create the dictionary with the Term Extraction transformation, these two transformations do not need to be connected in any way. You can also edit the dictionary extracted with the Term Extraction transformation manually.

 Quick Check

- Which languages are supported by the two text mining transformations?

Quick Check Answer

- Both the Term Extraction and Term Lookup transformations are limited to the English language only.

PRACTICE **Performing Text Mining**

In this practice, you will perform some simple text mining.

If you encounter a problem completing an exercise, you can install the completed projects from the Solution folder that is provided with the companion content for this chapter and lesson.

EXERCISE 1 Use the Term Extraction Transformation

In this exercise, you create a data flow that uses the Term Extraction transformation.

1. If you closed SSDT, open it and open the TK 463 Chapter 18 solution in the TK463\Chapter18\Lesson2\Starter folder. Add a package to the TK 463 Chapter 18 SSIS project. Rename the package **TextMining**.

2. Add a data flow task to the control flow and rename it **TermExtraction**.

3. Add another data flow task to the control flow and rename it **TermLookup**. Connect the two tasks with a precedence constraint defining that the TermExtraction task has to finish successfully before the TermLookup task can start.

4. Click the Data Flow tab. Select the data flow for the TermExtraction task.

5. Add an OLE DB data source. Rename the source **ProductReviews**. Configure the source to connect to the AdventureWorks2012 database on your SQL Server instance. Use the SQL command data access mode. Write the following query to the SQL command text box.

```
SELECT ProductReviewID,
 ProductID,
 ReviewerName,
 Rating,
 Comments
FROM Production.ProductReview;
```

6. Click the Columns tab and review the columns. Then click OK.

7. Add the Term Extraction transformation to your data flow. Connect it to the source with the gray arrow. Double-click it to open the editor.

8. On the Term Extraction tab, in the Available Input Columns table, select the check box near the *Comments* column. You are going to extract terms from this column. Leave the default output column names (*Term* and *Score*).

9. Click the Exclusion tab. Review the options, but do not change anything.

10. Click the Advanced tab. Review the options, but do not change anything.

11. Click the Configure Error Output button. By default, erroneous rows are redirected. Change the value of the *Error* column in the grid from Redirect Row to Fail Component. If anything goes wrong, the package execution will fail. You are not going to catch erroneous rows. Click OK to close the Configure Error Output window. Then click OK to close the Term Extraction Transformation Editor.

12. Add an OLE DB destination. Rename it **Terms**. Connect it to the Term Extraction transformation with the gray arrow. Double-click it to open the editor.

13. Use the connection manager to your AdventureWorks2012 database. Click the New button near the Name Of The Table Or The View drop-down list to create a new table for the Term Extraction results. Check the code in the Create Table pop-up window, and click OK to create the table.

14. Click the Mappings tab to map the input columns to the destination columns. Then click OK to close the OLE DB Destination Editor.

EXERCISE 2   Use the Term Lookup Transformation

In this exercise, you count how many times a term appears in a document by using the Term Lookup transformation, and you analyze the results.

1. If you closed SSDT, open it and open the TK 463 Chapter 18 solution you opened or created in the previous exercise. Open the designer for the TextMining package. Open the TermExtraction data flow.

2. Right-click the ProductReviews OLE DB source and select Copy.

3. Select the TermLookup task from the Data Flow Task drop-down list at the top of the Data Flow working area to open the TermLookup data flow.

4. Right-click in the TermLookup data flow working area and select Paste. This copies the source for the Term Lookup transformation.

5. Add the Term Lookup transformation to your data flow. Connect it to the source with the gray arrow. Double-click it to open the editor.

6. On the Reference Table tab, make sure that the OLE DB connection manager to your AdventureWorks2012 database is selected. Select the *dbo.Terms* table for the reference table in the Reference Table Name drop-down list.

7. Click the Term Lookup tab. Click the *Comments* column in the Available Input Columns table. Drag the column and drop it on the *Term* column in the Available Reference Columns table.

8. Select the check boxes for the *ProductReviewID*, *ProductId*, *ReviewerName*, and *Rating* columns in the Available Input Columns table. These columns should appear as the pass-through columns in the grid in the lower part of the editor. Your Term Lookup Transformation Editor should look like the one shown in Figure 18-6.

9. Click the Advanced tab. Review the options, but do not change anything.

10. Click the Configure Error Output button. By default, erroneous rows are redirected. Change the value of the *Error* column in the grid from Redirect Row to Fail Component. If anything goes wrong, the package execution will fail. You are not going to catch erroneous rows. Click OK to close the Configure Error Output window. Then click OK to close the Term Lookup Transformation Editor.

11. Add an OLE DB destination. Rename it **TermsInReviews**. Connect it to the Term Extraction transformation with the gray arrow. Double-click it to open the editor.

12. Use the connection manager to your AdventureWorks2012 database. Click the New button near the Name Of The Table Or The View drop-down list to create a new table for the Term Lookup results. Check the code in the Create Table pop-up window, and click OK to create the table.

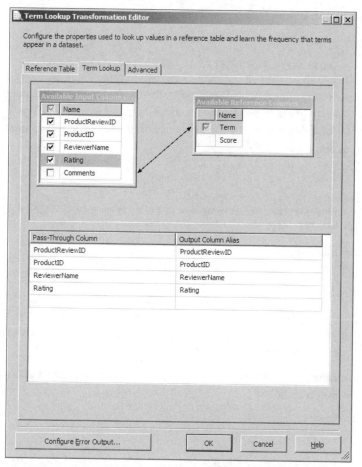

FIGURE 18-6 Configuring the Term Lookup transformation.

13. Click the Mappings tab to map the input columns to the destination columns. Then click OK to close the OLE DB Destination Editor.

14. In Solution Explorer, right-click the TextMining package and select the Execute Package option. When execution is complete, switch to design mode.

15. Open SSMS and connect to your SQL Server instance. Open a new query window and change the context to the AdventureWorks2012 database.

16. Use the following query to check the terms extracted and their frequency.

```
SELECT Term, Score
FROM dbo.Terms
ORDER BY Score DESC;
```

The most popular term should be the term "bike." You already learned something about the reviews: apparently, most of the reviews are about bikes.

17. Check the results of the Term Lookup transformation. Start with a simple query.

```
SELECT ReviewerName, Rating, Term, Frequency
FROM dbo.TermsInReviews
ORDER BY ReviewerName, Frequency DESC;
```

18. Now you will use a somewhat sophisticated query to see what the reviewers are dis-satisfied with. You are going to extract the two most frequent terms in each review and order the results by the rating and by the frequency of terms, in descending order. Use the following query.

```
WITH TermsCTE AS
(
SELECT ReviewerName, Rating, Term, Frequency,
 ROW_NUMBER() OVER(PARTITION BY ReviewerName ORDER BY Frequency DESC) AS RN
FROM dbo.TermsInReviews
)
SELECT ReviewerName, Rating, Term, Frequency
FROM TermsCTE
WHERE RN <= 2
ORDER BY Rating;
```

From the results, you should see that when the rating is not excellent (less than 5), the term "pedal" appears as one of the two most frequent terms. You can conclude that some bike models might have problems with pedals.

19. When you finish analyzing the data, clean up the AdventureWorks2012 database by running the following code.

```
DROP TABLE dbo.Terms;
DROP TABLE dbo.TermsInReviews;
```

> **NOTE** **CONTINUING WITH PRACTICES**
>
> Do not exit SSMS and SSDT if you intend to continue immediately with the next practice.

Lesson Summary

- You can extract terms with the Term Extraction transformation.
- You can count how many times a term appears in a document with the Term Lookup transformation.

Lesson Review

Answer the following questions to test your knowledge of the information in this lesson. You can find the answers to these questions and explanations of why each answer choice is correct or incorrect in the "Answers" section at the end of this chapter.

1. What are the default columns returned by the Term Extraction transformation?

   A. *Term* and *Score*

   B. *Phrase* and *Score*

   C. *TFIDF* and *Term*

   D. *Term* and *TermFrequency*

2. What are the default columns added to the output by the Term Lookup transformation?

   A. *Score* and *Frequency*

   B. *Score* and *Term*

   C. *Term* and *Frequency*

   D. *Term* and *Phrase*

3. What are exclusion terms?

   A. Exclusion terms are the exclusive terms to extract.

   B. Exclusion terms are terms that you already extracted.

   C. Exclusion terms are terms that you want to extract manually.

   D. Exclusion terms are terms you do not want to extract.

Lesson 3: Preparing Data for Data Mining

As with most data warehousing activity, most of the time in a data mining project is spent preparing the data. This preparation involves extracting the data from your sources, cleansing it, and loading it to a destination database. If you already have a data warehouse with cleansed data, this data might be appropriate for mining models immediately. However, more often you have to prepare the data in some special ways for data mining. This preparation involves defining the cases, creating derived variables, and—a very important part—creating appropriate *samples*. You will learn about data preparation for data mining in this lesson.

> **After this lesson, you will be able to:**
> - Understand the need for derived variables.
> - Use the SSIS Percentage Sampling and Row Sampling transformations.
>
> **Estimated lesson time: 30 minutes**

Preparing the Data

You start preparing data for data mining by determining the case you want to analyze in your data. Sometimes the definition of the case is simple; it might just be a customer from a customer dimension in your data warehouse. Other times, defining the case is trickier. For example, for credit risk management, the case might be a family and not just a single customer. In this example, you would need to find a way to define what a family is and create a new table in your data warehouse for families.

Before you even start preparing the data, you must understand it. You must realize how data values are measured in different variables. There are many ways to measure data values:

- Discrete Values
  - Categorical or nominal columns have no natural order; a value is just a name for a category. For example, you can have product categories that, regardless of whether they are denoted by a code or by a name, are always categorical.
  - Ranks have an order but do not permit arithmetic. Typical ranks include opinion ranks.

- Continuous Values
  - Intervals have an order and allow subtraction but do not always allow summations. Intervals can be closed or open on one side. In business scenarios, there are many one-side-closed intervals such as income, for which negative values usually cannot appear.
  - True numeric values support all arithmetic operations and are not limited in any way. In accounting, for example, you can have both positive and negative values.

You achieve the insight into your data with the data overview. You can use T-SQL queries, OLAP cubes, reports, graphs, all kinds of statistical analysis, and more to reach this understanding. For example, suppose you need to find outliers. Outliers are rare values that are far out of bounds. Because they are so far out of bounds, they can have a big impact on the analysis. You might want to check whether an outlier is actually an erroneous value. You might decide to filter the rows (cases) with outliers. You can discretize continuous values and hide outliers in the leftmost and rightmost bin.

> **REAL WORLD** DATA OVERVIEW AND DATA MINING
>
> The data overview for data mining is very similar to data profiling for estimating data quality. We have managed to lower expenses by joining two distinct projects into a single one more than once.

Simple facts are not often useful enough. Often you can improve analyses by introducing derived variables. For example, height2/weight is defined in medicine as the obesity index and gives much more information about your health than just plain height and weight. Maybe you do not have enough variables to analyze. Don't give up; you can often extract features from existing variables. For example, in many countries you can extract geographic locations from postal codes. Web addresses, Universal Product Codes (UPCs), and dates can be very useful for extracting features as well.

In order to prepare good data for data mining, you need creativity, experience, domain knowledge, technical knowledge, and more. Fortunately, you do not always meet all of the issues mentioned in this section. However, you nearly always meet one problem when you prepare the data for data mining: sampling.

SSIS Sampling

Selecting an appropriate sample is one of the most important tasks of a data mining project. Many times predictions and forecasts from mining models return weird values because they are used on a different population than the population represented by the sample used for model training. For example, if you use a website to collect answers to your questionnaire, you have to realize that your sample does not represent the entire population. Your sample represents people with web access who are willing to answer your questions. If you use data from cashiers of a retail store, then your sample probably does not include enough people who use online applications for their purchases.

In a data warehouse, you might have a lot of historical data. You might have data for, perhaps, the past 10 years. You might decide not to use all of the history and analyze recent data only. For example, imagine you have 10 years of data about sales of mobile phone models. If you use all of this data for forecasting, you might get a forecast that the best-selling model for the next year in the business world is going to be a model that was popular several years ago. You probably want to filter data and use the past year only, or more cases from the past couple of months and fewer cases from older data.

Data mining algorithms are quite complex. When you process a mining model, SSAS typically performs many passes through the whole dataset. In SQL Server query execution terminology, SSAS performs many scans on the same table. In addition, complex calculations take time. Therefore, there is some limit to how much data you can feed a mining model. If you use millions of cases, it could take days for SSAS to finish processing. Fortunately, you do not need that many cases. Statistical sampling is well known and defined. It would be out of the scope of this book to delve deeper into statistical sampling; we'll just mention a rule of thumb here. In order to get results with a fairly high level of confidence, you need approximately 20,000 cases. Usually, 50,000 cases is too many. Therefore, after you have defined and filtered your data, you typically need to further select a smaller sample. The important factor here is to select the cases in a statistically *random* fashion.

EXAM TIP

You typically train data mining on a sample from a large data set.

You can also measure the efficiency of predictive models. You can split your sample into two distinct datasets: the training set and the test set. You train the predictive models by using the training set. Then you perform predictions with the test set. However, because the test set comes from the existing data, the actual values of the variable you are predicting are known. You can compare how many times each of the models gives you correct predictions and how many times they give you incorrect predictions. Then you can select the best model for deployment in production. Using 30 percent of data for the test set is considered a best practice. It is important to do the split of the data randomly; you do not want to create a pattern with an inappropriate split.

Achieving a statistically random sample is not an easy task. There is a lot of mathematics behind randomness. Fortunately, SSIS can help you. With the Percentage Sampling transformation, you can select a specific percentage of rows for a sample. With the Row Sampling transformation, you can define exactly how many rows you want to have in your sample. Both transformations select the rows for the output in a statistically random manner. And both are very simple to use, as you will see in the practice for this lesson.

 Quick Check

- How can you select a predefined number of rows randomly?

Quick Check Answer

- You can use the SSIS Row Sampling transformation to select a predefined number of rows randomly.

PRACTICE **Performing Random Sampling**

In this practice, you will split the data from the dbo.vTargetMail view into a training set and a test set.

If you encounter a problem completing an exercise, you can install the completed projects from the Solution folder that is provided with the companion content for this chapter and lesson.

EXERCISE 1   Create a Training Set and Test Set

In this exercise, you use the Percentage Sampling transformation for a split.

1. If you closed SSDT, open it and open the TK 463 Chapter 18 solution in the TK463\Chapter18\Lesson3\Starter folder. Open the ProbableBuyers package you created in the Lesson 1 practice.

2. In the Connection Managers pane, right-click the connection manager for your AdventureWorksDW2012 database and select the Convert To Project Connection option. Save the solution and close the designer for this package.

3. Add a new package and rename it **TrainingTestSetSplit**.

4. Add a data flow task to the control flow and rename it **PctSampling**. Click the Data Flow tab to design the data flow.

5. Add an OLE DB Source to the data flow and rename it **vTargetMail**. Double-click it to open the editor. Use the project connection manager to the AdventureWorksDW2012 database. In the Name Of The Table Or The View drop-down list, select the dbo.vTargetMail view. Click the Columns tab to review the external and output columns mappings. Click OK to close the OLE DB Source Editor.

6. Add the Percentage Sampling transformation to the data flow. Connect it to the source with the gray arrow. Double-click it to open the editor.

7. In the Percentage Sampling Transformation Editor, change the Percentage Of Rows value from the default, 10, to 30. Rename the sample Output Name to **Test Set** and the Unselected Output Name to **Training Set**. Note that you can also fix the random seed. If you fix it, the transformation always selects the same rows for each of the outputs. Click OK to close the editor.

8. Add an OLE DB Destination and rename it **TM30**. Connect it with the Percentage Sampling transformation with the gray arrow. In the Input Output Selection pop-up window, select the Test Set output and click OK. Double-click the TM30 destination to open the editor.

9. Use the project connection manager to your AdventureWorksDW2012 database. Click the New button near the Name Of The Table Or The View drop-down list to create a new table for the test set. Check the code in the Create Table pop-up window, and click OK to create the table.

10. Click the Mappings tab to map the input columns to the destination columns. Then click OK to close the OLE DB Destination Editor.

11. Add another OLE DB Destination and rename it **TM70**. Connect it with the Percentage Sampling transformation with the gray arrow. Note that this one automatically uses the Training Set output. Double-click the TM70 destination to open the editor.

12. Use the project connection manager to your AdventureWorksDW2012 database. Click the New button near the Name Of The Table Or The View drop-down list to create a new table for the training set. Check the code in the Create Table pop-up window, and click OK to create the table.

13. Click the Mappings tab to map the input columns to the destination columns. Then click OK to close the OLE DB Destination Editor. Your data flow should look like the one shown in Figure 18-7.

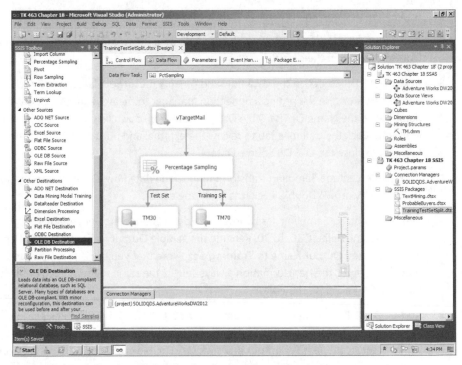

FIGURE 18-7 Data flow for splitting the data into training and test sets.

14. Execute the package. Switch to design mode after the execution.

EXERCISE 2   Test the Split

In the final exercise of this chapter, you check the split of the data into the training set and the test set with the SSIS package you created in the previous exercise.

1. Open SSMS and connect to your SQL Server instance.

2. Open a new query window and change the context to the AdventureWorksDW2012 database.

3. Use the following query to check the percentage of data in the test set.

```
SELECT (SELECT 100.0 * COUNT(*) FROM dbo.TM30) /
 ((SELECT COUNT(*) FROM dbo.TM30) +
  (SELECT COUNT(*) FROM dbo.TM70)) AS TestPct;
```

4. The percentage should be very close to 30. It is impossible to get exactly 30 percent, because the number of rows from the dbo.vTargetMail view is not divisible by 10.

5. After you have finished analyzing the split, you should clean up the AdventureWorks-DW2012 database by running the following code.

```
DROP TABLE dbo.TM30;
DROP TABLE dbo.TM70;
```

6. Close SSDT and SSMS.

Lesson Summary

- You have to have a lot of knowledge to prepare data for data mining.
- The SSIS Percentage Sampling and Row Sampling transformations help you select rows randomly.

Lesson Review

Answer the following questions to test your knowledge of the information in this lesson. You can find the answers to these questions and explanations of why each answer choice is correct or incorrect in the "Answers" section at the end of this chapter.

1. How much data should you use for the test set for predictive models?

    A. 1,000 rows

    B. 50 percent

    C. 10 percent

    D. 30 percent

2. Which transformations would you use to select data randomly? (Choose all that apply.)

    A. Conditional Split

    B. Row Sampling

    C. Percentage Sampling

    D. Multicast

3. What kind of continuous values can occur in a data mining project? (Choose all that apply.)

    A. True numeric values

    B. Categorical values

    C. Intervals

    D. Ranks

Case Scenario

In the following case scenario, you apply what you've learned about SSIS and data mining. You can find the answers to these questions in the "Answers" section at the end of this chapter.

Case Scenario: Preparing Data for Data Mining

A company that you are consulting with uses a predictive data mining model to predict customers' income. They prepared the data themselves. They complain that the predicted values are nearly always too high when they test the model on the test set. They want you to help them improve the predictions.

1. What do you suspect is the reason for the incorrect predictions?

2. How could you improve the predictions?

Suggested Practices

To help you successfully master the exam objectives presented in this chapter, complete the following tasks.

Test the Row Sampling and Conditional Split Transformations

To realize how hard it is to select rows randomly, try to create your own expression that returns random values between 0 and 1 and use it in the Conditional Split transformation.

- **Practice 1** Try to create your own expression that returns random values between 0 and 1 and use it in the Conditional Split transformation. Select rows from the dbo.vTargetMail view for which the expression is less than or equal to 0.3.

- **Practice 2** Select 5,544 random rows from the dbo.vTargetMail view with the Row Sampling transformation.

- **Practice 3** Use T-SQL queries to compare the mean and the standard deviation for the *YearlyIncome* column in the data you selected with the Conditional Split transformation and the data you selected with the Row Sampling transformation. If you managed to select rows randomly, the values should be very similar.

Answers

This section contains answers to the lesson review questions and solutions to the case scenario in this chapter.

Lesson 1

1. **Correct Answer: B**

   A. **Incorrect:** You use Decision Trees for predictions.

   B. **Correct:** You use the Time Series algorithm for forecasting.

   C. **Incorrect:** You use Association Rules for market basket analysis.

   D. **Incorrect:** You use Naïve Bayes for predictions.

2. **Correct Answer: D**

   A. **Incorrect:** MDX is the language for expressions and queries of an SSAS Multidimensional OLAP cube.

   B. **Incorrect:** T-SQL is the database engine language.

   C. **Incorrect:** DAX is the language for expressions and queries of an SSAS Tabular OLAP cube.

   D. **Correct:** DMX is the data mining language.

3. **Correct Answer: C**

   A. **Incorrect:** You use Decision Trees for predictions.

   B. **Incorrect:** You use the Time Series algorithm for forecasting.

   C. **Correct:** You use Association Rules for market basket analysis.

   D. **Incorrect:** You use Naïve Bayes for predictions.

Lesson 2

1. **Correct Answer: A**

   A. **Correct:** The Term Extraction transformation returns two columns, named by default *Term* and *Score*.

   B. **Incorrect:** The Term Extraction transformation returns two columns, named by default *Term* and *Score*.

   C. **Incorrect:** The Term Extraction transformation returns two columns, named by default *Term* and *Score*.

   D. **Incorrect:** The Term Extraction transformation returns two columns, named by default *Term* and *Score*.

2. **Correct Answer: C**

   A. **Incorrect:** The Term Lookup transformation adds two columns to the output, named by default *Term* and *Frequency*.

   B. **Incorrect:** The Term Lookup transformation adds two columns to the output, named by default *Term* and *Frequency*.

   C. **Correct:** The Term Lookup transformation adds two columns to the output, named by default *Term* and *Frequency*.

   D. **Incorrect:** The Term Lookup transformation adds two columns to the output, named by default *Term* and *Frequency*.

3. **Correct Answer: D**

   A. **Incorrect:** There is no concept of exclusive terms in text mining.

   B. **Incorrect:** The exclusion terms are terms you do not want to extract, not the terms already extracted.

   C. **Incorrect:** The exclusion terms are terms you do not want to extract, not the terms you would extract manually.

   D. **Correct:** The exclusion terms are terms you do not want to extract.

Lesson 3

1. **Correct Answer: D**

   A. **Incorrect:** There is no predefined number of rows for a test set.

   B. **Incorrect:** By selecting 50 percent of your data for the test set, you could leave too few cases for the training.

   C. **Incorrect:** By selecting 10 percent of your data for the test set, you would have too few cases in the test set to rely on the measured efficiency of your predictive models.

   D. **Correct:** Using 30 percent of the data for the test set is considered a best practice.

2. **Correct Answers: B and C**

   A. **Incorrect:** You could hardly get a really random split with the Conditional Split transformation.

   B. **Correct:** The Row Sampling transformation selects the configured number of rows randomly.

   C. **Correct:** The Percentage Sampling transformation selects the configured percentage of rows randomly.

   D. **Incorrect:** The Multicast transformation does not filter rows.

3. **Correct Answers: A and C**

   A. **Correct:** True numeric values are continuous values.

   B. **Incorrect:** Categorical values are discrete values.

   C. **Correct:** Intervals are continuous values.

   D. **Incorrect:** Ranks are discrete values.

Case Scenario

1. You should suspect that something is wrong with their sample. They probably selected richer customers only for the training set. Maybe they created a pattern by incorrectly splitting the data into the training and the test set and included richer customers in the training set and poorer customers in the test set.

2. You should re-check the sample and the split and correct them as needed.

CHAPTER 19

Implementing Custom Code in SSIS Packages

Exam objectives in this chapter:

- Extract and Transform Data
    - Design data flow.
    - Implement script tasks in SSIS.
- Load Data
    - Design control flow.
    - Implement script components in SSIS.
- Configure and Deploy SSIS Solutions
    - Deploy SSIS solutions.

There are many tasks, data sources, destinations, and transformations available in Microsoft SQL Server 2012 Integration Services (SSIS) out of the box. However, at times you might find yourself needing to perform an action that is not covered by the available tools. Fortunately, SSIS allows you to extend its capabilities by implementing your own code in a package.

There are many extension points in SSIS. For example, you can use the Execute SQL task to execute any T-SQL code, and you can use the Execute Process task to execute any application outside a package. In this chapter, you will learn how to extend a package with custom Microsoft .NET (or, if you prefer, common language runtime [CLR]) code. You will use the Microsoft Visual C# language to extend your packages.

You can use the script task to execute a custom .NET script in your control flow. You can use the script component in your data flow to define custom data sources and destinations with .NET code. You can use the same component to define custom transformations.

You might realize that some of your custom code implemented in a script task or script component could be useful in many packages. Maybe you could even share this code with other SSIS developers. Instead of copying and pasting the code from a package to another package, you can create a custom task or a custom component. You can deploy this custom code on an SSIS development machine; after that, an SSIS developer can use your component just like any built-in one.

Lessons in this chapter:

- Lesson 1: Script Task
- Lesson 2: Script Component
- Lesson 3: Implementing Custom Components

Before You Begin

To complete this chapter, you must have:

- SQL Server 2012 Database Services and Integration Services installed.
- Windows Software Development Kit (SDK) installed.
- Intermediate Transact-SQL skills.
- Intermediate Visual C# skills.
- The AdventureWorks2012 and AdventureWorksDW2012 sample databases installed.

Lesson 1: Script Task

Both the script task and the script component have two design-time modes: you begin editing by specifying properties using the common editors for tasks and components that you are already familiar with, and then switch to a development environment to write the .NET code. The second environment is the Microsoft Visual Studio Tools for Applications (VSTA) environment. You can write code in Microsoft Visual Basic or Visual C#.

The script task provides the entire required infrastructure for the custom code for you, letting you focus exclusively on the code. You can use any .NET class library and namespace in your code. In addition, from your code you can interact with the containing SSIS package through the global Dts object. For example, the Dts object exposes package variables, and you can read and modify them in your custom code. You will learn how to use the script task in this lesson.

After this lesson, you will be able to:

- Determine when to use the script task.
- Extend SSIS control flow with custom actions.

Estimated lesson time: 30 minutes

Configuring the Script Task

There are many uses of the script task. For example, you might need to browse Active Directory Domain Services, and there is no such task out of the box. You might need to generate a custom list of objects for the Foreach Loop. You might want to check whether a file you need to import is empty before starting the import. Another good example is using the results of the Data Profiling task further in your package. As you already know, the Data Profiling task writes results to an XML file. You can use the Data Profile Viewer application to view the results; however, you cannot incorporate the results in your package directly.

You start using the script task by dragging it from the SSIS Toolbox to your control flow. On the General page of the Script Task Editor, you specify the task name and description. On the Script page, you specify the most important properties of the task. This is the default page of the Script Task Editor. You first decide on the language you are going to use. You can choose between Visual Basic 2010 and Visual C# 2010. After you create the script, you cannot change the language anymore.

You must specify the method with which the script should start executing. You use the EntryPoint property for this. By default, a method called Main in the ScriptMain class is the starting point. The ScriptMain class is the default class generated by the script template. If you change the name of this method in the script, you have to change the value of the EntryPoint property appropriately.

On the Script page of the Script Task Editor, you also define the SSIS variables you are going to refer to in your script. You define Read-Only and Read-Write variables. You use the ReadOnlyVariables and ReadWriteVariables properties to enable the variables in your script. You use the Variables property of the Dts object to access SSIS variables in your script.

The Script Task Editor exposes property expressions on the Expressions page as other task editors do. You can use expressions to define the values for the properties exposed on the General and Script pages, and some other properties of the task as well.

After you define the task properties, you start writing the script. You begin by clicking the Edit Script button on the Script page of the Script Task Editor. Clicking this button opens the VSTA IDE with some code already created for you. Of course, you typically spend the vast majority of time needed for developing the script task in this environment.

EXAM TIP

Before coding the script, you need to configure the script task.

Coding the Script Task

When you open the VSTA environment, there is already some code created for you. There are many help regions with help comments. You can expand these regions and learn how to use variables or connection managers, or how to fire events directly, without using Books Online for SQL Server 2012. There is also a class named ScriptMain that includes the default starting method Main created for you. The ScriptMain class is the entry point; you should not rename it or change its attributes. The most common namespaces are already listed in the Namespaces region as well.

You can add your own classes and methods to the project. You can add references to .NET assemblies, COM components, other projects, or references to web services by right-clicking the References folder in the VSTA Solution Explorer, just as you would add references to other components in any .NET project. In the task, the global Dts object, which is based on the ScriptObjectModel class, is already instantiated. You can interact with package objects, such as variables and connections, through the Dts object.

 You can also debug your script. You need to set at least one *breakpoint* in the code by using the Debug menu or by clicking in the thin gray area on the left side of the script. When you execute the task, the VSTA IDE reopens and shows you the code in Read-Only mode. You can use standard debug windows to get the information you need to determine any error. For example, you can use the Locals window to read the current values of the local variables of your script.

To interact with package variables, you use the Variables property of the Dts object. Remember that you need to list the SSIS variables you want to use in your script in the ReadOnlyVariables and ReadWriteVariables properties of the script task. Variable names are case-sensitive. You read or change the value of a variable through its value property.

You can access the connection managers you use in your package through the Connections property of the Dts object. You can call the AcquireConnection method of a connection manager to connect to a data source. This method also returns the connection information for you if you need to use it later in your script. The connection is returned as a general object of type Object; in order to use it, you need to cast it to the appropriate connection type. The script task always requests strict data types. The AcquireConnection method can return managed .NET objects only. You cannot use unmanaged connections directly. However, you can read the ConnectionString property of a connection manager with the AcquireConnection method and connect to the data source directly in your code by using the connection string with an OledbConnection from the System.Data.OleDb namespace.

The Dts object also exposes the Events property. You can fire different kinds of events. The Events property exposes methods to fire an error, get information, get the progress of the task, fire the query cancel event that returns a value that indicates whether the package needs the task to shut down prematurely, or fire warnings or custom events. You can also use the Log method of the Dts object to log these events by using the common SSIS logging infrastructure.

When the script task finishes execution, you need to inform the parent package of the execution status, in order to determine the correct control flow. The Dts object uses the TaskResult property to report whether the task succeeded or failed. You can return even more information to the parent package by using the Dts object ExecutionValue property. This property returns a user-defined object. You can use the value returned to define the flow based on your own expressions.

> **Quick Check**
>
> ■ Can you log the execution of your script in the script task?
>
> **Quick Check Answer**
>
> ■ Yes, you can use the Log property of the Dts object to log the execution of your script.

PRACTICE Using the Script Task to Read Data Profiling Results

In this practice, you will profile data using the Data Profiling task. Then you will read the results with the script task.

If you encounter a problem completing an exercise, you can install the completed projects from the Solution folder that is provided with the companion content for this chapter and lesson.

EXERCISE 1 Use the Data Profiling Task

In this exercise, you use the Data Profiling task to profile your data and save the profiling results in an XML file.

1. Open SQL Server Data Tools (SSDT). Create a new solution named **TK 463 Chapter 19** and a new project in this solution named **TK 463 Chapter 19**. For the project, use the Integration Services Project template.

2. Rename the default package **ScriptTaskComponent**.

3. Create two package variables. Name them **EmailRegEx1** and **EmailRegEx2**. Use the String data type for both variables.

4. Add a project-level ADO.NET connection manager. Note that you need an ADO.NET and not an OLE DB connection manager. Connect to your SQL Server instance with the AdventureWorksDW2012 database, and select this database.

5. Add a package-level File Connection connection manager. Change the Usage Type property to Create File. In the File text box, enter **C:\TK463\Chapter19\Lesson1 \Solution\EmailProfiling.xml**. You will use this file to store the results of the Data Profiling task.

6. Drag the Data Profiling task to your control flow. Rename it **ProfileEmail**. Open the editor.

7. On the General page of the Data Profiling Task Editor, use the EmailProfiling.xml connection manager for the Destination property. Change the value of the Overwrite-Destination property to True.

8. On the Profile Requests page, add a Column Pattern Profile Request. Configure the ConnectionManager request property to use the ADO.NET connection manager to your AdventureWorksDW2012 database. Use the dbo.vTargetMail view for the TableOr-View property, and the EmailAddress column for the Column property of the request. When you are done configuring the request, close the task editor.

9. Execute the ProfileEmail task. After the execution is finished, open the EmailProfiling.xml file with the Data Profile Viewer application. Note that the Data Profiling task extracted two patterns, expressed as two regular expressions. Note also that the two extracted patterns do not cover all possible email addresses. The Data Profiling task does not extract very rare patterns by default. You will use this information in the practice for Lesson 2 of this chapter to find the email addresses that are not covered by these two most common patterns.

10. Close the Data Profile Viewer. Do not close SSDT.

EXERCISE 2   Use the Script Task to Process the Data Profiling Results

In the second exercise of this practice, you use the script task to read the results of the Data Profiling task you created in the previous exercise.

1. Drag the script task to your control flow. Rename it **ReadPatterns**. Connect it to the ProfileEmail task with the green arrow (use the On Success constraint for the flow). Open the editor for this task.

2. On the Script page of the Script Task Editor, make sure that the Visual C# language is selected. Do not change the entry point. Add the **User::EmailRegEx1** and **User::EmailRegEx2** variables to the ReadWriteVariables property. Figure 19-1 shows the correct settings for the script task.

3. Click the Edit Script button. When the VSTA IDE opens, expand the help regions and read the help information.

4. Expand the Namespaces region. Add the System.Xml namespace as follows.

```
using System.Xml;
```

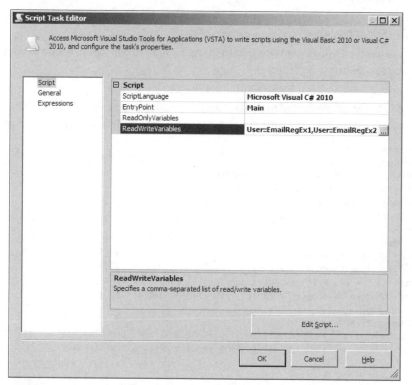

FIGURE 19-1 Script properties of the script task.

5. Declare private variables for the ScriptMain class. These private variables will point to the Data Profiling task result XML file, to the XML namespace URI for the Data Profiling task results, and to the two nodes in the XML file with the extracted regular expressions. Enter the following code right after the class definition and before the first help region in the class.

```
private string fileName = @"C:\TK463\Chapter19\Lesson1\Solution\EmailProfiling.
xml";
private string profileNamespaceUri = "http://schemas.microsoft.com/sqlserver/2008/
DataDebugger/";
private string erx1Path = "/default:DataProfile/default:DataProfileOutput/
default:Profiles" +
    "/default:ColumnPatternProfile[default:Column[@Name='EmailAddress']]" +
    "/default:TopRegexPatterns/default:PatternDistributionItem[1]/
default:RegexText/text()";
private string erx2Path = "/default:DataProfile/default:DataProfileOutput/
default:Profiles" +
    "/default:ColumnPatternProfile[default:Column[@Name='EmailAddress']]" +
    "/default:TopRegexPatterns/default:PatternDistributionItem[2]/
default:RegexText/text()";
```

6. Modify the Main method of the class. Add the following code after the // TODO:... comment and before the last command of the method, the Dts.TaskResult =... command.

```
// Local variables
string profilePath;
XmlDocument profileOutput = new XmlDocument();
XmlNamespaceManager profileNSM;
XmlNode regExNode1;
XmlNode regExNode2;

// Open output file.
profilePath = fileName;
profileOutput.Load(profilePath);
profileNSM = new XmlNamespaceManager(profileOutput.NameTable);
profileNSM.AddNamespace("default", profileNamespaceUri);

// Get regExNodes
regExNode1 = profileOutput.SelectSingleNode(erx1Path, profileNSM);
regExNode2 = profileOutput.SelectSingleNode(erx2Path, profileNSM);

// Assign variable values
Dts.Variables["User::EmailRegEx1"].Value = regExNode1.Value;
Dts.Variables["User::EmailRegEx2"].Value = regExNode2.Value;

// Show variable values
MessageBox.Show(Dts.Variables["User::EmailRegEx1"].Value.ToString());
MessageBox.Show(Dts.Variables["User::EmailRegEx2"].Value.ToString());
```

Note that this code reads the data profiling results, loads the XML file, and then assigns the extracted regular expression patterns to the values of the two SSIS package
variables you created in the first exercise for this lesson. Finally, the code shows the
variable values in two message boxes.

7. Save the script and close the VSTA environment. In the Script Task Editor, click the OK
button to close the editor.

8. Right-click the ReadPatterns task and execute it. Check the two message boxes with
the two regular expressions extracted by the Data Profiling task. Click OK in each of the
boxes to close them. Stop debugging the package.

Lesson Summary

- You can extend the control flow of your packages with the script task.
- Before writing the code, you configure the script task.

Lesson Review

Answer the following questions to test your knowledge of the information in this lesson. You can find the answers to these questions and explanations of why each answer choice is correct or incorrect in the "Answers" section at the end of this chapter.

1. What do you need to do to use the SSIS package variables in the script task?

   A. Nothing. You see all of the SSIS variables inside the script task by default.

   B. Enlist the variables you want to use in the ReadOnlyVariables and ReadWrite-Variables properties of the script task.

   C. You cannot use SSIS variables in the script task.

   D. You need to use SSIS project parameters instead of the SSIS variables.

2. Which method is the default starting method of the script in the script task?

   A. Start

   B. StartHere

   C. Main

   D. The first method you write

3. Which programming languages are supported by the script task? (Choose all that apply.)

   A. Visual C++

   B. Visual Basic

   C. Visual C#

   D. Visual F#

Lesson 2: Script Component

Similar to the script task, the script component provides the entire required infrastructure for the custom code, letting you focus exclusively on the code. However, you use the script component in your data flow. Again, you can use any .NET class library and namespace in your code. In addition, you can interact with the containing SSIS package and the containing data flow.

In the script of the script component, you get access to the data flow buffers and to SSIS package objects, such as variables and connections, through the ComponentWrapper and BufferWrapper project items. These are automatically instantiated objects of the Script-Component and ScriptBuffer classes.

Configuring the Script Component

When you add the script component to your data flow, you have to make the first decision immediately. You can use the script component as a custom data source, a destination, or a transformation. When you add it to the data flow, you will be asked which script component type you are creating.

Although there is a huge number of data sources and destinations supported in SSIS out of the box, you can still encounter a situation for which you need to create your own custom source or destination. For example, SSIS does not have an out-of-the-box web service source or destination. You can use the script component to use web services in your SSIS package data flow.

The next step of designing a script component, after you have decided the type of the component, is to configure its metadata. In the metadata configuration part, you use the Script Component Editor to define the component properties such as the name and the language you are going to use. You also have to enlist the SSIS package variables you are going to use in the script in the ReadOnlyVariables and ReadWriteVariables properties. Note that variable names are case-sensitive.

The script component metadata configuration is slightly more complex than the script task configuration. You need to define the input and output columns of the data flow buffers for the component as well. If you use the script component as a data source, then you define the output columns only. The script component is then responsible for creating the data flow buffers. If you use the component for a transformation, then you have to configure input and outputs. If you use it for a data destination, you configure the input only. You have to select which columns from the input buffers you are going to use in the script, and which columns you are going to send to the output buffers or to the data destination. The following are possible inputs and outputs for the script component:

- If you use it as a source, the script component has no input; however, you can define multiple outputs.
- If you use it as a transformation, the script component supports one input (inherited from the component earlier in the data flow) and multiple outputs.
- If you use it as a destination, the script component supports one input (inherited from the component earlier in the data flow) and no outputs.

When SSIS generates the default code for the component, it uses this metadata to create a class for each input and output. The classes have a property for each input or output column. You can use these properties to access or assign the values of the data flow buffers.

An output of an SSIS component can be synchronous or asynchronous, and thus the component can be non-blocking or blocking. Each output of the component has the SynchronousInputID property. If the value of this property is None, then the output is asynchronous, and you can completely redefine it. In addition, you can also define whether the output is sorted. If the value of the SynchronousInputID property is the component's input ID, then the output is synchronous. You process input row by row, and you cannot change the sort order of the input rows for the output. If you use synchronous outputs, then you can also configure the ExclusionGroup property to identify redirections of rows to different outputs. For example, you could redirect part of the rows to the regular output and part to the error output.

If you use the script component for a source or a destination, then you need to define the connection managers you will use in the script in the component's metadata as well. Of course, if you use the component as a transformation, you can enlist existing connection managers in the component metadata and then use them in the script as well.

Coding the Script Component

As with the script task, all of the code written for the script component resides inside a package; there is no separate deployment file. However, while you design the script, the script is stored in a temporary file. The power of the script component, compared to a custom component, is in the generated script that serves as an infrastructure for your enhancements. This is possible because inputs and outputs with all columns and properties are known in advance; this is the component metadata that you configure before writing the actual script.

A script component has three main items, stored in separate temporary files, which you can observe in the VSTA Solution Explorer:

- Main, which contains the ScriptMain class, where you write your own code. This class inherits from the UserComponent class.

- ComponentWrapper, which contains the UserComponent class. This class inherits from the ScriptComponent class, a class that contains the methods and properties that you need to process the data flow data. The ComponentWrapper class also contains Connections and Variables collection classes, which enable you to interact with package connection managers and variables.

- BufferWrapper, which contains the classes for each input and output. These classes inherit from the ScriptBuffer class. These classes include properties for each column of inputs and outputs.

Figure 19-2 shows this structure of the script of the script component.

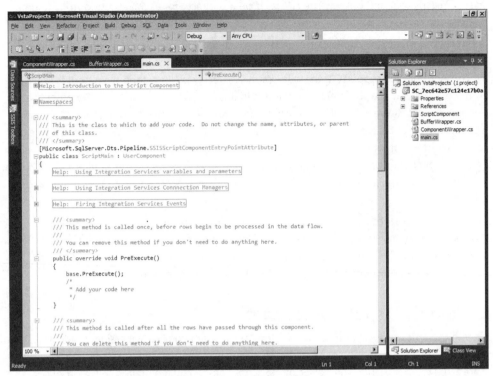

FIGURE 19-2 The structure of the script in the script component.

The run-time methods of the component are the same as the run-time methods of a custom component and are explained in detail in Lesson 3 of this chapter. Here is a list of some of the most important ones:

- Use the AcquireConnections method to retrieve the connection or the connection information from a connection manager. This is a method of the ScriptComponent base class, which you override.

- If you need to perform an action once before processing the rows, override the PreExecute method of the ScriptComponent base class.

- If you need to perform an action once after processing the rows, override the PostExecute method of the ScriptComponent base class. You can change a value of a package variable only in this method. Therefore, if you need Read-Write variables when processing the rows, you have to use local variables.

- Your processing code goes to the <InputX>_ProcessInputRow method to process each row of an input, <InputX>_ProcessInput to take some action for a complete input (for example, after all input rows have been processed), CreateNewOutputRows when you need to create rows in an asynchronous output, and the FinishOutputs method when you have to do something to an output before you close it. You will learn more details about these methods in Lesson 3 of this chapter.

- You need to release the connections you acquired when you do not need them anymore. Override the ReleaseConnections method of the ScriptComponent base class to close and release the connections.

The ComponentWrapper project item has, as you already know, a Variables collection class with a property for the value of each variable you configured as a Read-Only or Read-Write variable in the component metadata. You can use the variables through the Variables property of the ScriptMain class.

The ComponentWrapper project item also has a Connections collection class with an accessor for each connection manager you configured in the component metadata. You can use the variables through the Connections property of the ScriptMain class.

As with the script task, you can also raise events in the script component. In order to raise an event, you need to call the ComponentMetaData property of the ScriptMain class. You can also log the events.

In short, you can use the script component for almost any kind of extension to your data flow. The component gives you the infrastructure for fast development. However, if you need to reuse the component in multiple packages, you might prefer to develop a custom component.

EXAM TIP

Note that the script component can return synchronous or asynchronous outputs.

 Quick Check

- What does it mean if the value of the SynchronousInputID property of a script component is the component's input ID?

Quick Check Answer

- This means that the component returns synchronous outputs.

PRACTICE **Using the Data Profiling Results to Process Data Flow Rows**

In this practice, you will use the regular expressions for email addresses you extracted with the Data Profiling task and read into package variables with the script task in the practice for the previous lesson.

If you encounter a problem completing an exercise, you can install the completed projects from the Solution folder that is provided with the companion content for this chapter and lesson.

EXERCISE 1   Prepare the Environment

In this exercise, you prepare everything you need in the package and the AdventureWorks-DW2012 database for the script component.

1. If you closed SSDT, open it and open the TK 463 Chapter 19 solution. If you didn't finish the practice for the previous lesson, open the solution from the Starter folder for this lesson. Open the package designer for the ScriptTaskComponent package.

2. Open SSMS, connect to your SQL Server instance with the AdventureWorksDW2012 database, and open a new query window. Change the context to the AdventureWorks-DW2012 database.

3. Create a table to save the results of the validation of email addresses. The table should have three columns: *CustomerKey*, *EmailAddress*, and *EmailValid*. Use the same data types and NULL setting for the first two columns as are used for these two columns in the *dbo.DimCustomer* table. Use the BIT data type for the third column, and allow NULLs in this column. The code looks like the following.

    ```
    CREATE TABLE dbo.EmailValidated
    (
      CustomerKey    INT           NOT NULL,
      EmailAddress   NVARCHAR(50)  NULL,
      EmailValid     BIT           NULL
    );
    ```

4. Switch to SSDT. Open the editor for the ReadPatterns script task. You don't want to leave the message boxes in production. Click the Edit Script button. In the Main method, comment out the following two lines of code.

    ```
    MessageBox.Show(Dts.Variables["User::EmailRegEx1"].Value.ToString());
    MessageBox.Show(Dts.Variables["User::EmailRegEx2"].Value.ToString());
    ```

5. Save the script and close the VSTA IDE. Close the Script Task Editor.

EXERCISE 2   Use the Script Component

In this exercise, you use the script component to validate email addresses against regular expressions.

1. Add a data flow task to your control flow. Rename it **ValidateEmail**. Connect it to the ReadPatterns task with the green arrow. Switch to the Data Flow tab.

2. Add an ADO.NET source. Rename it **ReadEmails**. Use the project ADO.NET connection manager to connect to the AdventureWorksDW2012 database. Select the SQL Command data access mode. In the SQL Command text box, enter the following query.

    ```
    SELECT CustomerKey, EmailAddress
    FROM dbo.DimCustomer;
    ```

3. Click the Preview button to check the results of the query. Then click the Columns tab and review the columns. Click OK to close the ADO.NET Source Editor.

4. Add a script component to the data flow. Select the Transformation component type in the pop-up window and click OK. Rename the component **ValidateEmails**. Connect it with the gray arrow to the ReadEmails source. Open the component editor.

5. On the Script tab of the Script Transformation Editor, add the **User::EmailRegEx1** and **User::EmailRegEx2** variables to the ReadOnlyVariables property.

6. Click the Input Columns tab. Select both the CustomerKey and the EmailAddress input columns.

7. Click the Inputs And Outputs tab. Expand Output 0. Click the Output Columns folder. Click the Add Column button to add a column to this output. Name the column **EmailValid**. Use the Boolean [DT_BOOL] data type, as shown in Figure 19-3.

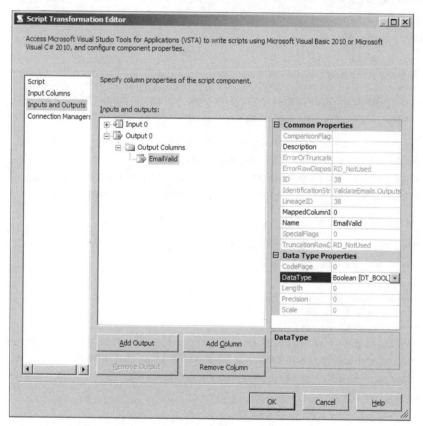

FIGURE 19-3 Adding an output column to the script component.

8. Click the Script tab. Review the scripts created by the component. In the Main script, expand the Namespaces region and add a reference to the System.Text.Regular-Expressions namespace, as follows.

```
using System.Text.RegularExpressions;
```

9. You need to validate the email addresses in the Input0_ProcessInputRow method. Add the following code after the Add Your Code Here section.

```
Row.EmailValid =
    Regex.IsMatch(Row.EmailAddress, Variables.EmailRegEx1,
                RegexOptions.IgnoreCase | RegexOptions.Compiled) |
    Regex.IsMatch(Row.EmailAddress, Variables.EmailRegEx2,
                RegexOptions.IgnoreCase | RegexOptions.Compiled);
```

> **NOTE** **CODE SNIPPETS**
>
> You can use the Snippets.txt file provided in the Solution folder for this lesson to copy the code snippets.

10. Save the script and close VSTA. Click OK to close the Script Transformation Editor.

11. Add an ADO.NET destination to the data flow. Rename it **EmailValidated** and connect it with the gray arrow to the ValidateEmails component. Open the editor.

12. Use the project ADO.NET connection manager to connect to the Adventure-WorksDW2012 database. In the Use A Table Or View drop-down list, select the *dbo.EmailValidated* table. Click the Mappings tab and check the column mappings. Then click OK to close the ADO.NET Destination Editor. Save the solution.

13. Execute the package.

14. When the package execution finishes, stop debugging. Switch to SSMS to check the results. Use the following query.

```
SELECT *
FROM dbo.EmailValidated
WHERE EmailValid = 0;
```

15. You should get three rows with email addresses that did not pass the validation. Note that the addresses are OK; it was the Data Profiling task that did not extract patterns for all possible email addresses. The regular expressions extracted allow only the following two forms:

- Unicode string + single digit + @adventure-works.com
- Unicode string + two digits + @adventure-works.com

Because there are more than 99 Richards in the AdventureWorksDW2012 database, some email addresses use three digits after the first name.

16. After you finish checking, clean up the AdventureWorksDW2012 database by running the following code.

```
DROP TABLE dbo.EmailValidated;
```

> **NOTE CONTINUING WITH PRACTICES**
>
> Do not exit SSMS and SSDT if you intend to continue immediately with the next practice.

Lesson Summary

- For the script component, you need to configure inputs and outputs.
- An output of an SSIS component can be synchronous or asynchronous.
- The run-time methods of the script component are the same as the run-time methods of a custom component.

Lesson Review

Answer the following questions to test your knowledge of the information in this lesson. You can find the answers to these questions and explanations of why each answer choice is correct or incorrect in the "Answers" section at the end of this chapter.

1. How can you use the script component? (Choose all that apply.)
   A. As a connection manager
   B. As a source
   C. As a destination
   D. As a transformation

2. Which property of the script component output is not empty if the output is synchronous?
   A. ReadOnlyVariables
   B. ReadWriteVariables
   C. SynchronousInputID
   D. ScriptLanguage

3. When does the script component not have an input?
   A. When you use it as a source.
   B. When you use it as a destination.
   C. When you use it as a transformation.
   D. It always has an input.

Lesson 3: Implementing Custom Components

When you use Script tasks or Script components, you can implement custom programmatic logic in an SSIS package quickly and efficiently. The definition of a Script task or component is embedded in the definition of the SSIS package itself, allowing it to be deployed and maintained as part of the package. As long as a particular custom operation can be encapsulated within an individual Script task or component in its entirety, a script task or a Script component without doubt provides the perfect alternative.

However, as soon as the same custom operation needs to be implemented in more than one SSIS solution, or be deployed to multiple destination environments, Script tasks and components cease to be the most appropriate alternatives.

To help you decide when to use Script tasks or components, consider the following guidelines:

- Can the custom operation be encapsulated in its entirety within an individual task or component?

- Can the component's dependencies on external resources be restricted to those found on any server where the SSIS package will be deployed, or can they be eliminated altogether?

- Is the operation so specific that it is only ever going to be used in a single SSIS package, and reusability is not an issue?

If, in a particular business problem, all of these statements are true, you can use Script tasks or components; otherwise, you should consider developing a custom task or component.

In contrast to Script tasks and components, custom tasks and components can be developed, deployed, and maintained independently of the SSIS package in which they are going to be used, meaning that any updates to the task or component can be performed without having to redesign and redeploy every package in which it is being used—of course, as long as the change has not affected any of the exposed interfaces.

On the other hand, compared to Script task and component development, the approach to custom task and component development is a bit more complex and requires more development efforts.

After this lesson, you will be able to:

- Develop custom components.
- Install custom components and tasks.

Estimated lesson time: 60 minutes

Planning a Custom Component

After you have determined that the business problem cannot be solved by using any of the standard, built-in SSIS data flow components, and after you have determined that due to complexity, dependency, or reusability requirements (or restrictions), a Script component may also not be appropriate, you can use the following guidelines to plan the design of the custom component:

- **Role** Is the component going to be used as a data source, a data destination, or to transform data?

  Typically, a *custom source* would be needed if none of the existing sources support the specific connection manager that you are using, or if an appropriate connection manager is not available. For instance, if the source data is extracted from an incompatible source or is stored in an incompatible format, you could develop a custom data source. Similarly, a *custom destination* could be designed if such an incompatible data store is used as the data flow's destination.

  In most cases, when custom development is needed, it is to design a *custom transformation*—to support a particular data management operation that is not supported by any of the standard, built-in transformations.

- **Usage** Is the source or transformation component going to use multiple outputs? Is the transformation or destination component going to use multiple inputs?

  A source or a transformation component can send data to multiple outputs, and a destination or a transformation component can receive data from multiple inputs. For instance, a transformation component used in merging data from multiple sources would have to support multiple inputs. A source component accessing a composite data set could be programmed to produce multiple, normalized row sets, instead of a single de-normalized one.

- **Access to external data** Is the component going to use additional data sources, or will it consume only data in the data flow buffer?

  If the component will perform lookup operations or will need to access data that is not available in the current data flow, it will require access to external data sources. To access data stored in variables or parameters, the component will also need access to those variables and parameters.

- **Behavior** Is the component going to be a blocking, a partially blocking, or a non-blocking component? Is it going to use synchronous or asynchronous outputs?

  If the component is going to pass rows to the destination without having to retain them, such as to calculate running totals (partially blocking), or to sort them (blocking), the component will not block the data flow (and is a non-blocking transformation).

If the transformation produces a single output row for each input row, where the result of the transformation can be written to one or more columns of the source row, a synchronous output can be used. However, if the transformation could produce one or more output rows for each input row, or even not produce a row at all, an asynchronous output would have to be used.

New rows cannot be added to a synchronous output and cannot be removed from it.

- **Configuration**   How will the component be configured?

   To improve the reusability of a custom component, specific settings used to control its operation should be exposed, allowing the developer to set them at design time, or even expose them to the environment. For instance, a transformation performing data extraction or data validation using Regular Expressions should allow the developer to set the expressions at design time, or even allow them to be determined automatically at run time.

Developing a Custom Component

Custom components are built in Visual Studio 2010, using the Class Library template, or even a blank solution template. The only vital prerequisite for custom SSIS development using the .NET Framework is to create references to the appropriate SSIS libraries:

- Microsoft.SqlServer.DTSPipelineWrap, containing classes and interfaces used to create data flow objects and automate data flow operations

- Microsoft.SQLServer.DTSRuntimeWrap, containing classes and interfaces used to create control flow objects and automate control flow operations

- Microsoft.SqlServer.PipelineHost, containing managed classes to access SSIS data flow objects and methods

Typically, custom components are developed separately from SSIS packages; mostly due to the fact that they are developed by a different developer or developer team. Nonetheless, they could also be part of the same solution (for example, they could be developed together with other SSIS projects) but placed in separate projects.

There are two principal classes that you should be familiar with when designing components:

- All data flow components are derived from the Microsoft.SqlServer.Dts.Pipeline .PipelineComponent base class, available in the Microsoft.SqlServer.PipelineHost class library. This class contains all built-in component properties, as well as design-time methods used to configure the component at design time and run-time methods to perform its operations at run time.

- The Microsoft.SqlServer.Dts.Pipeline.PipelineBuffer class, also available in the Microsoft .SqlServer.PipelineHost class library, provides access to the data being passed into, or being created by, the component. The PipelineBuffer represents an in-memory data store organized in rows and columns.

Design Time and Run Time

Custom tasks and components are used at design time, when developers are designing SSIS packages, as well as at run time, when an SSIS package using the component is being executed. This duality is reflected in the SSIS component object model and should be considered throughout development.

The customization of custom tasks and components is achieved when existing members of the component base class are overridden with custom code. There are two groups of methods that need to be customized when designing custom components:

- The *design-time methods* are used at design time, when the SSIS package developer adds the component to a data flow task and configures it.

  Design-time methods allow the developer to access the component and its properties when designing the SSIS package. They are used to create one or more instances of the component inside the data flow, to configure an instance, to validate it, and/or to reset the component to its initial state.

- The *run-time methods* are invoked by the SSIS engine when the package is run.

  Run-time methods allow the computer to perform the operations when packages implementing the component are being executed. They contain the actual business logic required by the particular data management process.

Design-Time Methods

Design-time methods facilitate the interaction between the SSIS developer and the data flow component, allowing the component to be placed in the data flow and configured appropriately.

The principal design-time methods are listed in this section, and you can find out more about the rest of the design-time methods in Books Online for SQL Server 2012.

> **MORE INFO** **DESIGN-TIME METHODS**
>
> More information about design-time methods can be found in Books Online for SQL Server 2012, in the article entitled "Design-time Methods of a Data Flow Component" at *http://msdn.microsoft.com/en-us/library/ms135969(SQL.110).aspx.*

ProvideComponentProperties

This method is used to initialize the component and is invoked when the component is dragged from the SSIS Toolbox and placed inside the data flow task.

This method should provide all the elements needed by the component at design time: inputs and outputs, custom component properties, and any external data sources.

Validate

This method is used to validate the state of the component and is invoked automatically when the component's editor is accessed and when changes to its configuration are confirmed by the SSIS developer.

The method is also called once at run time, before the component is executed.

This method should provide the programmatic logic used to verify whether the component has been configured correctly and can therefore be used at run time. It should not change the component's metadata, such as by adding, modifying, or removing any of its elements.

> **IMPORTANT VALIDATION**
>
> Only the component developer can be certain which properties, settings, or other elements should be configured, and how; therefore, only the component developer will know for certain what needs to be validated, how, and what steps must be taken to correct a particular problem.

The method returns one of the four validation results, as shown in Table 19-1.

TABLE 19-1 Validation Results

Validation status	Description
VS_ISVALID	The component is correctly configured and ready for execution.
	Use this status only if the component is configured correctly and can be executed.
VS_ISBROKEN	The component is incorrectly configured; for instance, a property is set incorrectly or an expected element is missing.
	Use this status to help the package developer configure the component appropriately.
VS_NEEDSNEWMETADATA	The component's metadata is outdated or corrupt, which can be corrected by invoking the ReinitializeMetaData method.
	Use this status to prompt the package developer to refresh the component's metadata.
VS_ISCORRUPT	The component is irreparably damaged and must be completely reset by invoking the ProvideComponentProperties method.
	Use this status when the component has been misconfigured and should be reinitialized.

ReinitializeMetaData

This method is used to update metadata describing the external data sources referenced by the component.

This method is invoked automatically when the component editor has been opened, after the VS_NEEDSNEWMETADATA result has been returned in an earlier validation.

Use this method to correct the metadata when changes have been made in the underlying data stores referenced by the component, and the changes have not yet been reflected in the component's metadata.

FireError, FireWarning, and FireInformation

These methods are used to facilitate communication between the developer who designed the component and the developer using the component when designing an SSIS package. Some of these methods may be invoked automatically by the base Validate method and should be invoked by the overridden Validate method to convey information about the state of the component to the package developer.

Package developers should understand how the component needs to be configured in order to perform the operations as expected, and the SSIS engine should prevent a misconfigured component from being executed at all.

These methods could also be invoked at run time: all of them are reported to the calling environment, but FireError will even prevent or stop execution.

By using FireInformation and FireWarning, the component developer can communicate to the package developer that the component has been set up in a certain way, or that it could have been set differently. By using the FireError method, the component developer can prevent the execution of the component until it has been configured correctly.

Run-Time Methods

Run-time methods represent the component's operational programmatic logic, which is executed when the component is used at run time. These methods provide the complete operational capabilities of the component; without them, the component performs no actions other than being validated and returning a validation result.

The run-time methods in this section are listed in the order of operation—from validation, through row processing, to cleanup.

MORE INFO   **RUN-TIME METHODS**

More information about run-time methods can be found in Books Online for SQL Server 2012, in the article entitled "Run-time Methods of a Data Flow Component" at *http://msdn.microsoft.com/en-us/library/ms136101(SQL.110).aspx*.

AcquireConnections (for Validation)

The method is invoked at design time whenever connections are needed—for instance for validation—and at run time to establish connections with external data sources.

This should be the only method used in establishing connections; once established, each connection should then be cached in a local variable and reused without the need to be re-established.

Connections should be released by using the ReleaseConnections method, described later in this lesson.

Validate

This method has already been described earlier in this lesson. At run time, it is executed at the beginning of the execution.

ReleaseConnections (after Validation)

This method is invoked after the validation has completed and is used to release the connections. It is executed again later, after the execution has completed.

This method is explained in more detail later in this lesson.

PrepareForExecute

After the validation has completed successfully, execution begins with this method. The BufferManager is not yet available when this method is executed, so PrepareForExecute can be used to initialize all the settings and variables that can be set before the data from the data flow is available to the component.

Typically, PrepareForExecute is used to initialize variables that will be used throughout the execution and that are not usually affected by the data received from the buffers.

AcquireConnections (for Execution)

After the execution has actually started, the connections are acquired again, this time to be used for data processing.

This method was discussed in more detail earlier in this lesson.

PreExecute

This method is invoked after the connections have been established and after the Buffer-Manager has been initialized, allowing access to the data in the data flow.

This method should be used to complete the initialization of variables and other settings needed to perform the operations.

If data sources provide access to sets of data that are small enough to fit into memory completely, the data they provide could now be cached in a variable, and the corresponding connections released.

PrimeOutput

If the component uses asynchronous outputs, these are initialized by using the PrimeOutput method; after this initialization, rows can be added to the output.

If multiple asynchronous outputs are used, appropriate programmatic logic must be implemented to prepare all outputs. Outputs that have not been primed cannot be written to.

This is the final method before row processing begins. Any resources that have already been consumed and will not be needed later—especially if they are not required for row processing—should now be released.

ProcessInput

This is the principal method used in processing the rows in the data flow; it is invoked after all preceding methods have completed successfully and when rows from an input buffer become available to the component.

The input buffers contain rows passed from upstream components and allow access to all columns returned by the upstream component. Synchronous outputs share the buffer with the corresponding input; therefore, the output columns are also already available when processing inputs with a corresponding synchronous output. Rows must be added manually to asynchronous outputs by using the NewRow() buffer method.

The ProcessInput method will be called repeatedly as data is received from upstream components, until the last row has been processed, which is reflected in the EndOfRowset property. Data processing is performed in batches, which means that multiple buffers will be sent to the component. Therefore, you should not assume that the processing has been completed solely based on the fact that all the rows in the current buffer have been processed.

This method will also be called multiple times for multiple inputs; therefore, appropriate programmatic logic must be implemented to process all inputs.

To process rows continuously as they are passed to the component, the data management operation must be implemented as a loop by using the NextRow() buffer method. This method returns each row from the buffer, to be processed one at a time, until the entire buffer has been consumed. As long as new buffers are being sent from upstream components, row processing continues.

When the entire input has been exhausted, synchronous outputs are completed automatically, whereas asynchronous outputs must be completed manually by using the SetEndOfRowSet() buffer method. Only by understanding the nature of SSIS data flow processing well can you ensure prevention of data loss or data corruption .

PostExecute

This method is called after all the data from the data flow has been processed. If any data needs to be passed to the package—via variables—or passed to external data sources, these operations should be performed in PostExecute.

Any resource that has not yet been released (such as component variables), except for external connections, should also now be released.

ReleaseConnections (after Execution)

This method is used to release any connections to external data sources used by the component that have not already been released earlier in the process.

This method should be used to release all connections acquired by using the AcquireConnections method; even if the connections have been released in other methods, the ReleaseConnections method should guarantee that no resources will remain active after the processing has completed.

In fact, whenever the AcquireConnections method is used in a component, the ReleaseConnections method must also be implemented; otherwise, a run time error will occur during each validation, and execution will not be possible.

Cleanup

After the processing has completed and any external connections have been released, the rest of the resources should also be released.

This method can also be used to assign values to package variables.

> **MORE INFO**   **DEVELOPING CUSTOM DATA FLOW COMPONENTS**
>
> More information about custom SSIS development, specifically about custom components, can be found in Books Online for SQL 2012, starting with the article entitled "Developing a Custom Data Flow Component" at *http://msdn.microsoft.com/en-us/library /ms136078(SQL.110).aspx.*

Quick Check

1. When should custom components be used instead of script components?

2. When is it necessary to use asynchronous outputs?

3. Why do custom components need design-time programmatic logic?

Quick Check Answers

1. Generally, the number-one reason for using custom components is reusability. If the same custom operation needs to be implemented in multiple SSIS packages, custom components with package-independent development, deployment, and maintenance capabilities provide a more appropriate alternative.

2. Whenever a data transformation operation produces zero, one, or more rows per each input row, asynchronous outputs need to be used, because additional rows cannot be added to a synchronous output, nor can they be removed from them.

3. Before being used in an executing SSIS package to perform the principal data management operation, each custom component is used by the SSIS package developer—it needs to be placed in the data flow, configured, and validated.

PRACTICE **Designing, Deploying, and Using a Custom Data Flow Component**

In this exercise, you will develop a custom data flow transformation component, deploy it to your local machine, and then use it in an SSIS package.

To successfully complete the exercises, you will need to have the Windows Software Development Kit (SDK) installed on your machine. The installation can be downloaded from the Microsoft website at *http://www.microsoft.com/en-us/download/details.aspx?id=8279.*

If you encounter a problem completing an exercise, you can install the completed projects from the Solution folder that is provided with the companion content for this chapter and lesson.

EXERCISE 1 **Prepare the Environment**

1. Start SSMS, and on the File menu, under Open, select File, then navigate to the C:\TK463\Chapter19\Code folder, and open the TK463Chapter19.sql Transact-SQL script.

2. After you have reviewed the script, execute the part for Lesson 3. The script creates the database and the objects you will be using in this lesson.

EXERCISE 2   Develop a Custom Data Flow Transformation

1. Start SSDT. On the Start page, select Open Project, navigate to the C:\TK463
   \Chapter19\Lesson3\Starter folder, and open the TK 463 Chapter 19.sln solution.

2. On the File menu, select Add | New Project, and create a new Visual C# Class Library, us-
   ing the Class Library template found under Installed Templates | Visual C# | Windows.
   Use the information provided in Table 19-2 to configure the new project.

TABLE 19-2 New Class Library

Property	Value
Name	TK463.CalculateCheckSum
Location	C:\TK463\Chapter19\Lesson3\Starter\
Solution Name	TK463 Chapter 19
Create Directory For Solution	(Selected)

3. In the Solution Explorer pane, locate the class file with the default name Class1.cs,
   right-click it, and on the shortcut menu select Delete to remove it.

4. In the Solution Explorer pane, right-click the newly created project, and on the short-
   cut menu, select Add | Existing Item to add a class file to the project. Use the Add
   Existing Item dialog box to navigate to the C:\TK463\Chapter19\Code folder, and then
   select the CalculateCheckSum.cs file. When you are ready, click OK to add the file.

5. In the Solution Explorer pane, right-click the newly created project, and the select
   Properties on the shortcut menu to access the project properties. On the Application page of the properties editor, set the project properties, using the information
   provided in Table 19-3.

TABLE 19-3 Project Properties

Property	Value
Assembly Name	TK463.CalculateCheckSum
Default Namespace	Microsoft.TK463
Target Framework	.NET Framework 4
Output Type	Class Library
Startup Object	(Not set)

6. When you are done, save the project, and then close the properties editor.

7. In the Solution Explorer pane, under the newly created project, right-click References, and select Add Reference on the shortcut menu to add references to the following SQL Server 2012 Integration Services libraries:

- Microsoft.SqlServer.DTSPipelineWrap
- Microsoft.SQLServer.DTSRuntimeWrap
- Microsoft.SqlServer.PipelineHost

You can find all these libraries among the .NET components, on the .NET tab of the Add Reference dialog box.

8. Open the CalculateCheckSum.cs file and review the definition.

The component implements the following design-time methods:

- ProvideComponentProperties
- Validate
- DeleteOutputColumn

The DeleteOutputColumn method is invoked when output columns are removed at design time. By overriding it you can, for instance, control which columns can actually be removed.

The component implements the following run-time methods:

- PrepareForExecute
- PreExecute
- ProcessInput
- PostExecute

Follow the comments in the code to see how the methods are implemented, what other functions are used when the component is configured, and when the operation is executed.

9. When done, save the solution and build the TK463.CalculateCheckSum project in debug mode.

10. Leave the solution open, because you will need it in the following exercises.

EXERCISE 3   Deploy a Custom Data Flow Component

Before you can deploy the component, it needs to be released. If you were able to build the project successfully in the preceding exercise, you can now complete the building process by creating a release build.

1. Before deploying the component, it needs to be released. If you were able to build the project successfully in the preceding exercise, you can now complete the building process by creating a release build. However, in order for the component to be used in production, it also needs to be digitally signed; for instance, using a strong name key.

2. In the Solution Explorer pane, right-click the TK463.CalculateCheckSum project, and in the context menu select Properties.

3. In the project properties editor, switch to the Signing tab at the bottom left. Check the Sign the assembly option; this will allow the component to be digitally signed. Expand the Choose a strong name key file list box, select Browse..., and in the Select file dialog navigate to the C:\TK463\Chapter19\Lesson3\Solution\TK463 Chapter 19\TK463.CalculateCheckSum folder. In the folder, locate the TK463.snk file, select it, and confirm the selection by clicking Open.

4. Save the solution, and close the project properties editor. Switch the solution configuration to Release, and build the TK463.CalculateCheckSum project again..

5. By default, the release version of the assembly should be placed in the C:\TK463 \Chapter19\Lesson3\Solution\TK463 Chapter 19\TK463.CalculateCheckSum\bin \Release folder. Use Windows Explorer to verify this.

EXERCISE 4   Configure and Use a Custom Data Flow Component

After the component has been deployed successfully, it can be used in SSIS packages.

1. In SSDT, open the FillStageTables.dtsx package of the TK463 Chapter 19 project, which is part of the TK 463 Chapter 19.sln solution that you used in Exercise 1 earlier in this lesson.

2. Open the Insert stgCustomer data flow component in the data flow editor, and remove the data path leading from the Customer data flow source to the Data Conversion data flow transformation.

3. Drag the Calculate Checksum transformation from the SSIS Toolbox onto the data flow editor surface.

   The Calculate Checksum component should be listed in the Common group.

   If the component is not displayed, right-click the SSIS Toolbox and select Refresh Toolbox on the shortcut menu to refresh the toolbox.

4. Connect the output of the Customer data source to the input of the Calculate Checksum transformation. Double-click the newly added transformation to open the Advanced Editor.

Use the Advanced Editor to configure the component. On the Component Properties page, use SHA256 as the HashAlgorithm property value. On the Input Columns page, select all input columns to be processed and passed to downstream components. On the Input and Output Properties page, explore the available settings, but make no additional changes. The dialog box should look like the one shown in Figure 19-4.

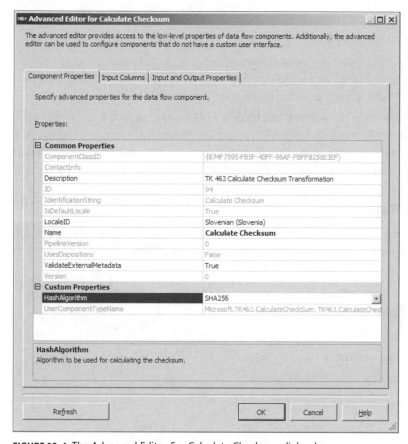

FIGURE 19-4 The Advanced Editor For Calculate Checksum dialog box.

5. When you are done, click OK to confirm the configuration.

6. Connect the output of the Calculate Checksum transformation to the input of the Data Conversion transformation.

7. Edit the stgCustomer data flow destination, and correct the column mapping so that the results of the Calculate Checksum transformation can be stored in the *RowCheckSum* column of the destination table.

8. When you are done, save the solution, and then execute the FillStageTables.dtsx package in debug mode.

9. After the execution has completed, review the contents of the *stg.Customer* table by using SSMS.

10. Optionally, you can repeat steps 2 through 8 of this exercise to implement the Calculate Checksum component in the Insert stgPerson and Insert stgCustomerInformation data flows as well.

Lesson Summary

- If a particular problem cannot be solved by using any of the standard built-in SSIS data flow components, you can design your own custom component: a custom source, a custom destination, or a custom transformation component.

- Before custom components can be used in SSIS development, they need to be deployed; this means that they must be copied to the workstation and registered in the workstation's global assembly cache. Of course, to be used in deployed SSIS processes, the components must also be deployed on the target server.

Lesson Review

Answer the following questions to test your knowledge of the information in this lesson. You can find the answers to these questions and explanations of why each answer choice is correct or incorrect in the "Answers" section at the end of this chapter.

1. Which of the following data flow roles can custom components be used for? (Choose all that apply.)

   A. Data sources

   B. Data destinations

   C. Data connection managers

   D. Data transformations

2. What are design-time methods used for? (Choose all that apply.)

   A. To allow the components to be executed

   B. To automate data flow design

   C. To allow the components to be configured

   D. To allow the components to be validated

3. What are run-time methods used for? (Choose all that apply.)

   A. To allow the components to be configured

   B. To allow internal variables to be set

   C. To allow external sources to be accessed

   D. To allow data to be processed

4. Which of the following statements describe the reasons why a custom component should be considered, instead of implementing the same programmatic logic in a Script component? (Choose all that apply.)

   A. Custom programmatic logic that will be used in multiple SSIS packages should be placed in a custom component, rather than a script component.

   B. Custom components should always be used, regardless of the complexity of the custom operation.

   C. If the custom solution requires access to external libraries, the script component cannot be used; only a custom component can be used in this case.

   D. Custom components can be developed, deployed, and maintained, independently of the SSIS package.

Case Scenario

In the following case scenario, you apply what you've learned about implementing custom code in SSIS packages. You can find the answers to these questions in the "Answers" section at the end of this chapter.

Case Scenario: Data Cleansing

You have been asked to implement data extraction by using Regular Expressions in SSIS.

1. Can this even be achieved by using SSIS? If so, how?

2. What SSIS features would you use for this operation? Considering the fact that more than one substring of the same input string can be matched by a particular regular expression pattern, how will you handle this in your data flow?

3. How will you allow SSIS package developers to use this component?

Suggested Practices

To help you successfully master the exam objectives presented in this chapter, complete the following tasks.

Create a Web Service Source

To master the usage of the script component, try to use it for a web service source.

- **Practice 1** Create a simple web service exposing a single result set from a stored procedure that reads the *dbo.DimCustomer* table from the AdventureWorksDW2012 database.

- **Practice 2** Create an SSIS package. Use the script component to connect to the web service, call the method, and get the data from the web service.

Answers

This section contains answers to the lesson review questions and solutions to the case scenario in this chapter.

Lesson 1

1. **Correct Answer: B**

    A. **Incorrect:** You need to enlist the variables you want to use in the ReadOnly-Variables and ReadWriteVariables properties of the script task.

    B. **Correct:** You need to enlist the variables you want to use in the ReadOnlyVariables and ReadWriteVariables properties of the script task.

    C. **Incorrect:** You can use SSIS variables in the script.

    D. **Incorrect:** You don't need to use project parameters in order to use SSIS variables in the script.

2. **Correct Answer: C**

    A. **Incorrect:** There is no Start method by default in the script.

    B. **Incorrect:** There is no StartHere method by default in the script.

    C. **Correct:** Main is the starting method by default.

    D. **Incorrect:** Although you can change the starting method, Main is the starting method by default.

3. **Correct Answers: B and C**

    A. **Incorrect:** Visual C++ is not supported by the script task.

    B. **Correct:** Visual Basic is supported by the script task.

    C. **Correct:** Visual C# is supported by the script task.

    D. **Incorrect:** Visual F# is not supported by the script task.

Lesson 2

1. **Correct Answers: B, C, and D**

    A. **Incorrect:** You cannot use the script component as a connection manager.

    B. **Correct:** You can use the script component as a source.

    C. **Correct:** You can use the script component as a destination.

    D. **Correct:** You can use the script component as a transformation.

2. **Correct Answer: C**

   A. **Incorrect:** You use the ReadOnlyVariables property to enlist the package variables you are going to use for reading only in your script.

   B. **Incorrect:** You use the ReadWriteVariables property to enlist the package variables you are going to use for reading and updating in your script.

   C. **Correct:** If an output is synchronous, then the SynchronousInputID value points to the synchronous input.

   D. **Incorrect:** The ScriptLanguage property is never empty. You can choose between the Visual Basic and Visual C# languages.

3. **Correct Answer: A**

   A. **Correct:** The script component doesn't have an input when you use it as a source.

   B. **Incorrect:** The script component doesn't have an output when you use it as a destination.

   C. **Incorrect:** The script component has both input and multiple outputs when you use it as a transformation.

   D. **Incorrect:** The script component doesn't have an input when you use it as a source.

Lesson 3

1. **Correct Answers: A, B, and D**

   A. **Correct:** Custom data flow sources can be developed.

   B. **Correct:** Custom data flow destinations can be developed.

   C. **Incorrect:** Connection managers are not data flow components.

   D. **Correct:** Custom data flow transformations can be developed.

2. **Correct Answers: C and D**

   A. **Incorrect:** Components are not executed at design time.

   B. **Incorrect:** Data flow development cannot be automated simply by using component design-time methods.

   C. **Correct:** Design-time methods allow the SSIS package developer to configure the custom component.

   D. **Correct:** The Validate design-time method is used to validate the component at design time, as well as at run time.

3. **Correct Answers: A, B, C, and D**

   A. **Correct:** Run-time methods can be used to configure the component automatically at run time.

   B. **Correct:** Run-time methods can be used to set internal variables.

   C. **Correct:** Run-time methods can be used to provide access to external data sources to the component.

   D. **Correct:** Run-time methods are used to process data in the data flow.

4. **Correct Answers: A and D**

   A. **Correct:** Custom components are designed once and can then be deployed multiple times.

   B. **Incorrect:** Custom components require more development efforts compared to those required by a Script component. If a particular problem can be solved with just a few lines of custom code, the Script component will allow the solution to be developed more quickly and efficiently.

   C. **Incorrect:** The Script component can reference external libraries just like the custom component can; in both cases, these external resources must be available at the target server.

   D. **Correct:** To modify and re-deploy a script component, the entire SSIS package must be opened in SSDT, modified, and re-deployed. To modify and re-deploy a custom component, no SSIS package that uses it needs to be re-deployed.

Case Scenario

1. Yes. SSIS can be used to implement data extraction by using Regular Expressions. The most appropriate method would be to design a custom data flow transformation component, using the .NET Framework Regular Expressions implementation.

2. The transformation component would have to read the string from an appropriate column, pass it to the Regular Expressions engine, and receive the results, which should then be stored in the appropriate columns. To allow multiple substrings to be extracted from a single row of source data, the component would have to implement an asynchronous output for the results of the transformation. After all, it is possible that the Regular Expression pattern in question could not find any matches in the source string at all.

3. The SSIS package developers should be allowed to pass the Regular Expression pattern to the transformation via a custom component property; they could, for instance, store the pattern in a package variable, or use the component to connect to an external data source and use Regular Expressions patterns stored in a table in a SQL Server database.

## CHAPTER 20

Identity Mapping and De-Duplicating

Exam objectives in this chapter:

- Extract and Transform Data
  - Design data flow.
  - Implement data flow.
- Build Data Quality Solutions
  - Create a data quality project to clean data.

Two of the most challenging problems with maintaining master data are identity mapping and de-duplication.

In an enterprise, you frequently have more than one source of master data. Sometimes you have to import master data from outer sources. Different sources can include older applications; relational databases used by OLTP applications; analytical databases; semi-structured data, such as XML data from a web service; and even non-structured data in Microsoft Excel worksheets and Microsoft Word documents. Typically, you do not have unique identification of entities in all of these different sources. However, you would like to get a complete picture of an entity (a customer, for example) in order to properly support your applications, such as a Customer Relationship Management (CRM) application. Therefore, you have to identify which objects (such as rows in a table or XML instances) represent the same entity. You need to match the identities based on similarities of entity attributes.

Even if you have a single source of data, you are not without problems. Master data is often duplicated. For example, multiple operators could insert the same customer multiple times, each time with a name or address that is written slightly differently. Again, you would like to identify such duplicates and get rid of them.

In this chapter, you will learn details of both problems and about possible solutions.

Lessons in this chapter:

- Lesson 1: Understanding the Problem
- Lesson 2: Using DQS and the DQS Cleansing Transformation
- Lesson 3: Implementing SSIS Fuzzy Transformations

Before You Begin

To complete this chapter, you must have:

- Microsoft SQL Server 2012 Database Services, Integration Services, and Data Quality Services installed.
- Excel 2010 with the SQL Server Master Data Services (MDS) Add-in for Excel installed.
- An understanding of data quality problems.
- Intermediate Transact-SQL skills.

Lesson 1: Understanding the Problem

One of the most challenging tasks an enterprise faces is *identity mapping*. A very similar problem is *de-duplicating*. Typically, these problems arise with customer data. Enterprises frequently have the data for one customer inserted twice, with a slightly different name or address. Or an enterprise can have multiple independent business systems, with the same customer data but different identification (keys). In this chapter, you will learn how to deal with these problems.

> **After this lesson, you will be able to:**
>
> - Understand why mapping identities and de-duplication are tough problems.
> - Understand how you can mitigate these problems.
>
> **Estimated lesson time: 30 minutes**

Identity Mapping and De-Duplicating Problems

The problem with *identity mapping* arises when data is merged from multiple sources that can update data independently. Each source has its own way of entity identification, or its own keys. There is no common key to make simple joins. Data merging has to be done based on similarities of strings, by using names, addresses, email addresses, and similar attributes. Figure 20-1 shows the problem: there are three rows in the first table in the upper-left corner, and two rows in the second table in the upper-right corner. The keys of the rows in the left table (the *Id1* column) are different from the keys of the rows in the right table (the *Id2*

column). The big table at the bottom shows the result of approximate string matching. Note that each row from the left table is matched to each row from the right table; similarities are different for different pairs of rows.

Id1	FullName1
17	Ken Sanchez
55	John Campbell
21	Diane Glimp

Id2	FullName2
21	Kren Canpez
49	Riane Glimpbell

A x B

Id1	FullName1	Id2	FullName2	Similarity
17	Ken Sanchez	21	Kren Canpez	0.778
17	Ken Sanchez	49	Riane Glimpbell	0.056
55	John Campbell	21	Kren Canpez	0.211
55	John Campbell	49	Riane Glimpbell	0.445
21	Diane Glimp	21	Kren Canpez	0.138
21	Diane Glimp	49	Riane Glimpbell	0.664

FIGURE 20-1 The identity mapping problem.

Many problems arise with identity mapping. First, there is no way to get a 100-percent accurate match programmatically; if you need a 100-percent accurate match, you must match entities manually. But even with manual matching, you cannot guarantee 100-percent accurate matches at all times, particularly when you are matching people. For example, in a database table, you might have two rows for people named John Smith, living at the same address; you cannot know whether this is a single person or two people, maybe a father and son. Nevertheless, when you perform the merging programmatically, you would like to get the best matching possible. You must learn which method to use and how to use it in order to get the best possible results for your data. In addition, you might even decide to use manual matching on the remaining unmatched rows after programmatic matching is done.

The next problem is performance. For approximate merging, any row from one side, from one source table, can be matched to any row from the other side. This creates a cross join of the two tables. Even small data sets can run into huge performance problems, because a cross join is an algorithm with quadratic complexity. For example, a cross join of 18,484 rows with 18,484 rows of the AdventureWorksDW2012 *dbo.DimCustomer* table to itself means dealing with 341,658,256 rows after the cross join! Different techniques for optimizing this matching (such as search space reduction techniques) are discussed later in this lesson.

EXAM TIP

When doing the matching, you have to avoid large cross joins.

Another problem related to identity mapping is *de-duplicating*. Actually, one problem can be translated to the other and vice-versa. You can union two tables that need identity mapping and then perform de-duplicating. Or you can join a table that needs de-duplicating to itself and perform identity mapping. In DQS, you can actually perform de-duplication. With SSIS, you can perform identity mapping with the Fuzzy Lookup transformation and de-duplication with the Fuzzy Grouping transformation.

The list of the problems with identity mapping and de-duplication is still not exhausted. If you have an authoritative source, then you know which data is correct. You know which row to keep after de-duplication, and you know which source to update with correct data after identity mapping. However, without an authoritative source, it is very hard to find the correct data automatically. The problem is hard because there are only a few, in many cases only two, rows to analyze. Therefore, it is really hard to learn which one is the correct one. Most of the time you have to decide interactively which piece of data is correct. Even with such sophisticated tools like DQS and the Fuzzy Lookup transformation, automatic results are not satisfactory. Nevertheless, with an authoritative source, there is no problem with finding the correct data. To complete the picture, MDS could be your authoritative source. Therefore, SQL Server gives you all the tools you need out of the box.

Solving the Problems

Finding similar strings is a problem that has been researched a lot in the past. There are many public algorithms available.

DQS matching uses *nGrams*. This algorithm tokenizes strings to all possible substrings of length *n*. These tokens are called nGrams. Then it checks how many different nGrams two strings have in common. The more they have in common, the more similar the strings are. By dividing the number of nGrams in common with the number of all possible nGrams, you can get a coefficient with a value between 0 and 1 that estimates the similarity of the strings. The closer the coefficient is to the value 1, the more similar the strings are.

SSIS fuzzy transformations use a much more sophisticated algorithm. The algorithm was developed by Microsoft Research and is not public. However, some details are described in the Books Online for SQL Server 2012 article "Fuzzy Lookup Transformation" at *http://msdn.microsoft.com/en-us/library/ms137786.aspx*.

In addition to DQS and SSIS, MDS has some public string similarity algorithms as well. You can find these algorithms implemented in the MDS database through the mdq.Similarity function. The function implements the following four public algorithms:

- Levenshtein distance (also called edit distance)
- Jaccard index
- Jaro-Winkler distance
- Simil (longest common substring; also called Ratcliff/Obershelp)

In addition, you can get nGrams with the mdq.NGrams function, also provided in the MDS database. Finally, there is also a function that finds similar dates called mdq.SimilarityDate. You can use all of the MDS functions in Transact-SQL queries.

As mentioned, because of the possible cross join, identity matching is a quadratic problem. The search space dimension is equal to the cardinality of A x B of the Cartesian product of the sets included in the match. There are multiple search space reduction techniques.

A *partitioning* or *blocking* technique partitions at least one set involved in the matching into blocks. For example, it might take the target rows in batches and match each batch with a full master table. With 10,000 rows in each table, you could have 10 iterations of joins with 1,000 x 10,000 = 10,000,000 rows instead of one big row with 10,000 x 10,000 = 100,000,000 rows. The important thing here is that you do not bloat the memory and exceed your hardware resources. In order to prevent this, you can change batch sizes appropriately.

A *sorting neighborhood* technique sorts both sets and then moves a window of a fixed size on both sets. You do the matching on that window only, one window after another. The problem with such a technique lies in the fact that you can have objects from one set in a window that is not compared to the window from another set, where objects that should actually be matched reside. The same problem could arise with blocking techniques implemented on both sets. You do not want to lose the matches you might find by optimization of the mapping methods.

A *pruning* or *filtering* method intelligently pre-selects a subset of rows from one table for a match with all rows or a single pre-selected batch from the other table. The problem here is how to pre-select these rows. You need to be sure that you do not exclude a row that should be matched with one or more target rows. Besides that, you need reasonably sized subsets; if you pre-select a subset of 9,000 rows from a set of 10,000 rows, you will hardly gain anything, because you would get a nearly full cross join again. In addition, you will want to select batches intelligently from the target table; for example, select the rows that have more chances to match well with master rows first, and then rows with a little less of a chance, and then rows with even fewer chances, and so on. Finally, you could leave some rows for manual matching.

The first step in optimizing the mapping procedure is to standardize and clean the data as much as possible. You can use DQS or the SSIS DQS cleansing transformation for this purpose. The next step is to start with exact matches. You can find exact matches with T-SQL INNER JOIN or EXISTS operators, or you can use the SSIS Lookup transformation. Then the path splits, depending on whether you use DQS or SSIS fuzzy transformations.

With DQS, you can use partitioning methods and manually, with T-SQL queries, split a table from one side into multiple partitions. Then you can union the other table with one partition from the first table at a time and perform DQS matching. Save the results of each matching in SQL Server tables and use the results in T-SQL queries to update the data to the correct values.

SSIS fuzzy transformations have more built-in heuristics. They use a filtering method. It is very simple to use this method. In both Fuzzy Lookup and Fuzzy Grouping transformations, you can use the similarity threshold parameter that takes values from a domain between 0 and 1. The closer the value is to 1, the closer the resemblance of the lookup string to the source string must be to qualify as a match. By increasing the threshold, you can improve the speed of matching, because the fuzzy transformations consider fewer candidate records for matching. You can start with a high threshold value when you have a lot of rows to match, and then proceed with a lower value on fewer rows, and so on.

SSIS fuzzy transformations are more sophisticated than DQS matching. SSIS fuzzy transformations are especially useful when you have huge amounts of data to match and you do not have a reference data source. However, DQS can be more useful with a reference data source. With a reference data source, you could translate the identity mapping problem to a data cleansing problem, by simply correcting the values with reference values. After you implement all of the DQS cleansing, there will probably not be many unmatched records left. Finally, DQS matching is used by MDS Add-in for Excel. If you are using Excel for updating MDS data, you can simply check for duplicates by using a DQS matching knowledge base.

 Quick Check

- Which two SSIS transformations are useful for identity mapping and de-duplication?

Quick Check Answer

- The SSIS Fuzzy Lookup transformation is useful for identity mapping, and the SSIS Fuzzy Grouping transformation is useful for de-duplication.

PRACTICE **Preparing the Data**

In this practice, you will prepare data for identity mapping and de-duplication.

If you encounter a problem completing an exercise, you can install the completed project and code from the Solution folder that is provided with the companion content for this chapter and lesson.

EXERCISE 1 Prepare Clean Data

In this exercise, you use T-SQL queries to prepare a clean version of the customer data found in the AdventureWorksDW2012 demo database.

Because some of the queries in this exercise are long and complex, you might prefer to use the code from the Solution folder for this practice.

1. Open SSMS, connect to your SQL Server instance, open a new query window, and change the context to the DQS_STAGING_DATA database.

2. Create a table for clean customer data in the *dbo* schema. Name it **CustomersClean**. Include only columns for the customer key, full name, and street address. Use the following code.

```
CREATE TABLE dbo.CustomersClean
(
 CustomerKey    INT          NOT NULL PRIMARY KEY,
 FullName       NVARCHAR(200) NULL,
 StreetAddress  NVARCHAR(200) NULL
);
```

3. Populate the table with every tenth customer from the *dbo.DimCustomer* table from the AdventureWorksDW2012 database by using the following query.

```
INSERT INTO dbo.CustomersClean
 (CustomerKey, FullName, StreetAddress)
SELECT CustomerKey,
 FirstName + ' ' + LastName AS FullName,
 AddressLine1 AS StreetAddress
FROM AdventureWorksDW2012.dbo.DimCustomer
WHERE CustomerKey % 10 = 0;
```

4. Create a table with a structure similar to the one for *dbo.CustomersClean* and call it **CustomersDirty**. Add two integer columns to this table called *Updated* and *CleanCustomerKey*. The first one will be used by the query that makes the data dirty and the second one to populate the table with the customer key from the clean table after identity mapping. Populate this table with the same data; multiply the *CustomerKey* column by –1 and populate the *Updated* column with zero. Do not populate the *CleanCustomerKey* column. This will allow you to track the accuracy of matches in later practices in this chapter. Use the following code.

```
CREATE TABLE dbo.CustomersDirty
(
 CustomerKey      INT          NOT NULL PRIMARY KEY,
 FullName         NVARCHAR(200) NULL,
 StreetAddress    NVARCHAR(200) NULL,
 Updated          INT          NULL,
 CleanCustomerKey INT          NULL
);
GO
INSERT INTO dbo.CustomersDirty
 (CustomerKey, FullName, StreetAddress, Updated)
SELECT CustomerKey * (-1) AS CustomerKey,
 FirstName + ' ' + LastName AS FullName,
 AddressLine1 AS StreetAddress,
 0 AS Updated
FROM AdventureWorksDW2012.dbo.DimCustomer
WHERE CustomerKey % 10 = 0;
```

EXERCISE 2 Prepare Dirty Data

In this exercise, you use T-SQL queries to prepare a dirty version of the customer data found in the AdventureWorksDW2012 demo database.

1. Making changes that resemble real life is very tricky. The following code performs these changes. This code makes changes with a slightly controlled randomness, in a loop that repeats three times. In every loop, the code makes three updates on 17 percent, 17 percent, and 16 percent (for a total of 50 percent) of the rows. Rows to be updated are selected with Bernoulli's formula for sampling, which provides statistically good randomness. In the first two passes, 50 percent of the rows are selected from all rows; in the third pass, the code selects 50 percent of the rows from the rows that were updated in the previous two passes only. This way, you get more errors on fewer rows. Because this code is very lengthy, you might want to use the code provided in the Solution folder for this practice.

```
DECLARE @i AS INT = 0, @j AS INT = 0;
WHILE (@i < 3)        -- loop more times for more changes
BEGIN
 SET @i += 1;
 SET @j = @i - 2;    -- control here in which step you want to update
                     -- only already updated rows
WITH RandomNumbersCTE AS
 (
  SELECT  CustomerKey
         ,RAND(CHECKSUM(NEWID()) % 1000000000 + CustomerKey) AS RandomNumber1
         ,RAND(CHECKSUM(NEWID()) % 1000000000 + CustomerKey) AS RandomNumber2
         ,RAND(CHECKSUM(NEWID()) % 1000000000 + CustomerKey) AS RandomNumber3
         ,FullName
         ,StreetAddress
         ,Updated
     FROM dbo.CustomersDirty
 )
UPDATE RandomNumbersCTE SET
        FullName =
        STUFF(FullName,
             CAST(CEILING(RandomNumber1 * LEN(FullName)) AS INT),
             1,
             CHAR(CEILING(RandomNumber2 * 26) + 96))
       ,StreetAddress =
        STUFF(StreetAddress,
             CAST(CEILING(RandomNumber1 * LEN(StreetAddress)) AS INT),
             2, '')
       ,Updated = Updated + 1
 WHERE RAND(CHECKSUM(NEWID()) % 1000000000 - CustomerKey) < 0.17
       AND Updated > @j;
WITH RandomNumbersCTE AS
```

```
    (
     SELECT  CustomerKey
            ,RAND(CHECKSUM(NEWID()) % 1000000000 + CustomerKey) AS RandomNumber1
            ,RAND(CHECKSUM(NEWID()) % 1000000000 + CustomerKey) AS RandomNumber2
            ,RAND(CHECKSUM(NEWID()) % 1000000000 + CustomerKey) AS RandomNumber3
            ,FullName
            ,StreetAddress
            ,Updated
        FROM dbo.CustomersDirty
    )
    UPDATE RandomNumbersCTE SET
            FullName =
            STUFF(FullName, CAST(CEILING(RandomNumber1 * LEN(FullName)) AS INT),
                0,
                CHAR(CEILING(RandomNumber2 * 26) + 96))
            ,StreetAddress =
            STUFF(StreetAddress,
                CAST(CEILING(RandomNumber1 * LEN(StreetAddress)) AS INT),
                2,
                CHAR(CEILING(RandomNumber2 * 26) + 96) +
                CHAR(CEILING(RandomNumber3 * 26) + 96))
            ,Updated = Updated + 1
      WHERE RAND(CHECKSUM(NEWID()) % 1000000000 - CustomerKey) < 0.17
            AND Updated > @j;
    WITH RandomNumbersCTE AS
    (
     SELECT  CustomerKey
            ,RAND(CHECKSUM(NEWID()) % 1000000000 + CustomerKey) AS RandomNumber1
            ,RAND(CHECKSUM(NEWID()) % 1000000000 + CustomerKey) AS RandomNumber2
            ,RAND(CHECKSUM(NEWID()) % 1000000000 + CustomerKey) AS RandomNumber3
            ,FullName
            ,StreetAddress
            ,Updated
        FROM dbo.CustomersDirty
    )
    UPDATE RandomNumbersCTE SET
            FullName =
            STUFF(FullName,
                CAST(CEILING(RandomNumber1 * LEN(FullName)) AS INT),
                1, '')
            ,StreetAddress =
            STUFF(StreetAddress,
                CAST(CEILING(RandomNumber1 * LEN(StreetAddress)) AS INT),
                0,
                CHAR(CEILING(RandomNumber2 * 26) + 96) +
                CHAR(CEILING(RandomNumber3 * 26) + 96))
            ,Updated = Updated + 1
      WHERE RAND(CHECKSUM(NEWID()) % 1000000000 - CustomerKey) < 0.16
            AND Updated > @j;
    END;
```

2. You can check the dirty data after changes. A little bit more than 40 percent of data should be updated. Because there is randomness in updates, you get a different number of rows and different rows updated every time you run the previous code. You can check the changes with the following query.

```
SELECT  C.FullName
       ,D.FullName
       ,C.StreetAddress
       ,D.StreetAddress
       ,D.Updated
  FROM dbo.CustomersClean AS C
       INNER JOIN dbo.CustomersDirty AS D
        ON C.CustomerKey = D.CustomerKey * (-1)
 WHERE C.FullName <> D.FullName
       OR C.StreetAddress <> D.StreetAddress
ORDER BY D.Updated DESC;
```

3. Finally, update the row for the customer with a key equal to -11010. Set the FullName to **Jacquelyn Suarez** and StreetAddress to **7800 Corrinne Ct.** This gives you a row that can be corrected with the DQS Cleansing transformation in the practice for the next lesson. Use the following code.

```
UPDATE dbo.CustomersDirty
   SET FullName = N'Jacquelyn Suarez',
       StreetAddress = N'7800 Corrinne Ct.'
WHERE CustomerKey = -11010;
```

Your data is prepared for identity mapping and de-duplication.

> **NOTE CONTINUING WITH PRACTICES**
>
> Do not exit SSMS if you intend to continue immediately with the next practice.

Lesson Summary

- You can use DQS and SSIS from the SQL Server suite for identity mapping and de-duplicating tasks.
- Data merging has to be done based on similarities of strings.
- When performing the matching, you have to avoid cross joins of huge amounts of data.
- You can even use MDS functions for your own mapping procedures.

Lesson Review

Answer the following questions to test your knowledge of the information in this lesson. You can find the answers to these questions and explanations of why each answer choice is correct or incorrect in the "Answers" section at the end of this chapter.

1. What are some of the problems with identity mapping and de-duplicating? (Choose all that apply.)

   A. It can be hard to find a good string similarity algorithm.

   B. No tools are provided in the SQL Server suite.

   C. The SSIS data flow fails when a record is duplicated.

   D. It is difficult to get good performance.

2. Why can you encounter a performance problem with identity mapping?

   A. Because you are not using stored procedures

   B. Because any row from one side can match any row from the other side, and thus you can get a full cross join

   C. Because you always have to do the matching interactively, and you work record by record

   D. Because SSIS Fuzzy Lookup can only handle one row at a time

3. Which string similarity algorithm is used for DQS matching?

   A. Jaccard index

   B. Levenshtein distance

   C. nGrams

   D. Jaro-Winkler distance

Lesson 2: Using DQS and the DQS Cleansing Transformation

The *DQS Cleansing transformation* is useful for cleansing batches of data inside the SSIS data flow. It should be a starting point for identity mapping and de-duplication, in order to minimize the number of rows that need approximate matching. You can use DQS to do the matching by creating a matching policy knowledge base.

> **After this lesson, you will be able to:**
> - Use the DQS Cleansing transformation.
> - Create a DQS matching policy KB.
> - Create a DQS matching project.
>
> **Estimated lesson time: 40 minutes**

DQS Cleansing Transformation

The DQS Cleansing transformation uses Data Quality Services (DQS) to correct data. You need to have a DQS knowledge base created in advance. You connect to a data source, select the columns to correct, and map the columns to the appropriate DQS KB domains. You learned how to create a DQS knowledge base and a DQS cleansing project in Chapter 17, "Creating a Data Quality Project to Clean Data."

In order to map the source columns to a KB domain, you need to create a connection to your DQS service. Then you select the knowledge base. Remember that you can have a single domain or composite domains. If you map multiple columns to each column of a composite domain, then the composite domain rules are applied. If you don't map to all domains from a composite domain, then single domain rules are applied, and each column is processed and cleansed individually.

Some advanced configuration options for the DQS Cleansing transformations are also available:

- **Standardize output**   Use this option to standardize the output as you define in domain settings. You can standardize strings to uppercase or lowercase, or capitalize each word. In addition, the values are standardized to the leading value.
- **Confidence**   If you select this option, you also get the confidence level for a correction or a suggestion.
- **Reason**   You can include the reason for a correction or a suggestion.
- **Appended data**   This setting is valid only if you are using a reference data provider. Some reference data providers can include additional information, such as geographic coordinates when you check an address. You get this additional information in the field called Appended Data.
- **Appended data schema**   If you append a reference provider's data, you get information about the schema for this data in this field.

The DQS Cleansing transformation, like other transformations, includes an error output allowing you to handle potential row-level errors.

EXAM TIP

Remember that you should cleanse your data before matching.

DQS Matching

For DQS matching, you need to prepare a separate *matching policy* KB. You cannot use knowledge bases created for a domain policy. For a matching policy, you define one or more matching rules. In a *matching rule*, you define which domains will be used for the matching process. Composite domains can be very useful for matching—for example, if you want to match customers based on their name and address together.

You can have additional influence on the matching process. You can specify the importance of each domain used for matching by specifying the weight that each domain value carries in the matching process. In addition, you can specify that one or more domains used for matching have to be an exact match and not just similar. If you specify that a domain can just be similar, you can define the degree of similarity. Finally, you can define that one or more domains are a prerequisite for matching. With all of these options, you can create a KB with very strict rules for initial matching, and then lower the similarity thresholds for consequent matching. This way, you can reduce the search space for less similar rows, and thus improve the performance of DQS matching assessment.

When building a matching KB, you can use sample data to speed up the learning process. You can define different rules and test them. You do not need to reload the data for each test. You reload the data only if you know that your sample data has changed substantially. When the test is finished, matching results are grouped in clusters for an overview. Matching results are not added to the KB; you use them interactively to find the best matching rule.

When you use strings for matching, you should normalize them when you load your data. Normalization improves matching accuracy. You can also compare numbers and dates. For numbers, you can define similarity as the percentage of the value or as an integer that defines the interval in which two numbers are treated as similar. For dates, you can define the similarity tolerance in the number of days, months, or years.

You also define the minimum score for matching. This is an overall score for complete rows. The default score is 80 percent. You can raise this number to get more accurate matches first, and then lower it for the next iteration.

You can run a matching DQS project on a different data set. Actually, this is very common, because you typically create KB rules on a sample. A matching project, like a cleansing project, consists of computer-assisted and interactive phases. During the computer-assisted phase, DQS searches for matches, calculates the similarity, and groups similar records into clusters. In the interactive phase, a data steward can define survivorship rules. You can export the matching and the survivorship results to a SQL Server table or to a .csv file.

 Quick Check

- How can you influence which column in a table should be more important for matching than other columns?

Quick Check Answer

- When creating a matching KB, you can define weight for each domain. Give higher weight to the domain mapped to the column you want to be more important for matching.

In this practice, you will use the DQS Cleansing transformation. Then you will create a DQS matching policy KB and use it to perform de-duplication.

If you encounter a problem completing an exercise, you can install the completed projects from the Solution folder that is provided with the companion content for this chapter and lesson.

EXERCISE 1   Use the DQS Cleansing Transformation

Before you start matching your data, you should cleanse it. In this way, you can improve the quality of the matches. In this exercise, you use the DQS Cleansing transformation.

1. Start SQL Server Data Tools and create a new Integration Services project. Name the project **TK 463 Chapter 20**. Rename the default package named Package to **DQSCleansing**.

2. Drag a data flow task to the control flow working area. Click the Data Flow tab to open the data flow working area.

3. Right-click the Connection Managers folder in Solution Explorer and select New Connection Manager.

4. Select the OLEDB connection manager type and click Add. In the Configure OLE DB Connection Manager window, click New.

5. Select Native OLE DB\SQL Server Native Client 11.0 Provider. Provide the name of your SQL Server instance and authentication information, and select the DQS_STAGING_DATA database. Click OK. When you are back in the Configure OLE DB Connection Manager window, click OK.

6. Add an OLE DB source to your data flow. Rename it to **CustomersDirty**. Double-click it to open the editor. Select the *dbo.CustomersDirty* table. Click the Columns tab in the left pane to get the column mappings. Check the mappings and click OK.

7. In the SSIS Toolbox, expand Other Transforms. Drag the DQS Cleansing transformation to the data flow. Connect it to the CustomersDirty data source with the normal data flow (gray arrow). Rename the transformation **Cleanse StreetAddress**. Double-click it to open the editor.

8. In the DQS Cleansing Transformation Editor, make sure that the Connection Manager tab is selected. Then click New. Enter your server name in the DQS Cleansing Connection Manager pop-up window and then click OK.

9. Select the TK463Customers knowledge base. You created this KB in the practices in Chapter 17. If you didn't create it yet, you can import it from the Starter folder for this practice. Refer to Chapter 17 for information on how to import a DQS KB.

10. Click the Mapping tab. In the Available Input Columns list, select the check box near the *StreetAddress* column. Then map it to the StreetAddress domain and rename the *StreetAddress_Output* column to **StreetAddress**, as shown in Figure 20-2. You are going to use this column with corrected data in downstream flow.

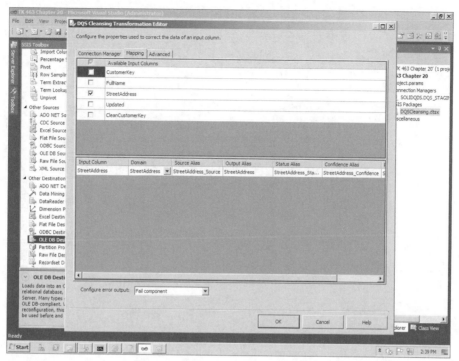

FIGURE 20-2 Mappings between columns and domains in the DQS Cleansing Transformation Editor.

11. Click the Advanced tab. Select the Confidence and Reason check boxes. Then click OK.

12. The next step in preparing for identity mapping is to perform the exact matches. Drag the Lookup transformation to the working area and connect it to the DQS Cleansing transformation. Name it **Exact Matches** and double-click it to open the editor.

13. In the Lookup Transformation Editor, click the Connection tab in the left pane. Use the connection manager for the DQS_STAGING_DATA database. Select the *dbo.Customers-Clean* table. Then click the Columns tab.

14. Drag the *FullName* and *StreetAddress* columns from Available Input Columns onto the columns with the same name in the Available Lookup Columns table. Select the check box near the *CustomerKey* column in the Available Lookup Columns table. In the Lookup Operation field in the grid in the bottom part of the editor, select the Replace 'CleanCustomerKey' option. Rename the output alias **CleanCustomerKey**, as shown in Figure 20-3.

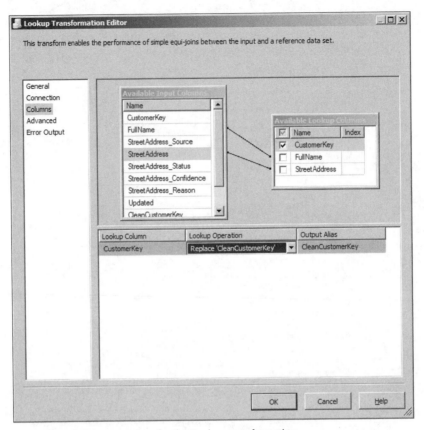

FIGURE 20-3 Column mappings for the Lookup transformation.

15. Click the General tab. For Specify How To Handle Rows With No Matching Entities, select the Redirect Rows To No Match Output option. Then click OK to close the Lookup Transformation Editor.

16. Drag two Multicast transformations to the working area. Rename the first one **Match** and the second one **No Match.** Connect them to the Lookup transformation, the first by using the Lookup Match Output and the second by using the Lookup No Match Output. You do not need to multicast the data for this exercise; however, you are going to expand the package in later exercises.

17. In SSMS, create a new table in the DQS_STAGING_DATA database in the *dbo* schema and name it **CustomersDirtyMatch**. Use the following code.

```
CREATE TABLE dbo.CustomersDirtyMatch
(
CustomerKey            INT              NOT NULL PRIMARY KEY,
FullName               NVARCHAR(200)    NULL,
StreetAddress_Source   NVARCHAR(200)    NULL,
StreetAddress          NVARCHAR(200)    NULL,
```

```
StreetAddress_Status      NVARCHAR(100)  NULL,
StreetAddress_Confidence  NVARCHAR(100)  NULL,
StreetAddress_Reason      NVARCHAR(4000) NULL,
Updated                   INT            NULL,
CleanCustomerKey          INT            NULL,
Record_Status             NVARCHAR(100)  NULL
);
```

18. Add another new table in the *dbo* schema and name it **CustomersDirtyNoMatch**. Use the same schema as for the previous table, as in the following code.

```
CREATE TABLE dbo.CustomersDirtyNoMatch
(
CustomerKey               INT            NOT NULL PRIMARY KEY,
FullName                  NVARCHAR(200)  NULL,
StreetAddress_Source      NVARCHAR(200)  NULL,
StreetAddress             NVARCHAR(200)  NULL,
StreetAddress_Status      NVARCHAR(100)  NULL,
StreetAddress_Confidence  NVARCHAR(100)  NULL,
StreetAddress_Reason      NVARCHAR(4000) NULL,
Updated                   INT            NULL,
CleanCustomerKey          INT            NULL,
Record_Status             NVARCHAR(100)  NULL
);
```

19. Add a new OLE DB destination and rename it **CustomersDirtyMatch**. Connect it to the Match Multicast transformation. Double-click it to open the editor. Select the *dbo.CustomersDirtyMatch* table. Click the Mappings tab to check the mappings. Note that the last column is ignored on the input side. Click the <Ignore> value and select the *Record Status* input column to map it to the *Record_Status* output column. Click OK.

20. Add a new OLE DB destination and rename it **CustomersDirtyNoMatch**. Connect it to the No Match Multicast transformation. Double-click it to open the editor. Select the *dbo.CustomersDirtyNoMatch* table. Click the Mappings tab to check the mappings. Note that the last column is ignored on the input side. Click the <Ignore> value and select the *Record Status* input column to map it to the *Record_Status* output column. Click OK.

21. Save the project. Execute the package and resolve any errors. When the package executes successfully, check the content of the *dbo.CustomersDirtyMatch* and *dbo.CustomersDirtyNoMatch* tables. Check the corrected *StreetAddress* column value for the customer with CustomerKey equal to -11010.

22. You are finished with the first exercise. Keep SSMS and SSDT open, because you will use them in the next exercise.

EXERCISE 2   Use DQS Matching

In this exercise, you use DQS to match data; that is, to perform the de-duplicating. For this you need to create a DQS KB and then a matching project.

1. In order to create a matching policy, you need to have some data to match. You have the *dbo.CustomersClean* table with clean data and the *dbo.CustomersNoMatch* table with data that didn't get a match after cleansing and using the Lookup transformation in the previous exercise. Create a view that unions this data by using the following code.

   ```
   CREATE VIEW dbo.CustomersDQSMatch
   AS
   SELECT CustomerKey, FullName, StreetAddress
   FROM dbo.CustomersClean
   UNION
   SELECT CustomerKey, FullName, StreetAddress
   FROM dbo.CustomersDirtyNoMatch;
   ```

2. Start Data Quality Client and connect to your DQS server.

3. Create a new knowledge base. Name it **TK463CustomersMatching**. Make sure that the Matching Policy activity is selected. Click Next.

4. In the Knowledge Base Management window, on the Map tab (the first one), select SQL Server as the data source. Select the DQS_STAGING_DATA database and the *CustomersDQSMatch* view.

5. Create a domain named **FullName**. Use the data type String, and select the Use Leading Values, Normalize String, and Disable Syntax Error Algorithms check boxes. Clear the Enable Speller check box. Set Format Output to None and English Language. Click OK.

6. Create another domain named **StreetAddress** with the same settings as for the FullName domain.

7. Map the *FullName* column to the FullName domain and the *StreetAddress* column to the StreetAddress domain.

8. Create a new composite domain (click the second icon from the right above the column/domain mappings grid in the left pane). For matching, you typically use a composite domain, which encompasses all columns involved in an approximate match. Name the domain **NameAddress** and add the *FullName* and *StreetAddress* columns from the Domain List window to the Domains In Composite Domains window. Click OK. Your screen should look like the one in Figure 20-4. After you are sure you have the correct domains and mappings, click Next.

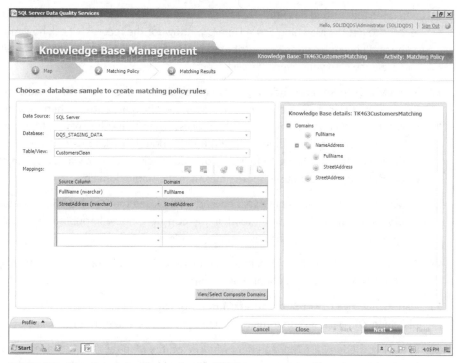

FIGURE 20-4 Domains and mappings for the TK463CustomersMatching KB.

9. On the Matching Policy tab, click the Create A Matching Rule button in the left pane. In the Rule Details pane on the right side, change the name of the rule to **Composite100**.

10. In the Rule Editor area on the right, click the Add A New Domain Element button in the upper-right corner. The NameAddress domain should appear. Scroll to the right of the *Similarity* column (leave the value Similar in it) to show the *Weight* column. Change the weight to 100% for the NameAddress composite domain. You could also start with exact matches for one domain by requesting this domain as a prerequisite— for example, by selecting the check box in the *Prerequisite* column for the FullName domain—to lower the number of rows for matching in one pass. When you are done defining the rule, click the Start button in the Matching Results section of the screen to run the matching policy.

11. When the matching policy run has finished, check the results. Filter matched and un-matched records by selecting the appropriate option in the Filter drop-down list.

12. You should test multiple rules. Create a new rule and name it **Name40Address60**. In the Rule Editor section, click the Add A New Domain Element button. Scroll to the right of the *Similarity* column (leave the value Similar in it) to show the *Weight* column. Change the weight to 40% for the FullName domain and to 60% for the StreetAddress domain. Click the Start button to test this rule.

13. When the rule testing has finished, review the results. Double-click some matched records to get the Matching Score Details window for the records. Check how much name and how much address contributed to the score. Then close the window. When you are done with your overview, click Next.

14. In the Matching Results window, you can check all rules at once. Make sure that the Execute On Previous Data option is selected below the Start button. Then click the Start button. Wait until DQS finishes the process. Then check the Profiler, Matching Rules, and Matching Results. In Matching Results, double-click some matched records to show the Matching Score Details window and check which rule was used. The composite domain should be used more times than the single domains.

15. When you are done with your overview and have closed the Matching Score Details window, click Finish. Then click Publish in the pop-up window to publish the KB. When it is published, click OK in the next pop-up window.

16. The next step is to create a DQS matching project. Click the New Data Quality Project button in the Data Quality Client main screen.

17. Name the project **TK463CustomersMatchingProject**. Select the TK463Customers-Matching KB. Make sure that the Matching activity is selected. Then click Next.

18. In the Knowledge Base Management window, on the Map tab (the first one), select SQL Server as the data source. Select the DQS_STAGING_DATA database and the CustomersDQSMatch view. Note that in a real project, you would have a separate table with sample data for learning during the KB creation, and then another table for real matching.

19. Map the *FullName* column to the FullName domain and the *StreetAddress* column to the StreetAddress domain. Then click Next.

20. On the Matching tab, click the Start button. Wait until matching is finished, and then review the results. When you are finished reviewing, click Next.

21. On the Export page, choose SQL Server as the destination type and choose the DQS_STAGING_DATA database. Select both the Matching Results and Survivorship Results check boxes. Export the matching results to a table named **DQSMatchingResults** and survivorship results to a table named **DQSSurvivorshipResults**. Select the Most Complete And Longest Record survivorship rule. The click the Export button.

22. When the export is finished, click Finish.

23. Check the exported results. You can quickly see that the survivorship policy is not sophisticated enough, because many customers with negative CustomerKey values are selected as survivors. You should use matching results and define your own survivorship rules or select the survivors manually.

24. Close Data Quality Client.

NOTE **CONTINUING WITH PRACTICES**

Do not exit SSMS and SSDT if you intend to continue immediately with the next practice.

Lesson Summary

- You can use the DQS Cleansing transformation to take advantage of DQS knowledge bases to correct data in the SSIS data flow.
- For DQS matching, use a matching policy DQS knowledge base.
- You can use sample data to speed up the learning process when creating a matching policy DQS knowledge base.

Lesson Review

Answer the following questions to test your knowledge of the information in this lesson. You can find the answers to these questions and explanations of why each answer choice is correct or incorrect in the "Answers" section at the end of this chapter.

1. How can you influence DQS matching rules? (Choose all that apply.)

   A. You can define the weight of each domain.

   B. You can define the overall minimum matching score for rows to be considered as a match.

   C. You can select a string similarity algorithm.

   D. You can define similarity tolerance for numbers and dates.

2. Which of the following is a DQS survivorship rule?

   A. Strings without special characters

   B. Most complete and longest record

   C. Numbers divisible by a specific integer

   D. Strings without a repeating substring

3. How do you use the matching results when building a matching DQS knowledge base?

   A. You use the matching results interactively to find the best matching rule.

   B. You add the matching results to the knowledge base.

   C. You export the matching results to a SQL Server table.

   D. You export the matching results to a .csv file.

Lesson 3: Implementing SSIS Fuzzy Transformations

You might be slightly disappointed with the results of DQS matching in the previous exercise. You might have millions of rows to match, and you cannot imagine doing an interactive survivorship process. This is where you should consider using SSIS fuzzy transformations. SSIS Fuzzy Lookup and Fuzzy Grouping can handle much bigger data sets than DQS. Still, DQS is not useless. You can use DQS matching for smaller amounts of records, probably sets of at most a couple of thousand records. Fuzzy components are limited to character data comparisons, whereas DQS matching can compare numbers and dates as well. In addition, you can use DQS matching interactively when you edit master data by using MDS Add-in for Excel.

> **After this lesson, you will be able to:**
> - Use SSIS Fuzzy Lookup and Fuzzy Grouping transformations.
> - Use MDS Add-in for Excel and a DQS matching KB for interactive matching.
>
> **Estimated lesson time: 45 minutes**

Fuzzy Transformations Algorithm

Fuzzy transformations use a quite advanced algorithm for approximate string matching. It actually comprises some public algorithms with algorithms developed by Microsoft Research. The algorithm starts by using the Jaccard similarity coefficient.

The *Jaccard index* (similarity coefficient) measures similarity between sample sets. When used for strings, it defines strings as sets of characters. The size of the intersection is divided by the size of the union of the sample sets. However, the fuzzy transformations version is much more advanced: It is actually weighted Jaccard similarity for tokens.

For example, the sets {a, b, c} and {a, c, d} have a Jaccard similarity of 2/4 = 0.5 because the intersection is {a, c} and the union is {a, b, c, d}. You can assign weights to each item in a set and define the weighted Jaccard similarity as the total weight of the intersection divided by the total weight of the union. For example, suppose you added arbitrary weights to the elements of the sets from the previous example to get the weighted sets {(a, 2), (b, 5), (c, 3)}, {(a, 2), (c, 3), (d, 7)}. For these two sets, the weighted Jaccard similarity is (2 + 3) / (2 + 3 + 5 +7) = 5/17 = 0.294.

Tokens are substrings of original strings. Fuzzy transformations convert strings to sets before they calculate the weighted Jaccard similarity. The transformation used for converting an internal component is called a *tokenizer*. For example, the row {"Ruben Torres", "5844 Linden Land"} might be tokenized into the set {"Ruben", "Torres", "5844", "Linden", "Land"}. The default tokenizer is for English text. You can change the LocaleId property in component properties. Note that this is an advanced property, and you need to open the Advanced Editor for the transformation in order to get to this property (right-click either the Fuzzy Lookup or the Fuzzy Grouping transformation in SSIS Designer and select the Show Advanced Editor option).

Fuzzy transformations assign weights to tokens. Tokens get higher weights if they occur infrequently and lower weights if they occur frequently. In database text, for example, frequent words such as "database" might be given a lower weight, whereas less frequent words such as "broker" might be given a higher weight. In the Excel version of Fuzzy Lookup, you can even override the default token weights by supplying your own table of token weights.

Fuzzy components are additionally enhanced with token transformations. Tokens are converted from one string to another. There are many classes of such transformations that fuzzy components handle automatically, such as spelling mistakes, string prefixes, and string merge/split operations. In the Excel version, you can also define a custom transformation table to specify conversions from a token to a token. For example, you can specify that the "Inc" token has to be converted to the "Incorporated" token.

The Jaccard coefficient is further enhanced by comparing transformations of sets. The maximal Jaccard coefficient between any two transformations of each set is called the Jaccard similarity. With a specified set of transformation rules (either from your table in Excel or built-in rules in SSIS), all possible transformations of the set are considered. For example, for the sets {a, b, c} and {a, c, d} and the transformation rules {b=>d, d=>e}, the Jaccard similarity is computed:

- Variations of {a, b, c}: {a, b, c}, {a, d, c}
- Variations of {a, c, d}: {a, c, d}, {a, c, e}
- Maximum Jaccard similarity between all pairs:
  - J({a, b, c}, {a, c, d}) = 2/4 = 0.5
  - J({a, b, c}, {a, c, e}) = 2/4 = 0.5
  - J({a, d, c}, {a, c, d}) = 3/3 = 1.0
  - J({a, d, c}, {a, c, e}) = 2/4 = 0.5
- The maximum is 1.0.

Fuzzy components also use Edit (Levenshtein) distance. *Levenshtein distance* measures the minimum number of edits needed to transform one string into the other. It is the total number of character insertions, deletions, or substitutions that it takes to convert one string to another. Fuzzy components include an additional internal transformation provider called EditTransformationProvider, which generates specific transformations for each string and creates a transformation from the token to all words in its dictionary that are within a given edit distance. The normalized edit distance is the edit distance divided by the length of the input string.

As you can see, Fuzzy transformations use quite an advanced algorithm, which combines many public algorithms and some internal components. Because of this advanced logic built into the transformation, you get more matches and better accuracy of the matches than you would get with a single string comparison algorithm.

Versions of Fuzzy Transformations

As you probably noticed in the text of this chapter so far, fuzzy transformations are mentioned in an SSIS and in an Excel context. There are three flavors of fuzzy transformations:

- The SSIS Fuzzy Lookup transformation
- The SSIS Fuzzy Grouping transformation
- The Excel Fuzzy Lookup Add-in

You use the Fuzzy Lookup transformation for identity mapping. You can control the matching through three parameters: maximum number of matches to return per input row, token delimiters, and similarity thresholds.

You can have zero or more matches. It is not guaranteed that you would always get the maximum number of matches you specify; if the similarity threshold is not passed, rows are not treated as matches. Fuzzy Lookup has a default set of delimiters used to tokenize the data. However, you can define your own set of delimiters, which is especially useful if you have data in different languages that might use different delimiters.

You can define a similarity threshold for the component as a whole or for a specific join of two string columns. A lower similarity level means that the component will try to match more rows. This means that fewer rows are pre-selected, and you are closer to a full cross join. Therefore, you should start with a higher similarity threshold and then lower it in the next iterations, when you deal with a smaller number of unmatched rows.

The output of the Fuzzy Lookup transformation includes two additional columns:

- *_Similarity*, which indicates the similarity between values in the input and reference columns
- *_Confidence*, which indicates the quality of the match

You use the Fuzzy Grouping transformation for de-duplicating. Just like you can reduce the search space for Fuzzy Lookup by performing exact matches first with a Lookup transformation, you can reduce the search space for Fuzzy Grouping by finding exact matches first with an Aggregate transformation. Then you can control the behavior of Fuzzy Grouping with a similarity threshold and token delimiters.

The Fuzzy Grouping transformation adds the following columns to the output:

- *_key_in*, a column that uniquely identifies each row for the transformation
- *_key_out*, a column that identifies a group of duplicate rows
- *_score*, a value between 0 and 1 that indicates the similarity of the input row to the canonical row. For the canonical row, *_score* has a value of 1

The *_key_out* column has the value of the *_key_in* column in the canonical data row. The *canonical row* is the row that the Fuzzy Grouping identified as the most plausible correct row and that was used for comparison (that is, the row used for standardizing data). Rows with the same value in *_key_out* are part of the same group. The *_key_out* value for a group corresponds to the value of *_key_in* in the canonical data row.

In addition, Fuzzy Grouping adds columns used for approximate string comparison with clean values. Clean values are the values from the canonical row. For example, you can have *FullName_clean* and *StreetAddress_clean* columns in the output for the *FullName* and *StreetAddress* input columns. Finally, the transformation adds columns with similarity scores for each character column used for approximate string comparison. For example, these could be *_Similarity_FullName* and *_Similarity_StreetAddress* columns.

Both SSIS fuzzy transformations use the connection to the SQL Server database to create temporary tables that the fuzzy matching algorithm uses.

Finally, you can get a free Fuzzy Lookup Add-in for Excel from the Microsoft Download Center at *http://www.microsoft.com/en-us/download/details.aspx?id=15011*. Note that this add-in works with Excel 2010 only. After you download and install the Fuzzy Lookup add-in for Excel, you can perform identity mapping for Excel tables as well. There is nothing much to add from the algorithm perspective—of course, this is the same Fuzzy Lookup algorithm as was described earlier in this chapter. Exhaustive instructions on how to use the add-in are provided in a PDF document and in a demo Excel file, both of which come with the Fuzzy Lookup for Excel download.

 Quick Check

- Which SSIS transformation is useful for de-duplication?

Quick Check Answer

- You can use the SSIS Fuzzy Grouping transformation for de-duplication.

PRACTICE **Using the SSIS Fuzzy Lookup Transformation and MDS Add-in for Excel with the DQS Matching KB**

In this practice, you will use the SSIS Fuzzy Lookup transformation for identity mapping of batches of data and MDS Add-in for Excel for interactive de-duplication with the help of the DQS matching policy KB.

If you encounter a problem completing an exercise, you can install the completed projects from the Solution folder that is provided with the companion content for this chapter and lesson.

EXERCISE 1   Use Fuzzy Lookup

In this exercise, you enhance the package you created in the practice for the previous lesson.

1. If you did not finish the previous practice, open the **TK 463 Chapter 20** project in the Starter folder for this lesson. Otherwise, continue with your project from the previous practice. Edit the data flow of the DQSCleansing package.

2. In SSMS, create a new table in the DQS_STAGING_DATA database in the *dbo* schema and name it **FuzzyMatchingResults**. Use the following code.

```
CREATE TABLE dbo.FuzzyMatchingResults
(
CustomerKey                 INT             NOT NULL PRIMARY KEY,
FullName                    NVARCHAR(200)   NULL,
StreetAddress_Source        NVARCHAR(200)   NULL,
StreetAddress               NVARCHAR(200)   NULL,
StreetAddress_Status        NVARCHAR(100)   NULL,
StreetAddress_Confidence    NVARCHAR(100)   NULL,
StreetAddress_Reason        NVARCHAR(4000)  NULL,
Updated                     INT             NULL,
Record_Status               NVARCHAR(100)   NULL,
CleanCustomerKey            INT             NULL,
_Similarity                 REAL            NULL,
_Confidence                 REAL            NULL,
_Similarity_FullName        REAL            NULL,
_Similarity_StreetAddress   REAL            NULL
);
```

3. Add a Fuzzy Lookup transformation below the No Match Multicast transformation. Rename it **Fuzzy Matches** and connect it to the No Match Multicast transformation. Double-click it to open the editor.

4. On the Reference Table tab, select the connection manager to your DQS_STAGING_ DATA database and select the *dbo.CustomersClean* table. Do not store a new index or use an existing index.

> **NOTE** **MATCH INDEX**
>
> When the package first runs the transformation, it copies the reference table, adds a key with an integer data type to the new table, and builds an index on the key column. Next, the transformation builds an index, called a match index, on the copy of the reference table. The match index stores the results of tokenizing the values in the transformation input columns, and the transformation then uses the tokens in the lookup operation. The match index is a table in a SQL Server database. When the package runs again, the transformation can either use an existing match index or create a new index. If the reference table is static, the package can avoid the potentially expensive process of rebuilding the index for repeat sessions of data cleaning.

5. Click the Columns tab. Delete the mapping between the two *CustomerKey* columns. Clear the check box near the *CleanCustomerKey* input column. Select the check box near the *CustomerKey* lookup column. Rename the output alias for this column to **CleanCustomerKey**. You are replacing the original column with the lookup one. You should have mappings like those shown in Figure 20-5.

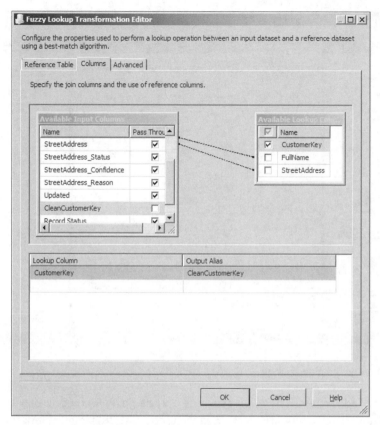

FIGURE 20-5 Fuzzy Lookup column mappings.

6. Click the Advanced tab. Raise the Similarity threshold to **0.50**. Click OK.

7. Drag the Union All transformation below the Fuzzy Lookup transformation. Connect it with an output from the Match Multicast transformation and Fuzzy Matches Fuzzy Lookup transformation. You combine the exact and approximate matches in a single rowset.

8. Drag an OLE DB Destination below the Union All transformation. Rename the OLE DB Destination **FuzzyMatchingResults** and connect it with the Union All transformation. Double-click it to open the editor.

9. Connect to your DQS_STAGING_DATA database and select the *dbo.FuzzyMatching-Results* table. Click the Mappings tab. Note that there is one column that is ignored on the input side and is not mapped to the *Record_Status* column from the destination side. Click the <Ignore> value and select the *Record Status* input column to map it to the *Record_Status* output column. Click OK. Your data flow should look like the one shown in Figure 20-6.

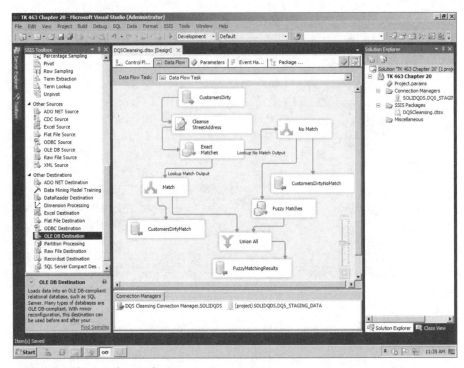

FIGURE 20-6 The complete package.

10. You need to add restartability to your package. You are going to truncate all destination tables. Click the Control Flow tab. Drag the Execute T-SQL Statement task above the data flow task. Connect the tasks with the green arrow from the Execute T-SQL Statement task to the data flow task. The Execute T-SQL Statement Task must finish with success in order to proceed with the data flow task.

11. Double-click the Execute T-SQL Statement task. Create a new connection to your SQL Server instance. Enter the following code in the T-SQL statement text box, and then click OK.

```
USE DQS_STAGING_DATA;
TRUNCATE TABLE dbo.CustomersDirtyMatch;
TRUNCATE TABLE dbo.CustomersDirtyNoMatch;
TRUNCATE TABLE FuzzyMatchingResults;
```

12. Save the solution. Run your package to test it. Check the results of the Fuzzy Lookup transformation. Check for rows for which the transformation didn't find a match, and for incorrect matches. Use the following code.

```
-- Not matched
SELECT * FROM FuzzyMatchingResults
WHERE CleanCustomerKey IS NULL;
-- Incorrect matches
SELECT * FROM FuzzyMatchingResults
WHERE CleanCustomerKey <> CustomerKey
```

13. When you are done checking, close SSDT. Use the following code to clean up the DQS_STAGING_DATA database.

```
DROP TABLE dbo.CustomersClean;
DROP TABLE dbo.CustomersDirty;
DROP TABLE dbo.CustomersDirtyMatch;
DROP TABLE dbo.CustomersDirtyNoMatch;
DROP TABLE dbo.FuzzyMatchingResults;
DROP TABLE dbo.DQSMatchingResults;
DROP TABLE dbo.DQSSurvivorshipResults;
DROP VIEW dbo.CustomersDQSMatch;
```

14. You can exit SSMS.

EXERCISE 2   Use the MDS Add-in for Excel and DQS Matching

In the last exercise of this book, you test how you can use the DQS matching policy KB to perform interactive matching of master data in Excel with MDS Add-in for Excel installed If you did not enable MDS integration with DQS yet, the Data Quality group of the Master Data tab might not be activated within Excel. If this is the case, open the Master Data Services Confirguration Manager console. You can find it in All Programs | Microsoft SQL Server 2012 | Master Data Services. Click "Web Configuration" in the left pane. In the Website drop-down in te right pane, select MDS. Lastly, click the "Enable integration with Data Quality Services" button in the bottom of the right pane. Click the "Exit" button.

1. If you did not create the TK463CustomersMatching DQS KB in the practice for the previous lesson, use Data Quality Client to import it from the Starter folder for this lesson.

2. Create a new Excel file named **TK463Chapter20Excel** and open it. Click the Master Data tab.

3. Connect to your MDS server. In Master Data Explorer, select the TK463Customer model, version 1. You created and populated this model in Chapter 16, "Managing Master Data." If you did not finish the practices for Chapter 16, deploy the TK463Customer-Data package provided in the Starter folder for this lesson. Note that this package includes data, so you need to use the MDSModelDeploy command prompt utility.

4. After you are connected to the TK463Customer model, click the TK463Customer entity in the Master Data Explorer area.

5. Click the Filter button in the Connect And Load group. In the Filter pop-up window, select only the Name, Code, and StreetAddress attributes. Add a row filter to filter rows with Code lower than 11020 (you are selecting two records with the lowest codes only). After you have created the filters, click the Load Data button.

6. Add a new customer. Enter **Jacquelin Suarez** for Name, **-11010** for Code, and **7800 Corinne Court** for StreetAddress. Note the typos in the name and street address.

7. Click the Match Data icon in the Data Quality group of the Master Data tab. Select the TK463CustomersMatching KB, and map the *Name* column to the FullName domain and the *StreetAddress* column to the StreetAddress domain. Note that if you have only one DQS matching KB, then the KB selection and the mappings are done automatically. Click OK. The DQS matching process should start.

8. When matching is done, check the results. DQS should properly match the two rows for Jacquelyn Suarez. Click the Show Details icon in the Data Quality group and check the similarity score. Your Excel worksheet should look like the one shown in Figure 20-7.

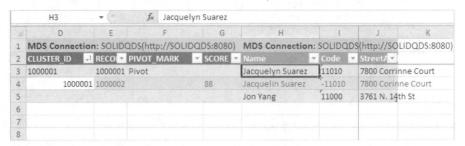

FIGURE 20-7 Results of DQS matching in Excel with MDS Add-in for Excel.

9. Save the Excel file and exit Excel.

Lesson Summary

- SSIS Fuzzy Lookup and Fuzzy Grouping can handle bigger amounts of data than DQS can.
- DQS matching is very useful for master data matching when you are using MDS Add-in for Excel to edit your master data.

Lesson Review

Answer the following questions to test your knowledge of the information in this lesson. You can find the answers to these questions and explanations of why each answer choice is correct or incorrect in the "Answers" section at the end of this chapter.

1. How can you influence Fuzzy Lookup matching rules? (Choose all that apply.)

   A. You can select a string similarity algorithm.

   B. You can define a maximum number of matches per input row.

   C. You can define custom token delimiters.

   D. You can define similarity thresholds.

2. Which additional columns do you get from the Fuzzy Lookup transformation?

   A. _Similarity and _Confidence

   B. _key_in and _key_out

   C. _DQS_Score and _SSIS_Score

   D. _MDS_Similarity and _MDS_Key

3. Which SSIS transformation is useful for de-duplicating?

   A. The DQS Cleansing transformation

   B. The Fuzzy Lookup transformation

   C. The Merge Join transformation

   D. The Fuzzy Grouping transformation

Case Scenario

In the following case scenario, you apply what you've learned about identity mapping and de-duplicating. You can find the answers to these questions in the "Answers" section at the end of this chapter.

Case Scenario: Improving Data Quality

A company for whom you are consulting needs to match a huge amount of customer data with existing MDS data. MDS data serves as the authoritative source. In addition, the company complains that sometimes even the MDS data is duplicated, especially when advanced end users use Excel as an MDS client tool. Answer the following questions:

1. What would you suggest to use for identity mapping of large amounts of data?

2. How would you prevent the insertion of duplicate data in MDS through Excel?

Suggested Practices

To help you successfully master the exam objectives presented in this chapter, complete the following tasks.

Research More on Matching

To get used to DQS and SSIS matching, you should practice using them.

- **Practice 1**   Create a DQS matching knowledge base for *dbo.DimProduct* from the AdventureWorksDW2012 demo database. Play with different rules. Use product names for matching. Change some product names. Create a DQS project and try to match the products.

- **Practice 2**   Try to match the products with an SSIS Fuzzy Lookup transformation.

Answers

This section contains answers to the lesson review questions and solutions to the case scenario in this chapter.

Lesson 1

1. **Correct Answers: A and D**

    A. **Correct:** You cannot perform good matching with a poor algorithm.

    B. **Incorrect:** There are many tools provided in the SQL Server suite for identity mapping and de-duplicating, including DQS, MDS, and SSIS.

    C. **Incorrect:** SSIS Data Flow does not fail on duplicates.

    D. **Correct:** You can import domain values from an Excel file.

2. **Correct Answer: B**

    A. **Incorrect:** Using or not using stored procedures is a minor issue for the identity mapping problem.

    B. **Correct:** Without any optimization, identity mapping with brute force means using a full cross join.

    C. **Incorrect:** With SQL Server tools, you can perform identity mapping in batches.

    D. **Incorrect:** SSIS Fuzzy Lookup can handle batches of rows.

3. **Correct Answer: C**

    A. **Incorrect:** You can get the Jaccard index with MDS functions, not in DQS.

    B. **Incorrect:** You can get the Levenshtein distance with MDS functions, not in DQS.

    C. **Correct:** DQS uses nGrams for matching.

    D. **Incorrect:** You can get the Jaro-Winkler distance with MDS functions, not in DQS.

Lesson 2

1. **Correct Answers: A, B, and D**

    A. **Correct:** You can define the weight of each domain for DQS matching.

    B. **Correct:** You can define an overall minimum matching score.

    C. **Incorrect:** You have no influence on the string similarity algorithm for DQS matching.

    D. **Correct:** You can define a similarity tolerance for numbers and dates.

2. **Correct Answer: B**

   A. **Incorrect:** There is no such survivorship rule.

   B. **Correct:** The most complete and longest record is a survivorship rule in DQS.

   C. **Incorrect:** There is no specific survivorship rule for numbers.

   D. **Incorrect:** There is no such survivorship rule.

3. **Correct Answer: A**

   A. **Correct:** You use the matching results for an interactive overview to find the best matching rule.

   B. **Incorrect:** You cannot store the matching results to the knowledge base.

   C. **Incorrect:** You cannot export the matching results when you are building a matching knowledge base.

   D. **Incorrect:** You cannot export the matching results when you are building a matching knowledge base.

Lesson 3

1. **Correct Answers: B, C, and D**

   A. **Incorrect:** You cannot select a string similarity algorithm.

   B. **Correct:** You can define the maximum number of matches per input row.

   C. **Correct:** You can define custom token delimiters.

   D. **Correct:** You can define similarity thresholds.

2. **Correct Answer: A**

   A. **Correct:** The Fuzzy Lookup transformation returns two additional columns, _Similarity_ and _Confidence_.

   B. **Incorrect:** The _key_in_ and _key_out_ columns are returned by the Fuzzy Grouping transformation.

   C. **Incorrect:** There are no _DQS_Score_ and _SSIS_Score_ columns.

   D. **Incorrect:** There are no _MDS_Similarity_ and _MDS_Key_ columns.

3. **Correct Answer: D**

   A. **Incorrect:** You use the DQS Cleansing transformation for data cleansing with the help of DQS and a DQS cleansing knowledge base. You cannot use a DQS matching knowledge base with this transformation.

   B. **Incorrect:** Fuzzy Lookup is intended for identity mapping. Although you could translate the de-duplication problem to identity mapping, there is another transformation in SSIS, namely the Fuzzy Grouping transformation, that can be used for de-duplicating directly.

   C. **Incorrect:** The Merge Join transformation is intended for regular joins.

   D. **Correct:** The SSIS Fuzzy Grouping transformation is intended for de-duplication.

Case Scenario

1. You should suggest that the company use the SSIS Fuzzy Lookup transformation.

2. You should suggest creating a DQS matching policy KB and using it in Excel.

Index

Symbols

32-bit data providers, 137
64-bit data providers, 137
64-bit vs. 32-bit environments
  Excel files and, 647
  in project validation, 471
  SSIS component installation, 427
@data_filename, 508
@dataflow_path_id_string, 507
@data_tap_id argument, 508
@execution_id, 507
@max_rows, 508
@task_package_path, 507

A

abstract entities, 467
abstraction, defined, 534
access permissions, 429
accounts. *See* storage accounts
accuracy, measurement of, 532
AcquireConnections method, 702, 722, 724
acting, in data mining, 669
Active Directory Domain Services, browsing, 701
Active Directory users, 617
Active Operations dialog box, 469
Active Solution Configuration, 359
adaptability, 240
adapters
  ADO Net source
    dynamic SQL, 302–304
  CDC source, 305
  data flow destination, 178–179
    defining, 184–187
  data flow source, 178–179

  adding with Source Assistant, 181–182
  defining, 180–183
  OLE DB Destination
    column mapping, 230
  OLE DB Source
    dynamic SQL, 300–302
Add Copy Of Existing Package dialog box, 113
Add Existing Item command, 407
additivity of measures, 29–31
Add New Item command, 407
Add New Source dialog box, 181
Add Parameter button, 364
Add Parameter icon, 357
Add Parameters To Configurations toolbar button, 357
Add Parameters window, 360
Add SSIS Connection Manager dialog box, 140, 141
Add SSIS Connection Manager window, 192
Add Users page, 621
Add Variable dialog box, 158, 159, 244
Add Watch, 502
administration operations (SQL Server), 132
administration tasks, 151
administrative stored procedures, accessibility of, 481
administrators, in MDS, 617
Administrators user group, 617
ADO connection manager, 134
ADO.NET connection manager, 134, 136
ADO.NET dataset consumer, Object type variable, 247
ADO.NET destination, 184–185
ADO.NET source, 180
ADO Net source adapter, dynamic SQL, 302–304
advanced configuration, SQL server installation, 428
advanced data preparation transformations, 204
Advanced Editor
  Fast Parse property, 189–190
  for Calculate Checksum dialog box, 729
  Input and Output Properties tab, 188
  specifying sorted output data, 225

Advanced Editor dialog box, 189
AdventureWorks2012 sample database
  configuring data flow source adapters, 182–183
  extracting data from views and loading into ta-
    bles, 91–98
  implementing transactions, 334
AdventureWorksDW2012 sample database
  aggregating columns in tables, 59–62
  conformed dimensions, 8
  database schema, 14–15
  DimCustomer dimension, 19–20, 49
    attributes, 19–20
  DimDate dimension, 9
    attributes, 20
  dimensions
    diagrams, 24–26
  fact tables, 32–33
  lineage, 36–37
  many-to-many relationships, 31–33
  master data, 573
  normalized dimensions, 9–10
  reporting problems with normalized relational sche-
    mas, 5–7
  SCD (Slowly Changing Dimension) problem, 36–37
  Star schema, 7–10
Aggregate data flow, 398
aggregated tables, indexed views, 58–61
aggregate functions, 29–30
  AVERAGE, 29
  COUNT_BIG, 59
  LastNonEmpty, 30
  SUM, 29
Aggregate transformation, 202, 399, 400, 758
aggregation, 146
aggregation functions, 399
alerts
  for package failure, 347
  specificity of, 381
algorithms
  for data mining, 668
  hash functions
    implementing in SSIS, 291–292
aligned indexes, 72
All Connections report, 506
All Connections validation report, 469
All environment references, validation mode, 467
All Executions report, 506
All Executions validation report, 469, 470

All Operations report, 506
All Operations validation report, 469
All process mode option (CDC), 306
All Validations report, 506
All Validations validation report, 469
All with old values process mode option (CDC), 306
ALTER INDEX command, 56
Analysis Services connection manager, 134
Analysis Services Execute DDL task, 153
Analysis Services Processing task, 153
analysis services tasks, 153
analytical applications
  dimensional model, 567
  hierarchical data, 566
analytical systems, presentation quality of, 533
annotations, adding, 626
Application log providers, 384, 385
application programming interface (API), SSIS management, 423
applications
  analytical
    dimensional model, 567
    hierarchical data, 566
  LOB
    transactional data, 566
approximate merging, 737
approximate string matching, 737, 756
architecture
  ETL (extract-transform-load), 217–218
  MDS (Master Data Services), 576–577
artificial intelligence, data mining algorithms, 668
A single environment reference
  validation mode, 467
asynchronous output, 709, 718
asynchronous transformation
  blocking vs. partial-blocking, 513
  execution trees, 513–514
atomic units, 328, 395
attribute completeness, 532
Attribute groups metadata, 606
Attribute Properties button, 627
attributes, 17–18, 18–19
  Business Key, 284
  checking changes, 291–292
  Code, 590, 591
  columns, 589
    DimCustomer dimension (AdventureWorksDW2012
      sample database), 19–20
  completeness of, 654

defining attribute types, 284
DimDate dimension (AdventureWorksDW2012 sample database), 20
discretizing, 17
    automatic discretization, 18
domain-based, 590
entities, 590, 591
file, 590
Fixed, 284
free-form, 590
Manager, 590
Name, 590
naming conventions, 21
pivoting, 17
Type 1 SCD, 22, 284
    set-based updates, 292–293
    updating dimensions, 290–293
Type 2 SCD, 22, 284
    set-based updates, 292–293
    updating dimensions, 290–293
Type 3 SCD, 23
Attributes metadata, 606
audit data
  correlating with SSIS logs, 401–402
  storing, 396
Audit data flow transformation, implementing, 402–405
auditing
  correlation with SSIS logs, 401–402
  customized for ETL, 342, 344, 347
  data lineage, 73
  defined, 394
  implementing, 394–395
  implementing row-level, 402
  Integration Services Auditing, 382
  master data, 568, 569
  native, 399
  tables, 13
  techniques, 395–402
  varied levels, 412
  vs. logging, 398
Audit transformation, 199
  elementary auditing, 401
  system variables, 400
Audit Transformation Editor, 404
authoritative sources, for de-duplication for, 738
authority, for MDM (master data mangement), 572
autogrowing, prevention of, 43
automated execution, 456, 462–464

automatic cleansing methods, 537
automatic discretization, 18
automation
  adaptability, 240
  determinism and, 239
  predictability, 240
Auto Shrink database option, 43–45
autoshrinking, prevention of, 43
Average aggregate function, 29, 399

B

backpressure mechanism, 514
Back Up Database task, 152
balanced tree. *See* B-trees
base entities, 590
Basic logging level, 468, 506
Batch_ID column, in stg.entityname_Leaf table, 608
batch processing, 62–64
BatchTag column, in stg.entityname_Leaf table, 608
BEGIN TRAN statement, 332
BIDS (SQL Server Business Intelligence Development Studio), 102, 179–180
binary large object (BLOB), 516
BISM (Business Intelligence Semantic Model), 30–31
bitmap filtered hash joins, 57
blocking
  selecting data transformations, 198–199
  transformations, 203
blocking (asynchronous) transformations, 513
blocking technique, 739
blocking transformations, 199
Boolean data type, 246
Boolean expressions, in precedence contraints, 256
break conditions, 500–501
breakpoints
  debugging with, 500–503
  in script task, 702
B-trees (balanced trees), 56–57
Buffer Memory counter, 520
buffers, data
  allocation with execution trees, 513–514
  architecture of, 512–513
  changing setting, 516
  counters for monitoring, 520
  fixed limit of, 514
  optimization of, 515–516
  synchronous vs. asynchronous components and, 513

Buffers in Use counters, 520
buffers, rows, 178
Buffers Spooled counter, 520
BufferWrapper, 707
build configurations, 358–361
  creating, 359
  uses for, 354, 358
  using, 359–361, 365–366
Build Model group, 627
Bulk Insert task, 150
Bulk Logged recovery model, 43
Business Intelligence Development Studio (BIDS), updating package settings in, 367
Business Intelligence Semantic Model (BISM), 30–31
business key, 23, 28–29
Business Key attribute, 284
business problems, schema completeness, 534
business rules
  data compliance, 529
  documentation of, 534
Business rules metadata, 606
Byte data type, 246

loading fact tables, 322
loading large dimensions, 322
MDM solutions, 600
MDS (Master Data Services), 600–601
prediction improvement, 694
remote executions, 491
single vs. multiple packages, 276–277
slow data warehouse reports, 79
Snowflake schema, 34–38
SQL Server installation, 451
Star schema, 34–38
strictly structured deployments, 451
tuning SSIS packages, 523
case sensitivity, in Lookup transformation, 220
cases, in data mining, 668, 688, 689
catalog.add_data_tap stored procedure, 507
catalog.configure_catalog stored procedure, 442, 481
catalog.create_execution stored procedure, 442, 507
catalog.deploy_project stored procedure, 442
catalog.extended_operation_info stored procedure, 465
catalog.grant_permission stored procedure, 481
catalog.operation_messages catalog view, 465
catalog.operations catalog view, 465
Catalog Properties window, 506
catalog.restore_project operation, 442
catalog.revoke_permission stored procedure, 481
catalog SQL Server views, 654
catalog.start_execution stored procedure, 507
catalog.stop_operation operation stored procedure, 442
catalog.validate_package stored procedure, 442
catalog.validate_project stored procedure, 442
catalog views, 63–64
cdc.captured_columns system table, 305
CDC (change data capture), 299
  components, 305–306
  enabling on databases, 304–305
  implementing with SSIS, 304–307, 308–316
  packages
    LSN (log sequence number) ranges, 305
  processing mode options, 306
cdc.change_tables system table, 305
CDC Control task, 149, 305
CDC Control Task Editor, 306
cdc.ddl_history system table, 305
cdc.index_columns system table, 305

C

Cache connection manager, 218, 517
cache modes, 218–219
CACHE option, creating sequences, 46
Cache Transform transformation, 199, 223–224
Calculate Checksum dialog box, advanced editor
  for, 729
calculation (data), 146
Call Stack debugging window, 503
Canceled operation status, 466
Candidate Key, profiling of, 657
canonical row, in fuzzy transformations, 758
case scenarios
  batch data editing, 633
  connection manager parameterization, 125
  copying production data to development, 125
  data cleansing, 731
  data-driven execution, 277
  data flow, 232
  data warehouse administration problems, 79
  data warehouse not used, 559
  deploying packages to multiple environments, 491
  improving data quality, 660, 765

cdc.lsn_time_mapping system table, 305
CDCSalesOrderHeader table, 304–305
CDC source, 180
CDC source adapter, 305
CDC Source Editor dialog box, 306
CDC splitter, 305
CDC Splitter transformation, 201
cdc.stg_CDCSalesOrderHeader_CT, 305
central MDM (master data management), 571
central metadata storage, 571
   continuously merged data, 571
   identity mapping, 571
change data capture. *See* CDC (change data capture)
Changed column, on create views page, 609
Changing Attributes Updates output, 290
Chaos property, IsolationLevel, 331
Character Map transformation, 199
Char data type, 246
Check Database Integrity task, 152
CheckPointFileName property, 337, 340
checkpoints
   creating restartable, 336–339
   setting and observing, 340–341
CheckpointUsage property, 337, 339, 340
child packages, 20, 328, 330, 344
   logging, 411
   parameterization of, 269
CI (compression information) structure, 62
Class Library template, 718
Clean Logs Periodically property, 439, 470
cleansing (data), 145–147, 570, 571
cleansing projects, 646
   quick start, 639
   stages of, 648
Cleansing Project setting, 552
Cleanup method, customization of, 724
clean values, 759
Client Tools SDK, development vs. production environments, 425
closed-world assumption, 532
CLR integration, 445
clustered indexes, 56–57
clustering keys, 56
code. *See also* listings
   adding foreign keys to InternetSales table, 75
   adding partitioning column to FactInternetSales
     table, 74
   creating columnstore index for InternetSales table, 75

   creating partition schemes, 74
   Customers dimension, 50
   dbo.Customers dimension table, 209
   enabling CDC on databases, 304–305
   InternetSales fact table, 53
   loading data to InternetSales table, 75
   loading data to partitioned tables, 76–78
   Products dimension, 51
Code attribute, 590, 591
Code column, in stg.entityname_Leaf table, 608
code snippets, 706, 714
collections, 591
collection settings (Foreach Loop Editor), 157
Collections metadata, 606
Column Length Distribution, profiling of, 656
column mappings, in fuzzy lookup, 761
Column Mappings window, 95
Column Null Ratio, profiling of, 656
Column Pattern, profiling of, 656
columns
   aggregating in AdventureWorksDW2012 sample
     database tables, 59–62
   <Attribute name>, 609
   attributes, 17–18, 18–19, 589
     DimCustomer dimension (AdventureWorksDW2012
       sample database), 19–20
   computed, 46
   Customers dimension, 49–50, 65
   Dates dimension, 52, 67
   dimensions, 17–18
   fact tables, 28–29, 47–48
     analyzing, 33–34
     lineage type, 29
   hash functions, implementing in SSIS, 291–292
   identity
     compared to sequences, 45–46
   in fuzzy lookup output, 758
   in stg.entityname_Leaf table, 608
   InternetSales Fact table, 67
   keys, 18
   language translation, 18
   lineage information, 18
   mapping
     OLE DB Destination adapter, 214, 230
     OLE DB Destination Editor, 187
   mappings, 95
   member properties, 18, 18–19
   name, 18

package-level audit, 398
Products dimension, 51, 66
references
errors, 208
resolving, 207–208
Remarks, 50
third normal form, 9
Type 2 SCD, 22
Type 3 SCD, 23
updating, 229–231
Valid From, 284
Valid To, 284
Column Statistics, profiling of, 657
columnstore indexes, 62–68
catalog views, 63–64
fact tables, 64
InternetSales fact table, 68–69
segments, 63
Column Value Distribution, profiling of, 657
column values, 400
Combine Data button, 626
combining data flows vs. isolating, 120
commands
ALTER INDEX, 56
OLE DB, 226
TRUNCATE TABLE, 71
T-SQL
data lineage, 73
COMMIT TRAN statement, 332
common language runtime [CLR]) code. See Microsoft.
NET
communication, importance of, 537
compatibility, data types and, 247
complete auditing, 395, 396
Completed operation status, 466
completeness
measurement of, 531–532
of attributes, 654
completion constraints, 165
complex data movements, 88, 145–147
complexity, of master data, 568
compliance with theoretical models, measurement
of, 534
components, parameterization of, 254
ComponentWrapper project item, 707, 711
composite domains, 638, 640
composite joins, Lookup transformations and, 220
compression. See data compression

compression information (CI) structure, 62
computations, elementary, 256
computed columns, 46
computedPackageID variable, 271
Computer-assisted cleansing stage, 648
Computer event property, 386
concepts, 567
conceptual schema, documentation of, 534
concrete instance, 467
Conditional Split transformation, 201, 214, 291, 694
confidence level, in data mining, 689
Configuration File Name text box, 371
Configuration Filter setting, table location, 373
Configuration Manager, creating additional projects
with, 359
configuration properties
setting multiple, 375
storage of, 375
Configuration Table setting, 373
configuration types, for packages, 370
configuration usage, described in debugging, 499
Configured Value property, 375
Configure Error Output dialog box, 318
Configure Project dialog box, 487
configuring
connections for SSIS deployment, 120–123
data destination adapters, 185–186
data source adapters, 182–183
Flat File connection manager, 138–140
OLE DB connection manager, 140–142
conformed dimensions, 8
connection context, of execution errors, 506
Connection Manager Conversion Confirmation dialog
box, 143
Connection Manager dialog box, 141
connection manager editor, 121–122
connection managers, 133–144
64-bit data providers, 137
accessing, 702
ADO, 134
ADO.NET, 134, 136
Analysis Services, 134
Cache
Lookup transformation, 218
creating, 138–143
event handlers, 345
Excel, 134
File, 134

file formatting, 140
Flat File, 134
    assigning property values dynamically, 160–161
    creating, 138–140
for 64-bit data provider, 427
FTP, 134
how to use, 702
HTTP, 134
manually handling transaction, 332
MSMQ, 135
Multiple Files, 134
Multiple Flat Files, 134
names, 136
ODBC, 135
OLE DB, 135
    creating, 140–142
    Lookup transformation, 218
package-scoped, 136–137
package templates, 407
parameterization, 137
    case scenario, 125
parameterization of, 254
parameters and, 354
project-level, 354–355
project-scoped, 136–137
SMO, 135
SMTP, 135
SQL Server Compact Edition, 135
WMI, 135
Connection Managers pane, 120, 142, 143
Connection Managers property, 374
Connection Managers window, 355
Connection Manager tab, 186, 471, 473
connection properties
    in package configurations, 368
    updating, 363
connections
    defining, 355
    SSIS (SQL Server Integration Services) deploy-
        ment, 111
Connections collection class, 711
connection setting, table location, 373
connection string paramaterization, 363–364
ConnectionString property, 702
connection strings
    Flat File, 142
    OLE DB, 142
    sharing, 372
    storing in a single location, 367

consistency
    measurement of, 532
    solutions for, 537
consolidated members, 591
constraints
    foreign keys, 47
    NOT NULL, 186
    precedence, 164–169
        completion, 165
        creating, 118
        failure, 165, 167–169
        success, 165
container editors, property expression with, 362
Container property (Foreach Loop Editor), 159
containers, 145, 155–163
    Foreach Loop, 156
    For Loop, 156
    logging configuration, 388–391
    Sequence, 156
container-scoped variables, 248, 249, 251
Continuous Values, 688
control flow. *See also* data flow
    debugging, 498, 500–503, 505
    determining, 156–163
    external processes, 171
    master package concept, 265–266
    parallel execution management, 517
    tasks, 145, 147–155
        administration, 151
        analysis services, 153
        Analysis Services Execute DDL, 153
        Analysis Services Processing, 153
        Back Up Database, 152
        Bulk Insert, 150
        CDC Control, 149, 305
        Check Database Integrity, 152
        custom, 154–155
        data flow, 177, 178–197, 190–192
        Data Flow, 150
        Data Mining Query, 153
        data movement, 150
        data preparation, 148
        Data Profiling, 148
        Execute Package, 149
        Execute Process, 149
        Execute SQL, 150, 226, 292, 292–293
        Execute SQL Server Agent Job, 152
        Execute T-SQL Statement, 152
        Expression, 149

File System, 148, 161, 167, 168
FTP, 148
History Cleanup, 152
maintenance, 151–152
Maintenance Cleanup, 152
Message Queue, 149
Notify Operator, 152
precedence constraints, 164–169
Rebuild Index, 152
Reorganize Index, 152
Script, 154
Send Mail, 149
Shrink Database, 152
Transfer Database, 151
Transfer Error Messages, 151
Transfer Jobs, 151
Transfer Logins, 151
Transfer Master Stored Procedures, 151
Update Statistics, 152
Web Service, 148
WMI Data Reader, 149
WMI Event Watcher, 149
workflow, 148–149
XML, 148
Control Flow Designer, 105–107
Control Flow tab, 336, 340, 502
Convert To Package Deployment Model, 368
Copy Column transformation, 199
copying
  data
    compared to specifying queries, 94
  production data to development, 125
Corrected status, in cleansing, 648
Count aggregate function, 399, 656
COUNT_BIG aggregate function, 59
Count distinct aggregate function, 399
Count distinct operation, 400
Country/Region domains, in default KB, 639
covered queries, 56
CPU utilization condition, job scheduling with, 463
Create A Domain button, 642
Create A New Data Source To SQL Server dialog
  box, 192
Create Catalog dialog box, 445
Created operation status, 466
Create Entities button, 627
Create Environment editor, 485
Create New Data Source dialog box, 192

Create New Parameter option, 358
CREATE_OBJECTS permission, 482
Create Views tab, 609
Create Website window, 584
credit risk management, defining cases for, 688
CRM (Customer Relationship Management) applications
  identity mapping, 735
  integrating master data, 569
  master data, 567
cross-domain rule, 640
cross joins, problems with, 737
CRUD cycle (create, read, update, and delete)
  master data, 568
  MDM (master data management), 569
custom code, 699–730
  custom components, 716–730
  script component, 707–715
  script task, 700–707
custom components
  developing, 718
  interaction with SSIS developer, 719
  planning, 717–718
  vs. script components, 716
custom data flow transformation component
  configuring, 728–730
  deploying, 727–728
  developing, 725–727
custom data flow transformations, 226
custom data source, script component as, 708, 709
custom destinations, in custom components, 717
customer complaints, 531
Customer dimension table
  columns, 49–50, 65
  creating, 49
  loading data to DW, 209–212
  loading data with SCD tranformation, 293–296
  loading into DW, 212–214
  set-based update logic, 292–293
  updating, 229–231
Customer Relationship Management (CRM) applications. See CRM (Customer Relationship Management)
  applications
Customers entity, schema correctness, 534
custom logging events, 469
custom reports, for SSIS monitoring, 470
custom source, in custom components, 717
custom SSIS components, 291
custom tasks, 154–155
custom transformation, in custom components, 717

D

daily frequency, job schedudle, 463
data. *See also* master data
  auditing, 395
  automatic removal, 402
  batch editing, 624–626, 633
  batch import, 612–614
  cleansing, 646–648
  combining, 626
  copying
    compared to specifying queries, 94
  copying production data to development, 125
  correcting with DQS, 746
  correlating audit with logs, 401
  currency of, 533
  de-duplicating, 626
  determining correct automatically, 738
  editing and publishing, 627
  extracting from views, 94
  extracting from views and loading into tables, 91–98
  filtering, 629–630
  finding inaccurate, 654
  hierarchical, 566
  importing/exporting master data, 606–616
  importing from flat files, 194–197
  improving quality, 660
  improving quality of, 765
  isolating inaccurate, 532
  loading, 64–68
    auditing with data lineage, 73
    changing from T-SQL procedures to SSIS, 227
    creating data warehouses, 42–44
    data lineage, 73
    foreign key constraints, 47
    incremental loads, 299–316
    into Customer dimension table with SCD tranfor-
      mation, 293–296
    preparing data transformations, 209–212
    to InternetSales table, 75
  loading with Excel, 629–630
  management in buffers, 512–513
  master, 566
    AdventureWorksDW2012 sample database, 573
    auditing, 568, 569
    complexity, 568

    CRM (Customer Relationship Management) ap-
      plications, 567
    CRUD cycle (create, read, update, and delete), 568
    defining, 573–574
    definition, 567–568
    dimensions, 567
    ERP (enterprise resource planning) applica-
      tions, 567
    hierarchical data, 569
    HRM (Human Resources Management) applica-
      tions, 567
    MDM (master data management), 569–572
    nouns, 567
    reusage, 568
    versioning, 568, 569
    volatility, 568
  merging from multiple sources, 736
  metadata, 566
  partition switching, 72
  preparation of, 667, 687–690
  profiling, 654–660
  reading
    dynamic SQL, 299–304
  retaining audit, 401–402
  reusing with master data management, 609
  semi-structured, 566
  source
    incremental loads, 299
  sources for DQS projects, 647
  splitting for test set, 690
  status modification during cleansing, 648
  transactional, 566
    verbs, 567
  unstructured, 566
  validating, 646
  validating in advance, 626
  viewing in pipeline, 503–505
  XML, 566–567
data aggregation, 146
Data Analysis Expression (DAX), 30
Database Engine
  SQL Server feature choice, 424
  SSIS solutions storage, 423, 429
  upgrading, 430
Database Engine Services, limited SSIS functionality
  of, 425
database roles, administrative tasks, 481

databases
  AdventureWorks2012 sample
    extracting data from views and loading into
        tables, 91–98
  AdventureWorksDW2012 sample
    aggregating columns in tables, 59–62
    conformed dimensions, 8
    database schema, 14–15
    DimCustomer dimension, 19–20, 49
    DimDate dimension, 9
    dimensions, 24–26
    fact tables, 32–33
    lineage, 36–37
    many-to-many relationships, 31–33
    master data, 573
    normalized dimensions, 9–10
    reporting problems with normalized relational
        schemas, 5–7
    SCD, 36–37
    Star schema, 7–10
  creating, 42–44
  enabling CDC on, 304–305
  in Data Quality Server, 541
  log providers, 385
  of Data Quality Services, 547
  relational
    master data, 567
  shrinking, 153
  space
    calculating requirements, 43
  SQL Server
    creating, 48–49
  TK463DW
    enabling CDC on, 304–305
database schemas
  AdventureWorksDW2012 sample database, 14–15
  unintended usage of, 533
data buffers
  allocation with execution trees, 513–514
  architecture of, 512–513
  changing settings, 516
  counters for monitoring, 520
  fixed limit of, 514
  optimization of, 515–516
  synchronous vs. asynchronous components, 513
DataBytes event property, 387
data calculation, 146
data cleansing, 145–147, 537, 541, 551–552, 570, 571

DataCode event property, 387
data compatibility, 247
data compression, 61–62, 64–68
  dictionary compression, 62
  InternetSales fact table, 68–69
  page compression, 62
  prefix compression, 62
  row compression, 61
  Unicode compression, 62
data conflicts, in MDM (master data management), 572
Data Conversion transformation, 199, 247
data destination adapters, 177
  configuring, 185–186
  defining, 184–185
data encryption, in deployed SSIS solutions, 480
data error correction vs. prevention, 536
data extraction, 265, 268, 731
data files, 43, 44
data flow. *See also* control flow
  adding system variables to, 382
  Aggregate, 398
  BIDS (SQL Server Business Intelligence Development
    Studio), 179–180
  Cache Transform transformation, 223
  controlling with expressions, 262
  data path arrows, 206
  debugging, 498, 505
  defining data sources, 178–197
  defining destinations, 178–197
  design tips, 516–517
  error flows, 317–321
  error output, 382
  error outputs, 317
  Lookup transformations, 218–224
  Row Count, 398
  SCD (Slowly Changing Dimension), 286–291
  set-based updates, 225–227
  Sort transformation, 224–225
  tuning options, 514–516
  visualizing with data viewers, 503–505
data flow buffers
  accessing, 707
  data types, 246
  in scripting, 708
data flow destination adapters, 178, 184–187
Data Flow Path Editor, 503–505, 507
data flow rows, processing with profiling, 711–716
data flows, combining vs. isolating, 120

data flow source adapters, 178
  adding with Source Assistant, 181–182
  defining, 180–182
data flow task, 150, 177
  buffer optimization, 515
  capturing data from, 507
  checkpoints, 339
  components SSIS (SQL Server Integration Services)
    Toolbox, 178–179
  creating, 178–180
      for Person.Person table (TK463DW), 190–192
  defining data destination adapters, 184–187
  defining data source adapters, 180–183
  design tips, 516–517
  event handlers, 344
  package templates, 407
  parameterization of, 255
  rows, 177, 178
  transactions, 330, 332, 333
data flow transformation components
  Aggregate, 399
  Row Count, 399
data flow transformations, 178
data governance, 537, 570
data history, SCD problem, 21–23
data integration, data types and, 247
data integrity
  accuracy, 570
  defined, 529
  RDBMS (relational database management sys-
    tem), 569–570
data latency, 3
data life cycle, 535
data lineage, 73
data loading, 268
data loads, 265–266
data management, SSIS vs. LOB, 87
DataMarket account ID, 550
data merges, business keys, 23
data mining, 668–687
  algorithms for, 670–671
  defined, 668
  predictions, 671–679
  techniques of, 668
  uses for, 667, 669
data mining (DM) models
  additional uses for, 669
  storage of, 668

Data Mining Extensions (DMX) query, 672
Data Mining Model Training destination, 184
data mining projects
  SSIS sampling, 689
  steps of, 669
data mining queries, 132
Data Mining Query task, 153, 667
Data Mining Query transformation, 204
data modification language (DML) statements. See DML
  (data modification language) statements
data movements
  complex, 145–147
  complex data movements, 88
  DW, 88
  modifying movements, 112–123
      adding existing SSIS packages to projects, 112–114
      configuring connections, 120–123
      editing SSIS packages creating by SQL Server
        Import and Export Wizard, 114–116
      running SSIS packages in Debug mode, 120–123
  planning, 89–99
  simple data movements, 88
      creating, 91–98
  SQL Server Import and Export Wizard, 88, 89–99
      creating simple data movements, 91–98
      transformations, 89
  SSDT (SQL Server Data Tools), 88
  SSIS (SQL Server Integration Services), 87
  tasks, 150
data normalization, 145–147
data overview, 688
data path arrows, 206
data pivoting, 146
data platforms
  SSIS (SQL Server Integration Services) deploy-
    ment, 111
data preparation tasks, 148
data profiling, 132, 530, 535, 552
  processing data flow rows with, 711–716
  with SSAS cubes, 656
Data Profiling task, 148
  incorporating results, 701
  using, 703
data providers
  32-bit, 137
  64-bit, 137
  data types, 246
  third-party, 660

data quality
  assessment of, 535–536
  checking for issues, 538–539
  cleansing methods, 537, 551–552
  defined, 529
  dimensions of, 531–532
  goals of master data managment, 530
  improvement plan for, 536–537
  MDM (master data management), 572
  measuring solutions, 537–538
  planning data quality projects, 535
  root causes of bad, 536
  schema dimensions, 534–535
  soft dimensions, 533
Data Quality Client
  administration with, 549–552
  cleansing and mathching, 551–552
  functions of, 541
  installation requirements, 542–543
  location of log file, 552
  log settings, 552–553
  main screen, 547
  monitoring DQS activity, 555–558
data quality data warehouse, schema for, 537. *See
  also* data quality warehouse
data quality dimensions
  accuracy, 532
  completeness, 531–532
  consistency, 532, 537
  defined, 530
  information, 532
  inspection of, 531
data quality projects
  creating, 646–653
  opening existing, 646
data quality schema dimensions, 534–535
Data Quality Services (DQS)
  architecture of, 540–541
  databases of, 547
  installation of, 542–547
  knowledge bases in, 540
  maintaining with Data Quality Client, 549–552,
    555–558
  maintaining with other tools, 553–555
  security administration, 553–554
data quality soft dimensions, measurement of, 533
data quality warehouse, schema for, 538. *See also* data
  quality data warehouse

DataReader destination, 184
dataset size, estimating, 515
data source adapters, 177
  configuring, 182–183
  defining, 180–183
data sources
  connection managers
    creating, 138–143
    file formatting, 140
    Flat File, 138–140
    OLE DB, 140–142
  defining, 178–197
  selecting, 91
data staging area (DSA), 44
data stewards, 537, 570
data stores
  auditing, 396
  connection managers, 133–144
    64-bit data providers, 137
    ADO, 134
    ADO.NET, 134, 136
    Analysis Services, 134
    Excel, 134
    File, 134
    Flat File, 134
    FTP, 134
    HTTP, 134
    MSMQ, 135
    Multiple Files, 134
    Multiple Flat Files, 134
    names, 136
    ODBC, 135
    OLE DB, 135
    package-scoped, 136–137
    parameterization, 137
    project-scoped, 136–137
    SMO, 135
    SMTP, 135
    SQL Server Compact Edition, 135
    WMI, 135
data taps
  adding, 509–510
  using, 507–508
data tap stored procedure, 507
data transformations, 177, 198–214, 265, 268
  advanced data preparation, 204
  blocking, 199, 203
  Cache Transform
    Lookup transformation, 223–224

Conditional Split, 214, 291
custom, 226
Derived Column, 206, 212
loading data, 209–212
logical-row, 199–200
Lookup, 200–201
  cache modes, 218–219
  Cache Transform transformation, 223–224
  case sensitivity, 220
  composite joins, 220
  connection managers, 218
  ETL (extract-transform-load), 218–224
  merging outputs with Union All component, 220–221
  replacing Union All transformation, 228–229
  rows with no matching entities, 220
Merge Join, 211
multi-input, 200–201
multi-output, 200–201
multi-row, 202–203
non-blocking, 199
partial-blocking, 199
resolving column references, 207–208
SCD (Slowly Changing Dimension), 285–290
Script Component, 291
selecting, 198–204
Sort, 224–225
Union All
  replacing multiple Lookup transformation out-puts, 228–229
Data type property, 244, 357, 639
data types
  Date, 284
  DateTime, 284
  of variables, 245–248
  purpose of, 247
  SSIS (SQL Server Integration Services), 187–189
data unpivoting, 146
data validation, 146
data values, variables measurement, 688
data viewers
  removing, 505
  visualizing data flow with, 503–505
Data Viewer tab, 503–504
Data Viewer window
  Detach, 505
  Play button, 505
data warehouses (DW), 3
  auditing, 396

creating databases, 42–44
data history
  SCD (Slowly Changing Dimension) problem, 21–23
data movements, 88
design
  queries, 4
Dimensional Models, 6
loading data to, 209–212
maintenance of, 265, 462
metadata storage w/ continuously merged data, 571
naming conventions, 17–18, 21
performance
  batch processing, 62–64
  columnstore indexes, 62–64
  data compression, 61–62
  indexed views, 58–61
  indexing dimensions, 56–59
  indexing fact tables, 56–59
data warehousing
  automation of, 239–240
  individual elements of, 267
  operations included, 265–266
Date data type, 284
date functions, 258
Dates dimension
  columns, 52, 67
  creating, 52–53
DateTime data type, 246, 284
DAX (Data Analysis Expression), 30
DBNull data type, 246
db_owner database role, 481
debugging
  control flow, 498, 500–503
  data flow, 498
  icons, 498
Debug logging level, 552
Debug menu, 505, 702
Debug mode, for SSIS packages, 120–123
Debug toolbar, 503
Decimal data type, 246
Decision Trees mining model, 671–673
de-duplicating
  and data cleansing, 646
  and identity mapping, 738
  in domain management, 640
  problems with, 738
  with fuzzy grouping, 758
default knowledge, in DQS, 639

DefaultMaxBufferRows parameter, 515
DefaultMaxBufferSize parameter, 515
default permissions, 483
default value parameter, 356
defining
   attribute types, 284
   data flow destination adapters, 184–187
   data sources, 178–197
   destinations, 178–197
   ETL (extract-transform-load) strategy, 217
delayed validation, 259
DelayValidation property, 259
Delete All Breakpoints, 505
Delete Parameter toolbar button, 357
deleting fact tables, 71–73
delimited files, Flat File source, 196
denormalized dimensions
   DimDate table, 9–10
   partially denormalized dimensions, 11
Deny permission, 618
deployment environment
   SSIS (SQL Server Integration Services)
      development environments, 111
      production environments, 111
   SSIS (SQL Server Integration Services) projects, 110–124
deployment environments, switching between, 360
deployment files, 443
Deployment Wizard, 442–443, 446
Derived Column transformation, 200, 206, 212, 401
Derived Column Transformation Editor, 206
derived hierarchies, 590
derived variables, in data mining, 688
Description property, 244, 357
design
   data flow, 516–517
   dimensions, 17–27
      column types, 17–18
      hierarchies, 19–22
      SCD (Slowly Changing Dimension) problem, 21–24
      Type 1 SCD, 22
      Type 2 SCD, 22
      Type 3 SCD, 23
   fact tables, 27–33
      additivity of measures, 29–30
      columns, 28–29
      many-to-many relationships, 30–32

   logical, 3
      Snowflake schema, 3, 4, 9–11
      Star schema, 3, 4, 7–10, 11
   queries, 4
design environment, data providers for, 137
design flow, parallel execution and, 517
design-time methods, customizatin of, 719–721
design-time troubleshooting, 498–505
design time validation, delaying, 259
destination adapters
   debugging, 505
   execution trees, 513–514
   optimization of, 517
Destination Assistant component, 184
destination environment
   determining, 421, 424
   preparing, 422
destination, script component as, 708, 709
destinations, defining, 178–197
destination tables, truncating, 117
Detach, Data Viewer window, 505
determinism, 239, 240
development environment
   copying production data to, 125
   SSIS installation choices, 424
   SSIS (SQL Server Integration Services), 110
   troubleshooting, 498
development execution, speeding, 505
development vs. production environments
   SSIS package deployment, 421, 437
Diagnostic event, 386
diagrams, dimensions, 24–26
dialog boxes
   Add Copy Of Existing Package, 113
   Add New Source, 181
   Add SSIS Connection Manager, 140, 141
   Add Variable, 158, 159
   Advanced Editor, 189
   CDC Source Editor, 306
   Configure Error Output, 318
   Connection Manager, 141
   Connection Manager Conversion Confirmation, 143
   Create A New Data Source To SQL Server, 192
   Create New Data Source, 192
   Execute SQL Task Editor, 191
   Input Output Selection, 214
   Load Package, 113
   OLE DB Source Editor, 182, 191

Set Breakpoints, 500–501
Set Query Parameters, 300–301
dictionary compression, 62
DimCustomer dimension
  AdventureWorksDW2012 sample database, 19–20, 49
  attributes, 19–20
DimCustomer.dtsx SSIS package, log confirmation
  template, 392
DimDate denormalized dimension, 9–10, 20
Dimensional Models, 6
dimensional storage, in SSAS, 30
dimension primary key, joins, 57
Dimension Processing destination, 184
dimensions, 3, 8–9, 567
  additivity of measures, 29–30
  columns, 17–18
  conformed, 8
  creating, 49–52
  Customers
    columns, 49–50, 65
  Dates
    columns, 52, 67
    creating, 52–53
  denormalized
    DimDate, 9–10
    partially denormalized dimensions, 11
  design, 17–27
    column types, 17–18
    hierarchies, 19–22
    SCD (Slowly Changing Dimension) problem, 21–24
    Type 1 SCD, 22
    Type 2 SCD, 22
    Type 3 SCD, 23
  diagrams, 24–26
  DimCustomer (AdventureWorksDW2012 sample
    database), 19–20
  DimDate (AdventureWorksDW2012 sample database)
    AdventureWorksDW2012 sample, 9
    attributes, 20
  DimProduct (AdventureWorksDW2012 sample data-
    base), 10
  granularity, 12
  implementing, 45–47
  indexing, 56–59
  intermediate, 32
  late-arriving, 48, 285
  multiple fact tables, 8
  naming conventions, 17, 21

  private, 9–10
  Products
    columns, 66
    creating, 51
  shared, 8–9
    DimProduct, 8
    POC projects, 9–10
    SSAS (SQL Server Analysis Services), 9
  Type 1 SCD, 22
  Type 2 SCD, 22
    surrogate key, 284
  Type 3 SCD, 23
  updating, 290–293
    checking attribute changes, 291–292
    set-based updates, 292–293
dimension tables, 396
  history, 287
  selecting, 287
DimProduct dimension (AdventureWorksDW2012
  sample database), 8, 10
direct assignments, 467
directed algorithms, in dining mining, 668
Disable Data Viewer, 505
DisableEventHandlers property, 346
Discrete Values, 688
discretizing
  attributes, 17
  automatic, 18
  groups, 17
disk storage, filegroups, 44
disk-swapping, 516
distributed transactions, 328
distribution of values, determining, 655
DML (data modification language) statements
  testing execution of, 43
DMX query builder, 677
DMX Query Editor, 672
documentation
  MDM (master data management), 573
  measurement of, 534
domain accounts, 426
domain-based attributes, 590
Domain management, 638
Domain Management setting, 552
domain rules, 640
Domain Rules tab, 644

domains
  changing values of, 640
  copying, 640
  creating linked, 640
  default KB, 639
  importing/exporting, 639
  in knowledge bases, 638
  management, 639–641
  manual editing of, 643–645
  MDM (master data management), 573
domain user accounts, insatlling MDS, 577–578
domain values, weighting in DQS matching, 747
Double data type, 246
DQLog.Client.xml, 552
DQS activities, life cycle of, 647
DQS Administrator role, 553
DQS cleansing project, creation of, 649–652
DQS Cleansing transformation, 204
DQS Cleansing transformations
  advanced configuration for, 746
  using, 745–746, 748–751
DQS databases, backup and restore, 554–555
DQS Data knowledge base, default storage, 639
DQS (Data Quality Services), de-duplication with, 626
DQServerLog.DQS_MAIN.log, 552
DQSInstaller application, actions of, 543
DQSInstaller.exe, 543
DQS KB Editor role, 554
DQS KB Operator role, 554
DQS log files
  deleting, 555
  location of, 552
DQS_MAIN, 541
DQS matching, 746–747
  algorithms in, 738
  using, 752–755
  vs. fuzzy transformations, 740, 756
DQS notification, 552
DQS projects
  creation of, 646
  knowledge bases requirements, 647
  management activities, 646–647
DQS_PROJECTS, 541
DQS_STAGING_DATA, 541
drillthrough, enabling in data mining, 668
DSA (data staging area), 44
DTExec command-line utility, 461–462, 518
DTExecUI utility, 458, 474

DTSExecResult enumeration, event properties, 387
Dts object, 700, 701, 702
Dump On Errors check box, 473
duplicate values, as inaccurate data, 532
dynamic packages, uses of, 353
dynamic pivoting, 203
dynamic SQL
  reading data, 299–304
    ADO Net source adapter, 302–304
    OLE DB Source adapter, 300–302

E

early-arriving facts, 285, 288
ease of use, measurement of, 533
Edit Breakpoints, 500
editing, SSIS (SQL Server Integration Services) pack-
  ages, 99, 114–120
Edit Value, 502
effective permissions, determining, 619
elementary auditing, 395, 396
email, 132
Empty data type, 246
Enable Data Viewer check box, 503
Enable Data Viewers, 503
Enable Inferred Member Support check box, 288
Enable Notifications value, 552
Enable Package Configurations check box, 368
Encryption Algorithm Name property, 439
encryption, in SSISDB catalog data, 438, 439
Ended unexpectedly operation status, 466
EndTime event property, 387
EngineThreads property, 517
English text, in term extraction, 680
enterprise resource planning (ERP) applications. *See* ERP
  (enterprise resource planning) applications
entities, 589
  attributes, 590, 591
  base, 590
  creating with Excel, 627–628
  de-duplicating, 735
  keys, 18
  MDS (Master Data Services) models, 589–590
  populating, 596–599
  StateProvince
    members, 597
  tables, 589

Entities metadata, 606
entity-relationship diagrams, 534
entity sets, 567
entropy, measurement of, 532
EntryPoint property, 701
Enumerator property (Foreach Loop Editor), 157
Environment list box, 471
environment, overriding values, 467
Environment Properties dialog box, 486
Environment references, 441
environment reference validation, 466–467
Environments node, 485
Environments object, 482
environment variables, 370, 371, 373, 441
ERP (enterprise resource planning) applications
  master data, 567
erroneous values vs. outliers, 688
Error Code column, 505, 608
error codes. *See* HTTP Status Codes
error detection, automatic execution of, 239
error flows, ETL, 317–321
Error logging level, 552
error outputs, 317
  debugging with, 505
  in data flow components, 382
error paths, 317–318, 319
errors
  allowing in package execution, 499
  capturing with continuous monitoring, 506
  column references, 208
  correction vs. prevention, 536
  described in debugging, 499
  identifying in Data Viewer window, 505
  truncation, 508–509
Estimated Row Size parameter, 515
ETL (extract-transform-load), 88, 177
  architecture, 217–218
  defining strategy, 217
  determining strategies/tools, 216–231
    landing zones, 217
    Lookup transformations, 218–224
    set-based updates, 225–227
    Sort transformation, 224–225
  for data preparation, 667
  Lookup transformations, 218–224
ETL (extract-transform-load) process, 13
  batch cleansing during, 646
  custom solutions for, 342–344

error flows, 317–321
hash functions, 291–292
incremental loads, 307–308
EvaluateAsExpression property, 244
event handlers
  defined, 342
  implementing, 344–346
  in debugging, 505
  package templates, 407
  turning off, 346
  types of, 343
  using, 342–344
Event Handlers tab, 342, 345
events
  extending data, 383
  identifying, 382
  logging groups, 386
  possible properties, 386–387
  raising in script component, 711
Events property, exposing, 702
Event Viewer, accessing, 392
Excel Add-in, for MDM, 624–631
Excel connection manager, 134
Excel destination, 184
Excel files, as source for DQS project, 180, 647
Excel Fuzzy Lookup Add-in, 758
Excel, modifying data in, 630
exceptions
  detecting, 382
  identifying, 382
exclamation point tooltip, 552
ExclusionGroup property, 709
exclusion terms, defining, 680
executable component, event handlers, 342
Executables property, 374
EXECUTE AS Transact-SQL statement, 489
EXECUTE_OBJECTS permission, 482
Execute Package dialog box, 458, 473
Execute Package task, 149, 265, 269
Execute Package tasks, 517
Execute Package Utility, default invocation, 427
EXECUTE permission, 482
Execute Process task, 149, 270, 699
Execute SQL Server Agent job task, 269–270
Execute SQL Server Agent Job task, 152

Execute SQL task, 133, 150, 226
  checkpoints, 338
  data types for, 247
  for T-SQL code, 699
  implementing event handlers, 344, 345
  manually handling transactions, 332
  package templates, 407
  property parameterization, 251
  set-based update logic, 292, 292–293
Execute SQL Task Editor, 115, 362
Execute SQL Task Editor dialog box, 191
Execute SQL Task properties, 116
Execute T-SQL Statement task, 152
execution
  automated, 462–463
  monitoring, 465–470
  new execution instance, 467
  observing for troubleshooting, 498–499, 500
  of SSIS solutions, 456
  on-demand, 457–462
execution boundaries, 385, 398
execution boundary events, 386, 387
execution data, storing, 396
execution engine, Integration Services, 421
execution environment, data providers, 137
execution errors
  displaying connection context, 506
  identifying, 382, 384, 386
  jobs vs. master packages, 464
execution events, 342
execution exception events, 386, 398
ExecutionID, event property, 387
execution instance, 467–468, 507
Execution instance GUID variable, 400
Execution Performance report, 519
execution progress events, 386
Execution Results tab, 499
execution speed, establishing, 518
Execution start time variable, 400
execution times, described in debugging, 499
execution trees, 513–514, 520–521
Execution value, parameter value, 356
EXISTS operator, 739
explicit assignment, property parameterization, 251
explicit hierarchies, 591
Explorer area, access to, 618
Export Column transformation, 200
Export stage, of cleansing projects, 648

Expression Builder, 262
expressions
  date and time functions, 258
  mathematical functions, 257
  null functions, 258–259
  operators, 255–256
  property expressions, 259
  setting properties, 303
  string functions, 257–258
Expressions property, 244, 302, 361
Expressions tab, property expressions, 362
Expression task, 149, 259
  parameterization with, 254
  setting variables with, 356
extension points, 699
external audit table schema, 397
external processes, 131, 171, 270
extracting
  data from views, 94
  data from views and loading into tables, 91–98
extraction processes, 267
extract-transform-load. See ETL (extract-transform-
  load)

F

FactInternetSales table, adding partitioning column
  to, 74
fact tables, 3, 396, 567
  additivity of measures, 29–30
  AdventureWorksDW2012 sample database, 32–33
  business key, 28–29
  columns, 28–29, 47–48
    analyzing, 33–34
    lineage type, 29
  columnstore indexes, 64
  creating, 52–54
  deleting large parts of, 71–73
  design, 27–33
    activity of measures, 29–30
    columns, 28–29
    many-to-many relationships, 30–32
  early-arriving facts, 285, 288
  foreign keys, 28
  granularity, 12
  implementing, 47–48
  indexing, 56–59

inferred members, 47
inserting unresolved records, 285
InternetSales table
    creating, 52–53
loading
    partitions, 71–73
loading data
    guidelines, 308
    incremental loads, 299–316
loading incrementally, 378
many-to-many relationships, 30–32
partitioning, 44–45, 74–76
partition switching, 76–78
Star schema, 7–8
surrogate keys, 28
Failed operation status, 466
failover cluster, 426
FailPackageOnFailure property, 337, 338, 340
Fail Transformation option, 317
failure precedence constraints, 165, 167–169
failures
    avioding, 381
    identifying, 382, 384
    jobs vs. master packages, 464
    logging, 385
Fast Load option, 517
Fast Parse property (Advanced Editor), 189–190
Fatal logging level, 552
Feature Selection screen, 433
file attributes, 590
File connection manager, 134, 384
File Connection Manager Editor, 162
file formatting, connection managers, 140
filegroups, 44
    partition schemes, 72
    Primary
        creating partition schemes, 74
    SQL Server Customer Advisory Team (SQLCAT) white
        papers, 44
files
    delimited
        Flat File source, 196
    flat
        importing data from, 194–197
    processing with SSIS (SQL Server Integration Services)
        packages, 157–159
Files property (Foreach Loop Editor), 157
file systems, 131

File System task, 148, 161
    general settings, 161, 167, 168
    transaction failure, 330
File Transfer Protocol. *See* FTP
Fill Stage Tables container, 390
FillStageTables.dtsx SSIS package, 389, 392
filtered indexes, 57
filtered nonclustered indexes, 57
filtering method, 739
final destination, described in debugging, 499
FireError method, 721
FireInformation method, 721
FireWarning method, 721
"five whys" method, 536
Fixed attribute, 284
Fixed Attribute output, 290
flags, Type 2 SCD, 22
Flat File connection manager, 134
    assigning property values dynamically, 160–161
    creating, 138–140
Flat File Connection Manager Editor, 139, 196–199, 346
flat file data sources, column configuration, 515
Flat File destination, 184
Flat File destination adapter
    in debugging, 505
    in event handling, 345
flat files
    importing data from, 194–197
    multiple
        merging, 225
Flat File source, 180
floating-point numbers, 590
Folder property (File System task), 161, 168
Folder property (Foreach Loop Editor), 157
folders, in SSISDB catalog, 440
Folders object, 482
Foreach File Enumerators, logging, 411
ForEach Loop container, 156
    debugging, 501
    in debug environment, 499
    logging variables, 411
    package templates, 407
    properties update, 363
    TransactionOption, 330
    unique identifier, 386
ForEach Loop Editor, 157–159
ForEach loop, generating object lists, 701

foreign keys
  adding to InternetSales tables, 75
  constraints, removing, 47
  fact tables, 28–29
  implementing fact tables, 47–48
foreign languages, term extraction for, 680
For Loop containers, 156
  debugging, 499, 501
  TransactionOption, 330
  unique identifier, 386
Format output property, in domains, 639
FOR XML directive, 248
free-form attributes, 590
Frequency column, in term lookup, 682
frequency distribution of values, 532
Frequency threshold, in term extraction, 681
fresh installation, 428
FTP connection manager, 134
FTP (File Transfer Protocol), 131
FTP task, 148
full-cache lookups, 517
Full Cache mode (Lookup transformations), 218
Full recovery model, 43
functional area access, 618–619
Functional area access permission, 617
Functional Dependency, profiling of, 657
functions
  aggregate, 29–30
  AVERAGE aggregate, 29
  COUNT_BIG aggregate, 59
  hash
    implementing in SSIS, 291–292
  LastNonEmpty aggregate, 30
  NEXT VALUE FOR, 45
  Partition, 72
  SUM aggregate, 29
  T-SQL HASHBYTES, 291
Fuzzy Grouping, 756
Fuzzy Grouping transformation, 204, 740
Fuzzy Lookup, 756
Fuzzy Lookup Add-in for Excel, obtaining, 759
Fuzzy Lookup transformation, 205, 740

G

General tab (Lookup Transformation Editor), 219
governance (data), 570
granularity dimensions, 12

graphs, pivot, 17
Group by aggregate functions, 399, 400
grouping, tasks, 155
groups, discretizing, 17
GUID, audit transformation, 400

H

hard dimensions
  defined, 531
  measurement of, 535, 537
hard disk space requirements, 425
hardware, monitoring consumption of, 519–520
hash functions, implementing in SSIS, 291–292
hash joins
  bitmap filtered, 57
  Query Optimizer, 57
help, in script task, 702
heterogeneous data, integration of, 247
hierarchical data, 566, 569
hierarchies
  derived, 590
  dimensions, 19–22
  explicit, 591
  levels, 20
    members, 20
  recursive, 590–591
  Snowflake schema, 21
  Star schema, 21
  Type 1 SCD, 22
Hierarchies metadata, 606
hierarchy member permissions, 617, 619
high determinism, 240
Historical Attributes Inserts output, 290
history
  defining attribute types, 284
  dimension tables, 287
History Cleanup task, 152
history (data), SCD, 21–23
Hit Count breakpoint, 501
Hit Count Type breakpoint, 501
home pages, Master Data Manager, 585
HRM (Human Resources Management) applications, master data, 567
HTTP connection manager, 134
hypercubes. *See* Star schema

I

icons
  in debug environment, 498–499
  for breakpoints, 501
ID column, in stg.entityname_Leaf table, 608
IdentificationString property, 507
identity columns, compared to sequences, 45–46
identity mapping
  and data merging, 736
  and de-duplicating, 738
  central metadata storage, 571
  preparing data for, 740–744
  problems with, 736–738
  with fuzzy transformations, 758
IDEs (integrated development environment), for
  SSDT, 110
Ignore Failure option, 222, 317
IIS (Internet Information Services), Master Data Manager, 577
implicit permissions, 483
Import Column transformation, 200
importing, data from flat files, 194–197
ImportStatus_ID, in stg.entityname_Leaf, 608
ImportType, stg.entityname_Leaf, 608
inaccurate data, isolated, 532
IncludeInDebugDump property, 244
incremental loads, 299–316
  creating incremental load packages, 312–314
  ELT (extract-transform-load), 307–308
  implementing CDC with SSIS, 304–307
  reading data with dynamic SQL, 299–304
indexed views, 58–61
indexes
  aligned, 72
  clustered, 56–58
  columnstore, 62–68
    catalog views, 63–64
    fact tables, 64
    InternetSales fact table, 68–69
    segments, 63
  filtered, 57
  nonclustered
    filtered, 57
  partition, 72
indexing
  dimensions, 56–59
  fact tables, 56–59
  testing methods, 79

indirect configurations, using, 372
indirect file location approach, 371
inferred dimension members, 285, 288
inferred members, 47
Inferred Member Updates output, 290
Info logging level, 552
information, measuring quality, 532
INFORMATION_SCHEMA ANSI standard view, 654
Information Theory, 532
inherited permissions, 483, 618
Initial Staging, ETL, 217
in-place upgrade, 428
Input and Output Properties tab (Advanced Editor), 188
inputFileName variable, 249
Input Output Selection dialog box, 214
inputs for script component, 708–709
INSERT statement, 73
installation footprint, minimizing, 424
Installation Type screen, 432
installing
  MDS (Master Data Services), 575–587
    domain user accounts, 577–578
    installation operations, 581
    post-installation tasks, 582–586
    pre-installation tasks, 579–581
    SQL Server Setup, 578
    user accounts, 577
    Windows Web Server roles, 577
  Silverlight 5, 586
Int16 data type, 246
Int32 data type, 246
Int64 data type, 246
integrated development environment. *See* IDEs (integrated development environment)
Integration Management
  access to, 618
  creating subscription views in, 609
Integration Services
  dashboard, 469, 506
  default database choice, 429
  deployment, 371
  Deployment Wizard, 442
  development vs. production environment, 425
  initialization operation, 442
  operations report, 506
  performance tuning, 422
  row level security, 483
  security model, 422
  SQL Server feature choice, 424
  SSIS process hosting, 421, 422

Integration Services Auditing, 382
integration services catalog, 461
  accessing SSISDB catalog, 506
  project deployment, 356
Integration Services Logging, 382
integrity (data)
  accuracy, 570
  RDBMS (relational database management system), 569–570
intention, measurement of, 533
Interactive cleansing stage, 648
interactive survivorship process, 756
intermediary-level audits, 396
intermediate dimensions, 32
Internet Information Services. *See* IIS (Internet Information Services)
InternetSales fact table
  adding foreign keys, 75
  columns, 67
  columnstore indexes, 68–69
  creating, 52–53
  creating columnstore index, 75
  data compression, 68–69
  loading data, 75
Invalid status, in cleansing projects, 648
IsDestinationPathVariable property (File System task), 161, 167
isolating vs. combining data flows, 120
IsolationLevel property, 331
isolation levels, for transactions, 331
IsSourcePathVariable property (File System task), 161, 167
Itanium-based operating systems, feature support on, 427

hash
  bitmap filtered, 57
  Query Optimizer, 57
merge loops, 58
nested loops, 58
non-equi self joins, 60
SQL Server, 58–59
SQL Server Query Optimizer, 57

K

keys, 18
  business, 28–29
    merging data, 23
  clustering, 56
  foreign
    adding to InternetSales tables, 75
    fact tables, 28–29
  surrogate, 23–24
    fact tables, 28
    Type 2 SCD, 284
keys, primary and secondary. *See* primary and secondary keys
key terms, retrieving, 680
knowledge base (KB)
  creating additional, 661
  creating and maintaining, 638–645
  for DQS matching, 746–747
Knowledge Base Management screen, 642
knowledge bases, preparation of, 541
knowledge discovery
  initiating, 638
  using, 641–643
KnowledgeDiscovery setting, 552

J

Jaccard similarity coefficient, 738, 756
Jaro-Winkler distance algorithm, 738
jobs, in SQL Server Agent, 463
joined tables
  indexed views, 58–61
  staging area, 227–228
joins
  composite
    Lookup transformations, 220
  dimension primary key, 57

L

landing zones, ETL, 217
language translation, 18
LastNonEmpty aggregate function, 30
late-arriving dimensions, 48, 285
latency, 3
leading value
  defined, 639
  uses of, 640
leaf-level members, 591

levels (hierarchies), 20
Levenshtein distance algorithm, 738
lineage information, columns, 18
lineage, tables, 13
lineage type, fact table columns, 29
line-of-business. *See* LOB
Line of Business (LOB). *See* LOB (Line of Business)
linked domains, creating, 640
listings. *See also* code
  Flat File connection string, 142
  OLE DB connection string, 142
loading
  data, 64–68
    auditing with data lineage, 73
    changing from T-SQL procedures to SSIS, 227
    creating data warehouses, 42–44
    data lineage, 73
    foreign key constraints, 47
    incremental loads, 299–316
    into Customer dimension table with SCD tranfor-
      mation, 293–296
    preparing data transformations, 209–212
    to InternetSales table, 75
  data into tables, 91–98
  dbo.Customers dimension table, 212–214
  fact tables
    partitions, 71–73
Load Package dialog box, 113
load processes, 267
LOB (Line of Business)
  data latency, 3
  data management operations compared to SSIS, 87
  naming conventions, 3
  OLTP applications, 566
  tables, 5
Locals windows, viewing variables, 502
locked projects, access to, 647
log configuration templates, 388, 392
Log Entry screen, 514
Log Events window, 514
logging
  benchmarking performance with, 518–519
  correlating data, 401, 402
  customized for ETL, 342, 344
  Integration Services Logging, 382
  multiple levels, 411
  packages, 383–388

production-time troubleshooting, 506
  SSIS (SQL Server Integration Services), 13
  vs. auditing, 398
Logging Level list box, 473
logging levels, 468–469
LoggingMode property, 387–388
logical design, 3
  Snowflake schema, 3, 4, 9–11
    case scenarios, 34–38
    hierarchies, 21
  Star schema, 3, 4, 7–10
    case scenarios, 34–38
    hierarchies, 21
    queries, 11
logical-row transformations, 199–200
logic, controlling w/ variables, 502
log providers
  configuring, 386–388, 388–391
  package templates, 407
  selecting, 384–385
  types of, 383–384
Log Providers property, 374
log sequence number (LSN) ranges, CDC packages, 305
Lookup transformation, 200–201
  cache modes, 218–219
  Cache Transform transformation, 223–224
  case sensitivity, 220
  composite joins, 220
  connection managers, 218
  ETL (extract-transform-load), 218–224
  merging outputs with Union All component, 220–221
  replacing Union All transformation, 228–229
  rows with no matching entities, 220
Lookup Transformation Editor, 213, 218–219
loop containers, TransactionOption, 330
low-level audits, 396
LSN (log sequence number) ranges, CDC packages, 305

M

Machine name variable, 400
Maintenance Cleanup task, 152
maintenance tasks, 132, 151–152
managed service account (MSA), SSIS installation, 426
management activities, on existing projects, 646

Management Tools
  Complete installation option, 427
  development vs. production environment, 425
Manage My DataMarket RDS Providers, 550
MANAGE_OBJECT_PERMISSIONS permission, 482
Manage Parameter Values dialog box, 360
MANAGE_PERMISSIONS permission, 482
Manager attribute, 590
Manage Users page, 621
manual cleansing methods, 537
manual matching, 737
many-to-many relationships
  fact tables, 30–32
  schema correctness and, 534
mapping
  columns, 95
    OLE DB Destination adapter, 230
    OLE DB Destination Adapter, 214
    OLE DB Destination Editor, 187
  optimizing, 739
  parameters to SSIS variables, 301
Mappings tab (OLE DB Destination Editor), 186
Mapping stage, of cleansing projects, 648
Mapping tab, 346
master data, 566. See also MDM (master data management)
  AdventureWorksDW2012 sample database, 573
  auditing, 568, 569
  complexity, 568
  CRM (Customer Relationship Management) applications, 567
  CRUD cycle (create, read, update, and delete), 568
  defined, 529
  defining, 573–574
  definition, 567–568
  dimensions, 567
  ERP (enterprise resource planning) applications, 567
  hierarchical data, 569
  HRM (Human Resources Management) applications, 567
  identity mapping/de-duplicating, 735–766
  MDM (master data management), 569–572
    authority, 572
    central, 571
    central metadata storage, 571
    challenges, 572
    data conflicts, 572
    data quality, 572
    data stewards, 570
    documentation, 573
    domain knowledge, 573
    no central MDM, 570
  nouns, 567
  reusage, 568
  versioning, 568, 569
  volatility, 568
master data management. See MDM (master data management)
Master Data Manager, 576–577, 623
  home page, 585
  IIS (Internet Information Services), 577
Master Data Manager web application
  creating subscription views with, 609
  functional access for, 618
  initiating staging process, 608
Master Data ribbon tab, 627
Master Data Services. See MDS (Master Data Services)
Master Data Services (MDS). See MDS (Master Data Services)
Master Data tab, 625
master package concept
  configuring, 274–275
  creating, 270–274
  for advanced control flow, 265–266
  vs. SQL Server Agent jobs, 464
MasterPackageID, 271
match index, 760
matching
  attaining 100% accurate, 737
  attaining the best, 737
  controlling in fuzzy lookup, 758
Matching policy, 638–639
Matching Policy And Matching Project setting, 552
matching policy KB, 746
matching projects, 646, 747
matching rules, 639, 746
mathematical functions, 257
MaxBufferSize parameter, 515
MaxConcurrentExecutables property, 517
Maximum aggregate function, 399
MaximumErrorCount property, 499
Maximum length in term extraction, 681
Maximum Number of Versions per Project property, 439
MaxProjectVersion operation type, 442
MDM (master data management), 569–572

authority, 572
central, 571
central metadata storage, 571
    continuously merged data, 571
    identity mapping, 571
challenges, 572
data conflicts, 572
data quality, 530, 572
data stewards, 570
documentation, 573
domain knowledge, 573
no central MDM, 570
RDBMS (relational database management system), 569
MDM (master data management) solutions, 605–633
defining security, 616–624
Excel Add-in for, 624–632
importing and exporting data, 606–616
quality data, 529, 537
mdm.tblUser table, 617
mdm.udpSecurityMemberProcessRebuildModel stored procedure, 617, 619
mdq.NGrams function, 738
mdq.SimilarityDate function, 738
MDS Add-in for Excel, using, 763–764
MDS Configuration folder, 607
MDS Configuration Manager, 577–578, 608
MDS connections, in Excel, 625
MDS (Master Data Services), 541
architecture, 576–577
case scenarios, 600–601
creating MDS models, 588–599
installing, 575–587
    domain user accounts, 577–578
    installation operations, 581
    post-installation tasks, 582–586
    pre-installation tasks, 579–581
    SQL Server Setup, 578
    user accounts, 577
    Windows Web Server roles, 577
models, 588–589
    entities, 589–590
objects, 588–589, 589–592
permissions in, 617
security settings in, 616
MDS metadata, in model deployment, 606
MDS model deployment packages
creating and deploying, 606, 610–611

exporting data, 609
importing batches of data, 607–609
MDSModelDeploy utility, 606–607
MDS Objects, creating in Excel, 627–628
MDS security
defining, 620–622
users and permissions, 617
MDS (SQL Server 2012 Master Data Services), 572
MDS string similarity functions, 739
MDS System Administrator, changing, 617
MDS web service, 609
member properties, 18, 18–19
members
consolidated, 591
hierarchy levels, 20
inferred dimension, 285
    setting, 288
StateProvince entity, 597
memory buffers. See data buffers
Merge Join transformation, 201, 211
Merge Join Transformation Editor, 211
merge loop joins, 58
MERGE statement, 293
Merge transformation, 201
MERGE T-SQL statement, Execute SQL task, 226
merging
data
    business keys, 23
    Lookup transformation outputs with Union All component, 220–221
    multiple flat files, 225
MessageBox.Show method, in debugging, 505
Message Queue task, 149
MessageText event property, 387
metadata, 566
and master data, 606
configuring for script component, 708
folder, 440
parameter, 441
project, 440
Microsoft CodePlex, custom SSIS components, 291
Microsoft Distributed Transaction Coordinator (MSDTC)
cross-host communication, 330, 332
transaction definition, 328–329
Microsoft.NET Framework 4, 542
Microsoft.Net Framework System.TypeCode enumeration, 245–246

Microsoft Silverlight 5
  installing, 586
  Master Data Manager, 577
Microsoft.SQLServer.DTSPipelineWrap namespace, 718
Microsoft.SQLServer.DTSRuntimeWrap namespace, 718
Microsoft.SQLServer.PipelineHost namespace, 718
Microsoft Visual Studio, breakpoint functionality, 500
Microsoft Visual Studio Tools for Applications (VSTA),
  scripting with, 700
migration, 429, 451
MinBufferSize parameter, 515
minimalization, measurement of, 534
minimal rights principle, 426
Minimum aggregate function, 399
mining models
  creating, 672
  limiting data feed in, 689
Min Record Score value, 551
Min Score For Auto Corrections value, 551
Min Score For Suggestions value, 551
Model Administrators, 617–618
Model Data Explorer pane, 626
model deployment packages
  creation of, 606, 610–611
  deploying, 611
Model Deployment Wizard, 606–607
model object permissions, 617, 618
model permission, assigning, 622
models, MDS
  creating, 588–599
  entities, 589–590
modifiedRecordCount variable, 271
MODIFY_OBJECTS permission, 482
MODIFY permission, 482
modules, defined, 553
movements (data)
  complex, 145–147
  DW, 88
  modifying movements, 112–123
    adding existing SSIS packages to projects, 112–114
    configuring connections, 120–123
    editing SSIS packages created by SQL Server Im-
      port and Export Wizard, 114–116
    running SSIS packages in Debug mode, 120–123
  planning, 89–99
  simple data movements
    creating, 91–98
  SQL Server Import and Export Wizard, 88, 89–99
    creating simple data movements, 91–98
    transformations, 89

SSDT (SQL Server Data Tools), 88
SSIS (SQL Server Integration Services), 87
  tasks, 150
msdb database, 429, 443
MSMQ connection manager, 135
Multicast transformation, 201, 400
Multidimensional mode, for data mining, 670
multidimensional processing, 266, 267
multi-input transformations, 200–201
multi-output transformations, 200–201
multiple configurations, 375
multiple fact tables, dimensions, 8
Multiple Files connection manager, 134
Multiple Flat Files connection manager, 134
multiple flat files, merging, 225
multiple result sets, retaining, 248
multiple tasks, execution of, 517
multi-row transformations, 202–203

N

Name attribute, 590
name columns, 18, 608
Name property, 244, 357
Name property (File System task), 161, 167
Name property (Foreach Loop Editor), 157, 159
names, connection managers, 136
Namespace property, 244
Namespace property (Foreach Loop Editor), 159
naming conventions
  attributes, 21
  dimensions, 17, 21
  DW, 17–18, 21
  LOB applications, 3
  OLAP, 17–18
Navigational Access, 619
nested loop joins, 58
nested tables, in data mining, 671
Net process mode option (CDC), 307
Net with merge process mode option (CDC), 307
Net with update mask process mode option (CDC), 307
NewCode column, in stg.entityname_Leaf table, 609
New Connection Manager option, 355
new execution operation, 458
New output, 290
newRecordCount variable, 271
New Solution Configuration dialog box,, 359

New status, in cleansing project, 648
NEXT VALUE FOR function, 45
nGrams algorithm, 738
No Cache mode (Lookup transformations), 219
No environment references, validation mode, 467
non-blocking transformations, 199, 513
nonclustered indexes, filtered, 57
None logging level, 468
non-equi self joins, 60–61
non-key columns, third normal form, 9
normalization, 5, 145–147, 747
normalized schemas
    measurement of quality, 534
    reporting problems, 5–7
Normalize property, in domains, 639
Notify Operator task, 152
NOT NULL constraint, 186
NotSupported property, TransactionOption, 329, 330
nouns, 567
NULL function, 200, 258
nulls, 400, 654
number series, sequences, 45
numbers, floating point, 590

O

Object Browser, SSIS monitoring reports, 469–470
Object data type, 246, 247
Object Explorer, accessing SSISDB catalog, 506
object hierarchy
    inheritance, 387
    permission inheritance, 483
    variable access, 248
objectives, separation of, 267
objects
    icons in debug environment, 498
    MDS (Master Data Services), 588–589, 589–592
    parameterizing with expressions, 261–262
    SSAS (SQL Server Analysis Services), 132
obsolete information, 533
ODBC connection manager, 135
ODBC destination, 184
ODBC source adapter, 180, 181
OLAP cubes, in data mining, 688
OLAP (online analytical processing), 9, 17–18
OLE DB command, 226
OLE DB Command transformation, 204, 290

OLE DB connection manager, 121, 135
    creating, 140–142
    log providers, 384
    Lookup transformation, 218
    parameterization, 122
OLE DB destination, 184
OLE DB Destination Adapter, column mapping, 214, 230
OLE DB Destination Editor
    column mapping, 187
    Connection Manager tab, 186
    Mappings tab, 186
OLE DB source, 180, 181
OLE DB Source adapter, dynamic SQL, 300–302
OLE DB Source Editor, 364
OLE DB Source Editor dialog box, 182, 191, 345
OLE DB transformation, 517
OLTP applications, SCD problem, 21–24
on-demand execution, 456
    DTExecUI utility, 458, 461–462
    programmatic execution, 458–462
    SQL Server Management Studio, 457–458
    uses for, 457
OnError event, 386, 391, 402
OnError event handler, 343, 344, 345
one-to-many relationships, auditing, 397
one-to-one relationships
    auditing, 396
    schema correctness, 534
OnExecStatusChanged event, 343, 386
OnInformation event, 343, 386
online analytical processing (OLAP), 9
on line transactional processing applications. See OLTP
    applications
OnPostExecute event, 343, 386, 391
OnPostValidate event, 343, 386
OnPreExecute event, 343, 386, 391, 501
OnPreValidate event, 343, 386
OnProgress event, 343, 386
OnQueryCancel event, 343, 386
OnTaskFailed event, 343, 386, 391
OnVariableValueChanged event, 343, 386
OnWarning event, 343, 386
open-world assumption, 531
operating system inspection, 132
operating system, log provider choice, 385
operation, 442
operational applications, auditing, 396

Operation property (File System task), 161, 167
operations
  and execution monitoring, 465–466
  SSISDB reports on, 506
  types of, 441–442
operation status values, 465–466
Operator event property, 386
operators
  batch mode processing, 63
  in expressions, 255
optimizing queries, 60–61
Order Details table, 28
outliers, finding, 688
outputs
  adding column to script component, 713
  error, 317
  for script components, 708–709
  Lookup transformation
    merging with Union All component, 220–221
  SCD transformation, 289–290
overall recurrence frequency, SQL Server Agent
  jobs, 463
overlapping permissions, 619
OverwriteDestination property (File System task), 161,
167

P

Package Configuration Organizer, possible tasks, 368
package configurations, 367–375
  creating, 369–371
  elements configured, 368
  in Execute Package task, 269
  modifying, 375
  ordering, 375
  parameters, 371
  sharing, 373, 375
  specifying location for, 371–372
  using, 375–377
Package Configurations Organizer, 368–369
Package Configuration Wizard, 369, 372, 373
package deployment model
  package configuration and, 368
  passing package variables in, 371
Package deployment model, 269

package execution
  monitoring, 521–522
  observing, 520–521
  performance tuning, 511–520
  troubleshooting, 498–509
Package ID variable, 400
package-level audit, table schema, 398
package-level connection managers, converting to
  project-level, 355
package-level parameter, filtering source data
  with, 364–365
Package name variable, 400
package parameters, 303
package performance
  benchmarking, 518–519
  monitoring, 519
package properties, in package configurations, 368
packages
  CDC (change data capture)
    LSN (log sequence number) ranges, 305
  design-time troubleshooting, 498–499
  ETL (extract-transform-load)
    error flows, 317–321
  executing, 456–470
  execution and monitoring, 473–474
  incremental loads, 312–314
  in deployment model, 440
  Integration Services Logging, 382
  logging, 383–388
  master package concept, 265–266
  parameters, 303
  restartability, 762
  securing, 480–484
  SSIS (SQL Server Integration Services)
    Control Flow Designer, 105–107
    creating, 91–98
    developing in SSDT, 101–108
    editing, 99, 114–120
    ETL (extract-transform-load), 218
    importing into SSIS projects, 112–123
    parameterization, 137
    parameters, 122
    preparing, 162–163
    preparing for incremental loads, 299–316
    processing files, 157–159
    running, 96
    saving, 96
    verifying, 162–163
    viewing files, 98

starting and monitoring, 470–479
validation in SSMS, 470–472
validation of, 466–467
package-scoped connection managers, 136–137
package-scoped errors, log providers, 385
package-scoped variables, 271
  as global, 248, 249
  default setting, 250
package settings, updating across packages, 367
package status, viewing in Locals window, 502
package templates
  preparing, 406–407, 408–409
  using, 408, 409–410
package transactions
  creating restartable, 336–339, 347
  defining settings, 328–330
  implementing, 333–335
  manual handling, 332–333
  transaction isolation levels, 331–332
package validations, 466–467
package variable properties, in package configurations, 368
package variables, interacting with, 702
page compression, 62
parallel execution, 517
parallel queries, 58
parameterization
  applicable properties, 241
  connection manager
    case scenario, 125
  connection managers, 137
  OLE DB connection manager, 122
  of properties, 251
  reusability and, 240
  SSIS (SQL Server Integration Services), 111, 123
Parameterize dialog box, 358
Parameterize option, 358
parameters
  adding in build configurations, 359–360
  and running packages, 363
  connection managers, 354
  defining, 356–358
  editing, 357
  for connection strings, 363–364
  implementing, 363–366
  in Execute Package task, 269
  mapping to SSIS variables, 301
  package, 303

packages, 303
project, 303
project and package, 441
read-only, 242
SSIS (SQL Server Integration Services) packages, 122
uses for, 356
validating, 466–467
values available, 356
vs. variables, 242
Parameters tab, 364, 471, 473
parameter values, for data taps, 507
parameter window, creating parameters in, 357
parent events, 344
parent level, 20
parent object, log settings, 387
parent packages, 269, 328, 330
Parent Package Variable, 370–371
partial-blocking transformations, 199, 513
Partial Cache mode (Lookup transformations), 219
partially denormalized dimensions, 11
partition elimination, 72
Partition function, 72
partition indexes, 72
partitioning, 44–45
  fact tables, 74–76
  tables
    testing, 80
partitioning technique, 739
Partition Processing destination, 184
partition schemes, 72
partitions, loading fact tables, 71–73
partition switching, 72, 76–78
PATH environment variable
  in 64-bit installation, 427
  SQL Server Agent, 428
pattern distribution, 532
Pending operation status, 466
people, 567
Percentage Sampling transformation, 202, 505, 690
performance
  DW
    batch processing, 62–64
    columnstore indexes, 62–64
    data compression, 61–62
    indexed views, 58–61
    indexing dimensions, 56–59
    indexing fact tables, 56–59
  queries, 60–61

performance counters, 519–520
Performance logging level, 468
Performance Monitor, 519–520
Performance property value, 518
performance tuning, of package execution, 511–520
Periodically Remove Old Versions property, 439
permission assignments, testing, 489
permission inheritance, 483
permission-related problems, operator ID, 386
permissions
    assigning, 480, 481, 482–484
    Bulk Insert task, 150
    implicit, 619
    testing assignment of, 622–623
    testing security settings, 633
Permissions page, 488
Person.Person table (TK463DW), creating data flow
    tasks, 190–192
PipelineComponentTime event, 386
PipelineExecutionTrees event, 513
Pivot editor, 203
pivot graphs, 17
pivoting
    attributes, 17
    dynamic, 203
pivoting (data), 146
pivot tables, 17
Pivot transformation, 202
places, 567
Play button, in Data Viewer window, 505
POC projects
    automatic discretization, 18
    shared dimensions, 9–10
point of failure, restarting packages from, 336, 347
policies, data governance, 570
populating entities, 596–599
population completeness, 531
pop-up message window, in debugging, 505
PostExecute method, customization, 724
Precedence Constraint Editor, 118, 119
precedence constraints, 119, 164–169
    Boolean expressions in, 256
    completion, 165
    creating, 118
    expressions and, 259–260
    failure, 165, 167–169
    and multiple tasks, 517
    success, 165

precedence, controlling w/ variables, 502
predefined reports
    benchmarking performance with, 519
    monitoring execution with, 506
predictability, 240
predictions
    and training, 690
    in data mining, 668
predictive models
    efficiency of, 689–690
    in SSIS, 667
PreExecute method, customization, 723
prefix compression, 62
PrepareForExecute method, customization, 722
presentation quality, measurement of, 533
primary data
    overgrowth, 401
    storage, 396
Primary filegroup, creating partition schemes, 74
primary keys, joins, 57
primary table schema, 397
PrimeOutput method, customization, 723
principals, implementing, 481
privacy laws, and completeness measuement, 531
private dimensions, 9–10
problem detection, execution monitoring, 465
problems, reporting w/ normalized schemas, 5–7
procedures, T-SQL data lineage, 73
processes, external, 131, 171
processing files, SSIS packages, 157–159
processing mode options (CDC), 306
ProcessInput method, customization, 723–724
Produce Error task, 345
production data, copying to development, 125
production environments
    SSIS (SQL Server Integration Services) projects, 111
    troubleshooting, 498, 506–508
production server
    SSIS installation choices, 424
    SSIS package deployment, 437
production systems, defining master data, 574
Products dimension
    columns, 66
    creating, 51
product taxonomies, 566
Profiler trace, log providers, 385
profiling data, methods for, 654
Profiling tab, exclamation point tooltip in, 552

programmatic execution, 458–462

Progress tab, execution details, 499–500, 509

project configurations, 358

Project Deployment model, 269, 437, 440
  build configurations in, 358
  moving solutions with, 371

project-level connection managers, 136–137, 354–355

project parameters, 303, 363–364

Project.params window, 356

Project Properties dialog box, 488

projects
  checking for problems, 466
  SSIS (SQL Server Integration Services)
    creating, 103–105
    deploying, 110–124
    development environments, 111
    importing SSIS packages into, 112–123
    production environments, 111
    properties, 139
  validation in SSMS, 470–472

Projects object, 482

proof-of-concept (POC) projects. *See* POC projects

properties
  Execute SQL Task, 116
  Expressions, 302
  File System task, 161, 167, 168
  Foreach Loop Editor, 157, 159
  member, 18, 18–19
  setting with expressions, 303
  SqlCommand
    modifying for data flow task, 303
    setting expressions for, 303–304
  SSIS (SQL Server Integration Services) projects, 139
  updating, 363
  ValidateExternalMetadata, 183

Properties property, 374

Properties To Export, 373

Properties window, editing with, 357

Property Expression Editor, 160, 361

property expressions, 259
  applying, 361–362
  evaluation of, 362

Property Expressions Editor, 302

Property Overrides grid, 473

Property Pages dialog box, 359, 360–361

property parameterization, by explicit assignment, 251

property paths
  assigning at run time, 468
  vs. parameters, 242

ProvideComponentProperties, customization, 719

pruning method, 739

Publish And Validate group, 626

Publish button, 626

purposes, separation of, 267

Q

queries, 3
  aggregating columns in AdventureWorksDW2012
    database tables, 59–62
  batch mode processing, 63
  clustered indexes, 56
  covered, 56
  creating, 626
  data mining, 132
  data quality measurement, 531
  in data mining predictions, 672
  indexed views, 58–61
  multiple lookups, 517
  non-equi self joins, 60–61
  optimizing, 60–61
  for package execution, 506
  parallel, 58
  profiling data with, 654–656
  Snowflake schema, 11
  specifying
    compared to copying data, 94
  Star schema, 11
  testing indexing methods, 79

Query Optimizer
  columnstore indexes, 62–64
  hash joins, 57
  joins, 57
  partition elimination, 72

R

RaiseChangeEvent property, 244

random samples
  achieving, 690
  performing, 690–693

Ratcliff/Obershelp algorithm, 738

Raw File destination, 184

Raw File source, 180

RDBMS (relational database management system), data integrity, 569–570

ReadCommitted property, IsolationLevel, 331

READ_OBJECTS permission, 482

Read-Only permission, 618

Read-only property, 159, 244

ReadOnlyVariables, 701, 708

READ permission, 482, 484

ReadUncommitted property, IsolationLevel, 331

ReadWriteVariables, 701, 708

real-world objects, correct representation of, 534

Rebuild Index task, 152

REBUILD option, 56

reconstruction, rows, 62

records
  inserting into fact tables, 285
  updating, 226

Recordset destination, 184

recovery models
  Bulk Logged, 43
  of DQS databases, 555
  Full, 43
  Simple, 43
  transaction logs, 42–43

recursive hierarchies, 590–591

Redirect Rows option, 318

red squiggly line, in spell checker, 640

reference data providers, 541

Reference Data Services (RDS), 638
  configuring, 549–550
  logging setting, 552

reference dictionary, for term lookup, 682

reference relation, in measuring completeness, 531–532

references
  adding, 702
  columns
    errors, 208
    resolving, 207–208
  in custom component development, 718

Registry Entry, package configuration type, 370

Regular Expressions, data extraction with, 731

regular users group, 617–618

ReinitializeMetaData, customization, 721

relational database management system (RDBMS).
  See RDBMS (relational database management system)

relational databases
  master data, 567
  nulls in, 654

relation completeness, 532, 654

relations, 589

ReleaseConnections method, customization, 724

Reliability And Performance Monitor, 384, 386

Remarks column, 50

Reorganize Index task, 152

REORGANIZE option, 56

RepeatableRead property, IsolationLevel, 331

reports
  aggregate functons, 29–30
  reporting problems with normalized relational schemas, 5–7
  slow DW reports, 79
  for troubleshooting packages, 506

Required property, 329, 330, 332, 339, 357

Resolve References editor, 207–208, 208

resource planning, execution monitoring, 465

RetainSameConnection property, 332

retention period, 402, 470

Retention Period (days) property, 439

Retention window operation, 442

Retrieve file name property (Foreach Loop Editor), 157

return on investment (ROI). See ROI (return on investment)

reusability
  defined, 240
  improving, 480, 492
  master data, 568
  master package concept and, 266
  maximizing, 242
  of custom components, 711

Reuse Existing button, 373

ROI (return on investment), MDM, 569

roles
  data stewards, 570
  Windows Web Server
    MDS (Master Data Services), 577

root causes, finding, 536

row-based (synchronous) transformations, 513

row compression, 61

Row Count data flow, 398

row counts, described in debugging, 499

Row Count transformation, 200, 399, 505

row-level auditing, 396–397, 398, 402

row-level security, 483

rows
  buffers, 178
  capture count of, 505
  capturing with data taps, 508
  data flow task, 177

displaying in data viewer, 503–504

error paths, 319–321

filtering, 626

filtering with package-level parameters, 364–365

identifying problems, 503

nulls, 400

reconstruction, 62

shrinking size of, 515

standardizing data in, 758

storage in buffers, 512

in transformations, 513

unique identifiers, 401

row sampling, testing, 694

Row Sampling transformation, 202, 505, 690

row sets

    retaining multiple, 248

    reusing, 248

    storing, 243, 247

    variables and, 243

Run64BitRuntime setting, 137

Running operation status, 466

run time engine, parallel execution in, 517

run-time methods

    customization, 719, 721–725

    of script component, 710

S

Sales Fact table, 28, 29

same-table row-level audits, 396

samples

    in data mining, 687

    selecting appropriate, 689–692

    testing row sampling, 694

SaveCheckpoints property, 337, 340

SByte data type, 246

scalar values, variables and, 243

SCD (Slowly Changing Dimension), 21–24, 284, 285–290

SCD transformation, 285–290

    implementing SCD logic, 293–298

    modifying to include set-based updates, 296–298

    outputs, 289–290

    updating dimensions, 290

SCD Wizard, 287

schedules, in SQL Server Agent, 463

SCHEMABINDING option, 59

schemas

    database

        AdventureWorksDW2012 sample database, 14–15

Dimensional Models, 6

documentation of, 534

measurement of quality, 534

measuring completeness, 534

measuring correctness, 534

normalized relational

    reporting problems, 5–7

Snowflake, 3, 4, 9–11

    case scenarios, 34–38

    hierarchies, 21

    queries, 11

Star, 3, 4, 7–10

    case scenarios, 34–38

    dimensions tables, 8–9

    fact table, 7–8

    hierarchies, 21

    queries, 11

scope

    ambiguity resolution, 250

    changing, 250

    function of, 248

    overriding variables with, 250

Scope property, 244

score, in term extraction, 681

Script Component, 205, 707–711

    coding, 709–711

    configuring, 708–709

    custom components and, 716

    debugging, 503, 505

    reusing row sets, 248

    using, 712–715

Script Component Editor, 708

Script Component transformation, 205, 291

scripting

    debugging, 702

    uses for, 699

ScriptMain class, 701, 702

ScriptObjectModel class, 702

Script page, 701

Script properties, 705

script task, 154, 700–707

    coding, 702–703

    configuring, 701

    custom components and, 716

    debugging, 505

    parameterization with, 254

    reading profiling results with, 704–706

    reusing row sets, 248

Script Task Editor, 701
Script transformation, 517
search space
   reducing, 747
   reduction techniques, 739
secondary keys. *See* primary and secondary keys
securables, 481, 482
security
   and storing connection information, 371, 375
   complex settings, 617
   governance policies, 570
   MDS security, 633
   of master data, 616–624
   of SSIS packages, 480–484
   overlapping permissions, 619
   SSIS component installation, 426, 431
   SSISDB catalog, 423, 437
   SSIS solutions, 455
   SSIS (SQL Server Integration Services) deploy-
      ment, 111
security model, Integration Services, 422
segments, 63
Select Destination wizard page, 447
Select New Scope pane, 250
Select Properties To Export page, 374
Select Source wizard page, 448
semi-structured data, 566
Send Mail task, 149
Sensitive property, 357
Sequence container, 156, 329
sequences, 45
   CACHE option, 46
   compared to identity columns, 45–46
   creating
      syntax, 46
   SQL Server, 45
Serializable property, IsolationLevel, 331
series, sequences, 45
Server default parameter value, 356
server variables, 441
Server-wide Default Logging Level property, 439, 506
service accounts, 426–427
Service Accounts Step-by-Step Guide (Microsoft), 426
set-based updates, 229
   updating Customer Dimension table, 229–231
   updating dimensions, 292–293
Set Breakpoints dialog box, 500–501
Set Parameter Value dialog box, 488

Set Query Parameters dialog box, 300–301, 364
shared dimensions, 8–9
   DimProduct, 8
   POC projects, 9–10
   SSAS (SQL Server Analysis Services), 9
Show Explorer button, 626
Show System Variables option, 245
Show Variables Of All Scopes option, 249
Shrink Database task, 152
shrinking databases, 153
side-by-side upgrade, 428
Silverlight 5
   installing, 586
   Master Data Manager, 577
Simil algorithm, 738
similarity scores, 759
similarity threshold, 747, 758
similarity threshold parameter, 740
similar strings, finding, 738
simple data movements, 88
   creating, 91–98
   planning, 89–99
Simple recovery model, 43, 555
simple sequential integers, surrogate keys, 45
Simple Table Quick Profiling Form dialog box, 658
Single data type, 246
64-bit environments, 427
   migration, 429
   tools available, 431
Slowly Changing Dimension. *See* SCD
Slowly Changing Dimension transformation, 204
SMO connection manager, 135
SMTP connection manager, 135
Snapshot property, IsolationLevel, 331
Snippets.txt file, 706
Snowflake schema, 3, 4, 9–11
   case scenarios, 34–38
   hierarchies, 21
   queries, 11
soft dimensions
   defined, 531
   measurement of, 533, 535, 537
solution configurations, 358
solution deployment, 437. *See also* SSIS project deployment
Solution Explorer, 103–104, 355, 356
   assigning project properties in, 360
   build configurations in, 359

sorted input, data flow tips for, 516

sorting neighborhood technique, 739

sort tables, staging area, 227–228

Sort transformation, 202, 224–225, 513, 516

source adapters

  debugging, 505

  execution trees, 513–514

  optimization of, 517

Source Assistant

  adding data flow source adapters, 181–182

  creating data flow source adapters, 181

source columns, mapping of, 556

SourceConnectionOLEDB connection manager, 121

source control, SSIS templates, 407

source data

  filtering with package-level parameter, 364

  incremental loads, 299

SourceID event property, 386

SourceName event property, 386

Source Order Details table, 28

Source Orders Header table, 28

source speed, 518

source systems, data quality solutions, 537

source tables, selecting, 95

source threads, default value of, 517

SourceVariable property (File System task), 161, 167

space

  databases

    calculating requirements, 43

  data files, 43

specific duration, job schedule, 463

Speller property, in domains, 639

spelling checker, 640

Split Transformations, 694

sp_sequence_get_range system procedure, 45

SQLCAT (SQL Server Customer Advisory Team), 44

SqlCommand property

  modifying for data flow task, 303

  setting expressions for, 303–304

SQL, reading data, 299–304

SQL Server

  autogrowing, 43

  autoshrinking, 43

  batch mode processing, 63

    operators, 63

  creating DW databases, 42–44

  data compression, 61–62

  indexed views, 58–61

  joins, 58–59

  log provider, 384

  maintenance, 132

  native auditing, 399

  sequences, 45

  SSIS option, 423

  SSIS solution deployment, 421

  transactions in, 328

SQL Server 2005/2008, upgrade paths, 429

SQL Server 2012

  data viewer display, 503

  package configuration type, 370

  solution deployment, 437

  SSIS server, 437

  SSIS Toolbox, 179

SQL Server 2012 Database Engine Services, DQS installation, 542

SQL Server 2012 Master Data Services (MDS). *See* MDS (Master Data Services)

SQL Server 2012 Upgrade Advisor, 429

SQL Server Agent, 462–464

  cleanup operation, 439

  development vs. production environment, 425

  PATH environment variable, 428

  schedules, 463

  SSIS execution automation, 455

  SSIS package creation, 475–476

  SSIS package scheduling, 477–479

  SSIS process execution, 455

  vs. master package concept, 464

SQL Server Analysis Services. *See* SSAS

SQL Server Business Intelligence Development Studio (BIDS), 102

SQL Server Business Intelligence suite, in data mining, 669

SQL Server Compact destination, 184

SQL Server Compact Edition connection manager, 135

SQL Server Configuration Manager

  service accounts, 427

  shortcut location, 434

SQL Server configuration, options available, 372

SQL Server Customer Advisory Team (SQLCAT), 44

SQL Server Database Engine

  accessing SSISDB catalog, 506

  development vs. production environmnet, 425

  SSIS functionality, 425

SQL Server databases, creating, 48–49

SQL Server Data Tools. *See* SSDT (SQL Server Data Tools)

SQL Server destination, 184
SQL Server Import and Export Wizard, 88, 89–99, 430, 431
  64-bit installation, 427
  creating simple data movements, 91–98
  editing SSIS packages created in, 114–116
  transformations, 89
  T-SQL scripts, 116
  viewing SSIS package files, 98–99
SQL Server Installation Center, 428–429, 432
SQL Server instance, CLR integration, 445
SQL Server Integration Services 11.0 properties, 435
SQL Server Integration Services Deployment Wizard, 430, 442
SQL Server Integration Services Execute Package Utility, 427, 430, 431
SQL Server Integration Services Package Installation Utility, 430
SQL Server Integration Services Package Upgrade Wizard, 430
SQL Server Integration Services Package Utility, 427, 430, 431
SQL Server Integration Services Project Conversion Wizard, 430
SQL Server Integration Services (SSIS). *See* SSIS (SQL Server Integration Services)
SQL Server Management Studio (SSMS)
  administering DQS with, 553–555
  management capabilities, 423
  on-demand execution, 457–458
  package deployment, 448–449
  project deployment, 442
  SSISDB settings, 438–439
  SSIS validation in, 469–471
  vs. Deployment Wizard, 442–443
SQL Server Management Tools, DQS database administration, 542
SQL Server permissions, 426, 429
SQL Server Profile, log provider, 384
SQL Server Profiler trace, log providers, 384
SQL Server service accounts, 426, 435
SQL Server services, account recommendations, 426
SQL Server Setup, installing MDS, 578
SQL Server table, storing package configurations, 372
SQL statements, set-based update logic, 292–293
SSAS (SQL Server Analysis Services), 9, 132
  additivity of measures, 30–31
  data mining engine, 668

data mining installation, 670
data mining support, 670
discretizing attributes, 17
for frequency of distributions, 656
multidemensional auditing, 398
storage types, 30
SSDT (SQL Server Data Tools), 88
  32- vs. 64-bit environments, 427
  Complete installation option, 427
  connection manager scope, 136–137
  creating SSIS (SQL Server Integration Services) projects, 103–105
  developing SSIS packages, 101–108
  development vs. production environment, 425
  IDE (integrated development environment), 110
  implementing event handlers, 344
  Log Events window, 513
  vs. Deployment Wizard, 442–443
ssis_admin role, 481
  default permission, 483
  folder creation, 484
SSIS component installation
  64-bit vs. 32-bit environments, 427
  development vs. production, 424–425, 433
  hardware/software requirements, 425
  preparing, 424
  security considerations, 426–427
  SQL Server Installation Center, 428–429, 432
  SSIS server functionalities, 423
  SSIS tools, 430
  upgrading SSIS, 429–430
SSIS Data Flow Engine, 512–514
SSIS data flow mining model, 675
SSIS Data Profiling task, 656–657
  using, 657–659
  vs. cleansing, 657
SSISDB catalog, 459
  as deployment target, 480
  benchmarking performance with, 518–519
  configuration, 438–439
  execution data, 465–466
  functions of, 423
  native auditing capabilities, 399
  package storage in, 467
  parameter access, 441
  parameter value control, 441, 507
  SSIS package deployment, 437, 438, 444
  timeout property, 467

troubleshooting with, 506
upgrades and, 430
SSISDB configuration, project deployment, 444–446
SSISDB objects, project deployment, 440–442
SSISDB permissions, 481, 484–489
SSISDB principals, 481
SSISDB securables, 481, 482
SSISDB security, 455, 480–484
SSIS Designer
  Control Flow tab, 336
  Execution Results tab, 499
  log providers, 384
  Progress tab, 499–500
  viewing execution information, 500
SSIS development
  automated execution of, 239
  package templates, 406–408
SSIS DQS Cleansing component, 646
SSIS DQS Cleansing transformation, 541
SSIS fuzzy transformations
  algorithm for, 756–757
  built-in filtering, 740
  finding similar strings with, 738
  implementing, 756–763
  versions of, 758–759
SSIS installation paths, 428
SSIS Legacy Service
  availability of, 423
  earlier SSIS packages, 443
  manual configuration, 429
SSIS logs, correlating w/ audit data, 401–402
SSIS managed API, programmatic execution with, 458, 460–461
SSIS management assembly, 460
SSIS packages
  creating dynamic, 378
  custom code for, 699–730
  from previous SQL versions, 443
  in 64-bit environments, 428
  mining model for, 675
  storage, 421, 422
  uses in data mining, 671
SSIS processes, automatic vs. manual, 455
SSIS project deployment
  Deployment Wizard vs. SSDT/SSMS, 442–443, 446, 448–449
  development vs. production environments, 421, 437
  SSISDB catalog, 438, 444

SSISDB configuration, 438–439, 444–446
SSISDB objects, 440–442
SSIS runtime
  for SSIS execution, 456
  SSIS processes, 421
SSIS server
  development vs. production environment, 425
  functionalities, 423
SSIS solutions, 421–423. See also SSIS project deployment
  advantages of separate packages, 266
  storage, 423
SSIS (SQL Server Integration Services), 87
  administration operations, 132
  CDC implementation, 304–307, 308–316
  connection managers, 133–144
  containers, 155–163
    Foreach Loop, 156
    For Loop, 156
    Sequence, 156
  data flow task. See data flow task
  data management operations compared to LOB, 87
  data mining queries, 132
  data profiling, 132
  data types, 187–189
  development, 110
  email, 132
  event handling, 342–344
  external processes, 131
  extract-transform-load. See ETL (extract-transform-load)
  file systems, 131
  FTP access, 131
  logging, 13
  logging/auditing, 382
  measuring performance, 386
  operating system inspection, 132
  package execution monitoring, 506–508
  packages
    Control Flow Designer, 105–107
    creating, 91–98
    developing in SSDT, 101–108
    editing, 99, 114–120
    ETL (extract-transform-load), 218
    importing into SSIS projects, 112–123
    parameterization, 137
    parameters, 122
    preparing, 162–163

preparing for incremental loads, 299–316
processing files, 157–159
running, 96
saving, 96
verifying, 162–163
viewing files, 98
parallel execution in, 517
parameterization, 111, 123
predictive models in, 667
projects
creating, 103–105
deploying, 110–124
development environments, 111
production environments, 111
properties, 139
set-based updates, 225–227
SQL Server Import and Export Wizard, 88
creating simple data movements, 89–99
viewing SSIS package files, 98–99
SSAS (SQL Server Analysis Services), 132
SSDT (SQL Server Data Tools), 88
creating SSIS projects, 103–105
developing packages, 101–108
IDE (integrated development environment), 110
SSIS Toolbox, 105–107
tasks. *See* tasks (control flow)
transaction isolation levels, 331–332
transaction support, 328–329
updating dimensions, 290–293
SSIS (SQL Server Integration Services) Toolbox
data flow task components, 178–179
event handlers, 342, 344, 345
script task, 701
SQL Server 2012, 179
SSIS tools, stand-alone tools, 430
SSIS transformations, in test mining, 679
stage maintenance processes, 267
stage preparation, 265
staging area
join tables, 227–228
sort tables, 227–228
Sort transformation, 225
Staging Batch Interval setting, 608
staging process, 607–609, 613
staging tables, 633
data set storage in, 243
implementing, 44
populating, 607

stale data, 533
Standard Reports, 506
Star schema, 3, 4, 7–10
case scenarios, 34–38
dimensions tables, 8–9
fact table, 7–8
hierarchies, 21
measurement of quality, 534
queries, 11
StartTime event property, 387
statements
INSERT, 73
MERGE, 293
Execute SQL task, 226
set-based update logic, 292–293
UPDATE
Execute SQL task, 226
StateProvince entity, 597
statistical sampling, 689, 690
stg.entityname_Consolidated, 607
stg.entityname_Leaf, 607
stg.entityname_Leaf table, 608
stg.entityname_Relationship, 607
Stopping operation status, 466
storage
disk storage
filegroups, 44
of SSIS solutions, 423
of rows in buffers, 512
SSAS (SQL Server Analysis Services), 30
SSIS packages, 421
String data type, 246, 247
string functions, 257
string length distribution, 532
string similarity algorithms, 738
subroutines, implementing, 291–292
subscription view
creating, 613–615
exporting master data with, 609
Subscription views metadata, 606
subsets, 567
Succeeded operation status, 466
success constraints, 165
Suggested status, in cleansing projects, 648
SUM aggregate function, 29, 399
Supported property, TransactionOption, 330
surrogate keys, 23–24
fact tables, 28
simple sequential integers, 45
Type 2 SCD, 284

suspicious values, discovering, 655
swapping to disk storage, 516, 520
switching data, partition switching, 72, 76–78
SynchronousInputID property, 709
synchronous (non-blocking) transformations, 513
synchronous output, 709
synonyms, creating, 640
Syntax algorithms property, 639
syntax, creating sequences, 46
sysadmin fixed server role, 543
System Administration
    access to, 618
    changing administrator, 617
System namespace, 251
system variables, 243, 251
    adding to data flow, 382
    to specify file location, 371
System.Windows.Forms namespace, 505

T

Table Lock check box, 185
Table Or View - Fast Load option, 185
tables
    aggregated
        indexed views, 58–61
    aggregating columns in AdventureWorksDW2012
     sample database, 59–62
    audit data, 396–397, 397
    audting, 13
    cdc.captured_columns system table, 305
    cdc.change_tables system table, 305
    cdc.ddl_history system table, 305
    cdc.index_columns system table, 305
    cdc.lsn_time_mapping system table, 305
    cdc.stg_CDCSalesOrderHeader_CT, 305
    cleansing errors, 344
    columns
        updating, 229–231
    complete auditing, 395
    cross join of, 737
    Customer dimension
        loading data with SCD tranformation, 293–296
        set-based update logic, 292–293
    Customer Dimension
        updating, 229–231

Customers Dimension
    loading data to DW, 209–212
    loading into DW, 212–214
defining location of, 373
destination
    truncating, 117
dimension
    history, 287
    selecting, 287
dimensions, 3, 8–9
    conformed, 8
    private, 9–10
    shared, 8–9
entities, 589
extracting data from views and loading into, 91–98
fact, 3, 567
    activity of measures, 29–30
    AdventureWorksDW2012 sample database, 32–33
    business key, 28–29
    columns, 28–29, 47–48
    columnstore indexes, 64
    creating, 52–54
    design, 27–33
    early-arriving facts, 285, 288
    foreign keys, 28
    granularity, 12
    implementing, 47–48
    incremental loads, 299–316
    inferred members, 47
    inserting unresolved records, 285
    loading, 71–73
    many-to-many relationships, 30–32
    partitioning, 44–45, 74–76
    partition switching, 76–78
    Star schema, 7–8
    surrogate keys, 28
FactInternetSales
    adding partitioning column to, 74
InternetSales
    adding foreign keys, 75
    creating columnstore index, 75
    loading data, 75
InternetSales fact
    columnstore indexes, 68–69
    data compression, 68–69
InternetSales Fact
    columns, 67

join
    staging area, 227–228
joined
    indexed views, 58–61
lineage, 13
LOB applications, 5
mdm.tblUser table, 617
multiple fact
    dimensions, 8
normalization, 5
Order Details, 28
package templates, 407
partitioning, 44–45
    testing, 80
Person.Person (TK463DW)
    creating data flow tasks, 190–192
pivot, 17
records
    updating, 226
rows
    reconstruction, 62
Sale Facts, 29
Sales Fact, 28
sort
    staging area, 227–228
source
    selecting, 95
Source Order Details, 28
Source Orders Header, 28
staging
    implementing, 44
staging tables, 243, 633
stg.CDCSalesOrderHeader
    enabling CDC, 304–305
stg.entityname_Leaf table, 608
table schema, package-level audit, 398
tabular mode, data mining and, 670
tabular storage, in SSAS, 30
target variables, in data minig, 668
task editors, property expressions, 362
Task ID variable, 400
Task name variable, 400
TaskResult property, 703
tasks
  breakpoint icons, 501
  parameterization of, 254
  variable access and, 248

tasks (control flow), 145, 147–155
  administration, 151
  analysis services, 153
  Analysis Services Execute DDL, 153
  Analysis Services Processing, 153
  Back Up Database, 152
  Bulk Insert, 150
  CDC Control, 149, 305
  Check Database Integrity, 152
  custom, 154–155
  data flow, 177
    creating, 178–180, 190–192
    defining data destination adapters, 184–187
    defining data source adapters, 180–183
    rows, 177, 178
    SSIS (SQL Server Integration Services) compo-
      nents, 178–179
  Data Flow, 150
  Data Mining Query, 153
  data movement, 150
  data preparation, 148
  Data Profiling, 148
  Execute Package, 149
  Execute Process, 149
  Execute SQL, 150, 226
    set-based update logic, 292, 292–293
  Execute SQL Server Agent Job, 152
  Execute T-SQL Statement, 152
  Expression, 149
  File System, 148, 161
    general settings, 161, 167, 168
  FTP, 148
  grouping, 155
  History Cleanup, 152
  maintenance, 151–152
  Maintenance Cleanup, 152
  Message Queue, 149
  Notify Operator, 152
  precedence constraints, 164–169
  Rebuild Index, 152
  Reorganize Index, 152
  Script, 154
  Send Mail, 149
  Shrink Database, 152
  Transfer Database, 151
  Transfer Error Messages, 151
  Transfer Jobs, 151
  Transfer Logins, 151

Transfer Master Stored Procedures, 151
Update Statistics, 152
Web Service, 148
WMI Data Reader, 149
WMI Event Watcher, 149
workflow, 148–149
XML, 148
task-scoped errors, 385
task transactions, defining settings, 328–330
taxonomies, product, 566
templates, SSIS package, 407–408
term-based relations, creating, 640
Term-Based Relations tab, 644
term columns
in term extraction, 681
in term lookup, 682
Term Extraction Transformation, 205, 667, 679–681, 682
Term Frequency/Inverse Document Frequency
(TFIDF), 681
term frequency (TF), 681
Term Lookup Transformation, 205, 667, 679, 681, 684
test sets, 690
text columns
in term lookup, 681
retrieving key terms from, 680
text file log provider, 384
text mining
defined, 679
performing, 682–686
transformations in SSIS, 670
with transformations, 667
theoretical models, measuring compliance with, 534
things, 567
third normal form, non-key columns, 9
third-party data providers, 660
32-bit environments, 427
migration, 429
tools available, 431
threads, allocation w/ execution trees, 513
timeliness, measuring, 533
tokenizer, 756
token transformations., 757
token weights, 757
top-level audits, 396
Toyoda, Sakichi, 536
Toyota Motor Corporation, 536
trace files, log providers, 384
training
of data in data mining, 668
of predictive models, 689

training sets, 690
transactional data, 566, 567
transaction inheritance, 328
transaction isolation levels, 331
transaction logs, recovery models, 42–43
TransactionOption property, 328, 330, 339
transactions
defined, 328, 626
defining settings, 328–330
implementing, 333–335
manually handling, 332–333
rollback, 333, 347
Transact-SQL
administering SQL with, 553–554
data quality measurement, 531
executing data taps, 507
profiling data with, 654
programmatic execution with, 458–459
SSISDB settings, 438
SSIS management, 423
Transfer Database task, 151
Transfer Error Messages task, 151
Transfer Jobs task, 151
Transfer Logins task, 151
Transfer Master Stored Procedures task, 151
Transformation Editor, 212
transformation processes, 267
transformations, 177
advanced data preparation, 204
backpressure mechanism for, 514
blocking, 199, 203
buffer architecture and, 512–513
Cache Transform
Lookup transformation, 223–224
Conditional Split, 214, 291
custom data flow, 226
data flow tips, 516
Derived Column, 206, 212
design-time debugging, 505
loading data, 209–210
logical-row, 199–200
Lookup, 200–201
cache modes, 218–219
Cache Transform transformation, 223–224
case sensitivity, 220
composite joins, 220
connection managers, 218
ETL (extract-transform-load), 218–224

transformations (*continued*)

merging outputs with Union All component, 220–221

replacing Union All transformation, 228–229

rows with no matching entities, 220

Merge Join, 211

multi-input, 200–201

multi-output, 200–201

multi-row, 202–203

non-blocking, 199

OLE DB Command

updating dimensions, 290

partial-blocking, 199

resolving column references, 207–208

SCD (Slowly Changing Dimension), 285–290

implementing slowly changing dimension logic, 293–298

modifying to include set-based updates, 296–298

outputs, 289–290

updating dimensions, 290

Script Component, 291

script component as, 708

selecting, 198–204

Sort, 224–225

SQL Server Import and Export Wizard, 89

types of, 512

Union All

replacing multiple Lookup transformation outputs, 228–229

transformation speed, 518

transform step, in data mining, 669, 670

Traverse subfolders property (Foreach Loop Editor), 157

troubleshooting

automation of, 239

execution monitoring, 465

of package execution, 498–508

TRUNCATE TABLE statement, 71

Truncate Update Table task, 339

truncating destination tables, 117

truncation error, repairing, 508–509

trust, measuring, 533

T-SQL commands, data lineage, 73

T-SQL HASHBYTES function, 291

T-SQL INNER JOIN operator, 739

T-SQL procedures, data lineage, 73

T-SQL queries

exporting master data with, 609

in data mining, 688

vs. SSAS, 656

T-SQL scripts, SQL Import and Export Wizard, 116

T-SQL statements, 332. *See also* statements

tuples, 531, 532, 654

Type 1 SCD, 22, 292–293

Type 1 SCD attribute, 284, 290–293

Type 2 SCD, 22

set-based updates, 292–293

surrogate key, 284

Type 2 SCD attribute, 284, 290–293

Type 3 SCD, 23

U

UDM cubes, as measurement tools, 669

UInt16 data type, 246

UInt32 data type, 246

UInt64 data type, 246

Unchanged output, 290

undirected algorithms, in data mining, 668

Unicode compression, 62

Unicode strings

in term lookup, 681

retrieving key terms from, 680

unintended usage, 533

Union All component, merging Lookup transformation outputs, 220–221

Union All transformation, 201, 228–229, 513

unique identification, lack of, 735

units, atomic, 328

unknown values (NULLs)

in measuring compliance, 534

in measuring completeness, 531–532

unmanaged connections, 702

unpivoting (data), 146

Unpivot transformation, 202

Unspecified property, IsolationLevel, 331

unstructured data, 566

unstructured sources, integration of, 533

unsupported data types, storage of, 247

Update permission, 618

UPDATE statement, Execute SQL task, 226

Update Statistics task, 152

updating

columns, 229–231

dimensions, 290–293

checking attribute changes, 291–292

set-based updates, 292–293

set-based updates, 225–227, 229
    updating Customer Dimension table, 229–231
upgrades, SSIS, 428–430, 451
Usage type property (File System task), 161, 168
US Counties, default KB, 639
Use A Single Column To Show Current And Expired
    Records option, 287
Use case-sensitive term extraction, 681
Use leading values property, 639
UseParentSetting property, 387
user accounts, installing MDS, 577
User and Group Permissions, access to, 618
user-defined variables, 243, 251–252
User namespace, 251
User name variable, 400
user perception, 533
Use Start And End Dates To Identify Current And Ex-
    pired Records option, 287
US Last Name domain, 639
US Places domain, 639
US State domain, 639

V

ValidateExternalMetadata property, 183
Validate method, customization, 720, 722
Validate Project dialog box, 471
validation, 146
    following data import, 608
    in SSMS, 470–472
    limits of, 472
validation errors, identifying, 382
Validation Report prompt, 472
validation results, 720
validations
    and execution monitoring, 466–467
    SSISDB reports, 506
validation step, described in debugging, 499
Validation Timeout property, 439, 467
Valid From column, 284
Valid To column, 284
value comparisons, 256
value completeness, 532
Value Inclusion, profiling of, 657
Value property, 244, 357, 502
Value property (Foreach Loop Editor), 159

values
    determining with expressions, 255
    direct assignment of, 467
Value type property (Foreach Loop Editor), 159
VARCHAR(MAX) columns, 516
variableA variable, 249
variableB variable, 249
Variable Grid Options dialog box, 244–245, 249
variables
    creation of, 244
    data types, 245–248
    in data mining, 668–669
    learning how to use, 702
    mapping parameters to, 301
    measurement in data mining, 688
    namespaces for, 251
    naming, 250
    vs. parameters, 242
    properties of, 244
    scope of, 248–250
    types of, 243
    uses for, 241
Variables collection class, 711
variable settings, Foreach Loop Editor, 159
Variables page, 486
Variables pane, 244, 250
Variables property, 374, 701, 702
variable values
    changing, 502
    debugging script components, 503
    viewing in Locals window, 502
verbose logging, 469
Verbose logging level, 468, 506
verbs, 567
verifying
    SSIS (SQL Server Integration Services) packages, 162–
    163
Version flags metadata, 606
Version ID variable, 400
versioning, master data, 568, 569
Version Management, access to, 618
viewing
    SSIS (SQL Server Integration Services) package
    files, 98
views
    catalog, 63–64
    extracting data from, 94
    extracting data from and loading into tables, 91–98
    selecting, 95

virtual accounts, SSIS installation, 426
virtual memory allocation, buffer size and, 515
Visual Studio 2010
  build configurations in, 358
  building custom components in, 718
Visual Studio Tools for Applications (VSTA). *See* VSTA
Visual Studio Tools for Applications (VSTA) IDE, 503
volatility, of master data, 568
VSTA Solution Explorer, 702, 709
VSTA (Visual Studio Tools for Applications), 154

W

warnings, in debugging, 499
Warn logging level, 552
watch windows, adding variables to, 502
web service source, creating, 731
web services, scripting for, 708
Web Service task, 148
windows
  Add SSIS Connection Manager, 192
  Column Mappings, 95
  Create Website, 584
Windows 7, account recommendations, 426
Windows Application Log, logging errors, 411
Windows Azure MarketPlace DataMarket, 541, 551
Windows Control Panel, component changes, 428
Windows Event Log
  configuring logging, 390
  log provider, 384
Windows Event Viewer, 384
Windows operating system, Performance Monitor, 519
Windows PowerShell, programmatic execution
  with, 458, 459–460, 474
Windows Server 2008/2008 R2, account recommenda-
  tions, 426
Windows user
  checking a name, 621
  creating, 620
Windows user groups
  in administration, 618
  permissions, 633
Windows Vista, account recommendations, 426
Windows Web Server roles, MDS, 577
wizards
  Slowly Changing Dimension
    selecting dimension tables, 287

SQL Server Import and Export Wizard, 88, 89–99
  creating simple data movements, 91–98
  editing SSIS packages created in, 114–116
  transformations, 89
  T-SQL scripts, 116
  viewing SSIS package files, 98–99
WMI connection manager, 135
WMI Data Reader task, 149
WMI Event Watcher task, 149
worker threads, required by execution trees, 513
workflow
  debugging, 503
  designing in advance, 268–269
workflow tasks, 148–149
workloads, separation of, 267
work threads, parallel execution of, 517

X

XML Configuration File
  package configuration type, 370
  sharing, 372
XML data, 566–567
XML data type columns, measuring completeness, 532
XML documents, for multiple result sets, 248
XML File Configuration, creating, 371–372, 376–377
XML file, log provider, 384
XML source, 180
XML task, 148, 330

About the Authors

DEJAN SARKA is a mentor with SolidQ who focuses on developing database and business intelligence applications. He is a frequent speaker at international conferences such as Tech-Ed, SqlDevCon, and SQL PASS, and is the founder of the Slovenian SQL Server and .NET Users Group. Dejan has authored or co-authored 11 books about Microsoft SQL Server. He has also developed three courses for SolidQ: Data Modeling Essentials, Data Quality and Master Data Management, and Data Mining.

MATIJA LAH is an independent consultant in the general and legal information management domains. Data warehousing represents an essential data management element in practically any business domain, and Matija has had the opportunity to solve a variety of data warehousing problems since he started working with data warehouses in 2001. He is one of the authors of the popular book series *SQL Server MVP Deep Dives* (Manning Publications). He is a frequent speaker at conferences related to Microsoft technologies, particularly those dedicated to SQL Server. Matija has been a Microsoft Most Valuable Professional for SQL Server since 2007 and is a mentor at SolidQ, a trusted global provider of advanced consulting, mentoring, and education solutions for the Microsoft platforms.

GREGA JERKIČ is an independent consultant and trainer for SolidQ. For the past 12 years, he has developed, architected, and managed projects focusing on data warehousing, MDM, data integration, analytical/planning solutions, and predictive analytics—primarily using Microsoft and IBM technology. He invented and was lead architect for BI4Dynamics, a predefined business intelligence solution on top of ERP Microsoft Dynamics NAV that is now used worldwide by more than 150 clients and has earned two Microsoft awards for best business intelligence solution for the CEE region. Grega currently provides training and mentoring for SQL Server and the IBM Business Intelligence platform around the world. He is a coauthor of the course *MOC 10774 - Querying Microsoft SQL Server 2012*.

What do you think of this book?

We want to hear from you!
To participate in a brief online survey, please visit:

microsoft.com/learning/booksurvey

Tell us how well this book meets your needs—what works effectively, and what we can do better. Your feedback will help us continually improve our books and learning resources for you.

Thank you in advance for your input!